# HISTORY OF THE
# GREAT WESTERN RAILWAY

Charles Russell, Chairman 1839–1855, by Sir Francis Grant, R.A. (" The Picture ")

# HISTORY
## of the
# GREAT WESTERN
# RAILWAY
## Volume One 1833-1863

E. T. MACDERMOT MA
Revised by C. R. CLINKER

LONDON
**IAN ALLAN LTD**

210489 30 1

First revised edition published 1964
Reprinted 1982

ISBN 0 7110 0411 0

Published by Ian Allan Ltd, Shepperton, Surrey;
and printed by R. J. Acford, Chichester, Sussex

# Contents

## VOLUME I

# Foreword

The *History of the Great Western Railway* compiled by E. T. MacDermot covering the period from the time of incorporation up to the grouping under the Railways Act, 1921, presents a picture of railway development during the Victorian era and portrays the heyday of the Great Western during the time when, in common with other railways, they were not beset by competition from road and air.

The Western Area Board of the British Transport Commission and the Management of Western Region welcomed Mr C. R. Clinker's offer to complete the history of the Company which had ceased to exist as the result of the Nationalization of Railways on 1st January 1948. In writing this Foreword, it is my pleasure to make a very small contribution to the admirable task he has performed in revising the two volumes of MacDermot's work. Mr Clinker, in his customary thorough manner, has taken the opportunity of expanding the locomotive history of the Company,* and the gradual elimination of steam motive power by diesel power makes it all the more imperative that there should be preserved for posterity the triumphs of the celebrated Locomotive Engineers responsible for the design and building of the famous types ever to be associated with Swindon and the Great Western.

The pattern of railways is now being drastically changed to comply with the demands of industry and to combat the ability of motor transport to carry traffics which were formerly rail-borne, and also to reduce working costs. In consequence, many unremunerative services are being either eliminated entirely or curtailed. This means that quite a number of the smaller lines which formed part of the old Great Western system have already been closed and more will follow. For this reason alone the work of MacDermot, revised now by Mr Clinker, in telling the story of the Great Western as it used to be, will prove to be an invaluable contribution to railway literature.

R. F. HANKS

---

* See Volume II.

# *Author's Preface*

The story of the Great Western has always had an extraordinary fascination for me, and its study has been a hobby of mine for many years. Hence, though published with the sanction of the Company, this book is by no means an 'official' history, as I am wholly unconnected with the railway world, but as it was desired to make the book an authentic history of the Company, I have used my best endeavours to ensure that nothing unsupported by authority is asserted.

I have to thank the Chairman and Directors for allowing me access to the records of the Company, and many Officers and members of the staff for invaluable assistance.

I am specially indebted to Sir Felix Pole for his encouragement; to the late Mr E. L. Ahrons, who wrote the chapters on the early engines and carriages, of which subject he had an unrivalled knowledge, and to Mr A. C. W. Lowe, who has kindly consented to complete this portion of the story; to Mr G. F. Bird for the use of his authentic drawings of the old engines; to Mr W. E. Edwards for information as to early signals; and last, but not least, to Mr G. T. Milford, of Bristol, who did much heavy spade-work in connection with the history.

E. T. MacDermot

August 1927

[MacDermot died at his home, Porlock, Somerset, on 17th May 1950, in his 77th year—*C. R. Clinker.*]

# *Preface to Revised Edition*

As a very junior member of the Great Western staff, I was given the pleasant task of helping the late E. T. MacDermot to sort an unwieldy and very dusty collection of Bristol & Exeter Railway books and papers stacked away, long forgotten, in a building which was formerly that Company's head office. From these and other sources he took many pages of notes. Some, not used in the History, were later made over to me, together with a number of timetables and other original material he had collected.

Since the publication of his now classic two-volume History in 1927 and 1931, railway history has established itself as a subject in its own right and there has been a notable increase in the serious study of this form of transport. Indeed, it is probable that MacDermot's painstaking researches encouraged, if not actually engendered, this development. His was the second full-scale, detailed history of a large railway company and students owe much to his work and example.

But they should not forget that the foundations of MacDermot's work were firmly and accurately laid by a clerk on the staff of the Great Western Audit Accountant from 1874 to 1908, Albert Robert Burnell. This remarkable man filled a large volume with minutely detailed parliamentary, legal, and general historical data covering the period from the Company's inception to April 1908. He died in November 1909, aged only 49 years, but not before the Directors had granted him a gratuity for his 'exceptional ability in compiling a history of the Great Western Railway'. MacDermot drew extensively on Burnell's work; I have done so, too.

The desirability of having a fully written-up, published, history of the Company seems to have originated with the late Sir Felix Pole, one of the greatest of Great Western men and General Manager from 1921 to 1929. In November 1924, he requested the head of each department to send him an annual report on the work of the department. These could, he said, be used *inter alia*, 'for the purpose of maintaining a history of the Company . . .' On Pole's recommendation, the Directors enlisted the services of MacDermot to write such a book.

In revising MacDermot's volumes I have made only such factual alterations as have come to light in the results of later research, following strictly the standard he laid down—'to ensure that nothing unsupported by authority is asserted'. The changes made have come from a variety of unimpeachable sources, including the corrections authenticated by MacDermot himself and published in *The Journal of Transport History* for May 1954. In a few instances, recent research has shown that the information given by MacDermot needed substantial re-writing. Paragraphs particularly affected were those dealing with the Royal Albert Bridge and Severn & Wye Railway.

Save the addition of a new appendix in Volume II, I have resisted the temptation to expand the original work, even the 1900–1922 portion to which MacDermot devoted only 43 pages, but a few unresolved queries have been cleared up and a certain unevenness of treatment adjusted. In short, only necessary changes have been made. Substantial portions of the text remain untouched.

In this revision, the Company's locomotive history has received special attention. Readers wishing for more information than that given in the condensed accounts in chapters by the late E. L. Ahrons (Volume I) and the late A. C. W. Lowe (Volume II), should consult the excellent series of booklets, *The Locomotives of the Great Western Railway* published by the Railway Correspondence & Travel Society, and H. Holcroft's *The Armstrongs of the Great Western.*

Specialization in various aspects of railway history is now commonplace and I have taken full advantage of the available expert knowledge. In this connection I am especially indebted to my friends who have given liberally of their time and patience—L. T. C. Rolt (Brunel and the Royal Albert Bridge), H. W. Paar (Severn & Wye Railway), Hamilton Ellis (Coaches), P. J. T. Reed and the late H. M. Le Fleming (Locomotives), Charles Hadfield (Canals), H. V. Borley, M. D. Greville, W. J. Skillern and J. G. Spence.

My particular thanks are due to Mr R. F. Hanks, former Chairman of the Western Area Board, and Mr J. R. Hammond, formerly General Manager of the Western Region of British Railways, for their encouragement and facilities given to me for carrying out this work. I have received indispensable help from many Headquarters, Divisional and District Officers and their staffs throughout the Western Region, many of them old Great Western men. I hope that all will think the results worthy of their efforts on my behalf.

C. R. CLINKER

Harlyn Bay,
Padstow, Cornwall

# I

# *Birth*

## *1833–1835*

The first proposal of a railway to be worked by locomotives between London and Bristol, then the second town in the kingdom, was made in the autumn of 1824, nearly a year before the opening of the Stockton & Darlington Railway. It originated among some Bristol merchants and was adopted at a meeting held in the London Tavern on the 27th December, Thomas Wilson, M.P., in the Chair, when the formation of a company for the purpose, with a capital of £1,500,000 in £100 shares was resolved upon. 'The London and Bristol Rail-Road Company' was accordingly formed, apparently without much difficulty. The Chairman was Richard Hart Davis, M.P., and among the Directors were John Fairlie, Sir Robert Farquhar, Sir John Lubbock, Hon. Leslie Melville, Donald Maclean, John Loudon McAdam, Sir Charles Price, and Sir John Reid. McAdam was of course the famous road engineer, at that time Surveyor to the Bristol Turnpike Trust and many other similar bodies all over the country. Although a Director, he was employed as engineer to lay out the line, and in little more than a fortnight produced a plan for a railroad from Bristol via Mangotsfield, Wootton Bassett, the Vale of White Horse, and Wantage to Wallingford, whence it *might* be carried on along the right bank of the Thames by Reading, Wargrave, and Bray to Brentford, or on the other side by Ewelme, Turville, Wooburn, and Burnham to the same place. Either of these routes, he asserted, would be shorter than any road then in use between Bristol and London, and peculiarly favourable for a railroad on which the expense of locomotive power would be very reasonable, owing to so few elevations occurring. As he describes the Cotswold ridge as 'a small swell of the country near Dodington', we can only assume that he took no levels. He recommended that a turnpike road should be made on the same line but 'passing through the towns instead of near them, as the Railroad must necessarily do'. Evidently the latter was intended only for the conveyance of goods, and there was no intention of bringing it nearer London than Brentford. At a meeting held, again at the London Tavern, on 2nd February 1825, the Directors adopted his scheme and resolved to apply for an Act of Parliament for both the rail and turnpike roads but, though all the shares were stated to have been taken up, no such application was ever made, and the project died a very natural death. Other schemes of this same year that never came to anything were 'The General Junction Railroad from London to Bristol', 'The London and Reading Railroad', a 'Proposed Railroad from Bristol to Bath', 'The Bristol Northern and Western Railway', and 'The Taunton

Grand Western Railroad'. After this violent outbreak, the railway fever in the west seems to have completely subsided for seven years, during which only the two horse tramways to Coalpit Heath, respectively entitled the Bristol & Gloucestershire Railway and the Avon & Gloucestershire Railway, were inaugurated.

The success of the Liverpool & Manchester Railway, opened in September 1830, and of the Stockton & Darlington five years earlier, having become generally recognized, and lines having already been proposed and surveyed between Liverpool and Birmingham and London and Birmingham, the project of a railway between Bristol and London was again brought before the public in 1832.

Two engineers, William Brunton and Henry Habberley Price, were the first in the field with a practical proposal for a line by Bath, Bradford, Trowbridge, near Devizes, and through the Pewsey Vale to Hungerford, Newbury, and Reading, and on near Datchet and Colnbrook, by Southall 'to a vacant spot within three or four hundred yards of Edgeware Road, Oxford Street, and the Paddington and City-Road Turnpike. A short branch may unite this line with the intended Birmingham Railway, and thereby proceed towards the City as far as Battle-Bridge.' This scheme was announced by a circular headed 'Bristol and London Railway' dated from Lombard Street 7th May 1832, amplified by another in June, estimating the expense of the undertaking at £2,500,000 and showing that 'an interest of 15 per cent. will be insured to subscribers'. Although this project was still alive in January 1833, sufficient financial support was not forthcoming, and we hear no more of Messrs Brunton and Price.

Meantime the topic had been frequently discussed in commercial circles in Bristol and in the press without any definite result till one day in the autumn of 1832 four influential business men—George Jones, John Harford, Thomas Richard Guppy, and William Tothill—foregathered in a small office in a main street called Temple Backs, long since swept away to make room for the Temple Meads Goods Depot, and resolved to press the matter forward. They forthwith proceeded to stir up their fellows with such success that before the end of the year a committee of prominent merchants and others, representing the five corporate bodies of Bristol, was appointed to investigate the practicability of a railway to London. These bodies and their deputies were the following:

Bristol Corporation—John Cave, Charles Ludlow Walker, and John Evans Lunnell.

Society of Merchant Venturers—George Gibbs, Peter Maze, and Henry George Fowler.

Bristol Dock Company—Humphry Jefferies, John Howell, and Nicholas Roch.

Bristol Chamber of Commerce—William Singer Jacques, Edward Harley, and William Tothill.

Bristol & Gloucestershire Railway—John Harford, George Jones, and Joseph Storrs Fry.

The Committee held its first meeting on 21st January 1833, John Cave in the Chair and William Tothill acting as Secretary, when they considered the matter generally and advertized for information. In the course of the following month the Deputies reported favourably on the prospects of the undertaking to their constituent public bodies, who thereupon provided funds for a preliminary survey and estimate, and Messrs Harford, Jones, Roch, and Tothill were appointed a sub-committee to arrange for this, which of course involved the selection of an engineer.

There were several candidates for the post, among them a young man of twenty-seven, Isambard Kingdom Brunel, son of the Engineer of the Thames Tunnel and himself well known in Bristol as the author of the chosen design for the Clifton Suspension Bridge and engineer to the Dock Company for the improvement of the Floating Harbour. Though some of the other candidates had considerable local interest behind them, Brunel was appointed engineer on 7th March, and at once set about surveying the country between Bristol and London in company with W. H. Townsend, a land surveyor and valuer.

Between Bath and Reading they first inspected the route by Bradford, Devizes, the Pewsey Vale, and Newbury, afterwards that north of Marlborough Downs, by Chippenham, Swindon, the Vale of White Horse, and the Thames Valley, and soon decided to recommend the latter. East of Maidenhead two or three lines of approach to the Metropolis were surveyed, one of them crossing the Thames by Kingston, and left for later decision. The expense of the undertaking was estimated at slightly over £2,800,000.

Their surveys and estimate having been completed and delivered to the Committee of Deputies, that body drew up an elaborate report on the whole subject, and a public meeting was held in the Guildhall, Bristol, on 30th July 1833, presided over by Mr Robert Bright in the absence of the Mayor. The Committee's report having been read and discussed, it was resolved that 'a Company should be formed for the establishment of Railway communication between Bristol and London, and for that purpose that a body of Directors for Bristol be appointed, who, in conjunction with a similar body to be appointed in London, shall constitute a General Board of Management for securing subscriptions and obtaining an Act of Parliament for effecting the same object'. No less than thirty Bristol Directors, including all the Deputies, were accordingly elected, with power to add to their number; bankers were appointed to receive subscriptions; and votes of thanks passed to the five public bodies for setting the undertaking on foot, and especially to a Mr Francis Fortune 'for his unremitting endeavours to arouse the attention of the Citizens of Bristol to the advantages to be derived from a railroad to London'.

Meanwhile the Bristol merchants who had become interested in the project had been working up support among their friends and business acquaintances in London, with the result that by this time an influential Committee had been formed there, largely by the able co-operation of

George Henry Gibbs, head of the firm of Antony Gibbs and Sons of London, and cousin of George Gibbs, one of the deputies of the Society of Merchant Venturers on the original Bristol Committee, and senior partner of Gibbs, Bright and Co., of Bristol and Liverpool. This London Committee engaged as their Secretary a remarkable man, who was destined to do more towards founding the Great Western Railway system than any other single individual, Brunel himself not even excepted.

Charles Alexander Saunders was born in December 1796, the fifth son of Robert Saunders of Southend, Lewisham, Kent, and descended from a family long settled in Banffshire. After five years at a preparatory school he was admitted scholar of Winchester College in May 1810, where he was soon joined by his younger brother Augustus, afterwards head master of Charterhouse and Dean of Peterborough. Though Charles duly gained a provisional right to a scholarship at New College, he never went to Oxford, but left Winchester in February 1814 to accept an offer of a Government clerkship. At twenty-one he married Miss Mary Rowlandson, and after a few years resigned the Civil Service for mercantile pursuits, which took him for some time to Mauritius. Hence he had considerable experience of life and business when he became Secretary to the London Committee at the age of thirty-six.

The first joint meeting of the London and Bristol Committees was held in the Counting House of Messrs Antony Gibbs and Sons, 47 Lime Street, in the City of London, on 19th August 1833. The title 'Great Western Railway' was there and then adopted instead of 'Bristol and London Railroad', by which the scheme had hitherto been known, and the first Prospectus of the Company settled.

This document was issued before the end of the month under the new title. The capital is stated as £3,000,000 in shares of £100 each, deposit £5 per share. The Board of Directors consisted of two Committees of twelve each:

| LONDON COMMITTEE | BRISTOL COMMITTEE |
|---|---|
| John Bettington. | Robert Bright. |
| Henry Cayley. | John Cave. |
| Ralph Fenwick. | Charles Bowles Fripp. |
| George Henry Gibbs. | George Gibbs. |
| Robert Fred. Gower. | Thos. Richard Guppy. |
| Riversdale W. Grenfell. | John Harford. |
| Robert Hopkins. | Wm. Singer Jacques. |
| Edw. Wheler Miles. | George Jones. |
| Benjamin Shaw. | James Lean. |
| Henry Simonds. | Peter Maze. |
| William Unwin Sims. | Nicholas Roch. |
| George Wildes. | John Vining. |
| C. A. Saunders, *Secretary*. | W. Tothill, *Secretary*. |
| Office, No. 17 Cornhill. | Railway Office, Bristol. |

The cost of the line of about 120 miles is estimated at £2,805,330, and the prospective revenue at £747,752 per annum. A map shows the course of the railway much as it was afterwards made between Bristol and the neighbourhood of Taplow, whence alternative routes into London are shown, one direct into the west end, the other crossing the Thames below Kingston and terminating south of the river somewhere about Waterloo Bridge. The latter was soon abandoned and does not appear in the later prospectuses. Three 'Probable Branches', from Didcot to Oxford, Swindon to Gloucester, and Chippenham to Bradford, also appear on the map.

Saunders was indefatigable in his efforts to replace the Company on a firm footing. He travelled about the country enlisting support for the scheme, and succeeded in obtaining the views of many members of the House of Commons and several peers. But time was short and the public apathetic and distrustful. By the end of October scarcely a quarter of the capital had been subscribed, whereas Parliament, by its standing orders, required at least half before the Bill could be proceeded with.

In consequence, the Directors issued a circular on 23rd October, stating their intention—

'. . . to make application in the approaching Session for authority to construct the sections of the main Railway extending between London and Reading (with a Branch to Windsor), and between Bristol and Bath, thereby rendering the ultimate completion of the whole line more certain, upon a further application to Parliament in the following year.

'The number of shares required for this part of the undertaking will be 12,500, of which 2,500 will be reserved for the proprietors of land, etc., and consequently no application for shares can be entertained so soon as 10,000 shall have been subscribed, of which a very considerable proportion has been already allotted.'

All this time Brunel and a staff of assistants had been busy on a detailed survey of the whole line.

His own duty of superintendence severely taxed his great powers of work. He spent several weeks travelling from place to place by night, and riding about the country by day, directing his assistants and endeavouring, very frequently without success, to conciliate the landowners on whose property he proposed to trespass.

His diary of this date shows that when he halted at an inn for the night but little time was spent in rest, and that often he sat up writing letters and reports until it was almost time for his horse to come round to take him on the day's work. 'Between ourselves', he wrote to Hammond, his assistant, 'it is harder work than I like. I am rarely much under twenty hours a day at it.'[1]

The plans deposited at the end of November showed a line of railway which, except at the London end, did not vary much from the existing line. Starting at Vauxhall Bridge, it was to be carried by a viaduct about 20 feet high for four miles, through Pimlico, Brompton, and Hammersmith to South Acton, thence by a short tunnel to the south of Ealing on to West Drayton, Slough, Maidenhead, and Twyford, and through a tunnel under Sonning Hill to Reading. Between Bristol and Bath it was to have crossed the Avon four times instead of twice, as it does now.

[1] *Life of I. K. Brunel*, by I. Brunel (Longmans Green & Co, 1870, page 65).

The second reading of the Bill in the House of Commons was moved on 10th March 1834 by Lord Granville Somerset, seconded by the Earl of Kerry and supported by several influential members, among them Daniel O'Connell, who saw in it 'the means of conferring great advantages on Ireland, the great granary and feeding farm of this country'. After a debate of some hours, it was carried by 182 votes to 92, and the Bill referred to a Committee of which Lord Granville Somerset was Chairman. The Windsor Branch was dropped at an early stage owing to the violent opposition of Eton College.

The Committee met on 16th April, and the proceedings occupied no less than fifty-seven days. Evidence to prove the public advantages of the railway was first taken. As far as passengers were concerned, these seem to have been generally acknowledged. Goods traffic between Bristol and London was then chiefly conducted by the Avon to Bath and thence by the Kennet and Avon Canal, opened throughout in 1810, and the Kennet and Thames. The evidence showed that, apart from frost, which closed the canal, winter floods and summer droughts caused great delays on the rivers and even held up the traffic occasionally for weeks. The worst delays from both causes occurred on the Thames between Reading and London, and so bad were they that goods which came by the canal were frequently sent on to London by road, of course at a greatly increased expense. The distance by river was nearly eighty miles, more than double that by the proposed railway, and even under the most favourable conditions goods in barges took at least three days, whereas the railway would bring them in three hours. Between Bath and Bristol the barges took a whole day, which the railway would reduce to one hour. Farmers and stock breeders, other than those quite near London, also had a good deal to say in favour of the railway.

Brunel was of course the chief engineering witness. Having given his evidence, he was cross-examined for eleven days by seven learned counsel, to whom a modern child of ten could have given points in simple railway knowledge. Questions of every conceivable kind, sensible and absurd, were asked him, many being suggested by a scientific theorist, Dr Dionysius Lardner, whose solemn theories as to railways were as a rule proved to be quite erroneous, but who enjoyed an ephemeral reputation as a great authority at this time. Brunel answered them all readily and patiently, and George Stephenson and other engineers who were present are said to have been much struck by the ability and knowledge he displayed. Stephenson himself, Joseph Locke, James Walker, and H. R. Palmer gave evidence as engineers in favour of the line laid out by Brunel, Stephenson saying: 'I can imagine a better line, but I do not know one so good'. It was established that the line through the Thames Valley and north of Marlborough Downs was the best course for a railway from London to Bristol, as the levels were much better than any possible south of the Downs, and, moreover, it provided for communication with Oxford, Gloucester, and South Wales, which the latter route did not.

At an early stage of Brunel's examination the Committee called on the promoters to declare whether they would proceed with their line to Vauxhall Bridge or terminate it at Brompton; so in view of the determined opposition of the landowners, who were influential members of the House of Lords, it was decided to abandon the last two miles of the viaduct, and look for communication with the River and Docks, which was the object in view in choosing the Vauxhall terminus, by means of the Kensington Canal to the Thames at Chelsea. A space at the back of the still existing 'Hoop and Toy' Public House in the Old Brompton Road was then selected for the site of the London Terminus. This did not please the Brompton owners and residents, who continued to oppose the line through their suburb with redoubled energy.

The chief opponents of the Bill were the landowners of Middlesex, Bucks, and Berks, including the Eton College authorities. At a meeting held by them in the previous November, the Provost of Eton said that no public good whatever could possibly come from such an undertaking, and he should be wanting in his duty to the establishment over which he presided if he did not oppose it to the utmost of his ability. These were only a part of the opposition. The inhabitants of Windsor opposed because the railway did not run as near their town as they wished; the Corporation of Maidenhead opposed because they feared the loss of tolls on their bridge over the Thames; the farmers near London opposed because produce from a distance would be brought to London to compete with their own; and the people interested in canals, rivers, and stage coaches opposed from fear of competition. Another kind of opposition came from the promoters of the London & Southampton Railway, who were seeking their own Act of Incorporation in this session, and went out of their way to attack the Great Western Bill, alleging that Bristol and the West of England could be equally well served by a branch from their line. This was the beginning of a long and bitter hostility to their great neighbour. There was also an insignificant rival project calling itself 'The London and Windsor Railway' in the field, the promoters of which did their little best against the Great Western Bill, although they had withdrawn their own as soon as the latter had passed its second reading.

All these opponents having had their say, the Committee at length, on the fifty-seventh day of hearing, declared their approval of the Bill, and it passed the House of Commons. The Lords, however, made short work of it. The second reading was moved in that august assembly by Lord Wharncliffe, and forthwith rejected on 25th July by 47 to 30, so the truncated scheme of 1834, which was described by an opposing Counsel as neither 'Great' nor 'Western', nor even a 'Railway', perished. The fifty-seven days before the Commons Committee were not, however, entirely wasted, as we shall see next year.

The Directors were not greatly dismayed by this defeat; they recognized that, owing to the time spent in the Commons, it was too late in the session to hope to get the Bill through the Upper House. Nothing daunted, they began preparations for bringing in a new Bill for the whole line next year, feeling that they now had public opinion behind them, and were sure of success provided only they could raise the necessary capital.

In September a Supplementary Prospectus, signed by the two Secretaries, was issued, inviting subscriptions for 10,000 additional shares, which, they said, with the 10,000 already subscribed, would enable the Directors to carry a Bill for the whole line through Parliament in the next session. After describing and drawing encouragement from the proceedings in Parliament, this document goes on as follows:

> The proposed line will pass through or near to Slough, Maidenhead, Reading, Wantage, Swindon, Wootton Bassett, Chippenham, and Bath, and thus intersect the South of England from East to West in the manner of a main Trunk, calculated to send branches to each district, North or South.
> This line has been preferred on account of the superiority of its levels, and the ultimate economy of working steam power upon it, as well as of its offering the greatest facilities for a junction with Oxford, Cheltenham, and Gloucester, the manufacturing districts of Gloucestershire and Wiltshire, and through Gloucester with South Wales.
> A branch of only twelve miles over a level country may connect the main line with Oxford, and a branch of 9 miles in length from the neighbourhood of Chippenham, passing by Melksham, may communicate with Bradford and Trowbridge, and confer on those important agricultural districts and manufacturing towns the benefits of the entire line, while the main Railway, as far as Swindon (a distance of 76 miles from London) will form the direct line to Gloucester, leaving only 28 miles to be hereafter added to complete a Railway communication between that City and London, reducing the total distance to 104 miles.
> As reference to the map might lead to the inquiry why a line by way of Hungerford, Devizes and Bradford was not chosen, it is right to state that a survey of that district was in the first instance made; but the difficulties and expence of such a Railway, owing to the altitude of the general levels of the country, were found to be so considerable that, even without reference to the reasons already adduced, the Directors cannot hesitate to prefer the northern line, which will scarcely exceed the other in length, and which, embracing Oxford, the clothing districts of Gloucestershire, the important towns of Stroud, Cheltenham and Gloucester; and thence leading eventually to Wales, may also be made to communicate, by a short branch as before stated, with Bradford, Trowbridge and other manufacturing towns on the southern line.
> . . . The expense of travelling and of carriage of goods by Railway will not exceed half the present charge; and the time occupied in passing from the Metropolis to Bristol will be about four hours and a half.
> The sum required for the construction of the entire line of 116 miles, including Depots, Locomotive Engines, etc., will be £2,500,000. The difference between this and the original estimate of £2,805,330 arises in a great degree from a change in the direction of the line in the neighbourhood of London, but principally from the Engineer having now sufficient data to calculate the cost with accuracy; in the absence of which data on the former occasion, the Directors preferred stating a sum which should exceed rather than fall short of the greatest probable cost.

Though the length of the whole line is precisely stated as 116 miles, one less than in October and four less than in August 1833, and a change of direction near London is alluded to, the eastern terminus is not specified, and so presumably had not been definitely fixed at this date. Negotiations with the London & Birmingham Company for a junction with their authorized line near Wormwood Scrubs were in progress. This having been arranged, a new edition of the Prospectus was issued in November, stating:

The Line of Railway is described in the annexed Plan. It will be 114 miles in length from Bristol to the point of junction with the Birmingham Line near Wormwood Scrubs. The station for Passengers in London is intended to be near the New Road in the Parish of St Pancras.

Thus was Euston Station indicated in 1834. A large portion of the new Prospectus was taken up by a very full 'Extract of Report of the Liverpool and Manchester Railway', showing in detail the receipts and expenses of that line and the alluring profits made. The Plan shows the main line exactly as in that of August 1833, except at the London end, and between Keynsham and Bristol, where two crossings of the Avon near Hanham are saved by the railway keeping to the Somerset bank. The 'Probable Branches' are also identical, except that to Bradford, which now throws off a fork to Trowbridge.

All through the autumn and winter of 1834–5 the promoters were busy stirring up support, financial and moral, all over the West of England and in South Wales. The towns to be served by the railway were very emphatic in their expressions of disapproval of the action of the Lords in rejecting the Bill. Public meetings for the purpose were held in many of them, including a big meeting in the Merchants' Hall, Bristol, in October, attended by several Members of Parliament, and people from London, Windsor, Reading, Gloucester, Stroud, Bath, Exeter, and other places. Later, meetings in support of the new Bill were organized in almost every town of any importance in the west, and petitions to Parliament extensively signed even in places as remote as Truro, Bridport, Hereford, and the County of Tipperary. Saunders and Brunel were the leaders in this campaign, but they had many helpers; even some of the Directors travelled the country.

The following letter from Saunders to Thomas Merriman Ward, his chief and for a time sole assistant at the London Office, 17 Cornhill, gives a good idea of the work.

3 COLLONADE
CHELTENHAM.
14 December 1834

MY DEAR SIR,

I find it impossible for me to be in London this week, having several appointments in this part of the Country which require attention. We had an excellent meeting at Cirencester on Friday, Mr Cripps in the Chair. Lord Ed$^d$ Somerset the other M.P. was present. The resolutions were passed unanimously and we had 90 shares taken at once. A Committee is formed for procuring Subscriptions, and we shall do very well in that Town. Here we are getting several Subscribers of 50 Shares each. Our days are wholly employed in canvassing and we have every reason to be pleased with our success. We are anxious however to say little or nothing about our doings, lest they should attract our opponents to disseminate in this quarter any false statements, etc. We certainly gain more by a quiet process, withdrawing from the observation of our Foes, and above all boasting as little as possible of success. I mention this as a caution to any of our own immediate Friends or Directors who may be enquiring from you.

We hope and believe that we have the means of getting up 3,000 Shares in Ireland, South Wales, Gloucestershire, etc., before the 20 January. At Bristol by great exertions 5,000 Shares in addition will be sold, and we must hope in London among old Proprietors, Friends, etc., to get rid of 2,000 Shares to complete the whole Affair.

We have a private meeting on Tuesday with 20 of the chief Merchants at Gloucester to form there a provisional Committee. Our public meeting is for 2$^d$ January. We shall

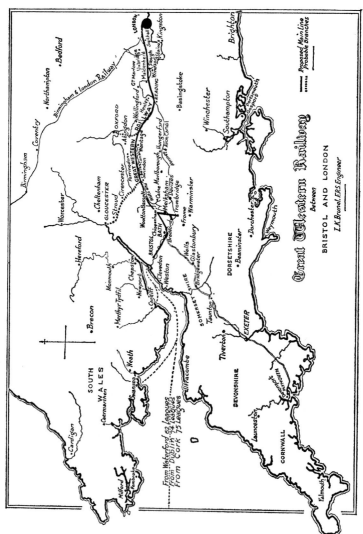

PROSPECTUS PLAN

be employed in Gloucester, Cheltenham, Stroud and Cirencester until that day. I must also go over to Dursley and Wootton-under-Edge, and probably to Chippenham.

After 2ᵈ January I expect Mr Maze and Mr Bright to accompany me for a week or 10 days into Sᵒ Wales. Mr Hunt will work towards London at the same time— through Wallingford, Abingdon, Oxford, etc.

Continue to address me at Cheltenham for the present.

Ever yours truly,
CHAS. A. SAUNDERS.

The 1st February 1835 finds him again at Cheltenham, at last confident of success. He writes to Ward:

> I leave this at 6 tomorrow for South Wales, where I shall be until this day week. My intention then is to leave Cheltenham on the evening of Monday the 9th, wait at Oxford to see what can be done there until Wednesday the 11th, upon which day I should return home. I hope you are preparing the Lists of Proprietors to be deposited in Parliament. This will be necessary, and I expect to have so much on hand when I return home in the form of Circulars, Letters, Accounts, Deeds to be executed, etc., that I wish to clear up such business beforehand.
>
> This last week has produced about 450 Shares, and I feel now quite sure that we shall effectually complete our List of Subscription in time for Parliament.
>
> It is however sad harassing work that I have encountered in calling upon and pressing perfect strangers to contribute. 'All's well that ends well.'

Out of such 'sad harassing work' of himself and others was the Great Western Railway born. His confidence was justified. Before the end of the month he and Tothill were able to announce to the public that the whole of the 10,000 additional shares required by Parliament for the entire railway from London to Bristol had been taken, making, with the previous 10,000, a capital of £2 million, and that the Petition for the Bill had been presented to the House of Commons.

The foes to whom he alludes in his December letter were the promoters of an abortive scheme for a line from Tring to Cheltenham, and the London & Southampton Railway Company, who, having obtained their Act, instead of proceeding quietly with their own business, at once began an active aggression on the Great Western by promoting a rival line from Basingstoke to Bath and Bristol, laid out by their engineer, Francis Giles, through Newbury, Hungerford, Devizes, Trowbridge, and Bradford. They met with some support from these townlets, but little or none from Bath and Bristol. At a meeting organized by them at Bath in September, after flowery addresses from several members of their deputation, Brunel got up and demolished their arguments, with the result that a resolution in favour of the Great Western was carried with acclamation, and the deputation retired discomfited. Notwithstanding this and other rebuffs, the Southampton Company proceeded with their Bill for the Basing, Bath and Bristol Railway, and in order to spike some of their guns, the Great Western added a forked branch from Chippenham to Bradford and Trowbridge to their own Bill.

This was read a second time without opposition in the Commons on 9th March 1835, again on the motion of Lord Granville Somerset, and committed, the Report of last year's proceedings being referred to the Committee.

The chief opponents were now the London & Southampton Company and the Eton schoolmasters, the landowners generally having either been conciliated or given up hope of defeating the railway.

Soon after the Committee had met, its Chairman, Charles Russell, member for Reading, announced that, inasmuch as the public advantages of a railway to Bristol were sufficiently established by last year's Report, referred to them by the House, they required no further evidence on that subject, and desired Counsel to confine the case to the merits of the line proposed. This decision, of course, took most of the wind out of the opponents' sails, and obliged them to try to show the superiority of their Basing and Bath Railway—a hopeless task.

The attack was mainly concentrated on the 'monstrous and extraordinary, most dangerous and impracticable' tunnel at Box, with its incline of 1 in 100. One opposing witness, calling himself an engineer, asserted his belief that the inevitable consequence of constructing such a tunnel would be the wholesale destruction of human life, and that no care, no foresight, no means that he was acquainted with could prevent it; another that 'no person would desire to be shut out from the daylight with a consciousness that he had a superincumbent weight of earth sufficient to crush him in case of accident'; and a third that 'the noise of two trains passing in the tunnel would shake the nerves of this assembly. I do not know such a noise. No passenger would be induced to go twice'! This sort of nonsense does not seem to have had much effect on the Committee, and the objections to the incline were defeated by the production of a report by George Stephenson and H. R. Palmer that Brunel had consulted them as to his two proposals, one of a long incline at 1 in 330 and the other of a shorter one of 1 in 100 confined to the tunnel, and that they agreed with him in preferring the latter, 'as by concentrating the rise at one point within a practicable length for working either by a stationary or assistant engine he reduced all the remaining inclinations on the line to the present favourable amount'. They anticipated no difficulties in the execution of the work, and added: 'The levels of the proposed line are undoubtedly superior to those of the Southampton or the Basing and Bath, or any of the extensive lines with which we have an acquaintance, and are therefore better adapted to the working of the locomotive engine both as regards economy and expedition.'

The opponents were obliged to admit that the gradients of the Basing and Bath were generally steeper than those of the Great Western, but maintained that they were so balanced that the rises and falls compensated one for another so as to render the line practically level; whereupon the Chairman remarked that on this principle the Highlands of Scotland would be as good as any other district for the construction of a railway.

The Committee eventually decided in favour of the Great Western Bill, and reported it to the House, where it was read a third time on 26th May, after a proposal by an earnest sabbatarian that no engine or carriage should be moved on the Lord's Day under a penalty of £20 had been defeated by 212 to 34.

Next day it was introduced in the Lords and read a first time, numerous petitions in its favour being presented by various peers. The second reading was carried by 46 to 34 on 10th June, and the Bill referred to a Committee presided over by Lord Wharncliffe. Although this Committee soon came to the same decision as the Commons that no more evidence of the need for a railway to Bristol was called for, the fight before them raged for forty days. Box Tunnel was again the chief point of attack, and our old friend, Dr Dionysius Lardner, the chief witness of its impracticability and danger. That great pundit soon gave himself away rather badly by producing some elaborate calculations, which proved conclusively—to his own satisfaction, at any rate—that if the brakes were to fail a train would run down the incline in the tunnel with a constantly increasing velocity, till it at last emerged at a speed of 120 miles an hour. Unfortunately for the philosopher's reputation, Brunel at once showed that he had entirely omitted the restraining forces of friction and air resistance from his calculations, and that these would have the effect of reducing his 120 miles an hour to 56. The assertions of the opposition party had already been considerably discounted by the Chairman having, during Brunel's cross-examination, drawn the attention of the Committee to a printed statement circulated by them just before the second reading of the Bill, which the actual evidence given showed to contain several gross falsehoods, as their Counsel was compelled to admit.

George Stephenson, Joseph Locke, and Messrs Palmer, Price, and Vignoles, called as engineers by the promoters, expressed their unqualified approbation of the line chosen by Brunel and of his estimates. On the other side, William Brunton, the pioneer of 1832, may be noted.

At last, towards the end of August, the Committee declared the preamble proved by 33 to 21, and having inserted some clauses proposed by the Eton lawyers for the protection of the morals and discipline of that famous school, which several masters said would be inevitably ruined by the proximity of a railway, reported the Bill for third reading. This was opposed by His Royal Highness the Duke of Cumberland, soon to be King of Hanover, and twenty-seven other peers, but carried by a majority of twenty-two, and the Bill received the Royal Assent on 31st August 1835.

Thus was the Great Western Railway Company at last incorporated, and empowered to make a railway 'commencing at or near a certain Field called Temple Mead within the Parish of Temple otherwise Holy Cross in the City and County of the City of Bristol, adjoining or near to the new Cattle Market there', passing through specified parishes in the Counties of Gloucester, Somerset, Wilts, Berks, Oxford, Bucks, and Middlesex, 'and terminating by a Junction with the London and Birmingham Railway in a certain Field lying between the Paddington Canal and the Turnpike Road leading from London to Harrow on the western side of the

General Cemetery in the Parish or Township of Hammersmith in the said County of Middlesex'; and also a branch railway from near Thingley Farm, in the parish of Corsham, to a field near the Gas Works in the part of the parish of Trowbridge called Islington, with another branch thereout from the south-western extremity of the village of Holt in the parish of Bradford, to the farmyard of Kingston Farm adjoining the town of Bradford. It is interesting to notice incidentally that part of Twyford, east of Reading, was then in the County of Wilts.

The Act contains two hundred and fifty-one sections, many of them for the protection of individual landowners, Canal Companies, and Turnpike Trusts. No diversion, branch, or station was to be made within three miles of Eton College, and besides 'a good and sufficient fence on each side' of four miles of the line, the Company were to maintain 'a sufficient additional number of persons for the purpose of preventing or restricting all access to the said Railway by the Scholars of Eton College aforesaid whether on the Foundation or otherwise', such persons to be under the orders of the Provost and Head Master. Compensation was to be paid to the Corporation of Maidenhead for any annual decrease in their Bridge tolls for six years after the opening of the railway; and to prevent loss of the Coal Duty payable to the City of London, a stone was to be placed on the East Bank of the River Colne, in the Parish of Hillingdon, and 1*s* 1*d* paid to the City on every ton of coal, culm, or cinders brought by railway towards London past such stone, 500 tons yearly for the use of the Company's engines only being allowed free of duty. Similar 'City Stones' already existed on the Thames at Staines Bridge and on the Grand Junction Canal at the north-east corner of Grove Park, Hertfordshire.

The First General Meeting of the new Company, held at the City of London Tavern on 29th October 1835, Benjamin Shaw in the Chair, was one of general congratulation and thanksgiving. Cordial votes of thanks were passed to Lord Wharncliffe, Lord Granville Somerset, and Charles Russell, M.P., for their invaluable help in Parliament, to the Directors, Brunel, the Solicitors, and St George Burke, the Parliamentary Agent, and especially to Secretary C. A. Saunders, to whom the Proprietors requested the Directors to present a gratuity in addition to his salary, 'entertaining a very high sense of his services and being desirous that some testimony of their esteem and approbation should be given him'.

The Directors reported that they proposed to push on at once with the sections of the railway between London and Maidenhead and Bristol and Bath; that they were negotiating with the London & Birmingham Board for the use of their line into London; and that they had secured premises in Prince's Street, near the Bank, 'with a large frontage to which all Public Conveyances will have access, constituting at once the General Office for the ordinary affairs of the Company, and the Receiving Station for passengers and light goods proceeding to and from the Railway'. Apparently the idea was that passengers would be booked in Prince's Street, and conveyed by coaches or omnibuses thence to the trains at

Euston; but why people from the railway should be 'received' in the City is not so clear.

The accounts show that £88,710 had been spent, the greater part of it in Parliamentary expenses.

Twenty-four Directors to replace the thirty named in the Act were elected at this meeting, half of them forming the London and half the Bristol Committee, each of which had considerable powers of action independently of the other. This first Board of the Company consisted of the following:

| LONDON COMMITTEE | BRISTOL COMMITTEE |
|---|---|
| Benjamin Shaw, *Chairman.* | Robert Bright, *Deputy Chairman.* |
| Ralph Fenwick. | Henry Bush. |
| George Henry Gibbs. | Charles Bowles Fripp. |
| Robert Frederick Gower. | Thomas Richard Guppy. |
| Riversdale William Grenfell. | William Singer Jacques. |
| Robert Hopkins. | George Jones. |
| Edward Wheler Mills. | Peter Maze. |
| Henry Simonds. | Thomas Pycroft. |
| William Unwin Sims. | Nicholas Roch. |
| William Tite. | Robert Scott. |
| George Wildes. | William Tothill. |
| John Woolley. | John Vining. |

Captain T. J. Chapman succeeded Tothill as Bristol Secretary.

## II

# *Construction*

## *1835–1838*

Immediately after the incorporation of the Great Western Railway Company, Brunel broached a subject to the Directors which was destined to have a momentous effect on its fortunes, and directly or indirectly on many other railways in England and elsewhere. This was the question of the most suitable width between the two rails, or, as it was called, the gauge of the railway.

The width of the old wooden tramways of the Northumberland collieries had originally been fixed by the distance between the wheels of the ordinary carts of the district, and when iron rails were adopted they were of course laid on the existing timbers. The space between the rails of these early railways varied slightly in the different collieries, but was generally somewhat less than five feet. At Killingworth, where George Stephenson was employed and where he made his first locomotive engine, the distance between the insides of the rails happened to be 4 feet 8 inches; so, when he was engaged to lay out the Stockton & Darlington Railway, he naturally adopted that gauge, especially as some of the waggons used in forming the earthworks came from a neighbouring tramway of the same width. Thus the first public railway was made with a gauge of 4 feet 8 inches, not from any deliberate choice or intrinsic advantage of this dimension, but merely because it chanced to be already established at some of the adjacent collieries. Perhaps it corresponded with an even five feet between the outer edges of the rails then in use.

The die was finally cast when Stephenson, apparently without any very deep consideration of the subject, adopted this same gauge for the infinitely more important Liverpool & Manchester Railway on the other side of England. An extra half-inch between the rails was added by some person unknown to fame about this time. His son Robert, asked by the Gauge Commissioners whether George Stephenson had proposed 4 feet 8½ inches for the Liverpool & Manchester, said: 'No. It was not proposed by my Father. It was the original gauge of the railways about Newcastle-on-Tyne, and *therefore* he adopted that gauge.' This explanation is far from satisfactory. There is no apparent reason why the gauge of these insignificant little private coal lines should decide or even influence that of an important public railway between two of the largest towns in England far away from Newcastle.

The Grand Junction Railway, from Warrington to Birmingham, necessarily adopted the gauge of the Liverpool & Manchester, which it joined, and this in its turn decided that of the London & Birmingham.

Thus the 4 feet 8½ inches gauge was established on the lines between Liverpool and Manchester and London, and as a necessary consequence on all the railways made or authorized to connect with any of them. It was also adopted for the London & Greenwich Railway, incorporated in 1833, and consequently for other lines south of London made later to connect therewith. In fact, it had already become the recognized gauge for all English railways, and was generally specified in the Acts of Parliament authorizing their construction.

Such was the state of the matter when Brunel was making his surveys for the Great Western line in 1833 and 1834. In the course of these, being endowed with a vivid imagination and distinctly original turn of mind, he became impressed with the great possibilities of the extraordinarily straight and level road he was laying out, and hence with the desirability of getting rid of the limitations imposed by rails less than five feet apart. In his own words to the Gauge Commissioners:

'Looking to the speeds which I contemplated would be adopted on railways and the masses to be moved, it seemed to me that the whole machine was too small for the work to be done, and that it required that the parts should be on a scale more commensurate with the mass and the velocity to be attained.

'I think the impression grew upon me gradually, so that it is difficult to fix the time when I first thought a wide gauge desirable; but I daresay there were stages between wishing that it could be so and determining to try and do it.'

Beyond discussing the subject casually with Saunders and one or two of the Directors, Brunel made no move till early in 1835, when he successfully persuaded Lord Shaftesbury, Chairman of Committees in the House of Lords, to allow the usual clause defining the gauge to be omitted from the Great Western Bill, on the ground that a wider gauge might be a great public advantage. As a precedent for the omission, he was able, curiously enough, to cite the London & Southampton Bill of the previous year, which had been passed without it, probably by an oversight. On the other hand, the Great Western Bill of 1834 is said[1] to have contained the clause, so that if that Bill had not been defeated, the wide gauge might never have been heard of.

Even at this time he had not definitely decided on the width to recommend, and it was not till after the passing of the Act that he first suggested seven feet in the following report:

53 PARLIAMENT STREET
15th September 1835

*To the Directors of the Great Western Railway Company.*

GENTLEMEN,

I beg to submit the following observations upon the subject of the width of the rails as explanatory of the grounds upon which I have recommended to you a deviation from the dimensions adopted in the railways hitherto constructed.

The leading feature which distinguishes railways from common roads is the great diminution of that resistance which arises from the friction at the axle trees, and more particularly from obstruction on the road; this latter is almost entirely removed in a well kept surface of a railway, and friction may be considered as the only constant resistance.

The effect of gravity when the load has to ascend any inclination is, of course, the same whatever the nature of the road, and depends only upon the rate of inclination.

---

[1] No copy of this Bill seems to have survived.

In the present state of railways and railway carriages the constant resistance, which we will call friction, amounts generally to about 1/250 or 9 lbs per ton, although under favourable circumstances it may be reduced to 1/280 or 8 lbs per ton. Assuming the latter as being the least favourable to the view which I purpose to take of the necessity of further improvement, I will apply this to the case of the Great Western Railway.

Upon the Great Western Railway from Bristol to Bath and from London to the Oxford branch, a total distance of about 70 miles, including those portions upon which two full thirds of the traffic will take place, there will be no inclination exceeding 4 feet per mile, which will cause a resistance of only 1 lb and seven tenths lbs per ton, calling it even two lbs, while the friction is taken at 8 lbs it appears that the latter will constitute 80 per cent. of the whole resistance. The importance of any improvement upon that which forms so large a proportion is obvious, but nevertheless, according to the present construction of railways, a limit has been put to this improvement, which limit is already reached, or at all events, great impediments are thrown in the way of any material diminution of the friction, and this serious evil is produced indirectly by the width of the railways.

The resistance from friction is diminished as the proportion of the diameter of the wheel to that of the axle-tree is increased; there are some causes which in practice slightly influence this result, but within the limits of increase which could be required we may consider that practically the resistance from friction will be diminished exactly in the same ratio that the diameter of the wheel is increased; we have here, therefore, the means of materially diminishing this resistance.

The wheels upon railways were originally much smaller than they are now. As the speed has been increased and economy in power become more important, the diameters have been progressively increased and are now nearly double the size they were but a few years ago—even upon the Liverpool and Manchester Railway I believe they have been increased nearly one-half, but by the present construction of the carriages they have reached their limit.

The width of the railway being only 4 feet 8 inches between the rails, or about 4 feet 6 inches between the wheels, the body of the carriage, or the platform upon which the luggage is placed, is, of necessity, extended over the tops of the wheels, and a space must also be left for the action of the springs; the carriage and load is raised unnecessarily high, while at the same time the size of the wheel is inconveniently limited.

If the centre of the gravity of the load could be lowered the motion would be more steady, and one of the causes of wear and tear both in rails and carriages would be diminished.

By simply widening the rails so that the body of the carriage might be kept entirely within the wheels the centre of gravity might be considerably lowered and at the same time the diameter of the wheels be unlimited.

I should propose 6 feet 10 inches to 7 feet as the width of the rails which would, I think, admit of sufficient width of carriages for all purposes. I am not by any means prepared at present to recommend any particular size of wheel or even any great increase of the present dimensions. I believe they will be materially increased, but my great object would be in every possible way to render each part capable of improvement, and to remove what appears to be an obstacle to any great progress in such a very important point as the diameter of the wheels, upon which the resistance, which governs the cost of transport and the speed that may be obtained, so materially depends.

The objections which may be urged against these alterations are:

(1) The increased widths required in the cuttings, embankments and tunnels and consequently the increased expenses;
(2) A greater amount of friction in the curves;
(3) The additional weight of the carriages;
(4) The inconvenience arising from the junction with the London and Birmingham Railway.

1st. As regards the increase of the earthwork, bridges and tunnels. This would not be so great as would at first sight appear; the increased width of each railway does not affect the width between the rails or on either side as the total widths of the bodies of the carriages remain the same, and as the slopes of the cuttings and embankments are the same, the total quantity would not necessarily be increased above one twelfth and the cost of the bridges and tunnels would be augmented about in the same ratio, and such addition has been provided for in the estimates.

2nd. The effect of the friction upon small curves. The necessary radius of curvature will be increased in the ratio of the widths between the wheels, viz., as 5 to 7, but the portions of the total length which is curved to such a degree as to render this effect sensible is so small (not being above 1½ miles upon the whole line except immediately at the entrance of the depots) that it is not worth considering when a great advantage is to be gained upon a total distance of 120 miles.

3rd. The additional weight of the Carriages. The axle-trees alone will be increased and these form but a small part of the Carriage. The frame will indeed be simplified and I believe this will fully counterbalance the increased lengths of the axle-trees. If the wheels are materially increased in diameter they must of course be stronger and consequently heavier, but this weight does not affect the friction at the axle-trees and not sensibly the resistance to traction, while their increased diameter affords the advantages which are sought for.

4th. The inconvenience in effecting the junction with the London and Birmingham Railway.

This I consider to be the only real obstacle to the adoption of the plan; one additional rail to each railway must be laid down. I do not foresee any great difficulty in doing this, but undoubtedly the London and Birmingham Railway Company may object to it, and in that case I see no remedy, the plan must be abandoned. It is therefore important that this point should be speedily determined.

I am, Gentlemen,
Your obedient servant,
I. K. Brunel.

The obstacle which Brunel feared might be fatal to the adoption of his plan was removed before the end of the year by the abandonment of the intended junction with the London & Birmingham Railway and the decision of the Great Western Board to seek an independent entry into London. According to the latter's statements, this was brought about, not, as has often been asserted, by the adoption of the wide gauge, but by the refusal of the London & Birmingham Directors to part for any reasonable and definite period with the land necessary for Great Western stations and depots at Camden and Euston. The official story of the negotiations is told at length in the Great Western Report to the First Half-yearly Meeting in February 1836. The Directors first stipulated for an absolute purchase or at least a building lease, and on these being refused went so far as to offer to accept a lease for twenty-one years. Even this was refused. All the Birmingham Board would do was to grant the land subject to resumption by them at any time on five years' notice; an offer 'which your Directors had no hesitation in declining, under the conviction that the permanency of the junction would be thereby defeated, entertaining also a confident belief that an excellent and independent terminus can be secured without much difficulty at latest in the next Session of Parliament'. This was in December 1835, just too late for the deposit of a Bill for the ensuing Session of 1836. On the other hand, Robert Stephenson, giving evidence before the Select Committee on Railways of 1839, said that if the same width of gauge had been adopted any other difficulties could have been arranged, and complained that his Company had been left with more land at Euston than they could use, bought to accommodate the Great Western. Saunders, on his part, told the same Committee that the causes were the conditions of tenure, the gauge, the danger of the junction, and the anticipated greater speed of the Great Western trains and difficulty of arranging their times; adding that 'the London and Birmingham were glad to get rid of us'.

After much consideration, Brunel's suggestion was accepted by a large majority of the Board, and the gauge of seven feet sanctioned on 29th October 1835. The fact soon became known, but was not officially published till August 1836, when their Report to the Half-yearly Meeting at Bristol, after alluding to the very favourable gradients of the now finally set out line 'unequalled upon any Railway of great extent now in progress' and the higher speeds that might consequently be obtained, proceeded:

Under these peculiar circumstances and with a view to obtaining the full advantage of the regularity and of the reduction of power effected by this near approach to a level, and also to remedy several serious inconveniences experienced in existing Railways, an increased width of Rails has been recommended by your Engineer, and after mature consideration has been determined upon by the Directors.

Difficulties and objections were at first supposed by some persons to exist in the construction of Engines for this increased width of Rails, but the Directors have pleasure in stating that several of the most experienced and eminent manufacturers of Locomotive Engines in the North, have undertaken to construct them—and that several Engines are now actually contracted for, adapted to the peculiar dimensions and levels of this Railway calculated for a minimum velocity of 30 miles per hour.

These Engines will be capable of attaining a rate of 35 to 40 miles per hour with the same facility as the speed of 25 to 30 miles is gained by those now constructed for other lines.

Acts authorizing several deviations of the original line were obtained without opposition in 1836 and 1837, whereby among other things two long tunnels in Berkshire, one of five-eighths of a mile under Holme Park in the parish of Sonning and the other of one mile at Purley, were avoided; an open cutting, the deepest on the line, a little further south, being substituted for the former with the consent of the landowner, Mr Palmer, M.P. for Berkshire, who had been an active and influential opponent of the railway.

Another Act of the latter year sanctioned the extension of the line from Acton to 'a certain space of ground adjoining the Basin of the Paddington Canal in the Parish of Paddington'.

Very soon after the breaking off of the negotiations with the London & Birmingham Company the Directors had decided on this extension, and in August 1836 were able to announce to the Proprietors that they had secured the general consent of the owners and occupiers to a line into Paddington, and ample space for the station there. The length of the new line from Acton would be about $4\frac{1}{2}$ miles, but allowing for the abandoned piece to the junction at Kensal Green, there would be only an additional $2\frac{1}{2}$ miles to construct. In order that the opening of the railway to Maidenhead, promised by Brunel for October 1837, might not be delayed, work was at once begun on the lands of the consenting owners without waiting for Parliamentary sanction, but of course no public roads could be interfered with. One result of the impossibility of getting the Act in 1836 was that the Birmingham, Bristol & Thames Junction, known later as the West London Railway Company, was authorized in that year to make a railway from the London & Birmingham near Willesden to the Kensington Canal, cutting right across the line of the intended Great Western

Isambard Kingdom Brunel, Engineer 1833–1859, by J. C. Horsley, A.R.A.

Front of original station, Paddington, with goods shed and sidings in foreground

Interior of Paddington Station about 1855, looking West

extension on the same level. However, that little Company was afterwards induced to surrender its prior rights and agree that the Great Western trains should have precedence over the crossing.

To complete the Parliamentary story of this early period, it must be noted that the Bristol & Exeter and Cheltenham & Great Western Union Companies obtained their Acts in 1836, the latter for a railway joining the Great Western at Swindon. This had been opposed by the London & Birmingham Company, who unsuccessfully promoted the rival line from Tring by Oxford to Cheltenham, which had come to nothing in the hands of independent parties in 1835. This was the first move in the hostilities which afterwards ensued between the two Companies, and was of course regarded by the Great Western as a wanton attack on their natural territory.

### CONSTRUCTION OF THE LINE

No time was lost after the safe passage of the Act in beginning work simultaneously at both ends of the line. On 3rd September 1835 Brunel writes to Osborne and Ward, the Bristol lawyers, and to Townsend, the surveyor, that he had been instructed to set out the line between Bristol and Bath, and London and Reading, and asking them to take immediate steps to get the thick underwood in Brislington cut, so that he may be able on his arrival next week to determine definitely the exact course of the line and fix the points for the shafts to ascertain the nature of the soil through which the tunnels were to go. He adds, 'We shall have our flags flying over the Brent Valley to-morrow. I should not wish that Bristol should fancy itself left behind. I shall be down on Tuesday or Wednesday.'

He had already got together a staff of assistants, and of these the chief, J. W. Hammond, was installed Resident Engineer at the London end, while G. E. Frere was despatched to take charge at Bristol. Little seems to have been left to them; Brunel himself, besides acting as Chief Engineer, was constantly dashing to and fro, keeping in close touch with every detail of the work and at once observing any faulty construction or bad workmanship on the part of contractors. In these early days and during the whole construction period the two Committees of the Board acted quite independently of each other in letting contracts and most other matters, the Bristol Committee being distinguished by its more lavish outlay on station buildings, architectural adornments and ornamental work generally. Evidence of this is noticeable at the present day, and early in 1839 we find the London members of the Board protesting against the unnecessary expenditure.

In view of this independence and the fact of the works going on simultaneously, it is convenient to take the sections of the line in the order in which they were eventually opened.

## London to Maidenhead

The first contract to be let was that for the viaduct across the Brent Valley, where, as we have seen, Brunel began operations. This was taken in November 1835 by Messrs Grissell & Peto, who began work in the following February. The viaduct is of brick with stone capitals, 300 yards long and 65 feet high, with eight arches of 70 feet span, each pier being composed of two slightly conical pillars. It was much the most important work between London and the Thames at Maidenhead, and was finished in the summer of 1837, when 'in acknowledgement of the zealous and indefatigable attention of Lord Wharncliffe, as Chairman of the Committee on the Act of Incorporation in the House of Lords, it was, by his Lordship's permission, named the Wharncliffe Viaduct',[1] and his coat of arms was carved on the centre of the south face. The viaduct is approached by high embankments, both of which gave much trouble for some time by continually slipping.

About a quarter of a mile west the line crosses the main Uxbridge Road and a by-road from Greenford towards Brentford at the point where they intersect. For this awkward situation Brunel designed a skew bridge of cast-iron girders, supported intermediately by two rows of eight pillars each between the main carriage road and its footpaths, the four in the middle adjoining the by-road being cast iron and the remainder brick. Apart from its peculiar design, this bridge is remarkable for the trouble it caused. Originally the spaces between the main and cross girders were filled by flat arches of brickwork but, one of the main girders having given way in March 1839, these were removed and a floor of six-inch planks substituted to lighten the weight. The timbers carrying the rails rested on the tops of the girders, and an upper floor, also of wood, covered the spaces between them. One day in May 1847 all this wood caught fire, probably from a piece of burning coke dropped by a passing engine, and burned fiercely, with the result that nearly every girder in the structure was broken by the heat. After being temporarily shored up from the road for some little time, the bridge was renewed with wrought iron. Two years later Brunel wrote to one of the Directors:

Cast-iron girder bridges are always giving trouble—from such cases as the Chester Bridge,[2] and our Great Western road bridge at Hanwell, which since 1838 has always been under repair and has cost its first cost three times over, down to petty little ones, which either in frosty weather or from other causes are frequently failing. I never use cast iron if I can help it, but in some cases it is necessary and to meet these I have had girders cast of a particular mixture of iron carefully attended to, and I have taught them at the Bridgewater foundry to cast them with the flange downwards instead of sideways.[3]

There were no other works of special interest on the 18 miles between Acton and the temporary terminus at Maidenhead or, strictly speaking, Taplow; it was on the Bucks side of the River.

[1] Directors' Report of August 1837.
[2] See Chapter VIII.
[3] Brunel's *Life*, page 190.

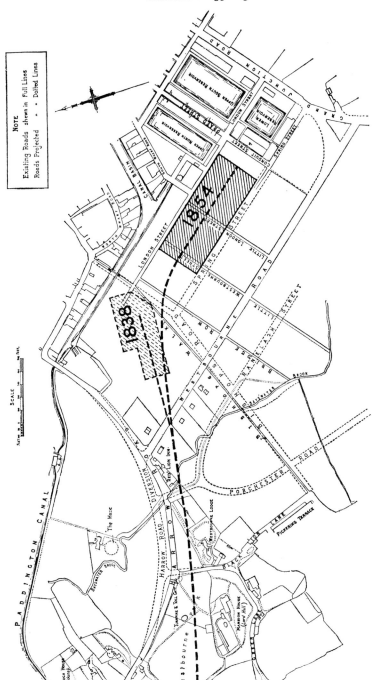

ENVIRONS OF PADDINGTON 1837
(showing centre line of Railway and Sites of Passenger Stations)

On the Extension Line from Acton to Paddington, most of the $4\frac{1}{2}$ miles consisted of clay cuttings. Wherever owners and occupiers were complaisant the works were begun in the autumn of 1836; elsewhere, and especially near Paddington where roads had to be altered, nothing could be done till the Act was at last obtained on 3rd July 1837. This provided for the northward diversion of the Harrow Road near the Westbourne Turnpike Gate, and the making of sundry bridges, including a wide road bridge in place of the existing footbridge over the Paddington Canal close to the intended depot of the railway and over the railway itself from the Harrow Road to Spring Street (now Eastbourne Terrace), whence a new road was to be made by the Company, in lieu of the footpath known as Bishop's Walk, to Black Lion Lane (Queen's Road and Porchester Road). Needless to say, this new road is the Bishop's Road of to-day.

A large quantity of land on both sides of the new bridge was acquired from the Bishop of London for the depot, Brunel's original intention being to make the passenger station where it is now, and to use the land north-west of the bridge for the goods depot and engine shed. The force of circumstances, however, compelled him at first to reverse their positions. There was no time after the passing of the Act to build the permanent passenger station without considerably delaying the opening of the line, so, to avoid occupying the site, the space west of the bridge intended for the goods depot was taken for a temporary passenger station, and later on, when the Company began to carry goods traffic, a wooden goods shed was set up east of the bridge in the corner between it and Eastbourne Terrace, or Spring Street as it was then. These temporary arrangements were destined to last for sixteen years.

Bishop's Road Bridge itself formed the front of the passenger station, some of its arches being used as booking hall, waiting rooms, and offices, and others for carriage entrance and exit roads. It was reached only by an approach road from London Street. The rest of the station was constructed almost entirely of timber, the platforms being roofed over. No plan of its original state has survived; that on page 25 shows the station as it was in 1845, by which time several additions and alterations had been made. For instance, the two arrival platforms on the north side had been added before 1840.

Westward of the station the course of the railway lay through open country. Westbourne Road had been laid out and some houses built, but beyond this there were only a few scattered cottages and one or two fair-sized residences with large grounds. One of these, Westbourne Place, immediately west of Black Lion Lane, was occupied by Lord Hill, Commander-in-Chief of the British Army, whose name is perpetuated in 'Lord Hill's Bridge' over the railway at Royal Oak. Opposite to it, east of the Lane, stood Westbourne Lodge, which the Company were obliged to buy, and which was for many years Charles Saunders' official residence.

By the end of August 1837 the works on several of the contracts between London and Maidenhead had been practically finished, and the Directors

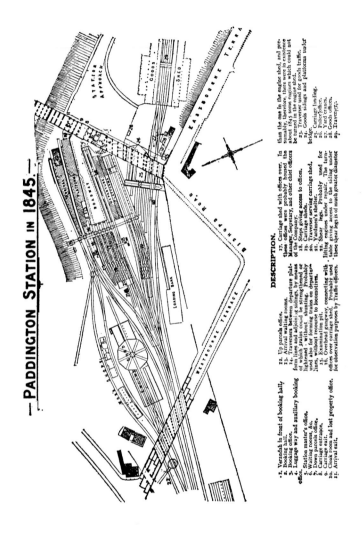

— PADDINGTON STATION IN 1845. —

## DESCRIPTION.

1. Verandah in front of booking hall.
2. Booking hall.
3. Booking office.
4. Luggage way and auxiliary booking office.
5. Station master's office, &c.
6. Waiting rooms.
7. Down parcels office.
8. Carriage entrance.
9. Carriage exit.
10. Cloak room and lost property office.
11. Arrival rail.
12. Up parcels office.
13. Arrival waiting rooms.
14. Traversers between departure platform lines and adjoining sidings, by means of which trains could be strengthened or lightened without shunting. Probably used also for forming trains on departure lines, without recourse to locomotives.
15. Examination pit.
16. Overhead gangway, connecting with offices over carriage shed. Probably used for observation purposes by Traffic officers.
17. Carriage shed with offices over. In these offices were probably housed the Manager, Secretary, and other chief officers of the Company.
18. Steps giving access to offices.
19. Carriage sheds.
20. Traverser serving carriage shed.
21. Yardman's shelter.
22. Shear legs. Probably used for lifting engines under repair. The turn-table giving access to the siding under these shear legs is of much greater diameter than the one in the engine shed, and presumably, therefore, there were in existence about 1845 some engines which could not be turned in the engine shed.
23. Traverser used for goods traffic.
24. Goods sidings and platforms under bridge.
25. Carriage landing.
26. Police office.
27. Yard cranes.
28. Goods offices.
29. Traverser.

announced that all would be completed early in October, but that the laying of the permanent way would probably postpone the opening until November.

For the formation of the permanent way Brunel of course had ideas of his own. He had no great opinion of the stone blocks and iron chairs adopted by Stephenson for supporting the rails at intervals, and as early as January 1836 had recommended the use of light rails on continuous bearings of timber. A year later he furnished a comparative estimate of the cost of the two methods of 65 lb rails on blocks and chairs and 40 lb rails on longitudinal timbers, admitting the additional expense of the latter to be about £500 a mile, but stating his confidence 'that the excess will be amply repaid, in the few first years of working, in the diminution of the mere cost of repair and maintenance of the way; while the gain in economy, facility and perfection of transport would be cheaply purchased at double the cost'.

The construction actually adopted is thus described by Nicholas Wood:[1]

Longitudinal timbers of a scantling of from 5 to 7 inches in depth and 12 to 14 inches in breadth, and about 30 feet long are placed along the whole line. Then these timbers are bolted to cross sleepers or transoms at intervals of every 15 feet; double transoms each 6 inches broad and 9 deep being placed at the joinings of each of the longitudinal timbers, and single transoms of the same scantling being placed midway between the joinings. These transoms stretch across, and are bolted to all the four lines of rails.[2] Within the two lines of rails of each track piles of beech are driven from the upper surface of the Railway into the solid ground, so as to retain a firm hold thereof, and the transoms are bolted to the heads of the piles.

There was of course nothing new in the longitudinal timbers to carry the rails. As Brunel said in more than one of his reports, this was the oldest form of railway in England. The novel feature was the piles, which were intended not to support the timbers, but to hold them down. Brunel's reasons for adopting them are given at length in his report of January 1838, and more concisely by Wood:

The principle of construction is this; the longitudinal timbers and transoms being firmly held down by the piles, gravel or sand is beat or packed underneath the longitudinal timbers for the purpose of obtaining a considerable vertical strain upon the timbers upwards, and consequently to effect a corresponding firmness of foundation of packing underneath them. Without piles, the longitudinal timbers could not be packed in this manner, as there would be nothing to resist the pressure of the packing except their own weight, and the piles were therefore introduced to hold down the timbers and to render it practicable to introduce a force of packing underneath.

The whole structure therefore formed a timber frame, pegged down to the ground by the piles, some 20 feet wide, made up of the two tracks of 7 feet[3] each and an intervening space of 6 feet. As the uniform width of the railway was 30 feet throughout, barely 5 feet were left outside each track. The rails were specially designed by Brunel, and from the shape of their section became known as 'bridge rails'. They weighed 43 lbs to the

---

[1] Report to Great Western Directors, 10th December 1838.
[2] This means the timbers which carried the rails.
[3] In laying the rails an extra quarter of an inch was allowed on the straight, making the gauge 7 feet 0¼ inches strictly speaking, but it was always referred to as 7 feet.

yard. To prevent their cutting into the timbers under the weight of the trains and also to cant them slightly inwards, a thin wedge-shaped layer of hard wood was interposed. All the timber was previously 'kyanized'. This was a process, then recently invented by a Dr Kyan, for preserving wood by saturating it with a solution of corrosive sublimate, otherwise bichloride of mercury, in wooden tanks. It was superseded by creosote about 1840.

Section of 43 lb.
Bridge Rail

The Directors' expectation of opening the line in November was far from being realized, for causes stated in their February Report as: (1) defective and leaky tanks for kyanizing such timber as had been delivered; (2) several months' delay in delivery of timber and rails—only half the quantity of timber contracted to be delivered in the summer had arrived by November, and much of the rails not till February; (3) the embarrassment caused by large quantities of timber arriving all at once; (4) the novel method of laying the permanent way requiring much care and supervision; and (5) the severe and prolonged frost, which 'paralyzed the exertions of the Engineer'. They do not mention the fact that the bridges and other works on the Extension Line to Paddington were very far from being finished, contenting themselves with saying that the 'Works at Paddington are going on with spirit'. Having learnt caution, they now only quote the Engineer as considering that the work will be completed and the traffic commenced in the course of May.

Meantime, the first Chairman of the Company, Benjamin Shaw, a shadowy figure of whom little more than his name is recorded, resigned in October 1837, and the Chair was offered to George Henry Gibbs, already mentioned as the leading London promoter of the railway. After taking advice of his Bristol relatives, Gibbs, 'not without regret, though it relieved my mind from rather a heavy burthen', declined the honour, and afterwards proposed his colleague on the London Committee, William Unwin Sims, another shadowy figure to-day, who took the Chair on 26th October.

Two Directors, Roch and Wildes, had already retired and been succeeded on the Bristol and London Committees respectively by Frederick Ricketts, first Chairman of the Bristol & Exeter Railway Company, and Charles Russell, M.P. for Reading, who, as Chairman of the Commons Committee on the Bill of 1835, had done much to help the birth of the Great Western, and was destined to do more in guiding its growth and development.

Another name destined to loom large in Great Western annals makes its first appearance about this time. An officer to take charge of the Locomotive Department under the Engineer being required, Brunel was authorized at the end of July to secure the services as 'Superintendent of Locomotive Engines' of a youth not yet twenty-one, whom he recommended, named Daniel Gooch. Happening to go north immediately after this to see to the progress of the engines then building at Liverpool and

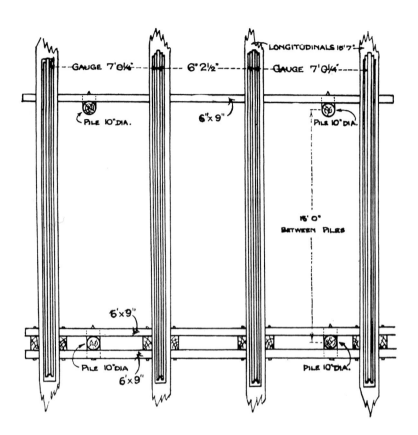

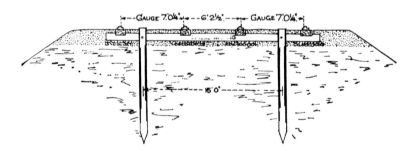

ORIGINAL PERMANENT WAY, 1838

Warrington, Brunel interviewed young Gooch at Manchester, where he was assisting an elder brother employed on the Manchester & Leeds Railway, and straightway engaged him. Gooch, of whom more will be said in another chapter, entered the Great Western service on 18th August 1837 and, there being as yet no engines for him to superintend, began work by preparing plans for the engine houses at Paddington and Maidenhead.

Early in November the first two engines were delivered by canal at West Drayton. They had come by sea from Liverpool to London Docks, one named *Premier* from Mather, Dixon & Co. of Liverpool, the other, *Vulcan*, from the Vulcan Foundry at Warrington. Like all the early engines made to Brunel's order, they were remarkable for very large wheels and very small boilers and cylinders. At first there was no road ready for them to run upon, but by Christmas a mile and a half between Drayton and Langley had been finished, and *Vulcan* made a trial trip on 28th December, so becoming the first engine to run on the Great Western Railway. Stephenson's famous *North Star* was delivered by barge on the Thames at Maidenhead at the end of November, but there she had to stay for lack of rails till May 1838.

The first official trial of the two engines in the presence of some of the Directors was made on 9th January. G. H. Gibbs, whose Diary[1] is a mine of information on Great Western affairs between 1836 and 1840, gives the following account of it:

Went down the line to West Drayton. Ealing Station is in a very unfinished state. The Hanwell embankment is not completed on either side, and none of the lines ballasted nor any piles driven; but I did not see anything to induce me to believe that everything might not be completed by the end of March. At West Drayton we were much pleased to find that the two engines were about to be tried. After walking with Brunel as far as the Chequers Bridge admiring the rails exceedingly, we returned to the Engine House. The Engines, after some delay in getting up steam, sallied forth, but the curve in the turn-out proving too sharp for them they got off the rail two or three times, and it was an hour before they could be got on the main line. When there, however, they performed beautifully and we had a very interesting drive.

After this, frequent trial trips were made by these and other engines at West Drayton, which was made the locomotive headquarters for the time being, an engine house, coke ovens,[2] and water supply being established there, as well as the office of the new Superintendent.

Progress with the laying of the permanent way was slow; according to Gibbs, only $5\frac{2}{3}$ miles of rails had been laid by 12th April.

In his reminiscences of this period,[3] Gooch states that *North Star* was first in steam on 15th January 1838, but says nothing of any trial trip. Gibbs wrote on 1st May:

Went to-day to Maidenhead and found two engines out *for the first time* with steam up. Brunel and his wife and Saunders were there and the trial went off exceedingly well. I

[1] Published in the Great Western Railway Magazine, 1909–10, and reprinted as a pamphlet.
[2] These ovens were superseded by those at Bristol soon after the opening of the whole line, and were eventually abolished as being useless and dilapidated early in 1850.
[3] *Diaries of Sir Daniel Gooch*, (Kegan Paul, 1892). As regards the period before 1865 this title is a misnomer; 'Reminiscences' would be more accurate.

rode on the '*North Star*', and found it very trying as I was not well, but the motion was very agreeable.

Soon he had a more exciting trip on *Thunderer*, that extraordinary locomotive freak with engine and boiler on separate carriages.

May 12th. Hammond came for me to Salt Hill[1] with Harrison's engine, and I went backward and forward on it twice. In some places we had the knocks which we had observed before at Drayton, but this we were told occurred only where the screws were not completely screwed down. Along the greatest part of the 4 miles the engine ran beautifully smooth and for some way we cleared 60 miles an hour.

Ten days later the Directors were able to travel on the railway from Bull's Bridge (Hayes), which even then was the chief depot for receiving from the canal and kyanizing the timber, over the eleven miles thence to Maidenhead Station. The latter was a wooden erection west of the Bath Road Bridge at Taplow, and about a quarter of a mile short of the river bridge, 22 miles 43 chains from the temporary terminus at Paddington. All traces of it have long since been swept away.

At last the line was ready. Again to quote Gibbs' Diary:

May 31st. This being the day appointed for the opening of our Railway, the Directors and the Company invited met at the Depot before 11. A very pretty sight it was. At 11.30 we entered the carriages of the first train, and proceeding at a moderate pace reached Maidenhead Station in 49 minutes, or at about 28 miles an hour. After visiting the works we returned to Salt Hill, where a cold luncheon for about 300 people was laid under a tent. After the usual complement of toasts we returned to the line and reached Paddington (19 miles) in 34 minutes, or 33½ miles an hour.

The engine employed on this first train was *North Star*, the only one of the ten at Gooch's disposal on which he could really rely. A Bristol Director, T. R. Guppy, distinguished himself by walking along the tops of the carriages from one end of the train to the other while it was going at full speed,[2] doubtless on the return journey after luncheon.

The public opening was fixed for the following Monday, 4th June 1838, and advertized in the London and Bristol papers.

Brunel's former chief clerk at 18 Duke Street, Westminster, a young man named Seymour Clarke, had been appointed Traffic Superintendent.

The stations at Ealing and Hanwell were not yet ready for use. They were opened in December, and another at Southall on 1st May 1839.[3]

It will be noticed that passengers were to be conveyed to and from Slough, though no station might be made there. The Directors had promised this in their Report of August 1837.

An enactment in the Bill precludes the Directors from constructing any Station or Depot within 3 miles of Eton College without the consent of the Provost and Fellows of that Establishment, which it is feared will deprive the Public of that accommodation to which they would otherwise be justly entitled at the hands of the Company.

The trains will of course convey any Passengers who may be desirous of travelling to and from the neighbourhood of Slough, and the Directors can only regret that they are not at liberty to provide the ordinary conveniences of a Station for Persons waiting there to be received on the Railway.

[1] Half a mile west of Slough.
[2] *The Times*, 2nd June 1838.
[3] Additional stations were opened as follows: Langley 1845, Hayes 1864, Acton 1868, Castle Hill (renamed West Ealing in 1899) and Westbourne Park 1871, a new Taplow (¼ mile east of the old 'Maidenhead', which was then abolished) 1872, Burnham Beeches 1899, and lastly Iver at the end of 1924.

GREAT WESTERN RAILWAY.—The public are informed that this RAILWAY will be OPENED for the CONVEYANCE of PASSENGERS only between London, West Drayton, Slough, and Maidenhead station, on Monday, the 4th June. The following will be the times for the departure of trains each way, from London and from Maidenhead, (excepting on Sundays,) until further notice :—

### Trains each way.

8 o'clock morning ; 4 o'clock afternoon.
9 o'clock ditto 5 o'clock ditto
10 o'clock ditto 6 o'clock ditto
12 o'clock noon 7 o'clock ditto

### Trains on Sundays each way.

7 o'clock morning ; 5 o'clock afternoon.
8 o'clock ditto 6 o'clock ditto
9 o'clock ditto 7 o clock ditto

Each train will take up or set down passengers at West Drayton and Slough.

### Fares of Passengers.

| | | First Class. | | Second Class. | |
| --- | --- | --- | --- | --- | --- |
| | | Posting Carriage. | Passenger Coach. | Coach. | Open Carriage. |
| | | s. d. | s. d. | s. d. | s. d. |
| Paddington Station { | to West Drayton | 4 0 | 3 6 | 2 0 | 1 6 |
| | to Slough........ | 5 6 | 4 6 | 3 0 | 2 6 |
| | to Maidenhead .. | 6 6 | 5 6 | 4 0 | 3 6 |

Notice is also given that on and after Monday, the 11th June, carriages and horses will be conveyed on the railway, and passengers and parcels booked for conveyance by coaches in connexion with the Railway Company to the west of England, including Stroud, Cheltenham, and Glocester, as well as to Oxford, Newbury, Reading, Henley, Marlow, Windsor, Uxbridge, and other contiguous places. By order of the Directors,
CHARLES A. SAUNDERS, } Secs.
THOMAS OSLER,

*From* The Times, 2nd June 1838.

*Note.*—The conveyance of Carriages was afterwards postponed to 4th August, and of Horses till the following month.

No sooner had the Company's intentions been advertized than the said Provost and Fellows, furious at this insidious attack on the morals of their school, applied to the Court of Chancery for an immediate injunction to stop such an evasion of the spirit of the Act. On 1st June their application was dismissed with costs. Of course they appealed, but the Lord Chancellor decided that the Directors were quite within their rights in stopping the trains, and were not even guilty of a breach of faith, as had been suggested, because they had made no agreement whatever with the College authorities; they had opposed the clause throughout; it was forced on them, and therefore they were clearly entitled to do anything not expressly forbidden by it.

The Eton masters were not long in recognizing the advantages of the railway, for, strange to say, within a month of their defeat and while the appeal was pending, they requested the Company to provide a special train to take the boys up to town for the Coronation on 28th June! It was duly provided.

Towards the end of the next year the Provost and Fellows gave way to the clamour of their neighbours—whether any Royal pressure was exercised we know not—and consented to the erection of a station and to the repeal of the forbidding clauses. A station was accordingly opened at Slough in June 1840. It consisted of two separate buildings, some distance apart, for Down and Up traffic respectively, both on the south side of the railway as at Reading, the Up station being the eastern of the two. In the meantime passengers were booked, first at the Crown Inn till September 1838, and afterwards at 'the New House in Stoke Lane'.

The opening for passenger traffic took place as advertized on Monday, 4th June. Gibbs recorded the event thus:

Our Railway opened to the public this morning. I went to Maidenhead by the first train and came back by the third, which started from Maidenhead at 10.15. I was disappointed with regard to the speed, as we were 1 hour and 20 minutes going down and 1 hour and 5 minutes coming up. If from the 65 minutes we deduct 4 lost at Drayton, 3 at Slough, and 4 between the two places in slackening and getting up the speed, there remain 54 minutes for 23 miles or 25½ miles an hour. We carried altogether to-day 1,479 people and took £226.

The opening was indeed far from auspicious; the road was very rough, the jolting of the carriages excessive, and the engines generally unreliable. By the end of the first week, during which 10,360 passengers were carried and £1,552 taken, it had become evident that Brunel's elaborate and expensive permanent way was anything but a success, though some of the trouble was attributed to faulty springs of the carriages.

All sorts of exaggerated reports were soon spread broadcast, and the shareholders naturally became excited and anxious. A considerable number, especially in Liverpool and the north, had from the first been opposed to Brunel and his wide gauge, and had only with difficulty been kept quiet by the Directors. They now became very demonstrative and troublesome.

At this stage we cannot do better than quote some extracts from Gibbs' Diary. As will be seen, he was Brunel's chief supporter during all this anxious time.

June 20th. Our position is this—at our opening there has been some little disappointment as to our speed and the smoothness of our line, and there is some difficulty in ascertaining how much of this defect is to be traced to the line and how much to the carriages. In the meantime shares have fallen to 16[1] and reports of all kinds have been set afoot by the advocates of the old system and by many interested parties to depreciate the whole concern. Brunel's character and reputation therefore, as well as our own peace and comfort, demand out best attention at this moment to the repacking of the line, the changes which have been suggested in the springs, etc.

June 21st. The most ridiculous reports were in circulation to-day about the bridge[2] and we were so pestered with inquiries that it became necessary to prepare some sort of

[1] 16 premium; they had been at 30 not long before the opening.
[2] Maidenhead River Bridge in course of construction.

report to tranquilize the shareholders. I went with Casson[1] and Sims to Paddington for that purpose and stayed there till 10 at night. Our difficulties were increased by the facts that the road is evidently deteriorating under the pressure of the trains, that the engines are getting out of order from too much use, and that our carriages are far from easy. Brunel acknowledged that the road was decidedly in a very bad state, arising as he believed from two causes—from his having ballasted with fine gravel instead of coarse and from his not having ballasted deep enough. It was agreed that two experiments should be tried, of half a mile each, one of relaying the ballasting with coarse gravel 18 in. deep well rammed, the other of releasing the timbers from the piles and relaying as above. Alterations were made in the trains to give rest to the engines and to allow of the above experiments being made. Alterations were also ordered in the carriages.

The tranquillizing report was issued at once in the form of a circular to shareholders signed by the Chairman. While admitting 'an uneasy movement' of the carriages, it alleges that this is confined to certain parts of the line, and is due to want of hard packing under the timbers. Wherever engines had been able to run previous to the opening, 'the rails answer all the expectations which could reasonably be entertained', but 'in other places and principally between Southall and London where no engines could run, from the Line only being completed just in time for the opening, the defective packing could not be discovered until the pressure of the trains manifested it. A very uneasy movement in some of the carriages has given rise to a rumour that the plan has totally failed, and the rails must be altered. The Directors entertain no such opinion. They are convinced that, as far as the rails are concerned, the remedy can and will be easily administered by a thorough repacking under the timbers with coarse gravel, which is now in progress, and with a favourable result.'

The circular goes on to attribute the chief cause of the 'roughness' to the springs of some of the carriages and the position of the axles under the bodies, all of which were being altered.

The Liverpool Proprietors, far from being tranquillized by this story, demanded a special meeting, whereupon the Directors offered instead to adjourn the ordinary half-yearly meeting in August to give time for consideration of their Report—in those days the Shareholders knew nothing of the reports till they were read to them at the meetings—and this was assented to.

July 13th. Went after dinner to the depot and saw Casson and Saunders there. The latter said he had not dined or breakfasted at home since our opening. He showed me a letter he had just received from Brunel expressed in a cool and very proper way, but showing great feeling with regard to the loss of confidence which he believes he has seen on the part of the Directors and even of Saunders. Poor fellow, I pity him exceedingly, and I know not how he will get through the storm which awaits him. With all his talent he has shown himself deficient, I confess, in general arrangement. There have been too many mistakes; too much of doing and undoing. The draining, I fear, is imperfect, and the carriages made under his direction have not worked well; but I cannot help asking myself whether it is fair to decide on a work of this kind within a few weeks of its opening; and is not the present outcry created in a great measure by Brunel's enemies. I hear that at the meeting Brunel's dismissal is to be moved. Now the strong bias of my mind is that our only chance of comfort and safety is that our line should be carried out by Brunel with

[1] J. L. Casson, an active Director who succeeded W. Tite in February 1838. Tite, afterwards Sir William, disapproved of Brunel and later promoted narrow-gauge lines in the West of England.

efficient assistance and on a more stringent system of control, unless Stephenson will join him on the principle of abandoning his granite blocks and following out Brunel's wide gauge. It can only be done by Brunel himself, and, even if Stephenson would join him, I doubt much if they would work well together.

A few days later Brunel himself suggested that two or three other engineers should be called in to survey the line and report on the permanent way. Casson proposed at the Board that Robert Stephenson should be associated with Brunel 'on a system of mutual concession', but Gibbs, Russell, Sims the Chairman, and two other Directors were for retaining Brunel, who offered to resign, and this was rejected. The same evening Gibbs, Casson, and Saunders went to inspect the London & Birmingham Railway,[1] on which a limited service throughout had started on 24th June.

July 17th. Went last night with Casson and Saunders to Denbigh Hall[1] by the Birmingham Railway in a first-class carriage to see and try the line, and having slept at Stony Stratford, we returned this morning in an open carriage. We were 2 hours going, stopping twice, being at the rate of $23\frac{1}{2}$ miles an hour, and $2\frac{1}{2}$ hours in returning, being at the rate of 18 miles an hour. The carriages and engines are much lighter than ours. The engines make much less noise and the general noise is less, but the wheels on the rails make more. The bumps or jolts at the joints are very frequent indeed, and are in some places very uncomfortable, and the joints show plainly the effect of the heavy blows they receive. The serpentine or lateral motion, of which we have none on our railway, is very striking; but, on the other hand, they have no pitching or see-saw motion whatever, produced with us by the yielding of the timber between the piles. The road is under repair in many places, 440 people being employed on it, and they have still an immense expense to incur in replacing the temporary transverse wooden sleepers on the embankments by stone blocks.

Gibbs was evidently much relieved at finding Stephenson's road very little, if at all, better than Brunel's. For the next month he and the other Directors were engaged in making arrangements to combat the opposition of 'the Liverpool people' at the coming Half-yearly Meeting.

---

[1] A mile north of Bletchley, and about 47 miles from Euston.

# III

# *The Fight for the Broad Gauge*

## *1838*

Towards the end of July the Directors decided to adopt Brunel's own suggestion and call in other engineers to inspect and report to them on the permanent way, the gauge, and generally on the novel system which had been adopted, including the construction and efficiency of the engines. Three of the most eminent authorities on railway construction of the time, James Walker, President of the Institution of Civil Engineers, Robert Stephenson, and Nicholas Wood were accordingly asked to undertake the task. Walker and Stephenson both declined, the former 'under the impression that the question would be controversially conducted', the latter 'on the ground that his opinions were known to be somewhat unfavourable to the methods adopted in construction of the permanent road, and that he did not wish to be engaged in a professional discussion upon them'. Wood alone accepted the invitation, but was unable to begin his inspection till September.

Meantime, Brunel was directed to report fully on all the matters at issue in time for the Half-yearly Meeting on 15th August. So much of his report as relates to the 7 foot gauge is as follows. His position had been somewhat strengthened by the decision of a Royal Commission in favour of 6 feet 2 inches as the standard gauge for all railways in Ireland.

The peculiarity of the circumstances of this railway, to which I would more particularly refer, and which have frequently been mentioned, consist in the unusually favourable gradients and curves, which we have been able to obtain. With the capability of carrying the line upwards of 50 miles out of London on almost a dead level, and without any objectionable curve, and having beyond this, and for the whole distance to Bristol, excellent gradients, it was thought that unusually high speed might easily be attained, and that the very large extent of passenger traffic which such a line would certainly command, would ensure a return for any advantages which could be offered to the public, either in increased speed or increased accommodations. With this view every possible attention was paid to the improvement of the line as originally laid down in the parliamentary plans; and after much labour bestowed in the setting out the line, we ultimately succeeded in determining a maximum gradient of 4 feet per mile, which could be maintained for the unusual distance before mentioned of upwards of 50 miles from London and also between Bristol and Bath, comprehending those parts of the line on which the principal portion of the passenger traffic will be carried. The attainment of high speed appeared to involve the question of the width of gauge, and on this point accordingly I expressed my opinion at a very early date.

It has been asserted that 4 feet 8 inches, the width adopted on the Liverpool and Manchester railway, is exactly the proper width for all railways, and that to adopt any other dimension is to deviate from a positive rule which experience has proved correct; but such an assertion can be maintained by no reasoning. Admitting, for the sake of argument, that under the particular circumstances in which it has been tried, 4 feet 8 inches has been proved the best possible dimension, the question would still remain— What are the best dimensions under the circumstances?

Although a breadth of 4 feet 8 inches has been found to create a certain resistance on curves of a certain radius, a greater breadth would produce only the same resistance on curves of greater radius.

If carriages and engines, and more particularly if wheels and axles of a certain weight, have not been found inconvenient upon one railway, greater weights may be employed, and the same results obtained on a railway with better gradients.

To adopt a gauge of the same number of inches on the Great Western as on the Grand Junction railway would, in fact, amount practically to the use of a different gauge in similar railways. The gauge which is well adapted to the one, is not well adapted to the other, unless, indeed, some mysterious cause exists which has never yet been explained for the empirical law which would fix the gauge under all circumstances.

Fortunately, this no longer requires to be argued, as too many authorities may now be quoted in support of a very considerable deviation from this prescribed width, and in every case this change has been an increase.

I take it for granted that in determining the dimensions in each case due regard has been had to the curves and gradients of the line, which ought to form a most essential, if not the principal, condition. In the report of the commissioners upon Irish railways, the arguments are identically the same with those which I used when first addressing you on the subject in my report of October 1835.[1]

The mechanical advantage to be gained by increasing the diameter of the carriage wheels, is pointed out, the necessity to attain this, of increasing the width of way; the dimensions of the bridges, tunnels, and other principal works, not being materially affected by this, but on the other hand, the circumstances which limit this increase being the curves on the line, and the increased proportional resistance on inclinations (and on this account, it is stated to be almost solely applicable to very level lines) and lastly, the increased expense, which could be justified only by a great traffic.

The whole is clearly argued in a general point of view, and then applied to the particular case, and the result of this application is the recommendation of the adoption of 6 feet 2 inches on the Irish railways. Thus an increase in the breadth of way to attain one particular object, viz.: the capability of increasing the diameter of the carriage wheels, without raising the bodies of the carriages, is admitted to be most desirable, but is limited by certain circumstances, namely—the gradients and curves of the line, and the extent of traffic.

Every argument here adduced, and every calculation made, would tend to the adoption of about 7 feet on the Great Western Railway.

The gradients of the lines laid down by the Irish commission are considerably steeper than those of the London and Birmingham railway, and four and five times the inclination of those on the Great Western Railway; the curves are, by no means, of very large radius; and indeed the commissioners, after fixing the gauge of 6 feet 2 inches, express their opinion that upon examination into the question of curves, with the view to economy, they do not find that the effect is so injurious as might have been anticipated, and imply therefore, that curves, generally considered of small radius on our English lines, are not incompatible with the 6 feet 2 inch gauge; and lastly, the traffic, instead of being unusually large, so as to justify any expense beyond that absolutely required, is such as to render assistance from government necessary to ensure a return for the capital embarked. As compared with this, what are the circumstances in our case? The object to be attained is the placing an ordinary coach body, which is upwards of 6 feet 6 inches in width, between the wheels: this necessarily involves a gauge of rail of about 6 feet 10 inches and a half to 6 feet 11 inches, but 7 feet allows of its being done easily; it allows, moreover, of a different arrangement of the body, it admits all sorts of carriages, stage coaches and carts to be carried between the wheels. And what are the limits in the case of the Great Western Railway as compared to those on Irish railways? Gradients of one fifth the inclination, very favourable curves, and probably the largest traffic in England.

I think it unnecessary to say another word to shew that the Irish commissioners would have arrived at 7 feet on the Great Western Railway by exactly the same train of argument that led them to adopt 6 feet 2 inches in the case then before them.

All these arguments were advanced by me in my first report to you, and the subject was well considered. The circumstance of the Great Western Railway, and other principal railways likely to extend beyond it, having no connection with other lines then made,

[1] The report referred to is dated 15th September 1835. See Chapter II.

*Vulcan*, the first engine to run on the G.W.R., after conversion into a tank engine

*North Star* as reconstructed in its original form for the Railway Centenary Exhibition at Darlington, 1925

West London Crossing, 1844

Ealing Station, 1839

leaving us free from any prescribed dimension, the 7 feet gauge was ultimately determined upon. Many objections were certainly urged against it; the deviation from the established 4 feet 8 inches was then considered as the abandonment of a principle; this, however, was a mere assertion, unsupported even by plausible argument and was gradually disused; but objections were still urged, that the original cost of construction of all the works connected with the formation of the line must be greatly increased; that the carriages must be so much stronger, that they would be proportionably heavier; that they would not run round the curves, and would be more liable to run off the rails; and particularly that the increased length of the axles would render them liable to be broken; and these objections were not advanced as difficulties which, existing in all railways, might be somewhat increased by the increase of gauge, but as peculiar to this, and fatal to the system.

With regard to the first objection, namely the increased cost in the original construction of the line, if there be any, it is a question of calculation which is easily estimated, and was so estimated before the increased gauge was determined upon. Here, however, preconceived opinions have been allowed weight in lieu of arguments and calculations; cause and effect are mixed up; and without much consideration, it was assumed at once that an increased gauge necessarily involved increased width of way and dimensions of bridges, tunnels, etc.

Yet such is not the case within the limits we are now treating of: a 7 feet rail requires no wider bridge or tunnel than a 5 feet; the breadth is governed by a maximum width allowed for a loaded waggon, or the largest load to be carried on the railway, and the clear space to be allowed on either side beyond this.

On the Manchester and Liverpool Railway this total breadth is only 9 feet 10 inches, and the bridges and viaducts need only have been twice this, or 19 feet 8 inches—9 feet 10 inches was found, however, rather too small, and in the London and Birmingham, with the same width of way, this was increased to 11 feet by widening the interval between the two railings.

In the space of 11 feet allowed for each rail, a 7 feet gauge might be placed just as well as a 5 feet leaving the bridges, tunnels, and viaducts exactly the same, but 11 feet was thought by some still too narrow; and when it is remembered that this barely allows a width of 10 feet for loads, whether of cotton, wool, agricultural produce, or other light goods, and which are liable also to be displaced in travelling, 13 feet (which has been fixed upon in the Great Western Railway, and which limits the maximum breadth, under any circumstance, to about 12 feet) will not be found excessive.

It is this which makes the minimum width, actually required under bridges and tunnels 26 feet instead of 22 feet, and not the increased gauge.

The earthwork is slightly affected by the gauge, but only to the extent of 2 feet on the embankment, and not quite so much in the cuttings; but what, in the practice, has been the result? The bridges over the railway, on the London and Birmingham, are 30 feet, and the width of viaducts 28 feet; on the Great Western Railway they are both 30 feet; no great additional expense is therefore incurred on these items, and certainly a very small one compared to the increased space gained, which as I have stated, is from 10 to 12 feet. In the tunnels exists the greatest difference; on the London and Birmingham Railway, which I refer to as being the best and most analogous case to that of the Great Western Railway, the tunnels are 24 feet wide. On the Great Western Railway the constant width of 30 feet is maintained, more with a view of diminishing the objections to tunnels and maintaining the same minimum space which hereafter may form a limit to the size and form of every thing carried on the railway, than from such a width being absolutely necessary.

Without pretending to find fault with the dimensions fixed, and which have, no doubt, been well considered, upon the works on other lines, I may state that the principle which has governed has been to fix the minimum width, and to make all the works the same, considering it unnecessary to have a greater width between the parapet walls of a viaduct which admits of being altered, than between the sides of a tunnel which cannot be altered.

The embankments on the London and Birmingham Railway are 26 feet, on the Great Western 30 feet, making an excess of about 6½ per cent. on the actual quantity of earthwork.

The difference in the quantity of land required is under half an acre to a mile. On the whole the increased dimensions from 10 feet to 12 will not cause any average increased expense in the construction of the works and purchase of land, of above 7 per cent.–8 per cent. having originally been assumed in my report in 1835 as the excess to be provided for.

With respect to the weight of the carriages, although we have wheels of 4 feet diameter, instead of 3 feet, which of course involves an increased weight, quite independent of the increase of width, and although the space allowed for each passenger is a trifle more, and the height of the body greater, yet the gross weight per passenger is somewhat less.

|  | Tons | cwt | qrs | lbs |
|---|---|---|---|---|
| A Birmingham first-class coach weighs . . . . | 3 | 17 | 2 | 0 |
| Which with 18 passengers at 15 to the ton . . . . | 1 | 4 | 0 | 0 |
|  | 5 | 1 | 2 | 0 |

Or 631 lbs per passenger.

|  | Tons | cwt | qrs | lbs |
|---|---|---|---|---|
| A Great Western first-class weighs . . . . . | 4 | 14 | 0 | 0 |
| And with 24 passengers . . . . . . . | 1 | 12 | 0 | 0 |
|  | 6 | 6 | 0 | 0 |

Or 588 lbs per passenger.

|  | Tons | cwt | qrs | lbs |
|---|---|---|---|---|
| And our 6-wheeled first-class . . . . . . | 6 | 11 | 0 | 0 |
| With 32 passengers . . . . . . . | 2 | 2 | 2 | 0 |
|  | 8 | 13 | 2 | 0 |

Or 600 lbs per passenger.

Being an average of 594 lbs on the two carriages.

This saving of weight does arise from the increased width and is notwithstanding the increased strength of the framing and the increased diameter and weight of the wheels; I have not weighed our second-class open carriages, but I should think the same proportion would exist.

As to the breaking of axles or running off the line, the practical result has been that, from some cause or other, we have been almost perfectly free from those very objections which have been felt so seriously on some other lines. Far from breaking any engine axles, not even a single cranked axle has been strained, although the engines have been subjected to rather severe trials. One of our largest having, a short time back, been sent along the line at night when it was not expected, came in collision with some ballast waggons, and was thrown off the line nearly 6 feet; none of the axles were bent, or even strained in the least, although the front of the carriage, a piece of oak of very large scantling, was shattered. After ten weeks running, one solitary instance has occurred of a carriage in a train getting off the line and dragging another with it and which was not discovered till after running a mile and a half. As the carriage was in the middle of the train, and one end of the axle was thrown completely out of the axle-guard, there must evidently have been some extraordinary cause—possibly a plank thrown across the railway by a blow from the carriage which preceded, and which might have produced the same effect on any railway; and at any rate it was a strong trial to the axle, which was not broken, but merely restored to its place, and the carriage sent on to London. The same mode of reasoning which has by some been used in favour of the 4 feet 8 inch gauge, if applied here, would prove that long axles are stronger than short, and wide rails best adapted for curves. All that I think proved however, is this—that the increased tendency of the axles to break, or of the wheels to run off the rails, is so slight that it is more than counterbalanced by the increased steadiness from the width of the base, and the absence of those violent strains which arise from irregularity on the gauge and the harshness of the ordinary construction of rails. In fact, not one of the objections originally urged against the practical working of the wide gauge has been found to exist, while the object sought for is attained, namely, the capability of increasing at any future period, the diameter of the wheels, which cannot be done, however desirable it may hereafter be found, with the old width of rail. This may be said to be only prospective; but in the meantime, contingent advantages are sensibly felt in the increased lateral steadiness of the carriages and engines, and the greater space which is afforded for the works of the locomotives: and here I wish particularly to call your attention to the fact that this prospective advantage—this absence of a most inconvenient limit to the reduction of the friction, which, with our gradients, forms $\frac{4}{5}$ths, or 80 per cent. of the total resistance—was the object sought for, and that at the time of recommending it, I expressly stated as follows:—'I am not by any means prepared at present to recommend any particular size of wheel, or even any great increase of the present dimensions. I believe they will be materially increased; but my great object would be in every possible way to render each part capable of improvement and to remove what appears an obstacle to any greater progress in such a very important point as the diameter of the wheels, upon which the resistance, which governs the cost of transport and the speed that may be obtained, so materially depends.'

These advantages were considered important by you, they are now considered so by many others; and certainly everything which has occurred in the practical working of the line confirms me in my conviction that we have secured a most valuable power to the Great Western Railway, and that it would be folly to abandon it.

Such was Brunel's defence of his 7 foot gauge. Much of it must be admitted to savour of special pleading. He founds his case on the wonderfully straight and level line he had laid out between London and Bristol with its possibilities of great speed and large passenger traffic, arguments which would not apply to the Cheltenham & Great Western Union, and still less to the South Devon and other broad-gauge railways of the future. On his showing, the gauge of each railway should be determined by its gradients and curves.

The report goes on to defend in somewhat guarded language the construction and efficiency of the engines, which, in Brunel's opinion, 'have proved to be well adapted to the particular task for which they were calculated, namely, high speeds; but circumstances prevent their being beneficially applied to this purpose at present, and they are, therefore, working under great disadvantages. An engine constructed expressly for a high velocity cannot, of course, be well adapted to exert great power at a low speed; neither can it be well adapted for stopping frequently and regaining its speed.'

The bad state of the permanent way is admitted, and attributed to defective packing under the longitudinal timbers, which caused the piles to aggravate the trouble by actually supporting the timbers at intervals instead of holding them down, as they were intended to do. That part of the road which had been laid under Brunel's own eye answered fully his expectations, and there the piles did answer their purpose and caused no inconvenience, but he was prevented by a serious accident—a bad fall into the hold of the 'Great Western' steamship on 1st April—from superintending the rest and seeing that sufficiently hard packing material was used and properly rammed under the timbers. This was in course of improvement by the gradual substitution of eighteen inches of coarse gravel under each timber, 'necessarily a slow expensive and laborious operation'. Though very loth to do so, Brunel had evidently already made up his mind to abandon the use of the piles in future. He writes:

I find that the system of piling involves considerable expense in the first construction, and requires perhaps too great a perfection in the whole work, and that if the whole or a part of this cost were expended in increasing the scantling of timber and weight of metal, a very solid continuous rail would be formed; for this as a principle, as for the width of gauge, I am prepared to contend and to stand or fall by it, believing it to be a most essential improvement where high speeds are to be obtained. I strongly urge upon you not to hesitate on these two main points, which, combined with what may be termed the natural advantages of the line, will eventually secure to you a superiority which under other circumstances cannot be attained.

This report of Brunel's, together with that of the Directors, was read at the Half-yearly Meeting held at the Merchants' Hall, Bristol, on 15th August 1838, and ordered to be printed and circulated. The Hall was crowded, and the opposition present in great force. Disarmed by the conciliatory spirit and good humour of the Chairman, Sims, they were very polite to the Directors and even went so far as to praise much of their work. Several objectionable resolutions were, however, proposed, such as that another engineer should be associated with Brunel and that a vacancy on the Board should be filled by their nominee, which, says Gibbs, 'would have been pressed to a division if they had known, as I did, that they had a majority'. The great increase in the probable cost of the line, now estimated at £4,568,928, exclusive of locomotive power and carriages, was even accepted as not extraordinary in the light of the experience of other railways and the necessarily conjectural nature of the former estimate. Eventually the meeting, after lasting seven hours, was adjourned to 10th October to give time for consideration of the voluminous reports.

In spite of their good humour at the Meeting, the Liverpool party were far from satisfied with the position, and during the next six months their leaders were in constant and often unpleasant communication with the Directors. At the end of August the latter agreed to meet their wishes by calling in John Hawkshaw, a young man of twenty-seven, then Engineer of the Manchester & Leeds Railway, as a second engineer with Wood to report and advise on Brunel's methods. Hawkshaw at once accepted, and during September he and Wood, the latter assisted by the egregious Dr Dionysius Lardner, were engaged separately in carrying out experiments on the line.

Meanwhile the leaders of the opposition, dissatisfied with Brunel's report, were pressing for the appointment of a consulting engineer and the admission of one at least of themselves to the Board. The Directors were divided; the Chairman and others were in favour of yielding to both demands, but Gibbs, who appears to have had more influence, though willing to agree to a consulting engineer, was adamant against any Liverpool colleagues on the Board, foreseeing a constant struggle and being loth, as he puts it, to abandon Saunders and Brunel. The latter, he writes on 17th September, 'is at present almost broken hearted, and in this state of mind he cannot exert himself, but if we treat him judiciously he will do what is right, and it will be our own fault if we do not make him an invaluable servant for the future'.

Reports were received from both Wood and Hawkshaw in the first week of October. That of the former was merely a statement of the course he was pursuing to arrive at a conclusion later on. He, or rather Dr Lardner on his behalf, had made many elaborate experiments on the Great Western, and was about to make similar experiments on other railways. Meantime he offered no opinion on any of the matters referred to him.

Hawkshaw's report on the other hand was a very definite condemnation of all Brunel's work, and a recommendation that the 4 feet 8½ inches gauge should be adopted and the line already open taken up forthwith and relaid accordingly. This proposal was backed by figures showing that more than £30,000 would thereby be actually saved on the whole line after making full allowance for scrapping the existing engines and other stock. He based his opinion more on commercial than on engineering grounds, assuming, as he says, that the Directors' object is to make a railway that will pay its proprietors, 'because it is one thing to design that which shall be pleasing in outline and grand in dimensions, and quite another thing to design that which under all the circumstances shall best answer the ends in view, one of those ends being to obtain a return for the capital invested'. Having reckoned the amount of traffic to be expected, he considered that the greatly enlarged capacity of the engines, carriages, and road was not warranted, and was in fact sheer waste of money.

His chief argument against the 7 foot gauge was, however—what alone was destined eventually to kill it—the isolation which he foresaw would be entailed, at any rate as to branch and collateral traffic, or any line of a different gauge from its neighbours.

> The main reason in my view for abiding by the 4 feet 8½ inch gauge in this country is that it has been generally adopted and that there are no very substantial grounds for altering it. I have never heard anyone, whose opinion I should esteem of great value from their experience of the working of locomotives on railways, wish for more than a few inches of additional width, five or six inches at the utmost; and even as to this increase, just in proportion as the parties had had much to do with the working of the locomotives on railways, so in the same proportion did they esteem even it to be of minor importance.
>
> Perhaps, if railways were just commencing in this country, an addition of a few inches, five or six at the most, might be made; but the advantage to be gained by making it now, in my opinion, would in no manner compensate the evil that will arise from a variety of gauges in the same country.

Hawkshaw is bold enough to question Brunel's axiom, which had been accepted by the Irish Commissioners, that friction was diminished by the use of large wheels. The engines he considered much too heavy and powerful—Gooch would hardly have agreed with him here!—and compares them to the building of 'a ship of 200 tons burthen when there was no probability of ever obtaining a cargo of half the weight'. On the permanent way he was specially curt and scathing.

> The mode adopted in laying the rails is, I think, attempting to do that in a difficult and expensive manner, which may be done at least as well in a simple and more economical manner.

This is all the young man has to say on one of the matters he was specially invited to report and advise upon. No wonder Gibbs characterized his report as 'a very ill-natured production from beginning to end, the greater part of which might have been written without coming near the line'.[1] Ill-natured or not, it made the Directors' position still more difficult. On the eve of the adjourned Meeting they showed it to the Liverpool deputation—who, needless to say, thought it quite conclusive— but decided to withhold it and Wood's preliminary statement from the Proprietors until the latter's full report was available. The Meeting on 10th October at Bristol consequently passed off fairly peaceably, the opposition ultimately withdrawing their amendment to the Half-yearly Report, which was adopted unanimously, and the Directors promising to

---

[1] Events have shown that Hawkshaw was absolutely right in his views except as regards the engines.

publish the Engineers' reports when both had been received and to call a Special Meeting to consider them and decide on future action.

Wood's report being still delayed, Brunel drew up a reply to Hawkshaw. To the latter's main objection to the exceptional gauge, he answers:

> The question of the disadvantage of differing in point of gauge from other railways, and the consequent exclusion from communication with them, is the first. This is undoubtedly an inconvenience; it amounts to a prohibition to almost any railway running northward from London, as they must all more or less depend for their supply upon other lines or districts where railways exist and with which they must hope to be connected. In such cases there is no alternative.
>
> The Great Western Railway, however, broke ground in an entirely new district, in which railways were unknown. At present it commands this district, and has already sent forth branches which embrace nearly all that can belong to it; and it will be the fault of the Company if it does not effectually and permanently secure to itself the whole trade of this portion of England with that of South Wales and the south of Ireland; not by a forced monopoly, which could never long resist the wants of the public, but by such attention to these wants as shall render competition unnecessary and hopeless. Such is the position of the Great Western Railway. It could have no connection with any other of the main lines, and the principal branches likely to be made were well considered and almost formed part of the original plan; nor can these be dependent upon any existing lines for the traffic which they will bring to the main trunk.
>
> The Great Western was therefore free to adopt its own dimensions; and none of the difficulties which would entirely prevent such a course in the north of England had any existence in the west. Consequently all the general arguments advanced and the comparisons made, on the supposition of such difficulties occurring—all excellent in case they did—are totally inapplicable to the particular case of the Great Western Railway, to which they have no reference whatever.

Such were Brunel's views in 1838; for a man gifted with such a lively imagination and so far-seeing in many ways, they seem to us to-day extraordinarily short-sighted. Elsewhere in the same report, he wrote:

> Railway carriages and waggons must belong to the particular line on which they run; and, except in such cases as the Grand Junction and London and Birmingham Railways, which form in fact one line, although they happen to be made by two Companies, it will never pay to trust them in the hands of others.

In reply to Hawkshaw's economic objections to the increased capacity of the railway generally, Brunel urges that higher speed and better accommodation will induce more people to travel, and so largely increase the Company's income, a point entirely overlooked by the critic. As to the engines, he answers with undeniable truth that 'our best engines, which are considered so unnecessarily powerful, have been barely sufficient to take the loads which we were obliged to carry'.

At last Wood's long delayed report was received on 12th December. It was a very long document, extending in print to eighty-two octavo pages, and was to have been followed by a still longer appendix with details of the elaborate experiments made by Dr Lardner on the Great Western, Grand Junction, London & Birmingham, Liverpool & Manchester, and Manchester, Bolton & Bury Railways to determine the amount of oscillation of the carriages on different forms of permanent way, the comparative power of the engines, and the effect of gradients, friction, and atmospheric resistance. The appendix, however, was not received until the whole controversy had been settled and so had no influence thereon.

Although he had made such a prolonged and extensive investigation of the matters referred to him, Wood was very chary of giving any unqualified judgments. On the most important point of all, the wide gauge, he dismisses Hawkshaw's chief objection, that it would prevent any junction with other lines, in a few words, 'the Great Western Railway being complete in itself between the two sides of the island'; but confesses himself incapable of judging how far this may be affected by the branches. The objection that there are no advantages gained commensurate with the increased expense and the possible inconvenience of such isolation, he considers substantially confirmed; but on the other hand, 'must be allowed to say that there are counteracting advantages incidental to an increased width of gauge above that of 56 inches, which should not be overlooked'. He sums up the matter in the same vacillating and indefinite way.

> Almost all the results arising from these enquiries go to establish a conclusion that 7 feet is beyond that width which may be considered the best; but these investigations are far from conclusive in the present state of our information as to what other width is, under all the circumstances, the most advisable to be adopted. Under these circumstances and considering the great sacrifice of property which would result by the removal of the present rails and the substitution of any other width, it appears to me that such a step would not be justified by the result of these enquiries.
> ... It is also necessary to state that the results elicited in the course of this enquiry show that considerable modifications may be beneficially made in both engines and carriages; and therefore until we have determined in the most satisfactory and conclusive manner the precise extent of the injury arising from the retention of the present width of gauge, and what width best effects all the objects required and which, under all the circumstances, is most conducive to the interests of the Company and affords the greatest accommodation to the public, it appears to me the present width should be retained.

This last paragraph alludes to the wretched results he, or rather Dr Lardner, had obtained from their experiments with the Great Western engines. For example, the best of them, *North Star*, was found capable of taking 82 tons at 33 miles an hour, only 33 tons at 37 miles an hour, and 16 tons at 41 miles an hour; and to obtain this last additional speed of 4 miles an hour, the consumption of coke was increased from 1·25 to 2·76 lbs per ton per mile. This phenomenon was ascribed by the learned Dr Lardner to atmospheric resistance, increased by the greater frontage of the wide carriages; and on the strength of his opinion Wood was actually led to conclude 'that it is not advisable to attempt an extreme rate of speed, and that 35 miles an hour, with the existing engine power, may be considered as the limit of practical speed for passenger trains'. Brunel and Gooch soon found it was due to quite another cause, and one easily remedied.

With regard to the permanent way, Wood does manage to make up his mind on one point: 'that the piles do not contribute to the firmness of base of the railway; their action seems to prevent the contact of the timbers with the ground; and it is unquestionably proved that the passage of the engines and carriages along the rails contributes with a more powerful effect to consolidate the road and produce a greater firmness of bearing to the rails than the packing connected with the piles'. He therefore had no hesitation in condemning the piles, and recommending that the scantling of the longitudinal timbers should be increased, as 'the present timbers are much too small for the loads that come upon them and do not present a sufficiently rigid and unyielding base for a railway'. They were only 5 to 6 inches thick, as we have seen. Continuous timber bearing of adequate strength, he considered superior to Stephenson's stone blocks, though somewhat more expensive, and both better than the cheaper cross sleepers of timber, 'which cannot be considered as a permanent description of road'.

Gibbs was not pleased with the report.

December 14th. I was a good deal troubled to-day by the great difficulty in which we are placed by the decidedly unfavourable tendency of Wood's Report. Our own conviction and Brunel's opinion and the weakness of Hawkshaw's reasoning all lead us to persevere in the wide gauge, when Wood's Report comes in, founded on hasty and imperfect experiments, not absolutely opposing our gauge but tending to show that we should be better without it.

Matters came to a crisis in the next few days; the whole future of the Great Western was at stake, and Brunel's position as Engineer hung by a thread. Even Saunders and Gibbs were shaken in their support, and favoured the appointment of a second or consulting engineer. Russell alone stood firm.

December 14th. To-day an attempt was made from within to bring the Committee[1] to the conviction that it was necessary to associate another engineer with Brunel. It came on in this way. On the 12th the unfavourable report of Wood placed us in a very awkward position, and at that moment Dr Squire's suggestion was received that we should call in Locke.[2]

I felt that under those circumstances, if the leading principles of the Railway could be previously settled, it might be shown to be necessary and not impracticable for the sake of peace to adopt some such plan as that suggested. Saunders was evidently very strongly of the same opinion.

To-day we learnt that Sims[3] and Mills had last night been talking the matter over and that the former had gone to Brunel to say that he felt some change of the kind would be necessary, and we were told that Brunel himself was very much of the same opinion. Saunders, Casson, Russell, and myself argued the matter after the Board broke up, Saunders supporting the proposition and Casson doing so in much stronger language, Russell resisting it in a very sensible way, and I siding in the main with him because our position has been again altered by the receipt of another letter from Dr Clarke.

We then repaired to Brunel's. He in a very modest way said that the evidence which was accumulating against him appeared to be too great to be resisted without injury to the Company, and therefore he was prepared to give way. He had no vanity of any kind. If it were necessary to yield, he had no objection to its being said that he had been defeated, for he felt confident in the correctness of his views and was sure that he should have opportunities of proving it. He spoke of the leading principles, for in other matters there had been errors and imperfections on our line as well as on others; but if it was proposed to connect another engineer with him, he could not see how such a scheme could possibly work, for which he gave his reasons, nor could he understand the meaning of a consulting engineer.

He gave us clearly to understand that he could not and would not submit to either of these alternatives, but that he would resign his situation as engineer whenever we pleased.

With respect to Wood's Report, he is perfectly convinced that a great fallacy pervades it, as may be shown and proved by experiment, and he proposed to devote all his mind and energies to show this in the next three weeks.

[1] The London Committee. The Bristol attitude will appear later.
[2] Joseph Locke, Engineer of the Grand Junction and London & Southampton Railways.
[3] The Chairman.

December 17th. I went to Paddington in the evening, and after the business was over the Chairman and Saunders talked to me about the proposal of Dr Squire that we should admit Locke as co-engineer with Brunel. They advocated this measure and I resisted it.

December 18th. Met in Princes Street at 12. Ricketts joined us with Fripp[1] and Brunel and we had a long talk till nearly 5. Brunel laid before us his remarks on Wood's Report and gave us great reason to hope that by Saturday next he should be able to prove that our engines could perform nearly double what Wood supposes, and that he is quite mistaken in attaching so much importance to atmospheric resistance.

After this we discussed Dr Squire's proposal. Fripp, Russell and I stoutly resisted the scheme, and I exerted myself to show its danger, the injustice we should be doing Brunel, and the hopelessness of our attaining peace by that means. It was at last settled that we should propose to appoint an engineer to whom to refer any new plans or experiments Brunel may suggest, and that if they[2] would give up the idea of Liverpool Directors we would appoint in February two out of six London men to be named by them.

The Bristol Committee seem to have been thoroughly frightened by the opposition and to have quite lost confidence in their Engineer. They were not satisfied with this decision of their London colleagues, so the full Board was summoned to meet immediately after Christmas. Gibbs records what passed as follows:

December 27th. Attended a Board at the Railway Office at 12, and having first heard and much approved the first part of Brunel's answer to Wood, we discussed the painful subject of our present position, and I was very sorry to hear that most of the Bristol gentlemen were in favour of concession.

Bright[3] judiciously suggested that these were points which would be better considered after the result of the Meeting had shown us how we really stood, and I urged at some length all the reasons which weighed with me against any concession. Upon the whole I was much disgusted with the view of the subject taken by our Bristol colleagues.

The Deputy Chairman's suggestion was adopted, and the matter left till after the Special Meeting, which, owing to the late arrival of Wood's report, had been adjourned from 20th December, the date originally fixed, to 9th January 1839, to give the Shareholders time to consider Wood's and Hawkshaw's reports, which were printed and circulated together with Brunel's replies.

In the meantime Brunel was at work to prove that Wood and Lardner were wrong in attributing the dismal failure of *North Star* to draw more than 16 tons at 40 miles an hour to atmospheric resistance, and thence arguing that high speed, one of the main objects of the wide gauge, was impracticable. He and Gooch were not long in finding that by increasing the size of the engine's blast-pipe, and at the same time taking care that the steam was discharged up the middle of the chimney, the power was greatly increased and the consumption of coke lessened. By this simple alteration they succeeded before Christmas in making her take 40 tons at 40 miles an hour, using less than a third of the quantity of coke.

On 29th December *North Star* took an experimental train with the Directors and a load of 43 tons to Maidenhead and back at an average speed of 38 miles an hour, the maximum being 45, consuming only ·95 of a lb of coke per net ton per mile, instead of 2·76 lbs, the quantity required for a load of 16 tons when Wood made his experiments in September.

---

[1] Both members of the Bristol Committee.
[2] The Opposition.
[3] Chairman of the Bristol Committee and Deputy Chairman of the Company.

This fact demolished Wood's arguments, founded on Dr Lardner's theories of atmospheric resistance, against the practicability of high speed, and inferentially against the wide gauge. Brunel was not slow to point this out and make the most of it in his printed reply to Wood's report, in which he also casts considerable doubt on the suitability and accuracy of Dr Lardner's instruments for measuring resistances and oscillation, and expresses regret that the experiments were not made by Wood himself with his practical, as distinguished from theoretical, knowledge of the subject.

About this time the rest of the engines seem to have become less efficient than ever, and poor young Gooch, who was in no possible way accountable for either their design or defects, came in for the blame. Gibbs writes on 26th December, 'Our engines are in very bad order, and Gooch seems to be very unfit for the superintendence of that department'! Two days later he is much worried by 'the total unfitness of Gooch for his situation'!! He must soon have changed his mind or found himself in a minority, for little more than a month later we find the Board sanctioning specifications and drawings for a large number of new engines, which Gooch had been directed to design quite independently of Brunel, his official superior.

The Special Meeting which was to decide the question of the gauge and, consequently, the whole future policy of the Company, assembled at the London Tavern in Bishopsgate Street on Wednesday, 9th January 1839. The Directors' Report consisted of short comments on the reports of the Engineers, which had been in the hands of the shareholders for a week, and a statement of the policy they recommended. Hawkshaw's advice is scouted in the following passage:

> Naturally expecting to find in his Report a clear and definite statement of the positive loss or disadvantage accruing from the increased width of gauge, the Directors could not fail to remark with some surprise that he enforces his recommendation, not upon any ascertained injury or failure in the plan, but almost exclusively upon the presumption that all railways, however disconnected or locally situated, should be constructed of one uniform width.
>
> . . . The objection that the wide gauge might prevent a junction with other lines seems both to Mr Wood and the Directors to have but little weight, as applied to the Great Western Railway. Already has the same width been contemplated and provided for in the extension lines through Gloucestershire to Cheltenham, and from Bristol to Exeter. Any local branches hereafter to be made would undoubtedly follow the same course, and the Proprietors therefore may be satisfied that no apprehension need be entertained by them on that head.

Wood's atmospheric arguments are shown to have been already upset by the performance of the altered *North Star*, and the importance of this 'in almost every relation of the inquiry' is emphasized. As to future policy—

> The Directors, upon a deliberate reconsideration of all the circumstances affecting the permanent welfare of the undertaking, divesting the question of all personal partialities or obstinate adherence to a system, unanimously acquiesce in the abandonment of the piles, in the substitution of a greater scantling of timber, and of a heavier rail, retaining the width of gauge with the continuous timber bearings, as the most conducive to the general interests of the Company.

The Report having been read, it was moved and seconded:

That this Report be approved and adopted: and that this Meeting, being deeply sensible of the disastrous consequences inevitably arising from the continual discussion of the principles acted upon in carrying on the Works, do request the Directors to adhere to the principles laid down in their Report, as the most conducive to the permanent welfare of the Proprietors.

Whereupon an Amendment was proposed and seconded by the opposition party:

That the Reports of Messrs Wood and Hawkshaw contain sufficient evidence that the plans of construction pursued by Mr Brunel are injudicious, expensive, and ineffectual for their professed objects, and therefore ought not to be proceeded in.

After much discussion, in which, according to Gibbs, 'our opponents made a wretched display', a show of hands on the amendment appeared decidedly in favour of the Directors, and a poll was demanded. The result was declared next day.

Votes against the Amendment:

| | | | | | |
|---|---|---|---|---|---|
| Present | . | . | . | . | 1,984 |
| Proxies | . | . | . | . | 5,808 |

Total 7,792

Votes for the Amendment:

| | | | | | |
|---|---|---|---|---|---|
| Present | . | . | . | . | 176 |
| Proxies | . | . | . | . | 5,969 |

Total 6,145

Majority against the Amendment  1,647

The original motion was then put and carried unanimously, and the Directors withdrew in triumph with the 'warm and cordial thanks of the Meeting for the zealous attention they have uniformly paid to the interests of the Proprietors'.

Thus, for good or ill, was Brunel's 7 foot gauge established on the Great Western Railway, and in consequence on other railways as yet unknown.

The opposition loyally accepted their defeat and gave no more trouble. Though all talk of concessions to them was soon dropped, at the Half-yearly Meeting in February they, writes Gibbs, 'treated us with respect and showed a disposition to co-operate with us cheerfully. This was very gratifying, particularly to me, as it showed that by firmness we had secured their respect, kept them out of the Direction, retained our Engineer, and preserved our gauge.'

# IV
# *Construction*
## *1839–1841*

### 1 MAIDENHEAD TO TWYFORD

The station called Maidenhead, though situated east of the Thames at Taplow a long mile from the town, was for more than a year the terminus of the Great Western Railway. Although the Directors resolved early in August 1838 to move it a mile westward as soon as the line had been extended, it remained the only main line station for both Maidenhead[1] and Taplow till November 1871, when a new Maidenhead station $1\frac{1}{2}$ miles to the west was opened.

A quarter of a mile beyond was Brunel's famous bridge over the Thames, which excited much heated controversy during its erection. The river at this point is not quite 100 yards wide between low banks with a small shoal in the middle. Brunel designed a brick bridge of two of the flattest and largest arches that have, or at any rate had, ever been constructed in brickwork. Each arch had a span of 128 feet with a rise of only $24\frac{1}{4}$ feet, the centre pier being placed on the shoal. Four semi-circular arches at each end to provide for floods, one of 21 and three of 28 feet span, completed the structure. Work was begun early in 1837 by the contractor, one Chadwick, and before the end of the year the arches had been turned. In February 1838 the Directors reported that the bridge was in a very forward state and the centering would shortly be eased. It was eased in the course of the spring, and to the delight of the critics, who had all along declared that such flat arches could not possibly stand, the eastern arch soon showed signs of distortion. The western arch, however, annoyed them by standing perfect. In June Brunel reported:

> The Contractor is now anxious to remove the centerings, as he feels confident that the arches have reached their maximum settlement, and proposes to remove and alter the external surface only of the distorted part, and thus prevent its being apparent to the eye. To this I have objected. I cannot say that I think the work unsafe, or that the Bridge would not stand very well in its present state, but the defect has been caused entirely by the fault of the Contractor, and while the centerings are in place he has still the means of removing this defective portion, and rendering the eastern arch as perfect as the western now is, and such as he contracted to make it. I propose therefore to direct Mr Chadwick to tighten up the centres of both arches and to remove and replace so much of the eastern arch as upon close examination during the progress of this work I may consider defective, but it would be more convenient to us that he should postpone this operation for a time, until we shall have completed so much of the embankment to the west as will enable Mr Oldham[2] to meet it within the required time, and we can then remove entirely our temporary roads which would interfere with the works of the Bridge.

[1] A small station entitled first 'Maidenhead (Wycombe Branch)' and later 'Maidenhead (Boyne Hill)' was opened with the branch in 1854 about a $\frac{1}{4}$ mile from the junction, close to the town but of course only served by the few branch trains. It was closed on the opening of the new main line station in 1871.

[2] Contractor for the adjoining section westward.

Earth was being brought from the Bucks side by these temporary roads to form the embankment immediately west of the bridge.

The distortion of the eastern arch, about which so much fuss was made, consisted of a separation of about half an inch between the lowest three courses of bricks for about twelve feet on each side of the crown of the arch. It was caused by the centering having been eased before the cement had properly set, and was worse at the two faces than in the interior. In July the contractor admitted that he alone was to blame and, as soon as the earth tipping was finished, set about replacing the defective part. At this time the attack of the Liverpool opposition party on Brunel and the Directors was at its height, and the apparently insecure state of the bridge was of course used as a weapon. Hence it formed one of the matters on which Wood and Hawkshaw were asked to report. The latter considered that more weight was required on the crown of the arch and accordingly recommended that some thirty feet of brickwork should be replaced by stone. Wood, on his part, found that the trouble was due merely to the cement not having had time to set and concurred in the remedy proposed by Brunel.

The necessary rebuilding was done and Gibbs records that the centres were eased on 8th October. They were, however, left in position, and the critics continued to declare that the bridge would fall down as soon as they were removed. Brunel had ordered that they should not be taken away till another winter had passed, but one night in the autumn of 1839 a violent storm blew them down. To the confusion of the critics and the triumph of the Engineer, the arches stood for all to see, and, needless to say, have been standing ever since. As a matter of fact, they had been quite clear of all support since the spring.

Westward from the bridge as far as Twyford, the works, for the most part a series of cuttings, were so far finished by February 1839 as to admit of the ballasting being proceeded with. For the permanent way Brunel decided to use bridge rails weighing 62 lbs to the yard, 19 lbs heavier than those east of Maidenhead, on longitudinal timbers 14 inches wide by 7 deep, with transoms and strap bolts, but of course no piles. The bulk of the piles between London and Maidenhead had already been cut off from the transoms and abandoned, but the light rails  and timbers remained for some years. The remaining stock of these light rails was got rid of at once. In February 1839 the sale of 500 tons of them to the Dutch Consul-General was sanctioned by the Board, and early in the following month all the remainder was ordered to be disposed of.

Section of 62 lb
Bridge Rail

Materials having become much cheaper, the relaying of the road between London and Maidenhead was begun in 1843. Timbers 14 by 7 inches, as on the rest of the line, and rails weighing 75 lbs to the yard, 13 lbs heavier, were used, making this stretch better instead of worse than the rest. The work was finished in 1846 and cost £97,266.

The permanent way being at last finished, and a temporary wooden terminus erected, the 8¼ miles between Maidenhead and Twyford were opened for traffic on 1st July 1839.

At the same time the classes of passengers were reduced to two. At the opening to Maidenhead there were four sets of fares—posting carriage, first-class coach, second-class coach, and second-class open carriage. The booking of single passengers for posting carriages was very soon dropped, and these were kept as saloons for special parties. Now second-class coaches were discontinued, and people who would not pay first-class fares had to be content with carriages roofed indeed, but with sides and doors only about three feet high, the rest being open to the weather. Needless to say, even these were vastly superior to the outside of a stage-coach, to which they corresponded.

Giving evidence before a Parliamentary Committee later in this same July, Saunders said the change had been made to lighten the trains, but it can scarcely be doubted that another weighty reason was to induce more people to go first-class. Questioned as to a third class of passengers, he replied that perhaps the Company would arrange to convey 'the very lowest orders of passengers' later on, but as yet no decision had been come to. Probably such people would eventually be taken once a day at very slow speed in carriages of an inferior description at a very low price, perhaps at night.

Goods traffic was begun in a small way in September, chiefly, it appears, through the agency of carriers, and these carriers soon began to take along with the goods that low class of passenger traffic which the Company so despised. One of them, Dibbin by name, told a Select Committee of the Commons, in February 1840, that he was carrying by the Great Western Railway, at a fare of 3s 6d each, 'persons in the lower stations of life' going on with the goods in his waggons from Twyford. So, indirectly and by sufferance only, third-class passenger traffic on the Great Western began.

## 2  Twyford to Reading

West of Twyford the great cutting through Sonning Hill was a source of much trouble and delay. Originally, as we have seen, Brunel intended to carry the line somewhat more to the north with a tunnel, five-eighths of a mile long, under Holme Park. He soon changed his mind and decided on a slight deviation and an open cutting. A short tunnel at the deepest part seems still to have been intended, for on 30th August 1838, more than a year after the substitution of a cutting had been announced, and the Act for the deviation obtained, Gibbs records in his Diary that the Directors had that day determined to substitute a bridge—doubtless that carrying the Bath Road—for the tunnel at Sonning Cutting.

The cutting, nearly two miles long and of a maximum depth of sixty feet, formed part of the Ruscombe-Reading contract taken by W. Ranger, and as early as February 1838 it was clear to the Directors that, though the work was proceeding steadily, he would not finish the excavation by the time appointed. Matters got worse during the spring, and at last, early in August, the Committee was obliged to take the work out of his hands, as we shall see the Bristol Committee had already done at their end of the line. Ranger then began proceedings in Chancery against the Company, which were destined to drag on for nearly twenty years.

The works were eventually sublet in three portions, and on 8th October Gibbs notes:

> At Sonning two of the Contractors were doing well, but the workmen have struck at the western end, and we had to threaten Knowles that we should instantly take the contract from him unless things were placed immediately in a more satisfactory condition.

Evidently the threat had no effect, for within a week Knowles was dismissed, and work resumed under the Company's Engineers. In February 1839 the Directors reported:

> The works at Sonning have been much retarded by the condition in which they were left by the late Contractor, and by the consequent difficulty of subletting them to sufficiently responsible persons in that state, especially in the winter season. This applies more particularly to the west end of that cutting. In the centre of the hill, which had not been commenced, the sub-contractor has steadily performed his engagement, and very considerable progress has been made. The Directors, finding that the only security for getting the earthwork completed in the course of the summer would be by taking it into their own hands, have done so, and are prosecuting the work with the utmost vigour to attain that object.
>
> By the last returns from the Resident Engineer, 1,220 men and 196 horses were employed on the Sonning Cutting, and the Company have purchased two locomotive engines to give the required assistance to the work. There are still 700,000 cube yards of earth to remove; and the quantity excavated and carried away by the above mentioned force exceeded 24,500 cube yards in the week. This quantity will be easily increased to 35,000 cube yards weekly when the locomotive power is brought into operation, and this will be in about a fortnight.

In the following August 145,000 cubic yards still remained to be excavated; these were finished by the end of the year.

Two bridges cross the cutting at its deepest part. Of these, the western, carrying the main road, is a brick bridge, 60 feet high, of three arches; the other, for a by-road, Brunel built of timber in the style which he afterwards adopted for some of his viaducts.[1] Between the end of the cutting and Reading Station the River Kennet was crossed by a brick arch of 60 feet span, with four 18 feet side arches.

Reading Station itself was the first—and was destined to be the last survivor—of the quaint one-sided stations which Brunel designed for certain towns lying wholly or mainly on one side of the railway; this happened in each case to be the south. The Up and Down platforms were practically separate stations, side by side a short distance apart on the south or Down side of the main lines, each on its separate loop, the Up station being the nearer to London.[2] The advantages of this plan were

---

[1] It was replaced by an iron bridge on brick piers when the line was widened in 1893.

[2] The Down station originally had a roof exactly similar to that of the Up station, but on the night of 12th October 1853 the open flap of a wagon in a goods train from Basingstoke cut away some of the pillars and caused its collapse. It was never reinstated, a "temporary" shed being erected to cover the platform only. This did duty till the new station was built, more than forty years later.

that passengers had not to cross the rails, and that non-stopping trains ran by clear of the station; while the disadvantages were that Up stopping trains crossed the Down main line twice, and also crossed the Down platform loop in entering the Up station, so that only one train either way could be admitted at a time, and no Down train could pass while an Up train was coming in. Some practical minds among the London Directors seem to have foreseen the inconvenience of this, for early in March 1839 the Engineer was directed 'to submit another plan for Reading Station with sheds on either side', but a week later they appear to have given way and the original plan was approved. Two years afterwards Brunel told a Parliamentary Committee: 'Nothing but experience could determine whether a one-sided station was more safe or more dangerous than an ordinary station; but it is a very convenient arrangement, it gives great accommodation to passengers'. Two or three years' experience at Reading and Slough evidently proved satisfactory, to the Engineer at any rate, and similar one-sided stations were established at Taunton, Exeter, and Gloucester.

The permanent way from Twyford to Reading, of the same construction as that between Maidenhead and Twyford, was laid by contract, and was ready in time for an engine with some of the Directors to run to Reading on 14th March 1840.

A fortnight later the first Great Western engine designed by Gooch, a 7 foot single named *Firefly*, which had been opportunely delivered on 12th March and made a successful trial trip on the 17th, took a train of two carriages and a truck with Directors and others to the number of about 40 from Paddington to Reading, $35\frac{3}{4}$ miles, in 45 minutes, and on the return journey covered the $30\frac{3}{4}$ miles from Twyford, where she stopped for water, in 37 minutes, at an average speed of 50 miles an hour with a maximum of 58.[1]

On Monday, 30th March 1840, the railway to Reading was opened for public traffic.

From this time onwards to the end of 1842 Gooch's engines were constantly being delivered by their various builders—three more came in April and six in May—and the trouble caused by the utter unreliability of almost all the original locomotives gradually passed away as they arrived. In Gooch's own words,[2] 'We could now calculate with some certainty, not only upon the speed they could run, but also upon their not breaking down on the journey. We had no difficulty in running at sixty miles an hour with good loads.' Previously breakdowns were of constant, almost daily, occurrence, and in January 1840, when the Company possessed twenty-two engines, we find Brunel writing to Gooch: 'We are to-day as badly off for engines as we have ever been'.

[1] *London Courier*, 1st April 1840.
[2] Gooch's *Diaries*, page 46.

Maidenhead Bridge. (*Bourne*)

Pangbourne Station. (*Bourne*)

Engine House, Swindon, about 1845. (*Bourne*)

First Class Refreshment Room, Swindon, about 1850

### 3  READING TO STEVENTON AND FARINGDON ROAD

Reading did not long remain the terminus; indeed, it had not been intended to be a terminus at all. Up to the autumn of 1839 the intention was to open the whole 32½ miles from Twyford to near Faringdon at once in the following spring, but the extraordinarily wet weather of the autumn and winter prevented this.

The contracts for the line as far as Didcot had been let early in 1838, that for the two bridges over the Thames being the first taken in February. Besides these, the chief works were the embankment west of Reading and several deep cuttings, among them that through Purley Park, where a long tunnel had been first contemplated. The Reading embankment was to have been formed with the earth from Sonning Cutting not required for the station and its approaches but, owing to the delay of the contractor there, much of it had to be made by side-cutting. By the end of August 1839 most of the work, including the river bridge at Basildon, had been finished, while the Moulsford Bridge and the line east of Pangbourne were expected to be ready by Christmas. These two bridges are very much alike, each consisting of four 62 foot arches of red brick, with Bath stone facings. West of Didcot, as far as Uffington, the contracts were let in March, and this comparatively light work was proceeding rapidly.

In February 1840 Brunel reported:

> Beyond Reading and up to Didcot, a distance of 17½ miles, the ballasting is completed with the exception of two short lengths, together about 2½ miles. The difficulty of procuring ballast for this part has been very great; the ground purchased for this purpose being under water, and it being necessary to resort to dredging the river to obtain gravel. The laying of the permanent rails is in a forward state, a single line being laid for 15 miles, upon which the materials for the second line are carried and distributed at all parts so that this work will proceed rapidly.

> Beyond Didcot, great exertions had been made to complete the line for opening to a point near Faringdon simultaneously with the opening to Reading, and there can be no doubt that this might have been accomplished during May, probably even in April, had the season permitted it. A few weeks will complete the earth-work, and preparations are making for ballasting. If no further delays should now occur from the indirect consequences of the late wet season, the opening to Faringdon may be calculated upon in June or the beginning of July; but although the embankments and cuttings are very slight in this part of the line, they will require dry weather before they can be ballasted. The further opening to Swindon will also necessarily have been delayed, but may still be looked for in the course of this year.

The 20½ miles from Reading to Steventon, with intermediate stations at Pangbourne, Goring, and Moulsford,[1] were opened to the public on Monday 1st June 1840. Steventon of course meant Oxford, only 10 miles off on a main turnpike road, and for four years it remained, by means of a frequent service of coaches and waggons, the Oxford Railway Station. Even to this day it is used as such by the Post Office for some of the northbound night mails.

---

[1] Renamed Wallingford Road by December 1840. This station was immediately west of the bridge over the Thames and on the main Reading–Wallingford road. On the opening of the Wallingford Branch in 1866 it assumed its original name of Moulsford, and in 1892 was superseded by a new station called Cholsey and Moulsford ¾ mile farther west. Didcot was opened in 1844, and Tilehurst in 1882.

Seven weeks later, on 20th July, the line was extended a further $7\frac{1}{4}$ miles to Faringdon Road Station,[1] some 5 miles from the little Berkshire town, and on a direct road to Cirencester, Gloucester, and Cheltenham.

Neither of these two openings had much effect on the Bath and Bristol traffic; the coaches continued to use their old London road and connect with the trains at Reading.

## 4  BRISTOL TO BATH

The works on this section were some of the heaviest on the line. The terminus at Temple Meads was to be built on arches 15 feet above the level of the ground, and in the first mile were bridges over the Floating Harbour, formed out of the original course of the Avon, a canal known as the Feeder, bringing water from the river at Netham to the same harbour, and the Avon itself. Then came at short intervals three tunnels through rock, respectively 326, 154, and 1,017 yards long, and officially known as Nos. 1, 2, and 3. For part of the way between No. 2 and No. 3 the railway was to be carried on a narrow shelf between the rocky hillside and the river, supported by a massive retaining wall, and eastward of No. 3 Tunnel the river had to be diverted for a short distance to the extent of half its breadth to form a similar shelf below a steep wood known then and now from its owner's name as Fox's Wood. East of Fox's Wood were two more short tunnels[2] and a deep cutting, soon followed by a long embankment across the low-lying Keynsham Hams. Two miles farther on at Saltford another tunnel of 176 yards and a deep cutting had to be made, and then nearly 2 miles of high embankment across the riverside meadows to an iron skew bridge carrying the Bath turnpike road, which is immediately succeeded by the short Newton Cutting, where the tessellated pavement of a Roman villa, long preserved at Keynsham Station, was unearthed. Twerton Tunnel, 264 yards long, comes next, followed by a walled cutting, and then the Twerton Viaduct of 28 arches. Bath Station was approached by another viaduct of 73 arches, two of them crossing diverging main roads, and a skew bridge over the Avon. This station was also to be built on arches somewhat higher than at Bristol between two bridges over the river.

Preliminary operations were begun in September 1835, immediately after the passing of the Act, by Brunel and his assistant, G. E. Frere, whom he installed as Resident Engineer for the Bristol Division of the line with a staff of five engineers under him. During the autumn and winter most of the land was bought or agreed for, and in March 1836 the first contract, comprising the Avon Bridge at Bristol and the three tunnels, was let by the Bristol Committee of the Board to William Ranger. Other contracts had been let by August, when the Directors reported that work had been begun at all the principal points. A year later considerable

---

[1] Renamed Challow in 1864 on the opening of Uffington and the branch to Faringdon. Wantage Road was opened in 1846.

[2] 53 and 37 yards long respectively; both had been opened out by 1894.

progress had been made; the Keynsham embankment was finished, as well as much of the Brislington Tunnel (No. 3) to its full dimensions, and the Avon Bridge, which had been delayed for some reason, was proceeding satisfactorily. Near Bath, difficulties in obtaining possession of the land had prevented anything being done, but these were overcome in August and the works begun. By this time the fond hope of opening the line in the spring of 1838, which had been expressed by the Committee as late as February 1837, had been abandoned. Brunel was having great trouble with Ranger, the contractor for the Bristol end of the line, who seems to have been quite unequal to the task he had undertaken, lacking both capital and energy. Having already relieved him from part of his engagements, to enable him to concentrate his resources on the remainder, without much result, the Directors were obliged in the spring of 1838 to get rid of him altogether and take possession of the works. The three tunnels were then taken in hand by the Company's Engineers, the work being sublet in small portions, and the remainder of Ranger's contracts let to a more competent man, David McIntosh, who was also employed in the London Division. These two contractors, Ranger and McIntosh, afterwards distinguished themselves from the rest by Chancery proceedings against the Company of the Jarndyce *v.* Jarndyce order, which dragged on till 1855 and 1866 respectively.

Ranger's failure and the other lesser troubles caused great delay, with the result that not till August 1839 were the Directors able to report much definite progress. Of the tunnels, No. 1, Saltford, and Twerton had been finished; No. 2 would be finished in three weeks, and No. 3, the longest and most difficult, in about two months. The Harbour Bridge had been much delayed, first by difficulty with the foundations, and secondly by bad work put in by the former contractor, which had to be almost entirely renewed. It was a stone bridge, slightly askew, of two main arches, each of 56 feet span with two smaller side arches, the centerings for which were then about to be erected. Beyond this, the viaduct and embankment were nearly finished, and the Feeder Bridge, which for some reason was made of timber,[1] was rapidly proceeding. The big Gothic arch of 100 feet span over the Avon and its two side arches had been completed for some time and the centerings lowered. Eastward from the long tunnel to the turnpike road at Newton St Loe, nine miles from Bristol, most of the line was nearly ready for the permanent way, and from this point onwards to 'the entrance to Bath' little or nothing remained to be done. The iron skew bridge under the said turnpike road, which had been long hindered by difficulties with the Bath Road Trustees, had just been begun and would be finished in a few weeks. At Bath matters were very much in arrear; neither the bridge over the river nor the station had yet been begun. On the whole, however, the Directors considered that most of the works would be completed during the autumn

[1] Replaced by iron 1879.

and a great part of the permanent way laid, for which a contract had already been let, so that they would be able to open the line from Bristol to Bath early in the spring of 1840.

They were again disappointed, this time by the very wet winter and consequent floods in the Avon. In February Brunel reported:

At the Bristol extremity the floods in the Avon have interfered with the supply of building materials; and at Bath and in its immediate neighbourhood the unprecedented continuation of a state of flood in the river for a long period and till within the last few days has rendered it impossible to carry on the works of the Bridges or even of the Station, the site of which has been flooded. Such a complete suspension of the works at some points and such delays at others have resulted from these and other causes indirectly consequent upon them that certainly not less than four months additional time will be required for the completion of some of these works, the whole of which would otherwise have been finished within a month or two of the present time, which must delay the opening to the end of the summer instead of the spring.

The works of the Station at Bristol, including the viaduct and offices, are rapidly advancing; but at Bath the causes I have referred to have prevented till within the last few days anything more than the commencement of the approaches.

Between these two extremities all the principle works—the Tunnelling, Cutting, and Embankments—are so far completed that, had the weather permitted it, the ballasting and permanent way would have been by this time in a very forward state. The excavation of the Tunnels is everywhere opened throughout, and the only work remaining to be done to them consists of the formation of the permanent drains and the finishing of detached parts of masonry, which in the general progress of the work had been injured or condemned, and the completion of one of the tunnel fronts. A few weeks will complete everything but the permanent rails, but many parts of the line, long since prepared, have not been in a state to allow of men or horses passing over them without destroying that portion of the forming which the rains had allowed to be completed, so that not more than $2\frac{1}{2}$ miles of ballasting have been actually finished.

The tunnel front alluded to—the west end of No. 2 Tunnel—remained unfinished till the end of the century. The continued wet of the winter brought down a portion of the hillside, and so made its completion and an intended retaining wall unnecessary. Struck by the resemblance of the unfinished masonry to a ruinous mediaeval gateway, Brunel then decided to leave it as it stood, and caused ivy to be planted to increase its picturesque effect. In this state it remained till 1900, when a less artistic successor completed it in the severely practical style of railway works of the present day.

Both Brunel and Stephenson built ornamental fronts to their tunnels, generally of the castellated kind. Those of the former between Bristol and Bath were of various imposing designs. The east end of the long No. 3 Tunnel was distinguished from the rest by having no front, the rock being left in its rough state like the mouth of a cave. Being cut through hard rock, this tunnel was not lined with masonry like the others. In excavating No. 1 Tunnel two very large specimens of the nodules often found in the sandstone were unearthed. These Brunel had set up on either side of the line near the east mouth; one of them is still to be seen at the end of the cutting there. Three shafts were used in boring No. 3 Tunnel, and no less than six smaller shafts were found necessary for purposes of ventilation to carry off the fumes of the blasting powder, large fans being erected on top to create a draught. Five of these nine shafts remain open to-day. Even the comparatively short No. 1 required four ventilating shafts, all of which were afterwards filled up.[1]

During the spring of 1840 great exertions were made to make up for lost time and get the line open, and in the summer these were redoubled, relays of men being employed on the work, which went on continuously by night as well as by day and even, to the horror of the citizens of Bath, on Sundays. The skew bridge over the Avon was the work most of all in arrear. Brunel had intended it to be of iron, and tenders for 500 tons of ironwork were invited in May 1839, but, as the Directors reported in August, difficulties in letting by tender occurred, which caused them to delay its beginning till they could make other arrangements. Eventually Brunel decided to make it of timber, perhaps with a view to getting it finished quickly. It is thus described in Bourne's *History of the Great Western Railway.*

The angle at which the Bridge crosses the River is so considerable that, although the space from quay to quay is only 80 feet, the space traversed by the railway is 164 feet. The bridge is of two arches, each of 80 feet span. Each arch is composed of six ribs placed about 5 feet apart and springing from the abutment and a central pier of masonry. Each rib is constructed of five horizontal layers of Memel timber held together by bolts and iron straps. The end or butt of each rib is enclosed in a shoe or socket of cast iron, resting with the intervention of a plate upon the springing stones, the shoes on the middle pier being common to the two ribs. The spandrils of the four external ribs are filled up with an ornamental framework of cast iron supporting the parapets. The interior ribs are connected by cross struts and ties. The cornice and parapet are both of timber; the latter is framed in open work of a lozenge pattern. The abutments are flanked by plain turretted piers, and the tow-path is carried on an iron gallery beneath the western arch.[2]

At last the various works and the laying of the permanent way, which like all that west of Maidenhead consisted of 62 lb bridge rails on longitudinal timbers, 14 inches by 7, were so advanced as to enable the Directors to announce the public opening for the last day of August. Meantime, six of Gooch's new engines had arrived, two named *Arrow* and *Dart* respectively built at Bristol by the firm of Stothert, Slaughter & Co., the others, *Fireball*, *Spitfire*, *Lynx*, and *Meridian*, from North country builders.[3] The latter are said to have been delivered in parts by river and put together in Saltford Tunnel.

Frederick Clarke, a brother of the London Traffic Superintendent, was appointed to a similar position at Bristol on 30th May 1840 in anticipation of the opening.

On 21st August five members of the Bristol Committee, accompanied by Brunel and one or two other officers of the Company, made a trial trip to Bath. As the rails were not yet laid at the station and no carriage was available, they started from the engine house, some 600 yards up the line, on *Arrow* and reached Keynsham in ten minutes. There they changed on to *Meridian* and after a delay of eight minutes proceeded on the other line

[1] No. 1 Tunnel was opened out in 1887 in connection with construction of a new marshalling yard at Bristol East Depot.

[2] It was replaced by an iron girder bridge in 1878.

[3] Some others came later; *Stag* is recorded to have killed a person at Keynsham on 23rd September.

of rails, stopping at the Newton Turnpike Bridge to pick up Frere, the Resident Engineer, and reached the Bath Viaduct—it and the river bridge were still unfinished—in a quarter of an hour from Keynsham, or 33 minutes from Bristol with two stops, a result which hugely delighted the five Directors. After inspecting the bridge they returned to Bristol in about the same time, changing engines and lines at Keynsham.

No special ceremony, beyond the flying of flags and ringing of church bells, marked the public opening of the line, which took place, as announced, on Monday, 31st August 1840, and caused much excitement in the two cities and the intervening country. The first train was advertized to start from the unfinished terminus at Temple Meads at 8 a.m., and start it did, only a few minutes late, although the last rail into the station had not been well and truly laid more than half an hour. It was drawn by *Fireball*, gaily decorated with flags, and made up of three first-class and five second-class carriages filled by the general public, who had previously obtained 'check tickets' in the large booking hall downstairs. The passengers, though much excited by the novel adventure and 'the shouts of the multitude which lined the road', seem to have controlled themselves—no one is recorded even to have jumped off after his hat, a not unusual occurrence in those days—and after dashing through Nos. 1 and 2 Tunnels 'in the twinkling of an eye', according to an enthusiastic reporter, and being somewhat terrified by the prolonged darkness and noise of No. 3, reached the only intermediate station at Keynsham in safety. Here a stop of three minutes was made, and then the train 'swept on in an incredibly short time' into Bath, which was reached in 33 minutes from Bristol. The station here was in a still less finished state than at Temple Meads, but had evidently been built up to rail level and provided with platforms. The first train from Bath, due to leave at 9, started more than half an hour late and arrived at Bristol at 10.8. Ten trains were run each way during the day, four of them not stopping at Keynsham, carrying 5,880 passengers and earning £476, of which £231 was taken at Bath, £224 at Bristol, and £21 at Keynsham. This service continued till December, when another train each way was added and stations were opened at Saltford and Twerton.[1] No reference to goods or third-class passengers was made in the announcements, either in August or December. Apparently this traffic was not provided for until the railway was opened throughout from London.

## 5 FARINGDON ROAD TO HAY LANE

For five months Faringdon Road Station, 63½ miles from Paddington, was the terminus of the London Division, and there the first recorded accident occurred on 25th October 1840. In the darkness of the early Sunday morning Brunel himself and one or two others, waiting for an engine to take them to London, saw the night goods train approaching at

[1] St Anne's Park was opened in 1898, and Twerton closed in 1917.

an unusual speed. In spite of their shouts and the efforts of the guard, who was in the open truck next the engine with four third-class passengers, the train rushed on unchecked through the station and the closed doors of the engine shed beyond, which it demolished. The driver, who was seen standing motionless on the engine—*Fire King*—was killed, and four others, including the guard, injured. It seems he was fast asleep at his post, and we are left wondering how long the poor man had been on duty.

The contracts for the rest of the London Division, which extended to Shrivenham, and for the portion of the Bristol Division thence to Chippenham, were let in the spring of 1839, but, as elsewhere, the work was much delayed by the wet winter of that year. In the summer following, the Directors determined to open a section of 16½ miles from Faringdon Road to a point between Swindon and Wootton Bassett, where the railway was within half a mile of the turnpike road between those places, and where a by-road called Hay Lane crossed the former at the entrance of the long Studley Cutting, evidently not yet finished, 80 miles from Paddington.[1] Although there are no works of any special difficulty or importance on it, even this was not ready till December.

Meantime the Railway Regulation Act of 1840, commonly known as Lord Seymour's Act, had come into force, providing, amongst other things, that all new railways must be inspected and approved by 'The Lords of the Committee of Her Majesty's Privy Council appointed for Trade and Foreign Plantations', called for short the Board of Trade, before being opened for the public conveyance of passengers. Accordingly Saunders gave the required notice of the intended opening to their Lordships, and their Inspector-General of Railways, Lieut.-Col. Sir Frederic Smith, R.E., came down early in December to inspect and report.

He found the embankments and cuttings finished off, except the central part of Marston Cutting, and most of the bridges complete or on the point of completion, save that under the Roman Ermin Street, near Stratton St Margaret, the arch of which had not yet been turned. About a mile and a half of permanent way remained to be laid, and more ballast was required at several places. 'The Signal Disks and Lamps, which are of a very satisfactory character on that part of the railway at present open to the Public, have not yet been put up on the new line.'

There were three level crossings of public highways, and as to these a legal question arose. The Great Western Act of 1835, in common with other early Railway Acts, provided that the gates should be kept shut across the railway and only opened to allow trains to pass. On the other hand, a public general Highway Act of 1839 provided that Railway Companies should maintain gates across each end of the road at such crossings, so that people passing along the road should not be exposed to danger from the trains. The point was whether the later general enactment

[1] About the present 80¼ mile post.

by inference repealed the special one. At these crossings the Company had erected gates across the roads not wide enough to close across the railway in accordance with their own Act. Sir Frederic Smith, being a man of common sense, contented himself with drawing attention to the fact and approving what had been done, while at the same time suggesting that the road gates should be of such dimensions as to meet across the railway when open and so prevent trespassing. A year later the point was again raised by a letter from Saunders to the Board of Trade, to which the Board replied that they agreed with the Directors that keeping the gates shut across the railway was much more dangerous than keeping them shut across the highway, and that several fatal accidents had recently occurred in consequence of the former practice; they also considered that Parliament had intended the general Act to supersede all inconsistent private Acts. The supposed intention of Parliament being, however, of little importance in law, Saunders had a test case brought before a bench of magistrates by causing one of his crossing keepers to be summoned for not keeping the gates shut across the railway. The magistrates adopted the view of the Board of Trade, and dismissed the case. The doubt was eventually set at rest by the Railway Regulation Act of 1842.

As to the terminus at Hay Lane, officially entitled 'Wootton Bassett Road' being nearly four miles by road from the little town, Sir Frederic remarked: 'Although Hay Lane Station is merely intended as a temporary terminus, the Company are forming it, in regard to sidings, switches and other mechanical arrangements, in the same extensive and substantial manner as is their ordinary practice at permanent terminals'.

Having received their Inspector's satisfactory report, the Board of Trade sanctioned the public opening as soon as his few requirements had been satisfied. This caused a delay of a day after that already advertized, and the extension to Wootton Bassett Road was eventually opened without any fuss on Thursday, 17th December 1840, for all kinds of traffic. The only intermediate station was at Shrivenham,[1] such inhabitants of the market town of Swindon as wished to venture on the new railway having to betake themselves to Hay Lane, three good miles to the west, until such time as the junction station to be established within a mile of the town should be ready.

Two months before the opening of the railway the founding of a new town in the fields between it and Swindon had been foreshadowed, when the Great Western Directors, by the advice of Brunel, who with Gooch had been down on a special visit of inspection, resolved on 6th October:

That the Principal Locomotive Station and Repairing Shops be established at or near the Junction with the Cheltenham and Great Western Union Railway at Swindon.

The following letter from Gooch to Brunel shows the grounds on which this decision was based.

[1] Uffington was added in 1864.

BRISTOL,
13th September 1840

MY DEAR SIR,

According to your wish I give you my views of the best site for our principal engine establishment, and in doing so I have studied the convenience of the Great Western Railway only, but also think the same point is the only place adapted for the Cheltenham and Great Western. The point I refer to is the Junction at Swindon of the two lines.

The only objection I see to Swindon is the bad supply of water. There is also an apparent inequality of distance or duty for the engines to work—but which is very much equalized when the circumstances attending it are taken into account. I find the actual distances are as 76½ to 41 and the gradients are for the short distance of 41 miles a rise of 318 feet or 7·75 feet per mile, and for the 76½ miles a rise of 292 feet or 3·8 feet per mile. Swindon being the point at which these gradients change, the different gradients necessarily require a different class of engine, requiring for the Bristol end a more powerful one than for the London end.

That power can only be obtained conveniently by reducing the diameter of the Driving Wheels, therefore, supposing we work between Swindon and Bristol with 6 feet wheels, and between Swindon and London with 7 feet wheels, there will actually be very little difference between the work required of the two engines, when the additional gradients and curves, and the increased number of revolutions per mile which the small wheeled engine makes are taken into account. It would also divide the pilot engines very nearly equally, as Reading being the first Station where a pilot engine would be kept, say 36 miles, the next distance, to Swindon, would then be 41 miles, and on to Bristol another 41, and which I think would be sufficiently near for pilot engines to be constantly ready, and with this arrangement the watering stations would work very well. Steventon, where plenty of water can be had, forming a central station between Reading and Swindon, and as our Oxford Traffic comes on there I should think it likely that all trains will stop there. A large station at Swindon would also enable us to keep our Bank engines for Wootton Bassett incline at Swindon instead of having a separate station for that purpose at the bottom of the incline, and in addition it would at any rate be necessary to have a considerable Station at Swindon to work the Cheltenham line, which would be saved if Swindon was our principal station.

It has also the great advantage of being on the side of a canal communicating with the whole of England, and by which we could get coal and coke, I should think at a moderate price. I am not sufficiently acquainted with the place to know how far we would be affected by the want of water, it might probably be collected in the neighbourhood, and as we have a great deal of side cutting they might be converted into reservoirs, and should even this fail us we have the canal. These reasons lead me to think Swindon by far the best point we have for a Central Engine Station. From the plans and sections there appear little or no difficulties with the nature of the ground for building upon, and by placing the Station somewhere as shown in the enclosed sketch,[1] it might be made in every respect very complete. I have not thought of the Bristol and Exeter line in the arrangement, as it is quite possible to work it very well by engines kept at Bristol as long as they are fit for work. In the same way we could work the additional Bath traffic, for when necessary they could always work their way to Swindon when any heavy repairs were required. The Engine House we are building at Bristol would be ample for any slight repairs that might be required during the time the engine was in working order, and that without any outlay of machinery beyond a few hundred pounds. I am not aware of any difficulties connected with Swindon more than the water.

I am, my dear Sir,
Yours very truly,
I. K. Brunel, Esq.                                    DANIEL GOOCH.

Concurrently with the extension of the line to Wootton Bassett Road, the Directors arranged with the proprietors of the Bath and Bristol coaches to work them at a fixed mileage rate between that station and Bath in connection with the trains, carrying passengers and parcels booked through by the Company, and also made similar arrangements for the

[1] The sketch plan shows an Engine Establishment of the roundhouse type in a triangle formed by the two railways and a western loop joining them.

conveyance of goods. The Cheltenham and Gloucester traffic continued to and from Faringdon Road, owing to the bad state of the roads in the Wootton Bassett neighbourhood and the existing arrangements of the coach proprietors. In their August Report the Directors said with reference to this:

Although nearer in distance to Cheltenham, the country roads from Hay Lane to Cirencester were in such bad repair as to be almost impassable, and consequently the whole of that branch of traffic continued to join or leave the Railway at Faringdon Road.

The same cause very greatly affected the direct Bristol and Bath traffic, and prevented any material increase of income from the more remote or collateral trade. Indeed, if the Directors had not decided to take the Bath and Bristol Coaches into their own hands, under an agreement with the Coach Proprietors at the time they did, it would probably have been impossible to secure their running to Hay Lane while the roads for some miles from that Station were permitted to remain in the condition so much and so justly complained of by every passenger.

This state of things continued for nearly six months, until the railway was opened simultaneously to Chippenham and Cirencester.

### 6   Hay Lane to Chippenham

The earthwork on the next section to be opened, from Hay Lane to Chippenham, was extensive; there were four cuttings of from 40 to 50 feet maximum depth and three embankments between 30 and 40 feet high, besides another $3\frac{3}{4}$ miles long though nowhere more than 20 feet high. Two of the latter near Wootton Bassett caused much difficulty and expense by constant slipping. As early as February 1840 Brunel scented trouble, and reported to the Board:

At Chippenham the works have proceeded well, but in the neighbourhood of Wootton Bassett such have been the effects of the weather that it is probable that time and expense might have been ultimately saved by totally suspending the works during the last autumn and winter.

The quantity of work done during this period has been so limited that it would have required a few weeks only of summer weather to form the same extent of earthwork in a more substantial manner without incurring the same risk of future delays in the progress of the contracts from the slipping of earth excavated and thrown into embankment in a wet state. Arrangements are now making for redeeming as far as possible the time which has been lost, by prosecuting the works by the use of locomotive engines and other means with every possible vigour and despatch during the coming season.

Six months later he had resorted to side cutting, though this involved the purchase of extra land, 'which has not only improved the quality of the earthwork, but has enabled me to expedite the final completion, and at the same time to perform the great bulk of the work during the Summer instead of the Winter months'. In spite of all his efforts, the clay, of one of these banks especially, continued to slip till at last in the spring of 1841 he was obliged to adopt the expensive and laborious plan of driving several rows of large piles through the mass into the solid ground below and chaining opposite piles together with chain cables. Even this, though it enabled the line to be opened, did not entirely cure the slipping, which continued to give more or less trouble for many years.

A sudden small slip during the night of 7th September 1841 in the western of the two embankments, that on the Wootton Bassett Incline, caused the derailment of the Up Mail train, consisting of three carriages drawn by two engines, *Rising Star* and *Tiger*. The former passed the slip in safety, but *Tiger* broke away from it and ran off the rails with the train, fortunately towards the Down line. Though all remained on their wheels, the first two carriages were badly damaged; one passenger had a leg broken, and three others as well as two servants of the Company were slightly injured.

The incline on which this accident occurred is the first of any importance on the line from London, and falls westward for 1 mile and 550 yards at 1 in 100. As far as Didcot the gradients, mostly rising, nowhere exceed 1 in 1,320, or 4 feet in the mile; thence to the summit level at Swindon, 270 feet above Paddington and 292 above Bristol Station, they vary from 6 to 7 feet in the mile, with two short pieces at 8 feet or 1 in 660. From Swindon to the top of the incline and on from its foot to just beyond the bridge over the Avon at Christian Malford the line falls gradually at 8 feet per mile, to rise at the same rate thence to the east end of Box Tunnel.

As soon as these two embankments near Wootton Bassett had been made secure and the bridge over the Avon at Christian Malford finished, the 13¾ miles from Hay Lane to Chippenham were ready for public use, all the remaining works having been already completed. This section was accordingly opened on Monday, 31st May 1841, having first been duly inspected by Sir Frederic Smith. On the arrival of the first train from London, the Chairman and several Directors, with Brunel, the two Secretaries and other officers of the Company, were entertained at a public breakfast by the Mayor and certain inhabitants of Chippenham.

The station at Chippenham was not yet quite complete, according to the Inspector's Report, which notes also that 'The temporary station at Hay Lane is to be abandoned as soon as the station-house and other buildings which are now forming at Swindon, shall be completed'. As the portion of the Cheltenham & Great Western Union Railway between Cirencester and Swindon was opened on this same 31st May, it is evident, notwithstanding the inference which might be drawn from these words, that the junction station at the latter place was already sufficiently formed to provide at any rate for the transfer of passengers. Indeed 'Wootton Bassett Road' appears in the timetable of 14th June 1841 in addition to Swindon and was not abandoned till the new station at Wootton Bassett itself, more than 2½ miles west of Hay Lane, was opened a month or two later.[1]

## 7 CHIPPENHAM TO BATH

The remaining section, from Chippenham to Bath, comprised the heaviest works on the whole line. On scarcely one of the thirteen miles were the rails within ten feet of the natural surface of the ground. A stone viaduct immediately west of the station is followed by a high embankment

[1] Dauntsey was opened in February 1868.

for more than two miles, and then come three miles of almost continuous deep cutting, with perpendicular sides for the last half mile, to the mouth of the great tunnel under Box Hill, not quite two miles long but then much the longest in the country. From the west end of the tunnel half a mile of embankment leads to a short tunnel, followed after a short interval by a cutting in the side of a hill and another long embankment for three miles to the village of Bathampton, with a bridge over the Avon at Bathford. Thence a cutting and embankment lead to the outskirts of Bath, where the Kennet & Avon Canal had to be diverted, a big retaining wall built, and two short tunnels under houses made. West of the second of these an embankment and viaduct, again crossing the Avon, bring the railway into Bath Station.

Preliminary work on Box Tunnel was begun early in 1836 by the sinking of trial shafts to ascertain the nature of the ground, and in September a contract was let for six permanent and two temporary shafts, 28 feet in diameter. Work on these started in November, and in February 1837 the Directors reported:

> Unfounded reports were circulated industriously during the first application to Parliament respecting imaginary difficulties to be encountered in the Tunnel through the Box Hill to the east of Bath, and it may be a satisfaction to the Proprietors to know that trial shafts have been sunk and the strata, through which it passes, fully ascertained; the result of which not only proves the incorrectness of such reports but gives full assurance of the work being free from all unexpected or unusual difficulties. The completion of the permanent shafts is now far advanced, and the works of the Tunnel will be commenced as quickly as possible.

The strata were found to be, successively from the east end, the great oolite or Bath stone, a thick bed of light coloured clay or fuller's earth, the inferior or lesser oolite, and the blue marl between that and the lias, all sloping from west to east at a steep angle to the tunnel, which was to be on a falling gradient of 1 in 100, 53 feet to the mile. Most of the shafts, which varied from about 70 to 300 feet in depth, having been sunk by the autumn of 1837, contracts for the tunnel itself were advertized. There seems to have been some difficulty in letting these, but eventually in February 1838 the greater part of the tunnel was undertaken by George Burge of Herne Bay, a big contractor of the day, and the remaining half mile, through Bath stone at the eastern end, by two local men, Lewis of Bath and Brewer of Box, who had already been engaged in sinking the shafts for this portion. The contracts provided for the work being finished in thirty months—by August 1840—and for defined monthly progress. Burge's part of the tunnel was to be lined with brickwork throughout, while Lewis and Brewer were to leave the bare rock to form the roof and sides. One of Brunel's assistants, William Glennie, was placed in charge of the whole tunnel as Resident Engineer, and remained so throughout its construction.

Lewis and Brewer had already had great trouble from water. In November 1837 one of the shafts was flooded to the height of 56 feet, and their steam pump being inadequate, work was suspended for some months till they installed a second, worked by a steam engine of 50 horse power.

The same thing recurred a year later but was overcome in less than a fortnight. Burge was luckier in this respect, though he also had to make use of a steam pump at one of his shafts.

Apart from these pumps, all the work was done by manual and horse labour, the material excavated being hoisted up the shafts by wretched horses walking round and round, turning drums on which the ropes were wound. A ton of gunpowder and a ton of candles are stated to have been used every week whilst the tunnel was making. For the greater part of the time, work went on night and day; 1,100 to 1,200 men and over 100 horses being employed by Burge alone; during the last six months these numbers were greatly increased, and 4,000 men and 300 horses are said to have been at work on the whole tunnel. The men lodged in the neighbouring villages and hamlets, where all available accommodation was fully occupied and beds never empty, the night shift turning in soon after the departure of the day shift. Drunkenness and fighting were very bad, and on Sundays the foremen were employed in endeavouring to keep the peace in the villages, there being of course no regular police force in those days. Altogether it is not surprising to read that there was much rejoicing among the inhabitants of the country-side when the tunnel was at last finished and the visitors took their departure. Nearly a hundred of the latter are said to have been killed on the works during the whole five years.

By the end of August 1839, 1,350 yards of the tunnel had been excavated, and 1,200 entirely finished. Six months later Brunel reported that, though the work had been again much hindered by an increase of water, 1,900 yards, nearly two-thirds of the whole length, had been done; to expedite matters, three additional shafts had been sunk and work begun from them in each direction.

Meantime the heavy work of the long cutting and embankment between the tunnel and Chippenham had been commenced in the summer of 1837 but made slow progress; two years later it was only about half finished. Then the wet winter caused slips in the embankment and more delay, but by the summer of 1840 this trouble had been overcome, and by the use of three locomotive engines the lost time was being made up.

Westward from the tunnel to Bath certain deviations from the original plan delayed the final setting out of the line and purchase of land till 1839. The works were begun in the summer, but the necessary diversion of the main turnpike and other roads in the Box Valley, and then the failure of a contractor early in the following year, caused more delay.

In February 1841 Brunel reported as to all this section as follows:

In the immediate neighbourhood of Bath much still remains to be executed on one contract. The diversion of the Kennet and Avon Canal, in the progress of which very serious difficulties had occurred, caused principally by continued wet weather at a critical period of the Works, requires most attention; the retaining wall, however, is nearly completed, and when the course of the Canal is diverted, which will shortly be done, the construction of the Railway itself at this point is a simple and easy operation.

With the exception of this one point, the Works are in a sufficiently forward state between Bath and Bathford. At Bathford the Bridge across the Avon is much in arrear, but the necessary means have been and shall be adopted for securing its early completion.

From this point to the Box Tunnel, the Works are in a forward state; the long embankment requires but a small additional quantity for its completion, and we are commencing to form the surface preparatory to ballasting.

The small Tunnel in Middle Hill and the adjoining cuttings are nearly finished.

The Works between Chippenham and the Box Tunnel, which have generally been considered as likely to be the latest, are now in such a state that by proper exertion their completion within the time required may be ensured; this exertion shall not be wanting on my part.

The Box Tunnel itself will be completed and open throughout from the Western Face to the Shaft No. 8, which has always been considered as the Eastern extremity, during the next month; and if the whole Tunnel cannot be then said to be finished, it is only because the Eastern end, which is entirely in rock and belonging more properly to the Contract last referred to, has been extended a few yards in order to diminish the quantity of excavation required in the open cutting. The permanent way in the Tunnel will shortly be commenced.

At this time Brunel anticipated opening the whole 27 miles from Hay Lane to Bath simultaneously early in June, but, in spite of continuous night and day work, bonuses to contractors and foremen, and all his efforts, it soon became evident that the western half would not be ready as soon as the eastern, so another partial opening, as far as Chippenham, was made on 31st May.

Some three weeks later notices appeared in the papers that the railway would be opened throughout from London to Bristol, and to Bridgwater— for the first section of the Bristol & Exeter Railway had been opened on the 14th—on Wednesday, 30th June. In view of the very unfinished state of the works, especially in the immediate neighbourhood of Bath, this notice seems to have been received with much scepticism by the public. Sir Frederic Smith, inspecting the line on the 28th, found several of the bridges, the fences, and the ballasting very far from complete, and only sanctioned the opening on Brunel personally undertaking that certain essential details should be completed before the running of the first train, and that every precaution for the public safety should be taken. Saunders also undertook that he and Gooch would personally superintend the traffic on the spot till everything had been fully completed.

The opening accordingly took place as advertized on 30th June 1841. No public ceremony seems to have marked this important historical event. A beflagged train with Directors and others left Paddington at 8 in the morning, and is stated to have reached Bristol in four and Bridgwater in five and a half hours, but the first train to use the new piece of line between Bath and Chippenham was one for the general public which left Bristol at 7 a.m. for London; when it got there is not recorded.

Box Tunnel was thus described to the Board of Trade:

The Tunnel is 3,193 yards,[1] rather more than 1¾ miles, in length, in forming which eight large shafts, numbered from west to east, were excavated, of which Nos. 1 and 8 were afterwards enlarged into the openings or deep cuttings for the entrances of the tunnel at each end, so that six only remained when the work was finished, which were about 25 feet in diameter and varied from about 85 to 260 feet in height above the top

[1] Its length is now officially stated to be 3,212 yards.

of the tunnel. The whole of the tunnel from the western extremity to about 100 yards beyond No. 6 Shaft is lined with brickwork. From thence to the eastern mouth of the tunnel a length of about 900 yards was formed by excavating the natural rock in the shape of a Gothic arch, no part of which is lined with masonry except at the eastern entrance and for a short distance in, where the sides are retained by walls and the roof by an arch built of the stone found near the spot.

As a matter of fact there were five or six smaller shafts open during the excavation, but these were all filled in when the work was finished. The tunnel is perfectly straight, and on an incline of 1 in 100 falling towards the west. When it is clear of smoke one can see through from either end, and it is said that on or about 9th April the sun is visible from the west end before it rises over Box Hill. To check the speed of trains descending the incline, Brunel adopted the curious expedient of substituting for the usual rails on the Down line two flat iron plates, an inch thick, laid on a thick layer of felt, and slightly inclined inwards. How far these answered their purpose, or how long they remained, we know not.[1]

At the opening, only a single line was ready through the tunnel, and for the first forty-eight hours on end Gooch, the Locomotive Superintendent, himself acted as pilotman to travel with every train. In his own words:[2]

At about 11 o'clock on the second night we had a very narrow escape from a fearful accident. I was going up the tunnel with the last up train when I fancied I saw some green lights in front.[3] A second's reflection convinced me it was the Mail coming down. I lost no time in reversing the engine I was on and running back to Box Station with my train as quickly as I could, when the Mail came down behind me. The policeman at the top of the Tunnel had made some blunder and sent the Mail on when it arrived there. Had the Tunnel not been pretty clear of steam, we must have met in full career and the smash would have been fearful, cutting short my career also. But, as though mishaps never come alone, when I was taking my train up again, from some cause or other the engine got off the rails in the Tunnel, and I was detained there all night before I got all straight again. I need not say I was not sorry to get home and to bed at Paddington, after two days and nights pretty hard work.

In order to allay, as far as possible, the public fear of this monstrous and terrible tunnel, it had been arranged to light it throughout with reflector lamps, and Sir Frederic Smith so reported to the Board of Trade. When he came down to enquire into the accident on the Wootton Bassett Incline in September, he discovered that it was not lighted, and reported the fact to the Board, adding that he believed 'the lighting would add essentially to the comfort of the travellers, and in some degree to their safety, for, as it is not the practice of this railway to have white lights at the head of the engines, the drivers have at present no means of discovering any obstructions that there might be on the rails in front of them'.

To this Brunel replied in his report to the Directors, which was sent to the Board of Trade:

It had originally been determined, as mentioned by Sir Frederic Smith, to light this tunnel, and the lamps were made and fixed, and for a short time the attempt was persevered in.

[1] The Down line was entirely relaid in June 1851, all trains being worked over the Up line for eight consecutive days.

[2] *Diaries of Sir Daniel Gooch*, page 49.

[3] All Great Western engines carried a green headlight at this time, and passenger carriages sidelamps showing green to the front.

I think Sir Frederic Smith saw some of the lamps tried; the attempt has been abandoned because it altogether failed. I should observe that I never hoped to be able to produce any great effect towards lighting the carriages; this would require the walls of the tunnel to be whitened and strongly illuminated; my object was to throw a light on the rails, both to assist the workmen engaged in packing, etc., and to enable the enginemen to see ahead. I soon found that the impurity of the air, whether from external fog or from the steam and vapours of the engines, rendered this quite impossible. At most times the lamps were of no use whatever, even to the men at work in the tunnel, and never to the engine driver, to whom of course it is necessary that, if he sees at all, he should see some considerable distance ahead. The lamps were therefore removed.

For the same reason no lamp has ever been used in front of our engines for the purpose of throwing a light ahead upon the line, and I am not aware that this has ever been successfully practised by others.

It must be a much more powerful lamp than any of those hitherto used for the purpose, that would under ordinary circumstances illuminate the road to a distance of 150 yards, yet this distance, being traversed in about 10 seconds, would be much too short to be useful, and the glare of the lamp thrown upon the foreground would unquestionably render the distance less clear, and in foggy or rainy weather quite invisible. The lamps in front of the engines are used merely as signals.

I am afraid there are no means of remedying the evil of darkness in tunnels (the extent of which evil, however, is this, that the tunnel is during 24 hours as dark as the rest of the line frequently is during the night, but is otherwise exposed to fewer casualties) unless by a general and brilliant illumination, which would of course be very costly.

The expedient of lighting the carriages themselves had not yet been thought of, or at any rate deemed feasible.

The intention of lighting the tunnel was not the only one to be abandoned. In 1839 Saunders told the Parliamentary Committee on Railways that it was intended to work the Box Tunnel Incline by a stationary engine, or possibly by water power. Needless to say, this idea was given up in the course of the next year or so, when the ability of locomotives to climb such banks had come to be recognized. For some time after the opening all trains were assisted up the incline by a bank engine behind. This practice with passenger trains was objected to by Sir Frederic Smith at the same time as the lack of lighting but defended by Brunel, who instanced two inclines on the Liverpool & Manchester which had been so worked for more than ten years without accident. However, whether in deference to the Inspector-General's views or not, it was soon afterwards abandoned, and the bank engine always attached in front of such passenger trains as needed assistance.

The constant rumours of the insecurity of Box Tunnel were much strengthened in the summer of 1842 by the opinions of an eminent geologist, the Reverend Dr William Buckland of Oxford, afterwards Dean of Westminster, expressed at a meeting of the Institution of Civil Engineers in May. Without having ever examined the tunnel, he asserted that the oolite rock was of such a nature that large pieces were likely to be loosened and brought down by the concussion of the atmosphere and vibration caused by the trains, and that there was great danger of a serious accident in the unlined portion of the tunnel. This drew a friendly though sarcastic letter from Brunel, in which, while lamenting his lack of scientific knowledge of geology, he ventured to claim, as a result of the very extensive excavations he had been making for several years, a more thorough and practical knowledge of the particular rock in question than even the

New Swindon, bird's-eye view looking East, about 1850

Box Tunnel, East end, with Bath Stone Firm's private siding, about 1904

Box Tunnel, West end, 1842. (*Bourne*)

Bath Station. (*Bourne*)

Bristol No. 1 Tunnel, East end. The tunnel was converted to open cutting in 1887

Bristol Station. (*Bourne*)

learned Professor himself, and of course insisted on the absolute safety of the tunnel. In this he was confirmed by Major-General C. W. Pasley, who had succeeded Sir Frederic Smith as Inspector-General of Railways and was sent down in August, in view of the fears so mischievously excited by Dr Buckland, to inspect and report upon the state of the Tunnel.

Brunel's half-yearly report, read at the General Meeting at Bristol on 18th August, thus alludes to the matter:

A report having been generally circulated that parts of the Box Tunnel were unsafe, and that such an opinion was entertained by an authority well competent to judge, I am happy to be able to assure you that such is not the case, and that there has been no foundation for any such report. A portion of this Tunnel, it is well known, is carried through very solid beds of Oolite, and at some parts a particularly sound and hard bed occurred immediately, or within a few feet above the top of the Tunnel. To have left the looser beds underneath and have lined it with masonry would indeed have been a waste of money, when by slightly varying the height of the excavation a perfectly solid and safe roof was afforded by nature. No precautions were spared in examining and ascertaining the quality of this bed, and the experience of the large quarries in the neighbourhood, joined to our own in carrying on one of the largest excavations hitherto made in the Oolite formation, enabled me to determine beyond doubt the security of the roof thus selected. In my opinion, and that of others well competent to judge and who were engaged in the works, has, I am glad to say, received a strong and a very satisfactory confirmation.

The reports referred to were considered by the Board of Trade sufficiently important to induce Lord Ripon to direct that a survey of the work should be made by General Pasley; that examination, made with the utmost care, has led to his expressing to me his perfect satisfaction of its security, and his opinion that it would have been an useless expense to have arched those portions of the Tunnel.

Not quite three years afterwards a very severe frost in March 1845 caused some scaling and brought down a piece of stone weighing about three hundredweight from a spot 160 yards west of No. 7 Shaft, where a temporary airshaft, made during the construction, had been blocked up. The stone happened to fall in front of a light engine on its way back to Box and threw it off the rails, causing some delay to the trains but no other injury. This determined J. W. Hammond, the Resident Engineer of the line under Brunel, and his assistant in charge of the tunnel, W. G. Owen, to turn brick arches under the blocked air shaft and also under No. 7 Shaft, and to fill up the latter. Major-General Pasley again came down and, while approving of these expedients and considering them all that was absolutely necessary, recommended that No. 6 Shaft should also be blocked up, as an extra precaution against frost; but making a second visit a month later, he changed his mind and withdrew the suggestion. On this last occasion he brought with him the redoubtable Dr Buckland himself, who, after spending several hours tapping and minutely examining the rock with his geological tools, was forced to admit that his former fears were groundless, and that the unlined tunnel was perfectly safe.

Curiously enough, almost exactly fifty years after this, another severe frost caused the tunnel to be closed to traffic in March 1895 for over a month, while more of it was lined with brickwork.[1]

[1] Subsequently it was closed for varying periods for relining and maintenance.

Returning to 1841 and the newly opened line, half a mile west of the long tunnel was a short one of 200 yards through Middle Hill. Beyond this, the deep Ashley Cutting was not yet finished off, and a siding had to be made to remove clay from the hillside. The bridges over the Avon at Bathford and immediately outside Bath Station were both handsome single arches of the local stone, of 54 and 88 feet span respectively.[1] Other works calling for mention are the long and high retaining wall supporting the canal above the railway between Hampton Row and the two short tunnels, respectively 77 and 99 yards long, under the houses of Bathwick Hill, and the viaduct of 37 plain arches leading to the river bridge. The only intermediate stations between Chippenham and Bath were at Corsham and Box.[2] Close to the former a high stone arch of 90 feet span carries a road across the cutting.

By this time the Bath Station was practically finished and covered with a roof of 50 feet span, supported on each side by a row of large iron columns, most inconveniently placed within four feet of the edge of the platform. The principal timbers of the roof were like the long arms of cranes meeting in the middle and resting on the columns, and short arms being held down by the side walls behind the platforms. This peculiar plan was adopted to avoid, without the use of cross ties, outward thrust on the walls, which were built on top of a viaduct of stone arches.[3] There were four lines of rails under the roof, the two in the middle used as sidings. The goods shed was a small building with several turn-tables on the Up side, immediately west of the station and at right angles to the main line.[4]

The Bristol Terminus, for the same reason, had a similar though more elaborate roof of 72 feet span covering five lines of rails, but here the columns were smaller and joined by arches.[5] At each place the booking office was below on the ground floor, and at Bristol the waiting rooms were also in the arches under the station. A sector-table was provided at the end of the arrival line to release the engines of incoming trains, and there were a traversing frame inside and several turn-tables just outside the terminus. At the west end was a large building with an ornamented front towards the street, containing the Board Room and Offices of the Bristol Committee and their Secretary, as well as a residence for the Station Superintendent. Here the united Board of Directors used frequently to meet, and the August Half-yearly Meetings of the Shareholders were regularly held from 1841 until 1858 inclusive.[6]

[1] Their appearance has been quite spoilt in modern times by unsightly patches of brickwork!

[2] Bathampton was opened with the Bradford branch in 1857.

[3] Save for the lengthening of the platforms at each end outside the building, this station remained without noticeable alteration till 1897.

[4] It remained in use till 1877, when a new Goods Station was established half a mile to the west. This was replaced by the existing station in 1926–7.

[5] The original terminus still exists unaltered save by the widening of the platforms, now known as Nos. 13 and 14. The ugly footbridge at the east end, which spoiled the vista of the original portion, was removed in October 1934.

[6] The rooms are now used as offices by the Bristol Goods Agent and his staff. The handsome old Board Room has been divided.

The goods shed, a large building 326 feet long by 138 wide, was north-east of the station on the ground level beside the Floating Harbour, 12 feet below the railway and at right angles to it. Access was afforded by turn-tables and a double lift resembling a pair of scales, worked by hydraulic power, whereby trucks were alternately raised and lowered. It was not finished till the autumn of 1842.

Not quite half a mile east of the terminus, on the south side of the line opposite the engine shed, a series of coke ovens was built, which soon began to supply all the Company's engines, superseding the original small establishment at West Drayton. The coal used came from the Rhondda Valley, of course by sea from Cardiff to Bristol. The engine shed over the way was a comparatively small building, accommodating only fifteen engines on its three lines.

Between the engine shed and the station, the bridge over the Floating Harbour, finished only the year before, was already being widened to provide for a direct junction with the Bristol & Exeter Railway. That line, for some reason, probably to avoid the purchase and demolition of expensive house property in the town, had been laid out by Brunel to commence at right angles to the Great Western just outside the terminus of the latter. Early in February 1841 the Great Western Board sanctioned the formation of a junction involving the widening of the Harbour Bridge and the adjacent land arches for some distance from the station to admit of four lines of railway instead of two, the piers and foundations for such increased width having already been built in anticipation. The Bristol & Exeter Company were to pay half the cost of this work, and the southernmost pair of lines were to be reserved for their permanent use after the expiry of the lease of their undertaking to the Great Western. The Bristol & Exeter Directors agreed to this, and proceeded forthwith to make the curve from their line to the bridge, but whether it was ready in time for the opening to Bridgwater on 14th June is a matter of doubt; it was certainly in use very soon afterwards.[1] Another connection between the two railways was afforded by turn-tables outside the Great Western Terminus, which for many years were used for the transfer of single vehicles and goods trucks. There was no separate Bristol & Exeter Station till 1845.

[1] Sir Frederic Smith's Report to the Board of Trade on the Bristol & Exeter Railway from Bristol to Bridgwater, dated 1st June 1841, states 'It *will* form a junction with the Great Western Railway at Temple Meads, Bristol', which suggests the junction was not then complete, but it is shown as open for traffic on an official plan dated August 1841. The Bristol & Exeter Company paid their share of the cost to the Great Western in October 1841. The legend that the turn-tables were for many years the only connection between the railways, as distinguished from the stations, turns out to be a myth.

# V

# Early Growth

## 1839–1846

It very soon became obvious that the broad-gauge railway from London to Bristol—let alone the branches to Bradford and Trowbridge, which had not been attempted—was not going to be made for anything like the capital authorized by the Act of Incorporation—2½ millions by shares and a third of that sum by loans, in all £3,333,333. Half the subscribed capital having been paid up by October 1837, a Special Meeting was held to sanction the issue of the mortgage debentures, and also the borrowing of the balance of capital by loan in anticipation of further calls on the shareholders.

In the following August the Directors broke to them that new estimates had been made, based on the cost of the portion already finished, which showed the total cost of the land and works on the whole line would be £4,280,928, exclusive of locomotive power and carriage stock. In addition, Parliamentary and general expenses would absorb £288,000 of capital. The necessary powers having been obtained from Parliament, a further 1¼ million was raised by the issue in June 1839 of half shares of £50 each, nearly all of which were taken up by the existing shareholders, and a third of that sum by more debentures early in the next year, bringing the total capital up to 5 millions. Still more being required, the Directors were authorized in August 1840 to create 37,500 fifth shares of £20 each, and to borrow £600,000 on loan notes, to be paid off at fixed periods in cash or debentures. A year later, when the line had been opened throughout, they announced that the total cost of it, including, besides engines and rolling stock and everything necessary for the completion of the works, the locomotive establishment at Swindon, and coke ovens at Bristol, would be £6,150,000. This enormous increase over the original estimate was ascribed to the expensive Paddington Extension, for which no provision had been made, the exorbitant sums paid for land, the costly means adopted for expediting progress, and various contingencies such as slips in cuttings and embankments, which often involved the purchase of additional land. By the end of 1841, £6,340,000 had been raised, more than half by debentures and loan notes, and £6,282,000 spent. At this time £35 remained to be called up on each original share and £16 on each fifth share, the half shares being fully paid. The original shares were not fully paid till 1849.

The autumn of 1839 saw several changes in the Directors of the Company. In November the Chairman, William Unwin Sims, who had succeeded Benjamin Shaw in October 1837, committed suicide. The tragedy is thus recorded in Gibbs' Diary:

> November 16th. On Tuesday I attended the usual Committee—Sims was in the chair. On Thursday Sims was in Princes Street and at the Bank. The next morning he was found dead in his bed, undressed and with a pistol in his hand, with which he had lodged a ball in his head. We were all dreadfully shocked with this most unexpected tragedy, as there was nothing in his manner or conduct or circumstances to create the slightest suspicion of such an event.

Sims does not appear to have been a strong Chairman. Though he had himself proposed his election, Gibbs frequently complains of his weakness and vacillation in the struggle with the Liverpool opposition, and, after that was over, wrote in April 1839:

> I was much annoyed to-day by the bad judgment shown by our Chairman Sims with respect to the attempt made in Parliament to make an *ex post facto* change in our Act. I have no confidence in his judgment at all and am afraid that we made a great mistake when we appointed him Chairman. Unfortunately he feels no diffidence on this subject himself.

Three other members of the London Committee, among them Shaw, the first Chairman, and one of the Bristol Directors, disappeared from the Board about this time. One of their successors was the sixth Viscount Barrington of Beckett Park, Shrivenham, M.P. for Berkshire 1837–57, who afterwards succeeded Robert Bright of Bristol as Deputy Chairman.

On Sims' death, Charles Russell was unanimously elected Chairman of the Company, whose growth and policy he was to rule with a strong hand for sixteen momentous years. In fact, he, Saunders, and Brunel, besides being the great champions of the Broad Gauge, may be regarded as the founders of the Great Western System of to-day. He was the second son of Sir Henry Russell, 1st Baronet, of Swallowfield Park near Reading, and was born in 1786. It is a curious coincidence that he was ten years older than Saunders, Saunders ten years older than Brunel, and Brunel ten years older than Gooch. After serving for some years as an officer in the East India Company's Bengal Army, Charles Russell returned home and entered Parliament as a Conservative member for Reading in 1830, sitting for that town till 1837, and again from 1841 to 1847, when he was finally defeated. As we have seen, he was Chairman of the Committee on the Great Western Bill of 1835, and did much to help its passage.

At this time there was some prospect of the Great Western Railway forming part of the line of communication between London and Dublin. Of the three schemes proposed, one was for a railway surveyed by Brunel, and of course intended to be on the Broad Gauge, from Didcot through Oxford, Evesham, Worcester, Ludlow, Newtown, Dinas Mawddwy, Dolgelley, Barmouth, and Portmadoc to Porth Dynlleyn near Nevin on the north-west coast of Caernarvonshire, where an entirely new harbour was to be constructed. Another, for which Vignoles was responsible, was to reach the same place, whence the passage to Dublin was supposed to have some advantages over that from Holyhead, by a railway from the Grand Junction at Wolverhampton by Shrewsbury, Llangollen, Bala, and Dolgelley. Robert Stephenson, for his part, proposed a line from Chester along the coast to Holyhead and the enlargement of the small harbour there. In view of the importance of the subject, the Government appointed a Commission of three with two naval advisers to report on the merits of the rival projects. Though Brunel's line was favourably regarded by the Commissioners, they eventually reported in favour of Holyhead and Stephenson, on the advice of the naval experts that a harbour at Porth Dynlleyn would be liable to be silted up and could not be made as satisfactory as one at Holyhead. Another attempt to reach Porth Dynlleyn with a broad-gauge railway from Worcester was made during the mania year of 1846 but failed, after which that potential port faded back into the obscurity in which it has ever since remained.

In 1840 the first extension of the Company's field of operations was undertaken by the leasing of two other railways. In April the Cheltenham & Great Western Union Company accepted the terms offered them in 1837, and agreed to lease the portion of their line between Swindon and Cirencester, which was now approaching completion, to the Great Western for seven years from its opening at a rent of £17,000 a year. Meantime negotiations were in progress with the Bristol & Exeter Company, who at this time were desirous of avoiding an outlay of capital on engines and rolling stock. These eventuated in August in an agreement for a lease of their railway, in the first instance as far as Bridgwater with a branch to Weston-super-Mare, which section they undertook to have ready for opening by 1st June 1841, at a rent of £30,000 a year and a toll of a farthing a mile on every passenger and a ton of goods or coal carried; all subsequent extensions of the main line to be included in the lease at a proportionate mileage increase of rent, and the lease to remain in force for five years from the completion of the railway to Exeter.

## SWINDON

As we have already seen, the fiat for the establishment of Locomotive Works at Swindon went forth on 6th October 1840. The Directors' Report of the following February thus alludes to the subject:

The final determination of working those two Railways[1] upon Lease has imposed upon the Directors the necessity of providing an increased stock of Locomotive Engines, Carriages, Waggons and other Plant adequate to the trade which may be reasonably expected.

It has also decided the Directors to provide an Engine Establishment at Swindon, commensurate with the wants of the Company, where a change of Engines may be advantageously made, and the Trains stopped for the purpose of the Passengers taking Refreshment, as is the case at Wolverton on the London and Birmingham Railway. The Establishment there would also comprehend the large repairing shops for the Locomotive Department, and this circumstance rendered it necessary to arrange for the building of Cottages, etc., for the residence of many persons employed in the service of the Company.

The Directors have, under these circumstances, made an arrangement with responsible Builders for the erection of Refreshment Rooms and Cottages, without the employment of any Capital from the Company. The profits of the refreshment business are to remunerate them for all the outlay in the accommodation required at Swindon by passengers,

---

[1] Cheltenham & Great Western Union and Bristol & Exeter.

consequent upon the trains stopping at that place. The Company are to provide the land for the cottages, and to secure to the Builders a fixed rent upon lease, which rent will of course be reimbursed by the tenants of the cottages.

The only increased demand, therefore, upon the Company for capital at Swindon, will be to defray the cost of that additional land, and of the Engine Establishment and Repairing Shops there, which are indispensably necessary.

The responsible Builders were Messrs J. & C. Rigby of Millbank, Westminster, who had already been employed by the Company to build all the stations between Steventon and Corsham, as well as that at Slough. They were now commissioned to build the refreshment rooms, locomotive establishment, and 300 cottages for workmen, which last formed the nucleus of the town of New Swindon.

It was the Directors' desire to avoid any further addition to the already swollen cost of the line that led them to make the unfortunate arrangement as to the refreshment rooms, which they were soon to regret, and which remained an almost intolerable incubus on the Company for more than half a century. To ensure remunerative profits to Messrs Rigby for their outlay in building the station at their own expense, it was agreed that all regular trains should stop at Swindon 'for a reasonable period of about ten minutes', and that no rival stopping-place for refreshments should be established between London and Bristol. This agreement was eventually embodied in a lease of the premises to Messrs Rigby for 99 years from Christmas 1841 at a rent of one penny a year.

Within a week of the completion of the lease in December, Messrs Rigby sublet the refreshment business to S. Y. Griffiths of the Queen's Hotel, Cheltenham, for seven years in consideration of a premium of £6,000 and a rent of £1,100 a year; and in August 1848 they sold the lease outright to one J. R. Phillips for £20,000.

From the very first the refreshment arrangements were most unsatisfactory. Pending the completion of the permanent buildings, Griffiths had evidently set out to make his profits in some temporary accommodation, for on 1st February 1842 the Great Western Directors resolved that the charges and management of Swindon Refreshment Rooms were most objectionable in every respect, and gave notice to Messrs Rigby that the quality and prices of provisions are so unsatisfactory they must make an immediate alteration. The power of supervising the quality of the food supplied and settling the prices to be charged had indeed been reserved to the Company by the lease, but apparently there was great difficulty in enforcing it. Complaints continued to be general for many years. In December 1842 we find Brunel himself writing a characteristic letter, evidently in reply to one from Griffiths.

Dear Sir,

I assure you Mr Player was wrong in supposing that I thought you purchased inferior coffee. I thought I said to him that I was surprised you should buy such bad roasted corn. I did not believe you had such a thing as coffee in the place; I am certain that I never tasted any. I have long ceased to make complaints at Swindon. I avoid taking anything there when I can help it.

Yours faithfully,
I. K. Brunel,

The permanent refreshment rooms were opened to the public on 14th July 1842. Two large three-storeyed stone buildings, each 170 feet by 37, were erected on either side of the main line, here consisting of four roads, and respectively between it and the departure and arrival lines of the Cheltenham Railway. The basements contained kitchens, offices, and attendants' rooms; the principal floor of each building was wholly occupied by a large refreshment room, surrounded by covered platforms 14 feet wide on each side and 7 feet at the ends, and divided into first- and second-class portions by columns and an oval counter in the middle at which the refreshments were sold. Needless to say, third-class passengers were not catered for. These rooms were heavily decorated in the terrible style of the period, 'the walls and ceiling Arabesque and the columns painted after a recent invention to resemble inlaid wood',[1] and were considered very magnificent.

The top storeys of both buildings, joined by a covered bridge, formed an hotel, the coffee and sitting rooms being on the south and the bedrooms on the north side of the railway. Until a subway was provided many years later, the bridge was also used by passengers requiring to cross the line. Apart from the addition of bay platforms at each end, the station layout remains unaltered to the present day.

The locomotive works, situated in the fork between the Great Western and the Cheltenham Railways, were at last finished and brought into regular operation on 2nd January 1843, Archibald Sturrock being installed as Manager under Gooch. The establishment is thus described by Bourne in the following year:

At some distance west of the passenger station, on the north side of the line, is the Engine depot; its arrangements are upon a large scale, and capable of accommodating about 100 engines; these consist of the engines in actual use, of the stock of spare engines and of those undergoing repair. At this station every train changes its engine, so that from this circumstance alone, at least twice as many engines are kept here as at any other part of the line.

The Engine Shed is a rectangular building, 490 feet long by 72 broad, and capable of holding upon its four lines of rails forty-eight engines and tenders; the two ends are open, the roof is of wood, slated, with louvres at intervals for the escape of steam. The engines standing here are all in serviceable condition, and a sufficient number of them are ready with their steam up to carry on the business of the Railway. In the centre of and at right angles to this shed and abutting against its northern side is the Engine House. This is an oblong room 290 feet by 140, divided by two rows of columns into three compartments; the engines stand in the side compartments transversely, as horses in the stalls of a stable; and the central part, 50 feet broad, is occupied by a large platform, travelling on wheels from one end of the house to the other, by means of which an engine can be readily transferred between the central part and any one of the stalls. Here the engines receive their lighter repairs, those which the enginemen themselves are for the most part capable of executing. The roof of this shed is of timber and wrought iron, covered in with slating; the stalls will contain thirty-six engines and tenders. At the northern end of the Engine House are placed the buildings employed in the repairs of locomotive engines. The Erecting House, in which the parts of the engine machinery when repaired are put together, is a building communicating with the Engine House, and capable of holding eighteen engines.

[1] Bourne's History.

Such were the original Swindon Works. They soon began to grow. Early in 1846 the first home-built engines were turned out, and in this and the next two years large sums were spent on new shops and machinery. Soon 1,800 men were employed, to be reduced to 600 in 1849, when the first wave of economy set in. Owing to this reduction, a large part of the works, which then covered $14\frac{1}{2}$ acres, and much costly machinery, were for a time rendered useless. The new town kept pace with the works. Speculative builders began almost at once to add largely to Rigby's 300 cottages, and very soon the Company were obliged to build more.

G. H. Gibbs, the Director whose Diary has afforded us so many glimpses of early days, died in August 1842, bequeathing £500 towards the erection of a Church and School at Swindon. This led the Directors in the following February 'to implore for individual contributions from the Proprietors to provide the means of religious instruction and worship for the men and families to be located there'. In August 1840 they had proposed, at 'the earnest representation of the Clergyman and Inhabitants of the Parish of St Philip and Jacob in Bristol', to devote half an acre of the Company's land there to the erection of a Church, in which 'a certain number of Sittings should be appropriated for the Servants of the Company'; but the Proprietors had naturally objected, and convinced them that such an application of the Company's property or funds was wholly beyond its powers. Their Swindon appeal for subscriptions was so successful that they were able to set about the erection and endowment of the Church and School forthwith, and these were completed in 1845.

To revert to the general affairs of the Company, an important step in organization was made by the Board on 3rd November 1840, when it resolved:

> That the present London Secretary be appointed Secretary and General Superintendent of the Line.

Their February Report contains the following paragraph on the subject:

> The Directors, considering it their duty to make an appointment for the general superintendence of the traffic in order that the responsibility might devolve upon an Officer of the Company, have nominated the present London Secretary for that purpose, who has consequently entered upon those duties.

In practice, Saunders seems 'to have entered upon those duties' from the first opening of the line; he told the Parliamentary Committee of 1839 that anything unusual in the way-bills of the trains was reported to him daily, and we find Seymour Clarke making constant reports to him throughout that year. However, this was the first formal step in making him what he soon became, the chief executive officer of the Company. It definitely raised him over the Bristol Secretary, Thomas Osler, who had resigned the secretaryship of the Bristol & Exeter Company to succeed Captain Chapman on the Great Western in May 1837, and also of course over Seymour Clarke, who had been appointed 'Chief Traffic Superintendent' at Paddington at the time of the opening to Maidenhead.

As soon as the railway had been completed throughout, a reduction of the number of Directors from twenty-four to eighteen was decided on; this was effected by one death and five resignations before the next Half-yearly Meeting in February 1842. Six months later, a further reduction to twelve was decreed, to be effected as vacancies by death or resignation should occur; it was not completed until the end of 1847.

Meantime great changes had been made by the adoption by the Board in October 1841 of a report made by the Chairman and Deputy Chairman as to the future management of the railway. The separate London and Bristol Committees were abolished and Traffic and General Committees appointed, Saunders becoming executive officer of the former, and Osler of the latter. These two Committees were to meet weekly. All meetings of the Board and of the Committees were to be held at Steventon, 'if the requisite offices can be provided there without material expense'. The two Traffic Superintendents, Seymour Clarke and his brother Frederick, were to act in the capacity of assistants to the General Superintendent of the Line for their respective districts.

Brunel was forthwith directed to prepare plans for the alteration of the rooms in the superintendent's house at Steventon to accommodate the Board and Committees, and in the following April the work there was ordered to be expedited. Part of the house is now occupied by the station-master.

Steventon was evidently chosen as being a halfway house between London and Bristol; until the opening of the branch to Oxford it was regarded as an important first-class station. It did not long remain the centre of Great Western government—for barely six months as events turned out. The first meeting was held there on 21st July 1842, and what appears to have been the last on 5th January 1843. By this time the Directors had decided, as a measure of economy, to consolidate the London and Bristol Offices and to concentrate all the Company's business in London. Reporting this to the Shareholders in February, they added that the abolition of the separate office at Bristol involved the retirement of Mr Osler from the service: 'The Directors feel it due to him to report that he has faithfully served the Company and devoted himself to the duties of his office with exemplary zeal, integrity and industry'. After this the Bristol Directors, of whom there were necessarily under the Company's Acts at least four, had perforce to travel all the way to London to attend the Board.

In 1843 the Company exhibited the first symptom of that appetite for swallowing lesser railway companies which it indulged at frequent intervals during the next eighty years till the craving was finally satiated by a surfeit of Welsh coal railways forcibly administered by Parliament. The appetiser was the unfortunate Cheltenham & Great Western Union Railway Company, whose sad story we must now relate.

Before doing so, the opening of the Bristol & Exeter Company's line from Bridgwater to Taunton, 163 miles from Paddington, on 1st July 1842, and its extension for 8½ miles to Beambridge beyond Wellington, where it crossed the main Exeter turnpike road, on 1st May 1843 must be recorded. For the time being these formed additions to the Great Western system under the existing lease.

### THE CHELTENHAM & GREAT WESTERN UNION RAILWAY

In the autumn of 1833, very soon after the issue of the prospectus of the Great Western, some enterprising residents in Cheltenham and its neighbourhood projected a railway from that town by way of Gloucester and Stroud to join the line from Bristol and so afford communication with London. No practical steps were, however, taken till after the Great Western Company had obtained their Act in 1835. Then, Brunel having made a survey of the proposed line, a public meeting was held in Cheltenham on 13th October, at which it was resolved that 'An Act having been obtained for making the Great Western Railway, it would be productive of important advantages to the town of Cheltenham and to the agricultural, manufacturing, and commercial classes of the City and County of Gloucester, that a Railway should be established from Cheltenham to join the Great Western Railway at or near Swindon in the County of Wilts'.

The Cheltenham & Great Western Union Railway Company was accordingly formed with a capital of £750,000, more than enough to cover the entire expense of the line according to Brunel's sanguine estimate, and a Bill deposited for the 1836 Session of Parliament with the warm support of the Great Western Company. Unfortunately it was not destined to have a calm passage like that for the Bristol & Exeter Railway. The London & Birmingham Company had already begun to think imperially and proposed to annex all the country north of the Great Western. With this object they supported, if they did not actually promote, a company to make a line from Tring to Cheltenham, passing by Aylesbury, Thame, north of Oxford with a short branch to that city, Witney, Burford, and Northleach. It would have had the advantage of being more than 20 miles shorter—99 miles from Euston as against 120 from Paddington by Swindon—but its gradients were incomparably worse all the way from Tring.

A strenuous fight in Parliament gave the Cheltenham & Great Western Union Company the victory, and the Tring attack was defeated, to be renewed a couple of years later and again defeated. The Thames & Severn Canal Company was another formidable opponent, as was Squire Gordon of Kemble, each of whom had to be bought off for £7,500 as 'compensation for damage to be sustained'.

The Bill for the Birmingham & Gloucester Railway was also before Parliament in this session, and as both Companies claimed the ground between Cheltenham and Gloucester, they very sensibly agreed to share it and make what was in effect a joint line. But the idea of a joint line as we know it seems to have been strange to the lawyers of the day, so they made the curious arrangement we shall find in the Act.

The two Companies also agreed to purchase jointly the old Gloucester

& Cheltenham Railway for £35,000, on which sum the tolls were then paying 6½%. This was a plate tramway, opened in 1811 from the Berkeley Canal Basin at Gloucester to Knapp Toll Gate, Cheltenham, with a branch to Leckhampton Hill, some 9 miles long in all, established under an Act of Parliament of 1809. It was worked by horses and used chiefly for the conveyance of coal. Only a small portion near Gloucester was used for the new railway; it continued to be worked and to pay small dividends down to 1859, when the Great Western and Midland Companies obtained an Act for its abandonment with power to sell the land.

The Cheltenham & Great Western Union Act, which received the Royal Assent on 21st June 1836, authorized railways from Cheltenham near a place called the Cold Bath in the tithing of Alstone, and from the east side of the new Cattle Market in Gloucester, to unite in a field in the Parish of Wotton St Mary, and thence through Stonehouse, Stroud, Chalford, and Kemble to a junction with the Great Western Railway where it crosses the North Wilts Canal near Swindon, with a branch from Kemble to a piece of land called Botany Bay in Cirencester. Clauses for the protection of Mr Robert Gordon, who evidently was no friend to the new-fangled method of travelling, provided that the railway should be in a covered way where it passed near Kemble House, and that no public station should be made on his estate. Hence Kemble Tunnel, 415 yards long, exists to this day, while for many years the junction of the Cirencester Branch was merely a junction with platforms to enable passengers to change trains, and did not appear in the public time-tables until 1872. The station for the neighbourhood was therefore established a mile farther on just across the ancient Fosse Way, which here formed the boundary of Mr Gordon's land and the counties of Wilts and Gloucester. Under the name of Tetbury Road it accommodated passengers as well as goods from the opening of the line till 30th April 1882, by which time a proper station had been built at Kemble, barely a mile off. It was rechristened Coates in 1908 and still exists as a goods station[1]. Another clause, also apparently to pacify the Squire of Kemble, enjoined the Company to build a new road-bridge over 'a stream called the Thames' in his parish.

With regard to the line between Cheltenham and Gloucester, the Act provided that the powers of the Birmingham & Gloucester Company under their Act, which had been passed two months earlier, should be inoperative, provided that upon tender by them to the Cheltenham & Great Western of half the actual cost incurred in making the line, the latter Company should become trustees for the former of the half of the line nearer Gloucester; after payment of that sum the Birmingham & Gloucester were to have the sole direction and control of such half, as if they had made it themselves. The Birmingham Company were to make the depot at Gloucester at their own cost for the use of both, the Cheltenham Company leasing them the land required, while the latter were to make the common depot at Cheltenham.

[1] It was closed on 1st July 1963.

Although the gauge of the Cheltenham & Great Western is not defined in the Act, it is clear that the broad had already been decided on, as the line between Cheltenham and Gloucester is directed to be formed 'in such manner and with rails of such shape and *width*' as was adapted for carriages running on the Birmingham & Gloucester and London & Birmingham Railways, subject to the power of the Cheltenham & Great Western to lay additional rails for its own traffic at its own expense. Afterwards each Company was to keep its own half in good repair, including the extra rails required for the other's traffic. The Cheltenham Company was bound to complete the line in readiness to be opened at the same time as that between Birmingham and Cheltenham.

Having obtained the Act, the Directors, of whom W. H. Hyett of Painswick House was Chairman, were in no hurry to proceed with the works. Hard times had set in and money was scarce. More than a year later, in November 1837, they reported that the condition of trade and the public credit had been so discouraging that they had been unable to make any material progress in the undertaking, but that these having then slightly improved, they were considering where to commence operations. After discussing the claims of the Cheltenham and Gloucester section, they recommended for reasons they gave at length that a start should be made on the portion between the junction with the Great Western and Cirencester, so that as soon as the Great Western had reached Swindon a continuous line would be open from London to Cirencester, whence coaches would complete the journeys to Stroud, Gloucester, and Cheltenham. They had accordingly made a conditional arrangement with the Great Western for a short lease to them of that portion when completed at a rent of £17,000 a year, which would give a satisfactory return on the £35 a share proposed to be called up for this purpose. As regards the rest of the line, they were applying to Parliament for an extension of time.

Needless to say, this course did not commend itself to the Directors of the Birmingham & Gloucester Railway, who had been getting on with their own line and were dependent on the Cheltenham Company for its completion to Gloucester. So they opposed the Bill in Parliament and obtained the insertion of clauses providing that if the Cheltenham Company had not purchased all the land required between Cheltenham and Gloucester by 21st March 1839, or had not completed the railway by 24th June 1840, then, in either case, the Birmingham Company should take over all the powers of the Cheltenham and do what was necessary themselves. If this should happen, the Cheltenham Company were empowered, provided they had completed their own line throughout from Swindon to Gloucester by 21st June 1845, to repurchase on payment of half the cost of the line, and thereupon the whole line between Cheltenham and Gloucester was to revest in them as if they had made it under the original Act, subject of course to their trusteeship of the half nearer Gloucester.

Besides giving two years extension of time, this Act of 1838 authorized a deviation at Frampton Common which shortened and straightened the Sapperton Tunnel, and provided that each Company should make its own separate station in Gloucester.

The Directors now felt obliged to proceed with the Cheltenham–Gloucester section, and at the next Half-yearly Meeting, held at Stroud—hitherto they had all been at Cheltenham—announced that two contracts had been let extending from the Lansdown Road at Cheltenham to the Barnwood Road at Gloucester, and that, all the land having been purchased, the contractors were at work. In the Cirencester Division two contracts covering the line to Minety had been let and the land bought with the exception of three acres, while two more contractors had taken the piece from Minety to Swindon. With the exception of Squire Gordon's portion, for which they had agreed to pay at an exorbitant rate to get rid of his opposition in Parliament, the Directors stated they had acquired the land on favourable terms. In one case near Cheltenham, which had to be referred to a jury, £1,056 was awarded, the claim having been for £2,200. Special thanks were accorded to Earl Bathurst 'for his kind assistance on all occasions in furthering the interests of the Company'. A quaint feature appears in the accounts for this half year entitled 'Income Account', showing a net receipt of exactly £100,318 17s 5d. A sub-title, however, reveals that the figures given represent 'Traffic *Expected* on the Cheltenham and Great Western Union Railway'!

Early in 1839 the Birmingham & Gloucester Board purchased four acres near the Cattle Market in Gloucester for their station, so the Cheltenham Company, as in duty bound, bought the land and let a contract for the railway between it and the Barnwood Road, using part of the old tramway for the purpose. The two Companies also agreed that each should have its own separate station in Cheltenham as well as in Gloucester.

All this time no attempt had been made even to begin work on the line between Kemble and Gloucester, beyond the sinking of five shafts for the Sapperton Tunnel. The shares of the Company were at a heavy discount, its credit very low, and the Directors most reluctant to make calls on the Shareholders. At the end of the year only about £200,000 had been received, and the arrears amounted to over £40,000.

Finances were so desperate that in November the Directors, considering that it was not even practicable to complete both ends of the line simultaneously, decided to concentrate their resources on the portion between Cirencester and Swindon, and suggested to the Birmingham & Gloucester Company that they should take steps to ensure the early completion of the line between Cheltenham and Gloucester. That Company, in conjunction with the new Bristol & Gloucester Company, which was to use the Cheltenham & Great Western between Stonehouse and Gloucester, then made a proposal to buy the whole line from Cheltenham to Swindon, and actually promoted a Bill in Parliament for power to do so, but early in the next year the proposal was dropped and the Bill withdrawn.

Soon afterwards the Birmingham Company decided to take over the Cheltenham–Gloucester line in exercise of their powers under the Act of 1838, and arranged with the Cheltenham & Great Western to pay off the money they had spent on it by instalments of £20,000 a month, besides the £17,500 they had contributed to the purchase of the tramway. The line was accordingly handed over to them on 18th June 1840, six days only before the opening of their own railway from Bromsgrove to Cheltenham. At the end of April Brunel had reported that all the principal works between the Lansdown Bridge at Cheltenham and the proposed station at Gloucester had been completed, except two road bridges which were three-quarters finished; so their Engineer, Captain Moorsom, had little to do but lay the permanent way. This and the Gloucester Station were ready by 4th November, when the line was opened as part of the Birmingham & Gloucester Railway.

The works between Cirencester and Swindon were now at last approaching completion, and the Directors obtained the sanction of the shareholders to lease that portion of the Great Western on the terms suggested in 1837. This lease was for seven years from the opening, at a fixed rent of £17,000. The opening, expected for January, was delayed for some months by slips in the embankment near Swindon. This embankment, about $1\frac{3}{4}$ miles long and averaging 20 feet high, was formed of clay obtained from side cuttings, much of it in the wet winter of 1839–40. Several small slips occurred in the following year, and in repairing these the interior of the bank was found to be saturated with water and in a very soft state. At one place it had subsided as much as 8 feet in 24 hours! To remedy this, Brunel first tried burning large masses of clay on the slopes, and then filled up portions of the side cutting where the foundation of the bank had given way and made the embankment good with large quantities of dry rubble and sand.

It was inspected for the Board of Trade by Sir Frederic Smith, who found it 'tolerably firm', but recommended careful watching. The rest of the line he found in good order and so sanctioned its opening, which took place on 31st May 1841, the same day as the extension of the Great Western from Hay Lane to Chippenham. As far as the intended junction at Kemble the line was double, thence to Cirencester single, all composed of bridge rails weighing 54 to 60 lbs to the yard on longitudinal timbers. There were stations at Purton, Minety, and Cirencester, and Disc-and-crossbar signals had been set up.

Very soon after the opening the Swindon embankment again began to move. Fortunately the slips were confined almost entirely to the east side, so it was possible by using the Up line for bringing materials to keep the Down line open for traffic as a single line, worked by a pilot engine. In spite of Brunel's efforts, matters got worse in the autumn, the Up line subsiding several feet below the level of the Down, which, however, was still kept passable and in use. Early in December an excitable traveller wrote from Cheltenham to the Board of Trade: 'I returned by the railway, and as far as Swindon all was very well, notwithstanding the wet, but from Swindon to Cirencester I was horrified at seeing the road I was passing over, and nothing shall tempt me to do it again. One line of rails has slipped for a mile or two completely away and the trains travel on the other line, which appears just hanging by a thread, and this on a precipice of 40 to 50 feet!'

The result of this was a visit of inspection by General Pasley, in January 1842, who, after observing on the gross exaggeration of the letter, and describing the embankment, reported as follows:

> Fortunately the ground on the western side of the embankment remained firm, so that the slips took place on the eastern side only, where the clay, almost in a fluid state, gave way and moved towards the adjacent cutting, this movement taking place below the surface, as was proved by the remarkable fact that some very strong piles, which had been driven at the bottom of the embankment, were forced forward out of their original line, moving along with the clay; and in one part in particular some of them are now to be seen 70 feet in advance of their former position. This movement was described to me as having been very slow, so that if carefully watched, and men be stationed to stop the trains, no danger can arise from it; but it was so powerful on the east side that the ground under the rails there sank no less than 3 feet in 24 hours in the worst part.
>
> To make good the embankment Mr Brunel has caused soil of a better quality to be brought from a hill at the north end of it, and to be continually laid on the east side, using the rails on that side for the transport of this earth; and, having found piling to be of little use, he has directed a dry wall of rubble stone, 12 feet thick, to be built at the bottom of the slope to the depth of 10 feet, which is equal to that of the cutting, as a retaining wall, to prevent the further movement of the base of his embankment towards the ditch or deep cutting on that side; which, as a further precaution, he has ordered to be filled up opposite to those places where the greatest movement of the moist clay took place. These measures will, no doubt, prove effectual, for, as I said before, the western line of rails is perfect throughout, and the eastern line is now only about 15 inches lower than the other in the worst part, and is being gradually brought up to its proper level, which Mr Brunel hopes to accomplish in four or five weeks.

The gallant General concludes his report by naively informing the Board that 'On my return from Swindon the rails were covered with snow, which had fallen continually during the day, and somewhat retarded but did not stop the progress of the train'!

Beyond having made conditional contracts for the land required for the whole railway and let a contract for a heading through Sapperton Tunnel, the Directors had done nothing towards proceeding with the line from Kemble to Gloucester up to the end of 1841. From this time onwards their main object, with the apparent assent of the Proprietors, seems to have been to get rid of the whole undertaking and their responsibilities as quickly as possible. Hyett had resigned the Chairmanship in the summer of 1840, to be succeeded by his Deputy, Norwood Trye of Leckhampton Court, who had had enough of the thankless office by November and gave place to C. F. Sage of Gloucester.

In 1842 the Company obtained an Act authorizing the sale or lease of the line to the Great Western, Birmingham & Gloucester, or Bristol & Gloucester Companies, and the raising of £750,000 additional capital; confirming the Swindon–Cirencester lease to the Great Western; allowing three years further time for completion of the railway; and enjoining the Birmingham & Gloucester Company to lay broad-gauge rails between

Bristol Goods Shed, 1842. (*Bourne*)

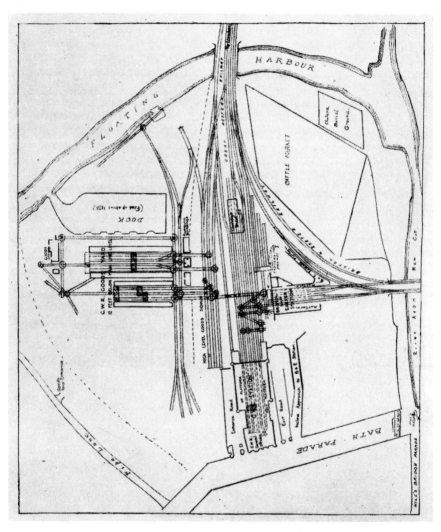

Plan of the Bristol Stations, 1845

Gloucester and Cheltenham at the cost of the Cheltenham & Great Western in time for the latter's traffic when it should be open to Gloucester. This same Act gave the Bristol & Gloucester Company power to make the portion they required to use between Standish and Gloucester themselves, and to lay narrow-gauge rails thereon, subject to the right of the Cheltenham & Great Western to repurchase, in which event the former Company were to have perpetual running powers over it.

After the passing of this Act the Directors lost no time in opening negotiations with the Great Western Board for the sale of the undertaking. For some months the latter would not consider anything beyond a lease of the line, when finished, with assistance in raising the necessary capital; but eventually in January 1843 they agreed, with the sanction of their shareholders, to buy the completed portion from Swindon to Cirencester and all the rights and powers of the Company, including that of repurchasing the moiety of the Gloucester–Cheltenham line and the tramway, for 3,000 Great Western half-shares of £50 each, fully paid, and £80,000 in cash. These terms were unanimously accepted by a Special Meeting of the unfortunate Cheltenham & Great Western Union Proprietors, held at the Company's Offices in Cirencester on 14th February, and finally ratified in detail at another meeting in August.

The transfer took effect on 1st July 1843. Thus for £230,000 additional capital the Great Western acquired the unfinished undertaking, on which the Cheltenham Company had managed to spend more than £600,000. A final Account of the latter, made up in December 1846, after all liabilities had been cleared off, shows that the shareholders received one Great Western half-share, worth in the market about £80, and 17s 6d cash for every 2 shares they held, on each of which they had paid up £83. Of the 5,693 existing shares the Great Western itself held 392; the rest of the original 7,500 had been forfeited for non-payment of calls.

The amalgamation of the two Companies was sanctioned by the Great Western Act of 1844, which also authorized an extension of $1\frac{1}{4}$ miles from the end of the 'joint' line at Lansdown Road to a station in the middle of St James' Square in the town of Cheltenham, and confirmed the power of repurchasing the moiety of that line from the Birmingham & Gloucester Company.

---

The Act of 1844, which confirmed the purchase of the Cheltenham & Great Western Union, also united the Oxford Railway Company with the Great Western. This Company never had more than a nominal existence, all its capital having been provided by the Great Western, and was finally dissolved by the Royal Assent to this Act on 10th May, just a month before the opening of its railway. The act also defined the capital of the united Company at £6,120,000, with power to borrow on debentures £2,040,000, the usual one-third of the fixed capital, and legalized the loan notes, by means of which the Company had raised £1,593,950 without Parliamentary authority

## THE OXFORD RAILWAY

A 'Probable Branch' of 12 miles to Oxford is shown on the map of the original Great Western Prospectus of 1833, but no steps towards making such a branch were taken till three years later. The Directors' Report to the Half-yearly Meeting in August 1836 states: 'A Branch to Oxford and a continuation of it to Worcester are promoted by the leading interests of those cities, and the best exertions of the Company will be devoted in co-operation with them to accomplish those objects'.

We hear nothing more at this time of the continuation to Worcester, but a Bill for the Oxford Branch was promoted in the Session of 1837. As originally laid out, the line, starting from Didcot, approached Oxford by the Cowley Road to a terminus near Magdalen Bridge and threw off a short branch to Abingdon. The proposed terminus was strongly opposed by Christ Church as owners of the land, so Brunel altered it to a site near Folly Bridge, east of the Abingdon Road, with an alternative in St Clement's. The University was pacified by clauses protecting the discipline of junior members and did not oppose, and the Bill had a peaceful passage through the Commons. In the Lords, however, it had a short shrift, the opposition of two landowners, Captain Pechell and Sir G. Bowyer, who owned $4\frac{1}{2}$ out of the total of $9\frac{1}{2}$ miles, being sufficient in that sanctuary of vested interests to stifle the project.

It was revived in 1838 without the Abingdon Branch—abandoned owing to the opposition of Mr Duffield, M.P. for that borough(!)—but again defeated in the House of Lords. This year the University was the chief opponent, and its Chancellor, the Duke of Wellington, led the opposition.

After another abortive effort in 1840, Oxford was left in peace with its station 10 miles off at Steventon, to and from which eight coaches ran daily, taking $1\frac{1}{2}$ hours on the journey for a fare of 3*s*. We learn that in 1842 77,567 passengers and 12,620 tons of goods were dealt with at that station.

By the autumn of that year the bulk of the residents seem to have discovered that this method of travelling might be improved on, and the 1838 project was revived in preference to a suggestion of George Stephenson for a line from Moulsford through Wallingford to Magdalen Bridge. Only two of the twenty-three members of the Hebdomadal Board, a committee formed of Heads of Houses which governed the University in those days, now opposed the railway, and of these two, the Warden of Wadham did so as Chairman of the Oxford Canal Committee. The Vice-Chancellor and the University generally were strongly in favour.

A Bill was accordingly deposited for the session of 1843 incorporating The Oxford Railway Company and authorizing the construction of a railway from the Great Western at Didcot to 'a certain field belonging to Brasenose College on the west of the Abingdon Turnpike Road in the Liberty of Grand Pont and Parish of St Aldate in the City of Oxford and

Counties of Oxford and Berks or one of them'. Clauses for the preservation of University discipline provided that the Vice-Chancellor, Proctors or Proproctors, Heads of Colleges and Halls or their deputies, and the Marshal of the University should have free access to all stations at train times to ascertain if any members of the University were travelling or attempting to do so, and forbade the Company to convey any such members below the degrees of Master of Arts or Bachelor of Civil Law as should be pointed out by such officers for a period of 24 hours, even if their fares had been paid, or to take up or set down any members below these degrees except at the regular stations, under a penalty of £5 for each offence. Power to sell or lease the line to the Great Western Company was taken, an early amalgamation being intended. The entire capital was put up by the Great Western in the names of ten of their Directors, there being no local shareholders.

Assents were obtained from all the landowners concerned, and the only petitions lodged in opposition were from the Corporation of Oxford and some 300 inhabitants of the town, both said to have been organized by the Oxford Canal interest; to counteract these a petition in favour bore the names of 1,500 citizens.

The Bill had an uneventful passage through Parliament, and received the Royal Assent on 11th April 1843.

Owing to difficulties in obtaining possession of parts of the land, work was not begun till October, but then proceeded rapidly through the exceptionally mild winter. The only engineering works of any importance were the bridges over the Thames at Appleford and Nuneham, and these were both constructed entirely of timber.

The whole branch, 9 miles 57 chains in length, was completed early in June, and on 10th Major-General Pasley, with Brunel and several Directors, came down to inspect it. The only fault the General had to find was the insecure state of the bridge carrying the Oxford–Abingdon turnpike road over the line. This brick arch with the road embankments approaching it had been left to the last moment for the curious reason given in General Pasley's report:

'Mr Brunel explained to me that the haste with which this arch was built was caused by the conduct of an individual in possession of part of the ground over which the embankment was carried, who after the site of the bridge had been decided on, erected what he called a "house", which I saw but should never have guessed the use of, being a small hut of timber framework covered with *brown paper*, with a fireplace in it, for the purpose of claiming compensation from the Railway Company for having diminished the value of his property; and the work was delayed as this person's unexpected claim could not be settled until near the period of the entire completion of all other parts of the railway.'[1]

Contenting himself with a direction that the old course of the road, crossing the railway on the level, should be maintained till the bridge and its approaches had been made good, the Inspector sanctioned the opening, which accordingly took place on 12th June 1844.

[1] The tradition of this paper house was current in Oxford at the end of the century.

On the same day a large junction station was opened at Didcot, consisting of four lines and five very narrow platforms under an 'all-over' roof, which did duty till burnt down on 11th March 1885. Intermediate stations were established at Appleford, 2 miles from Didcot, immediately south of the first overbridge on the branch, and 'Abingdon Road', 3 miles from Didcot. The former was abolished early in 1849, and the latter re-named Culham on the opening of the Abingdon Branch in 1856.

The Oxford terminus was a wooden erection with a large goods shed beyond it, and the line was continued almost to the bank of the river. It ceased to be used for passengers on the opening of the new station in 1852, but remained the Oxford Goods Station for another twenty years, after which it was finally abandoned and the land sold.

The Directors lost no time after the purchase of the Cheltenham & Great Western Union in proceeding to make the line from Kemble to Gloucester. There was need for hurry, as the power to buy back the moiety of the Gloucester–Cheltenham section from the Birmingham & Gloucester Company depended on its being completed from Swindon to Gloucester by 21st June 1845; moreover, as we shall see in the next chapter, they had agreed with the Bristol & Gloucester Company to have the portion between Standish and Gloucester ready for their use by April 1844. The whole was let in four contracts, and work begun in August 1843. A year later 7½ miles of the first of these had been finished as far as Standish and opened on 8th July as part of the Bristol & Gloucester Railway; of the second, from Stonehouse up the Stroud Valley to Sapperton Tunnel, about two-thirds had been completed and ballasted; of the third, limited to the tunnel itself, for which the heading and five shafts had been made by the Cheltenham Company 650 yards out of 2,227 remained unfinished; while from the tunnel to Kemble the line was ready for the permanent way. By February 1845 the tunnel and all the principal works were completed and the permanent way was being laid.

Early in May the new line was inspected by General Pasley, who was accompanied by Brunel's resident assistants, R. P. Brereton and C. Richardson. His report to the Board of Trade describes the tunnel.

The south entrance of the Sapperton Tunnel is 3 miles 71 chains from Kemble[1] in a cutting 47 feet deep. After a short portion of tunneling, on an ascending gradient of 1 in 95, 16 chains in length, is an open cutting of 3 chains in length on a level; after which the remainder of the tunnel, about 81 chains in length,[2] follows on a descending gradient of 1 in 90, except a short portion at the north end, which descends by a steeper gradient of 1 in 60. The whole length of the tunnel including the short cutting at the summit level is 2,212 yards, or rather more than 1¼ miles; about 80 yards at the north end of which are on the steeper gradient, and here the tunnel, which before was straight, has been laid out on a curve of 36 chains radius. At its north end it emerges in a cutting 64 feet in depth.

This tunnel has been cut through rock of the great and inferior oolites and fuller's earth formation, with shale and beds of shelly limestone. The rock being of an unsound quality with many wide and deep vertical and horizontal fissures, partly filled with clay or earth, it was deemed necessary to line it with masonry and brickwork throughout. The arch is a curve resembling an oblong segmental ellipse, of which the greatest span is

[1] This distance would make 'Kemble' 20 chains east of the present station.
[2] The two tunnels are actually 353 and 1,855 yards long.

28 feet at the height of 7 feet above the rails, diminishing to 27 at that level. Part of it, 443 yards, has been formed with an inverted arch, of which the span is 27 feet at rail level, with a versed sine of 2½ feet. The side walls and invert are of masonry and generally 2 feet thick, while 20 feet in width of the upper part of the arch have been built with brickwork varying in thickness from 18 to 27 inches, that is from two to three bricks thick. Ten shafts were opened in making the tunnel, all of which have been blocked up except one only in the middle of the long portion.[1]

From the tunnel the railway runs for 7 miles with many curves down the Golden Valley, following the course of the Thames & Severn Canal, to Stroud. In this distance there were nine timber viaducts,[2] described by General Pasley as follows:

| Distance from Kemble | Name | Description |
|---|---|---|
| 5.54 | Frampton . | Twelve 30 feet spans, |
| 6.65 | Slip[3] . . . | Twenty-two 30 feet spans, |
| 7.61 | St Mary's . | One span over the Canal of 75 feet on the skew, |
| 8.48 | Bourne . . | One span over the Canal of 67 feet on the skew, and sixteen others varying from 30 to 18 feet, |
| 10.16 | Capel's . . | Eighteen 30 feet spans, |
| 10.68 | Canal (in continuation of the above) | One span over the Canal of 51 feet on the skew and three others of 30, 28, and 22 feet, |
| 11.21 | Watt's . . | Eight 30 feet spans and four stone arches, |
| 11.31 | Stratford . | One 40 and seven 30 feet spans, |
| 12.10 | Cainscross . | Four 32 feet spans. |

After passing Stroud the line curves northward through Stonehouse to Standish, whence it runs almost due north to Gloucester.

There were four intermediate stations—Tetbury Road, Brimscombe, Stroud and Stonehouse—'all handsome stone buildings'.[4] At Gloucester the Company had as yet only a temporary station, and that not their own, made by adding a platform to the north side of the terminus of the Birmingham & Gloucester Railway, which the Great Western crossed on the level just outside the station. This platform had, of course, been used by the Bristol & Gloucester Company's trains since the opening of their line in the previous July. With the Inspector-General's sanction, the 15½ miles from Kemble to Standish Junction, completing the line from Swindon to Gloucester, were opened on Whit Monday, 12th May 1845.

Although the extension from the Lansdown Road into the town of Cheltenham had been begun early in 1844, and was by this time in a forward state, no attempt was made to open the broad-gauge line beyond Gloucester. In August the Directors reported:

The repurchase has been made of the moiety of the Line between Gloucester and Cheltenham, and the amount claimed has been paid or invested under the provisions of the Acts of Parliament relating thereto within the time prescribed; but the Directors have not thought it desirable yet to complete the line into Cheltenham, or to build the Station there, in consequence of the new Railway contemplated between that Town and

---

[1] There are now 2 shafts.

[2] From 1859 onwards they were gradually reconstructed with more durable materials.

[3] So called from a landslip which had occurred there some years before the railway was made.

[4] Chalford was added on 2nd August 1897.

the Oxford and Worcester Railway at Shipton under Wychwood, which would probably render the intermediate outlay of any buildings unprofitable, at all events until the future plans can be more distinctly defined.

Nothing was done for two years, when, the Shipton and other schemes having been laid to rest and disputes with the Midland Railway Company, who, as we shall see, had become possessed of the whole line between Birmingham and Bristol, settled, the Directors announced that they 'intended to work Great Western trains over the new line into Cheltenham in the course of next month, the rails for the Broad Gauge being already laid between Gloucester and Cheltenham, and the Station at the latter place nearly completed'.

As this was the first important instance of a mixed-gauge railway, the following extracts from Captain J. L. Simmons' report to the Railway Commissioners of 15th October 1847 are of interest.

On Monday last, the 11th instant, I inspected the double gauge line of railway from Gloucester to Cheltenham, as also the broad gauge extension into the latter town, and a short piece called the 'Avoiding Line' at Gloucester.

Additional rails have now been laid from Cheltenham to Gloucester, uniting the gauges in one line of railway, and a connection on the broad gauge has been made between the two lines leading into Gloucester Station called the 'Avoiding Line', thus throwing Gloucester off the direct line from London to Cheltenham by about half a mile.

The station arrangements at Gloucester will remain the same, as far as the separation of the two gauges is concerned, but the broad gauge to Cheltenham unites with the narrow gauge immediately outside the Station, the Down line to Cheltenham being laid with three rails throughout up to the point of separation of the gauges near that town, the Up line being laid with four rails as far as the junction with the Avoiding Line, from which point to the point of separation near Cheltenham it is likewise laid with three rails.

This point of separation is called the 'Cheltenham Junction'; the junction of the Avoiding Line with the line from Gloucester to Cheltenham is called the 'Barnwood Junction'; and the point of meeting of the Avoiding Line with the Bristol and London line is called the 'Millstream Bridge Junction'.

The combination of the gauges, where three rails have been used for both, has been effected by laying an additional rail outside each line of the narrow gauge, as if the latter had never been disturbed, so that carriages of either gauge may have a complete road, it not being contemplated to unite carriages of both gauges in one train, which for many reasons would be extremely dangerous and ill advised, but merely that each kind of stock should be able to work separately over the same ground. Between the Cheltenham and Barnwood Junctions, there is no station and only one 'through crossing', constructed for the narrow gauge only, so that the mixture of gauges causes not the slightest complication or difference as regards the running of the trains of either gauge between these points.

The permanent way where the gauges are combined is laid with transverse sleepers, $11\frac{1}{2}$ feet long, 12 inches broad by 6 deep, 3 feet apart, having chairs fixed to them by fang bolts, those to carry the joints of the rails weighing $60\frac{1}{2}$ lbs each, and the others 32 lbs. The rail weighing 83 lbs to the yard has a large upper flange and a small projection below to secure it, the fastening being by a timber wedge. Where the gauges are not combined or intermixed, the permanent way is of the same description as that adopted generally by Mr Brunel, and used upon the Great Western and other broad gauge railways.

The junctions were peculiar, and are described at great length by the Inspector.

On the Down line from Gloucester, the Barnwood Junction, where the broad-gauge Avoiding Line came into the mixed-gauge from the right, was formed by ordinary trailing points in the common and broad-gauge rails, there being no point in the middle narrow-gauge rail; at the Cheltenham or Lansdown (as it was even then generally called) Junction, where the Broad Gauge diverged to the right, there were no movable points at all, but only a fixed facing point in the common right-hand rail and a guard-rail inside the left narrow-gauge rail to draw the wheels of the narrow-gauge stock to the left of the fixed point, its operation being assisted by the same middle rail being lowered three inches, while the outer broad-gauge rail was raised three inches to throw the broad-gauge wheels to the right of the point.

On the Up line from Cheltenham, the union of the gauges at Lansdown Junction was effected merely by a single movable trailing point in the common right-hand rail; Barnwood Junction was still more peculiar— first, the Broad Gauge diverged to the left by means of a fixed facing point in the common rail as on the Down line at Lansdown, only that here it was the broad-gauge outer rail that was lowered and had the guard-rail while the narrow-gauge rail was raised; then, a few feet beyond the fixed point and while the right rail of the Broad Gauge was still between the two narrow-gauge rails, there were ordinary double facing points in the Broad Gauge to turn trains either along the Avoiding Line or towards Gloucester Station; in the latter direction there were then four rails, the right-hand broad-gauge rail continuing between those of the Narrow Gauge for several hundred yards till the Broad Gauge diverged to the left, of course without any points, and then swept round to the right to join the line from Swindon just east of the level crossing of the two railways.

These junctions were of course ordered to be passed at a slow speed— at first the limit was 8 miles an hour. Similar fixed-point junctions to that described at Lansdown, with some slight improvements, were afterwards installed at all places where the two gauges diverged from a mixed-gauge line, and were used for many years without any recorded accident.

The Millstream Junction at the south end of the Avoiding Line was an ordinary one, all lines there being broad-gauge only.

The Great Western trains began to run to their station in St James' Square, Cheltenham, on 23rd October 1847.

The Inspector alludes in his report to 'the new broad gauge station, which is to be on the Avoiding Line'. This station was built at the point where a short single line from Gloucester Station crossed the Avoiding Line at right angles, connecting with it by means of a turn-table in each of the running lines, and terminating in a short dead end beyond. Hence it came to be known as the 'T Station', and the short single line as the 'T Line'. As soon as these were ready for use, the Swindon trains were arranged to run direct to and from Cheltenham, calling at the T Station, and a shuttle service was run on the T Line from and to Gloucester Station to connect with them there, the through Gloucester vehicles being transferred by means of the appropriate turn-table. The Enginemen's Rule Book of 1848 contains the following rule:

All trains passing along the Main (or Avoiding) Line at Gloucester must stop before reaching the Turn-table, unless the Engineman sees that the T Line Engine has gone across and is standing on the opposite side of the line, and unless he also receives the Signal from the Policeman.

This quaint method of working the Gloucester traffic continued till the railway westward from Gloucester was opened in September 1851, after which the T Station and the Avoiding Line fell out of use and lay derelict for many years.[1] In addition to the local service via the T Station, the Great Western from the first ran some 'short trains' direct between Gloucester Station and Cheltenham.

The curious arrangement as to the ownership of the railway between Tramway Junction, Gloucester, and Lansdown Junction, Cheltenham, made by the Acts of 1836–44, survived until 1947 save that the Great Western were no longer trustees of the southern portion. On their re-purchase of the Cheltenham & Great Western Union Company's rights in 1845 they became the legal owners of the whole line, but, as regards the half nearer Gloucester, only as trustees for the Midland Company. This lasted till 1867, when a long-standing lawsuit between the Companies as to property and rights in the Gloucester district came at last to an end, and as one of the results,[2] the Great Western conveyed this southern half to the Midland. The northern half from the Halfway Post, just south of Churchdown Station,[3] to Lansdown was their absolute property, as well of course as the whole extension into St. James' Square Station. Each Company had free use of the other's half without payment of tolls, and each kept its own half in repair for the common benefit.[4]

Having made this excursion into the future in order to complete the story of the Cheltenham Branch, we will now return to the year 1844.

On 1st May the Bristol & Exeter Company completed their railway to Exeter, thereby giving the Great Western a main line of nearly 194 miles, longer far than that of any other Company in the Kingdom. Gooch gives his recollection of the opening in his *Diaries*:

> We had a special train with a large party from London to go down to the opening. A great dinner was given in the Goods Shed at Exeter Station. I worked the train with the '*Actaeon*' engine, one of our 7 feet class, with six carriages. We left London at 7.30 a.m and arrived at Exeter at 12.30, having had some detention over the hour fixed. On the return journey we left Exeter at 5.20 p.m. and stopped at Paddington platform at 10. Sir Thomas Acland, who was with us, went at once to the House of Commons, and by 10.30 got up and told the House he had been in Exeter at 5.20. It was a very hard day's work for me, as, apart from driving the engine a distance of 387 miles, I had to be out early in the morning to see that all was right for our trip, and while at Exeter was busy with matters connected with the opening, so that my only chance of sitting down was for the hour we were at dinner. Next day my back ached so that I could hardly walk. Mr Brunel wrote me a very handsome letter, thanking me for what I had done, and all were very much pleased.

At this time a Bill was before Parliament for a broad-gauge railway in continuation of the Bristol & Exeter from Exeter to Plymouth, to be made by a new company, to which the Great Western had agreed to subscribe

---

[1] The T Station House may still be seen, and the adjacent sidings are known to this day as 'Gloucester T Sidings'. The old Avoiding Line was reopened as the 'Cheltenham Loop' in 1901.

[2] Another result was the conveyance by the Midland to the Great Western of a considerable part of the land on which the latter's Gloucester Station stood.

[3] Opened January 1874.

[4] The line was quadrupled in 1942–44.

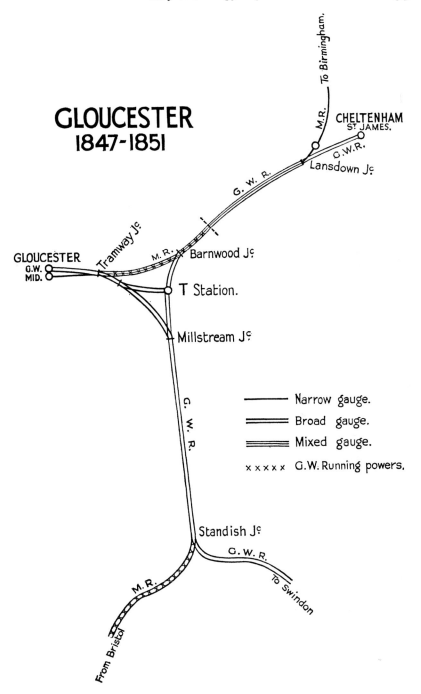

GLOUCESTER
1847-1851

£150,000. Two months later it received the Royal Assent and the South Devon Railway Company came into being, Russell and two of his colleagues representing the Great Western on its Board.

The general extension of railways in all parts of the country, which soon developed into the Railway Mania, was now beginning. Their utility was recognized; money was plentiful; and many of the established companies were paying good dividends, ten and even more per cent in several cases.

Companies were formed in the course of 1844, with Great Western assistance, to make the following broad-gauge lines:

The South Wales Railway, from Standish on the Cheltenham Branch through Chepstow, Newport, Cardiff, and Neath, and by Swansea and Carmarthen to Fishguard, with branches to the Forest of Dean, Pembroke, and from Newport to Monmouth; in all 211 miles.

The Cornwall Railway, from the South Devon at Plymouth to Falmouth; 66 miles.

The Wilts, Somerset & Weymouth Railway, from near Chippenham through Frome, Yeovil, and Dorchester to Weymouth, with branches to Devizes, Bradford, Salisbury, Radstock, Sherborne, and Bridport; in all 148 miles.

The Oxford, Worcester & Wolverhampton Railway, whose title is sufficiently descriptive, with some short branches; 97½ miles.

The Great Western Company itself promoted the following lines by means of subsidiary companies, as in the case of the Oxford Railway, providing the necessary subscription capital in the names of some of its Directors.

The Berks & Hants Railway, forking from Reading to Basingstoke and through Newbury to Hungerford; 39 miles.

The Oxford & Rugby Railway, through Banbury, Fenny Compton, and Southam; 51 miles.

The Monmouth & Hereford Railway, from Standish across the Severn at Framilode to Westbury and thence by Longhope, Walford, Ross, and Holme Lacy to Hereford, with a branch from Walford to Monmouth, there to join the South Wales branch from Newport, and another from a point in the Parish of Lea, north of Mitcheldean to join the other South Wales branch in the Forest of Dean; altogether 45 miles.

To connect the last-named railway with Gloucester, a company entitled the Gloucester & Dean Forest was projected locally, but, being reported against by the Board of Trade, was dropped for this year. The prospectus of a similar scheme, under the same title, had been published in 1842. Its object was to extend the Forest of Dean Railway from Churchway to Gloucester by a locomotive railway. The Engineer was Capt. Moorsom.

The Wilts, Somerset & Weymouth; Oxford, Worcester & Wolverhampton; Berks & Hants; and Oxford & Rugby were all projects over which the opening campaigns of the Gauge War were fought, and will be dealt with more fully in the next chapter, while the stories of the South Wales and Oxford, Worcester & Wolverhampton Companies, during their eighteen years of independence will be told later, when they eventually became parts of the Great Western. Here it is enough to say that Acts for all the railways named above, except the Cornwall, were obtained in the Session of 1845, but the South Wales and Monmouth & Hereford undertakings were confined by Parliament to the north side of the Severn, objections to the proposed bridges over the river being upheld, which of course cut them off from connection with the Great Western for the time.

The Great Western forthwith took over its three creature Companies, the Berks & Hants, Oxford & Rugby, and Monmouth & Hereford, and next year obtained an Act for their absorption. To connect the last named with their own system at Gloucester the Directors arranged with the promoters of the Gloucester & Dean Forest project to apply for an Act to carry it out, agreeing to take a long lease of their line on favourable terms, and to subscribe £50,000 capital. Another Act of 1845 authorized the leasing by the Great Western and London & Birmingham Companies jointly of the West London Railway. This was our old friend the Birmingham, Bristol & Thames Junction of 1836 under a new name adopted in 1840, which, starting from the London & Birmingham line near Kensal Green, crossed the Great Western on the level with a siding connection,

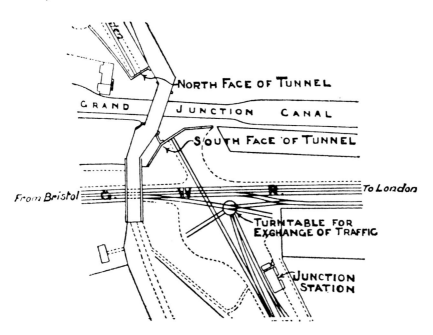

PLAN OF WEST LONDON CROSSING 1844

and terminated at the Kensington Canal Basin.[1] The Company had experienced all sorts of difficulties in getting its little railway finished. A short piece of it by Wormwood Scrubs had at one time been used by Messrs Clegg and Samuda for experiments with their Atmospheric system of traction, of which we shall have more to say hereafter in the story of the South Devon Railway. At last it was opened as a single line on 27th May 1844, and a ½-hourly service of passenger trains arranged. Some of these connected with Great Western trains at the crossing, where a small station[2] was made by the West London Company, but the service was not a success and was wholly discontinued at the end of November. From the Great Western crossing southward the single line was laid with three rails for the Mixed Gauge, but it does not appear to have been used by broad-gauge trains until the line had been doubled and reopened in 1863.

The Great Western Company was singularly unfortunate in the session of 1846, as far as schemes of its own promotion were concerned. Apart from the Gauge War projects described in the next chapter, these were only for short branches, one of them evidently intended to found a suburban traffic in the Thames Valley:

From Ealing through Brentford and Isleworth, and between Twicken-ham and Hounslow to Staines.

From Twyford to Henley.

From Twerton to the Collieries between Timsbury and Radstock.

On the other hand, Bills for the following lines, in which the Company was interested, were duly passed.

The Gloucester & Dean Forest Railway, from the Great Western at Gloucester to the Monmouth & Hereford in Westbury-on-Severn, and on to meet the South Wales Railway at Hagloe Farm beyond Awre; 15 miles.

The Cornwall Railway, from Plymouth to Falmouth, with branches from near Doublebois through Bodmin to Padstow, to the Liskeard and Caradon Railway, and to the quays at Truro and Penryn; altogether 81 miles.

The West Cornwall Railway, from Truro to Penzance with branches; 31 miles.

The Wycombe Railway, from Maidenhead to High Wycombe; 10 miles.

The Great Western & Uxbridge Railway, from West Drayton to Uxbridge; 2½ miles.

The last three were promoted locally without any assistance from the

[1] Corresponding nowadays to a point not quite half a mile south of Addison Road Station.

[2] The little station house, just south of the Great Western main line, remained until demolition between 1932 and 1934.

Great Western, who, however, afterwards agreed to buy the Wycombe and Uxbridge undertakings, and obtained an Act for the purpose in 1847. This purchase was never carried out, because the two Companies were unable to raise the half of their capital required by law to enable them to sell, so the powers lapsed.

In the next session the Company succeeded in getting power to make the Henley and Radstock Branches, and also one from Acton to the West London Railway, and to extend the latter to join the South Western at Vauxhall and make a branch from it to Hammersmith; but their suburban ambitions, now centered on a line from Acton to Staines and Egham, with branches to Brentford, Isleworth, and Twickenham, were again defeated, and those townlets delivered to the South Western enemy, who was authorized to invade Middlesex and even assault the Royal Borough of Windsor.

From one cause or another the Great Western had always been unsuccessful in their efforts to reach Windsor. At last in 1848 they got their Act for a forked branch 'from two points on the Great Western Railway near the western station at Slough' to Windsor. It bristles with provisions for the protection of Eton College: screens or planting to be provided to ensure the privacy of the Bathing Place; the Thames Bridge to have a clear waterway to the satisfaction of the Provost and Head Master; Provost and all Masters to have free access to the station to find any scholar, 'whether on the Foundation or otherwise'; Police along the line to prevent access of scholars;[1] in default, the College may appoint two at the expense of the Company; all such bridges as the College may require for passage to bathing places or other places of amusement and to carry flood water to be provided; no intermediate station or buildings to be erected *or passengers or goods taken up*[2] without consent of Provost and College under their common seal; special constables during construction to control workmen subject to the orders of the College; penalties for defaults, and their recovery by the College.

The branch was begun at once, and pushed on with quite unusual speed. The chief works were a long timber viaduct[3] and the Thames Bridge, one span of 202 feet, formed of three bow-and-string girders supported at each end on six cast-iron cylinders filled with concrete. Although the station was by no means complete, the branch was opened for traffic, together with the west fork at Slough, on 8th October 1849, two months before the enemy invaded the town from the other side.

As might be expected, more capital was required for the completion of the Cheltenham and Oxford Branches and to meet all these new engagements, so in August 1845 it was decided to raise £2,325,000 by the issue

---

[1] One man at least was employed for this purpose till October 1886, when the then Provost, Dr Hornby, agreed to his withdrawal on condition he was reinstated if required.
[2] They were not to be caught a second time!
[3] Reconstructed in brick 1861–65.

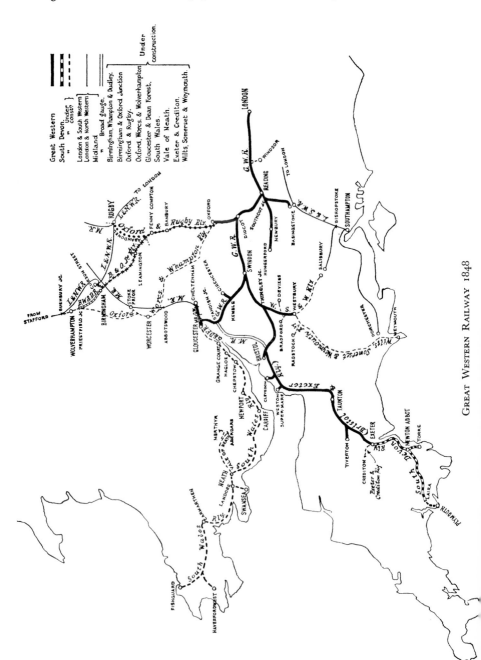

GREAT WESTERN RAILWAY 1848

of 93,000 quarter shares of £25 each, to be offered in the first instance to existing shareholders. A year later £1,185,000 was raised in shares of the curious amount of £17 each, bringing the share capital up to £8,160,000, and at the same time more debentures were authorized, making a total of £3,236,666 borrowed.

# VI

# *The Gauge War*

## *1844–1854*

### I  GENERAL SUMMARY

What has usually been called the 'Battle of the Gauges' was really a long war, lasting some ten years from the first meeting of the two gauges at Gloucester in 1844. During the war many battles were fought on different fronts with varying results before the Broad Gauge Forces were at last defeated by the mere multitude of their enemies.

The first of these was a short and sharp engagement over the body of the Bristol & Birmingham Railway, resulting in a victory for the Narrow Gauge. Later in the same year a long and hard fought contest gave the Broad Gauge lines from Oxford to Rugby and through Worcester to Wolverhampton, and raised hopes of its conquering even Liverpool and Manchester. But this victory and the inconvenience of the break of gauge at Gloucester, now made generally notorious and much exaggerated by the enemy in possession, led to the appointment by the Government of a Royal Commission to investigate the merits of the rival gauges, and the expediency of enforcing uniformity throughout the country.

A long struggle ensued, lasting through the autumn and winter of 1845, and resulting in the Report of the Commissioners, which, while admitting the superior capabilities of the Broad Gauge for speed and hauling heavy loads, was generally in favour of the Narrow as best suited to the general traffic of the country, and even went so far as to recommend that equitable means should be found of establishing uniformity by the compulsory extinction of the Broad Gauge.

The course of events has shown that it would have been much to the ultimate advantage of the companies concerned, though not of the public, had this recommendation been carried out at the time when less than 280 miles of broad-gauge railway were open, but the 'equitable means' were not forthcoming. It was felt that the companies could not fairly be called upon to bear the expense of altering their lines and rolling stock from the gauge they had been allowed or even authorized by law to adopt, and the Government naturally enough declined to provide any public money for the purpose. Moreover, the Commissioners had been far too ready to accept the mere oft-repeated assertions of interested witnesses as facts, and the Broad Gauge party had little difficulty in showing that many of their conclusions were based on errors.

Hence the Report was not adopted in its entirety by the Government or Parliament. Though the House of Commons passed a series of resolutions in favour of the general enforcement of the Narrow Gauge in future, the

Didcot Station, looking West, 1852

Oxford Old Station, looking North, 1852

Gloucester Station, looking North, 1852

Gloucester, Old " T " Station House

Gauge Act of 1846, which was the outcome of the whole business, excepted from this general rule any new railway whose gauge should be defined by its special Act, and so left matters, as far as the law was concerned, much as they had been before the agitation began. However, it cannot be denied that the result of the Commission was a distinct check, though by no means a decisive one, to the extension of the Broad Gauge.

The controversy was one of the public topics of the day, and a wordy warfare raged in pamphlets, newspaper articles, and even books. The general public, in the south at any rate, were strongly in favour of the Broad Gauge with its large, comfortable, and smooth running carriages, and its express trains, far faster and more punctual than those on the other lines, and, moreover, taking second as well as first-class passengers—the so-called expresses on the narrow-gauge lines took only first, and the London & North Western even limited the numbers of these. This popularity of the Broad Gauge was the cause of no little anxiety to the other party, and they did their best to counteract it. The late Sir Henry Cole tells us in his autobiography[1] that he was employed by the London & North Western Company 'to create a public opinion' in favour of the Narrow Gauge, and gives details of the pamphlets he caused to be published for the purpose. But fast and comfortable trains were stronger arguments than bushels of pamphlets, and the Great Western continued in general favour. The table on page 103, extracted from the 'Report of the Commissioners of Railways on Railway Communication between London and Birmingham, 1848', gives an interesting comparison of the speeds of the English express trains of this period.

Consequently, after yet another protracted inquiry and a bitter fight with the London & North Western, the Great Western were victorious in 1848 in obtaining power to extend the Broad Gauge to Birmingham and Wolverhampton by means of the Birmingham & Oxford Junction, and Birmingham, Wolverhampton & Dudley Railways, two narrow-gauge lines of 1846 purchased by the Company.

This was the last victory. Hard times set in, and though the war-cry of 'The Broad Gauge to the Mersey' was raised in the early 'fifties on the acquisition, after more desperate fighting, of the Shrewsbury & Birmingham and Shrewsbury & Chester lines with their powers over the Chester & Birkenhead, the Act of 1854 sanctioning this amalgamation specially forbade any extension of the Broad Gauge north of Wolverhampton, and enforced the completion and working of the Narrow Gauge throughout from Wolverhampton by Oxford to Basingstoke. As early as 1846 the Company had pledged itself to complete this chain of narrow-gauge communication from north to south, in order to defeat rival schemes.

Moreover, in 1851 the Broad Gauge was stabbed in the back and its ultimate defeat hastened by the mutiny of the Oxford, Worcester & Wolverhampton Railway, for whose very existence the first fierce battle

---

[1] *Fifty Years of Public Work* by Sir Henry Cole, K.C.B. 2 vols. 1884.

of 1845 had been fought. This rebellious daughter, in spite of Acts of Parliament and agreements, actually went over to the enemy, and though compelled to lay down broad-gauge rails laid narrow with them, and used the latter only. The story of this mutiny is told elsewhere. Here it will suffice to say that when the prodigal, after ten years in the wilderness, at last returned home, she succeeded in forcing the Narrow Gauge into the very citadel of Paddington.

While these battles were being fought on the northern front, warfare was also being carried on with the other enemy in the south. After a preliminary indecisive skirmish in 1844, a treaty was signed, and broad-gauge lines to Basingstoke, Hungerford, Salisbury, Yeovil, and Weymouth sanctioned in the following year. The next season saw the treaty broken by the enemy, and the beginning of the struggle for the country between Salisbury and Exeter. Neither side was victorious, and the country remained unoccupied. Then, after a campaign lasting over 1847 and 1848, it was captured by the Narrow Gauge and the Great Western attack utterly defeated. The Broad Gauge Forces, however—the Bristol & Exeter Company 'had joined in the fray on its own account—got some consolation in the power to make a direct line to Exeter by almost the exact route adopted nearly sixty years later. Owing to the extreme scarcity of money at this period, none of the lines so authorized was made by either side, and the powers lapsed. When times became somewhat brighter four years later, the Broad Gauge Allies determined on another assault on the still vacant district in Dorset and Devon, but were once more defeated in the session of 1853, and then finally abandoned the fight. This defeat was expressly on the question of gauge, the House of Commons Committee preferring for reasons of national defence a narrow-gauge line, continuous with that along the coast from Dover and Portsmouth, which the enemy pledged themselves to make forthwith. But, having obtained their object, they again broke their word, and made no attempt to redeem the pledge until compelled by Parliament to do so three years later.

In the far west also there was strife between the gauges for possession of the country beyond Exeter. In this the Broad Gauge Forces, represented not by the Great Western, but by the allied Bristol & Exeter and South Devon Companies, were for the time victorious. Some account of this local war will be found in the stories of those two railways.

By the end of 1854 the general war was over, though the fight with the mutinous Oxford, Worcester & Wolverhampton Company lasted nearly four years longer. The Great Western itself was no longer a purely broad-gauge railway, having become possessed of some 80 miles of narrow-gauge lines north of Wolverhampton, which it was expressly forbidden to widen. Two years later the Mixed Gauge was completed from the north to Basingstoke, and the portent of narrow-gauge goods and mineral trains appeared on the main line in the Thames Valley. Moreover, the Broad

# TABLE OF RATES OF TRAVELLING OF EXPRESS TRAINS

*Computed from Bradshaw's Time Tables for the Month of May 1848*

In the column headed 'Rate excluding Stoppages,' an allowance of five minutes has been made for each stoppage at stations in addition to the actual delay allowed by the Time Tables, and the stopping and starting at the termini have been considered as equivalent to one ordinary stoppage.

| Name | From | To | Distance | Stoppages | Delays | Time | | Rate including Stoppages | Rate excluding Stoppages | Remarks |
|---|---|---|---|---|---|---|---|---|---|---|
| | | | *Miles* | *No.* | *Min.* | *Hrs.* | *Min.* | *Miles* | *Miles* | |
| Great Western | London | Swindon | 77 | 2 | — | 1 | 25 | 54.35 | 61.60 | |
| Great Western | London | Exeter | 193¾ | 7 | 15 | 4 | 30 | 45.58 | 52.84 | |
| London and North Western | London | Liverpool | 201 | 14 | — | 6 | 45 | 29.77 | 36.00 | Mrng. Exp. |
| London and North Western | London | Liverpool | | 6 | — | 5 | 45 | 34.95 | 38.28 | A'noon Exp. |
| London and North Western and Midland etc. | London | Edinburgh | 377¼ | 13 | 60 | 12 | 25 | 33.04 | 36.50 | |
| London and South Western | London | Southampton | 78 | 3 | — | 1 | 45 | 44.57 | 52.00 | |
| London and South Western | London | Portsmouth | 88 | 4 | — | 2 | 10 | 40.62 | 48.00 | |
| South Eastern | London | Dover | 88 | 8 | — | 2 | 30 | 35.20 | 48.00 | |
| London, Brighton, and South Coast | London | Brighton | 50½ | 4 | — | 1 | 30 | 33.66 | 43.28 | |
| Eastern Counties and Norfolk | London | Norwich | 126 | 11 | 10 | 4 | 35 | 28.52 | 36.00 | |

Gauge cause suffered a heavy blow in the summer of 1855 by the retirement of its most powerful champion, Charles Russell, from the Chairmanship of the Great Western Company, which he had held for sixteen years. The next ten years saw a succession of no less than six short-lived Chairmen. In 1858 the Directors at last gave way to the Oxford, Worcester & Wolverhampton, and agreed to their release from the statutory obligation to complete their line as a broad-gauge railway. This was followed three years later by the extension of narrow-gauge rails from Reading to Paddington, chiefly to secure that Company's traffic, but also to obviate the break of gauge, which almost annihilated through goods traffic between London and the Great Western's own line north of Wolverhampton. These were, however, for several years used only by the few through trains to the Northern and West Midland districts, all others remaining broad-gauge.

The Great Western as yet manifested no intention of abandoning its distinctive gauge, though the ultimate necessity of this must have been foreseen. New branches and extensions, of no great length it is true, continued to be opened, 22 miles of them as late as 1864. In London itself, the costly Metropolitan Railway from Bishop's Road to Farringdon Street was opened as a broad-gauge line in 1863, and the same year saw broad-gauge trains in Victoria Station.

By the end of 1866 the broad-gauge rails ran from Paddington to Penzance, Milford Haven, Hereford, Wolverhampton, and Weymouth, and there were either open or under construction no less than 1,040 miles of broad and 387 of mixed-gauge lines, of which the Great Western owned or worked 592 and 240 miles respectively besides 462 miles of narrow-gauge. Breaks of gauge occurred at more than thirty places.

As we shall see, the gradual extinction of the Broad Gauge, as far as the Great Western was concerned, had by this time been decreed. Financial reasons, however, prevented any serious steps being taken till 1869. Six years later it had disappeared, except on three short branches and the main line to Bristol, where it was retained solely for the through traffic to and from the west. When the railways in the west were taken over in the following year, the Narrow Gauge had just reached Exeter. There it stopped for sixteen years till the South Devon and Cornish lines were altered and the Broad Gauge finally abolished.

But we are anticipating, and must now return to the outbreak of the war and give some account of the hard fought battles which failed to prevent the accidental gauge of the Northumberland colliery tramways being established on all the railways of England.

## 2   The Bristol & Gloucester Railway

The first so-called railway to be made in the neighbourhood of Bristol was a line from a point called Cuckold's Pill on the Floating Harbour, now known as Avon Street Wharf, through St Philips and by Lawrence

Hill, Fishponds, and Mangotsfield to the Collieries at Shortwood, Park-field, and Coal Pit Heath. It was authorized by an Act obtained in June 1828, and entitled The Bristol & Gloucestershire Railway. The line, some ten miles long, was single of a gauge of 4 feet 8 inches, and formed of fish-bellied rails fixed by means of iron chairs to square stone blocks. It was opened throughout on 6th August 1835, and was worked by horses and gravity, the gradients being with the load practically all the way. Needless to say, its sole object was the conveyance of coal to Bristol.

A similar though independent line from the River Avon opposite Keynsham, joined the Bristol & Gloucestershire Railway at a point 5¼ miles from Bristol, now Mangotsfield North Junction, and ran over it to Coal Pit Heath. This was the Avon & Gloucestershire Railway, belonging to the Kennet & Avon Canal Company, who used it to bring coal to Bath and places east thereof, as well as down the river to Bristol. It also was authorized by an Act of 1828, and opened, together with the Bristol & Gloucestershire north of the Junction, in July 1832.

These undertakings had not been at work many years when proposals were made in Bristol for forming a railway between that City and Gloucester by extending the Coal Pit Heath line to join the Cheltenham & Great Western Union near Stonehouse, and adapting the former for locomotives. A company for this purpose was promoted and, after an unsuccessful attempt in 1838, an Act obtained in the following year authorizing an extension, some 22 miles in length, of the Bristol & Gloucestershire Railway from Westerleigh, about two miles short of Coal Pit Heath, to a junction with the Cheltenham & Great Western at Standish, and the alteration of the existing line and ultimate absorption of its Proprietors in the enlarged Company entitled the Bristol & Gloucester Railway Company. At this time the gauge of the railway had not been decided, but at the General Meeting held at Bristol on 31st March 1840 the Directors reported that it appeared to them 'essential to the interests of the under-taking that the Line should be constructed of the same gauge as that of the Railway from Gloucester to Birmingham. On this Line the narrow gauge has been adopted.' They added that they had been negotiating with the Cheltenham & Great Western Company for the laying of addi-tional rails for the continuation of the Narrow Gauge from Standish to Gloucester. This matter had, however, been superseded by a proposal emanating from the Birmingham & Gloucester Company for a union with the Bristol & Gloucester, and the purchase by the united company of the Cheltenham & Great Western Union Railway. A Bill to authorize this union and purchase was actually introduced into Parliament, but the negotiations eventually fell through, and the Bill was abandoned.

A year later, when the works had been commenced, the Directors stated that they saw no reason whatever for altering their decision to adopt the Narrow Gauge, which had been unanimously confirmed by the Share-holders at the last General Meeting. In 1842, by arrangement with the Cheltenham & Great Western, the Bristol & Gloucester got Parliamentary powers to make the line between Standish Junction and Gloucester themselves and lay narrow-gauge rails thereon, subject to power of repurchase by the former Company.

Hence, up to the end of 1842, there was no intention on the part of the Bristol & Gloucester Directors of making their railway on a different gauge from the Birmingham & Gloucester, which had now been open more than two years. Early in the next year, however, they changed round completely. The acquisition of the Cheltenham & Great Western Union by the Great Western was imminent, and this seems to have thoroughly frightened them and made them feel that the friendship of that powerful Company must be secured at any cost. No doubt they were also urged on by their Engineer, who was no other than Brunel himself. The only member of the Board who was also a Director of the Great Western, George Jones, the Chairman, is said to have been opposed to the change.

Whatever the undisclosed motives, if any, may have been, the Bristol & Gloucester Board signed an agreement with the Great Western on 13th April 1843[1] to adopt the Broad Gauge, and make a branch in Bristol to join the Great Western near the bridge over Marsh Lane. The Great Western on their part undertook to complete a double line between the junction at Standish and Gloucester by April 1844, and to give the Bristol & Gloucester the use not only of that but also of the line between Gloucester and Cheltenham, and between the proposed junction at Marsh Lane and their Bristol Terminus, as well as of their passenger and goods stations at Bristol, Gloucester, and Cheltenham, with all requisite accommodation, including suitable sidings at Gloucester for the exchange of goods with the Birmingham & Gloucester Railway. The agreement was to last for twenty years from the day the Great Western began to work the Cheltenham & Great Western Union, and the Bristol & Gloucester Company were to pay by way of yearly rent £11,000 for the line between Standish and Gloucester, £4,000 for the line between Gloucester and Cheltenham, and £3,500 for the three stations; in all £18,500, to be increased by £1,000 after the first five years.

In a lengthy report to the Special Meeting of the Bristol & Gloucester Shareholders called to consider this agreement, the Directors, after emphasizing their fears of possible Great Western hostilities at both ends of the line, pointed out the advantages of avoiding a large outlay of capital on making the Standish–Gloucester line and providing a terminal station at Bristol, as to which no steps had yet been taken, and of a connection there with the Bristol & Exeter as well as the Great Western. They anticipated no trouble from the break of gauge with the Birmingham & Gloucester, as their Engineer had persuaded them that 'a very simple arrangement may effect the transfer of the entire load of goods from the waggon of one Company to that of the other', while the passengers will

---

[1] The Midland Company repudiated this agreement in 1858 on the ground that it was not sealed. Lengthy and acrimonious litigation followed.

'merely step from one carriage into the other in the same station and on the same platform'.

At the meeting the confirmation of the agreement was opposed by C. B. Fripp, who was a Director of the Bristol & Exeter, and had been one of the Great Western itself. He had few followers however, and the agreement was confirmed by a considerable majority.

Thus the Bristol & Gloucester became a broad-gauge railway,[1] and soon cemented its alliance with the Great Western and Bristol & Exeter by agreeing to subscribe £50,000 to the proposed line from Exeter to Plymouth, afterwards known as the South Devon Railway.

Negotiations for a working agreement with the Great Western having failed on the question of terms, the Bristol & Gloucester Directors contracted with Stothert, Slaughter & Co. of Bristol, to provide the entire plant and work the line for ten years from its opening.

This took place for passengers on 8th July 1844, from Temple Meads Station at Bristol to a temporary station at Gloucester made by adding a platform to the north side of the Birmingham & Gloucester Terminus, the Great Western having as yet no station there.

Goods traffic commenced on 2nd September, and at once the inconvenience of the break of gauge made itself felt. The bulk of the goods was through traffic to and from the Birmingham line, and of course all this had to be transferred from waggon to waggon at Gloucester. Brunel's 'very simple arrangement' for transferring entire loads was not forthcoming, or was found impracticable; at any rate, it was not used, and the congestion in the small and utterly insufficient transfer shed provided became worse and worse as the traffic increased.

The consequent delay and loss of packages by mis-sorting soon became notorious, and was much exaggerated by the Narrow Gauge faction as an argument for enforced uniformity of gauge. The Broad Gauge party, on the other hand, alleged that the trouble was due to insufficient accommodation and more or less intentional mismanagement.

G. P. Neele of the London & North Western in his *Railway Reminiscences*[2] relates that J. D. Payne, then Goods Manager of the Birmingham & Gloucester Railway, used to boast of having taken a leading part in checking the extension of the Broad Gauge. Hearing that the members of a Parliamentary Committee were coming to Gloucester to see for themselves the evil of which they had heard so much, Payne hurried down to prepare for them. 'Fearing lest the extent of the transfer work might be too small to impress the Committee, he arranged for the unloading of two trains already dealt with, as an addition to the usual work, and when the Members came to the scene, they were appalled by the clamour

---

[1] Owing to the works being already far advanced, the railway was never of the full broad-gauge width; for instance, the Wickwar and Staple Hill Tunnels were only 26 feet wide, and the underbridges the same between their parapets (Gauge Commission Evidence).

[2] McCorquodale and Co, Ltd, 1904.

arising from the well arranged confusion of shouting out addresses of consignments, the chucking of packages across from truck to truck, the enquiries for missing articles, the loading, unloading and reloading, which his clever device [*sic*] had brought into operation.'

Towards the close of 1844 negotiations for amalgamation with the Birmingham & Gloucester Company were renewed, and this time brought to a successful issue. An agreement was signed by the respective Chairmen on 14th January 1845, and ratified by the shareholders a fortnight later. A Bill to effect the union and constitute the Bristol & Birmingham Railway Company was carried into Parliament but withdrawn after the second reading through failure to comply with Standing Orders. In lieu of amalgamation, the two lines retained their separate identities but were worked as one until the Midland took over their working on 7th May 1845.

Immediately after the terms of union had been agreed on, the Directors were invited by the Great Western Board to negotiate on the subject of extending the Broad Gauge from Gloucester to Birmingham. Their consultations resulted in a proposal to amalgamate with the Great Western. At a meeting held at Bristol on 24th January the Great Western Deputation offered £60 of their capital, then worth at the price of the day £123, for each £100 of Birmingham & Gloucester worth £109. The representatives of the two Companies stood out for £65 Great Western capital, and the meeting was adjourned to the 27th, in London, when Saunders gave the final answer of his Board that they would not increase their offer.

The next day the lines were snapped up by the Midland Company!

How this dramatic event occurred is told us by the chief actor himself, John Ellis, the Deputy Chairman of that Company, in his evidence before the Committee of the House of Commons on the Oxford & Rugby Railway Bill. On 26th January Ellis happened quite by chance to travel to London in the company of Edward Sturge and Joseph Gibbons, Directors of the Birmingham & Gloucester Railway, who casually mentioned the negotiations going on with the Great Western, and told him that the matter was to be settled the very next morning. Having already had personal experience, in his business as a worsted spinner at Leicester getting wool from Bristol, of the delays caused by the break of gauge at Gloucester, he began, as he puts it, 'to look about my interest in the railway and to think the Broad Gauge would come too near'. Evidently a man of quick decision, he went at once to the Bristol and Birmingham negotiators and obtained a promise that if they did not settle with Saunders they would bargain with him. They came to him, and this bold and far-seeing Quaker, entirely on his own responsibility, pledged his Company to take a perpetual lease of the Bristol and Birmingham Companies' line from 1st July 1845[1] at a rent of 6% on the

---

[1] The Midland actually took over on 7th May.

united capital of £1,800,000, and to undertake all outstanding liabilities, estimated at nearly half a million.

'I took great responsibility on myself when I leased that line; I had not an opportunity of consulting with my colleagues, and I took a bold step to secure the interests of the Company I represented; I am satisfied I did right, and I am glad to say I had the concurrence of the whole of my colleagues in what I did. I had heard so much of the inconvenience of loss of packages and annoyance to the trade altogether, that when this thing was offered to me I considered I had better run the risk of losing a few thousand pounds than admit the plague of the Broad Gauge to Birmingham. It was from no feeling against the Great Western, but it seemed to me, somehow or other, that they have drawn the line themselves of demarcation between the two gauges; that Oxford and Bristol are the places where they ought to change.'

Having settled the business, Ellis at once went to the Board of Trade to inform them of the fact. At the door of the room he met Saunders! 'I spoke to him but did not tell him what I had done.' However, he made no secret of it, but let it be known in London the same day.

A meeting of the Midland Board was called to sanction the agreement. It was sanctioned unanimously and signed by the Chairman, the notorious 'Railway King', George Hudson; having already been signed by Samuel Bowly and George Jones, the respective Chairmen of the Birmingham & Gloucester and Bristol & Gloucester Companies. The date of this Agreement was 8th February 1845, less than a fortnight after Ellis's eventful journey with Sturge and Gibbons. It expressly states that it is made 'under the conviction of the absolute necessity of a uniformity of gauge between the northern and manufacturing districts and the Port of Bristol'. In the following month special meetings of the three Companies confirmed the arrangement, which was ratified by Parliament in 1846.

Thus the first battle of the gauges was won by John Ellis for the Narrow Gauge, and the Great Western lost the Bristol & Birmingham for a paltry difference of £5 a share. Poor Saunders and his Directors must have felt extremely sore over this sudden defeat, but they had no right to complain of Ellis's perfectly fair and straightforward action. It has been asserted[1] that the Bristol & Birmingham Directors carried on negotiations with both the Great Western and Midland simultaneously; the evidence, however, shows this was not so.

The only real ground of complaint the Great Western had was that making the Bristol & Gloucester a narrow-gauge line would be a breach of the Agreement of April 1843, their part of which they had duly carried out. On the strength of this, they succeeded in securing the insertion of a clause in the Midland Amalgamation Act of 1846, requiring that Company to maintain on the Bristol & Gloucester Railway, between the junctions at Bristol and Standish, 'two lines of railway of the same gauge as the

[1] By C. E. Stretton in his *History of the Midland Railway*. Methuen, 1901, not always a reliable source.

Great Western Railway', and giving the latter running powers over them. It was not till two years later that the Midland obtained an Act authorizing them to add narrow-gauge rails between the Bristol (G.W.) Terminus and Standish, and to make a separate narrow-gauge line thence into Gloucester. This Act gave the Great Western, in addition to their former powers, 'all proper and convenient accommodations in respect of stations, sidings, waiting and watering places, and other facilities'.

Until June 1854, when the Narrow Gauge was opened throughout between Bristol and Gloucester, the Midland Company continued to work the line on the Broad Gauge—they had taken over the working from Stothert, Slaughter & Co. and purchased their stock in July 1845—and to run over the Great Western between Standish Junction and Gloucester Station. They then got rid of the broad-gauge stock, selling some of the carriages to the Bristol & Exeter, but owing to the 1846 Act were unable to remove the broad-gauge rails. Though never used by the Great Western, these were maintained till 1872, when their use became impossible by the conversion of all that Company's lines in the Gloucester District. Between Bristol and Westerleigh they remained for another ten years after this, to accommodate a Bristol & Exeter coal train which, under an agreement with the Midland, ran daily to and from Parkfield Colliery until the end of January 1882.

Before leaving the story of the Bristol & Gloucester Railway, there is one item of interest worth notice. The right of the Avon & Gloucestershire Railway to use the line between Mangotsfield and Coal Pit Heath had been preserved by the Bristol & Gloucester Act of 1839. To provide for this, rails of the gauge of 4 feet 8 inches were added inside the Broad Gauge from the junction at Mangotsfield (now North Junction) to that at Westerleigh, a distance of about 2½ miles, and this section therefore became the first example of a mixed-gauge railway in the country. The old fish-bellied rails, which had been taken up, were used for the purpose, laid on cross sleepers instead of the former stone blocks between the longitudinal timbers carrying the broad-gauge rails, and to avoid the need of interfering with the latter at the crossings these inner rails were kept 2 inches above their level so that the only gaps necessary were in the narrow-gauge rails. The use of these for the horse-drawn traffic of the Avon Railway was actually sanctioned by Major-General Pasley, who reported to the Board of Trade that the safety of the public would be amply provided for by a rule that the horses should always start immediately after the passage of a passenger train, and that these should only run at intervals of not less than 1½ hours! This bright idea was, however, not acted on, and six months later we find the Canal Company complaining to the Board that their traffic was still prevented from using the line. The General then withdrew his suggestion, and said that the only safe way of providing for the Avon Railway's horse traffic was by laying an independent single line for it alongside the main line, but that the expense of this to the Bristol & Gloucester Company would be more than the traffic was worth, it being acknowledged to have averaged only 204 tons in 46 waggons a week during 1843. He therefore suggested that the two Companies should come to some agreement on the subject.

## 3 Oxford & Rugby, and Oxford, Worcester & Wolverhampton Railways

Owing to the depression in trade and tightness of money since 1836, the country between the Great Western and London & Birmingham main lines remained for some years without railways. Schemes had been projected in that year for lines from Rugby through Oxford to Basingstoke, called the North & South Junction Railway, and between Wolverhampton and Worcester with the high-sounding title of The Grand Connection Railway, both quite independent of the Great Western, and also, as we have seen, for a line from Oxford to Worcester with a probable continuation to Porth Dynlleyn.

The Oxford & Rugby project was taken up by the Great Western Directors in the spring of 1844, the importance of such a north and south communication having been brought out in the course of the Parliamentary proceedings on the two rival Newbury schemes,[1] when it became evident that if the Great Western did not provide it, some other company would. Rugby was at this period virtually the gate to the whole of the north, the Midland Counties Railway from Derby joining the London & Birmingham there and forming the principal route from Derbyshire, Yorkshire, and places beyond to London and the south. The original, but slightly longer, route of the Birmingham & Derby Junction Railway via Hampton was, of course, still open. At the August Half-yearly Meeting the Great Western Directors reported to the Shareholders:

> The necessity of the Oxford and Rugby line is universally admitted. It will form a direct communication from the North by the Great Western Junction at Basingstoke with Hampshire and the South Coast. The University Authorities have given their consent to it, and at meetings held in Oxford and Banbury unanimous Resolutions have been passed in favour of the Great Western Line being so continued towards the North. The principal Land owners have been seen and there is every reason to rely upon general support from them. The Line cannot fail greatly to enhance the value of the Junction Line to Basingstoke, both to the Public and to the Shareholders.

Accordingly the Meeting authorized them to take all necessary steps for applying to Parliament for an Act for making the line.

In this same spring of 1844 the Board was approached by representatives of the mining and manufacturing district of South Staffordshire, and parties connected with the earlier Worcester project, asking for their assistance towards a line, of course broad-gauge, from Oxford through Worcester to Wolverhampton. Before promising support the Great Western Directors required evidence that the local interests generally were in favour of the line, and it was suggested with a view to lessen the mileage and expense that the projected railway, instead of joining the

[1] See Section 6.

Great Western at Oxford, should join the Oxford & Rugby line north of Banbury. These terms being assented to, a conditional agreement was made in August for a lease of the line when completed to the Great Western Company. In the course of the next month, however, it was decided to carry the line direct from Oxford to Worcester, as originally proposed, and a new agreement was accordingly made on 20th September between the Great Western Directors and three representative members of the Committee of the Oxford, Worcester & Wolverhampton, whereby the capital was increased from 1 to 1½ million, the amount of Brunel's somewhat sanguine estimate of the total cost of the line, and the Great Western were to take a long lease of the railway, when completed as a broad-gauge double line, at a rent of 3½% on such capital and half surplus profits. This agreement was subject to four conditions: Satisfactory proof of a yearly traffic of £131,250, that two-thirds of the landowners were consenting or neutral, the Board of Trade's approval of the Bill, and a *bona fide* subscription list of £900,000. In the event, none of these conditions save the first were fulfilled, yet the Great Western continued their support and, in fact, became principals in the Parliamentary fight which ensued. Moreover, although it was no part of the arrangement with the promoters, on the latter finding themselves at the last moment unable to make up a sufficient subscription list, the Great Western Company arranged to take up no less than 7,500 shares, equivalent to £375,000 capital.

Though neither of the proposed railways would compete with them, directly at any rate, the London & Birmingham Company, who were in close alliance with the Midland, at once took steps to repel what they considered an invasion of their country. Under the title of the London, Worcester & South Staffordshire Railway, they promoted a line from Tring through Aylesbury, Bicester, Banbury, Fenny Compton, Kineton, Evesham, Worcester, Stourport, and Dudley to Wolverhampton, with branches from Bicester to Oxford, and from near Fenny Compton to Rugby; these branches of course forming a competing Oxford & Rugby line. They also projected an extension from Oxford to Didcot, parallel with the existing broad gauge line, to join the South Western's Basingstoke & Didcot Junction Railway, but on the abandonment of the latter the Oxford & Didcot Bill was withdrawn.

Here then were the makings of a very pretty fight for the Parliamentary Session of 1845, which came to be the second Battle of the Gauges.

Proceedings opened before the Board of Trade in the autumn. Anticipating an overwhelming rush of railway Bills, Parliament had ordered the Board to institute inquiries into the merits of competing projects and make reports to the ensuing session. These inquiries were conducted by Lord Dalhousie, who had succeeded Mr Gladstone as President of the Board, General Pasley, Inspector-General of Railways, Captain O'Brien, and Messrs G. R. Porter and S. Laing, afterwards Chairman of the

Brighton Railway. In railway circles these gentlemen became known as the 'Five Kings'.

Their Report on the Rugby and Wolverhampton schemes came out in January 1845, and proved to be dead against the northward extension of the Broad Gauge, and in favour of the district being given to the London & Birmingham Company.

The undeniable evil of a break of gauge, already experienced at Gloucester, is dwelt on, and Brunel's suggestion for obviating it by contrivances for transferring the bodies of goods waggons from one set of wheels to another declared to be impracticable, even if the mechanical difficulties were overcome, by reason of the large additional stock that would have to be kept to provide for journeys involving the transfer. As to the proposal of mixing the gauge, they say:

The second arrangement, of laying down additional rails, may be practicable under peculiar circumstances and, to a limited extent, but it is open to great objections.

It is very doubtful how far the addition of a single rail only would be consistent with safety, as in this case the centre of gravity of the carriages of different gauges in the same train would not be in the same straight line. If a complete double set of rails were laid down the expense would be very considerable. The complication of switches and crossings that would be necessary would involve considerable additional risk and great expense. The difficulty and expense of maintaining the permanent way and of keeping the double set of rails in proper adjustment would be greatly increased; and on the whole the expense, inconvenience and risk would probably be so great as to prevent the experiment being tried to any extent.

We cannot therefore consider the plan of laying down additional rails as applicable, unless perhaps to a limited extent and under special circumstances, such as enabling, for instance, mineral waggons constructed for the narrow gauge to pass for a short distance and at a slow speed over a wide gauge railway; with which view alone it is proposed to lay down extra rails upon the Oxford, Worcester, and Wolverhampton line, for a few miles south of Wolverhampton.

On the whole, therefore, we cannot consider the mechanical arrangements which have been proposed for obviating the inconvenience of a meeting of different gauges (even if we could assume their praticability, which in the present state of experience we should not be warranted in doing), as anything better than partial and imperfect palliatives of a great evil.

This is sound enough, save in one respect. It does not seem to have occurred to the 'Five Kings' that their objection to the single additional rail was founded on the fallacy that vehicles of both gauges would run in the same train. They go on:

Assuming this to be the case, and assuming also, as we are compelled to do, that an interruption of gauge must exist somewhere, the question is reduced to this: to ascertain at what points such interruption should be fixed in order to occasion the least inconvenience to the traffic and commerce of the country. From the fact that nearly 2,000 miles of railway are already made or sanctioned on the narrow gauge, while not more than 300 are sanctioned on the wide gauge, a disproportion which will be still more largely increased by the new railways now in contemplation, an inference might be drawn in favour of confining the gauge which is in such a decided minority within the narrowest possible limits; and this inference might be strengthened by referring to the obvious fact that the wide gauge has not realized those decided advantages over the narrow gauge which were at one time anticipated.

The actual speed of trains upon the Great Western Railway, as shown by the published time-tables and by official returns, is not so high as upon some narrow gauge Railways, and, notwithstanding the excellence of its gradients, very slightly higher than the average speed of other great Railways on the narrow gauge. In respect of safety, it is manifest that both gauges are alike unobjectionable, with due precaution and proper management;

and in respect of convenience and of economy, including the cost both of construction and working, the opinion of a great majority of the most eminent authorities is unfavourable to the wide gauge.

Without wishing to express any positive opinion ourselves upon the point, it is enough for us to say that we think there is nothing in the relative merits of the two gauges in themselves materially to affect the question between them, which turns upon commercial considerations.

That this statement as to the speed on the Great Western Railway at this time was a disgraceful truth was quickly realized at Paddington; so in March the original Exeter Express was put on to do the 194 miles in 5 hours—reduced to 4½ early in May when the battle had just begun in the Commons Committee—a speed far in advance of anything attempted on narrow-gauge lines for many years.

The Report proceeds to discuss the traffic passing and likely to pass over the proposed lines and the Bristol & Gloucester and Birmingham & Gloucester Railway, and recommends that the unavoidable breaks of gauge should be made at Oxford and Bristol, as the places where there would be the least through traffic, rather than at Rugby, Wolverhampton, Birmingham, or Gloucester.

Anticipating the objection that giving the district to the London & Birmingham would create a great monopoly, and stifle competition, the 'Kings' allege that 'to allow the Great Western Company to embrace by their influence not only the whole western communications of the island, but also the whole of South Wales, and the whole district up to Worcester and Birmingham, would be to establish a monopoly much more gigantic than that of the London & Birmingham'. The latter Company, they add, has voluntarily offered, on condition of their Worcester scheme being sanctioned, that the Act should provide for reducing the maximum rates for passengers and goods over the whole of their system, and to pledge their whole revenue for the completion of the proposed lines within a reasonable time. The competing scheme is expressly stated to have offered no such guarantees against any possible abuses of monopoly. As a matter of fact, the Great Western was never invited to do so, or afforded any opportunity of meeting the case set up by the other side. Saunders complained of this before the Commons Committee, but attributed it to the great pressure of business on the Board of Trade and not to any intentional unfairness.

In this preliminary skirmish before the 'Five Kings', the Broad Gauge party was thus thoroughly worsted by the enemy. Nothing daunted, they proceeded with the condemned projects, and in due course the Bills for the Oxford & Rugby and Oxford, Worcester & Wolverhampton broad-gauge Railways came before Parliament, and having safely passed the preliminary stages in the House of Commons, were referred to the same Committee, together with the rival narrow-gauge projects in the district.

The Committee opened their proceedings on 5th May, and on nineteen days between this and 4th June heard 102 witnesses answer 12,148 questions. Most of the witnesses were iron masters, colliery proprietors, and other commercial men of the Worcestershire and South Staffordshire districts. Engineers were represented by Robert Stephenson and R. B. Dockray of the London & Birmingham, Nicholas Wood, John Hawkshaw of the Manchester & Leeds, William Cubitt late of the South Eastern, J. Baylis of the Birmingham & Gloucester, and of course Brunel; Managers by W. Harding of the Bristol & Gloucester, J. D. Payne of the Birmingham & Gloucester, Captain Lawes of the Manchester & Leeds, Peter Clarke late of the North Midland, William Hansom of the Eastern Counties, Captain Mark Huish of the Grand Junction, and C. A. Saunders; and Locomotive Engineers by J. McConnell of the Birmingham & Gloucester, E. Bury of the London & Birmingham, and Daniel Gooch. George Hudson, the 'Railway King', Chairman of the Midland and other north country lines, John Ellis, Deputy Chairman of the Midland, and Charles Russell also gave their views.

It is quite impossible to attempt even to summarize the evidence, most of it of little interest nowadays; it was published by the Government, and can be read in a Blue Book of some 700 pages. Suffice it to say that on 4th June the Committee announced their decision that the preambles of the Oxford & Rugby and Oxford, Worcester & Wolverhampton Bills had been proved, and that of the London, Worcester & South Staffordshire had not.

This was, of course, a great victory for the Broad Gauge, but it was tempered by a clause obliging the Great Western to add the Narrow Gauge throughout the Oxford & Rugby line, if called upon to do so by the Board of Trade. The addition of Narrow Gauge on the Oxford, Worcester & Wolverhampton Railway between the junctions with the Birmingham & Gloucester line at Abbot's Wood near Worcester and the Grand Junction line at Wolverhampton and on the branch to Stoke Prior had been provided for in the original agreement between the promoters and the Great Western, and was included in the Bill as deposited.

The London & Birmingham authorities took this defeat very hardly and at once proceeded, with the aid of the Midland, to beat up opposition to the adoption of the Committee's Report by the House of Commons. Upon this the Grand Junction Company came to the aid of the Great Western by issuing the following interesting circular to their shareholders:

GRAND JUNCTION RAILWAY

The Directors beg to draw your attention to the decision, which after a long investigation, the Committee of the House of Commons has pronounced in the case of the Lines for connecting Oxford with Rugby on the one hand, and with Worcester and Wolverhampton on the other.

The decision, as you are probably aware, has been in favour of the Lines promoted by the Great Western Company, for which the Grand Junction have petitioned.

The Directors have been informed, through the medium of a circular from the London and Birmingham Company that an active canvas has commenced for the purpose of setting aside the decision; they consider it their duty therefore to urge you to meet this attempt by inducing such members of Parliament as you know to attend on the 17th inst., on the bringing up of the Report.

The question at issue has been represented as one entirely of Broad and Narrow Gauge; upon this point the Directors may observe that they do not anticipate any inconvenience whatever to arise from the introduction of the Broad Gauge among the Narrow Gauge Lines, or the mixture of gauges on the same Line. On the contrary, looking at Express Trains running at high speed, which are now being introduced on the leading roads, they deem it probable that many Companies possessing Trunk Lines on the Narrow Gauge principle may find it their interest to adopt both; and the Directors have ascertained the perfect practicability of adding the Broad Gauge on the Grand Junction at a very reasonable cost.

They consider, therefore, that any exclusive system south of Birmingham, which would deprive them of the power hereafter of adopting the Broad Gauge in addition to the Narrow would be a great evil to the public; but the question appears to them one of a much more comprehensive character—namely, whether the entire district between London, Bristol, and Birmingham shall be handed over to the absolute monopoly of the London and Birmingham Company, who, already, by purchase, lease, amalgamation, and arrangements with various Railways and Canals, are seeking to obtain, in addition to their Line from London to Birmingham, the entire control from Birmingham to Manchester, and Birmingham to Holyhead.

Such extensive powers would be in the highest degree dangerous to the public, and inconsistent with the fair interests of the Grand Junction Company.

It is on this ground, therefore, apart from the question of gauge, and convinced that from fair and open competition throughout between London, Liverpool and Manchester the Proprietors of the Grand Junction have nothing to apprehend; and feeling satisfied that no legislative enactments proposed by the London and Birmingham to be introduced into their Bill, will enable the Grand Junction so successfully to compete with that Company's extended schemes, as the formation of another Line, independent of the London and Birmingham Company, that the Grand Junction Directors, after exhausting every means in their power to avoid the present position of affairs, have resolved to solicit your aid with Members of Parliament in support of the Oxford and Rugby and the Oxford, Worcester, and Wolverhampton projects.

By order of the Board,

MARK HUISH, *Secretary.*

Liverpool. 11th June 1845.

Whether the Grand Junction really intended to lay the Broad Gauge on their line from Birmingham to Liverpool and Manchester may, perhaps, be doubted. The threat may have been merely an astute move on the part of Captain Huish in his war with the London & Birmingham. Anyhow, it soon brought that Company to its knees, and the birth of the London & North Western Railway, by the amalgamation of the London & Birmingham, Grand Junction, and Manchester & Birmingham Companies, was the result. We have Captain Huish's own words to a Parliamentary Committee in 1853: 'The effect of the circular was undoubtedly to bring about an immediate arrangement between the London and Birmingham and the Grand Junction, and to obtain for the Grand Junction a large sum of money as the price of it'. Probably this was its main intention!

The Committee's Report on the Oxford, Worcester & Wolverhampton Railway came before the House on 20th June, and was debated at some length. The opposition was led by Richard Cobden, of Free Trade fame, who proposed an amendment asking for a Royal Commission to enquire whether uniformity of gauge ought not to be insisted on in all future railway Acts, and as to the practicability of altering existing lines. This was negatived, and the Bill passed by 247 votes to 113, a majority of more than two to one. The Oxford & Rugby Bill was then passed by 79 to 43, and both Bills were read a third time on 24th June and sent up to the

Broad Gauge Engine *Ixion*

Narrow Gauge Engine " A "

Narrow Gauge Engine No. 54

Marlow Road Station about 1869.  It was renamed Bourne End in 1874

Bourne End Timber Viaduct over the Thames

Lords. The Lords' Committee, after a renewed investigation and protracted opposition, reported unanimously in favour of them, and they
finally received the Royal Assent on 4th August 1845.

## 4  THE GAUGE COMMISSION

Having failed in his efforts to defeat the Oxford & Rugby and Oxford,
Worcester & Wolverhampton Bills, Mr Cobden moved the following
resolution in the House of Commons on 25th June 1845:

> That it having been represented to this House by Petitions from various public bodies,
> as well as from Merchants, Manufacturers and others, that serious impediments to the
> internal traffic of the country are likely to arise from the 'breaks' that will occur in
> Railway communications from the want of an uniform Gauge, and these representations
> not having been fully inquired into by any of the Committees of this House upon private
> Bills, and it being desirable that the subject should be further investigated, an humble
> address be presented to Her Majesty, praying Her Majesty to be graciously pleased to
> issue a Commission to inquire whether in future private Acts for the construction of
> Railways, provision ought to be made for securing an uniform Gauge and, whether it
> would be expedient and practicable to take measures to bring the Railways already
> constructed or in progress of construction in Great Britain into uniformity of Gauge, and
> to inquire whether any other mode of obviating or mitigating the apprehended evil could
> be adopted, and to report the same to this House.

This was adopted without opposition, and a Royal Commission was
accordingly issued on 9th July to 'Our trusty and well-beloved Sir John
Mark Frederic Smith, Knight, Lieutenant-Colonel in Our Corps of Royal
Engineers, late Inspector-General of Railways; George Biddell Airy,
Esquire, Astronomical Observator in Our Observatory at Greenwich; and
Peter Barlow, Esquire, Professor of Mathematics in Our Military Academy
at Woolwich', directing them to conduct the inquiry prayed for.

The Commissioners began taking evidence on 6th August, and after
eleven days of it adjourned on 4th September for a six weeks' holiday till
17th October, when the Great Western champions made their first
appearance. They were Daniel Gooch, Locomotive Superintendent,
Seymour Clarke, Traffic Superintendent of the London Division, at this
time extending to Oxford and Gloucester, Charles Saunders, Secretary
and Manager, and Brunel. The sittings concluded on 18th December,
having occupied thirty days. Forty-eight witnesses were examined, of
whom fourteen were engineers, eight engine builders or locomotive
superintendents, sixteen directors, managers, or traffic superintendents,
and ten non-railwaymen, including the Inspector-General of Fortifica-
tions, the Quartermaster-General, and the Inspector-General of Railways.
Though many of them considered the accidentally fixed 4 feet 8½ inches
somewhat too narrow, the four Great Western officers were alone in
supporting the extreme width of 7 feet, and in attempting to make little
of the undeniable evil of breaks of gauge, which was emphasized and even
exaggerated by the other witnesses.[1]

Towards the close of the evidence Brunel suggested experiments to test

[1] The Minutes of Evidence and an Appendix of Documents and Statistics were published in two large Blue Books.

the power of the broad- and narrow-gauge engines with trains of similar weights and speeds. As no engine had been built for the Great Western since 1842, while the narrow-gauge engines had been much improved in the interval, this was a distinctly sporting offer. It was accepted somewhat unwillingly by the other party on condition that the broad-gauge experiments should be conducted first, and not both simultaneously, as Brunel suggested. Long distance tests were also declined by the Narrow Gauge representatives, who proposed Paddington and Didcot, 53 miles, and York and Darlington, 44 miles, as the rival courses, which had to be accepted.

Gooch chose *Ixion*, one of the seventy-two 7-foot single 6-wheeled engines then in daily use, as the broad-gauge champion. This engine had been built by Fenton, Murray & Jackson in October 1841, and had $15\frac{3}{4}$ inch cylinders with an 18 inch stroke. Three trips to and from Didcot with loads of 80, 70, and 60 tons respectively were made on 16th and 17th December. The narrow-gauge competitor was known as *Engine A*, a curious 6-wheeled affair just built by Stephenson and Co., with 6 feet 6 inch single driving wheels and outside cylinders 15 by 24 inches. With hot water in the tender and a flying start this engine took a load of 50 tons from York to Darlington and back in the morning and 80 tons to Darlington only in the afternoon of 31st December, an attempt on the previous day having been abandoned owing to bad weather. The trial of a North Midland engine No. 54, named *Stephenson*, on the following day terminated in its running off the line and falling over after covering 22 miles. Careful records of the speed and boiler pressure at each mile, and the coke and water consumed on the journeys were taken in each case by the Commissioners and both parties.[1] The general result was much in favour of *Ixion*, both for power and speed, though no exactly comparable tests were made. Further trials of two 6-coupled goods engines, each named *Hercules*, were made on 2nd and 10th January.

The Commissioners state in their Report that the experiments proved 'that the Broad Gauge Engines possess greater capabilities for speed with equal loads, and, generally speaking, of propelling greater loads with equal speed; and, moreover, that the working with such engines is economical where very high speeds are required, or where the loads to be conveyed are such as to require the full power of the engine'.

On the subject of speed and express trains, they say incidentally: 'We feel it a duty to observe here that the public are mainly indebted for the present rate of speed and the increased accommodation of the railway carriages to the genius of Mr Brunel and the liberality of the Great Western Railway Company'.

The Report, however, was generally dead against the Broad Gauge. It was laid before Parliament at the beginning of the 1846 Session. After discussing the subject in all its aspects, the Commissioners sum up their conclusions as to the need for uniformity of gauge by saying that 'they

---

[1] They were published in the Appendix to the Commissioners' Report.

consider a break of gauge to be a very serious evil', that 'no method has been proposed to them which is calculated to remedy in any important degree the inconvenience attending a break of gauge'; and, with reference to the expedient of mixing the gauges on the same line, that 'the general adoption of such a system ought not to be permitted'. Apart from this last, the methods proposed had been (1) wheels sliding on their axles adjustable to either gauge; (2) broad-gauge 'crocodile' trucks to carry narrow-gauge vehicles; (3) bodies movable from one set of wheels to the other; and (4) containers, of which a broad-gauge truck would carry two, a narrow-gauge one only. All these were condemned as impracticable in everyday working.

The Commissioners then examine the comparative advantages of the two gauges, and state that:

After a full consideration of all the circumstances that have come before us and of the deductions we have made from the evidence, we are led to conclude—

1st. That as regards the Safety, Accommodation, and Convenience of the Passengers, no decided preference is due to either Gauge, but that on the Broad Gauge the motion is generally more easy at high velocities.

2nd. That in respect of Speed, we consider the advantages are with the Broad Gauge; but we think the public safety would be endangered in employing the greater capabilities of the Broad Gauge much beyond their present use, except on roads more consolidated and more substantially and perfectly formed than those of the existing lines.

3rd. That in the commercial case of the Transport of Goods we believe the Narrow Gauge to possess the greater convenience, and to be the more suited to the general traffic of the Country.

4th. That the Broad Gauge involves the greater outlay; and that we have not been able to discover, either in the maintenance of way, in the cost of locomotive power, or in any other annual expenses, any adequate reduction to compensate for the additional first cost.

Therefore, esteeming the importance of the highest speed on Express Trains for the accommodation of a comparatively small number of persons, however desirable that may be to them, as of far less moment than affording increased convenience to the general commercial traffic of the Country, we are inclined to consider the Narrow Gauge as that which should be preferred for general convenience; and therefore, if it were imperative to produce uniformity, we should recommend that uniformity to be produced by an alteration of the Broad to the Narrow Gauge, more especially when we take into consideration that the extent of the former at present in work is only 274 miles, while that of the latter is not less than 1901 miles, and that the alteration of the former to the latter, even if of equal length, would be the less costly as well as the less difficult operation.

The Report concludes with the following recommendations.

1st. That the Gauge of 4 feet 8½ inches be declared by the Legislature to be the Gauge to be used in all public Railways now under construction or hereafter to be constructed in Great Britain.

2nd. That, unless by consent of the Legislature, it should not be permitted to the Directors of any Railway Company to alter the Gauge of such Railway.

3rd. That, in order to complete the general chain of Narrow Gauge communication from the North of England to the Southern Coast, any suitable measure should be promoted to form a Narrow Gauge link from Oxford to Reading, and thence to Basingstoke, or by any other route connecting the proposed Oxford and Rugby Line with the South Western Railway.

4th. That, as any junction to be formed with a Broad Gauge Line would involve a break of gauge, provided our first recommendation be adopted, great commercial convenience would be obtained by reducing the gauge of the present Broad Gauge Lines to the Narrow Gauge of 4 feet 8½ inches; and we therefore think it desirable that some equitable means should be found of producing such entire uniformity of gauge, or of adopting such other course as would admit of the Narrow Gauge carriages passing, without interruption or danger, along the Broad Gauge Lines.

The Great Western representatives at once set about preparing a reply to this unexpected report, which the Broad Gauge party considered grossly unfair and unwarranted by the evidence. With the help of Brunel and Gooch, Saunders soon produced his able 'Observations on the Report of the Gauge Commissioners', a folio publication of some fifty pages.[1] In this, general objection is first made to the acceptance of statements and opinions by interested witnesses, not subject to cross-examination or any other check, as facts.

Such repetition of statements and opinions unsifted could not fail, insensibly perhaps, to produce its effect on the minds of the Commissioners, who may have naturally received them as from impartial parties. A striking proof of this is to be adduced from the fact that, before any of the parties connected with the Broad Gauge had been examined, and at a very early stage of the proceedings, the Commissiners allowed an impression to be produced on their minds by Mr Locke and Mr Robert Stephenson, which led to a representation being made by the President of the Commission to the Government that the speed of Express Trains ought to be restricted by law, thereby seriously prejudging one of the most important points at issue between the parties before they had received even one word of evidence to prove the security of the Broad Gauge system of travelling at very high speed. This repression of speed was of course the main line of argument adopted by those who were conscious that they could not compete with the Broad Gauge in their rate of travelling and in safety at high velocities, both of which latter propositions have been since established in favour of the Broad Gauge, and are admitted in the Report itself. Yet this was prejudged. The opinion stated in the Report as that of many of the officers of Railways that 'there would be difficulty in maintaining with safety the present Express speed upon the great trunk Railways' must have emanated wholly from the Narrow Gauge advocates as to the capabilities of their own engines and railways. It certainly was never entertained by parties connected with the Broad Gauge . . . It does not appear, however, that the Government consented to commit themselves to any compliance with such a proposal, and this may be deemed a proof that they do not approve of such limitation on mechanical power.

The observations then proceed 'to consider the Report under the several heads into which it is divided by the Commissioners, from which it will be seen that their calculations and conclusions are not in accordance with the facts, and that very extraordinary mistakes have been introduced into the tables and figures, seriously affecting the character of the Report itself, and the correction of which controverts all their arguments and reasoning upon them'. Numerous real mistakes are then pointed out, and the whole report subjected to searching and detailed criticisms. In conclusion, it is submitted that 'the following results are clearly and fully established'. Though of some length, these are worth quoting as giving the official case for the Broad Gauge.

1. That the question of 'break of gauge' originated as a cloak to a monopoly, of a means of obtaining and holding a control over an immense traffic by an union of amalgamated companies, without the possibility of competition or interference with such traffic by any other contending system or separate interest.

2. That there has been no evidence given to prove, or any sufficient reason to assume, that even if the gauge were uniform throughout the country the Passenger Traffic could be carried on by sending the same carriages through, from the trains on the main and principal Railways, to all cross or diverging Lines or Branches or that the same inconvenience of a change at the principal towns or points of junction would not be experienced, whether it be a Break of Gauge or merely a change of line out of the main thoroughfare.

---

[1] Published by James Bigg and Son, Westminster, at 1s.

3. That such is the daily experience and practice now, where the lines converge at one point without any break of gauge, and that the Narrow Gauge Engines have not power to convey greater numbers of carriages to afford the accommodation of sending them through to each separate line of Railway (which is the assumed system), and still to maintain their rate of speed, inasmuch as they are now obliged to limit their quick Trains to First Class Carriages only.

4. That the Transfer of Merchandise, without unloading or disturbing the goods, may be effected by mechanical means, with perfect safety and facility:—that the same wagon with its wheels may be conveyed on a low platform or truck travelling on the Rails, in case it shall have to pass again to the same Gauge in the course of a journey—and that loose bodies or boxes may also be safely employed, as with the Diligences and Waggons in France, to be transferred to other wheels and axles, without delay or difficulty, at any Break of Gauge.[1]

5. That even if Goods had to be shifted from one waggon to another side by side, it would simply be a question of cost and of delay,—that such shifting by hand could be well performed for about sixpence per ton, and with far less delay than is now involved in the ordinary stoppage of Trains arriving at Birmingham, with Goods to be sent forward by other Lines.

6. That the commercial advantage of transporting goods in small waggons is quite as applicable to the Broad as to the Narrow Gauge, and that such waggons are actually running at this time on the Great Western Railway, although the Narrow Gauge may not be able, without considerable overhanging weight, to obtain such large waggons as the Broad Gauge—while proof is given by the Narrow Gauge witnesses that for certain purposes 'the larger the Truck the better'.

7. That the advantage of two systems, worked by two independent Companies, would tend greatly to secure the best and most economical management of such business, and to deprive the break of Gauge of its fancied inconveniences, whether to Passengers or to Goods—and that the time would be fully saved of any such interruption by the greater speed attainable on the Broad Gauge, that the fares and charges to the public would inevitably be lowered by the competition, while the accommodation would be improved by the rivalry.

8. That such rivalry and emulation of the two Gauges has already acted most powerfully to the improvement of both and, to the economical as well as rapid transport of Passengers and Merchandise throughout this country, and that it is calculated, if not prohibited, to extend in various ways the same and even still greater public benefits hereafter.

9. That any attempt to restrict improvement by annihilating the Broad Gauge would be in the highest degree impolitic, and would be a subversion of every principle which has hitherto stimulated science and mechanical skill, and would be most unfair and unjust as a punishment to those who have successfully and spiritedly pursued the course of improvement.

10. That the four recommendations of the Commissioners are wholly at variance with their separate conclusions on each branch of their inquiry, inasmuch as they have proved and admitted the superiority of the Broad Gauge, but have advised the adoption uniformly of the Narrow Gauge, if more than a million of money can be found to accomplish the extinction of the Broad and superior Gauge, on equitable conditions.

11. That under the first two recommendations, wherein they have advised the limitation of the Broad Gauge to Lines already made, specifically requiring every Line now making to be constructed on the Narrow Gauge, they would greatly multiply every inconvenience which can be sustained by the public from a Break of Gauge, introducing it at numerous points on direct Metropolitan Lines instead of a few only on Cross Lines, forgetting also that such recommendations must have the effect of reversing the most solemn decisions of the Legislature during the last and former Sessions of Parliament, which sanctioned certain Lines of Extension as those which could be worked most beneficially for the public, in connection with the Great Western system and upon which, as Broad Gauge Lines, specifically so enacted, large sums have been already contributed and expended.

---

[1] Gooch tells us in his *Diaries*: 'I never had any faith in any of these plans as workable in practice.' They were never adopted by the Great Western for the transfer in later years of their own traffic at Wolverhampton, Didcot, Swindon, Bristol, or Exeter.

12. That the inquiry before the Commissioners has not been conducted in a manner to enable them to obtain accurate and impartial information and sound evidence for their guidance; and that no legislation on the subject can be satisfactorily founded on such loose and erroneous evidence and calculations, without any proper investigation of accounts.

13. That the Commissioners have been misled by Tables which are altogether misstated; that their deductions of figures and reasoning upon figures are consequently wrong; that the arithmetical mistakes alone in the tables of speed and time and in the table of cost prove the very converse of all that they assume in respect of the Narrow Gauge capabilities, or their supposed equality of advantage in certain respects with the Broad Gauge.

14. That there is greater economy proved on the Broad Gauge, both in cost of stock (owing to the comparative fewness of Engines and greater capacity of Carriages, etc., for the same work), and that the expenses of Locomotive power are less on the Broad than on the Narrow Gauge.

15. That the greater power of the Engines does not involve waste, even when not required to be used—but on the contrary, the larger size of fire-box and boiler, producing greater power, are productive of economy, even with lighter loads.

16. That the greater power of the Engines, even at ordinary speeds, is essentially conducive to safety—by ensuring greater punctuality of time—and by taking more unlimited loads at all times of the day and seasons of the year, without unnecessarily sub-dividing the trains or using two or more Engines as assistant power excepting in extreme cases.

17. That the power of the Broad Gauge Engines has enabled the Great Western Company, without endangering the public safety by oscillation or by rocking motion (whether it arises from overhanging weight to acquire length or from outside cylinders to gain width of Engine), to attain a much higher speed than the Narrow Gauge Lines, and at such speed to benefit all classes of society without exception, of whom the Second Class travellers, although they cannot afford generally to pay as high fares as the First Class Passengers, probably considered speed as a commercial saving of time comparatively even more essential to themselves, while the higher classes are content to pay for the sake of this greater comfort and luxury in the better carriages at the same high speed.

18. That the Public will expect and pay for the highest speed by Express Trains; and that they do not partake of the fears or alarm, which have been expressed in the Report, as to the safety of such Trains, notwithstanding the strange representation made by the Commissioners to Government at so early a period of the inquiry, corroborating evidence is furnished by a demand recently made by the Merchants of Liverpool and Manchester for another Express Train to be dispatched at an early hour to London, and which has been granted by the Railway Company and that such Express Trains, if the Broad Gauge existed on those Lines, would convey both classes together at the same speed, and would also perform the journey with a saving in time of one hour at the very least to each passenger between Liverpool and London.

19. That the greater power of the Engines and capacity of the Carriages would enable the Great Western to convey, by means of the same number of Engines and Carriages, 15,000 troops on the Broad, to 10,000 troops on the Narrow Gauge in the case of any emergency for the defence of the Country, and that the transport would be effected in shorter time.

20. That the Broad Gauge, as admitted by the Commissioners, is more smooth as well as more safe at high velocities; and that the greater smoothness and freedom from oscillation and rocking motion mentioned in the Report must reduce the liability to accidents from the Engines running off the Line without any known cause of obstruction, as well as from defects in the permanent way, slips in Cuttings, subsidence of Embankments, loss of Gauge, broken or loose Chairs, and fractures of Wheels or Axles, etc., whether acting as the cause or the effect of those contingencies.

21. That no instance has occurred of a Broad Gauge Engine running off the Line, from excessive speed, or without known cause of obstruction, while instances are truly recorded in the Report of accidents from both on the Narrow Gauge Lines.

22. That accidents on the Great Western with their Passenger Trains, whether ordinary or express, have been extremely rare and have never proved fatal to any passenger (the Sonning accident, which occurred to a Luggage Train, alone excepted), their Carriages being constructed on six wheels and made far more solid and substantial in every respect than those on the Narrow Gauge, while from the circumstances of conveying in the extra width more passengers on the same number of wheels, this additional solidity

is gained without carrying as much deadweight for each passenger as on the Narrow Gauge.

23. That easy gradients, however desirable for other objects and principally of course for heavy luggage, do not account (as the Commissioners insinuate, by a wrong deduction from the Time Tables) for the higher speed of the Great Western, inasmuch as the lowest speed of their Express Trains is on the most level gradients of their Line, one of the Gauge Commissioners with their Secretary having ascertained personally by experiments that the highest speeds were maintained over the worst gradients between Taunton and Exeter, where the gradients are much steeper than those of either the London and Birmingham or Grand Junction or any of the lines referred to in the Report as running Express Trains; and in these experiments, all mention of which seems to be omitted in the Report, extra weights were added to the Express Trains by additional Carriages, so as to raise it to a load of 70 tons.

24. Finally.—That the Experiments made in the presence of the Commissioners have demonstrated beyond all controversy the complete success of the Broad Gauge System, which aimed at affording the utmost accommodation to the public by carrying large numbers of passengers of both classes at very high speeds with perfect safety and with comparative comfort and smoothness, taking precuations that by the additional power of the Engines the services should be performed with the greater precision and punctuality at all seasons of the year and in the varying state of the weather without limiting their loads or the public accommodation and without employing two Engines to Passenger Trains, excepting in extreme cases of necessity and never in Express Trains; also providing that the unnecessary multiplication of Goods Trains on main thoroughfares for Passengers should be avoided as much as possible by the capability to taking heavy roads of Goods in a few Trains at a sufficient speed so keep the Line more clear for Passenger Trains, and that the greater power of Engines, while producing economy of expense, should enable the Company to afford better Carriage accommodation and to convey when requisite more Carriages with each Train, to pass over Branch or Extension Lines without change of Carriage on the journey, still maintaining the highest speed of travelling which can be made consistently with safety, as essentially conducive to the comfort and enjoyment of this highest classes as well as tending to the commercial advantages of all individuals by a saving of time accompanied with the most unlimited facilities of locomotion; and the consequence of this greater capability of carrying heavy loads at high speeds must lead much more rapidly to the carrying of large numbers at lower fares.

The Observations were followed, soon after the publication of the Evidence and Appendix of Statistics taken by the Commissioners, by 'Additional Observations', criticising these. Both were presented to all Members of Parliament and widely circulated, and doubtless had their effect in the insertion in the Gauge Act of the saving clause, which will be referred to presently.

The Commissioners' Report was referred by the House of Commons to the Board of Trade for their views, and on 6th June 1846 the latter issued a Minute thereon giving the reasons which prevented them concurring with the full extent of the Commissioners' recommendations.

In this they say:

Adverting to the vast expense which must be involved in an entire alteration of the Broad Gauge, and having regard to the circumstances under which the Companies employing this gauge were established and to the interests they have acquired, my Lords cannot feel themselves justified in recommending that it should be proposed to Parliament to compel the entire reduction of the Seven Feet Gauge. They feel with the Commisioners that 'they cannot recommend the Legislature to sanction such an expense from the Public Monies, nor do they think that the Companies to which the Broad Gauge Railways belong can be called upon to incur such an expense themselves, having made all their works with the authority of Parliament, nor even the more limited expense of laying down intermediate rails for Narrow Gauge traffic.'

Still less can they feel themselves justified in proposing that the expense of such alteration should be defrayed by a contribution levied, as has sometimes been suggested, on the rest of the Railway Companies in Great Britain; and they are unable to suggest any other equitable or practical means by which the desired uniformity of Gauge could be obtained.

The conclusion to which my Lords have come respecting the reduction of the Broad Gauge on existing Lines necessarily affects their opinion with regard to the future Gauge of Lines now in course of construction.

If the Line now extending from London to Exeter be preserved on the broad gauge and yet all the railways in connection with it from the South, for which Acts have been obtained [*i.e.*, Berks and Hants and Wilts, Somerset, and Weymouth], are to be formed on the narrow gauge, then it is obvious that the inconveniences of the break of gauge will not only be continued but will be increased in amount.

Assuming that an absolute uniformity of gauge cannot now be obtained, they feel that the only practicable course to be pursued is to endeavour to effect such a settlement of the Gauges to be used on the several railways already sanctioned, and to lay down such general regulations for the future, as will prevent the increase and further extension of an evil they cannot altogether remedy, and will reduce the inconvenience inflicted on the Passenger and Goods traffic of the Country to the narrowest attainable limits.

They would therefore recommend that the Lines for which Acts have been obtained but which have not yet been completed to the South of the Line from London to Bristol should be permitted to be constructed on the Broad Gauge, as originally intended.

The Board then referred to the South Wales Railway, and stated that, though the case was attended with some difficulty, it was their opinion that on the whole it would be advisable that this line also should be made on the Broad Gauge, as originally sanctioned. With regard to the Oxford & Rugby Railway, they stated their intention to exercise the power given them by that Act to require the addition of narrow-gauge rails, and that therefore it was not necessary to interfere with the construction of the line on the Broad Gauge as authorized. The Oxford, Worcester & Wolverhampton Railway Act, it will be remembered, already provided for additional narrow-gauge rails north of the junction with the Birmingham & Gloucester at Abbot's Wood, near Worcester; so that also was not to be interfered with.

Thus the recommendations of the three Commissioners for the extinction of the Broad Gauge were considerably watered down by the Board of Trade, and, as we shall see, were destined to be still further diluted by Parliament.

The House of Commons having passed resolutions embodying almost in the same terms the suggestions of the Board, a Bill was brought in to give effect to them, and after passing through the usual stages in both Houses, obtained the Royal Assent on the 18th of August, and became the Gauge Act, 1846. Of this Act the first section forbids the future construction of any railway for the conveyance of passengers on any gauge other than 4 feet 8½ inches in Great Britain and 5 feet 3 inches in Ireland. The second section, however, excepts from this prohibition '*any Railway constructed or to be constructed under the provisions of any present or future Act containing any special enactment defining the gauge or gauges of such railway or any part thereof*,' or any Railway which is in its whole length southward of the Great Western Railway, or any Railway in any of the Counties of Cornwall, Devon, Dorset, or Somerset, for which any Act has been or shall be passed in this Session of Parliament, or any Railway in any of the last-mentioned Counties now in course of construction'. Branches just authorized from West Drayton to Uxbridge, Maidenhead to High Wycombe, and from the Oxford, Worcester & Wolverhampton Railway to Witney, are also excepted, and the South Wales and Monmouth & Hereford Railways ordered to be made on the gauge of 7 feet. Further sections provide 'that it shall not be lawful to alter the gauge of any Railway used for the Conveyance of Passengers'; that the Oxford & Rugby and Oxford, Worcester & Wolverhampton Acts shall not be affected; and for penalties of £10 per mile of any railway constructed or altered contrary to the Act 'for every day the same shall continue so unlawfully constructed or altered'.

Now it will be observed that the words in italics, which were not contained in the recommendations of the Board of Trade or in the resolutions of the House of Commons on which the Act was founded, completely took the sting out of the Gauge Act, leaving, as they did, the question of the gauge of any new line open for the decision of the Committee on the Bill for its construction, and only enjoining the Narrow Gauge in cases where such Committee has not been persuaded to sanction the Broad. This meant leaving matters much as they were before, so that the Royal Commission and the whole agitation ended, in effect, in a mere expression of opinion.

To quote from a Report of the Railway Commissioners in 1848:

'Supposing the object of Parliament to have been to ensure, in its future Railway legislation, a conformity with the Resolutions defining the limits of the two Gauges, it would appear that this object might have been more effectually secured by embodying the substance of those Resolutions in the Standing Orders of the two Houses, rather than by passing an Act of Parliament on the subject. It must be obvious that Committees of the Houses, when considering the provisions which they may deem expedient to insert in Bills, cannot be bound by previous Acts of Parliament. But had the Gauge Resolutions been embodied in the Standing Orders, no Committee could have inserted any clause in a Railway Bill in contravention of those Resolutions without having made a previous application to the House for the suspension of Standing Orders, and without having obtained its deliberate decision to that effect. . . . Under the present system Committees are at liberty to take any course they think fit respecting the choice of Gauge, and the only means possessed by the House of enforcing the rule it laid down is by rescinding the decision of the Committee on the Bill after the whole of its labour has been concluded— a course which the House is naturally and properly unwilling to adopt.'

Thus did the Broad Gauge party succeed in spiking the great gun of the enemy, to the intense annoyance of the latter. In the very next session a broad-gauge line from Oxford to Cheltenham as well as two short lines in South Wales were sanctioned by Parliament, with provisions, however, for the addition of the Narrow Gauge if required by the Railway Commissioners, and in 1848 the extension of the Broad Gauge to Birmingham and Wolverhampton was authorized on lines previously to be narrow-gauge only.

The facts remain, however, that these were all, potentially at any rate, double- or mixed-gauge railways, and that, although not forbidden by the Gauge Act, no exclusively broad-gauge lines outside the excepted district, other than short branches or extensions of branches, were passed by Parliament after 1846.

Moreover, the Board of Trade carried out the intention expressed in their Minute by an Order of 25th July 1846, in exercise of their power under the Oxford & Rugby Act, requiring the Company to lay down narrow-gauge rails on that line in addition to the Broad Gauge.

Upon this the Great Western Directors considered the subject of forming a continuous narrow-gauge line from Oxford to Basingstoke in order to comply with the recommendation made by the Gauge Commissioners and confirmed by the Board of Trade Minute and the Resolutions of the House of Commons. They had an additional inducement to do this by reason of a project with the grand title of 'The Manchester & Southampton Railway' then before Parliament; really it was for a narrow-gauge line from Cheltenham to Southampton. On 19th August they resolved:

That upon a careful review of all the circumstances of the case—taking into account the heavy expense now imposed on this Company by the Board of Trade in requiring them to lay down the Narrow Gauge for 50 miles from Rugby to Oxford, it is expedient to undertake to lay down in like manner Narrow Gauge Rails on the portion of the Great Western and Berks and Hants Railways between Oxford and Basingstoke, being about 40 miles, provided parliamentary sanction shall be refused to the Manchester and Southampton Railway Bill—which is projected for the purpose of diverting the North and South Traffic from the lines already sanctioned upon the plea of diversity of Gauge on such Lines.

That the Chairman be authorized to pledge this Company to such steps being taken to complete the chain of Narrow Gauge from North to South—in the event of the before-mentioned Bill now before parliament being rejected.

This pledge was accordingly given by Russell, and the Manchester & Southampton project extinguished. Thus was the thin end of the wedge inserted, which was destined to bring down the whole broad-gauge edifice he, Saunders, and Brunel were building up with such pains.

5 THE BIRMINGHAM & OXFORD JUNCTION RAILWAY AND THE BIRMINGHAM, WOLVERHAMPTON & DUDLEY RAILWAY

The Birmingham & Oxford line owed its origin entirely to the Grand Junction Company. Early in 1845 that Company determined on getting a communication with London independent of the London & Birmingham, with whom they had, as we have seen, long been at war. They accordingly projected a line from their Birmingham Terminus to join the Oxford Branch of the Great Western. In this they were supported by many of the iron masters, merchants, and manufacturers of the Birmingham District, who were thoroughly discontented with the London & Birmingham's alleged abuse of its monopoly, especially in the conduct of the goods traffic, extortionate rates, and refusal to afford much needed additional accommodation.

The Grand Junction naturally sought the co-operation of the Great Western Directors, and the latter, after some hesitation, eventually gave them cordial support. In this they were influenced—so Saunders told the Gauge Commissioners—by the bitter hostility shown by the London & Birmingham and Midland Companies in the matter of the Oxford & Rugby Railway, 'which was never intended to be a direct competing line adversely to the London and Birmingham', and in the promotion or encouragement of lines whose only object could be to prevent traffic coming on to the Great Western, and, last but not least, in the effort being made to force the Broad Gauge off from Gloucester to Bristol; by all of which they were driven to conclude that no friendly interchange of traffic was possible. The new railway was to be broad-gauge, and the Grand Junction even proposed to add broad-gauge rails on their own line to Liverpool and Manchester, and had estimates of the cost made by their Engineer, as we have already seen.

By the Subscribers' Agreement of 15th April 1845, power was given to their Committee to enter into contracts for the sale or lease of the undertaking to the Grand Junction or Great Western Company, each of whom was empowered to nominate three members of the Committee, and stipulations were made for securing the railway as a rival to the London & Birmingham and keeping it out of their hands.

Later, on the sanction of the Oxford & Rugby Line by Parliament being assured, the Birmingham & Oxford was shortened to join that Railway at Knightcote two miles north of Fenny Compton instead of the Great Western at Oxford.

Thus matters stood till the Grand Junction made up their quarrel with the London & Birmingham, and agreed to an amalgamation on very advantageous terms. They then, of course, deserted their Great Western allies, withdrew their support from the Birmingham & Oxford, and disclaimed the acts of their officers, asserting that the Directors, Solicitors, Secretary, etc., who had actually promoted the scheme, had done so in their private capacity only.

Undeterred by this defection of the Grand Junction, and the consequent accession of strength to the opposition for the coming fight, the other parties who had embarked on the Birmingham & Oxford project determined to proceed with it and accordingly lodged their Bill for the Session of 1846. At the same time they deposited another Bill for a short branch to an independent terminus in the town of Birmingham.

The London & Birmingham opposed with a projected system of loop lines to accommodate the chief portion of the district, but the Birmingham & Oxford based their case on the need of a competing line, and this consideration greatly influenced the Committees in both Houses to prefer their scheme.

The Bills provided for a sale or lease to the Great Western Company only, the alternative power in favour of the Grand Junction being of course omitted. Now it so happened that before the Bills had passed the Commons Committee, another Committee, which had been appointed to report on the expediency of granting powers of amalgamation and leasing to Railway Companies, made a recommendation to the House that in all such cases the tolls of the Companies should be revised and reduced to the lowest scale actually charged or authorized to be charged by either of them. The powers of sale or lease to the Great Western contained in the Bills brought that Company within the terms of this recommendation, but the technical difficulty that notice, necessary by Standing Orders, of an intended alteration of the Great Western tolls had not been given, of course not having been contemplated, prevented the Birmingham & Oxford Committee complying with the recommendation. The Bills were consequently reported to the House without any revision of the Great Western tolls. This gave the London & Birmingham opposition a chance, and they succeeded in obtaining a recommittal of the Bills in the hope of expunging the powers of sale or lease to the Great Western. The Committee, however, refused to oblige them, and got over the difficulty by inserting a proviso that such powers should take effect only when the tolls of the Great Western Railway should have been reduced by Parliament to the scale authorized by the Birmingham & Oxford Bills. They had another try at the Report stage in the House, but the Bills were passed and went up to the Lords without alteration.

In spite of violent opposition in the House of Lords, the two Bills passed all the stages, and received the Royal Assent on 3rd August 1846.

The Birmingham & Oxford Junction Railway Act authorized a railway from a junction with the London & North Western Railway, which, by the way, had only been constituted on 16th July, in the town of Birmingham, to a junction with the Oxford & Rugby Railway in the Parish of Fenny Compton, and also a branch from Finwood Green, in the Parish of Rowington, to a junction with the Oxford, Worcester & Wolverhampton's authorized Stratford Branch at Stratford-on-Avon.

The Birmingham Extension Act was for a railway in the town of Birmingham from a junction with the Birmingham & Oxford Railway at Adderley Street to Great Charles Street, with a station between Snow Hill and Livery Street and Monmouth Street and Great Charles Street, and provided that the portion between Moor Street and Monmouth Street should be covered by a tunnel with no opening therein, and that the whole railway should be amalgamated with the Birmingham & Oxford on the passing of the Act.

The capital authorized by the former Act was £700,000 and by the latter £300,000, making a total of £1,000,000, in £20 shares.

Neither Act makes any mention of the gauge of the railways; consequently under the Gauge Act there was no power to make them on any other than the Narrow Gauge. The reason for this was that, in view of the Gauge Commissioners' Report and the Government Bill to carry out their recommendations against the extension of the Broad Gauge, which was actually in Parliament at the time, it was not thought prudent to press a clause authorizing Broad Gauge on the Birmingham & Oxford.

On this same 3rd August the Royal Assent was also given to the Bill for the Birmingham, Wolverhampton & Dudley Railway. This line was first projected somewhat later in the year 1845 than the Birmingham & Oxford. Its promoters were to a great extent the same as those of the latter, and it was strongly supported by the mining and manufacturing interests of the Black Country, which it traversed, and also, it may be noted, by the Oxford, Worcester & Wolverhampton Company. This Bill also, of course, encountered desperate opposition from the united forces of the London & Birmingham and Grand Junction Companies, and was met by competing schemes of theirs, but eventually passed both Houses together with the competing Birmingham, Wolverhampton & Stour Valley Railway of the London & North Western and Shrewsbury & Birmingham Companies.

The Act authorized a railway from Monmouth Street between Livery Street and Snow Hill in Birmingham to a junction with the Oxford, Worcester & Wolverhampton Railway near Priestfield Furnaces, in the Parish of Wolverhampton, and from 'The Cross Guns', in West Bromwich Parish, to 'The Trindle House' in Dudley; but provided that, as the portion of the latter line between Great Bridge and Dudley was identical with the main line of the South Staffordshire Railway—authorized on the same day—the Birmingham, Wolverhampton & Dudley Company should not make that line unless the South Staffordshire failed to do so within three years. They were, however, to have running powers over that part of the South Staffordshire, and the latter Company was given similar powers between Wednesbury and Priestfield.

As in the case of the Birmingham & Oxford, and for the same reasons, no clause specifying the gauge appeared in the Act, though from the beginning this was intended to be the broad; hence the Birmingham, Wolverhampton & Dudley as originally sanctioned would have had to be a narrow-gauge line like the Birmingham & Oxford.

An important difference in the constitution of the two Companies was that no power of sale or lease to the Great Western or any other Company was contained in the Birmingham, Wolverhampton & Dudley Act.

It may be noted in passing that the two lines overlapped between Monmouth Street and Great Charles Street, Birmingham, so that each Company had equal rights over the site of the proposed station at Snow Hill. The authorized capital of the Birmingham, Wolverhampton & Dudley Company was £700,000 in £20 shares.

Very soon after the incorporation of the Companies it became obvious to their Directors that, one line being a continuation of the other, both starting from the same station in Birmingham, and both being rivals to the London & North Western and having many shareholders and directors in common, an amalgamation would be for the mutual interest. Accordingly they agreed to amalgamate on equal terms, and gave notice that the proposal would be submitted to the shareholders at the first meeting of each Company, appointed for 30th October.

The Birmingham & Oxford Directors made no proposal of selling their line to the Great Western at this time, being of opinion that the value of both lines would be enhanced by a previous amalgamation, but at the Meeting several shareholders advocated an immediate sale of the line. To this the Directors demurred. Eventually a resolution was passed sanctioning an amalgamation with the Birmingham, Wolverhampton & Dudley, and authorizing the Directors to apply for an Act to carry it out and to sell or lease the two lines when amalgamated to the Great Western, 'the Directors being requested and authorized at once to negotiate with that Company for some arrangement for that purpose'.

At the Birmingham, Wolverhampton & Dudley Meeting on the same day resolutions similar in effect were passed.

Deputations of the Directors of both Companies accordingly proceeded to negotiate with a Deputation of Great Western Directors, and terms were agreed to on 12th November, and afterwards confirmed by the Boards of the three Companies.

These terms were that the Great Western should buy the two undertakings by payment of £30 5s for each £20 share of the combined capital of £1,700,000, a premium of £10 5s per share, payable within six months of the opening or on 1st July 1850, with 5% interest from that date, and similar interest on all calls punctually paid during construction. Any further capital required was to be found by the Great Western, who were to have effectual control over the expenditure. Last, but not least, powers were to be obtained for the Broad Gauge.

As far as regards the Birmingham, Wolverhampton & Dudley, this agreement, of course, required the sanction of Parliament, but in the case of the Birmingham & Oxford it had been authorized in advance by their Acts, and therefore came into effect immediately it had been ratified by a General Meeting.

As soon as they had been confirmed by the respective Boards these terms were made public; and Special Meetings of the three Companies to consider them were called for 4th December.

At the Great Western and Birmingham, Wolverhampton & Dudley Meetings the proposed agreement was approved and confirmed without any difficulty, but at that of the Birmingham & Oxford there was opposition in favour of opening negotiations with the London & North Western.

On the very eve of the three meetings Russell had received a letter from G. C. Glyn, Chairman of that Company, enclosing a copy of a reply he had just sent to certain Birmingham & Oxford shareholders, in which he suggested a joint lease to his own and the Great Western Companies, and added that if the latter would not agree to this the North Western Directors would make proposals on their own account 'when the present offer of the Great Western is disposed of'. He asked for an immediate conference. To this Russell at once replied declining both the joint lease and the conference. This correspondence was read at the Birmingham & Oxford Meeting by the Chairman, P. H. Muntz, who then explained the negotiations with the Great Western Directors, and moved the confirmation of the agreement. An amendment was proposed for the adjournment of the Meeting to 14th January, on the ground that the sealed share certificates had not yet been issued, and that numerous purchasers of shares had therefore been unable to complete their purchases so as to vote at the Meeting. The opposition alleged that the delay in issuing the certificates was intentional on the part of the Directors. This was denied by them and the Secretary, who ascribed the delay entirely to the printers, and stated that he had registered all transfers sent in without certificates. As the charge was denied on oath in the subsequent lawsuits, and appears to have had no influence with the Courts, it may be disregarded. The leader of the opposition, Elias Mozley, a banker in Liverpool and a North Western shareholder, in support of the adjournment read a letter from Glyn, by which a premium of £15 per share was suggested on behalf of the London & North Western. Notwithstanding this, the amendment was eventually negatived, and the Chairman's motion ratifying the Great Western Agreement carried by the requisite three-fifths majority. This at once made the agreement binding as far as the Birmingham & Oxford and Great Western Companies were concerned, and the Directors then proceeded to draw up a more formal deed, which was sealed on 2nd January 1847.

Refusing to recognize this fact, Mr Glyn wrote to the Birmingham & Oxford Chairman shortly after the Meeting renewing the proposal of a joint lease and, failing that, offering on behalf of his Company to purchase the line at £15 premium on each share. In reply the following resolutions of the Birmingham & Oxford Directors were communicated to Mr Glyn by the Secretary:

18th December 1846.

*Resolved* that Mr Glyn be reminded that this Company has contracted to sell the Birmingham and Oxford Line to the Great Western Company and that he be informed that the Board is unanimously of opinion that under such circumstances the offer contained in his letter of the 16th instant ought not to have been made.

That the Board is further of opinion that Parliament, mindful of the policy which actuated it with reference to these Lines last Session, would refuse its consent to any such arrangement as that proposed by Mr Glyn on behalf of the London and North Western Company, and entertain no doubt of its sanctioning the arrangements completed by this Company for the purpose of carrying out this policy.

That the general interests of trade and the public imperiously call for the exclusion of the influence of the London and North Western Company from the management of any and every portion of a second line from London northwards.

On the receipt of this snub Captain Huish, who was now General Manager of the whole London & North Western Railway, and his Directors redoubled their efforts to acquire not only an influence but a controlling interest in the management of the rival line. They had begun buying shares in the Birmingham & Oxford about the time of the Meeting of 4th December, but were just too late, and this was no doubt the reason of the clamour about the non-issue of certificates and the proposal to adjourn the Meeting. From this time the purchases were carried on to such an extent that out of the whole 50,000 shares in the Birmingham & Oxford Company nearly 40,000 had very soon been acquired by their agents, many at as high a premium as £11 per share. To make things doubly sure by increasing their voting power, these purchases were split up in lots of ten—up to which number each share carried a vote—among their Directors, shareholders, officers, engineers, solicitors, clerks, and servants. Indeed, it was said at the time that most of the Euston porters were shareholders in the Birmingham & Oxford.

Having thus obtained a sweeping majority of votes in the Company, the next endeavour of Mr Elias Mozley and other North Western agents was to obtain a majority on the Board. The number of Directors at this time was twelve, but there was power in the Act to increase this to eighteen or lessen it to six.

Mr Mozley assumed that at the February Half-yearly Meeting four of the Directors appointed in October would retire by rotation, and that he could supply their places by nominees of his own. Still he would be in a minority of four to eight, so to overcome this it was intended to exercise the power of increasing the number to eighteen by electing six Directors of his own party, and so secure a majority of ten to eight. Accordingly he sent a requisition to the Directors to call an Extraordinary Meeting for the purpose of increasing the Board to eighteen, which they did for 13th March, the ordinary Half-yearly Meeting being already fixed for 27th February. Meantime the Directors took Counsel's opinion, and were advised that none of the Directors elected in October should retire in February, the only doubt being whether they should retire in the following October or February 1848. The Half-yearly Meeting on 27th February was adjourned after some talk to the day appointed for the Extraordinary Meeting. This was held on 13th March at Dee's Royal Hotel, Temple Row, Birmingham. Six new Directors were duly—and quite legally— elected, and various instructions to stultify all their former proceedings given to the Board by the Proprietors, most of whom had arrived by special train from Euston. The Half-yearly Meeting was then held; someone proposed that a third of the old Directors should retire at once, which was carried with acclamation when put to the Meeting by the Proposer on the refusal of the Chairman to do so. The Directors sat still, and the Proprietors, having on the motion of Mr Elias Mozley expressed their dislike of them and their behaviour in suitable terms, betook themselves to Curzon Street Station, where their special train was waiting.

Since the December Meeting three Bills had been lodged in Parliament for the Session of 1847 to carry out the Agreement of 12th November: one by the Birmingham, Wolverhampton & Dudley Company to authorize the sale of their line to the Great Western; another by the Great Western to enable them, among other things, to purchase that line and to effect the reduction of their tolls required by the Birmingham & Oxford Act as a condition of the amalgamation; and a third for amalgamating the Birmingham & Oxford and Birmingham, Wolverhampton & Dudley into one Company under the title of 'The Oxford, Birmingham & Wolver- hampton Railway Company', and empowering it to sell the Birmingham, Wolverhampton & Dudley to the Great Western. The first two duly passed and became Acts of Parliament in July, but the third, having passed the Commons, failed in the Lords on the Wharncliffe Standing Order, which required the approval of the Bill by a General Meeting of the Birmingham & Oxford shareholders, of course quite impossible to obtain. In the circumstances, however, its failure was not of much importance, as the Great Western had now obtained the power to purchase the Birmingham, Wolverhampton & Dudley, which had been lacking, and was as capable of making two mouthfuls of the Companies as of swallowing both at one gulp.

In the meantime the original Directors of the Birmingham & Oxford, feeling that their position at variance with the vast majority of their shareholders was somewhat curious and required public explanation, presented a Petition to the House of Lords in March setting out the facts of the case and praying for an inquiry into their allegations. This led to a Debate in that august assembly in which Lords Lyndhurst, Brougham, Lansdowne, and others supported a motion for an inquiry, while Lords Stanley and St Germans opposed it on behalf of the dissentient shareholders and the London & North Western Railway respectively. In the result, a Select Committee of five independent peers was appointed, but before they could take up the matter, Chancery proceedings were commenced by some of the opposition, so the inquiry was left to the Law Courts. The object of the suit was to upset the Agreement of November, to restrain the Directors from acting on it, and to force four of them to retire. The appointment of the six new Directors had not done the enemy much good, as the business of the Company was carried on by a committee of five, whom the old Directors had cunningly appointed for the purpose before the March Meeting. This was, of course, a special grievance.

The pleasant gatherings at Dee's Hotel were resumed at the requisition of the opposition on 12th June, adjourned to 19th then to 30th June and 12th July successively, in each case without any business being disposed of. It was not till a further adjournment to the King's Arms, Westminster, on 24th July, that the Euston troupe really got to work, and appointed a solicitor named Dobie to bring actions in the name of the Birmingham & Oxford Company against the old Directors for the cancellation of the Agreement, to restrain them from acting at all in the affairs of the Company, and to compel them personally to reimburse to the Company all sums expended in carrying out the Agreement or promoting the recent Bill in Parliament. Further, they 'deemed it highly unfit that any more of the funds of the Company should be placed under the control of such parties', and so protested against the call of £5 per share lately made by 'such parties' and recommended the shareholders not to pay it. To enable them to act in the name of the Company, they had even forged an imitation of the Common Seal, which was produced at the Meeting and duly declared to be the only common seal of the Birmingham & Oxford Junction Railway Company!

As the non-payment of the call would have the effect of suspending the works of the railway, and causing them much loss and inconvenience, the Great Western Directors thought it was now time for them to take a decisive hand in the fray. So towards the end of August the Great Western

Company filed a Bill in Chancery against the Birmingham & Oxford Company, all its eighteen Directors by name, and the Birmingham, Wolverhampton & Dudley Company, for specific performance of the Agreement of 12th November 1846, and an injunction restraining the Birmingham & Oxford Company and its Directors from attempting to make any arrangement for the sale or lease of the line to the London & North Western Company, or doing anything to prevent payment of the £5 call or inconsistent with the Agreement. The twelve old Directors and the Birmingham, Wolverhampton & Dudley Company were of course friendly but necessary Defendants.

On 4th December the Vice-Chancellor gave final judgment in favour of the Great Western on all points, and granted the injunction asked for. An appeal to the Lord Chancellor was dismissed with costs in January 1848, after which Captain Huish and his Directors threw up the sponge, and the civil war in the Birmingham & Oxford Company fizzled out.

Meantime, in consequence of the agitation carried on in and out of Parliament for a broad-gauge line to Birmingham, the House of Lords, in June 1847, ordered the Railway Commissioners, a short-lived Ministry of Transport of the period,[1] to inquire into the existing railway communication between London and Birmingham, and to report to the House early in the next Session how the interests of the public might best be secured, and whether it was expedient that the Broad Gauge should be extended to Birmingham.

This led to another battle, conducted on this occasion like a suit in Chancery by written statements and replies, between the Great Western and London & North Western champions. Each Company was invited by the Commissioners to submit a statement of its views, and this was forwarded to be contradicted and generally torn to ribbons by the other. The Great Western, while deprecating this method of inquiry as not likely to elicit the truth, dwelt on the necessity of Broad Gauge on the Birmingham & Oxford for effective competition and the absurdity of creating a needless break of gauge at Fenny Compton or Oxford, and forwarded an influentially signed memorial from many prominent manufacturing firms of Birmingham and the Black Country. The North Western objected to what they called a reopening of the Gauge question, supposed to be settled in their favour; expressed their desire for the amendment of the Gauge Act; were unable to see the need for any competing line—certainly not for a broad-gauge one; and pointed out that their Engineer, Robert Stephenson, had conclusively shown that a mixed-gauge line could not be worked. This last view, if really believed, should have led them to encourage its establishment. A very distant fear of the competitive value of the Broad Gauge on the rival line is manifest throughout their communications.

---

[1] They functioned from 9th November 1846 to 10th October 1851, when their powers were resumed by the Board of Trade.

This paper warfare having been brought to an end, the Commissioners in January 1848 sent to each Company, for the opinions of their respective Engineers and Locomotive Superintendents, a series of twenty-three questions as to the design, power, and speed capacity of engines and the resistance of trains at different speeds. The replies of the North Western officers, Stephenson, Locke, McConnell, and Trevithick, are singularly short and jejune, while Brunel and Gooch, especially the latter, went deeply into the subject and replied at considerable length. For estimating the resistance of trains, Gooch constructed an elaborate Dynamometer Carriage, and made a series of twenty-six experiments at various speeds on a mile of straight and level line west of Banwell Station[1] on the Bristol & Exeter, with his new *Great Britain* 8 foot single engine, and a train of nine carriages loaded with iron to make a total weight of 100 tons. The resulting diagrams were all printed by the Commissioners, and form the greater part of the Appendix to their Report.

In this document they agree with the Gauge Commissioners:

That a break of gauge is a most serious impediment in the transport of merchandize, and that the Broad Gauge does not offer any compensating advantage, so far as that description of traffic is concerned. They do not consider that the experience which has been obtained since that Report was made affords any grounds for modifying this opinion. No means have been adopted to mitigate the evil of a break of gauge; and although the power of the engines on both gauges may have been increased, particularly of those on the Broad Gauge, the effect of such increase has been principally shown by the increased speeds of the Express Trains; and it does not appear to have produced any material difference in the relative advantages of the two gauges for Merchandize Traffic.

As to passenger traffic they have a different story to tell. Since the Gauge Report the Great Western engines had been much improved, and seven of Gooch's great 8 foot singles were at work.

But it is notorious that higher speeds with larger and heavier Passenger Trains are regularly maintained on a part of the line of the Great Western Railway than on any other railway in the Country. The fact is known and greatly appreciated by a very large portion of the Public; and no opinion respecting the extension of the district within which the Broad Gauge should be adopted is likely to be received with confidence which is not founded on a full consideration of the circumstances to which the above fact is to be attributed, and of the extent to which, under differing circumstances, if attributable to the breadth of gauge, the gauge of the Great Western Railway offers this advantage.

The comparative efficiency of the broad- and narrow-gauge engines of the period is then discussed at some length, and the conclusion arrived at that the former 'can draw an ordinary Passenger Train of sixty tons weight with as much facility on a level at sixty miles per hour as the narrow gauge engines can at fifty'.

On moderately descending gradients the larger engine would possess a similar degree of advantage; but in proportion as the inclination increased and considerations of safety imposed a limit to the speed the advantage would diminish and disappear.

On rising gradients the Commissioners thought that the difference in power between the two engines diminishes gradually up to an incline of 1 in 170, on which 'the two engines would have nearly the same power over a train of 60 tons, and on steeper gradients the greater weight of the

---

[1] Now 'Puxton and Worle'.

larger engine would cause the difference to be in favour of the smaller engine'.

> Such appear to the Commissioners to be the advantages which the Broad Gauge at present offers; and although they cannot consider them sufficient to compensate the evils attendant on two gauges, if it were not possible to obtain uniformity, yet as two are established it appears to them that it might be expedient and for the public interest on account of those advantages to extend the Broad Gauge to Birmingham, although such extension is contrary to the strict interpretation of the Resolutions of the two Houses of Parliament on which the Gauge Act was founded. . . .

> There are strong reasons against the exclusive use of the Broad Gauge on the line between Fenny Compton and Birmingham; the injury that arrangement would inflict on the traffic of Aylesbury and the surrounding district and the complete change it would occasion in the conditions under which the Buckinghamshire Railway is being proceeded with, appear to the Commissioners to prohibit such a proposition from being entertained.

The Buckinghamshire Railway was formed in 1847 by the amalgamation of the Buckinghamshire & Brackley and the Oxford & Bletchley projects of 1846, relics of the system of loop lines with which the London & Birmingham Company sought to oppose the Birmingham & Oxford Junction Railway. It had powers to make lines from Aylesbury to Banbury and from Bletchley to Oxford, and was entirely a creature of the North Western, who had projected the extension to Banbury at the time they had hope of capturing the Birmingham & Oxford. The branch from Aylesbury, needless to say, was never made.

Moved by these 'strong reasons', which, as the Buckinghamshire had no running powers over either the Oxford & Rugby or the Birmingham & Oxford, are not so apparent as they seem to have been to the Commissioners, the latter 'consider it is only by the use of the Mixed Gauge that the disadvantages of the route between London and Birmingham by Oxford can be effectually removed'. Influenced obviously by Robert Stephenson's opinions on the subject, they were, however, very diffident about making this suggestion, and proceed:

> Although the Commissioners believe that the introduction of the Mixed Gauge on the Birmingham and Oxford Line will, if practicable, prove advantageous to the public interests, they cannot recommend to the House of Lords that it should be at once sanctioned. Its success has not been proved; and although they feel it difficult to believe that the same skill and energy, which has within the last few years so successfully surmounted the numerous impediments, which in the development of an entirely new means of communication must have arisen, will not also surmount the mechanical difficulties attending the details of the Double Gauge, they nevertheless consider that, while reasonable objections are expressed respecting its success by eminent engineers, they cannot advise the Legislature to act until a sufficient experiment has been tried.

Such is the gist of the somewhat timorous report which the Railway Commissioners presented to the House of Lords in May 1848.

When these Commissioners first took over the functions of the Board of Trade in November 1846, they found themselves faced with the problem of deciding how the narrow-gauge rails, ordered by their predecessors to be added to the Oxford & Rugby Railway, should be laid, the Oxford & Rugby Act having provided that these, if ordered, should be laid in a manner approved by the Board. They accordingly asked the Great Western for a description of the method proposed to be adopted, and in

January 1847 received Brunel's views on the subject, in which he recommended a single additional rail on each line and that the outer rail of each should be common to the two gauges. These they, strangely enough, then submitted to the London & North Western Company for the remarks of their Engineer, in order, they said, 'that the interests of the Narrow Gauge Companies, *who might require* to use the line, might be duly considered'. After taking six months to consider the matter—it was obviously not in the North Western's interest to accelerate progress— Stephenson sent in some very lengthy and elaborate 'Observations', in which he took advantage of the opportunity to inveigh generally against the mixture of the gauges and express his well-known strong opinions thereon, to foresee numerous difficulties, and to predict serious results.

To these 'Observations' Brunel replied curtly that the Mixed Gauge had never been proposed by the Great Western, but had been ordered by Parliament and the Board of Trade, and therefore the question now was not whether the London & North Western Engineer liked it, but simply as to the mode in which the Railway Commissioners might approve of such mixture being effected. He denied the correctness of nearly all Stephenson's calculations and figures and strongly deprecated the Commissioners having consulted him, an officer of a violently hostile Company, instead of some more impartial engineer. If, said he, the plans for the construction of some works by the North Western Company were submitted by the Commissioners to the Great Western for criticism, 'and if I as their Engineer were to avail myself of such an opportunity, I have little doubt that I could, without the exercise of much ingenuity, throw such doubts upon the safety or the expediency of those works as would seriously embarrass the decision of the Railway Commissioners who had thus consulted me, and thereby impede the progress of the London & North Western Railway Company'. He added that a portion of railway with crossings, switches, and sidings of the Mixed Gauge had more than six months previously been laid down for the inspection of the Commissioners on the Great Western main line at Ealing, where it had ever since been, and still was, subject to the constant passage of the whole of the traffic.

The matter was then referred by the Commissioners to Captain Simmons, R.E., who, after considering Brunel's proposals and Stephenson's criticisms, agreed with the former that the three rail system was the simplest mode of uniting the gauges, as being less intricate and expensive, more easily kept in repair, and with certain precautions more safe than four rails. In conclusion he 'conceived that the Gauges may be combined in one railway with perfect safety to the public', but suggested their separation in sidings used for standing spare vehicles, and the entire prohibition of running carriages of different gauges in the same train, which had never been intended or even suggested by anyone but the opposition.

Lacking courage to adopt the report of their own officer, the Commissioners then—November 1847—wrote to the Great Western Company that 'it would be very desirable to delay for a time the decision of the mode in which the two gauges were to be combined'. To this the Company naturally replied that it was important to them that it should be decided without any more loss of time; whereupon the Commissioners threw the responsibility on Captain Simmons by formally appointing him 'Inspector-General for the purpose of performing the duties of that [otherwise extinct] office under the Oxford and Rugby Act'.

So matters stood when the Great Western brought forward their Bill for further powers to carry out the Agreement of 12th November 1846 for the purchase of the Birmingham & Oxford Junction and Birmingham, Wolverhampton & Dudley Railways; this, of course, included the laying of Broad Gauge on those lines from Fenny Compton to Wolverhampton.

The North Western Chairman having promised that his Company would refrain from further hostilities, their opposition in the Commons was indirect in the name of the Buckinghamshire. Having heard evidence and considered the Railway Commissioners' Report, the Committee reported to the House on 6th June that they concurred with the Commissioners as to the expediency of extending the Broad Gauge to Birmingham and Wolverhampton on the grounds stated in the Report, especially 'inasmuch as it is only by the use of the Mixed Gauge that the disadvantages of the route by Oxford can be effectually removed, and the adoption of the Mixed Gauge will probably render the Line from Birmingham by Fenny Compton to London as a Broad Gauge Railway as rapid a communication as the direct line'. They recommended, however, that no extension beyond Wolverhampton should be authorized till the line had been completed and its practical working fully tested by experience. Pointing out that the mixed-gauge Line between Gloucester and Cheltenham had been worked with safety for several months by two hostile Companies, they disagreed with the characteristic suggestion of the Commissioners that the decision should be postponed, 'which appears to have been suggested to the Commissioners rather on account of objections still expressed by some eminent engineers than from any doubt as to the means of surmounting mechanical difficulties attending the details of the Mixed Gauge'. They thought, however, that the Commissioners should be given authority to supervise these mechanical details, and inserted a clause for that purpose.

Their report concludes:

The Committee attach much importance to the fact represented to them that this Bill will probably terminate a course of long and expensive litigation between public companies and individuals, to which the contest about the gauges has unhappily given rise; it has been proved in evidence that the dissentient shareholders of the Birmingham & Oxford Company, who had previously opposed the Great Western Company in respect to that Railway, have arranged all differences and consented to the powers being given for a mixed gauge over the line; and it seems to the Committee most expedient on that as well as the other more important grounds of public advantage already stated that no further delay should take place in giving Parliamentary sanction to carry out the Agreement between the Companies for the possession of the Line by the Great Western Company, and for the extension of the Broad Gauge over it as well as to secure the performance of every other condition in the purchase of the two undertakings, which object has been attained by other clauses in the Act to the satisfaction of the Committee.

The Bill passed the Commons and went up to the Lords, where the London & North Western joined the Buckinghamshire in opposing it, notwithstanding their Chairman's promise. By the Select Committee of the Lords their opposition to the preamble and to the laying of the Broad Gauge was dismissed, but they succeeded in obtaining running powers, with 'all proper and convenient accommodation in respect of stations, sidings, waiting and watering places and other facilities', over the narrow-gauge rails of the two lines, and also of the Oxford & Rugby Railway between Fenny Compton and Banbury, for 'engines and carriages to and from the several narrow-gauge railways which do or shall communicate therewith respectively'. In furtherance of these powers, they prevailed on the Committee to insert a clause that it should not be lawful for the Great Western to use the authorized broad-gauge rails until they had 'completed and opened a communication between the line of the said Birmingham & Oxford Junction Railway and the line of the London & North Western Railway in the town of Birmingham, or within one mile on the south side thereof, by means of a double line of Narrow Gauge rails'.

With these clauses the Bill passed the House of Lords, and received the Royal Assent on 31st August 1848.

The running powers were never exercised or intended to be exercised. They were inserted, nominally on behalf of the Buckinghamshire Railway, merely out of spite to hamper the victors; for this we have the authority of Robert Stephenson himself, in his evidence before the Committee on Railway and Canal Bills in February 1853, confirmed by the minutes of the Lords' Committee on the Bill. It is fair to add that Stephenson disclaimed all responsibility for the clauses, which he ascribed to the North Western Solicitor, Carter.

While on this subject, the story of this compulsory communication with the London & North Western in Birmingham may as well be related. It will be remembered that the Birmingham & Oxford Railway authorized by the Act of 1846 started from a junction with the London & North Western in Birmingham. This junction was close to the original terminus of the Grand Junction Line adjoining that of the London & Birmingham at Curzon Street. Soon afterwards the North Western obtained powers to extend their line farther into Birmingham and make a large passenger station at New Street, or Navigation Street as it was then called, in connection with the Stour Valley Line. This extension line cut across the authorized Birmingham & Oxford, almost at right angles outside the Curzon Street Stations, which were to be altered and abandoned for passenger traffic. It was owing to these circumstances that the line of the compulsory communication between the two railways was purposely left undefined by the Act of 1848, as it was necessarily dependent on the station arrangements of the North Western.

As the works of the Birmingham & Oxford progressed, it became essential that the mode of junction should be settled and the line made, in order to comply with the latter Act and enable the main line to be opened. Brunel accordingly planned a short line of only 14 chains to join the North Western near the mouth of the tunnel which forms the approach to New Street Station, and a Bill for the necessary powers was deposited for the Session of 1851. This was hotly opposed by the North Western on the grounds of the danger of such a junction and of an alleged insidious design of the Great Western to avail themselves of the new North Western Station and the Stour Valley Railway to Wolverhampton in order to save the expense of making their own line. The Great Western, they said, already had power to make the compulsory communication under the Act of 1846, and the point of junction authorized by that Act was a convenient one. The Bill, which also provided for a junction at Leamington, passed the House of Commons, but was thrown out by the Lords.

Hence the Great Western were driven to make the junction branch, originally sanctioned in 1846 as part of the main line of the Birmingham & Oxford Railway, from Adderley Street, where Bordesley Station now stands, to the site of the old Grand Junction Terminus at Curzon Street. This they forthwith proceeded to do, serving the usual notices on the parties interested. But the junction, described to the House of Lords as a convenient one in July, had become extremely inconvenient in August, and the North Western Company at once applied to the Court of Chancery to restrain the Birmingham & Oxford from taking possession of any of their land for the purpose. It was then arranged that the mode of crossing the North Western Extension Line to New Street on the level and the junction beyond should be referred to the Companies' Engineers, Messrs Stephenson and Brunel, for settlement, with power to appoint an arbitrator in case they disagreed. The construction of the branch, some 50 chains in length and wholly on arches over the town, was meantime proceeded with. At the opening of the main line to Snow Hill in October 1852 some of the arches were still in progress, but in the following February Brunel reported that it had been constructed up to the edge of the London & North Western Company's property. The junction was never made. Neither Company wanted it, but the Great Western was forced to make the branch as a condition of working their main line by the action of the North Western in 1848. And so the derelict Duddeston Viaduct or some of it still stands, a melancholy monument to the ill-conditioned spite of a great Railway Company against a victorious rival in the old fighting days.

The victory of 1848 did not quite put an end to the Gauge War in the Black Country. We have seen that, notwithstanding its name, the Birmingham, Wolverhampton & Dudley Railway reached neither Wolverhampton nor Dudley. The main line terminated at Priestfield, more than a mile from the former town, by a junction with the Oxford, Worcester & Wolverhampton, then regarded as a loyal member of the Broad Gauge family and leased to her parent, the Great Western. Two years later, however, the daughter rebelled, and by the end of 1851 was at open and bitter war with the parent. She even proposed to abandon her own line into Wolverhampton and to reach that town by running over the Stour Valley Railway of her new friend, the London & North Western, from Tipton. This would of course have left the Birmingham, Wolverhampton & Dudley in the air at Priestfield, so the Great Western applied to Parliament for powers to make this portion of the Oxford, Worcester & Wolverhampton themselves. These were denied them, the House of Commons Committee preferring instead to bind the Oxford Company under heavy penalties to complete their mixed-gauge line from Priestfield to Wolverhampton, and on to the point now known as Cannock Road Junction, rather more than $\frac{1}{2}$ mile beyond in the direction of Bushbury. In the same Session (1852) the Great Western obtained an Act authorizing the construction, also on the Mixed Gauge, of the Wolverhampton Junction Railway, about $\frac{3}{4}$ mile long, from this point to a junction with their Narrow Gauge ally, the Shrewsbury & Birmingham, at Stafford Road. It was not, however, till the following year that the Great Western secured statutory running powers over this intervening bit of the Oxford, Worcester & Wolverhampton between Priestfield and Cannock Road, although they and the Shrewsbury & Birmingham were equally interested with the Oxford in the joint Low Level Station to be constructed on it. In 1854 further powers were obtained to add broad-gauge rails on about a mile of the Shrewsbury & Birmingham line from the junction at Stafford Road into their Victoria Basin Depot, with sidings there for the convenient interchange of traffic.

This was the last extension authorized, so the farthest point towards the north ever reached by broad-gauge rails was about $\frac{1}{4}$ mile beyond the Stafford Road Junction. They were never laid from Wednesbury to Dudley. As we have seen, the Birmingham, Wolverhampton & Dudley Railway's proposed branch to Dudley coincided with the main line of the South Staffordshire Railway, and exclusive authority to make the line was given to the latter Company, the former having to be content with power to use it. This was in 1846 when the Birmingham, Wolverhampton & Dudley was to be a narrow-gauge line like the South Staffordshire. The Act of 1848 which authorized Broad Gauge on the Birmingham, Wolverhampton & Dudley made no reference to this piece of the South Staffordshire. In 1852 the Great Western applied to Parliament for power to lay the Broad Gauge on this section without success. The attack was renewed in the next year, only to be finally defeated by the opposition of the owning Company and their lessee, J. R. McClean, who, curiously enough, was also the Engineer engaged in the construction of the Birmingham, Wolverhampton & Dudley line itself.

In 1854 a projected mixed-gauge branch from the Great Western at Wednesbury to the Cannock Chase coalfield was also rejected by the House of Commons in favour of a rival South Staffordshire project, after which no further effort to extend the Broad Gauge in the Midlands was ever made.

## 6 THE FIGHT IN THE SOUTH

The long war between the Great Western and its ancient enemy the London & Southampton, which had changed its name to the London & South Western Railway in 1839, began in the Parliamentary Session of 1844 with a skirmish for the honour of providing railway accommodation to the town of Newbury. The Great Western proposed a branch from Pangbourne; the South Western one from Basingstoke with a suggested extension to Swindon. The fight was drawn, the Great Western Bill being thrown out by the Commons on landowners' opposition and the South Western by the Lords' Committee, who after a lengthy inquiry preferred the Great Western plan as the better route from London as well as forming with their Oxford Branch a link in a needed line of communication between the South Coast and the North of England far better than any by way of Swindon and Cheltenham.

With pacific intent Russell then wrote to the South Western Chairman, William Chapman, suggesting a joint line between the South Western at Basingstoke and the Great Western between Pangbourne and Reading with a branch from it to Newbury, the whole being laid with a third rail to form the Mixed Gauge and so take both Companies' stock.

This olive branch being rejected, each Company prepared for a general attack all along the front in the following Session.

At first the Great Western proposed lines from Reading to Basingstoke and Newbury, called the Berks & Hants Railway, and from Corsham to Salisbury with branches to Devizes, Bradford, and Frome and a 'coal line' from Frome to Radstock, called the Wilts & Somerset Railway. The main object of this Corsham and Salisbury line stated in the Directors' Report of August 1844 was to afford, in conjunction with the South Western's authorized branch from Bishopstoke to Salisbury, a communication between Bristol and Bath and Southampton, Portsmouth and the Isle of Wight, 'superior in every respect to any railway which could be made between Basingstoke and Swindon'. In addition to these Great Western proposals, the Bristol & Exeter Company were to make a line from near Taunton to Yeovil and on to Weymouth.

In the course of the autumn these projects were somewhat altered. The Newbury Branch of the Berks & Hants was extended to Hungerford, and, the Bristol & Exeter declining to go beyond Yeovil, the Wilts & Somerset was extended from Frome through Yeovil to Weymouth, with branches to Sherborne and Bridport, and its title altered to the Wilts, Somerset & Weymouth Railway.

Meantime the Great Western had carried their attack into the heart of the enemy's country by agreeing to take a lease of the Southampton & Dorchester Railway, an independent local project, vulgarly known as 'Castleman's Corkscrew' from its principal promoter Mr Charles Castleman, with which the South Western had till too late declined to come to any terms. It was, of course, to be broad-gauge.

The South Western projects were lines from Basingstoke to Didcot and through Newbury to Swindon; from a point on their main line some two miles north of Winchester to near Dunbridge on the Bishopstoke & Salisbury Branch—this was known as 'the Hook Pit Deviation', and its object was to shorten the distance from London to Salisbury; from Salisbury to Yeovil; and from Salisbury to Dorchester and Weymouth with a branch to Poole. They also gave support to the Cornwall & Devon Central Railway, a projected narrow-gauge line from Exeter by Oke-hampton, Launceston, and Bodmin to Truro and Falmouth. A proposed line to fill the gap between Yeovil and Exeter was abandoned for want of subscriptions.

Thus the rival schemes stood for the consideration of the 'Five Kings'. On the last day of the year the 'Kings' published their judgment in favour of the Great Western and other broad-gauge projects on all points, and against those of the London & South Western.

On this decision being known, the two Companies came to terms, and an agreement was drawn up between them whereby the Great Western, with the assent of the Southampton & Dorchester, gave up their interest in that line to the South Western and pledged themselves not to promote any competing lines from Basingstoke; and the South Western on their part pledged themselves to acquiesce in the decision of the Board of Trade by withdrawing their own projects, all connection with the Central Cornwall line, and their opposition to the lines sanctioned by the Board; not to promote any competing lines westward from Salisbury or Dorchester. The words of the Agreement, which was dated 16th January 1845, on this point are:

'As regards the future, the acquiescence of the Companies in the decision [of the Board] is to be shown by each Company pledging themselves not to encourage or promote, directly or indirectly, any future line of railway in opposition to, or tending to divert legitimate traffic from the lines of railway communication for the district as settled by the Report, unless under such a completely altered state of circumstances as would induce the Board of Trade to consider the principles which have guided them in that Report as no longer applicable.

'In order to preserve friendship between the Companies and to avoid unnecessary contention, no step shall be taken by either Company to bring any such line before the public, or in any way, directly or indirectly, to promote or encourage the same, without first applying to the Board of Trade after giving notice of their intention to do so to the other party, and ascertaining that the Board is favourable to such line on public grounds and does not think it inconsistent with the principles of its present decision; and if the opinion of the Board of Trade shall be ascertained to be unfavourable to such line, it shall at once be abandoned.

'In the above agreement reference has been had more especially to extension lines from Salisbury or Dorchester competing with the Great Western (including its branches) and the lines now sanctioned, on the one hand, and to extension lines from Basingstoke competing against the South Western Railway (including its branches) and the Coast Line to Dorchester, on the other.'

This Agreement was confirmed by the Directors of the two Companies, and afterwards approved and ratified by the Shareholders of both at their General Meetings in February.

Hence there was peace in the south during the 1845 Session, and the Broad Gauge Forces were left free to concentrate on the northern front, where they won a notable victory.

The rival schemes being all withdrawn, the Bills incorporating the Berks & Hants and the Wilts, Somerset & Weymouth Railway Companies had an easy passage through Parliament, as also did the Bristol & Exeter Company's Bill authorizing their branch to Yeovil. In passing the preamble of the Weymouth Bill, however, the Lords' Committee, impressed with the need of a direct line between London and the west, exacted a pledge from Counsel for the promoters that the powers given should not be used thereafter to prevent such a line being made. The actual pledge given was: 'The promoters of the Wilts, Somerset & Weymouth Railway Company are willing to assure the Committee that the extension of the line to Weymouth shall not be set up hereafter to defeat a direct line from London to Falmouth'.

The Southampton & Dorchester Company also got their Act of Incorporation with powers to lease or sell the railway to the South Western, the latter Company taking the place of the Great Western in accordance with the January Agreement. The intended Broad Gauge was of course altered to Narrow, and provision made for laying the latter on the Wilts & Somerset between the junction at Dorchester and Weymouth.

In view of the importance attached by Parliament to a direct line to the west and pledge to the Lords' Committee, the Great Western Directors instructed Brunel to prepare a scheme for the Session of 1846. In his evidence before the Gauge Commission in the autumn, Saunders tells us that it was always intended that the Wilts & Somerset should form part of a direct line to Exeter, and that the pledge asked for was therefore willingly given. As such a line would necessarily compete with and injure the Bristol & Exeter Railway, the Directors felt it would be only fair to make an arrangement with that Company before taking active measures to promote the direct line. Terms were accordingly arranged in October between the two Boards for the purchase of the smaller line by the Great Western. The Bristol & Exeter Proprietors, however, rejected the provisional agreement by a considerable majority, so the Great Western, having done their part, proceeded alone with the line. The proposals were to extend the Berks & Hants Railway from Hungerford to Westbury, with branches to Marlborough and Devizes; to straighten the Wilts & Somerset by making the junction between the Salisbury and Weymouth lines at Westbury instead of Upton Scudamore; and to promote a company to make a railway from Yeovil by Crewkerne, Axminster, Honiton, Ottery, and Stoke Canon to Exeter, with a connecting line from Bridport to Axminster and branches to Chard and Sidmouth, to be called the 'Exeter Great Western Railway'.

No sooner was this scheme made public than the South Western Directors seized on it as a pretext for breaking the Agreement, whereby they had secured the Southampton & Dorchester. For some months the promoters of the narrow-gauge projects west of Salisbury, led by their own Engineer, Joseph Locke, had been urging them to this course. So on 30th October their Secretary wrote to the Board of Trade alleging that the circumstances under which the Agreement was made had been materially altered by the Great Western proposal, and asking them to receive a deputation to urge that the South Western were now at liberty to promote a new direct line to Exeter by way of Salisbury and Yeovil. In their reply the Board 'admit that the numerous schemes which have been advertised for supplying railway accommodation through the districts referred to in the Agreement alter the circumstances in which it was made; but my Lords do not feel called upon to express an opinion whether this alteration of circumstances is sufficiently extensive to justify a departure from the Agreement by one or other of the two Companies'. The Board of Trade having thus declined to assist them with the sanction required by the Agreement, the South Western Directors took the responsibility on themselves and gave notice to the Great Western that 'they had come to the conclusion that in the present state of circumstances the London & South Western Railway Company are at liberty to act in such manner as shall seem best for the interests of this Company'. Upon this Russell wrote an indignant letter of protest to Chaplin, in which he described the conduct of the South Western as 'an unexampled breach of faith'; and a protest was also made by Lord de Mauley, Chairman of the Southampton & Dorchester Company, the third party to the Agreement.

For the 1846 Session the South Western promoted or supported a line from Basingstoke to Salisbury, which they had, of course, a perfect right to do, and also the Salisbury & Yeovil, Exeter, Yeovil & Dorchester, and Cornwall & Devon Central Lines. Of these, the first was passed, the last stopped by Standing Orders, and the remaining two defeated by the Great Western opposition in the House of Lords. On the other hand, the Great Western Bills, opposed by the Bristol & Exeter in addition to the South Western, were thrown out in the Commons. Broad Gauge interests were, however, consoled to some extent by the safe incorporation of the Cornwall and West Cornwall Railway Companies.

The fight was renewed in 1847, the Great Western reproducing the Berks & Hants Extension and the Exeter Great Western Railways, the latter slightly altered to provide a central station in Exeter and to join the South Devon Railway near St Thomas, with a fork to the Bristol & Exeter crossing over that line between St Davids Station and the River Exe, and joining it from the west a short distance north of the station. Branches to Charmouth and Crewkerne were added to those of the year before. They also projected the Compton & Wilton Line to connect Yeovil with Salisbury, from a point on the Weymouth line just north-east of Yeovil to Wilton on the Salisbury branch.

The Bristol & Exeter Company, for their part, again opposed the Exeter Great Western, and promoted a Bill for a line from Durston to

Castle Cary on the Wilts, Somerset & Weymouth, which with the Berks & Hants Extension would make a more direct line between London and Exeter than the former.

The South Western this year asked for powers to make a Salisbury & Yeovil line themselves, and supported the Exeter, Yeovil & Dorchester and Cornwall & Devon Central Companies, and also a new project—the Exeter & Cowley Bridge Junction Railway (not actually promoted until 1848) to join the Yeovil line with the Exeter & Crediton Railway, in which they had acquired a controlling interest by the indirect purchase of shares.

After a fifty-three days' fight in Committee the Berks & Hants Extension and the Bristol & Exeter line from Castle Cary to Durston, giving with the intervening portion of the Wilts, Somerset & Weymouth a direct broad-gauge line from London to Exeter, and the Salisbury & Yeovil, and Exeter, Yeovil & Dorchester, giving a similar narrow-gauge line, passed the House of Commons, the Exeter Great Western and the Cornwall & Devon Central projects being once more thrown out, while the Cowley Bridge Junction line was withdrawn. As it was then too late in the Session for the Lords to proceed with the Bills, the whole of them were suspended till the following year when, after another strenuous fight, the Peers confirmed the decision of the Commons.

Meantime the reaction after the Railway Mania had set in, and from the summer of 1847 onwards it became practically impossible to raise money on reasonable terms for railway enterprises of any kind. Hence no steps were taken to construct any of these lines sanctioned in 1848, and the powers given were eventually allowed to lapse by both sides. A competent witness, Joseph Locke, estimated that the four years' contest had cost between three and four hundred thousand pounds.

The same cause put a stop to the progress of the Wilts, Somerset & Weymouth Railway. As soon as they had got their Act, this Company took active steps to make the line throughout; land was bought and contracts let for the works on nearly all parts of the system. In 1846 a supplementary Act was obtained altering the junction between the Weymouth and Salisbury branches from Upton Scudamore to Westbury, and that of the Devizes Branch from near Melksham to Holt, and authorizing short deviations at Thingley, Frome, and near Dorchester, and extensions to the Quays at Weymouth and from Bradford to join the Great Western at Bathampton. This last had been forced on the Company by a clause inserted in their original Act compelling them to apply for and make a better line of communication with Bath and Bristol to the satisfaction of the Board of Trade. An improved line between Frome and Bruton was authorized by another Act in 1847. In this year the Directors' troubles began. Loans were unobtainable; calls were not paid, and as soon as one was made the value of the shares dropped almost to the full amount of the call. Matters were, of course, made worse by the success of the opposition lines from Basingstoke to Salisbury and Yeovil. Consequently no new contracts were let, and soon arrangements were made with existing contractors to reduce, and later to stop, the works, and with landowners to postpone completion of purchases. The section from Thingley Junction to Westbury, not quite 14 miles, was opened on 5th September 1848, but the remainder of the 120 miles of authorized railway was marked only by finished or unfinished bridges and earthworks scattered throughout its length, while in many cases the land was left in the hands of its former occupiers or re-let. The short branch from Staverton to Bradford was made and even the Bradford Station built, but for some reason the rails were left unfinished, and no attempt was made to open it. So matters remained for some years to the extreme discontent of the inhabitants.

Early in 1850, as the only hope of doing anything with the line, the Great Western Directors arranged to take it over from the local Company, giving the shareholders 4% guaranteed stock in lieu of their ordinary shares. As the Great Western had from the beginning guaranteed 4% on the capital, of which they held £545,000, this was only a paper transaction. The Wilts, Somerset & Weymouth Railway in its very incomplete state was accordingly handed over to the Great Western and became part of their system from 14th March 1850. The transfer was confirmed by Parliament in the following year, and the Wilts, Somerset & Weymouth Company dissolved.

The Great Western immediately proceeded to extend the line to Frome and Warminster, opening to the former place on 7th October 1850, and to the latter on 9th September 1851. They also began the branch from Frome to Radstock, which was expected to produce a considerable coal traffic, but this was not finished till November 1854 owing to difficulties in getting some of the land. Below Frome the remainder of the land was bought, and negotiations entered into with local people, who thought they could get the necessary capital for finishing the works. The result of these was the floating of the Frome, Yeovil & Weymouth Railway Company, for which an Act was obtained in 1852. As this Act contained a clause that the Agreement with the Great Western should be void unless the whole capital were subscribed within three months, and this was not done, the Company sank at once and the Great Western were left with no alternative but to find the money themselves. This they seem to have been very loth to do, in view probably of their engagements in the north at this period. The fever of the mania having passed, Saunders and Russell foresaw that it would be a long time before these extensive branches through purely agricultural districts would be likely to pay their way. At the same time they did not wish that country to fall into the hands of the South Western, with whom they felt after the experience of 1845 it was hopeless to try to make any binding agreement.

At this time the latter Company was a house divided against itself as regards the policy of western extensions. The branch from Bishopstoke to the Milford Station at Salisbury had been opened for goods traffic on 27th January 1847 (passengers 1st March), and the Southampton &

Dorchester line on 1st June in the same year, but no steps had been taken towards making the lines westward authorized in 1848; even between Basingstoke and Salisbury, though nearly all the land had been bought and most of the heavy works executed, the powers obtained in 1846 were allowed to lapse. At this the citizens of Salisbury were very irate, and an independent company was promoted by them and their neighbours to buy the works already made by the South Western and complete the line. This project failed in the Sessions of 1851 and 1852, but being brought in again in the next year was adopted by the South Western Company, who feared its becoming a broad-gauge line in connection with the Great Western Basingstoke Branch, and passed, with a clause suspending the South Western dividends if it was not finished in the time limited. Further progress westward was barred by the factions into which the Company and even the Board were divided. One party led by Locke, now no longer the Company's Engineer but M.P. for Honiton and owner of an estate nearby, was in favour of a central line from Salisbury through Yeovil to Exeter; another, led by Castleman and Captain Moorsom, the Engineer, was for the coast line from Dorchester by Bridport and Axminster; while a third was against all extension and advocated closing the capital account. The majority of the Directors favoured the central line. Bills for both schemes were deposited by independent parties at the end of 1851, and brought before a special meeting of the Shareholders in December. The Board recommended support for the central line, but a committee of shareholders was appointed who reported in favour of encouraging the coast line, and on a poll their report was adopted by a large majority. After this the central scheme collapsed for lack of subscriptions, and the Dorchester & Exeter Coast Extension Railway, to give Captain Moorsom's line its full title, was rejected on Standing Orders. Again, in the autumn of 1852 the central line was brought by the Directors before special meetings of the Shareholders as worthy of support, and again they refused, though by a smaller majority, to have anything to do with it.

Matters standing thus with their rivals, the Great Western Board determined to make one more effort to capture the country for the Broad Gauge, and announced their intention in their Report to the Half-yearly Meeting held on 12th August 1852, when their plans were duly sanctioned by the assembled Proprietors. These, as eventually matured for Parliament, were for a joint line with the Bristol & Exeter Company, entitled the Devon & Dorset Railway, from a forked junction at Maiden Newton on the Wilts, Somerset & Weymouth line, through Powerstock, Netherbury, Bettiscombe, and Chardstock to Axminster, and thence by Honiton and Ottery St Mary to join the Bristol & Exeter at the bridge over the Exe south of Stoke Canon, with branches from Netherbury to Bridport Harbour and from Ottery to Sidmouth.

Now it must be confessed that this line appears to have been a bold and, in view of the non-completion of the Wilts & Somerset, rather barefaced attempt merely to occupy the district to the exclusion of both the rival projects. As a through line to Exeter it had no merits, the distance from London being 203 miles, nearly ten longer than the existing route by Bristol; as a local line it left even Bridport 4 miles off on a branch. In his evidence before the Commons Committee, Brunel admitted it would be better to take the main line through that town, but stated that his endeavour had been to give the greatest accommodation to the district consistently with certain rules laid down from a military point of view. He had consulted the military authorities, who gave their opinion that for defence purposes the line should be kept some miles from the coast with branches to the ports. However, the two Companies had a genuine intention of making the line, offering to undertake an obligation under penalties to complete and open it in a limited time.

The Bill came before Parliament early in 1853 and was read a second time. Upon this, the South Western Directors took serious alarm and called a special meeting of their shareholders in May to consider the matter, telling them they must now decide once for all whether they would pledge themselves to make the coast line from Dorchester as advised by their own committee, or allow the whole district to pass into the hands of the Broad Gauge Companies, which, said the Board, would inflict a vital injury on the interests of the Company. At this meeting the Directors were definitely authorized to pledge the Company to apply for powers at the earliest possible period to extend their railway from Dorchester by Bridport and Axminster to Exeter, and to execute such powers forthwith by the creation of the necessary capital by the Company and not by independent parties.

The Committee of the House of Commons began taking evidence on the Devon & Dorset Bill on 17th June. Petitions against it had been lodged by landowners and occupiers, organized and backed by the South Western Directors, and by 'Inhabitants of Wilts, Somerset, and Dorset', who were angry with the Great Western for not proceeding with the long authorized lines in their districts. Saunders and Brunel were, of course, the chief witnesses for the Bill; they were severely attacked on this very vulnerable point. No representative of the Bristol & Exeter appeared, which suggests that that Company was somewhat half-hearted in the matter. It seems to have been very unpopular with the traders of Exeter, several of whom complained of its extortionate charges for goods, far higher than those of the Great Western and other lines, on account of which they got many things by sea to Torquay and even Plymouth, and thence by the South Devon Railway. The usual local witnesses were produced, a dozen by the promoters and sixteen by the opposition. Mr Locke urged the claims of the narrow-gauge central line from Salisbury, and Captain Moorsom those of the coast line from Dorchester, both uniting in attacking the Devon & Dorset as being laid out solely for the purpose of occupying the country without consideration for the needs of the public. The Chairman of the South Western, the Hon. Francis Scott, M.P., was examined at great length as to the past proceedings of his Company, and gave the definite pledge, authorized by his shareholders, that if the present Bill were rejected, the London & South Western Company would forthwith apply for powers, provide the capital themselves, and make the Coast Extension Line from Dorchester to Exeter. To ensure the defeat of the Bill, he had secured powerful allies. Lord Palmerston, Home Secretary, the Right Hon Sidney Herbert, Secretary at War and M.P. for South Wilts, Lord Malmesbury, late Foreign Secretary, Lieut.-General Lord Hardinge, Commander-in-Chief, and Sir James Graham, First Lord of the Admiralty, came to bear witness to the importance for the defence of the country of railway communication without break of gauge along the whole south coast from Dover to Plymouth. If a break was unavoidable, they would prefer it to be as far west as possible.

In view of the South Western Chairman's pledge that his Company would make a narrow-gauge line forthwith, this evidence decided the fate of the Devon & Dorset Bill, and on 30th June the Committee announced that the preamble was not proved.

Thus was the Broad Gauge decisively defeated in the South. Neither the Great Western nor the Bristol & Exeter made any further serious assault on the country between Salisbury or Dorchester and Exeter, which was, therefore, abandoned to the Narrow Gauge. The enemy were, however, very loth to reap the reward of their victory. Their subsequent proceedings are best related in the impartial language of the Railway Department of the Board of Trade. In his Report to the Board on the Railway Bills of 1855, Captain Galton wrote:

> The proceedings of the House of Commons with respect to the London and South Western Railway Bill also deserve notice.
>
> It will be in the recollection of your Lordships that in 1853 the London and South Western Railway Company opposed a Bill promoted by the Great Western and Bristol and Exeter Railway Companies, for a railway termed 'The Devon and Dorset Railway'; and that this Bill was thrown out by the House of Commons, upon a pledge given by the London and South Western Railway Company that they would introduce a Bill in the following Session for a continuation of their line to Exeter.
>
> But, having obtained their object, the London and South Western Railway Company repudiated their pledge. Consequently when the Company brought forward a Bill for other objects in 1855, the House of Commons referred the consideration of the Bill to a Committee of nearly the same Members to whom the Devon and Dorset Railway Bill had been referred in 1853. This Committee inserted clauses into their Bill by which the Company were bound, under the penalty of stoppage of their dividends, to introduce into and use their best endeavours to pass through Parliament a Bill for a narrow gauge line to Exeter.

After this the South Western were of course obliged to proceed to carry out their pledge. In the meantime Locke and his neighbours, disgusted with that Company's behaviour, had floated an independent Salisbury & Yeovil Railway Company with the assistance of Thomas Brassey, the famous contractor, who provided nearly half the necessary capital. They obtained their Act in 1854. This, with other things, turned the South Western scales in favour of the central line to Exeter and against the coast line, to which they were committed by the pledge of 1853. However, as the former was by this time generally admitted to be the better route, the

Company had little difficulty in obtaining an Act for their Yeovil & Exeter Extension in the Session of 1856, subject to the stoppage of their dividends if it was not open by the end of 1861. They also agreed to lease and work the Salisbury & Yeovil.

Their line was opened from Basingstoke to Andover on 3rd July 1854, and to Salisbury on 1st May 1857, ten months later than the Great Western branch from Warminster. The Salisbury & Yeovil reached Gillingham 2nd May 1859, Sherborne 7th May 1860, and was completed to a temporary terminus in the Bristol & Exeter's Hendford Station at Yeovil on 1st June in the same year. Seven weeks later, on 19th July, the first narrow-gauge train entered the City of Exeter.

# VII

# *General Progress*

## *1847–1854*

Of the three railways sanctioned by Parliament in 1845 and undertaken by the Great Western Company themselves, namely the Berks & Hants, Oxford & Rugby, and Monmouth & Hereford, the Berks & Hants was the first to be finished. The whole of it was let in one contract, and in August 1847 Brunel reported the works as 'all but completed', adding, as regards the general construction of the western branch, that 'the circumstance of its becoming in all probability the main line to the West of England has been attended to', and that a temporary terminus was being erected at Hungerford, so placed as not to interfere with the projected extension to Westbury.

This western section was opened for passenger traffic from Reading to Hungerford, 25½ miles, on 21st December 1847, with intermediate stations at Theale, Aldermaston, Woolhampton,[1] Thatcham, Newbury, and Kintbury; accommodation for goods was not ready till a year later. There were no works of any note on the line, save perhaps one high brick bridge of three arches near Reading, carrying the main Bath Road over a deep cutting; the numerous bridges over the canal and streams in the Kennet Valley were mostly, if not all, of timber.

The completion of the southern portion to Basingstoke was delayed by the necessary negotiations with the hostile London & South Western Company as to the terminus and method of communication—of course no junction was possible—with their station close by. These were eventually settled, and the 13½ miles from the junction at Southcote, not quite two miles from Reading Station, opened on 1st November 1848, with one intermediate station at Mortimer.[2]

Two months before this, on 5th September, the Wilts, Somerset & Weymouth Company had opened the first section of their line, and the only one they ever completed, from the junction with the Great Western at Thingley, 2 miles west of Chippenham, to Westbury, with stations at Melksham and Trowbridge, adding 13¾ miles to the Great Western system.

The Oxford & Rugby Line was let in one contract in the autumn of 1845 to a 'contractor of experience and responsibility', but there was much

---

[1] Renamed Midgham in 1873. A new station at Reading West was added in July 1906.
[2] Bramley, formerly a goods siding only, was opened as a passenger station in April 1895. Basingstoke GWR passenger station was closed on 1st January 1932, trains being diverted to the Southern Railway station into which one platform was merged.

delay in getting possession of the land. However, by the next August the works were in progress on nearly the whole of the line to Fenny Compton, at which point, it seems, the Directors had already determined to stop. A year later we find the experienced contractor had not been proceeding at all satisfactorily, and arrangements were being made to take the work out of his hands. This entailed an entire suspension till April 1848, when new contractors began operations. For financial reasons they were instructed to go slow and confine themselves mainly to necessary works such as public road and river bridges and culverts, and the rate of progress remained very limited till August 1849. By this time it had been definitely decided not to proceed farther than the point of junction with the Birmingham & Oxford Railway, two miles beyond Fenny Compton, and to abandon the remaining $15\frac{1}{2}$ miles to Rugby on which no work had been done save about $\frac{1}{4}$ mile of embankment at the point of junction.

It was also decided to open a single line to Banbury in the first instance, and, as there was no prospect of connection with any narrow-gauge line, to make this broad-gauge only, notwithstanding the Board of Trade order for Mixed Gauge on the Oxford & Rugby Railway. In April 1850 Saunders therefore wrote to the Railway Commissioners requesting their acquiescence in the postponement for the time of the addition of the useless third rail on such single line. The timid Commissioners thereupon sent a copy of his letter to the Buckinghamshire Company, in other words the London & North Western, requesting 'any observations they may have to offer on the subject'.

This led to another display of bad temper on the part of that Company, or perhaps we should say of Captain Mark Huish. That warrior's promising young subaltern, Edward Watkin, in his capacity of Secretary of the Buckinghamshire Railway Company, wrote from Euston requesting to be informed whether it was a fact that the Commissioners had, as he understood, ordered 'the national or 4 feet $8\frac{1}{2}$ inch gauge' to be laid down on the whole of the Oxford & Rugby Railway. On the Commissioners replying that such an order had been issued by their predecessors, the Board of Trade, he curtly replied that that being so his Directors considered it unnecessary to state their objections to the proposal of the Great Western Company; adding that, on hearing of the proposed opening of the latter's line, they applied to them to arrange for a narrow-gauge connection at Banbury. It need hardly be said that they had no intention of using any such connection, which could have been of no possible benefit to them.

Meanwhile Captain Simmons reported to the Commissioners that, considering there was no narrow-gauge railway communicating with this portion of the Oxford & Rugby, he did not consider the interests of the public would be injuriously affected by its opening on the Broad Gauge only, provided the Great Western Company undertook to lay the Narrow when the line was extended northward. He added:

The Buckinghamshire Railway is now nearly ready for opening,[1] having been inspected from Bletchley to Banbury; but although it approaches very near to the Oxford & Rugby line, it does not join it, and if it did so, the route would be very circuitous; and moreover, the more direct line from Oxford to Bletchley on the narrow gauge is in course of construction, joining the former at Claydon, which will obviate the immediate necessity for the narrow gauge being laid on this portion of the Oxford & Rugby Railway.

On this, the Commissioners plucked up courage and wrote to Saunders on 16th May that they had no objection to the proposed opening, provided his Company would undertake to add the third rail when required by them and before any extension northward from Banbury. The undertaking was given, and there matters rested for some two months till rumours of what had occurred reached the North Western Manager. The 24th July brought a truculent letter from Euston, this time signed by Sir Harry Verney, Bart., M.P., Chairman of the Buckinghamshire Company, desiring to be informed forthwith whether the Railway Commissioners had indeed given their permission for 'not merely an illegal act, but the evasion of the precautions for the advantage and security of the public which Parliament had enacted'! The Commissioners replied with an apologetic explanation of all that had passed, emphasizing the temporary nature of the arrangement and even offering to reconsider it. To this Sir Harry rejoined that he regretted to learn they had authorized a violation of the Oxford & Rugby Act, and must ask them to recall such authority. Thoroughly cowed by this bullying—Captain Huish evidently knew how to deal with them—they then sent copies of the correspondence to the Great Western, saying that in view of the Buckinghamshire's objections they must reconsider their position, and suggesting the Company should communicate with the latter for the purpose of removing these objections. Needless to say, the Great Western Directors did not attempt any such obviously hopeless task. What they did do was to take Counsel's opinion and, having obtained it, to reply on 21st August that they were advised that the Company had 'full power, in perfect consistency with the provisions of the Act, to open the line between Oxford and Banbury with rails of the same gauge as the Great Western Railway, without having previously laid upon that portion any rails of the narrow gauge'; and that the Railway Commissioners had no legal authority to postpone the opening of a railway on any other ground than a report from their Inspecting Officer that such opening would, in his opinion, 'be attended with danger to the public using the same'. In the same letter, Saunders gave notice that the line would be ready for inspection on 27th August, and expressed his Directors' intention of opening it at the end of the statutory ten days. The Commissioners answered that they would refer the matter to the Law Officers of the Crown, and meantime withdrew the

---

[1] It was opened to Banbury on the 1st May; from Verney Junction to Islip on 1st October, Islip to Banbury Road, 3½ miles from Oxford, on the 2nd December 1850; and to Oxford on 20th May 1851.

consent they had given in May but directed Captain Simmons to inspect the line in accordance with the notice.

Having inspected it, that officer reported that he was not aware of anything affecting the safety of the public to prevent its opening for traffic, so long as the single line was worked, as proposed by the Company, by one engine only. In forwarding his report to Saunders, the Commissioners, while admitting that they were advised they had no power to postpone the opening, stated that they could not approve of it in the absence of a narrow-gauge rail, and so the Company must act upon their own responsibility. Under the circumstances, they *trusted* the Company would defer the opening until the third rail had been added, but should they not do so, its addition should be made with all reasonable dispatch; if not made by the end of four months, 'the Commissioners will take such steps as may be necessary to protect the public interests and to enforce the provisions of the Act'! Though the rail was not added for more than two years they never attempted to carry out this dreadful threat.

With undaunted courage the Great Western Directors opened their broad-gauge single line between Oxford and Banbury on Monday, 2nd September 1850. It was $24\frac{1}{4}$ miles long from its commencement at the point named Millstream Junction,[1] on the Oxford Branch, $\frac{3}{4}$ mile south of the terminus and near the Abingdon Road Bridge. Captain Simmons wrote in his report:

> The works upon are not of a heavy character. One bridge over the River Isis near Oxford, consisting of three openings, is constructed of wrought iron. The railway is carried by three beams, one in the centre and two others on each side, each beam being continuous over the three openings, the centre opening being 62 feet, and the two end ones 32 feet. The other bridges carrying the railway are principally of timber framed, and so are of cast iron. They appear to be of ample dimensions and strength to perform the duties required of them.

Though only a single line of rails was laid, the works were all completed for a double line. There were only three intermediate stations, Woodstock Road, Heyford, and Aynho,[2] and trains from and to Oxford of course had to reverse at Millstream Junction.

Three days after the opening another outburst from Euston Square reached Whitehall, signed by Sir Harry Verney, protesting against 'the whole course of the Commissioners of Railways in the matter'; urging 'that they forthwith order and direct the Great Western Company not to open but to postpone the opening of the portion of the Oxford & Rugby Railway extending from Oxford to Banbury'; and stating the opinion of the Buckinghamshire Company 'that for the Inspector to report as complete, or fit for opening, or free from danger to the public, a railway which is upon a totally different gauge to that required by the Act under

---

[1] This was where the 62 mile post now stands, near the southern extremity of the reservoir, which was originally (1844–48), a Great Western ballast pit.

[2] A new Woodstock Road, 2 miles nearer Oxford, was opened in 1855, the old one being then renamed Kirtlington. In 1890 the former became Kidlington and the latter Bletchington. Somerton, renamed Fritwell & Somerton in 1907, was opened in 1855, and King's Sutton in 1872.

which it is constructed, and which cannot by possibility be traversed safely by narrow gauge engines, would be indeed a most extraordinary proceeding'. This effusion seems to have roused the Commissioners to some small sense of self-respect, for they replied curtly that having already informed the Buckinghamshire Company of their views as to the opening and the course they meant to pursue, they 'are not aware that they can give any fuller explanation of their intentions'.

Young Watkin returned to the attack in January 1851, but after patiently replying to several of his distinctly insolent letters the Commissioners at last had the spirit to inform him in April that 'after a full consideration of all the circumstances, they do not deem it expedient at present to take any further steps to protect the public interest or to enforce the provisions of the Act'. Even this snub did not quite choke him off, but the Commissioners stuck to their guns and Captain Huish's spiteful attempt to cause the Great Western useless expense was baffled.

The third Great Western line of 1845, the Monmouth & Hereford, never materialised. After the Act for the Gloucester & Dean Forest Railway to connect it with Gloucester was passed in the next year, it was set out, some land bought, and contracts advertised but not let, save one for shafts and headings of the tunnels. Work on this was soon stopped, and after 1847 we hear no more of the line, though £59,000 had been spent on it. Four years later the main portion between Grange Court and Hereford was revived in a slightly altered form by a local company, under the title of the Hereford, Ross & Gloucester Railway.

The Bristol & Exeter Company opened a branch to Clevedon on 28th July 1847, and another to Tiverton on 12th June 1848, thereby adding $3\frac{1}{2}$ and $4\frac{3}{4}$ miles respectively to the Great Western system; but, the lease of that railway coming to an end on 30th April 1849, the total mileage worked by the Great Western was reduced from 312 to 227 on 1st May.

From this time onwards for twenty-seven years the Bristol & Exeter Railway was totally distinct from the Great Western, with its own staff, engines, and rolling stock. Trains between Paddington and the west of course continued to run through, but were worked by Bristol & Exeter engines over that line and made up of both Companies' stock. The Companies themselves were quite independent of each other, not having even one Director in common.

Beyond Exeter the South Devon Company opened its main line to Teignmouth on 30th May 1846, to Newton on 30th December, to Totnes on 20th July 1847, to Laira Green, some 2 miles short of Plymouth, on 5th May 1848, and into Plymouth on 2nd April 1849; and its branch from Newton to Torre Station, Torquay, on 18th December 1848. It also had its own staff and rolling stock, but hired engines from the Great Western till the end of June 1851 and afterwards from contractors for fifteen years. It cannot, however, be said to have been really independent, as eleven Directors out of its original Board of twenty-one were nominated by other Companies who had subscribed capital; four by the Great Western, five by the Bristol & Exeter, and two by the Bristol & Gloucester or their successors, the Midland. In 1849 these were reduced to two, three, and one respectively, but as the whole Board was at the same time reduced to eleven, the nominated Directors still formed a majority.

After a year's interval the engines and stock rendered superfluous by the loss of the Bristol & Exeter came into use on the South Wales Railway, which the Great Western had undertaken to work, as far at least as the Locomotive and Carriage Department was concerned, the rest of the staff being employed by the South Wales Company itself. The first section, from Chepstow to Swansea, 75 miles long, was opened for traffic on 18th June 1850. This remained isolated for two years, till 19th July 1852, when a single line was completed over the Wye Bridge, uniting it with the portion between the east side of that river and Grange Court, which had been opened, together with the Gloucester & Dean Forest Railway between Grange Court and the Great Western at Gloucester, on 19th September 1851.

This opening of the through connection with the Great Western brought a so-called lease of the South Wales Railway into force, under which the line was managed by a joint committee of five Directors of each Company, the lessees providing power and rolling stock, and the lessors accommodation for the traffic. After being paid their part of the working expenses, the Great Western received one-third of the net profits in return for a fixed rent. This curious arrangement was the cause of endless disputes and trouble between the two Companies, as to which more will be said later in the story of the South Wales Railway.

The Gloucester & Dean Forest Railway of 1846 was, as we have seen, a line to connect the Great Western at Gloucester with the Monmouth & Hereford in Westbury-on-Severn and the South Wales at Hagloe Farm beyond Awre. Both the Great Western and South Wales Companies agreed to subscribe towards its capital, but the latter, in lieu of doing so, soon afterwards arranged to take over the seven miles between Hagloe and Grange Court, where the Monmouth & Hereford was to join, and make them part of their own Railway, leaving the Gloucester Company only 7½ miles to construct. These were begun early in 1847, but the hard times soon caused suspension of the works and very little was done for nearly two years.

The bridge at Over was reported as completed in August 1850, but that nearer Gloucester over the other branch of the Severn was not ready for another year. Although navigation on this branch was effectually stopped by the old stone bridge below, the Company was obliged by its Act to make an opening bridge to provide for the possibility of the road bridge being altered! Brunel accordingly designed a skew bridge of three wrought-iron girders, 125 feet long, to cover two openings of 50 feet each on the square, capable of turning on a central pier formed of five cast-iron columns filled with concrete. The construction of this bridge and the arrangements for the junction with the new Great Western Station both delayed the opening of the line, which eventually took place on 19th September 1851, together with that of the eastern section of the South Wales Railway to a temporary terminus on the east bank of the Wye.

The new Great Western Station at Gloucester was not fully completed until the autumn of the following year. It was another one-sided station on the south of the railway, but differed from those at Reading and Slough by consisting of one long continuous platform instead of two separate Up and Down stations.[1]

The Gloucester & Dean Forest Railway was leased to the Great Western from its opening in perpetuity at a rent of 4½ per cent on its capital, to be raised to 5½ on the opening of the railway to Hereford, which occurred in 1855; so this little Company did exceptionally well for itself. It maintained a nominal existence till 1875, when it was finally absorbed.

Besides the main line, this Company began the construction of a branch from Over to the Docks at Gloucester, for which it obtained powers in 1847, but its funds being exhausted, the Great Western was left to finish the branch, which was opened for goods traffic on 20th March 1854. There was another opening bridge of 70 feet span for a single line on this branch.

The effects of the reaction, which was bound to follow the mania of 1845–6 when the money had to be found for the many costly projects authorized in those years, began to affect the Great Western in the first half of 1847.

At the August Meeting the Directors announced that owing to the state of the money market, they intended to delay the construction of new works and spread it over as long a time as possible 'until some decided change shall have taken place in the aspect of the monetary affairs of the country'. They were, however, obliged to ask for authority to raise money to meet the subscriptions promised to other Companies, and proposed to do this by the issue of guaranteed securities rather than new shares. The authority was given them, to be exercised at their discretion as to time and manner.

To make matters worse, a deep depression of trade set in, and at the next General Meeting, 'influenced by the fact of an unusual stagnation in traffic perceptible during the last few weeks on this as on all other railways in England', they recommended that the dividend for the second half of 1847 should be reduced from the steady 8 per cent per annum of the last three years to 7, and a larger balance than usual be carried forward. Three-quarters of a century were destined to pass before the Company again paid 8 per cent.

All this time the value of the Company's shares was going down and down. By July 1848 the £100 shares, regarded as fully paid,[2] had fallen in twelve months from 146 to 95, and the other shares of course in proportion. The Great Western fared no worse than most other Companies in this

---

[1] It remained one-sided till 1889, when the new Up platform was built.
[2] They were not so in fact till January 1849, when the last call of £10 fell due.

respect; London & North Western fell from 184 to 120 in the same period.

In view of this serious state of affairs, deputations of the Boards of the London & North Western, Great Western, and London & South Western Companies met in September 1848 in order 'to adopt, as well for the sake of the Public as of the Proprietors, some immediate and efficacious measure for counteracting the prejudicial effect on the commercial and manufacturing interests (as affirmed by Committees of both Houses of Parliament), and the serious depreciation of Investments in Railways, occasioned by the unprecedented demand for additional capital to be employed in constructing simultaneously many new lines of railway not immediately or imperatively required'. After several conferences they finally resolved on 1st November that the most effectual plan would be an absolute and permanent amalgamation of the three Companies under the sanction of Parliament, and settled the preliminary arrangements for such amalgamation, including the immediate appointment of a Joint Board of seven Directors of each Company to promote the necessary Bill and meantime to control all expenditure. Their conclusions were announced to the shareholders and a Special Meeting of each Company convened for 13th December to consider them; but ten days before that another circular informed those of the Great Western that the North Western Directors had proposed an alteration in the terms, which was considered inadmissible by the two other Companies, and so had abandoned their Meeting; wherefore the Great Western Meeting would not be held. The North Western Directors were not content with an equal number of representatives of their Company on the United Board, and so this sensational amalgamation scheme was nipped in the bud.

For the first time, strict economy then became the order of the day, but in spite of the Directors' efforts and owing to the interest on additional capital, the dividend fell first to 6 per cent per annum in February 1849, and then to 4 in August. On the latter occasion the two Auditors suggested, in a report on the published Accounts, the appointment of two or three shareholders to confer with the Directors as to the future outlay of capital and general reduction of expenditure. This suggestion, which was evidently made with the connivance of the Directors, was 'cheerfully acquiesced in' by them, and they went so far as to offer that four of themselves should retire to make room for new Directors to be elected by the shareholders. Having cleared the ground by rescinding the old rule of the Company that at least four Directors must reside within 20 miles of London and four within 20 miles of Bristol, the August Meeting left the election of new Directors and of the committee of consultation to a Special Meeting to be held in September in London. At the Special Meeting a committee of four shareholders was appointed, and four new Directors were elected in place of the same number retiring, three of whom had been in office since the foundation of the Company.

The Committee of Consultation spent the autumn in a searching investigation of the Company's affairs, and in visiting all the fifty-two stations and goods depots on the system. At the end of January 1850 they produced a report, which was printed and sent to the Shareholders with the Half-yearly Accounts. It contained nothing very startling or new as to capital outlay and liabilities, the total of which they estimated at £17,300,000. They strongly recommended the completion of the northern line to Birmingham, Wolverhampton, and Dudley, but thought the Wilts & Somerset should not for the present be extended beyond Frome and Warminster. They had nothing but praise for the general administration and management of the different departments of the Company's business, beyond remarking that they did not think 'that sufficient means have been taken to bring Goods Traffic to the Line', and making a few suggestions as to details such as the provision of cottages at level crossings, 'which will save the expense of night watchmen', their idea evidently being that the wretched day watchman might then be called out of bed at any hour without being paid for it.

Their main recommendation for effecting economy was a general reduction of salaries, beginning from the top. Russell and most of the Directors strongly opposed this, but the Committee produced accounts of the salaries paid by other Companies, which seem to have had some effect, and a letter from Saunders, whose devotion to the Great Western far exceeded his self-interest, acquiescing in their proposal that his own salary should be reduced, disarmed the opposition and induced the Board, against their will, to agree to general reductions. 'With respect to the lower class of clerks, rather than recommend a reduction of their salaries, your Committee have suggested more activity on their part as a means of lessening their numbers.' As regarded the Police and Porters, the Committee 'considered the scale of periodical increase too great, particularly as they were clothed from head to foot at the expense of the Company'. They concluded by suggesting a reduction of the number of Directors and recommending that a quarter of the Board should retire annually and be ineligible for re-election for a year.

The Half-yearly Meeting in February passed a resolution recommending that the various propositions contained in the Committee's Report 'be considered by the Directors, to report their opinion thereon, with reasons, in case they do not carry them out, to be submitted to the decision of the next General Meeting of the Company'.

Two Special Meetings were held in April, one to raise £3,500,000 by the issue of 4½ per cent Guaranteed Stock, to provide for the purchase and completion of the Birmingham & Oxford and Birmingham, Wolverhampton & Dudley Railways, and the discharge of some existing loans; the other to consider the Board's reply to the Committee's Report.

With most of the Committee's suggestions the Directors heartily agreed; indeed, many of them had been adopted in advance. They had little difficulty in satisfying the assembled Proprietors that to reduce their own number below twelve, or to make an efficient Director with his intimate knowledge of the Company's affairs ineligible for re-election for even a year, would be distinctly prejudical to the Company's interests.

As to the question of salaries and wages, they stated that, having already made a considerable reduction in the number and thereby increased the duties and responsibility of the staff, they were very reluctant to make any reduction in the payment of 'those who had undertaken such increased duties and had proved themselves to be faithful and valuable servants'; and had only yielded at length by way of experiment to the opinion of the Committee nominated by the Proprietors, thereby proving that they were not influenced by any personal feelings.

It is with much regret the Board feels bound by its duty to the Proprietors to represent that the short experience of a few months has realized their apprehensions. Since the reduction was notified the whole establishment has become unsettled; the Officers and principal Clerks, with few exceptions, have been seeking other employment; some valuable servants have quitted and others are about to leave the service. Nor has the effect of the reduction been confined to those whose salaries were reduced, for several others, in despair of improving their position in the present service, have also resigned to obtain more lucrative employment elsewhere.

The Directors have thus had practical proof that serious prejudice to the Company has arisen, and they apprehend that still more must ensue, unless steps be now taken to give some assurance of an established scale of salary and pay, upon which your officers and servants can rely. If length of service with great experience and proved ability are essentials in managing affairs towards the prosperity and welfare of any important undertaking, success is not likely to be attained by the discouragement of those upon whom so much depends, nor can a reduction of reasonable salaries be expected to counteract pecuniary depression in times of difficulty.

The Board then recommended the adoption of a new scale of salaries and wages, which was eventually adopted by a 20 to 1 majority on a poll at another Special Meeting in May, and, generally speaking, remained in force for many years.

A new office, hitherto unknown on the Great Western, was created about this time, the Directors announcing in August that it had been thought desirable to engage the services of a gentleman in the capacity of a Goods Manager. For this post they had selected Mr A. J. Drewe, 'who has had long experience in the Carrying Trade of the West of England'. For some years the receipts from goods traffic had generally been about a third of those from passengers and parcels; for example, in the half-year to 30th June 1850 they were £99,850 as against £295,100.

In financial matters an important change was the conversion, as from 1st July, of the various denominations of shares into 'Consolidated Great Western Railway Stock'.

Towards the end of the year Saunders was approached by representatives of the Shrewsbury & Birmingham and Shrewsbury & Chester Railways, two little Companies engaged in a bitter and unequal fight with the London & North Western for some share of the traffic between the midlands and Liverpool and Manchester. Driven to look for outside help, they naturally applied to the only Company in a position to help them by means of its access to Wolverhampton from the south, now about to be constructed. The Great Western Secretary at once saw the prospect, not only of much additional traffic on the costly Wolverhampton line, but also of extending the Broad Gauge to the Mersey, originally proposed by Captain Huish himself in 1845. It so happened that negotiations with the North Western, which had been going on for nearly two years, for saving capital expenditure to both Companies by a common station in Birmingham and a joint line thence to Wolverhampton, as well as a joint piece of line through Leamington, had come to an end; so the Great Western was free from any obligations to them. The story of the two Shrewsbury Companies is told in the next chapter; here it will suffice to say that a traffic agreement with them was settled and finally sealed on 10th January 1851, and followed on 8th May by an agreement for their future amalgamation with the Great Western.

This prospective addition to the system came at a time when trouble with the Oxford, Worcester & Wolverhampton Company, which had been brewing since the autumn of 1848, came to a head and brought about the secession of that railway from the Broad Gauge family. How this trouble arose through the foolish conduct of the Oxford, Worcester & Wolverhampton Board, and how it developed into open hostility, is told elsewhere. In 1851 the Oxford, Worcester & Wolverhampton, which the Great Western had helped to create, became and remained for ten years an entirely foreign and bitterly hostile company, notwithstanding the fact that the Great Western held nearly £200,000 of its capital and appointed six Directors to its Board.

In anticipation of the opening of the Birmingham line and of through communication with South Wales, the question of additional accommodation at Paddington became pressing in 1850. For twelve years the increasing traffic had been carried on as best it might in the temporary station west of Bishops Road Bridge, to which only a few trifling additions had been made since its opening. Having come to the conclusion that any further additions would be neither effective nor economical, the Directors proposed at the February Meeting of 1851 to build 'a Passenger Departure Shed, with Offices, Platforms, etc., and proper approaches on the ground beyond the present Goods Shed', which was just east of the Bridge, and also a new 'Merchandize Building' north of the existing station to take the place of this goods shed, which would have to be cleared away. This partial commencement of the permanent station was estimated to cost £50,000. Nothing was said at this time about an 'Arrival Shed', the idea being to use the existing station for arrivals, as soon as the new departure platforms could be got ready.

At this same Meeting the Board were authorized, 'to agree for building on the Company's property an Hotel with Refreshment Rooms, Dormitories, Stables, and other conveniences adjoining the Paddington Station, and to procure the money, not exceeding £50,000, requisite for the purpose, either by Lease or Mortgage of the premises or upon the credit of their Undertaking, and to let the premises on lease when built'. A clause giving the needful power to build an hotel was included in the Company's Act of the ensuing session.

A year later the Directors came for £75,000 more, for general offices, goods warehouses, grain stores, goods offices, cattle and mileage depots, and a new engine house, as well as the additional land required. Brunel reported at this time that it had been found impracticable to get ready for use even a portion of the new Down platform, as had been intended, until the old goods shed had been removed, and that therefore the whole work depended on the completion of the new one, which was making good progress. Only a portion of it, however, had been finished after the lapse of another year, but enough to allow of the removal of much of the old shed and the consequent resumption of work on the Departure station and offices, which had been unavoidably suspended for want of room. The Directors had by this time, February 1853, decided to get on with the permanent 'Passenger Arrival Shed and Platforms', and so asked for and got another £75,000 for these and general purposes at the new station.

Other matters calling for notice in 1851 were: (1) The incorporation of the Hereford, Ross & Gloucester Railway Company, a local company assisted by the Great Western through the Gloucester & Dean Forest Company with a subscription of £25,000 to its capital of £275,000, formed to make a broad-gauge railway from the Gloucester & Dean Forest at Grange Court in Westbury-on-Severn, much on the line of the abandoned Monmouth & Hereford of 1845, to a junction with the Shrewsbury & Hereford Railway in the City of Hereford; and (2) the acquisition by the Great Western of the Kennet & Avon Canal as from 1st July.

The Great Exhibition of this year brought much additional traffic, and enabled the Company to add a modest 10s to the now usual dividend of £4%. It is pleasant to note that 'a gratuity was given to the Local Superintendents, Clerks, and other Servants of the Company as a reward for their greatly increased labors, and very meritorious conduct in carrying on the extra business of the season'.

The Great Western staff, from the highest to the lowest, were evidently a very loyal family in those days. This is shown by the following extract from the *Railway Times* of 10th January 1852:

> *Great Western.* At a meeting of the officers and servants of this Company, held last week at the Swindon Station, Mr Gooch, Locomotive Superintendent, in the Chair, it was stated that 1,900 officers, clerks, and servants in the employment of the Company had united in subscribing £420 for the purpose of obtaining a full-length portrait of Mr C. Russell, the Chairman of the Company, to be placed in the Board Room of the Paddington Station, as a testimonial of their grateful esteem for the high principles of honour, impartiality, and undeviating kindness he has ever displayed towards them; and also to record their sense of the eminent services rendered by him to the Company, over which he has so long and efficiently presided. Resolutions were passed appointing a Committee to carry out the object of the meeting.

The Committee accordingly waited on Russell soon afterwards and presented him with an address, which, after assuring him that he had 'endeared himself to every individual of the establishment', requested him to give sittings for a full-length portrait to some eminent painter, with a view to its being preserved in the new Board Room. Russell replied with a speech of deep feeling, in the course of which he said: 'I never have lost and I never can lose any opportunity of expressing my conviction that no public body was ever more ably, zealously, and honourably served than the Great Western'.

Francis Grant, R.A.,[1] was the eminent painter chosen, and the portrait dominates the Board Room to-day, as it did in the 'fifties and 'sixties, when appearing before the Directors at an inquiry, whether as culprit or witness, was commonly called by the staff 'Going to see the Picture'.

Of course in those days when every man in the service had been appointed after a personal interview and all delinquencies were investigated by the Board or a Committee, the Chairman came into much closer contact with the comparatively small staff than he has ever done since such matters were necessarily delegated to the officers.

Russell's reply at the Great Western General Meeting of February 1852 to the North Western Chairman's charge of aggression is worth recording.[2]

'I am far from denying that it is natural that the London & North Western should regard with feelings of uneasiness and dissatisfaction our approach towards the north; but they should not altogether forget that these results are the consummation of a policy which they themselves thought fit to pursue towards us. It was not to injure them, it was to defend ourselves against aggressions from the north and the south that we—how reluctantly those about me best know—were compelled to push forward our advanced posts to Birmingham and Wolverhampton, and make alliances with northern companies. I will not prefer one word that I am not capable of proving by written documents. At our early stages we were most desirous to make amicable arrangements with the London & North Western, if we could only secure to ourselves the positions we had actually obtained.'

Later, in reply to a shareholder, he was more explicit:

The Chairman was extremely sorry to say that no arrangement had been come to with the London & North Western; and proceeded to defend the policy of the Company with regard to the northern lines, and briefly adverted to the early opposition which the Great Western had experienced from the old London & Birmingham, who embarked in a project for a line from Tring to Cheltenham; to the Birmingham & Oxford line, which was promoted by the Grand Junction in opposition to the London & Birmingham; and stated that it was not until after repeated overtures from the former corporation that the Great Western consented to connect itself with the scheme; that the Shrewsbury & Birmingham line was projected by the London & Birmingham as an antagonistic one to the Grand Junction; and that they (the Great Western Directors) had offered to take one third of the Birmingham traffic and give two thirds to the London & North Western, and had done everything in their power to bring about a friendly settlement of the differences between themselves and that Company. The hon. gentleman also reminded the proprietors of the line promoted by the London & Birmingham, in conjunction with the South Western, to bring down a northern line through Oxford to run parallel to the Didcot branch, as far as Newbury, so as to intersect the whole Great Western district from north to south. He had done all in his power to forewarn Mr Glyn of the consequences of such an attack, and it was too much now to find fault with Great Western policy because they did not remain defenceless on their own ground but were driven to push forward their posts, as a security to their own traffic, in which they have happily succeeded. It would thus be seen that the aggression had clearly been upon the Great Western. He would ask, therefore, whether they were to stand with their hands behind their backs whilst repeated encroachments were made upon their traffic. It had been

---

[1] P.R.A. 1866–78.  Knighted 1866.
[2] *Railway Times*, 14th February 1852.

impossible for them to do otherwise than they had done. They would have been guilty of the greatest disregard to the interests of the shareholders if they had not taken the course they had adopted—if they had not advanced upon the enemy instead of letting him come among them. The honourable proprietor seemed to be frightened of a contest. He begged him to have no such fears.

At this same Meeting an agreement with the Electric Telegraph Company was announced. That Company were to lay and maintain wires on the Great Western lines, charging an annual rent for their use, and giving the Railway Company an option to purchase. The Bristol & Exeter Company having made a similar agreement and the telegraph being already in use on the South Devon, its completion between London and Plymouth was thus ensured. The wires were already up as far as Reading; they reached Bristol in May, Bridgwater in July, and were completed to Exeter in August. By the end of the year they extended from Swindon to Gloucester and throughout the South Wales Railway, and from this time their progress was rapid over the remainder of the Great Western system.

The Birmingham & Oxford Railway being nearly finished and all Captain Huish's desperate efforts to break the alliance between the Great Western and the two Shrewsbury Companies having failed, that warrior decided to try to capture the Great Western itself for his 'Euston Empire', which already embraced the Midland, Lancashire & Yorkshire, and Manchester, Sheffield & Lincolnshire, besides sundry smaller railways. From being, as Secretary and Manager of the Grand Junction, a strong opponent of monopoly, at any rate when in the hands of the London & Birmingham, he had become since his instalment at Euston its fierce upholder, and had striven by every means, lawful or unlawful, to block all competition. His methods were quite unscrupulous—to crush small opponents by ruinous rate-cutting; to upset sealed agreements on legal quibbles; to make secret treaties which, when disclosed, turned out to be *ultra vires*; to make 'pools' for certain towns and then evade the 'pooling' by some rebooking dodge; and even to use physical force against the servants of competing Companies and physical obstacles against their trains at junctions. Examples of most of these methods will be found in the story of his dealings with the two little Shrewsbury Companies told in the next chapter.[1]

The Great Western being too independent and powerful for such treatment, absolute amalgamation of the two great Companies, on the basis of North Western Ordinary Stock being worth £100 and Great Western £80,[2] was proposed in a letter to Russell dated 4th August 1852 from George Carr Glyn, the North Western Chairman, as the only means of putting an end to the strife between them.

The terms suggested appear in the main reasonable, but they involved the recognition by the Great Western of so-called agreements made by the North Western with certain shareholders of the two Shrewsbury

[1] See also Grindling's *History of the Great Northern Railway*, Methuen, 1898.
[2] The current prices were: London & North Western 132, Great Western 103.

Companies as of equal validity with their own agreements properly sealed and sanctioned by General Meetings of those Companies. Hence, if the amalgamation should be ultimately rejected by Parliament or the North Western shareholders, as was extremely likely, an important step would have been made towards breaking the Shrewsbury Alliance.

After consultation with his Board, Russell replied on 10th August that they were convinced that Parliament would never consent to the creation of such a vast monopoly, whatever it might have done to save the expenditure of capital in the financial stress of 1849; and that they could not therefore imperil their application to Parliament to carry out their contract with the Shrewsbury Companies, which had already been passed by the House of Commons and only defeated by the Wharncliffe Order of the Lords, by committing themselves to any such recognition. While equally anxious to put an end to the costly strife between the Companies, they did not agree that amalgamation was the only means of doing so, and proposed instead an agreement for equal fares and rates at competing points, with, if desired by the North Western, a fixed apportionment of the net receipts therefrom.

This proposal was at once curtly rejected—the rejection is dated 12th August—and the anger felt at Euston at the failure of what may quite probably, in view of his general conduct, have been intended as a trap by the astute and unscrupulous Captain Huish, was betrayed at the North Western General Meeting next day, when the Chairman actually suggested in so many words that, if their Directors would not carry out the amalgamation, the Great Western shareholders should take matters into their own hands. He also made some disparaging remarks as to the value and security of Great Western stock, which Russell felt obliged to contradict in a subsequent letter, at the same time strongly deprecating his attempt to create internal dissensions in another Company.

That the Great Western Board were absolutely right in their forecast of the policy of Parliament is shown by the adoption of the Report of the Cardwell Committee in 1853, condemning railway amalgamations save in special cases, and the consequent collapse of the agreed union of the London & North Western and Midland Companies.

The works of the Birmingham & Oxford Junction Railway, now nearly finished, were begun early in 1847 by Messrs Peto & Betts, the well-known contractors. Financial stringency soon caused them to be delayed, and very little was done for nearly two years. In August 1849 Brunel reported that though progress was still very slow, the viaduct into Birmingham had been finished, and thence as far as Warwick the whole line was in a forward state; the deep Harbury Cutting was also well advanced. Between Leamington and Warwick nothing had yet been done. The original line of 1846 was laid out to pass west of Leamington, but two years later the Great Western obtained power to deviate this from Whitnash through the town. The negotiations with the North Western, already alluded to, for a joint piece of line here to save the construction of two adjacent viaducts, and for a common station at Birmingham, caused further delay; so that work was not even begun on the Leamington Deviation or the Extension to Snow Hill Station till 1851, after all hope of any such arrangement had been abandoned. Snow Hill Station itself[1] was not commenced till the end of January 1852, owing to difficulties in obtaining possession of the houses and other buildings which had to be cleared away.

By this time the 11¼ miles of the Oxford & Rugby Railway, from Banbury to the commencement of the Birmingham & Oxford beyond Fenny Compton, had been finished and the permanent way was being laid. The second line of rails between Banbury and Millstream Junction, south of Oxford, had been laid but not brought into use, and the new Oxford Station on the west of the town was being built.

At last in September the whole line to Birmingham was ready for inspection. The chief works were: the Harbury Cutting, about ½ mile long and no less than 110 feet deep with a short tunnel of 73 yards, which would have been longer but for a big landslip in 1850; the Leamington Viaduct, alongside that of the London & North Western Rugby & Leamington Line,[2] with a bridge of 105 feet span over the High Street; an aqueduct carrying the Warwick & Napton Canal over the railway; a 160 foot bridge over the Avon; an iron girder bridge 150 feet long over the canal and a road at Warwick; a timber viaduct over the reservoir at Solihull 400 feet long; a high and long embankment near Acock's Green; a bridge under the Midland Company's Gloucester Line, which had, of course, to be made without stopping their traffic; another 150 foot iron bridge over the Warwick Canal at Sandy Lane; the Bordesley Viaduct of 58 brick arches; and last, the Snow Hill Tunnel, 596 yards long, on the incline of 1 in 45 from Moor Street up to the Terminus. Most of this was made as an open cutting and then covered, to comply with the Act of 1846. The land on top was afterwards sold.

Captain Douglas Galton was sent down by the Board of Trade on 14th September to inspect the line, with special instructions to see that the Mixed Gauge was complete. He found all the works sufficient as regards construction and strength, and the Mixed Gauge complete on both lines between Banbury and the junction with the branch to join the London & North Western in Birmingham, but on the remaining mile thence to the Snow Hill Station the narrow-gauge rails had not been laid though the longitudinal timbers to carry them were in position. The branch itself, already referred to as the Duddeston Viaduct, was far from finished, several arches being still in progress and no permanent way laid. He therefore reported that the line might be opened as far as the junction, but not beyond it, either towards Snow Hill or the North Western, 'by reason of the incompleteness of the works and permanent way'.

[1] The designation was not officially adopted until February 1858.
[2] Opened 1st March 1851. There was no L&NW Station at Leamington until February 1854.

Although there was no immediate prospect of their being used, the narrow-gauge rails into Snow Hill were forthwith laid, so after a second inspection a fortnight later the Board sanctioned the opening of the main line throughout. At the same time permission was given to open the second or Up line from Banbury to Millstream Junction, Oxford, which was laid with Mixed Gauge as far as the Isis Bridge ½ mile south of the new station, the addition of a narrow-gauge rail on the remaining mile being apparently dispensed with as useless. This second line was to be used as a single line for all traffic while the Down line, which had remained Broad only since its opening in 1850, was being altered to Mixed Gauge.

The original stations on the new line north of Banbury were Cropredy, Fenny Compton, Southam Road and Harbury, Leamington, Warwick, Hatton, Knowle, Solihull, Acock's Green, and Birmingham,[1] the last being merely a large wooden shed run up in a hurry for the opening; though intended to be only temporary, it did duty with little alteration for nearly twenty years. Those at Oxford, Banbury, and Leamington had all-over roofs of Brunel's usual style. At Leamington only broad-gauge trains could enter the station, the mixed-gauge line being carried outside it by a loop to the north-east, provided with narrow platforms and sheds of its own.

The opening of the new broad-gauge line to Birmingham was by no means auspicious. Public traffic being advertised to begin on 1st October 1852, a special inaugural trip of Directors, officers, and friends was arranged for the previous day, to leave Paddington at 9 and Oxford at 10.20, run to Birmingham, pick up more friends there and return to Leamington for the feast usual on such joyful occasions. The train consisted of ten carriages drawn by the famous *Lord of the Isles*, which had only begun work in July after a preliminary holiday at the Great Exhibition. Only one of these carriages, a second-class next the engine, empty save for a Guard, had a brake, and the special was actually timed to reach Banbury on the old Down line only five minutes after the ordinary train from Didcot, a notoriously unpunctual mixed train of passengers and goods. Needless to say, the Traffic Department was asking for trouble, and got it. Owing to delays at Reading and Didcot the special left the new station at Oxford, not yet open to the public, more than half an hour late, but the mixed train was later still by the time it reached Aynho. There it was engaged in detaching two goods waggons when the roar of the approaching special was heard. The driver at once put on steam to get away, the coupling between the carriages and waggons snapped, and a few seconds later *Lord of the Isles* dashed into the latter, smashing one to bits and driving the rest on to the receding carriages. These were not much damaged, but six passengers in them were a good deal shaken and hurt. The damage to the special was confined to the engine, neither the

[1] Kingswood (renamed Lapworth in 1902) and Bordesley were added in 1854 and 1855 respectively, Small Heath & Sparkbrook in 1863, Olton in 1869, Widney Manor in 1899, Tyseley in 1906, and Moor Street in 1909.

tender nor any of the carriages was injured, and the passengers escaped unhurt, a striking advertisement of the safety of the Broad Gauge. *Lord of the Isles* broke her buffer beam, was thrown off the rails by an axle of the smashed waggon, and tore up much of the stonework of the platform. It appears that none of the people on the engine, Gooch himself among them, knew the road, and so were misled by a disused signal a short distance south of Aynho, which had been left showing *All Right* after the temporary ballast siding it protected had been removed, and which they mistook for the Auxiliary or Distant Signal. Then when the Station Signal at *Danger* came in sight the brake power was utterly insufficient to stop the heavy train. The fact was that the signals, which had sufficed for the single line branch, had not been brought up to main line standard, and the Board of Trade Inspector had some unpleasant remarks to make on the recklessness displayed in the timing, formation, and speed of the special, and on the chronic unpunctuality of the ordinary train.

The delay caused by this accident put an end to the trip to Birmingham. The engine of the ordinary train, after taking its own two carriages on to Banbury, returned for those of the special and eventually dragged them to Leamington, whither another special train, ordered by telegraph, brought the Birmingham guests. 'At four o'clock about 180 ladies and gentlemen sat down to a sumptuous dejeuner in the Royal Hotel.'[1]

Next day, Friday, 1st October 1852, the line was opened for passenger trains only, and the expresses were timed to cover the 129 miles from Paddington to Birmingham in 2¾ hours. Goods traffic did not begin till February 1853, and remained very limited till after the opening of the railway to Wolverhampton.

The Mixed Gauge was laid in the manner proposed by Brunel and sanctioned by Captain Simmons on behalf of the Railway Commissioners in 1847, with three rails on each line and the common one outside so as to bring carriages of both gauges up to the platforms. Henceforth all mixed-gauge railways were made thus, and the Gloucester–Cheltenham piece remained the only one with common inner rails; on this the Broad Gauge had been added to an existing narrow-gauge line and there was no intermediate station.

Between Oxford and Birmingham the third rails were of course quite useless for traffic, there being no connection with any narrow-gauge railway; they were, however, used by the contractors for the permanent way, who did the necessary ballasting with narrow-gauge engines and trucks of their own. In June 1853 the Oxford, Worcester & Wolverhampton Company opened their railway to Wolvercot, some 3 miles north of Oxford, and were allowed to run their narrow-gauge passenger trains over the Great Western between the new junction there and Oxford Station, where sundry sidings were then laid in for their use. Until this time, and elsewhere, the third rails were confined almost exclusively to the running

---

[1] *Railway Times*, 2nd October 1852.

lines, being laid only to carry out the legal obligation. No further use was made of them till after the connection had been opened with the Shrewsbury lines north of Wolverhampton, and very little till they had been extended to Basingstoke at the end of 1856.

The opening of the Birmingham & Oxford Railway brought into force the general reduction of rates and fares over the whole Great Western system decreed by the Acts of 1846 and 1847, and this at a time when the capital was largely increased by the payment for that line and the traffic thereon was quite undeveloped, goods traffic not having even begun and the passenger accommodation at Birmingham being most inadequate. The Directors had, however, long foreseen that hard times would ensue on the first opening northward and had provided a small reserve fund, by drawing on which they were able to keep the dividend for 1853 up to the then normal figure of 4%.

The only addition to the system made this year was the first 5 miles of the Hereford, Ross & Gloucester Railway from Grange Court to a temporary station called Hopesbrook, just short of the Lea Tunnel, opened on 11th July. It was a single line worked by one engine.

In Parliament 1853 was a very bad year for the Broad Gauge. Proposals to lay it on the three Railways between Wolverhampton and Birkenhead and the Shrewsbury & Hereford line, and on the South Staffordshire from Wednesbury to Dudley, and Bills for new lines from Maiden Newton in Dorsetshire to Stoke Canon near Exeter—the 'Devon & Dorset Railway'—and from Worcester to Hereford, a mixed-gauge project, were all rejected. The only new powers the Great Western obtained were to revive the Henley and Uxbridge branches, to execute additional works at Reading, Chippenham, and elsewhere, and to run over the hostile Oxford, Worcester & Wolverhampton Railway between Priestfield and the junction with their own connecting line to the Shrewsbury & Birmingham, not far north of the joint Low Level Station at Wolverhampton.

The new Paddington Station made good progress during the year. In August Brunel reported:

> The works at Paddington Station for the passenger trains are still much in arrear, but are advancing towards completion.
>
> The alteration of the main lines, approaching Paddington, has been effected, and the Engine-house is in course of construction upon the site of the original line of Railway. As soon as it is completed, the old Engine-house may be removed and the extension of the Goods Department, so much needed, may be commenced.

Another £50,000 was required for the goods station, and at the same time the Directors took £25,000 for the construction of a new dock, canal wharfage, buildings, and sidings at Bull's Bridge (Hayes), for the transfer of coal, which was just beginning to come from South Wales, to barges going by the canal to the Thames and so down to the Docks.

The Departure side of the new station was at last ready enough to be brought into use on 16th January 1854, but the roof and Arrival side were still far from finished. In Brunel's words: 'the difficulties of proceeding successively with different portions of the new work on the site of old buildings, without interfering too much with the carrying on of the traffic in a Station, already far too small for the wants, have been very great; but after the removal of the Engine House we shall, I trust, be somewhat relieved from the present difficulties'.

On 29th May the Arrival Platforms were opened, and the passenger arrangements transferred to the new station, of which all the principal works had been by this time completed, but the new engine-house was not ready and so the goods station was still delayed. By the following February the passenger station had been finished except for painting, and the engine-house was ready for use but not yet occupied. Soon afterwards the old engine-house was pulled down and the second goods shed begun on its sight. Carriage repair shops commenced about this time were finished in the summer of 1856, but the goods station arrangements, including hydraulic machinery for lifting and moving trucks, were not finally completed for yet another year. From first to last the new station cost the Company over £650,000.

The passenger station is thus described in Brunel's *Life*:

> The interior of the principal part of the station is 700 feet long and 238 feet wide, divided in its width by two rows of columns into three spans of 68, 102, and 68 feet, and is crossed at two points by transepts 50 feet wide, which give space for large traversing frames. The roof is very light, consisting of wrought iron arched ribs, covered partly with corrugated iron and partly with the Paxton glass roofing, which Mr Brunel here adopted to a considerable extent. The columns which carry the roof are very strongly bolted down to large masses of concrete, to enable them to resist sideways pressure.

It is no small tribute to Brunel's foresight that this station of 1854 sufficed for the traffic without extension for more than fifty years. He was assisted in such few ornamental details as there are by Sir Matthew Digby Wyatt, a famous architect of the period.

The hotel was proceeded with at the same time as the station buildings, and leased to a Company formed for the purpose by some of the Great Western officers and shareholders. On 9th June 1854 H.R.H. Prince Albert, accompanied by the Prince of Wales, paid a visit of inspection and, according to the *Morning Post*, was much pleased with the house and general arrangements. It was opened for business the same day under the management of a Mr Wheeler, late steward of the Union Club. Brunel was one of the Directors, and soon became the Chairman of the Company.

The same Monday, 29th May, which saw the opening of the Arrival side of the new Station at Paddington, was marked by the invasion of the citadel at the other end of the line by the narrow-gauge trains of the Midland Company, who had at last finished their new line from Gloucester to Standish alongside the Great Western and the addition of narrow-gauge rails to the former Bristol & Gloucester Railway thence to Bristol, authorized in 1848. From their junction into and throughout both the passenger and goods stations at Temple Meads the additional rails were laid by the Great Western. Brunel reported this work in August as an effective reply to the oft-repeated assertions of Robert Stephenson and

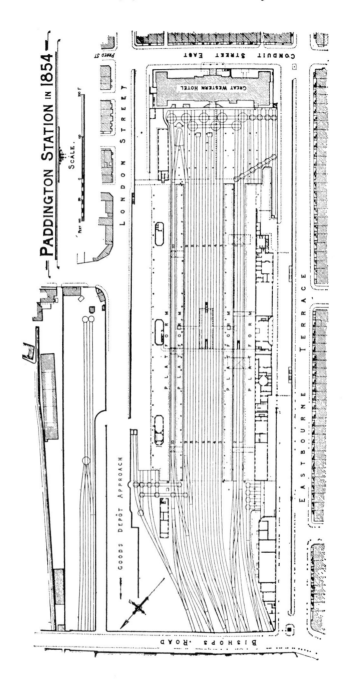

PADDINGTON STATION IN 1854

others that Mixed Gauge was altogether impracticable in a station yard. He wrote:

At the Bristol end of the line a considerable work, which for a length of time has caused great apparent confusion in the Station, has been carried on at the expense of the Midland Railway Company and for their use, the mixed gauge having been laid throughout this Station. The execution of this, without interruption to the large traffic of the Station, was a work of some difficulty, and was rather a severe test of the possibility of working the mixed gauge in a complicated Station not designed for the purpose. The whole has now been in use for some time.

Considerable additions were made to the locomotive workshops at Swindon at this time, in view of the opening of the northern line, £25,000 being voted for the purpose in August 1853, and £5,000 more for house accommodation at New Swindon a year later. It is worth recording that, when laying the foundation stone of the new shops in May 1854, Gooch took occasion to state that during the sixteen years he had been connected with the Company no strike or other symptom of disaffection between the workmen and Directors had occurred.

A branch to High Wycombe was opened on 1st August from 'Wycombe Junction', close to the town of Maidenhead and about 1½ miles west of Maidenhead Station. This was made by the Wycombe Railway Company of 1846, which had been revived by an Act of 1852, and leased to the Great Western at a fixed rent. It was a single line of cheap construction, not quite 10 miles long, laid with Barlow rails[1] weighing 90½ lbs to the yard and 12 inches wide at the bottom. There were two timber viaducts near Bourne End, one over the Thames, and the other over an adjacent meadow called Cock Marsh which was liable to floods, and five intermediate stations, named Maidenhead (Wycombe Branch)[2]—near but not at the junction—Cookham, Marlow Road,[3] Wooburn Green, and Loudwater.

The construction of the Birmingham, Wolverhampton & Dudley Railway between Snow Hill Station, Birmingham, and Priestfield, where it joined the Oxford, Worcester & Wolverhampton, 1½ miles from Wolverhampton, was begun in 1851, after the failure of the negotiations with the London & North Western Company for joint use of the Stour Valley Line.

Brunel was not the Engineer for this, but one John Robinson McClean, Engineer and Lessee of the neighbouring South Staffordshire Railway.

After a disappointment in the spring, this line and the short Great Western bit, authorized in 1852, to connect the Oxford, Worcester & Wolverhampton Railway, ½ mile north of Wolverhampton Station, with the Shrewsbury & Birmingham Railway at Stafford Road, were at last ready for inspection by the Board of Trade in August 1854. The intervening portion of the Oxford, Worcester & Wolverhampton Railway had already been finished, and it was of course of the utmost importance to

---

[1] See Chapter XI.
[2] Closed 1871.
[3] Renamed Bourne End in 1874.

get the line from Birmingham to the Shrewsbury Railway open by 1st September, when the amalgamation of the latter with the Great Western took effect and its running powers over the Stour Valley Line consequently ceased.

Captain Douglas Galton of the Board of Trade passed over the new line on 25th August, intending to return very soon to complete his inspection. Next day a large wrought-iron girder bridge, described by Captain Galton as a tubular bridge of 63 feet span, across the Winson turnpike road between Soho and Handsworth Stations fell into the road immediately after the safe passage of an engine with two ballast waggons!

Brunel was thereupon sent down to inspect all the works, with the result that no less than five of McClean's girder bridges were condemned as too weak, and had to be replaced or strengthened. This caused a delay of more than two months; the line was not again ready for inspection till November. Captain Galton's report then being satisfactory, it was opened for passenger trains without any ceremony on Tuesday, 14th November 1854, together with the short junction line to the Shrewsbury & Birmingham beyond Wolverhampton.

Both were double mixed-gauge lines, the former 11 miles, the latter ¾ mile long, as were also the intervening 2 miles of the Oxford, Worcester & Wolverhampton Railway. Between Birmingham and Wolverhampton there were intermediate stations at Hockley, Soho, Handsworth and Smethwick, West Bromwich, Swan Village, Wednesbury, and Bilston, and all Down trains stopped short of the junction at Priestfield for the collection of tickets. Bradley & Moxley was added in 1862. It was closed in 1915 and demolished two years later to make way for new loop lines. The joint Low Level Station at Wolverhampton was another one-sided station, even more peculiar, not to say dangerous, than those at Reading and Slough, in that the main passenger lines crossed each other twice— in the middle of the station and at the very mouth of the tunnel. The accommodation for goods traffic at many of the stations was not ready for nearly a year after the opening. There were two short tunnels, respectively 135 and 160 yards long between Birmingham and Hockley, and another of 412 yards north of Swan Village.

From the first day trains of both gauges were worked over the line, those from north of Wolverhampton running on to Birmingham and starting thence for Shrewsbury and Chester, while the local trains were broad-gauge. No difficulty was experienced in working the Mixed Gauge, as Brunel took care to point out in his report of February 1855:

The Birmingham, Dudley, and Wolverhampton Railway was opened in November last; the Mixed Gauge upon this Line, which is carried out to the fullest extent ever contemplated, or which is possible on any railway, both on the Main Line and in the numerous Stations and Sidings, has been worked from the day of opening with trains of both Gauges, and, as I fully expected, with perfect success, without any difficulty and indeed without requiring any effort or peculiar attention and without creating any observation.

In like manner, at Wolverhampton, in a Station occupied jointly with the Oxford, Worcester, & Wolverhampton Railway Company, while the Station has been in progress, and it is yet incomplete, the traffic of all our Narrow Gauge Lines from the North

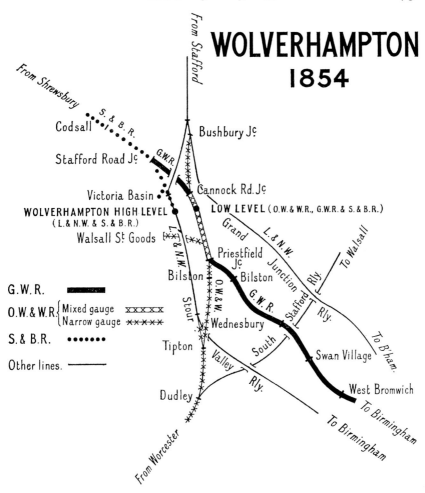

and all our Broad Gauge Traffic from the South, meet and cross each other; and together with the Narrow Gauge traffic of the Oxford, Worcester, and Wolverhampton Railway, have been carried on without difficulty, and without any interruption or accident, in a Mixed Gauge Station of a complicated arrangement.

The Goods Sidings and Stations are being completed as rapidly as possible; they will be of a very complete character, and afford a very large amount of accommodation. I expect that in a month or two we shall be able to enter into the use of a considerable portion of them.

The Engine and Carriage Establishment at Bordesley on the south side of Birmingham is nearly completed, and will be occupied by stock of both Gauges very shortly; and, with the Station making at Coventry Road, will add greatly to the facility of carrying on the very large local Passenger traffic of that neighbourhood.

There was extraordinary delay with these goods stations. In August 1855 they were 'in some cases completed and in use, and in others, with the exception of Wednesbury, nearly completed; the communications

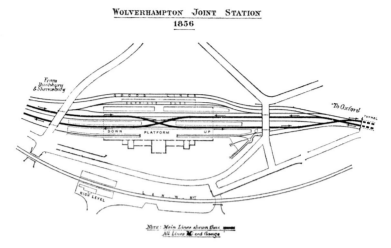

WOLVERHAMPTON JOINT STATION
1856

with the Birmingham Canal are also in a forward state'. They were not even finished in the following February, more than a year after the opening:

> Upon the Birmingham & Wolverhampton Line, the principal Works of the extensive Station accommodation and the communications with the Canal, which the probable future traffic upon this line appears to require, have been executed, and have more or less been brought into operation, and generally require only the extension and completion of Sidings and Permanent Way, Rails and Fittings, to render them thoroughly efficient.

It is not surprising to find that by this time some shareholders were beginning to complain that goods traffic was neglected on the Great Western. Of course no through traffic from north of Wolverhampton to London was possible owing to the break of gauge; all had to be transferred. For this purpose a transfer station, the first on the Great Western, was established in the Victoria Basin Depot of the former Shrewsbury & Birmingham Company, whither the broad-gauge rails were extended from the junction at Stafford Road. The Wolverhampton Town Goods Station for both north and south traffic was also established in the same yard at Herbert Street. Meanwhile the northern goods traffic continued to be dealt with at the High Level Station.

Down in Somersetshire the single line branch from Frome to Radstock, $8\frac{1}{2}$ miles, was opened for coal traffic on the same day as the line to Wolverhampton—14th November 1854.

# VIII

# The Shrewsbury Railways

## THE SHREWSBURY & CHESTER RAILWAY

A railway from Chester to the Wrexham and Ruabon coalfields was projected in 1839, George Stephenson being engaged as Engineer, but after the line had been laid out and plans deposited with the Clerks of the Peace, the scheme was abandoned owing to commercial depression. It was revived in 1842, only to be again stifled, this time by the opposition of landowners and general apathy.

Nothing daunted, the promoters, among whom the most active were Robert Roy and J. B. Ross, again took the field in the Parliamentary Session of 1844, and in spite of great opposition carried their Bill incorporating the North Wales Mineral Railway Company with power to make a railway from Chester to Wrexham. The Engineer was Henry Robertson,[1] and the line he laid out began at the River Dee at Saltney and terminated close to the old mansion of Bryn-y-fynnon at Wrexham, where the station was to have been. Instead of running into the City of Chester, it joined the Chester & Holyhead Railway, which had been authorized in the same session, not quite two miles from the already existing terminus of the Birkenhead Railway. Notwithstanding its title, the line had no connection with any of the coal or iron works, the intended branch for this purpose having been abandoned owing to the jealousies of rival mine owners. This was remedied in the following year, when, in addition to an extension of the main line from Wrexham to Rauabon, a branch from a point about 10 miles from Chester, known later as Wheatsheaf Junction, to Brymbo and Minera was authorized, to be followed in 1846 by further branches to Broughton and Gwersyllt.

The Extension Act of 1845 is noteworthy in having conferred on Sir Watkin Wynn and his successors, owners of Wynnstay, the right of appointing a director of the railway, a right preserved in all the subsequent amalgamations till it at last extended to a system considerably more than 100 times the size of the North Wales Mineral Railway.

In the mania year, 1845, a rival project for a direct line from Chester to Shrewsbury was promoted by the Chester & Holyhead Company and the Birkenhead interest, backed by the London & Birmingham in furtherance of its policy of encouraging lines to the north independent of the Grand Junction. The North Wales Mineral met this scheme by promoting a continuation of their own line to Shrewsbury under the title of the Shrewsbury, Oswestry & Chester Junction Railway with Henry Robertson as engineer and Messrs Roy and Ross prominent Directors.

[1] *Henry Robertson, Pioneer of Railways into Wales*, by George G. Lerry (1949).

The rival line being eventually abandoned and the landowners having been pacified, the Shrewsbury, Oswestry & Chester Junction Bill passed through Parliament unopposed and received the Royal Assent on 30th June 1845.

Next year the two Companies were amalgamated to form the Shrewsbury & Chester Railway.

Meanwhile the works of the North Wales Mineral had been steadily pushed on, and the line to Ruabon was opened to the public on 4th November 1846, together with the portion of the Chester & Holyhead Railway between the Birkenhead station in Chester and Saltney, which was used under an agreement by the Shrewsbury & Chester Company's trains.

Robertson's report to the first Meeting of the amalgamated Company, held a few days before the opening, describes the line as passing over a level country to 'the Rossett'—'the' was generally prefixed to the name of this place at the time—with remarkably light works; thence it proceeded up the side of the Gresford Vale with deep cuttings and embankments to Wrexham, and so on to Ruabon. At $2\frac{1}{2}$ miles from the Birkenhead Terminus in Chester there was a short branch to a wharf on the Dee at Saltney, and at 10 miles the branch to Minera, not yet finished, left the main line, passing through the centre of the coal and iron district to the lime rocks at Minera, with two tunnels respectively about 220 and 400 yards long. The North Wales Mineral Line terminated at a point near Rhosymedre, 1 mile beyond Ruabon, where the Shrewsbury, Oswestry & Chester Junction began; the length of the main line was 16 miles, and of the Dee and Minera branches $\frac{1}{2}$ mile and 6 miles respectively, making a total of $22\frac{1}{2}$ miles. An engine-house and workshops were established on the Dee Branch at Saltney.

The railway had only been open for six months when, on 24th May 1847, an evening train to Ruabon was precipitated into the River Dee by the collapse of the bridge just outside Chester. This bridge, for which Robert Stephenson, as Engineer of the Chester & Holyhead Railway, was responsible, was formed of cast-iron girders in three oblique spans of 98 feet each on stone piers, and the left girder of the span farthest from Chester broke in two places under the train. The engine got across safely with its tender off the rails, but the carriages all fell into the river 36 feet below. Of the thirty-five people in the train, five, including the fireman, who was jerked off the tender, were killed, all the rest except the driver, who alone escaped scot free, being more or less seriously injured. This accident caused a great stir at the time, and cast considerable doubt on the safety of cast iron as a material for railway under-bridges.

The Minera Branch with its two rope-worked inclines was opened for mineral traffic in July 1847, and two small branches out of it to the Brynmally and Ffrwd collieries in the following November.

On the portion of the main line between Ruabon and Shrewsbury the chief works, on which the completion of the whole depended, were the two great viaducts over the valleys of the Dee at Cefn and the Ceiriog at Chirk. Of these, the former is 510 yards long and 148 feet high, consisting of nineteen stone arches with a span of 60 feet each, and at the time was said to be the largest viaduct in the country. It was designed by the Company's Engineer, Henry Robertson, and built by the great contractor, Thomas Brassey. On 25th August 1848, the ceremony of keying the last arch was performed by W. Ormsby Gore, M.P., the first Chairman of the Shrewsbury & Chester Company, in the presence of a great gathering from Chester and the surrounding country; after which the company, to the number of 300, repaired to lunch in the goods shed at Ruabon, where no less than twenty-three separate toasts 'were enthusiastically responded to in eloquent and glowing terms'. The Chirk Viaduct, a somewhat smaller affair 283 yards long and 100 feet high, originally had twelve arches, ten of stone of 45 feet span and the extreme arch at each end of laminated timber with a span of 120 feet.[1]

These two viaducts being at length finished, the line between Ruabon and a temporary station at Shrewsbury, on the rest of which the works were mostly of a light nature, was opened for traffic on 14th October 1848, the first railway to enter Shrewsbury.

The original terminus of the Shrewsbury, Oswestry & Chester Junction Railway of 1845 was to have been at 'the junction of Chester Street and Cross Street, in the Parishes of St Mary and St Aulkmund in the Borough of Shrewsbury', but in the following year Parliament authorized a short extension 'from the authorized line near the Sun and Ball Inn in the Parish of St Aulkmund to a Yard in Castle Hill Street in Castle Foregate and the Parish of St Mary', and here a large joint passenger station was agreed upon by the four Companies—Shrewsbury & Chester, Shrewsbury & Birmingham, Shrewsbury & Hereford, and Shropshire Union. It was finished in time for the opening of the Shrewsbury & Birmingham and Shropshire Union's joint line from Wellington on 1st June 1849.

At the other end of the railway, the General Station at Chester, also the joint property of four Companies—Shrewsbury & Chester, Chester & Holyhead, London & North Western, and Birkenhead, Lancashire & Cheshire Junction—had been brought into use on 1st August 1848.

Notwithstanding the title of the Shrewsbury, Oswestry & Chester Junction Railway, the line as constructed left the town of Oswestry more than two miles off on the west. In 1846, just before its union with the North Wales Mineral, the Company obtained power to make two branches, one from Gobowen through Oswestry to join the authorized Crewe and Newtown line of the Shropshire Union Railway & Canal Company at Crickheath, near Llanymynech, the other from Leaton to the little town of Wem. The former was opened as far as Oswestry on 23rd December 1848, but the rest of it, as well as the whole of the Wem branch, was afterwards abandoned.

[1] These were replaced by masonry in 1858-9.

Accommodation for exchanging traffic with the Ellesmere Canal belonging to the Shropshire Union was provided at Rednal early in 1850, but the Canal Company's basin was not ready, and in view of the hostilities which had then begun it is not likely that much, if any, use was made of it for some years.

The stock with which the Company began work is stated in the Directors' Report of February 1849 as 21 engines, 16 first-class, 27 second-class, 16 third-class, and 4 'stand up' carriages, 6 luggage vans, 11 horse boxes, 10 carriage trucks, and 914 waggons.

For the first twelve months the life of the Shrewsbury & Chester Railway as a local branch from Chester was peaceful and uninteresting, and its relations with its neighbours, the London & North Western and Birkenhead Companies, friendly; but no sooner had it become part of a through line from Wolverhampton by the opening of the Shrewsbury & Birmingham than all this was changed and bitter warfare ensued, to last until both the Shrewsbury Railways had become part of the Great Western.

## The Shrewsbury & Birmingham Railway

In 1844 a railway from Birmingham through Dudley and Wolverhampton to Shrewsbury was projected by local people and warmly supported by the London & Birmingham Company, who went so far as to enter into a provisional agreement with the promoters to lease the line on a guarantee of $4\frac{1}{2}\%$ and half surplus profits, and at the same time urged its extension to Chester. This was a move in their warfare with the Grand Junction Company, the intention being ultimately to form a competing line for the South Staffordshire and some, at any rate, of the Liverpool traffic. The Grand Junction on their part, besides supporting lines southward to meet the Great Western as we have already seen, got up a rival project between Wolverhampton and Shrewsbury, and also proposed a branch from their main line at Stafford to join it. The former eventually became the Shrewsbury & Birmingham Railway, the latter the Shrewsbury, Wolverhampton & South Staffordshire Junction Railway. The 'Five Kings' having reported in favour of the London & Birmingham schemes and against those of the Grand Junction, both came before Parliament in the 1845 Session, but only to be thrown out, the Shrewsbury & Birmingham on Standing Orders.

Soon afterwards all the circumstances were completely altered by the agreement of the two chief combatants to amalgamate to form the London & North Western Railway Company. Upon this, the London & Birmingham repudiated its agreement to lease the Shrewsbury & Birmingham, and both withdrew their support from the rival Shrewsbury projects; they did not, however, oppose them save by continuing the promotion of the line from Stafford.

Left thus to their own resources, the Shrewsbury & Birmingham promoters agreed to a suggestion that they should leave the expensive

# SHREWSBURY AND CHESTER RAILWAY.

## TIME AND FARE TABLE, on and after 28th NOVEMBER, 1846.

Notice. *The time of arrival stated below, denotes when the Trains may be expected; but Passengers, to ensure being booked, should be at the principal Stations Five Minutes, and at the Road Stations Ten Minutes earlier, as the door of the Booking Office will be closed at the time fixed for the departure of the Trains.*

### Down Trains from Ruabon.

| Dist. from Ruabon | BIRKENHEAD, LIVERPOOL, MANCHESTER, BIRMINGHAM AND LONDON. | I. 1, 2, & 3 Class. | II. 1 & 2 Class. | III. 1 & 2 Class. | IV. 1 & 2 Class. | V. 1, 2, & 3 Class. | Sunday Trains I. 1, 2, & 3 Class. | II. 1, 2, & 3 Class. | Fares from Ruabon First Class. | Second Class. | P. Third Class. | Day Tickets First Class. | Second Class. |
|---|---|---|---|---|---|---|---|---|---|---|---|---|---|
| Mls. | RUABON ........... *Arrive* | H. M. | H. M. | H. M. | H. M. | H. M. | H. M. | H. M. | S. D. | S. D. | S. D. | S. D. | S. D. |
| 6 | WREXHAM ........... | 7 40 | 9 15 | 12 40 | ... 15 | 6 10 | 8 40 | 4 40 | 1 0 | 0 9 | 0 5 | ... | ... |
| 8 | GRESFORD ........... | 7 53 | | 12 53 | | 6 22 | 8 52 | 4 52 | 1 6 | 1 2 | 0 8 | ... | ... |
| 9 | ROSSETT ........... | 7 58 | 10 0 | 12 58 | | 6 23 | 8 56 | 4 56 | 1 10 | 1 4 | 0 9 | ... | ... |
| 11 | PULFORD & DODLESTON | 6 3 | | 1 | | 6 33 | 9 0 | 5 0 | 2 3 | 1 7 | 0 11 | ... | ... |
| 14 | SALTNEY ........... | 8 14 | 10 15 | 1 | 41 | 6 45 | 9 20 | 5 20 | 2 6 | 1 8 | ... | 4 6 | 3 9 |
| 17 | CHESTER ........... | 8 25 | 10 25 | 1 25 | 1 50 | 7 9 | 9 30 | | 3 6 | 2 10 | 1 8 | ... | ... |
| 20 | Mollington | 8 39 | | | | 7 21 | 9 51 | 5 51 | 4 2 | 3 5 | 2 0 | ... | ... |
| 24 | SUTTON | 8 51 | 10 51 | 1 54 | 21 | 7 24 | 9 54 | 5 54 | 4 6 | 3 6 | 2 1 | ... | ... |
| 25 | Hooton | | | 1 57 | | 7 27 | 9 57 | | 4 6 | 3 7 | 2 2 | ... | ... |
| 26 | Bromborough | | | 2 0 | | 7 33 | 10 3 | | 4 10 | 3 11 | 2 4 | ... | ... |
| 28 | Spital | | | 2 6 | 30 | 7 36 | 10 6 | 6 0 | 5 0 | 4 0 | 2 5 | ... | ... |
| 30 | Bebington | | | 2 9 | | 7 39 | 10 9 | | 5 2 | 4 2 | 2 6 | ... | ... |
| 30½ | Rock Lane | | | 2 13 | | 7 41 | 10 11 | | 5 4 | 4 3 | 2 7 | ... | ... |
| 32 | Lime Kiln Lane | | | 2 15 | 40 | 7 43 | 10 13 | 6 13 | 5 4 | 4 6 | 2 8 | 8 6 | 6 9 |
| | BIRKENHEAD | 9 10 | 11 15 | 2 30 | 5 55 | 8 0 | 10 30 | 6 25 | 5 8 | 4 8 | 2 10 | | |
| 69 | LIVERPOOL | 9 25 | 11 30 | | 6 0 | | | | 11 6 | 8 6 | 5 9 | | |
| | | | | P. M. | | | | | | | | | |
| 72 | MANCHESTER | | 1 16 | | | 7 35 | | 12 26 | 16 0 | 13 0 | 7 3 | | |
| | BIRMINGHAM | 1 15 | 3 20 | | | | | | | | | | |
| | | P. M. | P. M. | | | | | | | | | | |
| 205 | LONDON | 6 0 | 8 45 | | | | | 5 18 | 36 0 | 27 0 | 17 1 | | |

The Express Train for London leaves Chester, at 5. 10. p.m.; Birmingham, at 7. 35. p.m.; and arrives at London, at 11. 0. p.m.

### Up Trains from Chester.

| Dist. from Chester | LONDON, BIRMINGHAM, MANCHESTER, LIVERPOOL, AND BIRKENHEAD. | I. 1 & 2 Class. | II. 1 & 2 Class. | III. 1 & 2 Class. | IV. 1 & 2 Class. | V. 1, 2, & 3 Class. | Sunday Trains I. 1, 2, & 3 Class. | II. 1, 2, & 3 Class. | Fares from Chester First Class. | Second Class. | P. Third Class. | Day Tickets First Class. | Second Class. |
|---|---|---|---|---|---|---|---|---|---|---|---|---|---|
| Mls. | | H. M. | H. M. | H. M. | H. M. | H. M. | H. M. | H. M. | S. D. | S. D. | S. D. | S. D. | S. D. |
| 188 | LONDON ........... *Leave* | 8 45 | | 6 15 | | 11 0 | 8 45 | 10 0 | 33 6 | 24 6 | 15 8 | | |
| 75 | BIRMINGHAM | | | | | | | | | | | | |
| | | | | | | | H. M. | H. M. | | | | | |
| 52 | MANCHESTER | | 7 0 | 11 30 | | | 7 5 | | 9 6 | 6 6 | 4 0 | | |
| | LIVERPOOL | 8 30 | 10 30 | 1 30 | P.M. | | 6 30 | 5 30 | 9 0 | 6 6 | 3 9 | | |
| 15 | BIRKENHEAD | 8 45 | 10 45 | 1 45 | 4 15 | 7 15 | 8 15 | 5 45 | 2 6 | 2 0 | 1 3 | 4 6 | 3 2 |
| 15½ | Lime Kiln Lane | | | 1 50 | | 7 20 | 8 20 | 5 50 | 2 4 | 1 11 | 1 1 | | |
| 13½ | Rock Lane | | | 1 52 | | 7 22 | 8 22 | 5 52 | 2 2 | 1 9 | 1 1 | | |
| 13 | Bebington | | | 1 56 | | 7 26 | 8 26 | 5 56 | 2 0 | 1 8 | 1 0 | | |
| 11 | Spital | | | 2 0 | | 7 30 | 8 30 | 6 0 | 1 10 | 1 5 | 0 11 | | |
| 9 | Bromborough | | | 2 5 | | 7 36 | 8 38 | 6 4 | 1 7 | 1 1 | 0 9 | | |
| 8 | Hooton | | | 2 7 | | 7 38 | 8 42 | 6 6 | 1 6 | 1 0 | 0 8 | | |
| 5 | SUTTON | 8 11 | 11 10 | 2 12 | 4 33 | 7 42 | 8 48 | 6 12 | 1 2 | 0 11 | 0 7 | | |
| 3 | Mollington | 8 17 | | 2 23 | | 7 48 | 8 53 | 6 23 | 0 8 | 0 6 | 0 4 | | |
| | CHESTER ........ *Arrive at* | 8 42 | 11 40 | 2 45 | 5 15 | 8 15 | 9 30 | 6 40 | | | | | |
| 3 | SALTNEY | 8 48 | 11 48 | 2 53 | 5 20 | 8 23 | 9 38 | 6 48 | 0 6 | 0 4 | 0 3 | | |
| 6 | PULFORD & DODLESTON | 8 53 | | 3 1 | | 8 31 | 9 49 | | 1 2 | 0 10 | 0 6 | | |
| 8 | ROSSETT | 10 11 | 1 3 | 3 9 | 5 39 | 8 40 | 10 7 | 7 11 | 1 10 | 1 2 | 0 8 | | |
| 9 | GRESFORD | 10 15 | | 3 16 | | 8 45 | 10 11 | | 2 0 | 1 5 | 0 9 | | |
| 12 | WREXHAM | 10 27 | 1 27 | 3 22 | 5 48 | 9 0 | 10 27 | 7 27 | 2 6 | 1 8 | 1 0 | 5 0 | 3 9 |
| 17 | RUABON | 10 40 | 1 35 | 3 45 | 6 0 | 9 15 | 10 40 | 7 40 | 3 0 | 2 0 | 1 3 | | |

DAY TICKETS not transferable, and to return the same day by any Train, will be issued at Chester, Wrexham and Ruabon. Children under Ten years of age are charged half-price,—in arms, free.

SEASON TICKETS (not transferable) to pass between any of the Stations on the Line, will be granted at the following rates, viz:—

| | 12 Months. | 6 Months. | 3 Months. |
|---|---|---|---|
| First Class | 20s. per mile. | 12s. per mile. | 8s. per mile. |
| Second Class | 15s. per mile. | 9s. per mile. | 6s. per mile. |

Any fractional part of a mile will be charged the same as a whole mile, and parties under Fourteen Years of Age, one-half the above rates.

N.B.—The charge for conveyance between Monk's Ferry and Liverpool, is 2d. each way, or 2½s. for 12 months...17s. 6d. for 6 Months... 12s. 6d. for 3 Months.

Parcels under 15lbs. are charged 6d....6dlbs. 9d....and 112lbs. 1s....and above that weight, 1d. per lb. additional.

### COACHES IN CONNEXION WITH TRAINS.

| COACHES TO AND FROM | MEETING TRAINS UP DOWN | | AT |
|---|---|---|---|
| Overton, Ellesmere, Shrewsbury, Ludlow, Leominster, and Hereford | Nos. 1 | Nos. 5 | Ruabon. |
| Chirk, Oswestry, Llanymynech, Welshpool, Newtown, & Aberystwith | 2 | 3 | Do. |
| Chirk and Oswestry | 4 | 2 | Do. |
| Llangollen | 2 | | Do. |
| Barmouth Mail, Dolgelle, Bala, Corwen, Druid, and Llangollen | | 5 | Do. |
| Mold, Holywell, St. Asaph, Abergele, Conway, Bangor, Carnarvon, and Holyhead Mail | | | Chester. |
| Mold, Ruthin, Denbigh, &c. | 2, 4 | 2, 4 | Saltney. |

A supply of Carriage Trucks and Horse Boxes are kept at the principal Stations, but to prevent disappointment, previous Notice should be given, and it is required that Horses and Carriages be at the Station half an hour before the time of Departure. The Company will not hold themselves responsible for Luggage, unless booked and paid for according to its value; and Passengers are recommended, in all cases, to have their name and destination distinctly marked thereon. 100lbs weight of Luggage is allowed to each First and Second Class Passenger, and 56lbs. to each Third Class Passenger, and all above that weight will be charged at the rate of ½d. per lb.

*** Parcels received and delivered at Messrs. W. & G. Smith's, Mail Office, opposite the Royal Hotel, Eastgate Street, Chester.

Smoking is not allowed in the Carriages or at the Stations.

THE SERVANTS OF THE COMPANY ARE STRICTLY PROHIBITED FROM DEMANDING OR RECEIVING GRATUITIES.

By Order,

ROBERT ROY, Secretary.

PRINTED BY T. THOMAS, EASTGATE ROW, CHESTER.

Shrewsbury and Chester Railway Timetable, 1846

Wrexham Station, about 1870

Chirk Viaduct, Shrewsbury & Chester Railway

Birmingham–Wolverhampton portion of their proposed line to a separate company promoted jointly by themselves, the London & North Western, and the Birmingham Canal Company, each of whom was to subscribe a quarter of the capital, the remaining quarter being raised by public subscription. This was entitled the Birmingham, Wolverhampton & Stour Valley Railway, and commonly known as the Stour Valley. Though it retained its former title, the Shrewsbury & Birmingham undertaking was thus cut down to a railway from Shrewsbury to Wolverhampton only.

Bills for the Shrewsbury & Birmingham, Shrewsbury, Wolverhampton & South Staffordshire, Stour Valley, and Shropshire Union line from Stafford to Shrewsbury all came before Parliament in 1846, and all were passed. The first two provided for the amalgamation of the rival projects under the title of the Shrewsbury & Birmingham, which had been arranged at the last moment.

The Shrewsbury & Birmingham Company's Act authorized a railway 'from the Parish of St Mary in the town of Shrewsbury with a double terminus in the Parish of Holy Cross and St Giles, Shrewsbury, to New Mill Street in the Parish of Wolverhampton', with a branch from Shifnal through Madeley to the ironworks at Dawley. Of the whole 29½ miles, 10 between Shrewsbury and Wellington were to be the joint property of the Shrewsbury & Birmingham and Shropshire Union Companies, constructed at joint expense and managed by a committee of six Directors, three from each Company.

The final laying out and construction of the line was then taken in hand by the Company's Engineer, William Baker, one of Robert Stephenson's disciples, who was also Engineer for the Shropshire Union. It is interesting to find that as early as September 1846 the Shrewsbury & Birmingham Directors considered the advisability of making the bridges and tunnels wide enough to take the Broad Gauge, and directed him to report on the extra expense involved. Six months later they ordered the tunnel near Oakengates, the only one on the line, to be made 28 feet wide for that purpose, the ordinary width for two narrow-gauge lines being 24 feet. At this time the only authorized broad-gauge railway anywhere near was the Oxford, Worcester & Wolverhampton, but it was no doubt anticipated that that gauge would eventually be sanctioned on the new Birmingham, Wolverhampton & Dudley, as had been intended by its promoters, and traffic from both of these was expected.

In the autumn of 1846 the London & North Western Company took two steps which were destined to have an important effect on the destinies of the Shrewsbury & Birmingham, by arranging to lease the Shropshire Union and the Stour Valley Railways from the two owning Companies. The Shropshire Union Railways & Canal Company, to give it its full title, had been formed by an amalgamation of the Ellesmere & Chester Canal, Shrewsbury Canal, and Montgomeryshire Canal Companies, and authorized in the mad session of 1846 to make railways from Calveley, on the Chester & Crewe Branch of the North Western, to Wolverhampton; from

Shrewsbury to Stafford; and from Crewe to Newtown in Montgomery-shire; in all 155 miles, mostly to be formed by the conversion of the existing canals. It is hardly necessary to say that of all this extensive system only the Shrewsbury–Stafford line was ever made. To enable them to take the lease of this undertaking, the North Western Company promoted a Bill in the 1847 Session. This the Shrewsbury & Birmingham opposed, rightly scenting trouble from this competing line to Shrewsbury in the hands of that great Company. They were eventually induced to withdraw their opposition by an Agreement, put into formal shape and sealed by the three Companies in the following October, that all traffic between Shrewsbury and other stations on the joint line to Wellington and stations south of Rugby should be pooled and divided in certain proportions, and that the North Western should not convey any traffic between the same joint line stations and Wolverhampton or any station on the Stour Valley Line, or use the Stafford line to compete for traffic properly belonging to the Shrewsbury & Birmingham. The latter Company being content with this Agreement, the Bill was allowed to pass and in due course became an Act.

In the same Session the North Western Company sought powers to lease the Stour Valley Railway, in which by reason of their acquisition of the Birmingham Canal they now held half the capital and hence a controlling interest, and duly obtained them, subject to a clause in the Act giving full running powers over the line to the Shrewsbury & Birmingham. The possibility of the latter's union with the Great Western was evidently contemplated as early as this, 1847, though no move in that direction had yet been made, for the Act provides that these running powers should cease in case the Shrewsbury & Birmingham should be leased to or purchased by or amalgamated with the Great Western, Oxford, Worcester & Wolverhampton, Birmingham & Oxford, or Birmingham, Wolverhampton & Dudley Companies.

About this same time, July 1847, an Agreement was made between the North Western and the Shrewsbury & Birmingham that the station at Wolverhampton and the line between it and the point where the Stour Valley Railway to Bushbury diverged from the Shrewsbury line, which both Companies had powers to make, should be the joint property of the two Companies to be managed by a committee of three Directors of each. This arrangement was confirmed and elaborated by a clause in the Shrewsbury & Birmingham Act of 1849.

Of the two new railways to Shrewsbury, the Shropshire Union from Stafford was ready first. It was opened, together of course with the joint line between Wellington and Shrewsbury, on 1st June 1849. At this time Oakengates Tunnel was not quite finished, so the Shrewsbury & Birmingham were only able to open their own line as far as Oakengates Station, some $2\frac{1}{2}$ miles beyond the Wellington Junction. The rest of the line was opened throughout to a temporary station on the joint property at Wolverhampton (High Level) on Monday, 12th November following.

There were no engineering works of special interest on this railway; the Oakengates Tunnel is only 471 yards long.

From the day of its opening till it became part of the Great Western five years later, the life of the Shrewsbury & Birmingham Railway was one long and bitter fight with the London & North Western. In this fight the Shrewsbury & Chester was its close ally, and the fortunes of the two Companies were so inextricably interwoven that they are best related together, in one story.

### THE FIGHTING SHREWSBURYS

Long before the opening of the Shrewsbury & Birmingham line, that Company and the Shrewsbury & Chester had built hopes on carrying some of the traffic between Birmingham and the Black Country and Chester, Birkenhead, and Liverpool, hitherto monopolized first by the Grand Junction and then by the London & North Western. Indeed, this had been the intention of the London & Birmingham when in its war with the Grand Junction it had supported the Shrewsbury and Birmingham scheme and urged its extension by a direct line to Chester. The two Shrewsbury Companies therefore arranged to work such traffic through and divide the proceeds according to mileage. Not content with this, they rashly decided to induce passengers to use their line by charging less than normal fares. Needless to say this was a direct challenge to the North Western, and was quickly taken up as such. On 16th October 1849 Captain Huish wrote to Mr Roy, Secretary of the Shrewsbury & Chester, the following politely menacing letter:

DEAR SIR,
It is stated by the Shrewsbury & Birmingham Company that you are about to join them in opposing us, at low rates, between Birkenhead and Wolverhampton, and thence by coach to Birmingham for passengers, and by canal for goods; will you tell me candidly whether this is the case. I trust not, and that your Company and ours may avoid the competition which has brought so much loss on other parties. I need not say that if you should be unwise enough to encourage such a proceeding, it must result in a general fight both by our Railway from Shrewsbury to Liverpool and by our Shropshire Canal, the only gainers being of course the public and the Shrewsbury & Birmingham Company. Let me hope, however, that there is no truth in the statements; or, if there is, that you will reconsider your measures.
Yours truly,
MARK HUISH.

Nothing daunted by this, Mr Roy replied at once in an airy, not to say chatty, letter, the material parts of which are as follows:

This Company have always looked for a share of the through traffic on the opening of the lines to the south of Shrewsbury; the small difference in the length of the two lines making it a matter of course. It is a part, we think, of our legitimate traffic. It is intended to carry through passengers only, first, second, and third class, at reduced rates with each of our regular trains; the extent of the reduction will depend on the arrangements of your Company. For the present we look to 30 or 40 per cent, and you will be aware that as the addition of a few through carriages to our local trains occasions scarcely any expense, a much greater reduction would leave a handsome profit.
As to goods, you will learn from Mr Skey[1] that you are misinformed, this Company being prepared either to continue or give up the amicable arrangements with your

[1] Manager of the Shropshire Union.

Shropshire Union ally, which since the first opening of the line have been carried on. Indeed, our explicit refusal to break off these arrangements with them was assigned by the Birkenhead Company as the leading reason for declining to accept a mileage proportion of the through traffic instead of their ordinary fares, a matter of too small amount on their short length to affect so large a question in one way or other, although it and other considerations may deprive them permanently of our goods traffic, and place it on the Shropshire Union Canal into Liverpool; or, according to circumstances, by the Dee and steamers, as the Runcorn trade is conducted.

But although perfectly prepared to compete with you or them for whatever traffic we are entitled to, our Directors are equally prepared to arrange the whole questions that may arise, or any part of them separately by itself, on proper and reasonable terms.

I have thought it right to give you this explicit intimation of our views and position, and our disposition to arrange, in consequence of the terms of your letter, written, I have no doubt, in the hurry of business, in order that you may be perfectly aware that if a 'general fight', as you express it, arise, it is not of our seeking, nor from any unreasonable views on the part of this Company.

Such a letter as this to the redoubtable General Manager of the North Western meant nothing but war. The Shrewsbury Companies were, of course, absolutely within their rights in joining to compete for the through traffic, but to do so by cutting fares against the richest Company in England was, to put it mildly, questionable policy. In those days rate cutting was a by no means unusual form of competition. It was never approved of or willingly adopted by Saunders, but with Captain Huish, on the other hand, it was a frequent weapon, and in the war with the Shrewsburys only one of many at his command.

Chester Station was the scene of the first battle. There the Joint Committee, on which the North Western with its subject the Chester & Holyhead, and its terrorised ally, the Birkenhead, had a large majority, refused to allow passengers to be booked to Wolverhampton or beyond via Shrewsbury, and, on the Shrewsbury Company persisting, had their booking clerk dragged out of the office and his tickets thrown after him. The Birkenhead Company having declined to convey third-class passengers by more than two trains, one very early in the morning the other late at night, the Shrewsbury & Chester established a service of omnibuses to and from Birkenhead. These were excluded from the station by barricades of wood and chains across the approaches. Their time bills and notices also were torn down. All this in a station of which the Shrewsbury Company were part owners was, of course, quite illegal, and they had no difficulty in speedily obtaining an injunction to stop it, which was confirmed on appeal by the Lord Chancellor on 12th December.

Apart from this, relations with the Birkenhead Railway remained for the time comparatively peaceful, though that Company declined to join in any competition against the North Western, of whom they stood in great awe. A considerable quantity of goods traffic was exchanged between them and the Shrewsbury line at Chester, and this had not as yet been much affected by the war. In April 1850, however, their Chairman, James Bancroft, who gloried in the title of Alderman Bancroft, was frightened into making an agreement with Captain Huish to withdraw all facilities from the Shrewsbury Companies, except such as they could by law demand, in consideration of the London & North Western guaranteeing to the Birkenhead weekly receipts equal to those of the preceding year.

This agreement was acted on by a letter sent to the Shrewsbury & Chester late on Saturday, 4th May, refusing to continue through booking, forwarding their trucks for cattle, or interchanging carriages; so from the following Monday the passengers had to turn out at Chester to rebook, and the cattle trucks, which had been sent to Birkenhead in the usual course, were all returned empty, the cattle being loaded into North Western trucks and sent by that line. This effectually stopped the cattle traffic, of which the Shrewsbury had been carrying about forty trucks every Monday.

The latter Company then chartered a steamer to work flat-bottomed boats on the Dee to and from Saltney, and began to send their goods traffic that way, whereupon Captain Huish, his local Goods Manager, and the Traffic Manager of the Birkenhead met and concerted plans for attacking all their goods traffic by canal and road competition. The North Western were of course already doing all they could by means of their Shropshire Union Canal and their railway from Stafford, and were even running coaches and waggons from Chester to Wrexham and Oswestry. Now all goods from the Birkenhead Railway were to sent to Shrewsbury and Wellington by Stafford, to Wrexham by waggons, and to Ruabon, Ellesmere, and Oswestry by the Canal from Chester. All loss entailed by these proceedings was to be borne by the London & North Western. This plan of campaign was forthwith carried out, and continued in force for nearly six months, till 23rd October, 1850, when it was abandoned by the Birkenhead Company, whose Chairman had found considerable difficulty in defending it to his own shareholders at their Half-yearly Meeting. That the Birkenhead Company was fighting against its own interests was shown by the fact that the tonnage of goods received from the Shrewsbury & Chester during the half year to June 1850, was 38,795 as against 2,245 received from the North Western. The timid Alderman was also frightened by the proposal of the Shrewsbury Company to apply to Parliament for running powers over his railway. A sort of truce was therefore patched up and the worst obstructions withdrawn, the Shrewsbury at the same time discontinuing its boats on the Dee and the omnibuses to Birkenhead. They were, however, by no means satisfied with the position, and proceeded with their Bill for running powers.

While all this was happening in the Chester District, the North Western were by no means idle at the Wolverhampton end of the two Companies' line. In complete disregard of their Agreement of 1847, whereby they had got rid of the Shrewsbury & Birmingham's opposition in Parliament to their Bill for power to lease the Shropshire Union, they started a fierce competition at low fares and rates between Wolverhampton and Shrewsbury over that line round by Stafford, a distance of 46 miles against 29½ by the Shrewsbury & Birmingham. The loss of a few thousand pounds of course mattered little to Captain Huish as long as he could crush the insolent little Companies, who had dared to challenge him at his own game of rate cutting. He already had a reputation for finding pretexts to avoid agreements which had become inconvenient. On this occasion his pretext was that his Company had no legal power to make the Agreement of 1847, and that therefore, though they had received the consideration for it, they were entitled afterwards to dishonour their own signature, or rather seal. The Shrewsbury & Birmingham of course went to law and obtained an injunction to stop the competition from Lord Chancellor Cottenham; this was afterwards revoked by his successor, Lord Truro, subject to the condition that the North Western should keep an account of the traffic and that the validity of the Agreement should be tried by a common law action. This delayed matters till the end of 1851, when the Queen's Bench decided in favour of the plaintiffs, but on their then applying to Chancery for a new injunction, it was refused on another technical plea that the lease of the Shropshire Union to the North Western had never been completed and that therefore the Agreement had not come into operation. This was appealed against, but the Lords Justices eventually dismissed the appeal, without costs, however, at the end of June 1853, and the case does not appear to have been carried further.

All this time, save for an interval in 1850 while the injunction was in force, passengers were carried between Wolverhampton and Shrewsbury at ridiculous fares, eventually fixed at—first-class 1s, second 9d, and third 6d. Between Wellington and Shrewsbury, over the joint line, the fares were respectively 6d, 3d, and 1d for the 10¼ miles.

At first the Shrewsbury & Birmingham were unable to deal with goods traffic for places south of Wolverhampton owing to lack of communication with the Birmingham Canal, though this adjoined the last ½ mile of their line, which was joint property with the Stour Valley. In April 1850 they attempted to lay a siding for this purpose, whereupon their men were forcibly prevented by their late Engineer, William Baker, who had been succeeded by Henry Robertson of the Shrewsbury & Chester immediately after the opening of the line and beginning of the quarrel with the North Western, on the plea that the plan had not been sanctioned by the Joint Committee. This Committee met on 7th May and referred the plan to their two Engineers, Messrs Robertson and Baker, who settled it in time for the June meeting. No representative of the Stour Valley appearing at this, no business could, according to the Committee's by-laws, be done, but the plan having been signed by Mr Baker, the Stour Valley Engineer, the Shrewsbury Company proceeded to make the siding. A large force of London & North Western navvies, under the command of Mr Baker, thenceforth known in the district as 'General' Baker, and accompanied in the rear by the North Western lawyer, were then marched on to the ground to stop the work, and only the prompt calling out of the police and military prevented a free fight.

As at Chester, an injunction from the Court of Chancery soon put a stop to this illegal violence, and under its protection the Shrewsbury & Birmingham made the siding, and later, on their own land adjoining, the Victoria Basin with its wharves and sidings.

In July Mr Ormsby Gore, Chairman of the Shrewsbury & Birmingham and also of the Joint Committee of the two Companies formed to manage the through traffic, wrote to Mr Glyn, the North Western Chairman, deprecating the ruinous competition and suggesting that the traffic should be pooled and the share to which his Committee were entitled, as well as all other matters in dispute, referred to arbitration. This was peremptorily rejected by the North Western Board, who insisted on equal fares to all competing points. The Birmingham Company were disposed to agree to these terms, which seem to us eminently reasonable, but the Chester would not, chiefly on the ground that the handicap of crossing the Mersey by ferry boats would deprive them of any Liverpool passengers unless the inducement of cheaper fares was offered. For goods traffic the Shrewsbury Companies always had charged equal rates; in this case the North Western had been the first to reduce them at all competitive places.

All this time the London & North Western, as lessee from the Stour Valley Company, in which the Shrewsbury & Birmingham held a quarter of the capital, was going very slow in the construction of that railway, which would admit the latter's trains to Birmingham. The North Western had the old Grand Junction line to Wolverhampton, or rather to a station so called more than a mile from the town;[1] hence they had no need to hurry, and the convenience of the public was a very secondary consideration compared with keeping their wretched little rival out of Birmingham. The Stour Valley Representatives also stayed away from the Joint Committee from May 1850 till the end of August 1851, thereby preventing any progress being made with the station at Wolverhampton.

Having suffered all this opposition and obstruction for more than a year, and feeling the ruinous results of the unequal warfare and the hopelessness of arranging satisfactory terms with the enemy, the two little Shrewsbury Companies naturally looked for some ally who would have a common interest with them in developing traffic on their railways, and it is not surprising that they turned to the Great Western as the only Company able to help them and to face their oppressor on equal terms. Moreover, the Great Western was already by means of the Birmingham, Wolverhampton & Dudley Railway potentially at Wolverhampton, and the Shrewsbury & Birmingham were partners with them and the Oxford, Worcester & Wolverhampton in the proposed Low Level Station there under an Act of 1848.

To Paddington therefore went Mr Roy of the Chester and Mr Knox of the Birmingham, and there Saunders, having first satisfied himself that the two Companies were free to make arrangements with him, after several interviews settled a traffic agreement with them, which was adopted by

[1] It was aptly renamed 'Wednesfield Heath' in 1852.

the three Boards and sealed on 10th January 1851. This provided for the mutual interchange of all traffic for each other's districts, the division of net receipts according to mileage, and the appointment of a joint committee to manage the through traffic, composed of four Directors of the Great Western and two of each of the Shrewsbury Companies, with an umpire to decide cases of difference. Until continuous communication was established goods were to be forwarded over the interval by canal. At this time, as we know, the Great Western was actually open only as far as Banbury.

This alliance with his great rival naturally enraged Captain Huish, and made the strife with the Shrewsburys still more bitter. He now, again too late, began the tactics which had so signally failed in the case of the Birmingham & Oxford Company. First the Shrewsbury & Birmingham Company was attacked; shares were bought and divided among the denizens of the Euston Square and Camden Town districts, who had not long before figured as Birmingham & Oxford proprietors, circulars and proxy papers printed and broadcast, and much money spent in canvassing to strengthen the oposition to the Directors, which already existed. The fun began at the Half-yearly Meeting held at the Swan Hotel, Wolverhampton, on 12th February 1851, at which a Committee of Investigation was agreed to by the Board and proceedings adjourned for a month to await its report. This was duly forthcoming at a crowded gathering in the Wolverhampton Assembly Rooms on 12th March. After misrepresenting and censuring all the work of the Board, the Committee stated that they had reopened negotiations with the London & North Western and made a 'preliminary arrangement' with that Company, which they produced. By this the Shrewsbury & Birmingham were to cease being carriers and hand over their line with all its rolling-stock to be worked by the North Western for twenty-one years, and abandon all legal proceedings against that Company, who in consideration of this were to pay them, *out of the traffic receipts of the Shrewsbury & Birmingham line*, dividends beginning at 3 and rising after four years to 4%. The meeting was eventually adjourned for another month to enable the Proprietors to consider this and any reply the Directors might make. In the interval the Board issued a circular demonstrating the illegality of the proposed agreement without an Act of Parliament to authorize it, which there was not the remotest chance of their getting; and the fact that it guaranteed them nothing more than they had already in their own traffic, in view of the obvious absurdity of expecting a Company with a line of its own to their principal towns to rob itself by transferring traffic to theirs; and also defending the traffic agreement with the Great Western as their natural ally, who would have an interest in putting traffic on their line.

A special meeting demanded by the opposition to consider the North Western Agreement began on 4th April and lasted four days. The general uproar and confusion were terrific. Chairman, Directors, and Officers were unmercifully abused, especially Knox, the Secretary, who was an object of special hatred to the North Western party, he having taken a leaf out of their book by arranging the splitting of stock among the Company's staff, his own children, and friends. Mr Ormsby Gore, who was supported by a Q.C. engaged to advise him on points of law, preserved an impeturbable calm throughout, and allowed both sides to talk and abuse each other to their hearts' content. Every now and then someone proposed a resolution for adjournment or what not, and each time a poll was demanded by the other side, the proceedings being suspended while it took place. On the evening of the third day—

> The poll was proceeding and Mr Gore was about to leave the Chair, but Mr Scott rose and prevented him. He said—It is time a stop is put to this sort of thing. I object to your leaving the Chair; let the poll be taken in an adjoining room; we will remain here till the work is done.
> The business was entirely suspended. Mr Gore had however no alternative but to keep his seat. He quietly resigned himself to his fate. After sitting a couple of hours (most of the shareholders having gone away for refreshments) the honourable gentleman was relieved for a brief period by Mr Clive, the Deputy Chairman. At seven o'clock the Meeting was in a state of the wildest uproar, and loudly protested against any adjournment, upon which Mr Gore quietly sat down and began reading a volume of *Household Words*. At nine, Mr Gore brought from his pocket a white night-cap, which he drew over his head, and sank apparently into a peaceful slumber, upon which the meeting was convulsed with laughter and appeared for the time restored to good humour.
> The scrutineers shortly afterwards returned to the room, and said there was no probability of their being ready with the poll that evening, and a motion for adjournment till the morrow was submitted. The Chairman was awakened and asked to put it, which he did in drowsy tones and declared it carried.[1]

Next day the resolution accepting the North Western terms and handing over the railway to them was put to the meeting, after the Chairman had read Counsel's opinion that such an agreement would be totally illegal and void. It was carried with immense applause, and Mr Gore declared the special meeting over; notwithstanding which, the triumphant opposition proposed, put, and carried an adjournment thereof to the scene of their former Birmingham & Oxford fights—Dee's Royal Hotel, Birmingham, on 7th May.

The adjourned Half-yearly Meeting was then proceeded with, the Directors' Report rejected, and a batch of new opposition 'Directors'— quite illegally—appointed.

In the course of the following month the Great Western Company made an offer to the two Shrewsburys, which took the wind out of the sails of the opposition, and caused such genuine shareholders as had been misled by their assertions to reconsider their attitude. This was for a future amalgamation of all three in 1856 or 1857 at the choice of the small Companies on the basis of their net revenues in the preceding year, and in the meantime a guarantee out of the whole revenue from the London through traffic to places beyond Birmingham of a dividend beginning from January 1852 at 3% and rising to 4% in 1855. They also undertook, as the North Western had not, to obtain an Act of Parliament to sanction

---

[1] *Railway Times*, 12th April 1851.

the arrangement. This offer was accepted by the Shrewsbury & Birmingham Directors, and a Special Meeting of the Company called for 8th May to consider it.

At the opposition Meeting at Dee's Hotel on 7th May, Mr Gore having looked in for a moment to tell them it was not a legal meeting, the Chair was taken by Mr Geach, M.P., a Director of the Company at variance with his colleagues, and the North Western party had things all their own way. As in the case of the Birmingham & Oxford four years before, a forgery of the Company's seal was produced and the Agreement with the North Western solemnly sealed therewith 'amidst boisterous cheers'.

Next day the Special Meeting called by the Directors was held at Wolverhampton, at which, after the defeat of a motion for adjournment till July, the opposition leaders having entered a protest against the proceedings withdrew, and the Agreement for amalgamation with the Great Western and Shrewsbury & Chester was approved, and forthwith sealed with the genuine seal of the Shrewsbury & Birmingham Railway Company. The resolution passed in February appointing the Committee of Investigation was at the same time rescinded and their powers annulled.

The London & North Western made no serious use of the forged-seal Agreement with them, which Captain Huish and his astute advisers well knew was not worth the paper it was written on. They did indeed go so far as to file a Bill in Chancery to enforce it, but after various dilatory proceedings this was dropped. At one time in July 1851 a rumour that they intended to run a train from Wellington to Wolverhampton with the object of taking forcible possession caused the Shrewsbury & Birmingham authorities to station a strong force of platelayers at the junction, who removed two rails from the Wolverhampton line, only replacing them temporarily on the approach of a Shrewsbury & Birmingham train. However, no such attempt was made, if it had ever really been intended. The former hostilities by obstruction and competition of course continued unabated.

Having failed to break the middle link in the prospective rival chain of communication between London and the Mersey, Captain Huish now concentrated his efforts on the northern portion. The special meeting of the Shrewsbury & Chester Company to confirm the Amalgamation Agreement, which the Directors had already entered into, was appointed for 12th June, so a lively opposition was got up by the usual methods. A special train brought the famous Euston Troupe, 140 strong, to Chester, but the cunning Mr Roy, who was now a Director, had prepared for them by endowing a rival band of Shrewsbury & Chester employés with a share or two apiece, so their performance was not as brilliant as usual. After much noisy recrimination, the Meeting was adjourned for a month, and the interval devoted to a war of circulars and rival canvassing. So desperate had Captain Huish now become that an offer of a guaranteed dividend of $4\frac{1}{2}\%$ was actually held out to the Company, with which a few months before the North Western would have nothing but war. His most promising pupil, Edward Watkin, was put in charge of the campaign, and organized meetings to stir up trouble in London, Manchester, Edinburgh, and even as far away as Inverness. It seems that a good deal of Shrewsbury & Chester capital was held in Scotland, doubtless due to Henry Robertson's interests there. Watkin met with some success at the first two places, but at Edinburgh the Scots were almost unanimously against him, having recently, they said, had an example of his Company's bad faith in the case of an agreement with the Scottish Central. At Inverness only two or three shareholders troubled to attend, so the long journey was wasted.

The adjourned Meeting was held at the Royal Hotel, Chester, on 16th July, and lasted till 10 o'clock at night. There was, of course, great uproar and confusion between the contending parties, but when it came to voting 17,831 were cast in favour of the Great Western Agreement and only 7,040 against it. The North Western offer of $4\frac{1}{2}\%$ was not made directly to the Board, and does not seem to have been taken seriously; besides which, the probability of Parliament ever sanctioning such a monopoly was generally regarded as very remote, and without such sanction any guarantee would be quite illusory.

Thus was the Great Western Railway potentially extended as far afield as Chester, just ten years after its opening from London to Bristol. Three years of strenuous fighting were to ensue before it actually got there, but the ultimate certainty of this was now assured. By the irony of fate, the author of this undreamed of extension of the original system was no other than the General Manager of the London & North Western. He it was, as we have seen, who invited the Great Western to come out of their own country at Oxford to Wolverhampton and to Birmingham, and then not long afterwards, by his efforts to crush the two little Shrewsbury Companies, threw them into his great rival's arms. Captain Huish has been described as a great railway diplomatist, and no doubt the first step was a diplomatic one in his fight with the London & Birmingham Company, but that he did not foresee the obvious consequences of his treatment of the Shrewsburys is no testimony to his powers. That he did not foresee it is shown by the extravagant attempts he made, by offers of costly guarantees and otherwise, to break the alliance after it had been concluded. Yet the possibility of this very alliance had been contemplated by the North Western lawyers long before the fight with the Shrewsbury Companies began, when they provided in the Stour Valley Act of 1847 that the Shrewsbury & Birmingham's running powers should cease if they amalgamated with the Great Western.

It need hardly be said that the City of Chester was in itself no fitting termination of a main line of railway from London. Birkenhead with its docks and with Liverpool across the Mersey was the point aimed at, so as early as April 1851 the Associated Companies, as the Great Western and the two Shrewsburys came to be called, made overtures to the Birkenhead Company to join the Alliance.

The latter's full title was the Birkenhead, Lancashire & Cheshire Junction Railway, and it had, in December 1850, opened a line from Chester to a junction with the North Western main line at Walton near Warrington, whence under an agreement with the latter it worked its own traffic over their line into Manchester. Early in 1851 some through trucks from the Shrewsbury & Chester were sent over this line, only to be stopped by the North Western, who maintained that the agreement only covered the Birkenhead's own stock. Hence the Shrewsbury's traffic had to be transhipped into Birkenhead waggons to get to Manchester, which effectually hindered the passage of any quantity of it. Matters were little, if at all, improved by another Birkenhead-North Western Agreement in June 1851, allowing other Companies' waggons to pass to Manchester, but only on condition that the former charged the full local rates on such traffic.

So matters stood while the Bill asking for running powers, which the Shrewsbury & Chester had introduced on account of the obstructions of the previous year, was before Parliament. In spite of strenuous opposition from the Companies concerned, backed up by the North Western, this Bill duly became an Act conferring full running powers over the Chester & Holyhead between Saltney Junction and Chester, which had hitherto been by agreement only, and also over the whole of the Birkenhead Railway, both to Birkenhead and Walton Junction, and authorizing the Shrewsbury to make a station on the South Reserve at Birkenhead.

Influenced by the grant of these powers over his line and the views of his shareholders, Alderman Bancroft came to the conclusion that he had better make terms with the Associated Companies. The result of the negotiations was an Agreement between the four Companies, made in October 1851, and confirmed by the Birkenhead Proprietors in the following month, for a perpetual lease of the Birkenhead, Lancashire & Cheshire Junction Railway, with all its plant and the benefit of its agreements with other Companies, to the Associated Companies in return for a guarantee by them to the Birkenhead Company, of dividends, beginning at 3% and rising after three years to 4%, together with an option to the latter at any time after the amalgamation of the other three Companies and before January 1856 to amalgamate with them on a par basis. All this was subject to the necessary sanction of Parliament being obtained in 1852 or 1853, but meanwhile the Associated Companies were given power to convey any traffic over the Birkenhead, paying 60% of the receipts to the latter.

Hence at the end of 1851 an independent line from London to Birkenhead, as well as access to Manchester, seemed assured, and hopes of 'the Broad Gauge to the Mersey' rose high at Paddington. How the exclusive possession of the Birkenhead was lost to the Great Western, not by the machinations of the enemy but by their own act, will be seen later. We must now turn our attention southward to the 'Battle of Wolverhampton' and the long struggle to reach Birmingham from the north.

In spite of the dilatory construction of the Stour Valley Railway by the North Western Company, that line was practically finished early in 1851 if not before the end of 1850, but no attempt was made to open it, much to the annoyance of the inhabitants of the Black Country. In November 1851 the Shrewsbury & Birmingham gave notice of an application to Parliament for power to open the line themselves, whereupon the North Western published their intention of opening it on 1st December.

Captain Wynne having inspected it and reported satisfactorily, the Board of Trade, on 25th November, duly sanctioned its opening from the station at Navigation Street, Birmingham, to the junction with the former Grand Junction Line at Bushbury beyond Wolverhampton. This of course included the new joint (High Level) station at Wolverhampton.

As soon as the Shrewsbury & Birmingham Directors heard of this intended opening, they notified the London & North Western that they would forthwith exercise their running powers over the line. The latter replied contending that the Shrewsbury Company had now amalgamated with the Great Western Railway and that their powers had therefore ceased, as the Act conferring them provided in that event. The Shrewsbury of course answered that they had not amalgamated with the Great Western but only agreed to do so at a future date, and therefore their running powers were in full force and they intended to exercise them.

The North Western then decided to postpone the opening on the ground of 'imminent risk to the public from such a hostile attempt and the danger to be anticipated of a collision', and issued public notice to this effect late on Saturday, 29th November, whereupon the Shrewsbury issued a counter notice that their trains would arrive at the new station, Wolverhampton, at specified hours, 'and proceed over the Stour Valley Railway to Birmingham, as specially authorized by the Stour Valley Act of Parliament of 1847'.

Now, although the North Western pretence that their running powers had ceased was quite unwarranted, this proceeding of the Shrewsbury Company was distinctly ill advised, not to say foolish. They had no right to run into the Birmingham Station, which was situated on the North Western's own Birmingham Extension line immediately beyond the termination of the Stour Valley; no tolls or regulations for the use of the line had been settled; neither had their engines been inspected or the times of their trains arranged with that Company; all of which were essential preliminaries to the exercise of the running powers.

However, they were as good as their word, and attempted to force a passage. The following account of the ensuing battle is extracted from the *Wolverhampton Herald* of the time.

The first Shrewsbury & Birmingham train was to leave about 9.15, and on arriving at the Wolverhampton station from Shrewsbury several persons who were desirous of going through, and others who had booked from the new station, were waiting to be conveyed to Birmingham. The London & North Western had caused their powerful engine 'Swift' to be placed on the up line a little beyond the signal post upon the bridge leading to Mr Bayley's chemical works, thus causing an obstruction to the progress of the Shrewsbury

& Birmingham train. Several officials, policemen, and other persons connected with the London & North Western, surrounded the engine, quietly waiting for any further proceedings on the part of the Shrewsbury & Birmingham people. A little further up the line an engine and tender were placed across the up and down rails. Hundreds of people were congregated upon the line, and shortly after ten o'clock a strong body of the borough police were marched, under the command of Colonel Hogg, to the bridge on which the London & North Western engine rested. As a breach of the peace and a serious disturbance was expected when the train from Shrewsbury proceeded towards Birmingham, the military under the command of Captain Bellairs, stationed in the town, were ordered to be in readiness. The Mayor was also in attendance, and an army of police waited in the hall of the station.

About a quarter past 10 o'clock, the passengers having previously alighted, the engine of the Shrewsbury & Birmingham with guards and a 3rd Class carriage filled with men, who appeared to be servants of the Company, and with G. Knox, Esq., and several other Directors and gentlemen standing on the engine carriage, proceeded towards Birmingham, the whistle of the engine emitting its shrillest sound to signify their advance to the obstructing engine before them. When within 200 yards of the London & North Western engine, two fog alarm signals, which had been placed on the rails, exploded. No notice, however, was taken by the parties belonging to the London & North Western engine, save the continual waving of red danger flags, which a number of policemen held in their hands, and one of which had been also tied to the signal post.

The engine of the Shrewsbury & Birmingham slowly advanced in spite of the red flags hoisted, and amidst the cheers and shouts of the assembled multitude, bunted against that of the London & North Western, which, being a very powerful engine, and the brakes being screwed tightly down, received but a slight shock from the concussion. The parties in charge of the London & North Western engine were then requested to move on but declined, and Mr Baker, the engineer of the Stour Valley, who was on that engine, in reply to several questions knowingly shook his head. The two engines standing opposite each other in the closest proximity with the steam power of their gigantic bodies issuing from the various safety valves in voluminous quantities with a hissing noise presented an exciting spectacle, representing the antagonism of their respective proprietors.

As no satisfactory answer could be got from the London & North Western Officials, the Directors and other gentlemen on the opposing Company's engine got down and immediately obtained a summons from the Borough Magistrates against Mr Baker, the engineer who was in charge of the engine, and Thomas Newbold, the engine driver, for obstructing the free traffic of the line.

So the battle terminated without bloodshed and the combatants adjourned to the Town Hall, where the proceedings led to an arrangement that the North Western Directors should meet at once to consider the Magistrates' suggestions for peace and the Shrewsbury & Birmingham suspend the active assertion of their rights for a month.

The North Western then appealed to the Board of Trade, giving their version of what had happened and urging the extreme danger to the public of opening the line, caused of course solely by the action of the Shrewsbury Company. At the same time the Wolverhampton Town Council passed and sent to the Board a resolution complaining of the delay in opening, and pointing out that provisions might easily be made to prevent any such danger. Although they had already sanctioned the opening and had therefore exhausted their powers in the matter, the Board then sent Captain Simmons to reinspect the line, as a way out of the difficulty. He then found many elements of danger, especially a lack of certain signals, which had, curiously enough, escaped the notice of his colleague, Captain Wynne. The Board thereupon ordered the London & North Western to postpone the opening, which that Company had of course already done. After this they pretended to the public that they were anxious to open the line, but were prevented doing so by the Board of Trade on account of the wicked behaviour of the Shrewsbury & Birmingham. The signals required by the Inspector remained lacking till the end of March, when, the Shrewsbury Company having, in order to get the line opened, undertaken not to exercise their running powers without the decision of a court of law, the North Western proposed to open it on 2nd April, and so erected them. But another difficulty now arose. No regulations for the joint station and mile of line at Wolverhampton, binding on the servants of both Companies, had been drawn up, so the Board of Trade refused their sanction to the opening of the Stour Valley, which extended on both sides of the joint line.

A separate dispute on the subject of this joint station had been going on between the two Companies since August 1851. The North Western wished it to be divided into two separate stations, one for each Company; the Shrewsbury objected on the ground of expense and insisted on the original Agreement and Act of Parliament, which made it a joint station, being kept to. The joint Committee, consisting of three Directors of each Company, being equally divided on practically every subject, did nothing; so when the station was ready for opening in November, each Company appointed separate staffs for it, which, of course, created further unpleasantness. Both opponents then appealed to the Board of Trade, and the matter was eventually referred to the arbitration of Sir William Cubitt. He issued a preliminary report in April proposing to divide the station as the North Western wished, allotting the southern half to them and the northern to the Shrewsbury, whereupon the latter protested that he was exceeding his powers and repudiated the arbitration.

Needless to say, the inhabitants of the district through which the Stour Valley Railway passed were by no means pleased at its being kept closed, and their complaints increased as time went on.[1] Several memorials were sent to the Board of Trade and the matter was taken up by the local Members of Parliament, besides being thoroughly ventilated before the Commons Committee on the Shrewsbury & Birmingham Bill for power to open the line themselves.

Eventually the President of the Board arranged a meeting at his office on 8th June of a Wolverhampton Deputation and several M.Ps. with the Chairmen and solicitors of the two hostile Companies. After some discussion Mr Glyn, the North Western Chairman, somewhat unwillingly agreed to open the line and the joint station forthwith, on condition that it was clearly understood the Shrewsbury & Birmingham would not try to enforce their running powers till a judgment had been obtained. Mr Clive, who had succeeded Mr Ormsby Gore as Chairman of the latter Company, at once agreed to this, and the deputation withdrew.

All the objections of the Board of Trade to the opening vanished at once as if by magic. They themselves, under their general powers, settled

[1] It had been opened for goods traffic in February 1852.

the dispute as to the Wolverhampton Station, treating it as a joint one in accordance with the Act of Parliament, and appointing a station-master with entire control of the station and common piece of line; and also settled a code of rules binding on the servants of both Companies.

The Stour Valley Railway was accordingly opened at last for public passenger traffic on 1st July 1852 by the London & North Western Company, but, needless to say, the trains thereon were carefully arranged so as not to connect at Wolverhampton with those of the Shrewsbury & Birmingham and no through booking arrangements were allowed. The goods traffic of the latter Company continued to be transferred to and from the canal at the Victoria Basin.

At the time Mr Glyn agreed to open the line, the Shrewsbury Company's Bill for power to do so themselves and to use the North Western Station in Birmingham had already been unanimously approved by the House of Commons Committee, which fact doubtless influenced him and his advisers in no small degree. After the opening, the clauses relating to the Stour Valley were of course withdrawn; not so those for use of the Navigation Street, now New Street, Station, which passed both Houses in spite of the fiercest opposition of the owning Company.

Meantime the Shrewsbury & Birmingham's lawsuit to establish their running powers, and another, which they began later, to restrain the North Western from trying to enforce the Award for the division of the Wolverhampton Station, which Sir William Cubitt appears to have made in spite of the Shrewsbury Company's protest, were dragging on, every possible expedient for causing delay—and there were many in the old Chancery Court in those days—being adopted by the Defendants' lawyers, who knew they had a very weak case. At last both suits came up together for final judgment by the Lords Justices on 16th December 1852. Their Lordships declared that 'it was impossible to maintain that there had been a leasing or purchasing or amalgamating' with the Great Western, and that therefore the running powers were in full force; also that Sir William Cubitt had plainly exceeded the limits of his authority and his award was void.

After this apparently decisive victory, it may be thought that the unfortunate Shrewsbury & Birmingham Railway had at last reached its rightful southern terminus. Far from it; many means of delay remained open to an ill-conditioned opponent, sulky and spiteful in defeat. Tolls and by-laws had to be settled, engines inspected and passed, though these same engines were running daily over the joint Shrewsbury & Wellington line. Failing agreement, these matters had to be settled by arbitration; failing that, by an umpire appointed by the Board of Trade. Needless to say, no agreement could be come to, so after considerable delay arbitrators were appointed; they were of course unable to arrange a meeting for some time and at last met only to disagree. Meantime the North Western, to show the danger of Shrewsbury trains on the Stour

Bradford-on-Avon, 1848–1857. The station buildings are marked X

Dundas Aqueduct carrying the Kennet & Avon Canal over the River Avon near Limpley Stoke, 1926

ABOVE

*left* Shrewsbury and Birmingham Railway

*right* Newport, Abergavenny and Hereford Railway

BELOW

*left* West Midland Railway

*right* Oxford, Worcester and Wolverhampton Railway

Valley, commenced from 1st May 1853 a half-hourly passenger service between Birmingham and Wolverhampton.

In July the Board of Trade appointed John Hawkshaw umpire to settle the matter. He held his first meeting on 10th October! On 30th January 1854, the last day allowed by the Court, which had been appealed to, he published his award fixing the *maximum* tolls possible both on passengers and goods, and a heavy rent for the use of the North Western Station.

The Shrewsbury & Birmingham Company protested against this as illegal, the special Act having provided for *reasonable* tolls, but in their anxiety to get to Birmingham accepted it without prejudice, and their passenger trains at last began to run over the Stour Valley Railway into New Street Station on 4th February 1854, more than a year after their victory in the Courts and nineteen months after the opening of the line. From New Street a service of omnibuses took through passengers to the Great Western Station at Snow Hill.

At the end of May the Court of Chancery set aside Hawkshaw's Award and refused to refer the matter back to him, as it was pressed to do by the North Western. How the tolls were eventually settled is of little interest; the interesting point is that two engineers of the eminence of Sir William Cubitt and John Hawkshaw should have so strained their powers as arbitrators in favour of the London & North Western and against the little Shrewsbury & Birmingham as to have their awards declared illegal and void by the Courts.

The Wolverhampton Station dispute was settled by the adoption of an arrangement proposed by the Shrewsbury that each Company should have its separate goods station, the North Western on the south-east and they themselves on the north-west of the passenger station, which remained common to both.

This concludes the story of the fighting in the south. In the north we left the Birkenhead Company at the end of 1851 on friendly terms with the Associated Companies, having agreed to lease its line to them with a view to ultimate amalgamation. A Bill to authorize this was accordingly deposited for the 1852 Session of Parliament. But when the formal agreement came to be settled, the Great Western maintained that the arrangement was subject to the amalgamation of the three Companies being first effected. The Birkenhead denied this, and the Shrewsbury representatives agreed with them. Saunders had to admit that the preliminary agreement was not clear on the point, through his own fault, he said; however, it had all along been the intention of his Directors and he was obliged to insist on it. In view of the organized opposition among the shareholders of both Shrewsbury Companies, there was of course the possibility of a hitch in the amalgamation, and the Great Western could not undertake a guarantee to a line which in that event would be 70 miles off. On the other hand the Birkenhead would in the same event be left alone to the tender mercies of Captain Huish. The Chairman of the Birkenhead, whose personal sympathies were notoriously North Western, seized on this point as a pretext, and with some difficulty persuaded a majority of his Board to concur in breaking off the agreement. Moreover, the Captain had fairly terrified the Alderman by the magnificent bluff of promoting in this session not one but two competing lines between Chester and Birkenhead, by his own and the Chester & Holyhead Companies respectively. So the Bill for leasing the Birkenhead was withdrawn by that Company in spite of the protests of the other partners, and soon afterwards Alderman Bancroft had the satisfaction of arranging a lease of the line and the immediate handing over of its rolling stock to the London & North Western; in consideration of which Captain Huish graciously consented to withdraw the Bills for the two competing lines, which he must have well known had a very small chance of passing. This manoeuvre was promptly squashed as *ultra vires* by an injunction obtained by a shareholder, no doubt put up by the Associated Companies; so in the following December, after much internal squabbling, another agreement was made to carry it out as soon as power had been obtained from Parliament. A Bill for the purpose introduced in the 1853 Session was stopped for reasons affecting all railway bills for amalgamations or leases, and on being again brought forward in 1854 was ignominiously and unanimously thrown out by the Commons Committee as soon as the promoters had closed their case, without the opposition being called upon.

The Bill for the amalgamation of the three Associated Companies passed the House of Commons with flying colours in 1852 after a bitter fight in Committee, but was stopped by the Wharncliffe Standing Order of the House of Lords, which at that time required the approval of any such Bill by a majority of four-fifths of the shareholders present at a Special Meeting. The Euston Troupe were strong enough to prevent this being obtained at either of the Shrewsbury Meetings, and so the Bill was killed for that Session. Another Bill for the amalgamation of the two Shrewsbury Companies alone also passed the Commons only to be killed in like manner, this time by the Shrewsbury & Birmingham detachment of the same troupe. The Shrewsbury & Chester succeeded in obtaining an Act enabling them to make two branches to connect the Birkenhead, Lancashire & Cheshire Junction Line at Norton and Walton, near Warrington, with the Bridgewater Canal, and, amongst other things to employ steamers on the Mersey and the Dee.

Next year the two Amalgamation Bills were again brought in by the Associated Companies, and rival Bills for power to lease the two Shrewsbury lines by the London & North Western. At this time the House of Commons, in view chiefly of Captain Huish's all-embracing activities and especially the proposed amalgamation of the Midland Railway with the London & North Western, had appointed a Select Committee to consider the whole question of railway amalgamations, and the principles which ought to guide the House in such matters. On the recommendation of this Committee, all railway bills involving amalgamation or leasing of other lines were postponed for that Session of 1853, the above Bills of course among them.

The Great Western on their own account boldly applied for powers, irrespective of the amalgamation, to run over and use the Shrewsbury & Birmingham, Shrewsbury & Chester, Shrewsbury & Hereford, and Birkenhead, Lancashire & Cheshire Junction Railways, as well as the intervening piece of the Chester & Holyhead and the Birkenhead Docks, and for that purpose at their own expense to lay additional broad-gauge rails on those lines from Wolverhampton and Hereford to Birkenhead. The Bill was opposed by all the Companies concerned except the Shrewsbury & Birmingham—even the friendly Shrewsbury & Chester petitioned against it—and after a week's hearing was rejected by the Committee of the Commons. This was the first and only attempt to obtain power to extend the Broad Gauge north of Wolverhampton.

The London & North Western Company on their part succeeded in getting an Act for a branch from Crewe to Shrewsbury, which they opened in September 1858.

While these various proceedings were going on in Parliament, the Birkenhead Company under North Western influence and against their own interests once more declared war on their best customer, the Shrewsbury & Chester. From October 1851 the latter had been working their own traffic over the Birkenhead Railway under the Agreement then made, and continued to do so after the Birkenhead people had changed their minds and gone over to the enemy, the Associated Companies contending that the Agreement remained in force till two attempts to obtain Parliamentary sanction for it had failed. In August 1852 the Birkenhead gave notice to the Shrewsbury that from September onwards they would charge them 80 instead of 60% of the mileage receipts and half terminal charges as well; but, persisting that the Agreement was still in force, the latter continued to run, paying only the 60%. Eventually the Birkenhead Company brought an action claiming not the 80%, which they said had not been agreed to, but much more—the maximum tolls chargeable on the basis that the Shrewsbury Company had been exercising their statutory running powers. This came on for trial at the Summer Assizes of 1853, and resulted in the sum due being referred to arbitration. The Arbitrator, a learned barrister, decided that the maximum tolls could be exacted, and that the charges made to the London & North Western of about a quarter as much for similar traffic—for example they paid 7s 6d for a truck of cattle from Birkenhead to Chester compared with £1 8s 0d— were not an undue preference, for the comical reason that the Shrewsbury did their own haulage! Upon this, the latter ceased running over the line on 1st December, and began handing over their traffic at Chester, much to the annoyance of Alderman Bancroft, who complained bitterly that his Company were obliged to buy six new engines to work it and go to much other expense, all through the wickedness of the Shrewsbury & Chester Company.

The Arbitrator made his Award at the end of January 1854 of some £8,500 to the Birkenhead, and next day a new action was begun for similar tolls for the further period from July to November and the ordinary rates in December and January. The state of the Alderman's feelings may be judged by the fact that the very day the taxation of costs in the first action was completed, 2nd March, without any demand or even notice to the Shrewsbury & Chester's solicitor, who happened to be in London, writs were issued to the Sheriffs of Shropshire, Denbigh, Flint, Cheshire, and the City of Chester to levy execution. Next morning the bailiffs were in possession of all stations from Shrewsbury to 'the Rossett' and in Shropshire alone property to the value of £50,000, including engines, rolling stock, and goods in the warehouses, was seized for this debt of about £9,000. The money was of course at once paid, but the bailiffs remained in possession for two days, till the evening of the 4th. The responsibility for this exhibition of spite was afterwards disputed between Alderman Bancroft and his Company's solicitor, John Buck Lloyd of Liverpool, but there can be no doubt the latter had his instructions.

These proceedings were of course foolish and short-sighted. They led to Parliament granting further powers over the Birkenhead Railway to the Shrewsbury & Chester in the 1854 Session, and to the Birkenhead Shareholders taking matters into their own hands by appointing a committee of investigation, which reported strongly against the Alderman's policy of favouring the North Western and obstructing the Shrewsbury. A table in the report shows that in spite of the constant obstructions the latter had in the five years to the end of June 1854 sent 710,304 tons of goods traffic over the line, compared with 219,817 from the London & North Western and Chester & Holyhead combined. The report was adopted by a General Meeting in October, and four Directors were replaced by four members of the Committee. By this time the injured Shrewsbury & Chester Railway had become part of the Great Western.

The Shrewsbury & Hereford Railway was opened throughout to Hereford in December 1853 (it had been available for through goods traffic since 30th July 1852), and the Newport, Abergavenny & Hereford a month later. The latter line being for the time in the hands of the North Western and managed by Captain Huish, it need hardly be said that none of the traffic from South Wales to Birkenhead found its way over the Shrewsbury & Chester, but was all sent round by Stafford and Crewe. This, however, did not last long. The Directors of the Newport, objecting to being dragged into the Shrewsbury fight, pluckily rebelled and soon got rid of the warlike Captain and his Company, and began to work their line themselves.

It would be tedious to attempt to describe the ructions that went on at the frequent General Meetings of the two Shrewsbury Companies. Except that neither Chairman is recorded to have again had recourse to a nightcap or the opposition to a forged seal, the proceedings of the latter continued to be very similar to those of the early part of 1851, already

mentioned. Tempting offers from the London & North Western of 4 and—
to the Chester—even $4\frac{1}{2}\%$, without however any very certain guarantee,
were dangled before the shareholders by the opposition leaders to induce
them to throw over the Directors and break their Agreement with the
Great Western. Whenever an important division was anticipated the
Euston troupe of small capitalists, 130 strong, could be relied on to arrive,
sometimes by special train, at Wolverhampton, Shrewsbury, or even
Chester, in time to support by silent votes any resolution or amendment
calculated to embarrass the respective Boards. However, the latter were
generally ready for them with the home team of employés and others, to
the extreme anger of the opposition leaders, who regarded such retaliation
as most unfair. After the enemy had secured the defeat of the Amalgamation Bills of 1852, an inquiry into the matter was made by the House of
Lords, when the purchase and division of shares in the two Companies
and the payment of the expenses of circulars and proxies and of opposition
meetings were admitted and defended by the solicitor and other agents
of the North Western. This and other evidence of the misuse of the Wharncliffe Standing Order, originally intended for the protection of genuine
minorities, led to its being modified so as to prevent such practices as far
as possible.

The Directors and the majority of the Proprietors of both Companies
loyally stood by the Agreements with the Great Western, which at their
request had been altered so as to postpone the actual amalgamation to
January 1860, by which time they considered their through traffic would
have had more chance of being developed. But in August 1853, after the
adoption by the House of Commons of the resolutions of Mr Cardwell's
Committee on the subject of railway amalgamations in general, the
Great Western Chairman made a new proposal for immediate amalgamation, as soon as the necessary Act of Parliament could be obtained, with a
guarantee from 1st January 1854 of certain proportions in successive years
of the Great Western dividend. In the following month this guarantee was
altered to a fixed $3\frac{1}{2}\%$ from the same date, and half surplus profits. Upon
this all honest opposition suddenly collapsed, and the Euston troupe,
unable to perform without leaders, was kept to its ordinary duties at home.
Consequently the new terms were accepted by enormous majorities at the
meetings of both Companies held in September, and peace reigned at
last in their councils.

A third Bill for effecting the amalgamation of the three Associated
Companies was accordingly introduced for the Session of 1854. It was
opposed, of course fiercely by the London & North Western and its
subsidiary Companies the Chester & Holyhead and Shropshire Union,
also by the Oxford, Worcester & Wolverhampton, the Birkenhead,
Lancashire & Cheshire Junction, and the Newport, Abergavenny &
Hereford, which last had not yet got rid of Captain Huish. The opposition
called no witnesses but relied solely on their Counsels' eloquence and
powers of invective. After only five days' hearing the House of Commons

Committee unanimously passed the Bill, and made a special report to the House, in view of the Cardwell Resolutions against amalgamations in general, that they had decided on recommending this amalgamation 'as being of a special character and of great importance to the public interest'. Wonderful to relate, at the Wharncliffe Meetings of the two Shrewsbury Companies in June, the Bill was unanimously approved.

The Bill came before the Lords' Committee early in July to encounter a last and even more desperate attack, in spite of which the Committee decided on the seventh day that the preamble had been duly proved. Two more days were then taken up in settling the clauses. Although the Bill contained no provision for extending the Broad Gauge, the prospect of this, which always seems to have inspired terror in North Western minds, was much dwelt on by their Counsel. An attempt to extend it to Birkenhead had been made the year before, and Saunders admitted in his evidence that the Company would probably find it necessary in the course of a year or two to come to Parliament again for the necessary powers. To allay these fears as far as possible, the Great Western agreed that they would make no such application till the Board of Trade should have reported that the extension of Broad Gauge north of Wolverhampton was desirable in the interests of the public. They also agreed to become bound under penalties to complete the Narrow Gauge from Oxford to Basingstoke within eighteen months of the passing of the Act, and afterwards *to work it* in connection with the London & South Western, their own Birmingham and Chester line, and other narrow-gauge railways. Clauses to effect these objects were accordingly inserted in the Bill. With scarcely an exception the various objectionable clauses proposed by the opponents were rejected, but the North Western exhibited another of those displays of temper, without which that Company in the days of Captain Huish seems never to have been able to accept defeat. The guarantee of $3\frac{1}{2}\%$ to the Shrewsbury shareholders began from 1st January 1854, and owing to the treatment those Companies had received there was of course a big deficiency in their current revenue. To obviate this loss falling at once solely on Great Western receipts, the Bill provided that for the first two years the deficiency might be met temporarily by advances out of capital, to be repaid within the next seven years. This arrangement was sanctioned by the House of Commons but rejected by the Lords' Committee on North Western opposition, and the Bill eventually received the Royal Assent on 7th August without it. Thus the London & North Western succeeded in injuring the Great Western shareholders in their purely domestic affairs without any possible benefit to themselves.

The Amalgamation Act came into force on 1st September 1854, putting an end to the stormy existence of the plucky little Shrewsbury & Birmingham and Shrewsbury & Chester Railway Companies, and extending the Great Western to the City of Chester, with running powers to Birkenhead and the prospect of early access to Manchester. It is pleasant to be able to record, by way of a change, that when the failure of McClean's bridges delayed the opening of the Great Western Line to Wolverhampton till November, the North Western Authorities allowed the Shrewsbury trains to continue running over the Stour Valley into New Street Station during the interval, although the statutory running powers expired on the day the Amalgamation took effect. The trains ran for the last time on 12th November.

The two Shrewsbury Railways were of the usual narrow-gauge type of the period with rather light permanent way on cross sleepers. During the next ten years the whole of the Chester line was relaid with heavier materials, but on the Birmingham the substitution of fish-plates for joint-chairs seems to have been all that was necessary. Signals were of the ordinary semaphore pattern, a double-armed one for both roads some-where on the station platform, and auxiliary signals about a ¼ mile out in each direction. The telegraph was installed throughout both lines in 1852.

Of their internal economy there is not much to be said. Both Companies seem to have been fairly well provided with engines and rolling stock; the Chester, besides its traffic over the Birkenhead Railway, was able to work the Shrewsbury & Hereford from its first opening to Ludlow until Mr Brassey was ready to do so, and also to assist the Newport, Abergavenny & Hereford with locomotive power for a short time. Even before the opening of the Shrewsbury & Birmingham Line mutual arrangements for working through traffic were made between it and the Shrewsbury & Chester, and soon afterwards a Joint Committee for managing this was formed of representatives of both Boards. In 1851 this Committee was merged in a larger one with Great Western representatives, and a young Scotsman named James Grierson was appointed Secretary. Early in 1854 Grierson became Traffic Manager of both lines in succession to Captain Coddington, who had succeeded Dudley Parsons in 1852 on the latter's secession to the London & North Western.

The passenger train service was of the ordinary type, save that third-class passengers were catered for to an extent quite unusual in those days; in fact, the Shrewsbury Companies seem to have been pioneers in encouraging this traffic. Queen Victoria patronized their route on 12th October 1852 with Prince Albert and the Prince of Wales on her return from a visit of inspection to the new Britannia Tubular Bridge over the Menai Straits, which she made on her way from Balmoral to Windsor. The Royal Train did not enter Chester, but was taken on from Saltney Junction by Shrewsbury engines to Wolverhampton, where it was handed over to the London & North Western for conveyance over the Stour Valley Line. The three engines used on this occasion, one as pilot, were christened *Queen*, *Victoria and Albert*, and *Prince of Wales*; of these, *Queen* belonged to the Birmingham, the others to the Chester Company.

The engines of each Company seem from the first to have worked indis-criminately over both lines. Edward Jeffreys was Locomotive Superin-tendent of the Shrewsbury & Chester with headquarters at Shrewsbury and workshops at Saltney till April 1853, when he was succeeded by

Joseph Armstrong. The Shrewsbury & Birmingham engines, though the property of the Company, were worked by contractors, Messrs Johnson and Kinder, with William Marlow as Superintendent till the same date, when the contract was terminated and the Hon. Edmund Petre became the Company's Locomotive Superintendent for a year, after which he went to the North British and Armstrong took charge of the united stock of the two Companies. The Shrewsbury & Birmingham headquarters and repair shops were at Wolverhampton, Stafford Road.

William Ormsby Gore, M.P. of Parkington near Oswestry, was the first Chairman of both Companies, as well as of the Shrewsbury & Hereford; indeed he may be regarded as the father of railways in Shropshire. He became Chairman of the Joint Traffic Committee in 1850, and was succeeded on the Chester by William Wardell of that city, who gave place in 1852 to John Williams, also of Chester. On the Birmingham the Hon. Robert Clive, M.P., succeeded him in October 1851; and on the latter's death in 1853 Lord Bateman became the last Chairman.

The most active Directors and objects of the special hatred of the North Western party were Robert Roy of the Chester and George Knox of the Birmingham, each of whom had been the first Secretary of his Company. In this office Roy was succeeded first by W. S. Darkin and then by John Nicholl. Knox's successors were J. F. Nicoll, Thomas Hall, and J. F. Kirshaw.

It need hardly be said that the two Shrewsbury Companies were never exactly prosperous! Captain Huish's persecution made sure of that. The Chester did indeed pay its preference dividends and occasionally 1% on its ordinary stock, but the Birmingham never even succeeded in paying its preference shareholders in full.

# IX

## *Hard Times*

For the holders of Great Western ordinary stock at this time the Company's northern conquests were indeed Pyrrhic victories. Not only had the interest on more than 6 millions, the cost of the extension from Oxford to Birmingham and Wolverhampton, which had been raised by debentures and preference stock, to come out of current revenue before they got a penny, but the guaranteed $3\frac{1}{2}\%$ to the Shrewsbury shareholders had to be provided for. Owing to the cut-throat competition to which the two Shrewsbury Companies had been subjected by Captain Huish, there was a considerable deficiency in their receipts which would have to be made up by the Great Western. This had of course been foreseen and provision made in the Amalgamation Bill for spreading the liability over several years, but, as we have seen, this was defeated by the spiteful opposition of the vanquished enemy. Consequently the guarantee had to be met out of current revenue, and as it began from 1st January 1854 the Great Western shareholders were hit hard before they had even got possession of the Shrewsbury Railways, and their dividend for the half year reduced from the usual 2 to $1\frac{1}{2}\%$, although the net revenue from their own line showed a satisfactory increase.

Another liability hanging over the Company was the completion of the Wilts, Somerset & Weymouth Railway of 1845, which had been taken over in 1850. This was open from Thingley Junction between Chippenham and Corsham, to Frome and Warminster, and, although nearly $1\frac{1}{2}$ million had already been spent on these lines and unfinished works disfiguring the country here and there all the way to Weymouth and Salisbury, the only portion the Directors had expressed any intention of completing was the Radstock coal branch. Local agitation consequently sprang up, and committees were formed in 1852 to induce the Company to proceed with their undertaking. The Directors proving deaf to their appeals, legal proceedings were taken for writs of Mandamus to compel them to complete the unfinished portions, and petitions were presented in Parliament. The Mayor of Salisbury also gave evidence of the general complaints of the district before the Cardwell Committee of 1853, alleging that the Company would not make the line from Warminster to Salisbury because it suited them better to carry passengers between Bristol and Southampton or Portsmouth round by Reading and Basingstoke, as they were doing. The lawsuits were successfully defeated, except as regards the branch from Bradford to Bathampton, for the completion of which the Mandamus was made absolute by the Queen's Bench in Michaelmas Term 1853, after a trial at the Somerset Assizes. This the Directors seem to have intended to abandon altogether, so they forthwith appealed against the order, but the Exchequer Chamber decided in November that owing to the terms of the Act of 1845 the Company could be compelled to make the branch, and so dismissed the appeal.

Upon this the Directors, who had already recommenced some work on the Weymouth line, reconsidered the whole case and decided to promote a Bill for an extension of time and new powers to complete the Bathampton branch, the line from Frome to Weymouth, the Devizes branch, and the line to Salisbury. This Bill in due course became an Act of Parliament on 31st July 1854, giving the needful powers and providing for the suspension of the Great Western dividends if the lines were not completed and opened within two years, or such further period as the Board of Trade might allow. The Act also enforced a curious agreement made with the London & South Western that, on condition they laid the Broad Gauge on their Southampton and Dorchester line for 8 miles eastward from Dorchester, the Great Western would lay the Narrow Gauge on the 6½ miles between the junction there and the Weymouth Terminus, and gave each Company reciprocal running powers over these mixed-gauge sections. The importance to the South Western of access to Weymouth is obvious, but what possible use running powers to a point somewhere about half-way between the country stations of Moreton and Wool could be to the Great Western seems indeed an unfathomable mystery. Needless to say, they were never exercised. Surely the extra rails cannot have been insisted on merely to annoy!

This same Act empowered the Company to make a loop line a mile west of Reading to connect the main line from the north and west with the Berks & Hants branch to Basingstoke and Hungerford. The loop was to be mixed-gauge and form part of the narrow-gauge communication between Wolverhampton and Basingstoke, which the Company were now bound under penalties to complete within eighteen months.

On 1st September the Shrewsbury & Birmingham and Shrewsbury & Chester Railways became part of the Great Western, adding some 85 miles of narrow-gauge line, 10½ of which were joint with the London & North Western, to the system. Owing to the difference of gauge, signals, and other arrangements, they remained for some years an almost foreign section, known as the 'Northern Division'. For the first two months indeed they were quite isolated till the Wolverhampton line was opened in mid November.

Three representatives of each Company joined the Great Western Board, increasing its number to eighteen, and introducing a new feature in its composition in the shape of a Director appointed not by the shareholders but by the owner of Wynnstay near Ruabon in Denbighshire. Hitherto that gentleman, Sir Watkin Williams-Wynn, Bart., M.P., had been content to appoint his steward or some other representative to the Shrewsbury & Chester Board, but soon after the right had been extended to the Great Western he appointed himself, as he and his successor continued to do almost without intermission till the Railways Act of 1921 abolished all such rights. On the London & North Western the Duke of Sutherland, as owner of Trentham in Staffordshire, possessed a similar power.

The ruinous rate-cutting competition which Captain Huish had instituted in 1849 with the sole object of crushing the Shrewsbury Companies, and by which his own Company had lost quite a lot of money, went on till the end of the year, when it was at last terminated by an Agreement between the Great Western and London & North Western Companies to charge equal and remunerative fares and rates for all traffic between all competing points, with special provisions to prevent the special rates, discounts, allowances, and rebooking tricks, for which the Captain was notorious; in fact, the very terms Saunders had proposed in 1852, which were then contemptuously rejected. This of course also put an end to similar rate-cutting between Leamington and Birmingham and several other places where the two Companies came into contact.

Early in 1855 it became necessary to raise £1,325,000 more capital for the completion of the Wilts & Somerset lines, the Reading Loop, and the addition of narrow-gauge rails between Oxford and Basingstoke. Owing to the Crimean War and the general financial situation this had to be done by the issue of 5% preference stock, to the further detriment of the ordinary shareholders, who had received only 3% for the year just past, and were not to see even that meagre sum again for six years.

The Hereford, Ross & Gloucester Railway was completed to Hereford and opened by the Great Western, who had agreed to work it for 60% of the receipts, on 1st June. It was a broad-gauge single line, 22½ miles long from Grange Court Junction, of which the first 5 miles to Hopesbrook had already been open for nearly two years. The works were heavy, consisting on most of the line of a series of embankments and cuttings, following closely on each other and attaining a height of 40 feet and a depth of 72 feet respectively. There were four tunnels—Lea 771, Fawley 540, Ballingham 1,210, and Dinedor 110 yards long—and four viaducts over the Wye, each of timber on stone piers with six openings all of 44 feet span. The permanent way consisted of Barlow rails weighing 90 lbs to the yard in 20 feet lengths with iron ties at the ends of each rail to preserve the gauge. A new station was opened at Grange Court, and intermediate stations at Longhope, which superseded the temporary Hopesbrook terminus, Mitcheldean Road, Ross, Fawley, and Holme Lacy.[1] The station at Barr's Court, Hereford, as yet far from complete, was a joint one with the Shrewsbury & Hereford Company, provision being made at the south end for the broad- and at the north end for the narrow-gauge traffic. The single line was worked by telegraph from the first, with Ross as the only crossing station.

Charles Russell's long tenure of the Great Western Chair came to an end on 2nd August. He had told the subscribers to 'The Picture' more than

[1] Ballingham was added in September 1908.

three years ago that the time would soon come when he must retire from active life, and twice since then had his colleagues, with some difficulty, persuaded him to continue in office. Now increasing ill-health and age— he was in his seventieth year—compelled him to resign. During the sixteen years of his reign the foundations of the Great Western system of modern times were laid and its territory marked out. From a mere railway from London to Bristol the undertaking had been extended to embrace first Cheltenham and Oxford, then Weymouth, Birmingham, and Chester, with running powers to the Mersey, and by its daughter Company the whole coast of South Wales to Milford Haven; while its trains ran through over the lines of its allies to Plymouth, whence the jointly leased Cornwall Railway would ere long carry them on to Truro and Falmouth. It is not surprising that such rapid growth had somewhat exhausted the Company and that the shareholders of those days had to pay for it in the shape of sadly diminished dividends. They had only themselves to blame; in the wild years of the Mania and excitement of the Gauge War they had encouraged—indeed many of them had urged—the Board to undertake extensions both north and south of the original line. Moreover, Russell and his colleagues had to choose between going north of Oxford, which they were at first very loath to do, or abandoning all that district to the London & Birmingham Company, with the certainty of a rival line to Cheltenham, giving future narrow-gauge access to the whole of South Wales, and the almost equal certainty of narrow-gauge communication from Oxford to the London & South Western cutting across their original district from north to south. Once north of Oxford there was really no place to stop at, save Birmingham or Rugby, and they were invited to Birmingham by the Grand Junction Company. The Wolverhampton line followed naturally as a feeder, and the completion of both these lines was 'strongly recommended' by the independent Committee of Consultation appointed by the Proprietors in 1849, who also recommended 'such arrangements with other Companies north of Wolverhampton, as may produce the greatest possible traffic by this route'. Hence, in accepting the overtures of the two Shrewsbury Companies at the end of 1850 for traffic arrangements, the Board were only carrying out this express recommendation. The subsequent agreement for absolute amalgamation was unanimously approved by the Great Western shareholders, as was also the onerous $3\frac{1}{2}\%$ guarantee to those Companies. So the shareholders had no right to complain of the progressive policy adopted by Russell and his colleagues, though they paid dearly for it at the time. While he occupied the Chair, he invariably carried the Meetings with him and received loyal and general support; that this was chiefly due to his influence and personality is suggested by the fact that opposition and dissensions in the Company broke out almost immediately after he had gone. We have already had evidence of the respect and affection with which he was regarded by the Great Western staff, high and low. Altogether he was a great Chairman, worthy of the great Railway he did so much to found. Of

Brunel and the Broad Gauge he was of course the foremost champion in Parliament and before the world at large. It is sad to record that within a year of his resignation his illness affected his brain and like his predecessor, Sims, he died by his own hand—on 15th May 1856.

Russell was temporarily succeeded by the Right Hon. Spencer Horatio Walpole, M.P., a lawyer politician, who had been Home Secretary in Lord Derby's short-lived Government of 1852 and joined the Great Western Board in the following year. He now agreed to take the Chair during the interval of the Parliamentary recess till the following February.

The first act of the new Chairman was to suggest the appointment of a committee of the Board to investigate the financial position of the Company and its general condition and prospects. A Committee of seven was accordingly formed, consisting of himself, Russell, Lord Barrington, two of the Directors appointed by the Proprietors in 1849, and a representative of each of the late Shrewsbury Companies.

After an exhaustive investigation this Committee made a lengthy Report in January 1856, which was at once printed and circulated to the Shareholders. Among many other things, it shows that the capital of the Company, excluding the two Shrewsbury Lines, was then in round figures £23,500,000, of which only £8,300,000 consisted of ordinary stock, £4,900,000 of preference, and no less than £10,300,000 of debentures and loans at various rates of interest. This huge floating debt, besides being a heavy burden on the revenue, was a frequent cause of anxiety to the Board. Some 4 millions of it could be paid off at any favourable opportunity by the issue of stock and the sale of the shares held to the extent of £1,800,000 in other Companies, and power had been obtained from Parliament in 1853 to convert the remainder into 4% debenture stock; but no opportunity of taking either of these courses on reasonable terms had yet occurred. Of this capital, while £10,760,000 had been spent on the 216 miles of the Company's own lines open in 1849, the 82 miles of new railways connecting the Oxford Branch with the Shrewsbury & Birmingham north of Wolverhampton had cost £6,335,000, and £1,433,000 had already been spent on the Wilts, Somerset & Weymouth, of which only 31½ miles were open for traffic, £750,000 of this on land and works of the unfinished portions beyond Frome and Warminster; Paddington Station accounted for over £480,000, including £59,500 for the Hotel. The capital of the two Shrewsbury Railways was just over £3,000,000; £1,800,000 whereof consisted of ordinary stock, £775,000 of debentures, and the rest of preference shares, mostly at 8%.

The internal administration of the Company's business the Committee found generally satisfactory. Of the Engineering and Locomotive Departments and the establishment generally, they have not much to say. Since 1853, when a new arrangement had been made with Brunel, a permanent Engineering Establishment had been located at Paddington under his general superintendence—he had of course much work on hand for other Companies.

The annual increase in the traffic receipts was satisfactory and encouraging, especially as regards goods traffic, which had doubled itself in the five years since 1851. It was, however, still little more than half that from passenger traffic, the actual figures for 1855 being £436,394 and £848,880 respectively. This the Committee attributed 'to the fact that the Great Western Railway until recently had been principally dependent for its traffic on agricultural districts, and, with the exception of Bristol, had not any extensive communications with commercial towns'. They anticipated that the goods and mineral traffic would soon greatly increase. At this time the Goods Management was divided between three independent officers with co-ordinate authority: A. J. Drewe in the south, J. S. Forbes in the west, and W. L. Newcombe in the north. The last named, previously Goods Manager of the York, Newcastle & Berwick, now part of the newly formed North Eastern Railway, had been specially engaged at the beginning of 1855 to manage the new northern goods business. The Committee recommended that Newcombe should forthwith be appointed Chief Goods Manager for the whole system, and that 'a thoroughly competent and intelligent person' under him should be placed in the north to carry out the arrangements he had already made. The person chosen, when the Board adopted this recommendation soon afterwards, was James Grierson, a young man of twenty-eight, who had been successively Secretary to the Through Traffic Committee of the two Shrewsbury Companies from December 1851, Traffic Manager of those Railways from March 1854, and local Goods Manager at Wolverhampton from February 1855. When Newcombe resigned in September 1857 to become General Manager of the Midland Railway, Grierson succeeded him as Chief Goods Manager at Paddington, while still under thirty years of age.

The Committee summed up their views on the Company's prospects as follows:

To estimate fairly the real state and condition of the Company, they must look as much to its future prospects, founded on a calm and dispassionate view of its liabilities on the one hand and its expectations on the other, as to the actual circumstances which have recently depressed the undertaking. In doing this, there is good ground for encouragement. The improvement in the traffic of the Shrewsbury Lines exhibits during the last half year an average increase of £1,000 a week. The improvement in the traffic of the Great Western Lines exhibits during the same period an average increase of £3,000 a week. The Goods traffic with the North is only just about to commence. The Mineral traffic both of South Wales and Somersetshire, as well as of North Wales, is susceptible of large increase. The growing receipts of the general traffic, whether it be of Passengers or of Goods, is so uniformly diffused over all parts of the Line that, if all outstanding liabilities were now closed, the Committee would feel confident that the condition of the Company not only would not be worse but, as far as they are capable of judging, would steadily grow better. At the same time it ought not to be disguised that their liabilities are still large, and they must therefore be anticipated by every precaution which prudence can devise. During the current half year indeed they will not be felt to their full extent; but it may be anticipated with confidence that increasing receipts will balance them. In the next half year, most of the remaining liabilities will fall upon current revenue, because by that time the Wilts, Somerset, & Weymouth Line, as well as the Uxbridge and Henley Branches will be opened. The extent of new revenue to be derived from these sources will depend on the condition of the country, the activity of trade, and the influences which a state of peace or war may bring to bear upon the amount of traffic.

Evidently the Committee did not expect much from the completion of the Wilts & Somerset, especially now that a rival line between Salisbury and Yeovil had been authorized and was under construction. Reading between the lines of the report, it is clear that they took a somewhat gloomy view of general Great Western prospects for the immediate future.

Shortly before the issue of this report a bombshell was dropped among the shareholders by the publication of a circular letter from the two 1849 Directors on the Committee, Samuel Baker of Worcester and Richard Potter of Gloucester, attacking the Board and their administration of the Company's affairs. Their complaint was that the Board persisted in refusing to appoint committees to supervise the different departments, or to divide the offices of Secretary and General Superintendent, both of which changes they had proposed as early as 1851, and that more work was therefore imposed on Saunders than he was capable of doing. The recent Committee of Investigation had, they said, suggested the formation of a Traffic Committee, but even this was negatived by the Board. While both admitted Saunders' great ability and wholehearted devotion to the Company, they strongly urged that he should be relieved, without any reduction of salary, of the office of General Superintendent, and that a General Manager should be appointed, in conformity with the practice of nearly all other Railway Companies. Potter went so far as to allege that external relations with other Companies and the conduct of the goods traffic were injuriously affected by 'the peculiar organization of the Board and the anomalous position of the Secretary', who, he considered, had too much authority, owing to the lack of Departmental Committees. Being unable to induce their colleagues to agree with them, Messrs Baker and Potter announced their intention of resigning their seats at the Board, which they did after further expounding their views to the Shareholders at the February General Meeting without much effect.

At this Meeting there was a great deal of opposition and criticism owing to the dividend having fallen from 3 to $2\frac{1}{2}$% and especially over the formation of the Ruabon Coal Company, which the Directors announced in their Report. This undertaking originated in the desire to get a large regular coal traffic on the line. At first the Directors, acting on Gooch's advice, had proposed that the Great Western should acquire a colliery near Ruabon belonging to Mr Henry Robertson, with the view of bringing coal to London and other stations and selling it, but finding that such action would be beyond the Company's powers, the Chairman suggested to Gooch that he should form a limited company to buy the colliery and agree to send a large quantity of coal over the railway. The Ruabon Coal Company, consisting chiefly of Great Western officers and their friends with Gooch as Chairman, was the result. Before making the proposed agreement with the new Company, however, the Directors, anticipating opposition and accusations of undue preference from rival interests in the coal trade, decided to ask for the express approval of their Proprietors.

Having got this by a large majority at the Meeting, they afterwards made an agreement with the Coal Company for ten years from January 1857, whereby the latter undertook to send sufficient coal over the railway for more than 100 miles to produce a gross revenue of at least £40,000 a year, to be doubled after two years in certain events; in return for which the Great Western were to charge only agreed rates and afford various facilities, including the transfer from narrow- to broad-gauge trucks at the nominal charge of 1*d* a ton. This agreement was a stock bone of contention between certain shareholders, who considered their private interests in other collieries were affected by it, and the Board at all the Half-yearly Meetings till at last in November 1858 judgment was given in a Chancery suit brought by a coalowner of Lydney that it was perfectly legal and created no undue preference. It is satisfactory to learn from Gooch's Reminiscences that the colliery turned out a very good investment and brought profit to both parties to the arrangement.

The term for which Walpole had agreed to occupy the Great Western Chair coming to an end with this February Meeting, Viscount Barrington, who had been Deputy Chairman since 1843, was elected Chairman, with Walpole as his Deputy, but on the latter declining this post Mr John William Miles of Bristol accepted it.

The immediate effect of Messrs Baker and Potter's attack on Saunders, or rather in his dual office, for they made no attack on him personally, was a spontaneous outburst of loyalty and affection on the part of the Great Western staff. In a very short time some £400 was subscribed by about the same number of the officers and principal clerks. This sum was invested in a large silver centre-piece for the table and a pair of claret jugs, which were presented at a crowded gathering in the Paddington Board Room on 19th April 1856. In the course of his speech Saunders referred to the assertions of the two ex-Directors and expressly denied that he had ever interfered with the duties of the heads of departments or interposed between them and the Board, or taken on himself exclusively the management of the Company. As to this, he said: 'When I was asked some years ago whether I could undertake it I said it was impossible, and that all I could venture upon, in the position of a superior officer and as the organ of the Board, was to superintend the executive administration, and assist as far as possible those who had the management of affairs placed in their hands; and I have sedulously endeavoured to do so much and nothing more.' This view of his duties accords with a statement made in December 1854 by Russell himself, than whom no one could be better informed, that the title General Superintendent had been purposely chosen rather than that of General Manager, because the Board intended to retain the entire management in their own hands, and Saunders was to act only as their mouthpiece and superintend the carrying out of their orders by the various chief officers, all of whom had direct access to the Board.

Several extensions were completed in 1856, the first being the little Abingdon Railway, which the Company had undertaken to work, opened on 2nd June. This was a broad-gauge single line, constructed in less than a year by a local Company,[1] not quite two miles long from that town to a junction with the Oxford Branch a ¼ mile north of the Thames Bridge at Nuneham, where platforms to enable passengers to change trains were erected. Abingdon Junction, as these were entitled, was never a station in the ordinary sense of the word and did not appear in the public time-tables; like Kemble on the Gloucester Line in its early days, it was merely a changing place.[2]

On the last day of this same June the Salisbury Branch was completed by the opening of the remaining 19½ miles from Warminster. Like the section between Westbury and Warminster, this was a single line with no engineering works of special interest. Intermediate stations were established at Heytesbury, Codford, Wiley [*sic*], Langford,[3] Wishford, and Wilton, of which Wiley alone was a crossing station.[4] The whole branch from Westbury was worked by single-needle telegraph from the first. The original terminus at Salisbury is still in use,[5] one of the few remaining examples of Brunel's usual type of all-over roofed stations. It was somewhat damaged when only three months old by a cattle train with two engines, which did their best to run through it and out on to the road beyond, at the cost of the lives of two of the four men on the engines, none of whom had been over the new line before, and 108 sheep.[6] At this time the South Western Company's station was at Milford, a mile away on the other side of the city, to the great inconvenience of passengers for Southampton and Portsmouth. More than three years elapsed before their new station, adjoining the broad-gauge terminus, was opened with the Salisbury & Yeovil Railway, whereupon the Great Western provided a transfer shed and sidings for the transhipment of goods, which were brought into use in the summer of 1860.

A further 26 miles of the main Wilts, Somerset & Weymouth Line, from Frome to Yeovil, were opened for traffic on 1st September. Though all the works had been made wide enough for two lines only one was laid, to be worked by telegraph like the Salisbury Branch. The new stations were Witham, Bruton, Castle Cary, Sparkford, Marston,[7] and Yeovil, Pen Mill, to which the Bristol & Exeter Company were extending their Durston–Yeovil Branch from their station at Hendford on the other side

[1] The Abingdon Railway Company maintained a prosperous existence till 1904, when the shareholders got £20 Great Western ordinary stock for each £10 share.
[2] Superseded by a new station at Radley, ¾ mile north in 1873, the branch being prolonged beside the main line.
[3] 1¼ miles beyond Wiley; abolished in October 1857.
[4] It was doubled in sections, the last, between Wylye and Wilton, in 1901.
[5] As a goods station. It was closed to passengers from 12th September 1932 when all GWR trains commenced to use the adjoining Southern Railway station.
[6] On 6th October 1856.
[7] Renamed Marston Magna 1895.

of the town; there were crossing loops at all these places except Marston.[1]

A week later the branch from West Drayton to Uxbridge, $2\frac{1}{2}$ miles more of single line, was opened.

Finally, at the end of the year, the narrow-gauge rails between Oxford and Basingstoke, promised by the Board in 1846 and made compulsory by the Shrewsbury Amalgamation Act to provide through communication between the railways north of Wolverhampton and the London & South Western, were completed, and used for the first time by a narrow-gauge goods and coal train on 22nd December. The Avoiding Line at Didcot, to which the Mixed Gauge was confined, no additional rails being laid through the station there, and the western loop near Reading, also mixed-gauge, were opened at the same time. After this, narrow-gauge goods trains gradually became a common sight between Birmingham and Basingstoke, where they had hitherto been unknown, for though the third rails had been in existence as far as Oxford for more than four years no regular trains, either for goods or passengers, seem to have used them till this extension. Between Wolverhampton and Birmingham trains of both gauges had been run indiscriminately from the opening of that line.

In the north, Great Western goods trains had been running to Birkenhead since 2nd February. Relations with the Birkenhead Company had undergone several changes since the Shrewsbury Amalgamation. At that time, as we have seen, the Shrewsbury & Chester had ceased exercising its running powers over the line, and the Birkenhead Board, under the influence of Alderman Bancroft, had agreed to lease the railway to the London & North Western. Power to do this having been refused by Parliament, and a committee of investigation having reported strongly against the Alderman's policy of hostility to their best customer in the interests of another Company, and in favour of an agreement with the Great Western, the shareholders adopted their report at a General Meeting in October 1854 and elected four new Directors. The altered Board then concluded a working agreement with the Great Western with an option to lease the Birkenhead Railway in perpetuity, but this was defeated by North Western influence at the Half-yearly Meeting in February, and the Company's policy once more became hostile.

In August 1855 the Great Western Directors reported:

It has been a disappointment to find that some obstruction, similar to that previously complained of, has been continued to the traffic of the two Shrewsbury Railways passing over the Birkenhead Lines, in spite of the assurances given by their late Chairman to the contrary, and notwithstanding the efforts perseveringly made by Directors of both Companies to overcome that state of affairs.

The consequence has been that in the absence of all facilities for transmission of traffic either to or from Liverpool or Manchester, by means of friendly co-operation and aid from the Birkenhead Company, it has been hitherto found necessary to forego the advantages of soliciting or undertaking the conveyance of that merchandize, the Directors being unable to rely with certainty that it would be properly forwarded on equitable terms or punctually and correctly delivered.

[1] The line was doubled between Frome and Witham in 1875, thence to Castle Cary in 1880 and Yeovil, Pen Mill, in 1881.

They were therefore taking steps 'to procure independent premises in Birkenhead, with adequate local accommodation, both in Liverpool and at Timperley, near Manchester', and then proposed to exercise their running powers over the Birkenhead Lines. Timperley was to be reached by means of powers acquired in 1855 over the Warrington & Stockport Railway from Lower Walton, but there the powers ceased, some 6 miles from Manchester. In the course of the next half year the Company leased some premises and wharves in the Birkenhead Docks, and as soon as these were ready began to run their own goods trains from Chester on terms settled by arbitration. No attempt to reach Manchester via Timperley seems to have been made. At about the same time, according to the Report of February 1856, 'a considerable Mineral Traffic, from the interchange of Red Ore from Birkenhead for the Iron Masters of South Wales, with Steam Coals back from that district to the River Mersey', began. This was worked throughout from Pontypool to Birkenhead by the engines and waggons of the Newport, Abergavenny & Hereford Company, under an arrangement with the three other Companies concerned—Shrewsbury & Hereford, Great Western, and Birkenhead.

Great Western passenger trains began running through to and from Birkenhead on 1st May 1857 under an agreement with the Birkenhead Company, who by this time had thrown off their subservience to Captain Huish and taken up the more sensible attitude of welcoming traffic over their line, no matter whence it came.

The remainder of the Wilts, Somerset & Weymouth Line was completed in 1857. First, the 27½ miles from Yeovil to Weymouth were opened on 20th January, as a single line to Dorchester, and thence double, with additional narrow-gauge rails from the junction with the London & South Western, beyond Dorchester Station, to Weymouth. On this there were four tunnels: Holywell, near Evershot, 311 yards; Frampton 660; Poundbury, near Dorchester, 264; and Bincombe 814, besides two of 40 and 20 yards respectively; and nine viaducts from 22 to 102 yards long of stone or timber. Stations were provided at Yetminster, Evershot, Maiden Newton, Grimstone,[1] Dorchester, and Weymouth,[2] Evershot being at first the only crossing station on the single portion; until the completion of the telegraph, which was not quite ready, this was worked by two pilotmen, one on each side of Evershot.[3] All the works were wide enough for a double line throughout, and much of the earth work had been executed from six to ten years previously. The permanent way consisted

---

[1] Renamed Grimstone & Frampton in 1858.

[2] Upwey was added in 1871. It was replaced by a new station at the junction with the Abbotsbury branch in 1886.

[3] Between Yeovil and Evershot the line was doubled in 1858; Evershot and Maiden Newton in 1882, Maiden Newton and Grimstone & Frampton 1884, thence to Dorchester 1885.

of the usual bridge rails, varying from 61 to 68 lb to the yard, on longi-tudinal sleepers 12 inches wide by 8 deep. At the Weymouth Terminus, another of Brunel's all-over roofed stations like Salisbury, separate plat-forms were provided for the narrow-gauge South Western trains, which began running on the opening day. The curve connecting the two railways at Dorchester was a mixed-gauge single line, worked by a pilotman, and the Mixed Gauge was extended on the South Western line for the covenanted 8 miles from Dorchester towards Wareham.

The branch from near Trowbridge to Bradford and Bathampton should have been opened on the same day, but the Board of Trade Inspector, Colonel Yolland, finding the permanent way very rough, ordered it to be postponed. This having been made good, the line, 9½ miles long, through the Avon Valley was opened on 2nd February.[1] As far as Bradford, with the tunnel (159 yards) and even the station there, it had been practically ready, save for part of the permanent way, more than seven years, as we have seen. It left the main Wilts & Somerset line about 1¼ miles north of Trowbridge by a fork, on the southern branch only of which rails were laid,[2] and joined the Great Western main line 2½ miles east of Bath at Bathampton, where a station was built. The intermediate stations were the same as now—Bradford, Freshford, and Limpley Stoke; a platform at Avoncliff was opened in 1906. The Kennet & Avon Canal was carried over the line twice, at Avoncliff by means of a timber trough on brick abutments, and at the Dundas Aqueduct over the Avon by brick arches built in cement. The latter work had caused much trouble and delay, and was described by Brunel as 'a tedious and rather difficult operation'. There were seven viaducts on the branch, all of timber on piles, varying in length from 66 to 242 yards. All the works and even the ballast were wide enough for a double line. A notable feature was the permanent way, for which Brunel adopted, apparently as an experiment, the usual narrow-gauge practice of cross sleepers and chairs. About 1½ miles at the Bradford end consisted of 61 lb bridge rails on 14 by 7 inch longitudinals but, in Colonel Yolland's words,

The remainder of the line is laid on transverse sleepers 12 feet × 8″ × 5″. The rails, of the **T** form, are fixed in cast-iron chairs weighing 28 lbs by wooden keys, and these chairs are bolted to the transverse sleepers by fang-bolts. The sleepers are placed one yard apart. The rails average 71½lbs, per linear yard in lengths of 24 feet. The joints are fished.

Only the Devizes Branch now remained to finish the Wilts, Somerset & Weymouth undertaking. This had been delayed by a landslip and was not ready till 1st July, when it was opened as a single line without either an intermediate station or even one at Holt Junction, where it joined the main line between Melksham and Trowbridge.[3] It was 8¼ miles long.

---

[1] The single line section between Bradford and Bathampton was doubled in 1885.
[2] The northern curve was not used till March 1895.
[3] Seend Station first appears in September 1858; and Holt Junction in 1861, but only as a changing place till 1874.

The Bridport Railway from Maiden Newton to that town was made by a local Company[1] and opened on 12th November. It was a broad-gauge single line, 9¼ miles long, with one intermediate station at Powerstock.[2] On it we find yet another variety of permanent way, which Captain Tyler of the Board of Trade thus described:

Section of MacDonnells rail

It has been laid with MacDonnell's patent permanent way, consisting of bridge rails weighing 51 lbs and longitudinal rolled iron sleepers weighing 60 lbs to the lineal yard, which are secured to each other by screw bolts and nuts. The gauge is preserved by angle iron cross-ties, 9 feet apart; and a strip of wood has been inserted between the rails and sleepers to prevent rigidity. This description of permanent way has been already tried on the Bristol & Exeter Railway, and with such success as to induce the Company to lay down an additional portion of it.

The Bridport Railway was worked by the Great Western from the opening and afterwards leased to them.

The opening of the line to Salisbury and Weymouth necessitated considerable alteration and enlargement of the Chippenham Station, entailing the diversion of the main line there to new booking offices slightly nearer the town and the provision of an engine house and new goods shed; these were completed in the summer of 1858. The actual junction at Thingley,[3] two miles to the west, remained peculiar in having no facing points, so that trains for the branch had to stop and back into a siding before proceeding towards Melksham. Brunel had a prudent objection to facing points, especially at places away from stations where they would be passed at speed, and avoided using them wherever possible.

Yet another single line branch was opened in 1857—from Twyford to Henley on 1st June, 4½ miles long with a timber viaduct across the Thames and a station at Shiplake.[4]

Altogether the Company opened just upon 100 miles of country branches of their own in the twelve months from the end of June 1856, most of them in the autumn and winter. The result was of course another blow to the already hard-hit ordinary shareholders, the traffic on such lines, dependent as it was on the local population and produce, being small at the beginning and very slow in development, and yet requiring all facilities to stimulate its growth. Moreover, two of them, the Salisbury and Bathampton Branches, diverted traffic from and to the Bristol district, which had hitherto passed by Reading and Basingstoke or by Chippenham, to shorter routes, and so actually lessened the earnings of the main line.

[1] Absorbed in 1901; £6 cash for each £10 share.

[2] The railway adopted this spelling, though locally it was 'Poorstock'; Toller station was added in 1862.

[3] No evidence has been found that rails were laid on the western curve until a double-line connection over it was opened for war purposes on 2nd September 1943. It was probably formed before the construction of the Bathhampton Branch was made compulsory.

[4] Wargrave was added in 1900. The branch was doubled in 1896–98 and singled again in June 1961.

The dividend, which had risen from $2\frac{1}{4}\%$ for 1855 to $2\frac{3}{4}$ for 1856, fell to $1\frac{1}{2}$ for 1857 and to $1\frac{1}{4}$, the lowest ever paid by the Company, for 1858, when a general depression of trade had increased the burden of the recent extensions. For the first half of this wretched year nothing at all was paid; and for the second only $1\%$ was proposed by the Board, the additional quarter being insisted on by the shareholders at the Half-yearly Meeting.

The General Meetings of the Company at this period were far from peaceful. There was a strong opposition to the Directors, composed chiefly of Bristol business men and led by Mr William Miles of Leigh Court, M.P. for East Somerset, whose object was to replace some of the country gentlemen on the Board by commercial men, or, as they put it, 'to infuse a more mercantile element into the Board'. Other demands were for the reinstatement of Messrs Baker and Potter, who had recently resigned of their own accord, and the adoption of their policy of committees and a General Manager distinct from the Secretary. The Ruabon Coal contract was also a subject of much uncalled-for jealousy with shareholders interested in other collieries. At the August Meeting of 1856, held as usual at Bristol, the opposition succeeded in securing the appointment of a deputation of four to consult with the Directors as to the alteration of the Board. Failing to induce the Directors to accept any of their proposals the deputation circulated a report of their proceedings in a pamphlet of sixty pages, which called forth a reply of fifty-four pages from an anonymous Shareholder, and Mr Miles moved at the London Meeting of February 1857 that 'the present system of management of the Great Western Railway is defective and requires amendment'. This was defeated on a poll by a considerable majority, apart from the proxies which the Directors had obtained in large numbers, but the opposition was by no means quieted, and remained to be reckoned with, especially at the August Meetings in Bristol.

In May the Directors at last succeeded in finding a gentleman qualified and ready to relieve Lord Barrington from the onerous and not altogether pleasant duties of the Chair, which he had only consented to undertake for a few months on the withdrawal of Mr Walpole. This was the Hon. Frederick George Brabazon Ponsonby, third son of the 4th Earl of Bessborough,[1] aged only forty-two, a barrister of Lincoln's Inn and famous in the cricket field. He was elected a Director in Russell's place, which had been kept vacant for the purpose, and forthwith appointed to the Chair, Lord Barrington resuming his old post of Deputy Chairman, vacated for him by Mr John Miles.

The new Chairman was a man of peace. Now that the Great Western system had been completed and all its Parliamentary engagements fulfilled, what the Company wanted to recover prosperity was an end to fighting, both internal and external, and Ponsonby set himself to achieve it.

---

[1] He succeeded his brother as 6th Earl in 1880 while still a Great Western Director.

He began by holding out the olive branch to the Bristol opposition at his first Meeting there by a promise on behalf of the Board that if three or four gentlemen of commercial pursuits, willing to give their time as Directors, could be found, vacancies should be made for them. Up to the time of the next Half-yearly Meeting in February 1858 no suitable candidates had been found either by the Directors or the Opposition; then three were proposed and accepted, one of them being the ex-Director Samuel Baker; and three Directors, including Walpole the late Chairman, resigned their seats to admit them to the Board.[1]

The next August Meeting was the last held in Bristol. In February 1859 the Directors were authorized to insert a clause in the Company's Bill of that session repealing the provision in the original Act of 1835, which required the Half-yearly Meetings to be held in London and Bristol alternately, and in anticipation of its passing a Special Meeting on 31st March decreed that all future meetings of the Company should be held in London.

Of external enemies the first with whom peace was made was the Oxford, Worcester & Wolverhampton. In this case the overtures came from the Board of that Company, which had been remodelled in 1856, but from various causes nothing was effected till February 1858, when after prolonged negotiations Ponsonby and the Oxford, Worcester & Wolverhampton Chairman signed an Agreement releasing the Company from the obligation to complete the Broad Gauge on its main line, which it had been fighting against for nearly seven years, and providing for an interchange of traffic and the establishment of improved relations in general.

Next, an Agreement was come to with the South Eastern and London & South Western Companies in June for the termination of the insane rate-cutting competition between London and Reading, which they had been engaged in against the Great Western ever since the opening of their lines in 1849 and 1856 respectively, and a pool of the receipts from which the Great Western was to have roughly two-thirds of the passenger revenue and the other two Companies between them two-thirds of that from goods, after allowing for working expenses.[2]

Later in the year Ponsonby had the satisfaction of signing three Agreements with Lord Chandos, the London & North Western Chairman, for peaceful relations with that Company. The first of these, in July, provided for through bookings between Great Western stations and the Chester and Holyhead line; the second, in November, for an extension of the practice of equal rates and the division of traffic at all competitive places; and the third, also in November, giving Great Western traffic access to Manchester over the North Western from Walton Junction, via Warrington and the old Liverpool & Manchester Line, and the use of their Liverpool Road Goods Station there.

[1] Walpole rejoined in 1859.
[2] For details of this competition see, H. G. Lewin's *The Railway Mania and its Aftermath* (1936).

These last arrangements were facilitated by the entire collapse of Captain Huish's 'Euston Empire'—even the faithful Midland had at last rebelled and deserted him—and the abandonment of his fighting protectionist policy by the North Western Company, from whose service the old warrior retired in September.

How far Ponsonby was himself responsible for this general policy of pacification and how much Saunders had to do with it, we shall never know. Equal rates the latter had always advocated, but it is hardly likely that, loyal admirer of Brunel and foremost champion of the Broad Gauge as he was, he approved of the surrender to the rebel Oxford, Worcester & Wolverhampton; all the same, he must have recognized that any extension of the existing broad-gauge system, north of Oxford at any rate, was now wellnigh hopeless, and that the surrender was practically inevitable. However this may be, the Chairman, during whose short reign these various agreements were made and who put his name to them, is certainly entitled to be remembered in Great Western annals as Ponsonby the Peacemaker.

The only new railway in connection with the Great Western opened in 1858 was that of the East Somerset Company,[1] a broad-gauge single line 9 miles long from Witham on the Weymouth Branch to Shepton Mallet with an intermediate station at Cranmore.[2] This was opened on 9th November and worked by the Great Western. The permanent way on this line was of the usual broad-gauge type of the period—61 lb bridge rails on longitudinal sleepers; there were no engineering works worth mention.

The Narrow Gauge made a small but important encroachment on the broad-gauge system towards the end of the year. Two Bills were introduced into Parliament in the 1857 Session with the object of connecting the South Eastern Railway at Reading with the Great Western mixed-gauge line between Basingstoke and the north, which passed within little more than a mile of the town. One of these, promoted by the South Eastern Company itself, was opposed by the Great Western and defeated; the other, by the Staines, Wokingham & Reading Company, whose line with running powers over the South Eastern into Reading was worked by the London & South Western, was assented to on certain conditions, and passed by Parliament. It authorized the Staines Company to make a railway from a junction with the narrow-gauge rails of the Great Western in the parish of Tilehurst to the South Eastern, provided the Great Western did not within a year make a narrow-gauge line thence to a certain point east of their Reading Station; in which case the Staines Company might only complete the connecting link from that point. Preferring to do the work themselves, the Great Western accordingly proceeded to lay a single narrow-gauge line on the north side of the main line from the junction of the Basingstoke

---

[1] Absorbed in 1874.
[2] Wanstrow (unstaffed until 1909) was added in 1860; goods accommodation was not provided until 1926.

Loop for 1¼ miles past Reading Station and down to the ground level, curving round to pass under the main line at a very acute angle to join the Staines Company's short branch from the South Eastern Railway. This was finished within the time limited by the Act but not opened for traffic till the exchange sidings on the low level were ready in December 1858. Its completion inaugurated a new route between the midlands and north and the south-eastern ports, and through them with the Continent.

One other event remains to be recorded before we leave this year—the sale to the London & North Western for £80,000 of the Company's interest, as successors of the Shrewsbury & Birmingham, in the joint High Level Station at Wolverhampton and the concentration of the passenger and goods business at the Low Level Station, also joint but with the Oxford, Worcester & Wolverhampton Company, and the Victoria Basin Depot respectively. Since November 1854 both stations had been used by the Great Western for their passenger traffic northward, carriages being started from the High Level to join the trains from the new Low Level Station at Stafford Road Junction, where there was a platform.[1] This curious practice ceased from 1st March 1859 and as soon as the new goods sheds and warehouses at the Victoria Basin, to replace those of the late Shrewsbury & Birmingham at the High Level Station, were ready for use in the autumn of that year, the latter were handed over to the North Western and the connection between the two railways abolished.

Having done good work in his short term of office, Ponsonby relinquished the Chair immediately after the General Meeting of February 1859, at which he was accorded a hearty vote of thanks 'for his great services to the Company since he became their Chairman'. His successor was a connection by marriage, a year younger than himself, the second son and heir of the 3rd Marquis of Lansdowne, known by his father's title of Earl of Shelburne. Lord Shelburne, who sat in the House of Lords as Baron Wycombe and had been Foreign Under-Secretary in Palmerston's Government, joined the Great Western Board in the previous autumn, no doubt with a view to relieving Ponsonby.

The Great Western & Brentford Railway Company,[2] incorporated in 1855 to make a broad-gauge railway from the Great Western at Southall to the Thames at Brentford with a dock there, completed their line sufficiently to enable it to be opened for goods and mineral traffic on 18th July. It was, of course, of great importance to the Great Western in affording direct access to the river for the considerable traffic, hitherto carried to Bull's Bridge only and thence sent in barges by the Grand Junction Canal with much delay and expense. The Company therefore agreed to lease the new line, and transferred their hydraulic and other plant from Bull's Bridge to the new dock at Brentford. It was a double line

[1] There was no corresponding service in the opposite direction, all passengers from the north being landed at the Low Level.
[2] Absorbed in February 1872; £50 Great Western 5% Preference Stock for £100 Brentford Ordinary.

laid out by Brunel, and within a mile of Southall passes under the Grand Junction Canal at a point where this is crossed by a road bridge. Passenger traffic began on 1st May 1860.

In the far west the Cornwall Railway was opened from Plymouth to Truro on 4th May 1859, and carriages could now run through over the 300 miles from Paddington, but, though that line was largely financed by the Great Western in common with the Bristol & Exeter and South Devon Companies, the event was not of sufficient importance to find mention in the Directors' Half-yearly Report; probably it made little difference to the traffic receipts.

On 15th September Brunel died, worn out by hard work and worry at the early age of fifty-three. For more than two years his health had been failing, and latterly he had spent much time abroad in Switzerland and Egypt. Though he remained nominally the Great Western Engineer to the time of his death, his position for some years had been practically that of consultant, much as he hated the term, and the everyday work of the railway was left to his chief assistant, T. H. Bertram, as Resident Engineer.[1] It does not fall within the scope of this work to tell the story of his life and achievements; that has already been done by his son.[2] He was a great engineer of outstanding and original genius, too original perhaps in that he was sometimes given to trying costly experiments, for which the Company employing him had to pay dearly. Gooch wrote the following panegyric:[1]

By his death the greatest of England's engineers was lost, the man of the greatest originality of thought and power of execution, bold in his plans but right. The commercial world thought him extravagant, but although he was so, great things are not done by those who sit down and count the cost of every thought and act. He was a true and sincere friend, a man of the highest honour, and his loss was deplored by all who had the pleasure to know him.

Bertram continued to act as Great Western Engineer till April 1860, when he retired and another of Brunel's assistants, Michael Lane, who had once been a foreman bricklayer under his father on the Thames Tunnel, was appointed 'Principal Engineer'. A few months before this the Board had engaged John Fowler to succeed Brunel in the capacity of 'Consulting Engineer'.

Negotiations were opened in May 1859 with the Birkenhead Company, which was now anxious to get rid of the working and management of its railway, and had obtained powers from Parliament to make arrangements for that purpose with the Great Western *and* London & North Western, jointly but not separately. These eventually took the form of an agreement for the absolute transfer of the Birkenhead to the two Companies from 1st January 1860, but as this was not provided for by the Act another

[1] The last half-yearly Report signed by Brunel is that for August 1857.
[2] *The Life of Isambard Kingdom Brunel, Civil Engineer* by Isambard Brunel. Longmans Green & Co, 1870, and *Isambard Kingdom Brunel* by L. T. C. Rolt, the same publisher, 1957. The latter work is based on newly-found material which was not available to Isambard Brunel.
[3] *Diaries of Sir Daniel Gooch*. Kegan Paul & Co, 1892.

application to Parliament became necessary. This was made in 1860, but fell through owing to certain differences springing up between the two great Companies, the chief one being the North Western's desire to obtain the previous abandonment by the Birkenhead of its alternative running powers into Manchester over their Warrington & Stockport and South Junction Railways via Timperley, to which the Great Western naturally objected. These disputes were not settled till July, when the provisional agreement was finally sealed by all three Companies. It took effect as from the previous 1st January, but, owing to the approval of the Board of Trade being required, the Great Western and North Western did not actually obtain possession of the Birkenhead Railway till 20th November. The engines and rolling stock were then valued and divided between them, and in the following year an Act was obtained sanctioning the transfer and providing for the management of the joint line by a committee formed of three Directors of each Company with an independent Chairman.

The Birkenhead Railway consisted of the old Chester & Birkenhead Line opened as long ago as September 1840, from Chester to Grange Lane, with a single line branch to Monks Ferry added four years later, and an extension to the Docks, and also of the Birkenhead, Lancashire & Cheshire Junction Railway from Chester to Walton Junction near Warrington, opened in December 1850. The latter undertaking was originally intended and authorized in 1846 to connect the Chester & Birkenhead at Hooton and Chester with Altrincham and Stockport, but owing to the financial troubles of 1848 and 1849 it was cut down to a line from Chester to a junction with the North Western main line at Walton, with running powers thence to Manchester. The Chester & Birkenhead and Birkenhead, Lancashire & Cheshire Junction Companies amalgamated on 22nd July 1847 under the latter title, which was shortened to the plain Birkenhead Railway Company on 1st August 1859.

Extensions of the system in the north such as this were, however, of comparatively little value while it remained impossible to send a truck of goods through to London over the Company's line. There was no longer the remotest prospect of the Board of Trade being induced to report that 'it would be for the advantage of the public' that the Broad Gauge should be extended northward from Wolverhampton—the condition precedent to any application to Parliament for the purpose laid down by the Amalgamation Act of 1854. The only alternative, therefore, was to extend the Narrow Gauge from Reading to Paddington. Another event helped to force this uncongenial task on the reluctant Directors. Saunders explained the position in their Report of August 1860 as follows:

The Amalgamation of the Oxford, Worcester & Wolverhampton Railway with the Worcester & Hereford and the Newport & Abergavenny Railway Companies, under the title of the West Midland Railway, has been a subject of much consideration by your Directors, holding, as the Company does, so large a stake in the ordinary capital of the former Company, besides being deeply interested in the traffic of the District.

The Directors felt bound to resist that Amalgamation, until they were assured by the Chairman of the Oxford, Worcester & Wolverhampton Company that, by laying down the Narrow Gauge on the Great Western Line between Reading and London, great good would result to both Companies; and that, in his opinion, it would be difficult to over-estimate the amount of traffic which would flow off the Oxford and Worcester Lines from South Wales for London, when the Worcester and Hereford link shall be completed.

Facility clauses for the interchange of traffic were subsequently introduced into the West Midland Amalgamation Bill, and it becomes now a matter of importance to consider by what means the extensive traffic which should flow from that source can be best conducted.

The extension of Railways throughout England and Wales on the narrow-gauge system has made it more and more apparent that, for the convenient interchange of traffic, it is desirable that a continuous line of narrow-gauge rails should exist from the North to Brentford and Paddington, instead of ceasing, as they now do, at Reading.

To carry out such arrangements, a large expenditure would necessarily be incurred, and an application to Parliament required for powers to increase the capital of the Company.

The Directors promised to call a Special Meeting of the Company to decide the question, and to circulate a full report on the subject with estimates of the cost. This report was issued on 18th October and, as will be seen from the following extract, contains an acknowledgment of the evils of a break of gauge, which were so strongly contested and belittled in 1846.

The Directors have now been furnished with detailed Estimates stating what will be the cost of additional rails upon the Line between Reading and Paddington, including the branches to Windsor and Brentford, and at other stations, which show that the cost of those rails laid down, with all requisite Sidings, Crossings, and Switches, will amount to £225,000; and assuming that a new narrow-gauge traffic is thereby to be acquired, the narrow-gauge Locomotives, Carriages, and Waggons, employed for the conveyance of it, will probably require an outlay of an additional sum of £230,000; so that ultimately the aggregate capital employed under this head, the interest of which should be covered by increased traffic, will be £455,000.

The assurances which your Directors received from the Chairman of the West Midland Company, to which allusion has been made in a previous Report, entitles them to believe that, in the event of the proposed Narrow Gauge being laid down, a large additional traffic would flow over the Great Western system between Oxford and London from the Oxford, Worcester & Wolverhampton and other amalgamated lines, and your Directors naturally rely upon those assurances for obtaining such revenue from that source.

It should not be forgotten also that there are other narrow-gauge lines now in operation, or which may spring into existence in different parts of the country, more or less directly connected with your system, to which this Company should be able to afford, and from which they should be able to obtain, facilities for through traffic, rendered difficult during the present break of gauge.

Evidence has been given by competent Persons connected with the Goods Management of this Company that there exists at present inconvenience, expense, and delay in the Transfer of Goods and Coals from the narrow-gauge Waggons in the North to broad-gauge Waggons for conveyance to the Metropolis, which tends materially to fetter and restrict such trade over the Great Western Line; and those Witnesses anticipate an accession of narrow-gauge traffic from places beyond Wolverhampton, if the additional rails shall be laid in the manner proposed.

It appears that not only are Goods unavoidably delayed in their transit by the process of shifting, but that the Consignors of certain Goods object to the risk of breakage or injury, and are deterred from using this Railway by the break of gauge. An injury to coals in the removal from one waggon to another, the detention of plant by the employment of two waggons of different gauges for minerals destined for London, and the necessary distribution of coals of different descriptions in a manner which generally precludes the transmission of full loads in each broad-gauge truck, are likewise admitted disadvantages in the conduct of that trade, which could be effectually remedied by the continuation of narrow-gauge rails throughout to the Metropolis.

Faced with these convincing arguments the shareholders at the Special Meeting, which was held on 29th November, consented to the narrow-gauge rails being extended from Reading to Paddington, Brentford, and

Windsor, and authorized the Directors to apply to Parliament for power to raise an additional million of capital for this and various other prospective requirements, some of which, such as the rebuilding of Reading and Birmingham Stations and the doubling of the line between Frome and Yeovil, were not carried out for many years.

The work of laying the additional rails was not begun till the following May, by which time a sensational event had made immediate narrow-gauge access to Paddington even more essential. This was no less than the agreed amalgamation of the Great Western and West Midland Companies.

The story of that Company and of the events leading up to this agreement are fully told in the next chapter. Here it is enough to say that a Bill for a railway from Yarnton to London was deposited for the Session of 1861. Having at first officially denied any connection with the project, the West Midland Board afterwards openly adopted it with Teutonic disregard of their existing treaty with the Great Western, which provided that neither Company should promote or assist any new line competing with the other. This unscrupulous attack seems to have had the desired effect of thoroughly frightening the Great Western Directors. Notwithstanding that they had the London & North Western as allies in the coming fight, they at last decided to buy off the enemy, and did so on the very eve of the battle by agreeing to an amalgamation on terms distinctly favourable to the West Midland Company—$17\frac{1}{2}\%$ of the net revenue of the united systems. That the latter got the best of the bargain is shown by the fact that as soon as it came into force West Midland ordinary stock began to pay a dividend, which it had never done before, and continued to do so during the remaining nine years of its distinct existence, while on the other hand the Great Western dividend did not again reach the $3\frac{1}{4}\%$ of 1860 until the end of that period. This surrender to what he—probably rightly—regarded as a renewal of an old twice-defeated attempt to extort blackmail was entirely against all Saunder's feelings and prejudices, but he concurred in it because he was unwillingly convinced that the amalgamation was necessary for the future development and ultimate prosperity of the Great Western.

The Agreement was sanctioned by the Great Western shareholders at a Special Meeting on 30th May, and came into force, so far as it lawfully could without an Act of Parliament, on 1st July 1861, from which day the two systems were, as far as was practicable, worked as one under the management of a Joint Committee consisting of the eighteen Great Western Directors with the addition of six representatives of the West Midland Board.

Meantime good progress was being made with the narrow-gauge rails towards Paddington, which of course had to be laid without interfering with the traffic. In his Half-yearly Report of 12th August Lane wrote:

The Mixed Gauge between Reading and Paddington, and between Southall and Brentford, was commenced in May, and is now very nearly complete on the Main Lines, and will certainly be ready for traffic in a few weeks. The remaining portions yet to execute consists of sidings at all intermediate stations, and the Paddington Engine and Goods Sidings, where from the frequent arrivals and departure, and the reforming Goods Trains, the difficulties of construction will unavoidably be much increased. The time required to complete those portions and the Windsor Branch will occupy from four to six months. The total expenditure, notwithstanding the rapid progress of the works will be within the Estimate.

The main lines must indeed have been very nearly complete, for in the early morning of the second day after writing this Report, Lane and the District Engineer, G. D. Beynon, were able to make an inspection trip throughout on a narrow-gauge engine. They left Reading at 4.30 a.m. and travelling very slowly with frequent stops reached Paddington Platform at 8. Thus on 14th August 1861 did the first narrow-gauge engine enter the citadel of the broad-gauge stronghold, two days before the Half-yearly Meeting of the Proprietors, to whom Lord Shelburne announced this ominous event.

A narrow-gauge passenger service was inaugurated on 1st October in the shape of three through trains to and from the Northern and West Midland Lines, the first leaving Paddington for Birkenhead at 9.35 a.m. on that day.

To obviate additional rails through the complicated station at Reading narrow wooden platforms were erected on either side of the main line outside it, at which these trains stopped. At Didcot also there were no narrow-gauge rails through the station, so all such trains had to run through the Avoiding Line.[1] Although the siding accommodation was far from complete, narrow-gauge goods trains began running to and from Paddington and Brentford at the same time. On the Brentford Branch, a double line, only one road was mixed, and henceforth for many years the branch was worked as two single lines, one for the broad-gauge passenger trains, the other for goods trains of both gauges.

The Windsor Branch, with the Queen's Curve[2] at Slough, was not ready for narrow-gauge trains until the spring of 1862. Her Majesty travelled over the new rails in April on her way to Scotland.

This completion of narrow-gauge rails to Paddington gave the Great Western not only through access to Birkenhead and Manchester, but also by the West Midland through Worcester and Hereford an alternative route to much of South Wales, which, though somewhat roundabout, was capable of being used as a competing line for goods and mineral traffic with the South Wales Railway. This fact, combined with other matters to be mentioned later, led the Great Western Board to offer to unite with the South Wales Company also. The proposal was eventually accepted, and terms of amalgamation were agreed upon in November.

The existing Agreement or so-called Lease of 1851, under which the Great Western supplied locomotive power to the South Wales, was to be cancelled, and replaced by a lease of the usual kind at a fixed rent of £170,000 a year from 1st January 1862 until the Great Western and West

---

[1] Till June 1863. Reading Station was not mixed till April 1869.
[2] The western fork; so called because it was used almost exclusively by Royal Trains.

Midland amalgamation should be sanctioned by Parliament, when this was to be changed into a division of net receipts on the same principle as between those Companies and an amalgamation Act obtained. The South Wales Proprietors were to receive at first 10·7, and from 1868 onwards 10·9, per cent of the net revenue of the three united Companies, but never less than £170,000 a year, which would ensure them a minimum dividend of 3¼ per cent.

This treaty having been ratified by the shareholders of all three Companies, the South Wales Railway became for all practical purposes part of the Great Western on 1st January 1862, and four Directors joined the Committee of Management, increasing its number to twenty-eight.

Another railway taken over at this time in consequence of the West Midland amalgamation and the alternative route to Hereford thereby obtained, was the Hereford, Ross & Gloucester, but, as this had been leased to the Great Western from its opening, the effect of its absorption was purely financial.

The same eventful amalgamation also led to the joint acquisition of the Shrewsbury & Hereford Railway by the Great Western and London & North Western Companies. This was a narrow-gauge line 50½ miles long, promoted by much the same people as the Shrewsbury & Chester and sanctioned by Parliament in 1846, in preference to a broad-gauge line from the Monmouth & Hereford Railway to Shrewsbury laid out by Brunel. Its Engineer was Henry Robertson. Owing to the general financial troubles no serious beginning was made till the end of 1850, when the famous Thomas Brassey took a contract to make the line, and offered to work it at his own risk, paying 3½% on the cost. His offer was accepted and afterwards changed into a lease for eight years from 1st July 1854, during the last four years of which he was to pay the Company 4% and half surplus profits. The railway was opened as a single line from Shrewsbury to Ludlow, 27½ miles, on 21st April 1852, and throughout to Hereford, Barrs Court, on 6th December 1853. It had been open for through goods traffic since 30th July 1852. So successful was Mr Brassey that by 1860 he was handing over to the Company enough to enable them to pay dividends of 6% on the ordinary shares. In that year the Company opposed the formation of the West Midland Company, and as a result obtained running powers over the whole of the Newport, Abergavenny & Hereford in return for similar powers to the West Midland over the Shrewsbury & Hereford for traffic to and from the Newport Line.

The news of the Great Western and West Midland agreement fell like a bombshell into the peaceful existence of the Shrewsbury & Hereford Directors. The Great Western, with whom they had hitherto been on friendly terms, was already at both ends of their line, and the West Midland, whom they had frequently had occasion to oppose in Parliament, was about to open the Worcester & Hereford and Severn Valley lines, both of which, they feared, might be used to divert traffic. Moreover, Brassey's lease had little more than a year to run, and then they would have to purchase rolling stock and fend for themselves.

Disturbed by the prospect, they at once approached the London & North Western Board, and the latter, without much loss of time, offered to take a perpetual lease of the Shrewsbury & Hereford on terms which would guarantee 6% to the ordinary shareholders, but proposed for politic reasons that the Great Western should be invited to join with them in the lease. This proposal was forthwith communicated to the Great Western Board before the end of May 1861, and again more formally in August, but no definite reply was made till 13th December, when Saunders wrote that the Great Western and West Midland Joint Committee entertained 'so decided an objection that the Shrewsbury & Hereford Railway should pass from independent parties into the control and management of the London & North Western Company, that they cannot consent to become parties in any way to such a lease as proposed'. Their real chief reason for refusing was not so much on account of the Shrewsbury & Hereford itself, over which the North Western had already acquired running powers by agreement, as of the fact that even joint possession of that railway would give the North Western Company its powers of running over the whole of the Newport, Abergavenny & Hereford Line, and so obtaining access to the Monmouthshire, Taff Vale, and other railways in South Wales, for which they had been striving for the last ten years, as well as to the Merthyr, Tredegar & Abergavenny Railway, which they had lately succeeded in snatching out of the jaws of the West Midland.

In view of the Great Western attitude, the Shrewsbury & Hereford and London & North Western Companies jointly promoted a Bill in the session of 1862 to authorize the lease to the latter alone, but reserving power to admit the Great Western to participate on terms to be agreed. Though somewhat disarmed by this reservation the Great Western and West Midland fought the Bill fiercely for six days before the Commons Committee, but without success; the Committee would not even cancel the objectionable running powers. So, making the best of a bad job, they withdrew their opposition and agreed to share equally with the North Western in the lease. The Bill then passed, and the Shrewsbury & Hereford Railway became a joint line on 1st July 1862, half London & North Western and half Great Western and West Midland, for these two were of course not yet legally united. Mr Brassey's working stock was then purchased by the Shrewsbury & Hereford and handed over to the Lessees, and arrangements were made for doubling the line throughout, except the Dinmore Tunnel (1,056 yards long);[1] it had already been doubled between Shrewsbury and Ludlow. A joint committee of four North Western and four Great Western and West Midland Directors, with an independent Chairman, to be appointed in case of difference by the Board of Trade, took over the management.

[1] This was duplicated in 1893.

To return to the Great Western Railway itself, several extensions of the system were opened in the last few years before the great amalgamation, though none of these was constructed by the Company.

Of broad-gauge lines not yet mentioned the first was the branch from Hatton to Stratford, opened on 10th October 1860. This was a single line, $9\frac{1}{4}$ miles long, with a third rail for narrow-gauge trains, made by the Stratford-on-Avon Railway Company,[1] incorporated for the purpose in 1857, and was worked by the Great Western. Its broad-gauge life was very short. The Oxford, Worcester & Wolverhampton had opened their branch from Honeybourne to Stratford in July 1859, and the Stratford Company having opened a short connecting link between the two on 24th July 1861,[2] through trains, of course narrow-gauge, began to run between Worcester and Leamington in August; then from 1st January 1863 all regular trains on the branch became narrow-gauge, and though the broad-gauge rail seems to have remained for the next six years it can only have been used, if at all, by occasional special trains.

The Ely Valley Railway,[3] a coal line, from Llantrissant on the South Wales was opened for mineral traffic in August 1860 and leased by the Great Western quite irrespectively of the South Wales, though it could only be reached over the latter Railway. It extended about $7\frac{1}{2}$ miles to Tonyrefail, where the Great Western Company acquired the Cilely Colliery for the supply of coal for their engines. Some short extensions were opened in 1862.

Coming nearer home, the East Somerset Company extended their railway from Shepton Mallet to Wells on 1st March 1862, and the Wycombe Company theirs from Wycombe to Thame on 1st August, while the Berks & Hants Extension Company[4] of 1859—not to be confounded with the old Berks & Hants of 1845, which really did enter Hampshire—opened their line from Hungerford to Devizes on 11th November. All these were broad-gauge single lines worked by the Great Western; the last named had a short tunnel (190 yards) at Devizes.

Three short single-line branches were also added to the Northern Division during this period, all constructed by local Companies, and all of course narrow-gauge. These Companies were the Wellington & Severn Junction,[5] Vale of Llangollen,[6] and Wrexham & Minera;[7] particulars of their lines will be found in the chronological list in the Appendix.

In London itself two important railways were opened for traffic early in 1863—the Metropolitan and the West London Extension.

[1] Absorbed in 1883; £135 Great Western ordinary for £100 Stratford.
[2] The section between the present Goods Junction and passenger Station.
[3] Absorbed in 1903; £120 Great Western 5% guaranteed for £100 Ely consolidated.
[4] Absorbed in 1882; £87½ Great Western ordinary for £100 Berks & Hants.
[5] Absorbed in 1892.
[6] Absorbed in 1896; £145 Great Western 5% guaranteed for £100 Vale of Llangollen ordinary.
[7] Absorbed in 1871.

The former was originally sanctioned by Parliament in 1853 as a railway under the New Road between Paddington and King's Cross entitled the North Metropolitan. The Great Western Directors, who had already found that the distance of Paddington Station from the centre of London counteracted to a great extent the attraction of broad-gauge travelling to Birmingham, at once saw the value of such a line to the Company and alluded to it in their August Report of that year. In the autumn they agreed to subscribe £175,000 to the scheme, provided Parliament should sanction the extensions, at one end into the City and at the other to join the Great Western in Paddington Yard, and that the new railway should be broad-gauge. An Act of 1854 reincorporated the Company as the Metropolitan pure and simple with a capital of a million, to make a mixed-gauge railway from the Great Western to near the General Post Office, and authorized the Great Western subscription. However, nothing was done for some years. Apart from the war and general depression, people did not take kindly to the new idea of travelling underground and would not subscribe money for any such wild enterprise. At last the City Corporation was induced to take an interest in it to the tune of a £200,000 subscription, and by the end of 1859 the whole million had been obtained and the works commenced. An Act was passed this year making Farringdon Street the eastern terminus.

The formation of the junction branch at Paddington was at once put in hand to provide for the removal of spoil and conveyance of materials, and was practically completed by August 1860. About this same time the Corporation got powers to establish a new Central Meat Market at Smithfield, and the Great Western joined the Metropolitan in leasing the basement under the Market for a goods station. In November 1861 the Great Western Directors agreed to work the line, providing locomotive power and rolling stock; and Gooch at once set about designing engines which would consume their own smoke, while eight-wheeled carriages were specially ordered for the new service, which was expected to begin in the following summer. It did not begin, however, till 10th January 1863, when the Metropolitan Railway was opened from the new station alongside Paddington, entitled Bishop's Road, to Farringdon Street, not quite 4 miles, and worked by the Great Western with their new broad-gauge condensing engines and eight-wheeled carriages, which latter were lighted with gas, an entirely new departure, and carried twelve second- or third-class passengers in each compartment.

Very soon the two Companies began to quarrel, the first bone of contention being the refusal of the Metropolitan to allot any of its new stock, to be raised for the extension to Moorgate Street, to the Great Western in respect of their holding of the original stock, on the ground that they had no statutory power to subscribe more than they had already done. As the new stock was selling at a premium the Great Western Directors felt much aggrieved at being deprived of this opportunity of making a little money for the Company and went to law on the subject, but without success.

Then sundry disputes as to the working arose, the Metropolitan desiring more frequent trains than the four per hour, which Saunders with his somewhat old-fashioned notions considered the limit of safety although the line was worked by Block Telegraph. The Great Western officers on their part seem to have thought the Company were going to lose money by the working. The result was that the Great Western Board gave notice on 18th July that they would cease to work the railway at the end of September.

Nothing daunted, the Metropolitan replied they would take it over on 1st October, whereupon Saunders wrote that the Great Western stock would be withdrawn on 10th August. If, as appears to have been the case, the Directors thought this ultimatum would bring the Metropolitan people to their knees, they were sadly mistaken, for on the morning of the 11th that Company was ready to carry on with narrow-gauge trains borrowed from the Great Northern, and did so. For this it was indebted to an old Great Western man, Archibald Sturrock, the first Manager of Swindon Works and since 1850 Locomotive Superintendent of the Great Northern Railway, who quickly fitted some of his engines with condensing apparatus for the underground working. Henceforth the Metropolitan worked its own traffic with narrow-gauge stock, but as soon as the differences between the Companies had been composed in the autumn the Great Western began to run some through broad-gauge trains between Windsor and Farringdon Street, and later on worked a broad-gauge service on the Hammersmith line for a short time and then between Addison Road and the City, so the big coaches were not yet entirely banished from the line, for which their great carrying capacity was so eminently suited.

The other new London railway was the West London Extension from the old West London Railway at Kensington over the Thames to join the West End of London & Crystal Palace Line of the London, Brighton & South Coast Railway at Battersea and Clapham Junction, and the London & South Western at the latter place and also by an eastward fork in the direction of Waterloo.

The West London Railway[1] was leased to the London & North Western and Great Western Railways jointly for 999 years from 11th March 1845. Two years later the Great Western had designs of extending it across the River to join the South Western near Vauxhall and obtained an Act for the purpose, but the project perished in the general collapse of 1848–9, and the West London Line was left entirely in the hands of the North Western, who used it for a considerable coal traffic to Shepherd's Bush and Warwick Road Basin, Kensington.

As we have seen, the line from Willesden Junction crossed the Great Western on the level near Wormwood Scrubbs, not quite $2\frac{1}{2}$ miles from Paddington, immediately after passing under the Grand Junction Canal and at the foot of a steep incline. The crossing was therefore distinctly

[1] See Chapter V.

awkward, not to say dangerous. It was protected on the West London Line, in addition to Home and Distant signals in each direction, by heavy wooden barriers on each side of the Great Western, which were raised by ropes and pulleys to let the North Western trains pass, and also on the north by a catch siding on the single line half-way down the incline from Willesden. On the Great Western there were Up and Down signals at the crossing and an Up Distant $\frac{1}{2}$ mile to the west, to which another Distant signal in Acton Cutting was added in 1854 worked by a signalman stationed a mile from the crossing, who was expected to repeat the signal shown there, though the latter was only visible in clear daylight and he had no means of cummunication. Neither of these Distant signals was provided with a lamp, apparently because the crossing was only used between 6 in the morning and 6.15 at night. Hence it is not surprising that a collision occurred one dark morning at the end of November 1855 between a goods train[1] from Bristol and a North Western coal train in the act of crossing, whereby the guard of the latter was killed and the Great Western guard very severely injured. This accident caused the Directors of the two Companies to decide to divert the West London Railway over the Great Western and abolish the crossing, but for some reason nothing was done for three years, when work was at last begun in anticipation of Parliamentary powers obtained in 1859. The diversion was completed and the crossing abolished in October 1860.

In the same session of 1859 the West London Extension Railway Company was incorporated for the purposes already stated, the Great Western and North Western each subscribing a third of its capital of £300,000, and the South Western and the London, Brighton & South Coast each a sixth. Soon after this the Great Western Directors took steps to acquire a new London terminus in Westminster, from which they seem to have expected great things, by joining with the London, Chatham & Dover Company in a lease of the eastern half of the new station which the Victoria Station & Pimlico Company was constructing at the west end of Victoria Street, together with the use of the latter's railway from Stewart's Lane Junction, which was reached from the end of the West London Extension at Long-hedge Junction over the West End and Crystal Palace line of the London, Brighton and South Coast until 1st January, 1867, when the new London, Chatham and Dover line between these junctions and the widened Thames Bridge was opened. Broad-gauge rails for Great Western trains were laid at that Company's expense throughout from Kensington into Victoria Station, and at the same time steps were taken to double the mixed-gauge single line of the old West London Railway and to connect it with the Great Western main line westward at the point near Wormwood Scrubbs

---

[1] It is interesting to note that this train consisted of 68 waggons with the only guard's van in front next the second engine, and that from Twyford to Southall it had conveyed no less than 90 loaded waggons! The North Western train was actually being *propelled* by an engine behind, the guard's van leading! There were no means or running round on the West London.

long known as West London Junction.[1] This was completed in the summer of 1862 but not used for Great Western passenger traffic till 1st April 1863, when a service of trains, some broad- some narrow-gauge, was inaugurated between Victoria and Southall, where, or at Ealing, they connected with main line trains.[2] As this service became wholly narrow-gauge in little more than three years time—by October 1866—it would seem that the broad-gauge extension across the Thames, involving as it did the extra width of two long bridges, was in the circumstances a useless expense, which would probably never have been incurred had the work been begun even one year later than it was. As far as Chelsea Basin one or two broad-gauge coal trains continued to run daily for more than ten years, and excursion trains from the west occasionally landed their passengers at Kensington (Addison Road) Station, which in its early days consisted of one long platform on the east side of the line.

These were the last extensions of the old Great Western system prior to the completion of its amalgamation with the West Midland and South Wales to form what was in many ways a new Great Western, nearly half narrow-gauge.

A fight with the London & South Western Company in 1862 remains to be chronicled. For a long time certain people at Southampton had been agitating for a connection with the broad-gauge system, first at Basingstoke and later at Salisbury, and various ineffectual attempts had been made to form companies for the purpose. Although Russell had threatened reprisals for the breach by the South Western of the 1845 Agreement, nothing was done till 1856, when a line from Salisbury through Romsey and Redbridge to Southampton was surveyed by Brunel, only to be dropped.

In 1858 a local company was incorporated, without Great Western support, to make a railway from Andover to Redbridge, chiefly by the conversion of the existing Andover Canal. This was intended to be broad-gauge, but the gauge was left to depend on a connection being sanctioned with the Great Western. The first sod was cut by Lord Palmerston on 20th September 1859, and construction began in a rather half-hearted fashion. Two years later the Great Western was induced to take up the project, and Bills were promoted in the 1862 Session for broad- or mixed-gauge railways from Enborne, just west of Newbury, to Andover, and from Redbridge to the Royal Pier in Southampton, and also to sanction an agreed lease of the Andover & Redbridge Railway to the Great Western.

The South Western met this assault on their preserves with a Bill for a lease of the Andover & Redbridge to themselves; and counter-attacked with one for a narrow-gauge railway 40 miles long, entitled the Bristol & South Western Junction, from Buckhorn Western, between Gillingham

---

[1] Latterly Old Oak Common East Box. (abolished October 1962)
[2] The West London Extension Railway itself had been opened on 2nd March 1863.

and Templecombe on the Salisbury & Yeovil Line, through Wincanton and Shepton Mallet and over the Mendip Hills to Bristol.

After a thirty-eight days' fight before the Commons Committee all these Bills were thrown out, together with a Great Western one for a branch from Keynsham to the Radstock collieries. Another Bill, promoted locally with Great Western assistance, for a railway in Bristol from Temple Meads to a central station under Brandon Hill with connections to the Docks, was also rejected in this same session.

The result of this Parliamentary battle was a peace treaty made on 23rd October 1862 between the Great Western and South Western Companies, whereby the former relinquished the Andover & Redbridge Railway to the latter, and each Company bound itself not to promote or assist any new line in the other's district, such districts being defined by a map, and agreed to afford various facilities for through traffic. The South Devon Company was invited to join in the treaty and did so, its territory also being defined and provision made for through rates and fares with the South Western.

Soon after this the Bills for the amalgamation of the West Midland and South Wales Companies with the Great Western were deposited for the forthcoming Session of 1863. They were opposed by the London & North Western, Midland, Vale of Neath, and Taff Vale, as well as by the various little Companies which later on combined to form the Cambrian, and several others in Wales and its borderland, such as the Brecon & Merthyr and Hereford, Hay & Brecon. The first four were pacified by Agreements scheduled to the Bills, providing for mutual facilities and dealing satisfactorily with all matters at issue between them and the enlarged Great Western. These important Agreements of which those with the North Western and Midland remained in force for nearly 60 years were ably negotiated by James Grierson, the Chief Goods Manager. The principal opposition being thus got rid of, the two Bills had a comparatively easy passage through Parliament, the smaller opponents having to be content with provisions for through fares and rates, and received the Royal Assent on 13th and 21st July respectively, to come into force on 1st August 1863.

In the meantime changes had been made in the Great Western Board. Lord Shelburne succeeded his father as Marquis of Lansdowne on 31st January 1863 and was unable to preside at the February Meeting, though he signed the Directors' Report with his new title. The Chair at the Meeting was taken by Ponsonby the Peacemaker, who failed on this occasion to pacify the opposition. The latter was present in force and succeeded in carrying several resolutions limiting the powers of the Board in certain respects, and providing for its reconstruction by a shareholders' election of the Great Western members of the new Board of the amalgamated Company. A committee of seven shareholders was appointed to arrange with the Directors as to the best method of carrying out the resolutions, and the Meeting adjourned for a month to receive their report.

In the interval Lord Lansdowne resigned, and Spencer Walpole consented once again to act as a stop-gap Chairman till the Amalgamation.

At the adjourned Meeting the Committee reported, amongst other things, that the reconstruction of the Board was to be carried out by a clause in the Amalgamation Bill, by which the election of the Great Western contingent on the new Board would be vested in the shareholders, and that in the meantime the present Board had agreed to make vacancies for six new Directors and to fill them up with an equal number to be selected by the Committee and approved by the Board.

Among those who made way for the new-comers were the last two survivors of the original Board of 1835, E. W. Mills of London and H. Simonds of Reading, Lord Barrington, who had been Deputy Chairman for twenty years save for a short interval in the Chair, and Lord Lansdowne, Chairman for the last four years. Notable new Directors were Richard Potter, who had resigned his seat in 1856 and was now a Director of the West Midland, and Alexander Wood, destined to be Deputy Chairman for well-nigh a quarter of a century.

The Amalgamation Acts having passed, a Special Meeting of the old Great Western shareholders was held on 7th August to select seventeen Directors—Sir Watkin Wynn's right to nominate one having been preserved by the Act—to represent them on the new Board of twenty-eight. The eleven old and six new Directors in office were duly nominated but opposed by candidates put up by a recalcitrant minority of the opposition, whose spokesman demanded a poll on every name. This caused the Meeting to be adjourned to 10th and then to 13th August, when at last the existing Directors were declared elected by large majorities. Only one of them, J. W. Miles, had been on the Board in the 'fighting 'forties'.

A still greater break with the past was the retirement of the man who had done so much to nurse the Great Western Railway into life originally and to guide and foster its growth and development for thirty years, Charles Saunders, the first servant of the Company and later its chief executive officer. In the summer of 1862 Saunders, now aged nearly sixty-six, began to feel the first symptoms of heart trouble, caused by overwork and doubtless also by distress due to the embarrassed state of the Company's finances. A holiday brought temporary relief, but in December medical advice decided him to inform the Board of his wish to resign. The Directors, however, begged him to remain in office at any rate till the end of the forthcoming session of Parliament, on the distinct understanding that he was to take things easily and not work as he had done. They promised then to secure him 'such retiring pension as his long and highly valued services, to which in fact he may be said to have sacrificed his health, fully entitle him to expect'; and the Chairman was requested, with the help of his predecessors, Walpole and Barrington, to draft a paragraph for the February Report. It was as follows:

The Directors regret to add that it has now become their painful duty to announce to the Shareholders that their old and much valued Secretary and General Superintendent has

been constrained by the state of his health and advancing years to tender his resignation
Instead, however, of accepting that resignation it has seemed to them to be a matter of
so much importance that the Company should have the benefit of his knowledge and
experience in assisting them to pass the Amalgamation Bill through Parliament that they
have requested him to continue his services for a limited period.

To this Mr Saunders has consented. In the meanwhile the Directors feel that, after
thirty years of unwearied labour and conspicuous ability, they ought not to part with one
who has given them the best years of his life without recommending to the Shareholders
that such a retiring pension should be granted to him as his long and faithful services
fully entitle him to expect.

Although it was not to be decided at the Meeting, this hitherto unheard
of proposal of a pension to a retiring officer provoked some protests.
Moreover, a small but noisy section of the opposition, mostly from Bristol
and its neighbourhood, was animated by personal hostility to Saunders,
whom they regarded as the originator of the costly extensions to the north.
The Great Western Railway, in their opinion, should have remained
confined to its original purpose—of serving the City of Bristol and perhaps
South Wales, certainly not Birmingham, much less the rival port of the
Mersey.

Saunders therefore remained in office to see the Amalgamation Bills
safely through Parliament and was the chief witness for them before the
Committees, but most of the arrangements, such as the agreements with
other Companies, were left, subject to his general supervision, to his able
young coadjutor, James Grierson, aided by A. C. Sherriff, the General
Manager of the West Midland.

The first Meeting of the united Company in September was the scene
of a painful display of spite on the part of the hostile clique against the old
man who had worn himself out in the service of the Great Western and
was now made the scapegoat for its lack of prosperity. He was warmly
defended by, amongst others, Lord Lansdowne and Ponsonby, who as
ex-Chairmen bore witness that he had never been an advocate for
extensions in general, and that his advice had been by no means always
followed by the Board. When it came to voting, his enemies made a very
poor show, and a modest pension of less than half his salary, proposed by
the Directors, was carried by a large majority of the shareholders present.
He did not live long to enjoy a well-earned rest. His resignation took
effect at the end of the month, but he never recovered his health and died
at Westbourne Lodge on 19th September 1864, just a year and a day after
the Meeting.

How far Saunders was responsible for Great Western policy during his
long term of office it is now impossible to say. As regards the extension to the
north, it seems that after the defection of the Grand Junction Company in
1845 he doubted the wisdom of going on with the Birmingham & Oxford
and Birmingham, Wolverhampton & Dudley projects, but the Board
having decided on it he loyally accepted their decision, as he always did,
and carried the great fight to victory, thereby making many bitter enemies.
The subsequent acquisition of the Shrewsbury Railways he appears to

have favoured, recognizing their value as feeders for the line to Wolverhampton, though it is doubtful whether he approved of the costly guarantee eventually given to the two Companies.

Of Brunel and the Broad Gauge he was always an out-and-out supporter, and the weight which he soon acquired and held as a witness before Parliamentary Committees contributed largely to the victories of the Great Western over their Narrow Gauge opponents in the days of the Gauge War and afterwards. He remained a Broad Gauge man to the last, though he must have recognized that its ultimate extinction was only a matter of time.

In dealings with other Companies Saunders is said to have been in his later days somewhat cautious and difficult, and this was one of the accusations brought against him by the two Directors who resigned in 1856. His old adversary, Captain Huish, giving evidence before the Commons Committee on the South Wales Railway Bill of 1861, said: 'I do not know of any Company so difficult to come to an agreement with as the Great Western, or one which keeps so honourably to an agreement when once made'.

Though he was the chief executive officer of the Company with the title of General Superintendent, his position was not quite that of a General Manager because during all his time the Directors themselves took cognizance of and decided the most trifling details of management. Hence it is uncertain whether on any given occasion Saunders was acting independently or merely as the mouthpiece of the Board. Matters for which he must be given credit were the original organization and training of the staff, other than that of the Engineering and Locomotive Departments, and the general administration of the Company's business at a time when there was little or no experience to guide him. According to his successor, Grierson, he was specially insistent on two points—harmonious working between the officers of the various departments, and that unfailing courtesy to the public for which the Great Western staff has always been distinguished. No less than five General Managers of other railways were trained under Saunders at Paddington—Seymour Clarke of the Great Northern, W. O'Brien of the North Eastern, R. Underdown of the Manchester, Sheffield & Lincolnshire, J. S. Forbes of the London, Chatham & Dover, and P. Morris of the North Staffordshire.

Gooch wrote of his death:[1]

On September 22nd[2] 1864, my old and good friend Mr Saunders died. He was one of the most able of our railway men, and in his time had probably had a greater amount of influence than any other. He was a perfect gentleman and much liked by all the officers. We presented him with a very handsome testimonial in January. We had worked together for nearly my whole life and never had a disagreement. He was always a good friend to his brother officers and a man of high honour.

The testimonial alluded to was subscribed by 180 of the Directors, officers, station masters, and principal clerks, and took the form of a

[1] *Diaries of Sir Daniel Gooch*, page 84.
[2] This date is a mistake; probably it is that of the funeral.

valedictory address and a dressing case for Mrs Saunders containing the balance of the £575 collected.

In November Saunders had received from Queen Victoria a handsome silver centrepiece 'as a mark of Her Majesty's approval of your services in attendance on Her Majesty on every occasion for very many years past on which she has travelled on the Great Western Railway'.[1]

These tributes must have helped somewhat to soften the old man's pain at leaving the Company, to whose interests he was so devoted, at a time when its fortunes were at such a low ebb. Altogether the passing of this Great Western pioneer is rather pathetic. He sowed—or at any rate helped to sow—the seed from which his successors in better times were to reap prosperity.

---

[1] Extract from letter of Sir Charles Phipps, K.C.B., Keeper of the Privy Purse, dated Windsor Castle, 3rd November 1863.

# X

# *The West Midland Railway*

### THE OXFORD, WORCESTER & WOLVERHAMPTON RAILWAY

The Oxford, Worcester & Wolverhampton Railway, as constituted by
the Act for which the great Battle of 1845 was fought, was a line from a
junction with the Oxford Branch of the Great Western in the parish of
South Hinksey, some ¾ mile south of the Oxford Terminus, through
Moreton-in-the-Marsh, Evesham, Worcester, Droitwich, Kidderminster,
and Dudley to the Wolverhampton Station of the Grand Junction Railway
at Wednesfield Heath, with branches from Worcester to the Severn at
Diglis Basin, from Droitwich to the Salt Works at Stoke Prior, from
Amblecote to Stourbridge, and from Brettel Lane to Oak Farm, Kingswinford; it connected with the Birmingham & Gloucester Railway at Abbot's
Wood, south of Worcester, and at Stoke Prior. It was to be 'constructed
and completed in all respects to the satisfaction of the Engineer for the
time being to the Great Western Railway Company', and to be 'formed of
such gauge, and according to such mode of construction as will admit of
the same being worked continuously with the said Great Western Railway',
a somewhat roundabout way of saying that it was to be broad-gauge
throughout. Another clause of the Act, however, compelled the laying
down and maintenance between the junction with the Birmingham &
Gloucester Railway at Abbot's Wood and that with the Grand Junction
Railway near Wolverhampton and on the branches to Stoke Prior and
Kingswinford of additional rails adapted to the gauge of those railways;
in other words the Mixed Gauge on this part of the line.

Powers to lease or sell the railway to the Great Western, and for the
latter Company to appoint six Directors out of a total number of sixteen,
were conferred by the Act. The line was at this time regarded as already
practically leased to the Great Western under the Agreements of August
and September 1844, by which that Company guaranteed an annual
payment of £52,500, being 3½% on the authorized capital of £1,500,000,
and half the profits for a 999 years lease of the whole line when completed.
Indeed it was this guarantee, prominently set out in the Prospectus, that
attracted investors and on the safe passage of the Act sent the shares to a
premium. The Great Western were empowered to subscribe up to half
the whole capital. They had already, as we have seen in the story of the
battle, subscribed for 7,500 of the £50 shares, a quarter of the whole, at
the urgent request of the promoters, to enable the latter to make up the
necessary subscription list for Parliament, although this was no part of
their duty under the agreements. Rather more than half of these they
afterwards sold at a profit with the consent of the Oxford, Worcester &

Wolverhampton Board, retaining 3,620 shares, £181,000, as a permanent holding.

Another clause of the Act, which became important later on, was inserted in Committee. After reciting that the Great Western Company were willing to undertake, in case of need, the due completion of the railway, it empowered that Company, in the event of the Worcester Company neglecting or failing to complete their line within the period limited, to proceed to construct it themselves and to exercise all the powers of the defaulting Company. Further, the Great Western were to be obliged to do this if called upon by the Board of Trade.

Very soon after the Act was passed it became evident that Brunel's estimate of £1½ million was, or had become, utterly insufficient for the construction of the railway. During the progress of the Bill through Parliament considerable additional works had been imposed on the Company, and the cost of materials and labour had greatly increased in consequence of the number of new railways authorized. Consequently, in November 1845, Francis Rufford, the Chairman, a banker of Stourbridge, wrote to the Great Western Chairman asking that the rent for the lease should be increased from the fixed sum of £52,500 to 3½% on the legitimate expenditure found to be necessary. Russell replied at once:

'I will bring your letter before our Board on the first day we meet. I fully admit the reasonableness of the grounds on which you apply for an alteration in the terms of our agreement, provided the increased amount of capital be not excessive and that it is limited to some specific extent. Without such limitation I am satisfied our Board will not entertain the proposition, and I therefore think you will be wise to fix the amount as soon as you can'.

In consequence of this Brunel, in his capacity of that Company's Engineer, was directed by the Oxford, Worcester & Wolverhampton Board to make a revised estimate of the whole cost of the line.

His revised estimate, amounting to just under £2½ millions, was sent to the Great Western Company, and the Directors, after full consideration of the whole subject at their meeting on 10th February 1846, resolved:

That the sanction of the General Meeting, to be held on the 12th instant, shall be applied for to authorize the Directors to enter into an agreement with the Directors of the Oxford, Worcester & Wolverhampton Company for modifying the terms and conditions of the lease, by extending the guarantee to such sum as may be necessary for the completion of the said Railway and works, and fixing the rate of interest at 4 per cent in lieu of 3½ per cent per annum.

That, if such sanction and authority be obtained from the General Meeting, it will be expedient to increase the amount on which such guarantee shall be given to *a sum not exceeding £2,500,000*, and to pay a minimum interest of 4 per cent per annum. together with half the profits of the line.

This resolution was made subject to two conditions—that the new Oxford, Worcester & Wolverhampton shares should be offered rateably to the Great Western shareholders as well as to those of the Oxford, Worcester & Wolverhampton, and that no capital should be spent for purposes not included in Brunel's estimate without the written consent of the Great Western Board.

At the General Meeting of the Great Western shareholders on 12th February 1846 the following resolution was passed:

That the Directors be, and they are hereby *empowered* to enter into an agreement with the Directors of the Oxford, Worcester & Wolverhampton Railway Company for modifying the terms and conditions previously arranged for the lease of the said line, by extending the guarantee to *such sum as shall appear to them* necessary for the completion of the said railway and works, and fixing the rate of interest at 4 per cent in lieu of 3½ per cent per annum, subject to such conditions as may seem to them equitable between the two Companies.

The two resolutions have been fully set out because they lay at the root of the bitter quarrel which was to ensue between the Companies.

The resolution of the Great Western General Meeting was forthwith entered in their minutes by the Oxford, Worcester & Wolverhampton Directors, and published in their Report to the Half-yearly Meeting of the Company held a fortnight later; but no mention was made of the Directors' resolution limiting the guarantee they were prepared to make to £2½ millions. Hence the Oxford, Worcester & Wolverhampton shareholders and the general investing public were led to think that interest on the whole cost of making the line, whatever that might be, was guaranteed by the Great Western Company. The excuse, made three years later, of the Board for this curious and misleading behaviour was that the resolution of the Great Western General Meeting 'was transmitted to the Oxford, Worcester & Wolverhampton Company and entered in their minutes, but the minutes of the Great Western Directors do not appear to have been received by the Oxford, Worcester & Wolverhampton Company, although the contents were verbally communicated to the Chairman, Mr Rufford, and other Directors of the Company'. On their own showing, therefore, it is quite evident that they knew all about the limit, though they did not mention it to the shareholders.

Nothing was done towards making any proper formal agreement with the Great Western, and six months later, in consequence of some remarks by shareholders, the Directors passed the following curious resolution:

11th August 1846. The position of the Company with reference to the guarantee engaged to be given by the Great Western Railway Company having been taken into consideration;

Resolved—That this Board deem it most advantageous to the interests of this Company that the arrangement should be allowed to remain in its present state, and that no more defined settlement should at this time be pressed for.

The only possible explanation of this conduct seems to be that the Directors, or at any rate Rufford, who was said to be an absolute dictator at the Board, were banking on the hope of getting the Great Western Company to exceed their limit in spite of Russell's letter of November, and his Board's decision of February. In their apology of 1849 they went so far as to assert that there was at this time a *verbal* understanding to this effect with the Great Western Company. No evidence of any such understanding was ever produced, and it was utterly denied by the Great Western Directors.

While matters were left in this indefinite state as regards the Great Western the work of forming the line was proceeded with in a somewhat leisurely manner. In August 1846 Brunel reported that 'the three principal works—the tunnel through the town of Dudley, the tunnel and other works near Worcester, and the Mickleton Tunnel have been let, and the works are advancing as rapidly as the possession of land will allow'. The only other contracts actually let were for the portion from Abbot's Wood through Worcester to Stoke, which was to be used by the Birmingham & Gloucester Railway. Six months later he stated that the whole line from Tipton, 5 miles short of Wolverhampton, to Charlbury, some 72 miles, was in the hands of responsible contractors and upwards of 2,800 men were employed on it. North of Tipton a deviation through Wolverhampton was contemplated, while south of Charlbury difficulties with 'an important landowner' had impeded progress.

In the Parliamentary Session of 1846 the Company joined with the Great Western, the Shrewsbury & Hereford, and the Waterford, Wexford, Wicklow & Dublin Railway Companies in promoting a Bill for the broad-gauge route to Ireland, from Worcester to Porth Dynlleyn in Caernarvonshire, but this was withdrawn in consequence of the resolutions of the House of Commons on the Report of the Gauge Commission. Another Bill, joint with the Great Western, for a line from Shipton-under-Wychwood to Cheltenham was thrown out by the Commons, upon which the Great Western refunded the Oxford, Worcester & Wolverhampton subscription. The Company also supported the Birmingham & Oxford Junction Railway, as they had originally agreed with the Grand Junction and Great Western to do, and took shares to the extent of £100,000 in the Birmingham, Wolverhampton & Dudley, which latter line was intended to join the Oxford, Worcester & Wolverhampton at Priestfield and Dudley, and, the Directors said, 'will be of vast importance to the interests of this Company'. These shares they sold within the year at a profit of nearly £23,000. On their own account they obtained an Act for branches to Stratford-on-Avon and to Witney; to raise £220,000 further capital; and to purchase the Stratford and Stourbridge Extension Canals.

Next year they applied for powers to make branch lines connecting Halesowen with the main line at Stourbridge and Dudley; and a line, foreshadowing the Cheltenham and Honeybourne of modern times, from Evesham to Cheltenham. The Bill was, however, rejected in company with some competing schemes of the London & North Western in the Stourbridge district.

By this time the reaction after the Mania had set in. Railway property became greatly depressed and the means of obtaining additional capital to complete the line more and more difficult. So in August 1847 the Directors applied to the Great Western, asking them once again to increase the rate of interest payable under the guarantee, this time from 4 to 5%. It need hardly be said that the Great Western Board refused this naive request.

From the Report to the Half-yearly Meeting in February 1848, the shareholders learned that the chief object of the Directors during the past six months had been to curtail the expenditure of the Company's funds as far as they could consistently with the contracts, and that insurmountable difficulty had been experienced in the attempt to raise loans on debentures.

Nevertheless the Company sought and obtained powers from Parliament to raise a further £1 million, three-quarters by shares and the rest by debentures; and also to deviate the last $2\frac{1}{2}$ miles of line at Wolverhampton nearer to the town, make a joint station there with the Birmingham, Wolverhampton & Dudley and the Shrewsbury & Birmingham Companies, and join the London & North Western at Bushbury instead of Wednesfield Heath.

Owing to the state of the money market and of the Company's credit these capital powers, like those of 1846, were quite useless; so having called up all the original capital, except £5 a share to be called in September, the Directors applied to the Great Western in the summer of 1848 for advice. A conference was held but no means of raising money could be devised, and the only result was a suggestion that the expenditure should be confined to the line between Oxford and Worcester and that Brunel should be consulted as to this.

Consequently Brunel wrote to Rufford that he had already frequently urged the necessity of devoting the available funds of the Company to the early completion of some portion which could be rendered profitable, but that he was still without instructions from the Board and so had been unable to diminish the expenditure on any portion, and he feared that unless some steps were immediately taken the Company would get into very great difficulties. After admitting that a great deal might be said in favour of different portions of the line, he pointed out that the only one which could be worked by the Great Western with any profit to pay rent to the Oxford, Worcester & Wolverhampton Company was from Oxford to Worcester, and concluded by begging for authority to prevent the further waste of money upon such portion as the Board should decide had better be postponed. Upon this the Directors decided to prosecute the works between Oxford and Worcester in preference to those north of Worcester.

Meantime some inkling of the state of affairs between the two Companies seems to have leaked out, for at the Great Western Meeting on 17th August 1848, in reply to some questions, Russell explicitly stated that the Company's guarantee to the Oxford, Worcester & Wolverhampton was limited to 4% on a sum not exceeding £2½ millions. This public statement caused a sensation among the Oxford, Worcester & Wolverhampton Shareholders, who had hitherto been remarkably quiet, probably owing to the 4% interest regularly paid by the Company on the paid-up amount of their shares; and at their Meeting held a week later some pertinent questions were put to the Chairman, to which he replied that the guarantee of the Great Western Company was *intended* to cover the whole cost of the line. This statement was literally true, but gave a false impression. A few days after the Meeting, in his reply to a letter from a Mr Mortimer and some other members of the Stock Exchange who were interested in the Company, Rufford explained it by saying: 'The guarantee of £2,500,000 was agreed to by the Board of the Great Western Company as being sufficient to cover the amount of a re-estimate made in 1846 of the probable cost of the line, including interest and all other charges, and the limitation of the guarantee to this amount has been referred to at our General Meetings'. In a further letter to Mr Mortimer on 16th September he added: 'The Directors of the Great Western Company could not have been expected to grant to us a guarantee upon an unlimited expenditure, over which they had no direct control'.

Deputations from the two Boards met again on 29th September, when the Great Western Directors denied ever having agreed or intended to guarantee interest on more than the £2,500,000, but were willing to recommend to their Board that a proportionate rent should be paid for such portions of the Oxford, Worcester & Wolverhampton Railway in unbroken connection with the Great Western as should be opened for traffic.

Upon the result of this meeting being reported to them, the Oxford, Worcester & Wolverhampton Directors at a Board Meeting on 3rd October officially registered their own ineptitude in their minutes by the following resolution:

> That the local Directors on this Board feel bound to declare that, although aware that the Directors of the Great Western Railway Company had by resolutions limited the guarantee of that Company to an amount then estimated to be sufficient, they, the local Directors, have in their intercourse with the Great Western Railway Company and in all their proceedings acted under the conviction that the guarantee was intended to extend over such a sum as should be found necessary for the completion of the railway and works, including interest and expenses.
>
> That, under this impression, they have at the General Meetings of the Company, in the presence of the Directors of the Great Western Railway Company, made repeated declarations and statements in reply to the inquiries of shareholders, that the guarantee would extend to the whole cost of the line, and ensure the payment of 4 per cent interest to the original shareholders, and that no remonstrance nor observation to the contrary has at any time until the last month been made, either by the Directors present or by any other person on the part of the Great Western Company.
>
> That, acting under the same impression, they have entered into various expensive Parliamentary contests, at the suggestion or with the concurrence of the Great Western Company, which they would not have been justified in doing, and would not have consented to undertake, except under the belief that the guarantee was intended to cover the cost of the railway and of such Parliamentary contests.

These pathetic resolutions were sent to the Great Western, and the whole subject was very fully discussed at a Board meeting held on 19th October. The resulting minutes, which were communicated to the Oxford, Worcester & Wolverhampton Company, after affirming that the Directors had uniformly and unequivocally refused to give any guarantee on an unlimited sum, though this had been constantly urged on them by the various Oxford, Worcester & Wolverhampton deputations, and pointing out that in 1845–6 they had declined to increase the original limit till revised estimates of the maximum sum required had been made, which would have been quite unnecessary if the guarantee was to cover any sum expended by that Company, stated that the resolution of the Board of 10th February 1846 accurately recorded the terms agreed to, which had never been rescinded or altered by them.

In the opinion of this Board, the personal attendance of any individual Great Western Director at a general meeting of the Oxford, Worcester, & Wolverhampton Company cannot be assumed with fairness to recognize an alteration of terms and conditions previously agreed upon between the two Companies merely because he may happen to hear from the Chairman or any other Director, their statement of opinion on a subject at variance with his own, without controverting or contradicting them.

This Board learning, however, with satisfaction that Mr Rufford had recently stated that he had never represented at any meeting that the guarantee was unlimited, considers that fact to be the best refutation of the charge on any Great Western Directors, that such alleged representations by the Chairman, while presiding at a meeting of his own Company, were left unnoticed by them; and this Board considers it at least unusual, if not unjustifiable, for an individual Director to offer any direct contradiction to, or confirmation of, statements or opinions so communicated to a general meeting of proprietors, unless he shall be distinctly appealed to at the time.

The Board concluded by resolving that it was essential in order to preserve friendly and honourable relations with the Oxford, Worcester & Wolverhampton Company that the question should be finally determined. Accordingly, when the deputations of the two Companies met again on 8th November, the Great Western Chairman intimated that he would not treat with them any more until the Oxford, Worcester & Wolverhampton Directors admitted that the guarantee was limited to 4% on £2,500,000 and half profits.

There the matter rested till the General Meeting of the Oxford, Worcester & Wolverhampton Company in February 1849. At their preliminary Board Meeting the Directors resolved that, if their Report was adopted by the shareholders, their deputation should be authorized to recognize the Great Western minutes of 10th February 1846 as the basis of the existing agreement between the Companies and requested to confer with the Great Western Directors as to details, particularly with a view to the partial opening of the line. The Report, after stating that the Directors had made the final call on the original shares and had found it impossible to raise money on debentures to any adequate extent, and that it would not be in their power within any reasonable period to raise the money necessary to complete the whole line, asked the Proprietors for authority to make some arrangement with the Great Western Company for payment of a rent for a portion thereof. The 'difference which had arisen between the Directors of the two Companies' is alluded to, and the Meeting urged not to increase the difficulties by discussing the question. The 'postponement' of the payment of interest on the paid-up capital is for the first time recommended. Never again, as events turned out, was the Oxford, Worcester & Wolverhampton Company to make any such payment to its unfortunate ordinary shareholders.

This Report having been adopted, the Directors made the required admission and arranged a further conference with the Great Western deputation. At this they proposed that the Great Western should lease the portion of line between Oxford and Stourbridge, as soon as finished, at a rent of £84,000, proportionate to the agreed £100,000 for the whole line. The Great Western Board, however, 'with great regret felt compelled to decline the proposal, as quite incompatible with the just and equitable rights of their proprietors, being calculated materially to increase their risk, while it would deprive them of the principal traffic on which this Company has always relied as the consideration for the rent they engaged to pay for the whole line'. Instead, they suggested an arrangement similar to that agreed on with the South Wales Company: to work any portion of the line while partially open for the benefit and at the risk of the owners until the fixed rent should become payable for the whole line under the terms of the lease. This the Oxford, Worcester & Wolverhampton Directors declined, and negotiations terminated.

In this matter it may be thought that the Great Western dealt somewhat hardly with the Worcester Company, but they themselves were by no means as prosperous at this time as they had been, and the Directors dared not add to their existing heavy liabilities in the slightest degree. As regards the main question of the guarantee, they were consistent from the beginning in insisting on a defined limit, and it seems quite clear that the trouble arose solely from the foolish and unbusinesslike conduct of the Oxford, Worcester & Wolverhampton Directors themselves.

These gentlemen now found themselves at a deadlock. Practically all the Company's money had been spent, but not a mile of the railway was ready for opening and the works were of course suspended. There was nothing for it but to make a clean breast to their unfortunate shareholders, and this they did in a voluminous report dated 1st June 1849. Save for a very natural gloss, excusing themselves as far as was possible, and throwing the blame on the Great Western Board, they stated the facts fairly enough: indeed, most of the story already told has been gathered from this report. It was considered by a Special Meeting of the Company and a Committee of Investigation into all matters, past and present, appointed.

About this same time the Board sought Counsel's opinion on the position of the Company as regards the Great Western, and were advised that no valid contract, which could be enforced by either Company, existed, and that the relations between them had been left in too loose and ill-defined a state to make it advisable for either party to indulge in litigation.

In their report the Committee of Investigation state that another £1½ million will be required to complete the undertaking, and attribute 'this sad result to the connection with the Great Western Company and the want of foresight and policy of the Wolverhampton Board'. They state as a fact that it had been admitted again and again by Rufford and some of his colleagues that an unlimited guarantee had been asked and refused. After saying that the hope of carrying out any arrangement with the Great Western had failed, they recommend the completion of the line from the Midland at Abbot's Wood through Worcester to Tipton, where a junction could be made with the Stour Valley line, and the laying down of the Narrow Gauge, but made no practical suggestion towards raising the money required.

In the autumn of 1849 complaints were made to the Commissioners of Railways by many of the landowners and residents on the course of the unfinished line, led by the Duke of Marlborough and Lord Redesdale, of the injury and inconvenience they were suffering by the stoppage of the works, and calling on them to require the Great Western Company to exercise the power of completing the railway given by the Act of 1845. The Commissioners sent copies of the memorials to the two Companies. Saunders replied for the Great Western: 'that in the present depreciated state of railway property generally, such is the consequent difficulty of raising capital to construct new lines that it is out of the power of this Company to undertake the provision of funds to complete the Oxford, Worcester & Wolverhampton Railway, even if the Act had conferred upon them (which it has not) specific provisions for that object'. These wise men of Whitehall then actually wrote asking if, as the Great Western would in the circumstances be authorized to exercise all the powers of the Oxford, Worcester & Wolverhampton Company, the Directors did not consider they would be enabled to make calls on the wretched shareholders, inasmuch as, although all the original capital had been called up, that Company had been authorized to raise more by their Acts of 1846 and 1848! To this ridiculous enquiry Saunders patiently answered: 'I am desired to acquaint the Railway Commissioners that there is not, as the Directors of this Company believe, any compulsory power to call upon the Shareholders of the Oxford, Worcester & Wolverhampton Company to pay more capital for the completion of that railway than the sum they originally agreed to subscribe—which it is understood has been already called up and expended by the Directors of that Company. Under such circumstances it does not appear to this Board that they can possess any means of completing that railway in the manner suggested by your enquiry.'

Now it is a fact that the original Oxford, Worcester & Wolverhampton Act of 1845, which gave these powers to the Great Western and to the Board of Trade, contained no provisions for raising money to complete the line in the events which happened. It only authorized the Great Western to exercise the powers of the Worcester Company, which in this respect had been already exhausted. But it is also a fact that the Great Western, in order to win the battle for the Broad Gauge, had accepted the clause, to meet evidence given by the opposition in the Lords' Committee that Brunel's estimate of £1½ million was utterly insufficient and that the line could not be made for the money. The clause in question begins: 'Whereas the Great Western Railway Company are willing to undertake, in case of need, the due completion of the line'. Hence it may be said that the Great Western were bound in honour to find the money somehow. Russell and Saunders were men of their word and prided themselves on the Company carrying out all its engagements and promises, but at this time circumstances were too strong for them. The Great Western was already far too heavily committed by its extensions to north and south to accept further liabilities, and a Committee of Consultation on this very subject had just been appointed by the shareholders. Moreover, it was impossible for any railway company to raise capital at this time, save at a ruinous discount or very heavy rate of interest.

Feeling themselves obliged to enforce the provisions of the Act, the Railway Commissioners first directed Captain Simmons to make a report on the state of the Oxford, Worcester & Wolverhampton line, and an estimate of the sum required to complete it. That officer accordingly inspected the works and made a detailed report on 27th November 1849. He summed up by saying that 'at each end of the line a great deal of work remains to be done, but from Evesham by Worcester and Stourbridge to near Dudley the works are very far advanced and nearly ready for opening, with the exception of stations and the permanent way not being laid'. The 'works' included the Abbot's Wood and Stoke Prior branches. His estimate of the sum required was just under £1¼ million. Of the principal works, the tunnels at Worcester and Dudley were finished, while at Mickleton (Campden) a heading had been driven throughout, the shafts sunk, and the brickwork lining commenced at both ends; the abutments of the bridges over the Avon at Aldington, Evesham, and Fladbury were ready for the timber superstructures, as were also the Hoo Brook and Blakedown Viaducts on either side of Kidderminster, but at Stourbridge and Brettell Lane the piers were only partially begun.

Having considered this report and given the Great Western a month's notice of their intention, the Railway Commissioners sent that Company on 17th January 1850 a formal order, requiring them 'forthwith to enter upon the said Railway from Oxford to Worcester and Wolverhampton and to proceed with the construction thereof and to complete the same'. This Saunders acknowledged, saying that 'the subject will receive the deliberate consideration of the Directors of this Company' The Directors making no move, the Commissioners, having received further memorials from the Corporations of Worcester, Kidderminster, Droitwich, and Evesham, in May set the Attorney-General in motion, and he filed an information against the Great Western Company in the Queen's Bench. To this the Company pleaded that the powers of the Act of 1845 were insufficient to enable them to comply with the order, and the proceedings dragged on till 28th April 1851, when the Commissioners wrote that 'having satisfactory grounds for believing that the Railway is in progress towards completion and that it is probable it will be opened for public traffic at no very distant period, they no longer consider it necessary to continue the legal proceedings instituted to enforce their order'. To understand how this surprising state of things arose we must return to the doings of the Oxford, Worcester & Wolverhampton Company.

We left the Directors in 1849 unable to make any arrangement with the Great Western and at their wits' end to raise money to finish even part of the line. Sundry committees of shareholders investigated and consulted, or contented themselves with abusing the Directors, all without result, till the suggestion to issue preference shares was made and adopted. A Bill was then promoted and passed in the Session of 1850 enabling the Company to raise the additional capital authorized by the Act of 1848 by such shares. Meantime new blood was infused into the Board by the substitution of four new Directors selected by a shareholders' committee for four named by them to retire; the latter appear to have been those with Great Western sympathies. The Directors appointed by the latter Company had for some time ceased to attend the Board.

On 5th October 1850 the first section of the railway, 4 miles in length, from the junction with the Midland at Abbot's Wood to a temporary station in Worcester, was opened for traffic. It was worked entirely by the Midland Company as a single line branch, and superseded the omnibus service to and from their station at Spetchley, which for ten years had been the only connection between the City of Worcester and the railway system of the country.

About this time Messrs Peto & Betts, the famous contractors, tendered to complete the line from Oxford to Worcester and from Tipton to Wolverhampton within eighteen months, and Messrs Treadwells offered to do the same between Worcester and Tipton. Their tenders were accepted by the Directors subject to the Proprietors resolving to raise the necessary capital, which had now become possible by means of the lately authorized preference shares. The Contractors also proposed to find a portion of the capital required, provided they were allowed some control in the management. With them was associated John Parson, a London solicitor, who in November 1850 was appointed the Company's legal adviser, and became almost at once dictator of its policy. Rufford retired from the Chair though not from the Board, and Lord Ward of Dudley was persuaded to accept the office. Two more of the old Directors were also superseded.

A Special Meeting of the Company was held on 15th January 1851, at which the proposal of the Directors to raise £850,000 by new 6% preference shares was adopted. Incidentally Parson took occasion to inform the assembled Proprietors that 'he was very largely interested in the line, being perhaps the largest shareholder in the concern', admitting, however, that he had only recently bought his shares.

Immediately after this Meeting he and Peto, with the authority of the Oxford, Worcester & Wolverhampton Board, opened negotiations with the London & North Western and Midland Companies. The result was an agreement that the Oxford, Worcester & Wolverhampton Railway should be completed as a narrow-gauge line, double from Tipton to Moreton-in-the-Marsh (whither the North Western proposed a branch from Banbury) and single thence to Oxford, ready for working from the Buckinghamshire Railway (London & North Western) at Oxford, the whole to be worked by the London & North Western and Midland

Companies for twenty-one years on certain terms, which need not be specified. This Agreement was completed and sealed by the three Boards on 21st February, triumphantly announced in the North Western and Midland Half-yearly Reports, and adopted by their shareholders. At the Oxford, Worcester & Wolverhampton Meeting the Chairman, Lord Ward, would have nothing to do with it, telling the Proprietors it was beyond the powers of the Company and utterly illegal, and that he should resign at once if it were adopted. In this view he said he was opposed by the Solicitor of the Company and all his own colleagues but still maintained it, and so could not conscientiously continue to act with them. He added that the Board of Directors were virtually a nonentity, and that the whole of the business was transacted by the Solicitor and the Contractor, who permitted the Board to know only so much as they thought proper! The Agreement was, however, adopted by the Meeting, and Lord Ward resigned, being succeeded later on by Captain Rushout, M.P. for East Worcestershire.

One of Parson's first moves after the Meeting was to interview the Railway Commissioners to inform them of the state of affairs and ask them to withdraw their pending action to compel the Great Western to finish the line. This they eventually did, as we have seen, after one of their Inspectors had reported that the works were again in active progress, which promised completion in the course of the following year.

Meantime steps had been taken to show that Lord Ward was right and Parson and the rest of the Board wrong as to the legality of the North Western and Midland working Agreement. It was hardly to be expected that the Great Western would quietly allow the Oxford, Worcester & Wolverhampton line to fall into the hands of their Narrow Gauge foes. Within a month of the Meeting certain Oxford, Worcester & Wolverhampton shareholders, in the interests of the Great Western, filed a Bill in Chancery for an injunction to restrain the Directors from carrying out the Agreement and spending the Company's money on laying the Narrow Gauge. The case was argued before Vice-Chancellor Lord Cranworth on four days in May, and on the 29th he declared the Agreement to be in effect a lease, which the Company had no power to make, and therefore illegal and void, and granted the injunction asked for. In the course of his judgment he gave his opinion that there was no binding agreement with the Great Western, owing to the Oxford, Worcester & Wolverhampton never having closed with the former's offer of 4% on £2½ millions, and that that Company had never given or intended to give an unlimited guarantee.

Pending these proceedings the Great Western Board had been urged to offer the Worcester Company terms for a lease similar to those given by the North Western and Midland, a lease of the line to them being authorized by the Act of 1845. As soon as Lord Cranworth's judgment had put an end to their opponents' contract they consented to do this, and an Agreement was eventually concluded between the two Boards and sealed on 20th June 1851, subject of course to confirmation by the shareholders.

The Oxford, Worcester & Wolverhampton Railway was to be completed from a junction with the Great Western's Oxford & Rugby line at Wolvercot, near Oxford, to Wolverhampton with a double broad-gauge line throughout and additional narrow-gauge rails northward from Abbot's Wood, as prescribed by the Act, and leased to the Great Western, who were to provide stock and work the line on terms rather more favourable to the owners than those agreed with the rival Companies. Its confirmation was strongly recommended by the Oxford, Worcester & Wolverhampton Board in their Report to a Special Meeting of their Proprietors called for the purpose on 15th July. This Meeting was a stormy one. Parson spoke at great length in favour of the Agreement, but the opposition, made up of strong supporters of Narrow Gauge interests and of old shareholders, who had been taught to believe that all their misfortunes were due to the conduct of the Great Western, was too strong for him. In the end a committee was appointed to consider the Agreement, and the Meeting adjourned. This committee, as was to be expected from its composition, reported strongly against the Great Western Agreement, and suggested that when the Company had freed itself from the Great Western a beneficial arrangement *might* be made with the Narrow Gauge interest, or, failing this, that the line should be worked independently. On this Parson and the majority of his Board issued a circular exposing several misrepresentations and inaccuracies in the committee's report, reaffirming that the Agreement was certainly not less favourable to the Company than that with the North Western and Midland which had been sanctioned by the Proprietors, and stating in conclusion that the Board could not be parties to any proceedings which would involve its absolute rejection.

The adjourned Meeting, held on 27th August, was even more stormy than the last, a noisy opposition being present in greater numbers. Eventually the Agreement was confirmed, subject to a condition that at the end of four years the Great Western should buy the line, if called upon to do so, at a price, over and above all liabilities and preferential charges, of £30 for each £50 share, the market price of which at the time, it should be noted, was 14½–15. Parson, who had been the foremost champion of the Agreement as it stood, told the Meeting he held the proxies of nearly the whole Stock Exchange and would support the new condition, adding that he believed, when the Great Western knew it was the final determination of the Proprietors, they would accept it. In this he was again wrong, as he had been as to the legality of the North Western Agreement; the Great Western was not to be blackmailed.

Russell, who was up in Cumberland, on hearing the result of the Meeting, wrote to Saunders at Paddington:

By the proceedings of Wednesday it is shewn—indeed it was almost avowed—that it had been preconcerted between Parson and the Stock Exchange to throw over the Agreement with us, which he was pledged to carry, by annexing to it the conditions which we had actually rejected. But I do not infer from that fact a wish to throw themselves into the arms of the North Western. If that had been their object, they would have at once absolutely rejected the agreement with us, and thus have set themselves entirely free to act with others. They had strength enough to do so, and they were not deterred by scruples of conscience from using it. I infer rather, therefore, that they mistrust the practicability of an arrangement with the North Western; that they would prefer one with us; and that the course they have taken is merely with the view of intimidating us into better terms. . . . Under any circumstances my counsel is—do not yield. Either stand fast or advance. As a mere money question (and that after all is the light in which we ought to regard it) I believe it will be cheaper in the end to fight the battle than to purchase peace at such cost both of purse and character.

Turning aside for a moment from warfare, a sensational event in the domestic concerns of the Oxford, Worcester & Wolverhampton Company has to be recorded. This was the bankruptcy and final disappearance from this history of Francis Rufford, Chairman of the Company from its beginning till November 1850, and since then Vice-Chairman. On 26th June 1851 his Bank, Messrs Ruffords and Wragge of Stourbridge, stopped payment, and the Worcester Company lost in all about £24,000, which it could ill spare. Of Rufford, a co-director told a Committee of Investigation some five years later:

When I first joined the Company as a Director Mr Rufford was Chairman and, if I may say so, Dictator. He managed the concerns of other Directors; worthy, able, and respectable men deferred to him, and anything he proposed was carried. When I joined the direction, I opposed this with some degree of success, believing that Mr Rufford was acting for his own advantage rather than for the benefit of the Company, and his failure proved my views to be correct. The public had no confidence in this concern owing to his neighbours' knowledge of him and his affairs, of which the Directors seemed to be entirely ignorant. It appears to have been well known in the district that he was a man of straw using the railway for his own purposes.

If true, this explains much of the early history of the Company and its curious dealings with the Great Western in the matter of the guarantee, which left such a legacy of bitterness and ill feeling.

The Great Western Board met on 25th September and of course rejected the condition attached to the Agreement by the Oxford, Worcester & Wolverhampton shareholders. Their minutes, published as a circular, go fully into the grounds for rejection, pointing out the absurdity of asking them to buy the shares at double their value besides accepting liabilities over which they would have no control—in effect amounting to the unlimited guarantee which had always been refused; offer to modify specific terms of the lease or to purchase the undertaking at its real and not a fictitious value if the Company prefer to sell; and conclude by stating that any attempt to transfer the line to be worked on the Narrow Gauge would be strenuously resisted in Parliament.

To this circular Parson and his Board replied by a pamphlet of 56 pages full of misrepresentations old and new and bitterly abusing the Great Western Board. Saunders countered with another circular consisting of copies of letters of the late Oxford, Worcester & Wolverhampton Chairman and an extract from Lord Cranworth's judgment, which exposed the misrepresentations; and Parson had the last word by repeating them with some additions, and declaring war to the knife. He and his friends were evidently savage at the failure of their attempt to obtain £30 for shares they had lately bought for about £7.

For the proper understanding of the extreme bitterness of the fight which raged between the two Companies for the next five years, it is well to summarize once for all the grievances persistently charged by the Oxford, Worcester & Wolverhampton Company against the Great Western, together with the latter's case in reply to them. They were:

1. The old allegation of an unlimited guarantee afterwards repudiated when found inconvenient. This lay at the root of the quarrel and has already been sufficiently dealt with. There is no doubt the original shareholders in the Worcester Company were grievously deceived, but for this the blame lay with their Directors and not with the Great Western Board, who had from the beginning insisted on a defined limit.

2. The adoption and purchase by the Great Western of a more direct line to Wolverhampton, depriving the Worcester Railway of through traffic. This is disposed of by the following extract from a letter of the Worcester Chairman, written officially on behalf of his Board to Lord Redesdale in October 1846, and confirmed by the original Parliamentary traffic estimates of the Railway.

The traffic from Wolverhampton to London never was promised, and never was contemplated to pass through Worcester, and it was not included in our traffic estimates. When in 1845, we procured the assistance of the Grand Junction Company in our Parliamentary proceedings, it was upon the distinct understanding that we were to aid them in obtaining as direct a line as practicable from Birmingham to join the Great Western Railway, so as to render the northern traffic to London independent of the London & Birmingham Company. As regards the construction of the Birmingham and Oxford line, therefore, it cannot be alleged that the Great Western Company are depriving us of any harvest which they promised us.

The London traffic from Dudley was also excluded from the traffic estimates, it being considered certain that a direct line would be made; and, as we have seen, the Oxford, Worcester & Wolverhampton Board hailed 'as of vast importance to the interests of the Company' the promotion of the Birmingham, Wolverhampton & Dudley Railway. Indeed, they were among its chief promoters, three of them becoming original Directors, and the Company subscribing for £100,000 of its capital. Moreover, it may be noted that this objection to the Great Western applied equally to their hoped-for friends, the London & North Western Company.

3. The continued nomination by the Great Western of Directors of the Oxford, Worcester & Wolverhampton Railway although the Company had parted with some of the capital it had originally subscribed.

There was originally no connection between these two matters. The nomination of the six Directors was provided for by the Subscribers' Agreement of 1844, which did not contemplate the finding of any capital by the Great Western. It was only at the last moment and at the urgent request of the promoters that that Company subscribed for £375,000 to make up the Parliamentary subscription list. The Oxford,

Worcester & Wolverhampton Board, who were first consulted, saw no objection to their afterwards selling rather more than half of their shares, which they did, retaining the by no means inconsiderable sum of £181,000 as a permanent investment, on which of course they got no return. The fact that this sale was made at a profit of some £30,000 was specially thrown in their teeth.

4. The refusal of the Great Western in 1849 to lease a part of the line when opened. This has been already dealt with. They indeed refused to lease the part at the rent named by the Oxford, Worcester & Wolverhampton Board, but offered to work it for the owners on terms the South Wales Company had accepted in a similar case.

5. The refusal to complete the line, as they had undertaken in Parliament to do. This also has been discussed and some blame admitted, but the Worcester Company had no right to complain. Had the Great Western entered on the line and completed it as they were empowered to do, they would have been entitled to retain possession till all their expenses had been paid, and the Oxford, Worcester & Wolverhampton would have got nothing. Moreover, the proceedings taken by the Railway Commissioners to enforce this duty were abandoned at the special request of Parson himself.

These grievances were constantly paraded and urged on Parliamentary Committees and in the Law Courts during the next five years without producing much effect. They were, however, persisted in and of course firmly believed by the unfortunate shareholders.

After another Special Meeting of the Oxford, Worcester & Wolverhampton Company in October, at which a Committee of seven shareholders was appointed to consult with the Directors as to the best course to be pursued, the war began in earnest. The result of their joint deliberations was the promotion of no less than four Bills for the Session of 1852.

1. For extension of time, a junction branch at Tipton to the Stour Valley Line of the North Western, and a junction with the Great Western at Wolvercot.

2. For a short line and an independent station at Oxford, and the repeal of the provisions of the 1845 Act, which gave special powers to the Great Western.

3. For an extension line from Wolvercot by Thame, Risborough, Wycombe, Beaconsfield, and Uxbridge, to join the Hounslow Branch of the London & South Western at Brentford.

4. For power to lease the Railway to the London & North Western or the Midland Company.

Of these, No. 3 was the most sensational. Its proposal was originally merely another attempt by Parson to blackmail the Great Western. He told the shareholders at the Half-yearly Meeting in February: 'The Oxford & Brentford line was at first projected as a lever to obtain an agreement, but the support received convinced the Board that they must proceed to its construction'. The money necessary for the preliminary expenses and Parliamentary deposit was provided by the Contractors, Peto & Betts and Treadwells.

In the House of Commons all four Bills were referred to the same Committee, before whom the whole pathetic story of the Oxford, Worcester & Wolverhampton Company and its alleged grievous ill-treatment by the Great Western was thoroughly well aired. The inquiry lasted seventeen days and produced the following results. The Committee declined to interfere with the powers of the Great Western and rejected the second Bill; the fourth was withdrawn as likely to prejudice the success of the third; this, for the Oxford & Brentford line, encountered strenuous opposition from the Great Western and London & North Western and was also rejected; the first alone was passed, but with the addition of a clause imposing heavy penalties if the line between Priestfield and Wolverhampton were not completed by September 1853. The Great Western had promoted a Bill for power to complete this section themselves for their own Wolverhampton traffic, which was thrown out, this penalty clause being considered sufficient to effect the object in view. They also asked for running powers over the whole of the Worcester line, but did not get them. This sole survivor of the four Bills eventually became an Act authorizing, besides the junction with the Stour Valley at Tipton, the junction with the Great Western at Wolvercot 'at the point where the embankments meet'. The original Oxford, Worcester & Wolverhampton Act had given that Company concurrent powers with the Oxford & Rugby to make the line past Oxford, which had now already been done by the Great Western on behalf of the latter, but made no provision for a junction.

The London & North Western participated in the fight with a Bill for a junction branch from their Buckinghamshire line to the Oxford, Worcester & Wolverhampton and power to work the latter; this was thrown out by the House of Lords.

While this fight was pending in Parliament two fierce battles were waged in the Law Courts. The presence of six Great Western nominees at the Oxford, Worcester & Wolverhampton Board, resumed after an interval of more than a year, was, needless to say, extremely inconvenient to Parson and his 'local Directors', of whom there were generally ten. So the majority formed committees, from which the Great Western Directors were excluded, and delegated to these committees the functions of the Board. They even authorized the 'General Purposes Committee' to withhold their proceedings from confirmation by the monthly Board for so long as they should think fit. Upon this, the Great Western promptly obtained an injunction from the Court of Chancery putting a stop to this illegality, and incidentally restraining the Company from using their funds on the Oxford and Brentford Bill.

About this same time, February 1852, the Great Western Board became aware that the Directors were proceeding with the narrow-gauge rails and not the broad, and even laying them on the main line between the junction of the Abbot's Wood Branch at Norton and Evesham, where they were not authorized by Parliament. As early as the previous October the General Purposes Committee had issued instructions to the contractors to lay down the permanent way for both gauges as a single line, but not to lay the rail on the broad-gauge sleeper till further orders. It is quite evident they had already made up their minds not to complete the Broad Gauge at all if they could help it. So on 18th March the Great Western filed a Bill in Chancery to restrain the Company from spending their funds in constructing their railway in the first instance otherwise than on the Broad Gauge throughout, from laying narrow-gauge rails between Abbot's Wood and Evesham, and from laying them north of Abbot's Wood until they had completed the Broad Gauge throughout. Parson then swore an affidavit that the Directors intended to construct the whole of the main line on the Mixed Gauge so as to admit its being worked continuously with the Great Western in accordance with the Act, double between Wolverhampton and Norton Junction or perhaps Evesham, and single thence, to be doubled if and when the funds of the Company were sufficient. He specifically denied that they intended the railway or any portion of it should be permanently worked on the Narrow Gauge only, and stated his belief that the Company's funds were sufficient to complete the whole line on the Mixed Gauge. In this he was confirmed by W. H. Thomas, Chairman of the Finance Committee, who also swore to the sufficiency of the funds for this purpose. Vice-Chancellor Parker gave judgment on 21st April, refusing the injunction on the strength of these affidavits; and declaring his opinion that the Act, which prescribed that the railway should be of such gauge as to admit of being worked continuously with the Great Western, did not forbid its being adapted to another mode of working as well—in other words, that the Mixed Gauge might be laid south of Abbot's Wood at the option of the Company, nor did it make a double line compulsory. If, however, when the line was opened to Wolvercot, it was open as a narrow-gauge line only, he considered 'the law would furnish ample means to the Great Western Company of getting redress'.

Meantime a further section of the railway, from Worcester through Droitwich to the junction with the Midland at Stoke, nearly 9¾ miles, was opened on 18th February 1852 as a double narrow-gauge line, with room, however, for the addition of broad-gauge rails. It was worked with the piece between Abbot's Wood and Worcester entirely by the Midland Company as a loop from their Birmingham & Gloucester line.

In March Brunel finally resigned his office as Engineer to the Company. For the last year he had ceased to advise them and continued to act only in connection with the existing contracts. He was succeeded by John Fowler.

On 1st May 1852 the sections of the main line between Droitwich and Stourbridge and Norton Junction and Evesham, making with the intervening piece between Droitwich and Norton a total stretch of 36 miles, were opened by the Oxford, Worcester & Wolverhampton Company themselves. Having no stock and no money to spare to buy any, the Directors contracted, on the advice of Fowler, with 'Mr Williams, the carriage builder of Goswell Street, for the supply of the necessary loco- motive and carrying stock', on terms which their Engineer considered very reasonable. Between Worcester and Evesham and on some detached bits north of Droitwich, there was at first only a single line, but by the end of July the whole was finished throughout as a narrow-gauge double line 'with the requisite provisions for carrying out the Act of Parliament for the Broad Gauge'. A further 6 miles, from Stourbridge to Dudley, was opened for passengers on 20th December, in the first instance as a single line from Brettell Lane. It had been in use for goods traffic since 16th November.

In August Russell, thinking that the rejection by Parliament of all their designs for getting rid of the Great Western and for a competing line to London would have brought the Oxford, Worcester & Wolverhampton Board to their senses, wrote to Captain Rushout, the Chairman, a friendly letter, once more offering the Agreement of July 1851 with any reasonable modifications, a lease on joint account like that of the South Wales with or without a contract for future purchase, or lastly, to provide engine power on fair terms. To this no reply was vouchsafed till November, when the offers were spurned, with the statement that arrangements had been made to renew the application to Parliament for the Oxford and Brentford scheme, and that, as the Directors 'cannot see the possibility of reconciling therewith an amicable working of their line by the Great Western, they decline to attempt it'.

Not content with reviving the Brentford project, Parson and his friends proposed a line from Oxford to Cheltenham, each to be made by a separate company in alliance with the Oxford, Worcester & Wolver- hampton. Accordingly Bills were deposited for the session of 1853 to incorporate the London & Mid-Western and the Cheltenham & Oxford Union Railway Companies; the former for a line from the Oxford, Worcester & Wolverhampton near Wolvercot by much the same course as the ill-fated Oxford & Brentford of the previous year to the South Western at Brentford, but this time with a fork to the North Western at Willesden and a branch to Aylesbury; the latter for one from the Oxford, Worcester & Wolverhampton at Yarnton through Witney, Burford, and Northleach to the Midland at Cheltenham. The capital needed to float these bold schemes was again subscribed by Peto & Betts and Treadwells, Parson himself, and sundry London stockbrokers, with some slight local support. The poor Oxford, Worcester & Wolverhampton shareholders put up very little money in spite of pressing appeals from their Board, and the local support was chiefly moral.

As last year, before meeting in Parliament, the combatants had a stiff bout in the Law Courts. Preliminaries began in December with an acrimonious correspondence between the two Secretaries as to traffic arrangements at Oxford. Noel T. Smith, the Oxford, Worcester & Wolverhampton Secretary, wrote to Saunders:

> Our Line will be opened to Wolvercot in January next and will be worked upon the Narrow Gauge without narrow-gauge plant; and the question put to your Board really is—will you, for the convenience of the public, let your trains, on fair terms of remuneration to your Company, go on to the Oxford Station, the passengers being there transferred to and from our respective trains.
>
> If you decline this, will you let your trains stop at the point of Junction, and enable passengers to pass from one line to the other, or will you refuse both of these plans, and compel us to make arrangements for carrying the public by omnibuses and other road conveyances between Wolvercot and Oxford, to their discomfort and to your disadvantage?

To this Saunders replied on Christmas Eve that his Directors would not enter into any arrangements to assist the Oxford, Worcester & Wolverhampton Board to evade their statutory obligations, but were willing to accommodate any of their traffic on the Broad Gauge at Oxford, and offering 'if you have not a stock of engines and carriages adapted to that gauge'(!) to lend them on reasonable terms. Smith answered denying that the laying or working of the Narrow Gauge was a violation of the Company's engagements, and challenged the Great Western Board to 'appeal without delay to the Tribunals of the Country'.

The challenge was at once accepted, and within a week the Great Western lodged an appeal against Vice-Chancellor Parker's judgment, which allowed the Mixed Gauge south of Abbot's Wood, and a Bill for an injunction restraining the Oxford, Worcester & Wolverhampton from opening their line from Evesham to Wolvercot until they should have formed the whole railway on the Broad Gauge, and from spending their money on the Narrow Gauge.

Parson was soon ready with one of his strong affidavits. After referring to his effort of last year, which he reaffirmed, he swore that the Directors still intended to complete the whole line on the Mixed Gauge 'so as to admit of the same being worked continuously with the Great Western Railway', and that the completion of the second line of rails on the Mixed Gauge was no longer contingent on the funds being sufficient, as these were now ample for the purpose! Further he denied that his Company did 'in fact intend to *work* their said railway, either in its whole extent or any portion thereof, with rails on the Narrow Gauge only'!! He was again ably backed up by his friend Thomas, Chairman of the Finance Committee, who swore that 'the funds of the said Company are very much more than sufficient to construct the main line of the said railway from Wolverhampton to Wolvercot throughout the whole extent of such main line, including the necessary sidelines between Stourbridge and Wolverhampton with a double line of rails on the Mixed Gauge'!!! It is perhaps not surprising to learn that this gentleman soon afterwards had a stroke, and was unable to make a further affidavit required of him.

After all this hard swearing, what could the poor Lords Justices of Appeal in Chancery, who depended on written affidavits for their evidence, do? The Plaintiffs had, they said, delayed too long in appealing from the

Parker judgment, and so had encouraged the Defendants to believe there would be no appeal and that they might go on with their Narrow Gauge, and further, the injury to the latter if their line were not opened would be far greater than the injury, if any, to the Great Western if it were opened. 'The Defendants profess', said one of them, 'and I believe not fraudulently or dishonestly, an intention to complete, before the end of the two years allowed by the last Act, a double line of Mixed Gauge along the whole course along which the Plaintiffs require that they should make a double line of Broad Gauge. I am not satisfied that this alleged intention is of impossible or even of improbable execution, and the Defendants are not in my opinion shown to be acting *mala fide*.' So, without deciding the main question, they refused to interfere, and the Oxford, Worcester & Wolverhampton scored a victory. This was on 16th March 1853. The reason the Great Western had not appealed earlier from the Parker judgment was that they hoped the disputes would have come to an end after the rejection by Parliament of the Worcester Company's Bills.

Meantime the opening of the line southward from Evesham had been delayed, not by the fighting but by the extraordinary floods of the 1852–3 winter, which had caused serious damage to the timber bridge over the Avon at Aldington and large slips at several places, the worst near the Mickleton Tunnel.

This tunnel had been a constant trouble from its commencement in the summer of 1846. A few months later Brunel had to install a new contractor, and when the works were suspended in 1849 only a heading had been carried through and the brickwork begun at each end. In June 1851, not long after their resumption, the same contractor, who was again employed, had a dispute with the Company and stopped work. The Company decided to take possession of the works and plant and hand them over to Messrs Peto & Betts to complete with the rest of the line, whereupon the Contractor defied them and kept his men on guard. Sundry skirmishes took place, and eventually, on a Friday afternoon towards the end of July, Brunel himself with his resident assistant, R. Varden, came with a considerable body of men to take possession. Having had notice of his intention, the Contractor got two magistrates to attend, as he expected a fight. After a conference with them Brunel postponed action till the next day, 'when the magistrates were early on the ground, attended by a large body of police armed with cutlasses. Mr Brunel was there with his men, an Mr Marchant, the Contractor, also appeared at the head of a formidable body of navigators. A conflict was expected, but happily through the prompt action of the magistrates, who twice read the Riot Act to the men, they were dispersed.' During Sunday, Peto & Betts' men were collected from other parts of the line, and some even from the works of the Birmingham & Oxford Railway at Warwick and elsewhere which they were constructing for the Great Western, and marched during Sunday night to the scene of action, the idea being to overawe the refractory Marchant by an overwhelming display of strength and take possession before the arrival of the Gloucestershire magistrates to spoil the fun.

The first contingent from Evesham, some 200 strong, arrived at the north end of the tunnel at 3 a.m. on Monday, and the Battle of Mickleton began. It is difficult to gather from contemporary narratives just what did occur in the course of the argument, during which reinforcements to Brunel's Army kept pouring in from all quarters till at last it was 2,000 strong. According to one account several heads and limbs were broken, some shoulders dislocated, and one hero, who produced a pistol, 'was seized upon and his skull nearly severed in two' with a shovel. However, no one seems to have been killed, and eventually 'Marchant finding that all attempts at resistance were useless, from the vast majority in numbers of his opponents, gave in, and he and Mr Brunel adjourned in order to come to some amicable settlement'; and arbitration by Messrs Stephenson and Cubitt was agreed upon. So the battle was over before the arrival of the troops from Coventry, who had been sent for to aid the police. In their August Report the Directors asserted that they had taken possession of the Contract 'without absolute violence or injury to any individual, though the menacing conduct of the Contractor at one time rendered such an issue probable'. The tunnel was at last completed in the spring of 1852.

To return from this digression to the more important dispute with the Great Western; immediately after their defeat before the Lords Justices, the Directors of that Company consented that 'every facility should be given to the traffic of the Oxford, Worcester & Wolverhampton Railway, whether on Broad or Narrow Gauge, and that suitable arrangements should be made to admit their trains to and from the Great Western Station at Oxford, so that the public may have no impediment in the change of trains'. Accordingly steps were taken to provide the needful siding accommodation at the new passenger station.

As it was part of the mixed-gauge Oxford & Rugby line, narrow-gauge rails already existed between Wolvercot and Oxford and through the station as far as the Isis River Bridge, but, as there had been no intention of using them, they were confined to the running lines.

The opening of the line between Wolvercot and Evesham was first announced for 21st April, but this had to be altered, owing to some further slips, to 7th May. A few days before, Captain Douglas Galton came down to inspect it on behalf of the Board of Trade, and reported that it was laid as a mixed-gauge single line with short pieces of double line at stations; the Narrow Gauge was complete throughout, but the Broad Gauge incomplete in five or six places; broad-gauge cross-over roads existed at four stations besides Evesham, where one was being prepared, and narrow-gauge ones at seven stations, of which there were nine in all; the Stratford & Moreton Railway, a horse-worked tramway, crossed the line at Moreton by two inclines falling from sidings on each side; and at the Wolvercot Junction the points and crossings had not been laid, nor any signals erected. In consequence, the Board ordered the opening to be postponed for a month.

Smith, the Oxford, Worcester & Wolverhampton Secretary, having written to the Board of Trade that all the objections to the opening had been removed, Captain Galton went down again to Wolvercot on 28th May, but 'upon my expressing my readiness to proceed to Evesham with an engine and carriage adapted to the gauge of the line required by the Oxford, Worcester & Wolverhampton Act of 1845, the Engineer of the Company stated that the outer rail on that gauge had only been hand-packed, and that the ballast had not been packed under it sufficiently to admit of the passage of an engine, and that, as he could not therefore be responsible for the safety of an engine and train upon that road, it was not possible to proceed'. Captain Galton accordingly reported that the opening would 'be attended with danger to the public using the same, by reason of the incompleteness of the works and permanent way'.

However, this was made good forthwith, and on 2nd June the Inspector went to Evesham and back with his broad-gauge engine and carriage, and sanctioned the opening of the mixed-gauge single line, subject to its being worked, in the manner proposed by the Company, by two pilotmen, one between Wolvercot and Charlbury, and the other between Charlbury and Evesham. As the latter section is no less than 30 miles long, it is evident that the traffic was not expected to be heavy. There were semaphore station and distant signals at the stations, but Wolvercot Junction was of course furnished with the ordinary Great Western signals, including double Disc-and-crossbars for the Oxford, Worcester & Wolverhampton trains. A special Book of Rules for working the line between Wolvercot Junction, Oxford Station, 'and the point of Railway south thereof where it crosses the River Isis, so far as the rails of the Narrow Gauge are laid thereon' was compiled by the Great Western officers, and approved, in order to make it binding on the Oxford, Worcester & Wolverhampton men, by the Board of Trade.

So the line was at last opened on Saturday, 4th June 1853. The opening had been celebrated in advance on the prearranged 7th May, when the Directors and their friends started from Dudley in a special train of twenty-six carriages, enjoyed a champagne lunch at Evesham, changed at Wolver-cot into a broad-gauge train kindly provided by the hated Great Western, and finished the day with a 'sumptuous dinner' at Oxford, supplied by Peto, the Contractor, at which sanguine hopes of the success of the Mid-Western project were expressed. This was fortunate, as on the real opening day the spirits of the Company would have been considerably damped by the recent rejection by the Commons Committee of both that and the Cheltenham & Oxford scheme.

The session was an eventful one. The same Committee, which threw out these two Bills after a lengthy inquiry, passed the London & North Western Bill for a line from Tring to Oxford, but this was thrown out by the Lords. Another Bill of the same Company, which had failed in the previous year, for a branch, $1\frac{1}{2}$ miles long, from their Buckinghamshire line to join the Oxford, Worcester & Wolverhampton at Yarnton, became an Act, and so gave the latter the much desired narrow-gauge outlet to the south. But the two Companies were by no means friends, for the North Western promoted a branch to Stourbridge, which, though hotly opposed by the Worcester Company, passed the Commons; the Lords, however, gave the latter running powers over it, upon which the Bill was withdrawn. Strangely enough, the Great Western and the Oxford, Worcester & Wolverhampton, at daggers drawn in most things, joined in promoting a mixed-gauge line from Worcester to Hereford. This was, however, rejected in favour of a narrow-gauge line supported by the London & North Western and Midland Companies, as to which more will be said elsewhere. The Great Western were successful in obtaining statutory running powers over the portion of the Oxford, Worcester & Wolverhampton between Priestfield and Cannock Road Junction, north of the joint station at Wolverhampton, in spite of strenuous opposition, but a clause was inserted in the Act by the House of Lords' Committee giving similar powers to the Worcester Company from Wolvercot to the passenger and goods stations of the Great Western at Oxford, the latter being required to lay the necessary narrow-gauge rails between the two at the cost of the former Company. It will be remembered that the Oxford goods station at this time was the former terminus of the original branch from Didcot; hence this would have involved narrow-gauge rails for rather more than a mile to Millstream Junction, and thence for $\frac{3}{4}$ mile back into the terminus. They were never laid for the purpose, however; the Oxford, Worcester & Wolverhampton had no money to spare and were soon to find accommodation for their Oxford goods traffic at the North Western station by means of the latter's new branch from Yarnton. Until this was opened, the Company's goods service south of Evesham consisted of one train each night from Dudley to Handborough and back. Five passenger trains on weekdays and two on Sundays were run to and from Oxford throughout the summer of 1853.

During this summer the Company, in order to make pretence of carrying out their statutory obligations, added the broad-gauge rail to the Down line throughout from Evesham to Dudley, but no broad-gauge sidings or even crossing places were provided, and the Up line remained solely narrow. They also took steps to double portions of the 40 mile stretch of single line between Evesham and Wolvercot, which, apart from traffic needs, they were required to do in a limited period by a clause in one of their Acts. In November they had completed the sections between Evesham and Honeybourne and Handborough and Wolvercot to their satisfaction, and invited the Board of Trade to inspect the work. Captain Galton accordingly came down and, finding the latter section complete as a double mixed-gauge line, passed it for opening. Between Evesham and Honeybourne, on the other hand, he found the new up line laid on the Narrow Gauge only; so, explaining that it was not safe for a mixed-gauge line to be worked as a double line upon one gauge and as a single line upon the other, reported that its opening would be attended with danger to the public; and the Board accordingly 'directed the Company to postpone such opening for the period of one calendar month'.

However, as we have already had evidence of Parson's and his Directors' contempt for Acts of Parliament, it is not surprising to find that the new line was opened in spite of the Board's order, the Secretary meanwhile keeping them in play with letters explaining that there was no intention of working any portion of the line on the Broad Gauge, and undertaking before doing so to submit the line for further inspection. It is interesting to notice, by the way, that he states the broad-gauge rail will be laid when additional capital shall have been raised, in view of Messrs Parson and Thomas' affidavits that there was plenty of money for the purpose.

Unfortunately for the Company's proceedings, it happened that a week or so after this opening their Traffic Manager, W. T. Adcock, submitted his time bill to the Board of Trade for their necessary approval of the 'cheap train' arrangements, and some astute gentleman in Whitehall observed that an up train was timed so as to meet and pass a down train between Evesham and Honeybourne, whereupon the Board wrote to the Secretary requesting an explanation of this curious circumstance. Smith replied that 'Passenger trains on the Narrow Gauge are now daily running on the up line between Evesham and Honeybourne, the Directors being advised that Captain Galton's refusal to sanction the opening for the reasons he gave was not within his functions'. Upon this the Board took leisurely steps to convince the Directors that they had once more been wrongly advised as to the law. Having taken the opinion of the Attorney- and Solicitor-General on the subject, and caused a formal notice to be served on the Company, all of which took time, they requested the Attorney-General to take action. This he did early in March 1854, and at once obtained an injunction restraining the Company from using the Up line between Evesham and Honeybourne for passenger trains until it had been sanctioned by the Board of Trade. The heavy penalties, £20 a day, for its use since November do not appear to have been enforced. This Up line was accordingly closed for passenger traffic on 18th March, and single line working from Evesham to Handborough, 36 miles, resumed.

After this the proceedings degenerated into broad farce. Month by month Captain Galton re-inspected the line and made the same stereo-typed report, a copy of which was promptly passed on to the Company with a letter from the Board of Trade directing them 'to postpone the opening of the second line of rails referred to, for the public conveyance of passengers, for a further period of one calendar month from this date'. At first these monthly missives drew replies from the Secretary, affidavits of engineers, copies of Directors' minutes, even interviews with deputations, all to prove that the use of the line would be perfectly safe, that there was no prospect of broad-gauge trains being run, that the Company had no money to complete the extra rail; everything in fact except an intention to comply with the Act of Parliament. None of these made much impression on the Board of Trade officials; they were there to see the law was obeyed, and they intended to do it. After August the expostulations ceased, and by the end of the year the resistance was at length worn down, so that on his January visit Captain Galton found that steps were being taken to add the third rail. In March he was able to report that the Mixed Gauge was complete on the Up line from Evesham, not only to Honeybourne, but on up the bank and through the tunnel to Campden, and further that the line between Honeybourne and Campden was to be worked by telegraph. Accordingly the Board sanctioned its opening on 20th March 1855, almost exactly a year since it was closed. Meanwhile the line between Charlbury and Handborough had been doubled on the Mixed Gauge, duly sanctioned, and opened on 1st August 1854. The 20 miles between Charlbury and Campden remained single till 2nd August 1858, when the gauge fight was over.

Apart from this futile struggle with the Board of Trade, the war with the Great Western was renewed in the autumn of 1853. Brunel having inspected and reported the state of the line to his Directors, Saunders wrote to the Secretary early in November remonstrating on the neglect of the pledge given in Court that the double broad-gauge line should be completed, and asking whether it was really intended to carry it out. The tone of the ensuing correspondence may be gathered from the following paragraph of his concluding letter, which offered any reasonable assistance towards accomplishing that object:

My Directors, making allowance for the bitterness of repeated disappointments to certain parties influentially connected with the affairs of your Company, who have promoted constant contests in and out of Parliament, and have always sustained defeats, ascribe to their temper and to the ruinous consequences of their policy the calumnies contained in your letter, already so often refuted.

The 'certain parties' were, of course, John Parson and those of the Directors who had succumbed to his influence.

All attempts at conciliation proving fruitless, the Great Western filed a Bill in Chancery on 16th December for a declaration that the Oxford, Worcester & Wolverhampton Railway should be constructed with a double line of rails on the Broad Gauge throughout its entire length, and that the Company should not be permitted to construct a second or additional line of rails on the Narrow Gauge, nor to expend their capital or pledge their credit for such purpose, until they should have constructed and completed a double line on the Broad Gauge throughout the whole extent of their line. Saunders also wrote to the Board of Trade suggesting that the Board should take measures to enforce the law. To this 'my Lords' replied that the subject was then under their consideration. It had been brought before them in September by Lord Redesdale, whose seat, Batsford Park, was near Moreton-in-the-Marsh; and later they received memorials signed by the Duke of Marlborough, Lords Churchill, Redesdale, Dynevor, and Sherborne, and many other influential landowners and residents, complaining of the inconvenience of the needless break of gauge at Oxford, the refusal of the Company to work the Broad Gauge or allow it to be worked, and the proposal to send the London passengers round by Bletchley and the already overcrowded North Western line through several tunnels, instead of by the 10 miles shorter Great Western route without any tunnel, on which the trains were so much faster.

The matter remained 'under their Lordships' consideration' till they had been emboldened by the Attorney-General's success in March with regard to the Evesham and Honeybourne defiance of their authority. During the hearing of that case, Roundell Palmer, afterwards Lord Selbourne, counsel for the Oxford, Worcester & Wolverhampton Company, let the cat out of the bag by admitting in open court that his clients did not intend to lay the double broad-gauge line, and believed themselves under no obligation to do so. Of course, this had been obvious for a long time, though Parson had frequently sworn the contrary, but it was the first open admission of the Directors' intentions. They afterwards disclaimed their Counsel's statement, but as Parson himself and their solicitor were sitting close to Palmer and made no protest at the time, the admission turned out to be most inconvenient. In February Parson had become Deputy Chairman of the Company, which in effect meant Chairman as Colonel Rushout seldom attended the Board, and had turned over the legal work to his partner.

Soon after this disclosure their Lordships of the Board of Trade were advised by the Law Officers that it was incumbent on them to intervene for the purpose of obliging the Company to complete their railway on the Broad Gauge in accordance with their own Acts. So, in spite of urgent entreaties for further delay from the Company, towards the end of April they instructed the Attorney-General to take proceedings, which he did forthwith.

A few days later judgment was given in the suit brought by the Great Western. The usual strong affidavit had this time been sworn by Secretary Smith; in it he asserted that the Company had never refused to allow the Great Western broad-gauge engines and stock to work over the line, and once more that the Company's funds and resources were sufficient to complete the double mixed-gauge line throughout! But Oxford, Worcester & Wolverhampton affidavits had ceased to carry conviction, and in the course of his judgment, which was wholly in favour of the Plaintiffs, the Vice-Chancellor said: 'It is now admitted and beyond all controversy that the Defendant Company are not now in possession of funds sufficient to enable them to complete the whole of the up line both on the Broad and Narrow Gauge'. So he granted the injunction asked for, stopping the Company spending any more on narrow-gauge works till they had completed the double line of Broad Gauge over the whole of their railway. After this drastic decree the Attorney-General did not proceed with his similar action.

But the Great Western were not to have it all their own way. In the 1854 Session of Parliament they had promoted a Bill to enable them to advance money to the Worcester Company to be applied in completing the Broad Gauge under the supervision of the Board of Trade, and to give them running powers over the line. This was rejected in the Commons. On the other hand, an Oxford, Worcester & Wolverhampton Bill, applying among other things for extension of time to complete their works, had two clauses inserted in Committee; one binding them not to spend any money on new works till they had completed the doubling of their main line; the other requiring them under a penalty of £50 a day to complete *and open for traffic* the double Broad Gauge with proper sidings, etc., on certain sections by specified dates, and the whole by 1st January 1856.

While all this was going on in Parliament and the Law Courts, further portions of the railway were opened. The first of these was from Dudley to the junction with the Stour Valley Railway at Tipton on 1st December 1853. This had been reported as ready in July, but the Board of Trade Inspector had postponed the opening owing to the condition of some of the bridges and the lack of any information as to the state of the mines under the line. It was a double narrow-gauge line with a broad-gauge rail on part of one line.

On 1st April 1854 the London & North Western branch from the Buckinghamshire Line, 3½ miles north of Oxford, to the Oxford, Worcester & Wolverhampton at Yarnton was opened. In anticipation of this, Parson had lost no time after the passing of the Bill in negotiating a traffic agreement with Captain Huish. This was settled in September 1853, and provided that all traffic to and from London and places south and east of Oxford, accessible by the North Western and other narrow-gauge lines in connection, should be carried via Bletchley by that Company, the distance between Euston and the 'Bucks Junction' at Yarnton being taken as 65, instead of the real 76 miles; the North Western to accommodate the Oxford, Worcester & Wolverhampton traffic on the Bucks Line and at their Oxford Station, and do their utmost to develop the passenger traffic by 'express or other quick trains'. As between the two Companies, the North Western were to have the whole traffic between Wolverhampton and London and half that to and from Dudley and intermediate places, so the arrangement was by no means as beneficial to the Worcester Company as the rejected Great Western Agreement of 1851. It was to last for twenty-one years, but was one of those traffic agreements, for which Captain Huish was famous, without Parliamentary authority and therefore not legally enforceable by either party.

The new branch joined the Buckinghamshire at 'Banbury Road' by a fork, the southern curve towards Oxford being used by Oxford, Worcester & Wolverhampton goods and passenger trains. The latter ran only in October–December 1857, using the North Western station at Oxford; connections were given from 'Handborough Junction' to the Great Western station at the same time. The through passenger service from Euston to Worcester and on by Tipton to the High Level Station at

Wolverhampton began at once, and the London traffic was thus diverted from the Great Western. Connecting trains were, however, run between the Great Western Station at Oxford and 'Handborough Junction'—there was no station at Yarnton till the opening of the Witney Branch in 1861 —so it was still possible by re-booking at Oxford to travel from or to Paddington. In October 1854 the North Western opened a short curve to connect their main line with the Buckinghamshire south of Bletchley, so as to avoid the necessity of reversing through trains at that station. This was chiefly for goods traffic, only one passenger train running daily from Euston specially for the Worcester line, the rest of the service being by through carriages on main line trains. The fastest time between London and Worcester was 4 hours for the 129¼ miles by one train each way. It may be noted that the 'Worcester Curve' at Bletchley was relaid and again opened for goods traffic on 31st August 1942.

The section of main line from Tipton to a temporary station at Wolverhampton and on to the point of junction with the short Great Western line to join the Shrewsbury & Birmingham Railway, known later as Cannock Road Junction, was opened for passenger trains on 1st July 1854. It had been in use for goods traffic since April, but the Government Inspector was not then quite satisfied with the wooden viaduct at Bilston or a large wrought-iron tubular girder bridge near by, and so postponed the opening for passenger traffic. The mode of signalling trains through the Wolverhampton Tunnel, 375 yards long, is interesting:

When a train enters at one end of the tunnel, the signalmen stationed at that end rings a bell at the other end by means of a lever handle and wire, with which he is provided, and places his signal at danger until five minutes after his own bell, rung by the signalman at the other end, apprises him of the train having emerged from the tunnel.

This section was a double mixed-gauge line as the Great Western trains were to use it from Priestfield Junction; they made their first appearance in November. Meanwhile, the remaining mile to the junction with the London & North Western at Bushbury, or Snow Hill as it was sometimes called, was opened as a double narrow-gauge line for goods traffic in July and sanctioned for passenger trains in October. Save for a short-lived through service between Wolverhampton (GW) and Manchester in 1864–7, it has not carried regular passenger trains; Her Majesty Queen Victoria and suite, made their first journey over it, on their way from Balmoral to Osborne, on 17th September 1860. From 1862 onwards to the end of her reign it was regularly traversed by the Queen on her journeys between Windsor or Osborne and Scotland, and during the Great War it was part of the usual route for Ambulance trains from the Channel ports to the north.

Thus was the main line of the Oxford, Worcester & Wolverhampton Railway from Wolvercot to Bushbury Junction, 89¼ miles, at last opened throughout. Its state as regards gauge in the summer of 1855, after which no more broad-gauge rails were laid in spite of Acts of Parliament,

Decrees of the High Court of Chancery, and suchlike trifles, was as follows:

*Wolvercot Junction to Charlbury.*                                        1OM. 40C.
    Double Mixed Gauge with B.G. cross-over roads at Handborough and Charlbury.
*Charlbury to Campden.*                                                  2OM. 15C.
    Single Mixed Gauge with B.G. crossing places at Shipton, Adlestrop, and Moreton.
*Campden to Evesham.*                                                      9M. 6OC.
    Double Mixed Gauge with B.G. cross-over roads at those places only.
*Evesham to Brettell Lane.*                                               37M. 40C.
    Double Narrow Gauge with B.G. rail on the Down Line but no crossing places.
*Bettell Land to Cannock Road Junction.*                                 1OM. 30C.
    Double Mixed Gauge with B.G. cross-over roads at Dudley, Bilston, and Wolver-
hampton.
*Cannock Road Junction to Bushbury Junction.*                                 75C.
    Double Narrow Gauge.

Save in the joint station yard at Wolverhampton, there was only one broad-gauge siding on the whole line, at Bilston; the reason for its unique existence must remain a mystery.

The only recorded instance of a broad-gauge train running over any part of the line south of Priestfield was Captain Galton's inspection trip from Wolvercot to Evesham and back on 2nd June 1853. There was a legend, which the writer heard from an ancient Oxford, Worcester & Wolverhampton engine driver at Oxford in the early 'nineties, that a broad-gauge engine once penetrated thence as far as Dudley, but this can only be accepted with great doubt. It is most unlikely that the broad-gauge rail beyond Evesham was ever in a state to carry an engine, and even so the engine, if it went no farther, would have had to return up the Down line in face of the traffic nearly all the way.

By the end of 1854 the financial position of the Worcester Company had, as might be expected, been brought to the verge of ruin. Money had been raised by debentures at exorbitant rates and by 6% preference shares, and the receipts were barely sufficient to pay the dividend on these. The rolling stock was utterly inadequate for the traffic, and the ramshackle engines provided by the contractor were constantly breaking down; moreover, much traffic was lost owing to the want of access to the various works and canals. Altogether the wretched line had thoroughly earned its nickname of the 'Old Worse and Worse Railway'.

The Board was hopelessly divided, though Parson was still able to carry whatever he proposed. As early as May 1854 he was publicly attacked at a Special Meeting of the shareholders, over which he was presiding, by a fellow Director, not one of the Great Western nominees, who accused him among other things of jobbing in the Company's shares. To this he replied that next to the Great Western he was the largest shareholder, though he had to admit that no more than thirty shares were registered in his name. Later, particulars of his extensive operations in Oxford, Worcester & Wolverhampton shares from 1850 down to June 1854 were published in the *Railway Times* of 26th August, with the further accusations that he made use of his knowledge as solicitor to the Company to buy and sell shares; that he threw the Norton Hall Estate on the

Company when he found he could not make a profit out of the transaction for himself; and that, while professing to the shareholders to be acting gratuitously on their behalf, he made a charge of £2,500 for his personal services, in addition to the sum of £19,400 paid to his firm for legal work in 1851, 1852, and 1853. The Norton Hall Estate of 350 acres near Honeybourne was, it appears, bought by him in his own name early in September 1853, without the knowledge of any of the other Directors, who first learned six weeks later that this purchase had been made on behalf of the Company. These charges were not answered, at any rate publicly, and no proceedings were taken against the paper which published them.

We must, however, give the maligned gentleman credit for courage. Undeterred by the repeated disappointments, he announced from the Chair at the Half-yearly Meeting in August 1854 his intention of again promoting a Bill in the next session of Parliament to get rid of the Broad Gauge and all powers of the Great Western over the Oxford, Worcester & Wolverhampton, including of course that of nominating Directors.

The Bill, which this time offered the Great Western a preferential dividend of 3½% on their £181,000 holding in the Company, was passed by the Commons after a stiff fight, but thrown out by the Lords in the session of 1855.

The attitude of Parliament towards the Oxford, Worcester & Wolverhampton Company during these years certainly seems inexplicable. It consistently refused to release them from the obligation of laying the Broad Gauge throughout their line, yet would neither compel them to work it when laid nor allow the Great Western power to do so.

The Directors were now left with no alternative to completing the broad-gauge double line. They announced this to the Proprietors in their August Report, at the same time repeating their opinion 'that all money expended on the Broad Gauge will be unproductive to the Company, and that all works executed on that gauge will be found by experience valueless to the public'. This was of course very true; they had effectually made it so by their conduct during the last four years and their expressed intention of continuing to work their line 'in connection with the narrow-gauge system'. They now saw no possibility of raising money to complete the Broad Gauge except by the assistance of the London & North Western and Midland Companies, with whom they proposed to make an agreement for working the line. The fact that they had no more power to do this than they had in 1851 does not seem to have troubled Parson.

The Company being already liable, under their Act of 1854, to an accruing penalty of £50 a day since 31st May 1855 for not having laid the double broad-gauge line on the first section defined by that Act, the Directors appealed to the Board of Trade not to take steps to enforce the penalties. An interview was accordingly arranged between the President of the Board and deputations of the Great Western and Oxford, Worcester & Wolverhampton Directors on 15th November, which resulted in a minute signed by Walpole, the Great Western Chairman, and Parson, to the effect that the former Company did not object to a delay till the end of February, on the latter undertaking that their Bills in Parliament for 1856 should be confined to an application for extension of time, power to raise money, and relief from the penalties already incurred. The time was afterwards extended to 1st July at a further interview in March.

The traffic receipts of the railway remained most unsatisfactory, and the working expenses continued to increase till for the second half of 1855 they reached no less than 59% of the total income, a most excessive figure in those days. In the summer of 1854 the twenty-seven engines provided by Williams had been found wholly inadequate, even if they had been kept in good order, which owing to the amount of work put upon them was almost impossible; so, as he declined to furnish any more, the Company purchased twelve and hired three.[1] Consequently the traffic was worked partly by the Contractor, partly by the Company, and partly by the North Western, who worked the through trains south of Handborough and between Dudley and their Wolverhampton Station. It is not surprising therefore to find the locomotive expenses were 25% of the receipts; on the North Western line they were 15%. Williams' contract was consequently terminated by mutual consent on 1st February 1856, and his stock of engines, coaches, and waggons taken over at a valuation, David Joy[2] of valve gear fame, who had acted as Williams' representative at Worcester, giving place to F. Haward, the Company's Locomotive Superintendent.

The Report of the Directors to the Half-yearly Meeting held at the end of this month is a melancholy document. The agreement, proposed in August, with the North Western and Midland Companies had fallen through after much negotiation 'in consequence of those Companies requiring such an amount of control over the executive of this Company as your Directors thought it inconsistent with your interests to give'. There were no means of meeting the expenditure necessary to complete the Broad Gauge, they said, and the liabilities of the Company were estimated at £352,000, a purposely exaggerated figure, as we shall presently see. In the result, a Committee of Investigation was appointed consisting of Sir Morton Peto, the contractor, Mr William Fenton of Rochdale, and three others.

Before this Committee John Parson gave some illuminating evidence. First he admitted that he had been responsible for the policy of the Company ever since he became its solicitor in November 1850, and that the Parliamentary and law expenses were initiated by him and not by the Board generally. Notwithstanding their complaisance in such matters,

[1] The state of the locomotive stock came under the notice of the Board of Trade by reason of a delay of six hours near Hartlebury to the evening down 'express' train on 18th October 1855, caused by the successive failures of four engines: the regular engine for the train, the engine which took it on from Worcester, and two sent one after the other to its assistance!

[2] His experiences on the Oxford, Worcester & Wolverhampton were recorded from his Diaries in the *Railway Magazine* for July, August, and September 1908.

he was not pleased with his colleagues and considered the Board required to be entirely remodelled. He specially complained of the Chairman as unable to keep order, and only putting in an appearance once a month, he being a member of Parliament and with his Regiment at Aldershot. His own 'peculiar position' as solicitor to the Company prevented him having proper control as Deputy Chairman, he said. Other Directors confirmed his account of the Chairman's inability to attend to the Company's affairs, though their reason for regretting it was that in consequence too much power was exercised by one individual, and therefore the public had less confidence in the concern.

Asked for his plan to relieve the Company from its financial embarrassments, Parson said:

'I merely propose to carry my present Bills. If I could carry the two Bills now before Parliament in the form I desire, the Company would in a short time be in a very sound position. I am not at all ambitious of showing too great an amount of wealth. I have rather increased the liabilities of the Company or allowed them to be increased to a greater extent than I believe they will turn out to be, because I wish to show Parliament that it is impossible to go on with the Broad Gauge. If I were to show assets, the Great Western and the Board of Trade would compel us to fulfil the obligation, which at present is immediate, but while I can show that we cannot pay our debts, debentures, or interest on preference, all parties will agree that I must have more time and more money. I want to get from Parliament three years to execute the broad-gauge works. The Great Western have asked me if two years would not be sufficient, but I distinctly said "No", and I think I shall get the three years with their concurrence. If I can get the three years, I am of opinion that the work will never be executed at all. I think the Staines and Wokingham Line will within that period be connected with the Great Western at Reading and furnish another narrow-gauge access to London, and as soon as the Great Western see that, they will themselves lay down the Narrow Gauge and there will be no more Broad Gauge."

This passage well shows the speaker's absolute lack of scruples, and his cleverness in foreseeing what actually did occur.

The Committee published a lengthy report at the end of April, in which they show that the sum required for the discharge of liabilities and all necessary works including branches from Worcester to the Severn and from Brettell Lane to Kingswinford, and provision of £150,000 for completing the mixed-gauge rails, if required, need not exceed £350,000, instead of the £780,000 stated to be necessary by the Directors. This sum they recommend to be raised by a new first preference stock and not by borrowing. They conclude by recommending that all the Directors should place their seats at the disposal of the shareholders, being eligible for re-election, and that a policy of peace and friendly intercourse with all neighbouring Companies should be adopted.

Accordingly a new Board was elected at a Special General Meeting early in June 1856, consisting of five new and five old Directors. Of the former, Mr Fenton became Chairman and Sir Morton Peto Deputy Chairman, while a notable member was Edward Watkin, who had left Euston in 1853 to become General Manager of the Manchester, Sheffield & Lincolnshire Railway. Though Parson was re-elected among the latter, his reign as dictator was over, and the chief obstacle to friendship with the Great Western so removed. It comes out clearly enough in the evidence before the Committee that much of the bitter hostility was a personal matter on his part; Russell and Saunders had apparently taken his measure from the beginning.

The application to Parliament for more time to complete the Broad Gauge succeeded beyond Parson's most sanguine expectations. He hoped for three years; in spite of Great Western opposition, Parliament gave more than four. The Act provided that the Company should not be required even to proceed with the completion of the double broad-gauge line until the expiration of four years from its passing, nor should they be liable to the penalties of the 1854 Act unless they made default in such period after the four years as the Board of Trade should allow. Penalties incurred during the past year were remitted, but the broad-gauge rails already laid were not to be removed. Another Act gave the various capital powers asked for.

One of the first measures taken by the new Board was the appointment as General Manager with full powers and a percentage on increased profits of A. C. Sherriff, formerly Traffic Manager of the North Eastern Railway, who, they considered, would be better able than Adcock to meet Saunders, Captain Huish, and Allport of the Midland, on equal terms. Adcock succeeded Smith as Secretary. The Head Offices of the Company had been moved back to Worcester in the autumn of 1855 from Westminster, whither they were transferred, apparently for Parson's convenience, in 1851.

From the summer of 1856 the position of the Company began steadily to improve, and the new Board was able to report in the following February:

> The finances of the Company are in a healthier condition, its credit stands higher, traffic of every kind has increased, the working expenditure has diminished, and the Company has surmounted much of its former embarrassment.

The working expenses had, in fact, decreased from 68% for the first half of the year to 51% for the second, a striking commentary on the former management. A year later they had come down to 43%. The locomotive stock had been vastly improved. When the Board took charge, the Company possessed forty-two engines, of which twenty-two were usually in steam, a considerable portion of the remainder being 'laid away as incapable of running'. In their first half-year nine new engines were acquired, and many of the incapables thoroughly repaired; by the end of 1857 all the fifty-one were reported as in good working order. The permanent way, which consisted of bridge rails on longitudinal timbers like the Great Western, seems to have been kept in fair order from the beginning.

Soon after their appointment, the new Directors made approaches to the Great Western Board with a view to a friendly settlement of all differences. However, as they felt their hands were more or less tied by Parson's traffic agreement with the London & North Western, these led to no practical result for some time.

One matter long in dispute was decided in July 1857, when Captain Galton of the Board of Trade at last issued his Award as to the payments to be made by each Company for running over the other's line, between Oxford and Wolvercot on the one hand, and between Priestfield and Cannock Road Junction at Wolverhampton on the other. Parson had always contended that the latter section ought, owing to the cost of construction, to be reckoned as 6 miles, three times its real length, without allowing for the Great Western's two-thirds ownership of the joint Low Level Station. The question was referred to the Board of Trade, who appointed Captain Galton arbitrator in June 1854. After three years he now gave his decision that the real mileage should be adopted in each case. One cause of the delay appears to have been the unexercised right of the Oxford, Worcester & Wolverhampton Company to use the Great Western goods station at Oxford, involving, as it did, running over that Company's line for 2 miles beyond the passenger station. This right the Worcester Company agreed to abandon in April 1857.

At last, after many conferences and much correspondence, the general disputes between the two Companies were settled, as far as they could be in the circumstances, and Ponsonby the Peacemaker and Fenton set their hands to an Agreement in February 1858.

By this, the Great Western agreed to the Broad Gauge on the Oxford, Worcester & Wolverhampton Railway south of Priestfield being dispensed with, and to assent to an Act for the purpose; in return for which the Worcester Company were to pay the Great Western £2,000 a year for nine years. This cash payment has rather the appearance of blackmail, but was not really so. It was substituted for a clause providing that a defined minimum of traffic should be sent over the Great Western, only because this provision was thought to conflict with the Agreement between the Oxford, Worcester & Wolverhampton and the North Western. The first suggestion had been that the Worcester Company should supply rails and timber for the extension of the Narrow Gauge from Reading to Paddington, but this the Great Western Directors would not then hear of.[1] Other clauses provided that the Oxford, Worcester & Wolverhampton should run at least three passenger trains daily over their line in connection with the Great Western trains at Oxford; that each Company should use the other's line between Oxford and Wolvercot and Priestfield and Cannock Road respectively at nominal tolls; for a friendly interchange of traffic and equal rates between competing points; and that neither Company should promote or assist in any way any new line competing with the other. This Agreement, though acted on from 1st March 1858, was not put into formal shape and sanctioned by the respective share-holders till February 1859, in which year an Act was obtained by the Worcester Company confirming it and authorizing the removal of the broad-gauge rails from the line. Most of them had already been taken

[1] It was afterwards adopted to some extent, the materials being taken at a valuation in part discharge of the cash payment, but for use on the Wilts & Somerset.

up in 1858 and sold to the Worcester & Hereford Company and the Great Western, but some remained in position for many years, rusty memorials of the fierce struggles of the past and John Parson's triumph over Parliament, the Court of Chancery, and the Great Western Railway Company.

Its fighting days over, the monotony of the few remaining years of the life of the Oxford, Worcester & Wolverhampton Railway was only broken in August 1858 by what Captain Tyler of the Board of Trade described as 'decidedly the worst railway accident that has ever occurred in this country'. On the 23rd of that month an excursion at very low fares was run from Wolverhampton and the intervening stations to Worcester and back. It was advertized as for school children and teachers only, but in spite of this seems to have taken all comers to the number of 1,506, 767 adults and 739 children. On the forward journey the train eventually consisted of 2 engines, 37 carriages, and 2 vans, and no less than three times did a screw coupling break; on starting from Brettell Lane, Hagley, and Droitwich, the side chains also snapping except at the last place. However, it reached Worcester in safety three hours after leaving Wolverhampton. For the return in the evening two trains were provided, one of 28 carriages and 2 vans, the other of 14 carriages and 2 vans. The first took an assistant engine from Stourbridge and at length reached Round Oak. Scarcely had it stopped when a fourth coupling and its side chains broke with the rebound of the buffers, and 17 carriages packed with people and the rear van started back down the bank of 1 in 75 to meet the second train, which was about to start from Brettell Lane, 1¼ miles off. They met at Moor Lane Bridge, about half-way; the last three vehicles were smashed to pieces, 14 people killed and 50 more or less seriously injured, while over 170 afterwards claimed compensation for minor injuries. Captain Tyler laid the blame on the goods guard in charge of the train, who had evidently been very careless with his brake on both journeys, and doubted much whether he was in his van at all when it was running back, although the man declared he had the brake hard on and only left the train after calling on the passengers to save themselves by jumping out. The position of the nut on the bent brake screw after the collision showed that the brake was off when it occurred.

In consequence of this accident trials were made in the autumn of Fay's and Newall's patent brakes on experimental trains. These early brake trials took place near Evesham and were attended by representatives of several other railways, but did not lead to any change from the ordinary hand brake of the period, as far at least as the Oxford, Worcester & Wolverhampton line was concerned.

Only a passing reference has been made to the Stratford & Moreton Railway, an ancient horse tramway between Stratford-on-Avon and Moreton-in-the-Marsh, with a branch to Shipston-on-Stour, which was in existence long before the Oxford, Worcester & Wolverhampton Railway. It was authorized by an Act of Parliament in 1821, and owed its origin

to William James of Henley in Arden, one of the promoters of the Liverpool & Manchester Railway, who disputed with George Stephenson the
title of 'The Father of Railways'. The line from the canal at Stratford by
Atherstone and Preston-upon-Stour, Alderminster, Ilmington, Longdon
Road, and Stretton-on-the-Fosse to Moreton, 17 miles, was opened on
5th September 1826, and the branch from Longdon Road to Shipston-
on-Stour, 2 miles, authorized by Act of 1833, on 11th February 1836.
The gauge was probably 4 feet 8½ inches, and the railway consisted of
light fish-bellied malleable-iron rails, 15 feet long and weighing 30 lbs to
the yard, fixed by 6 lb chairs to small stone blocks a yard apart; some
wooden rails and sleepers were also used. The Oxford, Worcester &
Wolverhampton Railway was laid out to cut right through the yard of the
Moreton terminus, and that Company agreed in 1844 to take a perpetual
lease of the Stratford & Moreton, and were authorized to do so by their
original Act of the following year. They accordingly took possession on
1st May 1847 at a rent of £2,360 for the main line and £177 10s 0d for
the Shipston Branch. The receipts from that date, consisting of 'Tonnages,
Weighings, Wharfage, Rents, Licences for Passengers, Sand, Fines, etc.',
for several years averaged about £3,000 a year, and the expenses about
£400 more, so the acquisition was by no means profitable to the Company.
The tramway continued to be managed by its former officers till Christmas
1851, when the Company got rid of them and so considerably reduced the
working expenses. In the spring of 1853, in view of the increase of traffic
expected on the opening of the main line through Moreton, 'the Tramway
was closed for some weeks, and a considerable outlay was incurred in
order to adapt it to the passage of carriages for passenger traffic between
the Main Line and the towns of Stratford and Shipston-on-Stour, and
also for waggons and trucks of the gauge of the Main Line. The traffic
is now increasing, and as soon as the works in progress at Moreton,
connecting the Tramway with the Main Line, are complete, a considerable improvement in the receipts may be expected.' No such improvement was realised, however; quite the reverse, for in 1856 the annual loss
was stated to the Committee of Investigation to amount to over £1,600 a
year. From 1st August 1853 a passenger carriage was run twice daily from
Moreton to Stratford and back by Mr Bull of the George Hotel, Shipston,
on behalf of the Oxford, Worcester & Wolverhampton Company. This
ceased when the branch from Honeybourne to Stratford was opened on
12th July 1859. Goods traffic was conveyed by the traders themselves,
who were also allowed to take passengers in their waggons on payment of
£1 a month for a licence.[1]

The single line branch railway to Chipping Norton was opened on
10th August 1855, 'from a junction with the main line situated midway
between Shipston and Addlestrop Stations, where a house has been erected
for the issue of tickets to passengers, etc.' It was constructed as a separate

[1] A detailed account of this interesting early railway appears in *Waterways to Stratford*
by Charles Hadfield and John Norris (1962).

undertaking at a total cost of £26,000, of which local people subscribed £10,000 and Peto, the contractor, the remainder. The Oxford, Worcester & Wolverhampton Company worked the line from the opening and purchased it on a guarantee of 4% in 1859. The house at the junction afterwards became Chipping Norton Junction Station, re-christened Kingham in 1909.

Although a Company, sponsored by the Midland and North-Western Companies, had been incorporated in 1853 to make a railway from Worcester to Hereford, the needful capital was not forthcoming, and nothing was done for more than four years. The Newport, Abergavenny & Hereford Company then took the project up and induced the Oxford, Worcester & Wolverhampton and the Midland to join them in subscribing to it. An Act authorizing this arrangement was obtained in 1858 and soon afterwards the works were begun, the first section from Henwick to Malvern Link being opened in July 1859 and worked by the Oxford, Worcester & Wolverhampton Company though the actual connection between the two railways in Worcester was not effected till the following May.

The friendly relations thus begun between the Oxford, Worcester & Wolverhampton and the Newport, Abergavenny & Hereford Companies soon ripened into an agreement for amalgamation and the purchase of the Worcester & Hereford Railway. A Bill to amalgamate the three Companies under the name of the West Midland Railway Company was accordingly introduced in the session of 1860 and eventually became an Act of Parliament.

By this Act the Oxford, Worcester & Wolverhampton changed its name to West Midland, the other two being dissolved and merged in it under the new title. The Board was to consist of the existing sixteen Directors of the Oxford, Worcester & Wolverhampton with the addition of five representatives of the Newport, Abergavenny & Hereford, and two of the Worcester & Hereford; but the powers of the six Oxford, Worcester & Wolverhampton Directors nominated by the Great Western were to be strictly limited to the affairs of that undertaking as it existed before the amalgamation. The Worcester & Hereford shareholders were guaranteed 4% from the opening of their line, rising to 5 in the third year, and the balance of revenue was to be divided between those of the Oxford, Worcester & Wolverhampton and Newport, Abergavenny & Hereford sections, the former taking 78 and the latter 22% of the total. Special facilities were given to the traffic of the Midland Company, who had subscribed largely to the Worcester & Hereford, from Worcester towards South Wales, with conditional running powers if these were denied them. The Shrewsbury & Hereford Company obtained running powers over the Newport, Abergavenny & Hereford in exchange for similar powers over their line to the West Midland, and through booking arrangements were to be made with both the Great Western and London & North Western for all traffic.

Crumlin Viaduct—Newport, Abergavenny & Hereford Railway

Wye Bridge, Hereford—Newport, Abergavenny & Hereford Railway

Severn Bridge, Worcester—Worcester & Hereford Railway

THE NEWPORT, ABERGAVENNY & HEREFORD RAILWAY

During the Mania of 1844–6 a grand scheme, entitled 'The Welsh Midland Railway', was before the public for a line from the Birmingham & Gloucester in the neighbourhood of Worcester through Hereford and Brecon to Merthyr, where it was to connect with the Taff Vale and so reach Cardiff, and on to Swansea, with branches to other South Wales ports. This never materialized, but a separate company, originally promoted to connect it with Newport, obtained enough local support to go to Parliament in 1846 with a Bill to incorporate the Newport, Abergavenny & Hereford Railway Company, which received the Royal Assent on 3rd August, the same day as that for the Shrewsbury & Hereford Railway.

The Monmouthshire Railway & Canal Company having been empowered in 1845 to make a line from Newport to Pontypool, this Act authorized a railway—not from Newport but—'from a junction with the intended Newport and Pontypool Railway in the Parish of Llanvrechva, in the County of Monmouth, to the Widemarsh Turnpike in the Parish of St John the Baptist in the City of Hereford', with no less than six branches: (1) to the Newport & Pontypool Railway in Panteague, (2) to Llangeview, (3) to Llanbaddock, (4) from Penpergwm to Ragland, (5) to Abergavenny Gasworks, (6) to Portfields, Widemarsh Street Without in Hereford. None of these branches was, however, made.

The ground between Abergavenny and Hereford was already occupied by three distinct Tramway—legally Railway—Companies; these the new Company was empowered and indeed obliged to buy out. They were: first, the Llanvihangel Railway Company of 1811, from the Brecknock & Abergavenny Canal in the parish of Llanwenarth to Llanvihangel Crucorney; second, the Grosmont Railway Company of 1812, from the end of the last named to the 12th milestone on the road from Abergavenny to Hereford; and third, the Hereford Railway Company of 1826, from the Grosmont Railway at Monmouth Cap in the parish of Llangua to Wyebridge in the Liberties of the City of Hereford. The authorized capital of the new Company was £733,000 in £25 shares.

In the following year two more Acts were passed. One provided for certain deviations of the main line and a junction with the Shrewsbury & Hereford Railway near the Hereford & Gloucester Canal in Hereford as well as a joint station, the abandonment of the Portfields Branch, and the substitution of a different Gasworks branch at Abergavenny. The other authorized the important Taff Vale Extension line from the main line in Llanvrechva to a junction with the Taff Vale Railway near Quaker's Yard, and the raising of £400,000 additional capital for its construction. A Bill for a narrow-gauge line from Worcester to Hereford, promoted by the Midland Railway Company in the same session, failed to pass, as did also a rival broad-gauge project, surveyed by Brunel, to connect with the Monmouth & Hereford Railway of 1845. Meantime the purchase of the three tramways had been arranged and deposits paid, the Company becoming entitled to their revenue from October 1846. In 1847 proposals were brought before the shareholders for the purchase of the old Rumney Railway and a lease of Sir B. Hall's tramroads in the Monmouthshire Valleys, but these were eventually abandoned. A contract for the main line between Pontypool and Abergavenny was let to Messrs Rennie and Logan of Newport, the Company's Engineer being a Mr Miller, but by the end of the year the general monetary crisis caused its suspension. An extension of the time for purchase of land and completion of the railway was obtained from the Commissioners of Railways and arrangements made with the three Tramway Companies for postponement of the contracts with them, after which the Newport, Abergavenny & Hereford Railway Company sank into a sleep destined to last for three years, disturbed only by Half-yearly Meetings in London, at which the Director administered a further sleeping draught to such few Proprietors as were wakeful enough to attend.

At length, in February 1851, the latter were startled by the announcement that 'influential parties' were taking an interest in the undertaking, and so there were prospects of renewed activity. The 'influential parties' were no other than the authorities of the London & North Western Company, who, drawn by the prospect of the Great Western reaching Liverpool and Manchester through its recent agreement with the two Shrewsbury Companies, proposed to invade South Wales. At a Special General Meeting in May the Directors reported that they had engaged Mr Charles Liddell as Engineer, and intended to take immediate steps to purchase the land for the main line, which the owners had agreed in most cases to sell at its agricultural value. The Shrewsbury & Hereford Railway was now, they said, certain to be made, giving a direct line to Birkenhead, and a line between Worcester and Hereford was being arranged for by the London & North Western and Midland Companies, which would afford communication with Birmingham and the Midlands. At this meeting the number of Directors was increased from five to fifteen, by the addition of four representatives of the Monmouthsire mineral districts, three of the County of Hereford, and three London & North Western Directors.

Soon after this things began to move; the land was bought and a new contract for the whole line let to James Rennie of Newport, to be completed by the end of September 1853. In March 1852 the works were in active progress, and the Board had concluded a working agreement with the London & North Western to come into force on the opening of the Worcester & Hereford Railway, for which an ostensibly independent company was promoting a Bill in the current session of Parliament. This having been thrown out by the Lords, the North Western proposed to absorb the Newport Company and renew the Worcester & Hereford application next year.

Consequently the Newport, Abergavenny & Hereford Company went to Parliament in 1853 with no less than five Bills, three of them on behalf and at the cost of the North Western. These three were for powers to sell or lease the line to that Company, and to extend it to Swansea and Brecon respectively. The Report of the Cardwell Committee against such amalgamations caused the first to be dropped and the others went with it Of the two remaining Bills in the Company's own interests, one was for new junctions at each end of the line, with the Shrewsbury & Hereford and Newport & Pontypool Railways respectively, and the other for deviation of part of the Taff Vale Extension and short spurs therefrom to connect with the Newport & Pontypool in Panteague, and with existing tramways at Llanhilleth, Pontlanfraith, and Mynyddysllwyn. These duly passed. The Worcester & Hereford Railway Bill also passed, but with all clauses giving powers to the North Western and Midland Companies struck out, the Lords intending that the line should be in the hands of a really independent company.

Meantime the works of the main line had been progressing satisfactorily. The purchase of the three tramways between Abergavenny and Hereford was completed in 1852; they were closed to traffic on 20th April 1853. The tram-plates were sold soon afterwards at a price only 15s a ton less than that of new iron rails, and the remaining property of the old Companies disposed of by auction, except the first 2 miles of the 'Llanvihangel Railway' which were retained to form a branch from the Brecon Canal at Govilon to the main line near Abergavenny. This was conveyed to the Merthyr, Tredegar & Abergavenny Railway in 1859 and used to form part of their line. Early in 1853 the Directors began buying land for the Taff Vale Extension, and in the autumn work was begun on the tunnel at Hafodyrhynys and the great viaduct at Crumlin, stated then to be the largest viaduct in the world. It was to cross the Ebbw Valley at a maximum height of 200 feet, and to be 1,650 feet long in two sections divided by the apex of an intervening hill, the main eastern section being 1,066 feet. The contract for the viaduct was taken by Mr T. W. Kennard, whose design of braced cast-iron tubes and girders had been selected by Liddell the Company's Engineer. The first column of one of the principal piers was fixed with some ceremony on 8th December 1853 by the Chairman of the Company, the Hon W. E. Fitzmaurice, and his wife Isabella, after whom the pier was named.

Two days before this, the formal opening of both the Shrewsbury & Hereford and Newport, Abergavenny & Hereford Railways was celebrated with great demonstrations; prematurely in the latter case as, owing to an extensive slip in the deep cutting at Llanvihangel, the Board of Trade Inspector, Captain Wynne, ordered a postponement, and, moreover, the station buildings were far from complete. The actual opening for traffic of the double line of Barlow rails from the junction with the Monmouthshire Company's Newport and Pontypool Line at Coedygric, about a mile south of Pontypool, to the Barton Station in

Hereford took place on 2nd January 1854. There were no engineering works of note on the line, unless the iron bridges over the Usk near Penpergwm and the Wye at Hereford can so be described. A mile of single line from the Barton Station to the Shrewsbury & Hereford at what is now known as Barr's Court Junction was also ready, but was not sanctioned for passenger trains till a fortnight later owing to the lack of proper signals at the junction. This mile was part of the Worcester & Hereford Railway, and though the Newport, Abergavenny & Hereford had conditional power to make it they actually did so as agents for the former Company, who were to repay the cost. At the south end of the railway, arrangements had been made with the Monmouthshire Company for the trains to work through to Newport, passengers using their Mill Street Station. The Newport, Abergavenny & Hereford had no statutory running powers over the Newport and Pontypool line, which had been opened as a single line in 1852, and was doubled in April 1854.

From the opening the traffic was worked by the London & North Western Company under a temporary agreement pending the completion of the Worcester &. Hereford Railway, but this did not last long. Captain Huish, being bent on crushing the little Shrewsbury lines, refused to quote any through rates between Pontypool and Birkenhead or Wolverhampton by the direct routes, insisting on all the traffic being sent from Shrewsbury over his own line round by Stafford. The Newport, Abergavenny & Hereford Board considered this policy distinctly detrimental to the Company's interests, and, refusing to be drawn into the Captain's quarrels, decided, with the approval of the shareholders, to put an end to the working arrangement, which was accordingly terminated by mutual consent on 1st October. The renewed application to Parliament for power to sell the line to the North Western was also abandoned, and Captain Huish's action being brought before the Commons Committee on the Great Western and Shrewsbury Railways Amalgamation Bill helped to carry that measure.

The Directors then arranged with Mr Brassey, the lessee of the Shrewsbury & Hereford, to provide locomotive power, and took the traffic working into their own hands, the North Western kindly continuing to provide carriages and other rolling stock. Finding the traffic was still kept down by the very limited engine power which Brassey could spare, they decided to take over that department too, and began work on 1st January 1855, with four goods and three passenger engines. At the end of March the North Western withdrew their stock, and the contractor having failed to deliver the new carriages and waggons promised for the 1st of that month, the Company was for a short time in great difficulties and lost much traffic in consequence.

Work on the Taff Vale Extension had meanwhile been proceeding. In August 1854 the Directors reported that the line from Pontypool up the Glyn Valley had been altered by laying it along the bottom of the valley, the Glyn ponds being drained for the purpose, instead of cutting it out of the side of the hill along their margin, whereby the risk of landslips was avoided, and the worst gradient improved from 1 in 38 to 1 in 48.[1] The Blaendare Tramroad had been acquired, affording needful sidings to the ironworks and collieries. On 20th August 1855 the portion between Pontypool Road and the east side of the valley at Crumlin was opened, though the sanction of the Board of Trade was not obtained till two months later. It was at first a single line laid with Barlow rails, 112 lbs to the yard, to be worked by one engine, but was doubled soon afterwards. The branch to the Monmouthshire Company's Western Valleys Railway at Llanhilleth was completed at the same time, but not opened for passenger traffic.

The Crumlin Viaduct was finished in May 1857, and after being thoroughly tested with heavy loads by the Board of Trade Inspector was opened for traffic on 1st June, together with a further section of some 3 miles of single line to Tredegar Junction, now known as Pontllanfraith, where a connection was formed with the Sirhowy Tramway. On 11th January following the Extension was completed by the opening of the remaining portion to the junction with the Taff Vale Railway at Quaker's Yard (Low Level) Station. This also was originally a single line. Meantime power had been obtained in 1857 for a further extension to join the Aberdare Branch of the Vale of Neath Railway and also the Taff Vale Line there, but this was not effected till the Newport, Abergavenny & Hereford Railway had passed into the hands of the Great Western, by which time the line from Pontypool Road was double as far as Crumlin Station, and was being doubled thence onward.

The Coleford, Monmouth, Usk & Pontypool Railway Company was incorporated in 1853 to make the railway described by its lengthy title from a junction with the Newport, Abergavenny & Hereford at a spot known as Little Mill not quite 2 miles north of Pontypool Road. It was opened thence to the town of Usk on 2nd June 1856 and worked by the Newport Company till 12th October 1857, when the line was extended to Monmouth, Troy Station, and the owning Company took it into their own hands, hiring a couple of engines from the Newport, Abergavenny & Hereford. A further extension across the river to an interchange wharf with the Monmouth Railway's tramroad at Wyesham was brought into use on 1st July 1861.

Throughout the period of its independent existence the only connection between the Newport, Abergavenny & Hereford Railway and the northern and midland districts—indeed, with the English railway system in general, for those at Hereford and Newport involved a break of gauge—was the 50 mile stretch of single line of the Shrewsbury & Hereford. Hence the stagnation of the Worcester & Hereford Company was a serious matter. At last in 1857 the Board took steps with the aid of the Oxford, Worcester & Wolverhampton and the Midland to provide financial

[1] As a matter of fact, there are gradients there now of 1 in 42 for 500 yards, and 1 in 45 for 1½ miles.

support to that undertaking, and its works were commenced in the following year. Long before their completion, however, an amalgamation of the Newport, Abergavenny & Hereford with the Oxford, Worcester & Wolverhampton and Worcester & Hereford Companies was arranged, and, being sanctioned by Parliament, the Newport, Abergavenny & Hereford was merged in the West Midland on 1st July 1860.

Of its internal economy there is not much to be said. Save that the permanent way consisted of Barlow rails, it was an ordinary narrow-gauge line of the period, with semaphore signals. Its General Manager was Percy Morris, who had learned his business under Saunders at Paddington and became Goods Manager of the West Midland in 1860 and General Manager of the North Staffordshire some three years later. Charles Liddell was the Engineer, and Alexander MacDonnell succeeded Mark Carr as Locomotive Superintendent in 1857. The locomotive shops, as well as the chief office of the Company, were at Barton Station, Hereford. At the time of the amalgamation the Company possessed 19 Goods and 7 Passenger Engines, all, except three of the latter, built by E. B. Wilson & Co. of Leeds, and having that firm's characteristic fluted domes and safety valve covers. The passenger carriages were the usual wretched four-wheeled flat-sided vehicles of the period, one of them destined to cause the frightful Shipton smash fourteen years later.

### The Worcester & Hereford Railway

Two rival schemes for a railway between the Cities of Worcester and Hereford were projected in 1846; one, part of the Welsh Midland Railway, backed by the Midland Company, the other, a broad-gauge line laid out under Brunel's auspices, to connect the Oxford, Worcester & Wolverhampton with the Monmouth & Hereford Railway. Both were abandoned in the following year and nothing more was done till 1851, when Captain Huish and the London & North Western Directors took the matter up as a first step in their invasion of South Wales, to connect their ally, the Midland, with the Newport, Abergavenny & Hereford, which they had every hope of annexing.

A line was accordingly laid out by Charles Liddell from the south end of the Shrub Hill Station of the Oxford, Worcester & Wolverhampton Railway to cross the Severn and the Teme south of the City and, leaving Malvern Link well on the left, proceed by Cradley and Bosbury to the Herefordshire & Gloucestershire Canal, part of which was to be used for the railway, and so on to join the Newport, Abergavenny & Hereford Railway 'at or near Above Eign in the Parish of All Saints within the Liberties of the City of Hereford'. Both Malvern and Ledbury were thus left to be served by branches, from Leigh and Bosbury respectively, to the no small discontent of those towns. A Bill for this line was promoted in the session of 1852 ostensibly by an independent Company, but really by the London & North Western, Midland, and Newport, Abergavenny &

Hereford. It was opposed by the Great Western and Shrewsbury & Hereford. After a long and strenuous fight it passed the Commons, only to be rejected by the Lords, upon which the promoters announced their intention of trying again next year.

Preparations were accordingly made by both sides for a decisive battle in 1853. The Great Western joined with the Oxford, Worcester & Wolverhampton, whom they were fighting bitterly on everything else, to promote the Worcester & Hereford Junction Railway, in opposition to the Worcester & Hereford Railway of the North Western, Midland, and Newport, Abergavenny & Hereford Companies. The former, laid out by Brunel and Fowler, was to be a mixed-gauge line from the Oxford, Worcester & Wolverhampton south of Shrub Hill, crossing the Severn by an opening bridge at Diglis Lock and passing through Great Malvern to a tunnel close to that now existing, and thence north of Colwall and south of Bosbury, with a 3-mile branch to Ledbury, on to Hereford, where it joined the authorized broad-gauge Hereford, Ross & Gloucester as well as the narrow-gauge Shrewsbury & Hereford and Newport, Abergavenny & Hereford Railways. Liddell's rival narrow-gauge line was totally different from that of the previous year. To secure the support of the Corporation of Worcester it had been altered to leave the Oxford, Worcester & Wolverhampton Railway at the north end of the Shrub Hill Station, provide a central station in Foregate Street, and cross the river by a fixed bridge above the road bridge. Also for the sake of local support it was to pass through Malvern Link and Great Malvern and within a mile of Ledbury, thence bearing rather north of west to the Shrewsbury & Hereford at Shelwick Court, some 2 miles north of Hereford. These alterations involved the purchase of much house property in Worcester and two long tunnels vastly increasing the cost of the line.

Both projects came before the same Committee of the House of Commons in May 1853, and a stiff fight ensued, resulting in the defeat of the mixed-gauge Worcester & Hereford Junction and the success of the narrow-gauge Worcester & Hereford. This defeat was attributed by the Great Western party not so much to the confident assertions of Messrs Stephenson, Locke, and Hawkshaw of the practical impossibility of working a mixed-gauge line of any length—that between Gloucester and Cheltenham was the only working example at this date—as to the lack of local support and especially well-founded doubts of the truth of the Oxford, Worcester & Wolverhampton Company's declaration of surplus funds available for the purposes of the undertaking. However, the Committee refused to authorize the addition of a broad-gauge rail to the successful Worcester & Hereford at the instance of its defeated opponents. The promoters of the latter met with an unexpected reverse in the Upper House. The Lords passed the Bill but insisted on the line being really, as it pretended to be, in the hands of an independent Company, and struck out all clauses giving powers of subscription or working to the London & North Western or Midland. This result utterly upset the calculations of the promoters and the bulk of the subscribers, who, with the exception of a few local people and the usual contractors, solicitors, and bankers, were directors, officials, or other dependents of the North Western, Midland, and Newport, Abergavenny & Hereford, their intention being to sell the line forthwith to the North Western Company, and by no means to keep and pay calls on the shares standing in their names. Hence it is not surprising to find that no steps were taken to raise the capital subscribed or to proceed with the works, the state of the money market being alleged as an excuse. In the session of 1855 an attempt was made to induce Parliament to reverse its decision and allow the North Western, Midland, Newport, Abergavenny & Hereford, and Oxford, Worcester & Wolverhampton Companies—the last named having come over to them—to subscribe capital and work the line, but the Bill was ignominiously thrown out, and Captain Huish's assault on South Wales by this route finally defeated. It had already received a severe check by the refusal of the Newport, Abergavenny & Hereford to submit to his domination.

After this the Worcester & Hereford remained in a state of suspended animation for another year and more till it was again taken up by the Newport, Abergavenny & Hereford Company, whose representatives had retired in disgust at the beginning of 1854. Eight of them now came back to form a majority of the Board, which was almost entirely reconstructed, and negotiations were opened with the new rulers of the Oxford, Worcester & Wolverhampton Company. These resulted in an agreement to subscribe capital and work the line when completed. The Midland Company soon afterwards joined with them, and a Bill for the necessary powers was introduced in the 1858 Session. It was passed in due course, giving, besides the power for the three Companies to subscribe, an extension of time for completing the line and authority to the Worcester & Hereford Company to repurchase from the Newport, Abergavenny & Hereford the mile of line between the Shrewsbury & Hereford at Barr's Court Junction and their Barton Station. This part of the Worcester & Hereford Railway, authorized by the original Act of 1853, had been made by the Newport, Abergavenny & Hereford as agents for the Worcester & Hereford Company; and then the latter, being unable to pay for it, had ceded it to them subject to running powers.

Financial difficulties being at last overcome, the works were begun in earnest on a double line from Worcester to Malvern, including a short northward fork at Worcester, and a single line thence to a junction with the Shrewsbury & Hereford Railway at Shelwick Court. Here also a northward fork towards Shrewsbury had been authorized, but was not made.

The first section, 6 miles, from Henwick on the west bank of the Severn to Malvern Link was opened on 25th July 1859 and worked by the Oxford, Worcester & Wolverhampton Company. The iron bridge over the Severn was finished towards the end of the year, but the Board of Trade Inspector, finding a greater deflection in the two arched spans than he liked, insisted on their being stiffened before he would sanction the use of the bridge for passenger trains. This having been effected by temporary piles and struts, the line from the Oxford, Worcester & Wolverhampton at Tunnel Junction to Henwick was opened on 17th May 1860. Until the opening of the Shrub Hill–Rainbow Hill curve in July, the trains reversed at Tunnel Junction. On 25th May the other end was extended from Malvern Link for 2 miles through Great Malvern to Malvern Wells. There were stations at Foregate Street, Henwick, Malvern Link, Great Malvern and Malvern Wells; Bransford Road was opened on 1st September 1860.

The completion of the remaining 20 miles to Shelwick depended on the progress of the two tunnels at Colwall and Ledbury. In February 1860 Liddell reported that the syenite rock at the east end of the former was so hard that $2\frac{1}{2}$ yards was the best week's work yet done, 4 feet being the average, while on the west side of the hill 10 yards a week was the average rate through the shale there. In all 815 yards had been driven leaving 749 to be done, and a third shaft was being sunk to expedite the work. Of the Ledbury Tunnel 236 yards had been excavated from the west end and three shafts sunk the full depth, from each of which headings were begun on the remaining 1,128 yards.

At this time the days of the Worcester & Hereford Railway as a distinct undertaking were numbered, the Bill being already in Parliament for its amalgamation with the Oxford, Worcester & Wolverhampton under its new name of West Midland Railway. The Bill having passed, the Company was dissolved on 1st July 1869.

### THE WEST MIDLAND RAILWAY

At its birth on 1st July 1860 the West Midland Railway consisted of two as yet unconnected main systems:

    1. From Oxford, or strictly speaking Wolvercot, to Bushbury Junction, Wolverhampton; with branches to Chipping Norton, Stratford-on-Avon, the Midland at Abbot's Wood and Stoke Prior, Malvern Wells, and the London & North Western at Tipton.

    2. From the Shrewsbury & Hereford Railway at Hereford to the Monmouthshire Railway near Pontypool, with facilities—by agreement only—to Newport, and branches to the Taff Vale Railway at Quaker's Yard, and the Monmouthshire at Llanhilleth in the Ebbw Valley;

in all about 173 miles. There was also the more or less derelict Stratford & Moreton Railway with its branch to Shipston-on-Stour.

The connecting link between Malvern Wells and Hereford was in active progress—the Engineer reported in August that only 146 yards of the heading at Malvern Tunnel and 378 at Ledbury remained to be driven —and work had been begun on the Aberdare Extension from Quaker's Yard.

Besides these lines of its own the Company was interested, under agreements to lease or work, in the following railways, all in course of construction or authorized.

The Severn Valley Railway, from the Oxford, Worcester & Wolverhampton main line at Hartlebury to Shrewsbury, 40 miles.

The Witney Railway, from Yarnton to Witney, 8 miles.

The Bourton-on-the-Water Railway, from Chipping Norton Junction to Bourton, 6½ miles.

The Much Wenlock & Severn Junction Railway, from Buildwas on the Severn Valley Line to Much Wenlock, 3½ miles.

The Tenbury & Bewdley Railway, from the Severn Valley at Bewdley to Tenbury, 15 miles.

The Stourbridge Railway, from Stourbridge Junction to Old Hill, 3½ miles.

The Chairman of the Company was William Fenton, late Chairman of the Oxford, Worcester & Wolverhampton; the Deputy Chairman, W. P. Price, who had succeeded the Hon. W. E. Fitzmaurice as Chairman of the Newport, Abergavenny & Hereford in 1859; the General Manager, A. C. Sherriff; and the Secretary, W. T. Adcock.

Relations with the Great Western remained much as they had been since the Agreement of 1858, save that through bookings had been arranged, practically all the London traffic continuing to pass over the North Western by Yarnton and Bletchley. But events were to happen in the ensuing year which changed all this.

In the autumn the old proposal for a 'Mid-Western' direct line from Yarnton to London was once more brought before the public by certain promoters unknown to fame backed by Lord Carrington and other local people on its course, who had been active in support of the defeated projects of 1852 and 1853. The solicitors concerned were, oddly enough, Parson's old firm, who were still the solicitors for the West Midland Company, so we may suspect that that astute gentleman had some hand in the business, even if his colleagues on the West Midland Board knew nothing of it. However, as soon as the scheme was advertised in November, Fenton at once wrote to the Great Western and London & North Western Chairman to assure them that his Company had nothing at all to do with the project, and that the solicitors had at his request withdrawn from it. In view of the clause in the 1858 Agreement that neither Company should in any way assist any new line competing with the other, such action in this case by the West Midland would obviously be a gross breach of faith.

Two months later Fenton wrote to Lord Shelburne complaining that the Great Western were assisting the Wycombe Railway Company in the promotion of a Bill for the extension of their line from Thame to Oxford, which his Board considered hostile to their 'well recognized position and prospects', as it would occupy 'the ground known to Railwaymen as the

Mid Western District'. This, he maintained, apparently on the strength of Parson's defeated projects of 1852 and 1853, was neutral territory and could only be occupied by the Great Western by violating the Agreement with the Oxford, Worcester, & Wolverhampton Company! The Great Western Chairman replied that the line in question was purely a local branch and could not possibly be considered as in any way competing with the Oxford, Worcester & Wolverhampton Railway and so covered by the Agreement; if it could be viewed as a competing line at all, it would compete only with the Great Western main line to Oxford. Later, on 2nd March, Fenton, on behalf of his Board, invited the Great Western to withdraw the Thame and Oxford line on condition that the Yarnton–London line was also withdrawn for the current session. Lord Shelburne declined this course in view of the Great Western's engagements with the Wycombe Company, and expressed surprise that the West Midland were in a position to control a scheme with which they alleged that had nothing at all to do. It then came out that on that very 2nd March the West Midland Board, 'yielding to great pressure on the part of the public' (!), had adopted the line and made 'such arrangements with the promoters as practically gave us a control over the Bill'.

The London, Buckinghamshire & West Midland Junction Railway Bill, to give it its full title, was accordingly proceeded with. It provided for a main line from the West Midland at Yarnton, with fork connections from the Great Western respectively north and south of the existing junction at Wolvercot, passing by Thame, Risborough, Amersham, Beaconsfield, and Uxbridge to Kensington (Addison Road) and on to a terminus in the vicinity of Knightsbridge and Sloane Street, with a branch to Aylesbury and a fork to the West London Railway near Shepherd's Bush. All this was to be done on a capital of £1¼ million.

Counsel were briefed and everything ready for a battle royal between the promoters and the West Midland on the one side and the Great Western and London & North Western on the other, when on the last day of April 1861, just as the case for the Bill was to be opened before the House of Commons Committee, Parliamentary railway circles were electrified by the astounding news that the Great Western and West Midland had settled all their differences and were to be amalgamated! The news was confirmed by the immediate withdrawal of the Bill, and on 4th May Heads of Agreement between the Boards of the two Companies were concluded.

These provided that so much of the West Midland as could legally be leased to the Great Western—the original Oxford, Worcester & Wolverhampton line under the powers of the Act of 1845—should be so leased, and that the Great Western should have full powers of running over and using the remainder of the West Midland system, whether complete or in course of completion; the West Midland being given reciprocal powers over the Great Western, the two systems being worked as far as possible as one system, and the net receipts of the whole being divided in the proportions of 82½% to the Great Western Company and the remaining 17½% to the West Midland. A Joint Committee consisting of the eighteen Great Western Directors and six Directors of the West Midland was to be appointed to manage the whole undertaking. The Narrow Gauge was to be completed from Reading to Paddington and Brentford—this had already been determined on and a Bill for the necessary powers was in Parliament—so as to be ready for traffic, if possible, on the opening of the Worcester & Hereford and Severn Valley lines, and thereafter through and express trains were to be worked over the two systems as if they were one. Application was to be made to Parliament within five years for a complete amalgamation of the two Companies on the basis of the apportionment of net receipts already mentioned. The Lease and Agreement were to begin from 1st July 1861, and formal deeds to effect them to be submitted as soon as possible to special meetings of the two Companies.

These deeds were prepared with quite unusual speed, adopted by the respective Proprietors at their meetings on 30th May, and forthwith duly sealed by both Companies.

Parson's Agreement with Captain Huish of September 1853, binding the Oxford, Worcester & Wolverhampton to the London & North Western for twenty-one years, thus went by the board. It could not be enforced by law and some of the Oxford, Worcester & Wolverhampton Directors had complained of the neglect of its terms by the other Company as early as 1856. One of its clauses bound the North Western to assist the Oxford, Worcester & Wolverhampton in obtaining a direct line to London, and the breach of this condition by that Company's opposition to the Buckinghamshire project seems to have been the final pretext for its abandonment.

As it was not yet possible to run through trains from and to Paddington, the London service, viz. the Yarnton Loop and Bletchley was continued till the end of September, when Paddington finally succeeded Euston as the station for Worcester and the West Midland Railway generally. Meantime the Great Western connections from Handborough were slightly improved in July, and an express in each direction between Oxford and Worcester was put on; the Down train, off the 6.30 p.m. broad-gauge Birmingham express from Paddington, reaching Worcester at 9.25, and there overtaking and joining the 5 o'clock through train from Euston to Wolverhampton, London & North Western Station; while the new Up express from Worcester at 7.15 in the morning caught a Birmingham train at Oxford and enabled Worcester people to be in London at 10.30, an hour earlier than hitherto. These, as long as they lasted—not long—were the only good trains in point of time between Paddington and Worcester, for the new through narrow-gauge service inaugurated on 1st October was miserably slow, averaging well over 4 hours for the 120 miles, and remained so for nearly thirty years.

Since this time the London & North Western loop line at Yarnton has been used mainly for the transfer of mineral and goods traffic, and 'Handborough Junction' has lost the importance it once had and became an ordinary roadside station; the empty title remained, however, on the name-boards and even in the time-tables for several years.

For the next two years the West Midland, though worked in the closest co-operation with the Great Western, retained its own individuality and was managed by its own officers, of course under the Joint Committee. There was no certainty that Parliament would sanction the proposed amalgamation, which was sure to be strongly opposed by other interests.

In the 1861 Session the Company very nearly secured control of the Monmouthshire Railway & Canal system. The two Boards had agreed on a lease and a Bill to effect it was brought in by the Monmouthshire Company. Though opposed by the Great Western, until their agreement with the West Midland, and by the Shrewsbury & Hereford Company, it passed the House of Commons, but was eventually rejected by the Monmouthshire Proprietors at their Wharncliffe Meeting, and so failed in the Lords. The attempt was not renewed, but in the following year the West Midland succeeded, in spite of strenuous opposition from the Monmouthshire, in obtaining statutory running powers over that Company's Eastern Valley line between Coed-y-gric Junction, near Pontypool, and Newport.

In August 1861 the Directors reported that the Stratford Branch had been extended to join the Great Western branch from Hatton; a service of through trains between Malvern and Leamington by this route was inaugurated on 1st August.

The Coleford, Monmouth, Usk & Pontypool Railway, which had been worked independently since its opening to Monmouth, was taken on a long lease from 1st July 1861, adding 17 miles of single line to the system.

The opening of the line between Malvern Wells and Hereford—or rather the junction with the Shrewsbury & Hereford Railway at Shelwick —which had been somewhat delayed by the decision to brick the Colwall Tunnel throughout, took place on 13th September 1861, and so the Worcester & Hereford Railway was at last completed and the two sections of the West Midland united. The new line was single throughout[1] and worked by telegraph, but that from Shelwick Junction to the Barton Station, had by this time been doubled by the two owning Companies. The chief engineering works on the Worcester & Hereford were the Colwall and Ledbury Tunnels, respectively 1,567 and 1,323 yards long, and the Ledbury Viaduct.[2]

A fortnight after this opening the completion of the narrow-gauge rails between Reading and Paddington at once gave the Great Western a new through route to the whole of the West Midland system, the Taff Vale Railway, and much of South Wales.

Other lines opened during the next six months were the Witney Railway, from Yarnton to Witney, on 14th November; the Severn Valley Railway,

[1] It was doubled in 1867–68
[2] Because of deterioration in its condition, Colwall Tunnel was replaced by a new bore, 1589 yards long, brought into use on 2nd August 1926.

from Hartlebury to the Shrewsbury & Hereford at a point $\frac{3}{4}$ mile south of Shrewsbury, with running powers to the joint station there, and the Much Wenlock & Severn Junction Railway from Buildwas on the Severn Valley to Much Wenlock, both on 1st February 1862; followed by the Bourton-on-the-Water Railway from Chipping Norton Junction to Bourton on 1st March. All these were and remain to this day single lines, and though they added nearly 60 miles to the West Midland system, it is not likely that they yielded much revenue.

The chief event of 1862 was the leasing from 1st July, in circumstances already recounted, of the Shrewsbury & Hereford Railway, half by the London & North Western and half by the Great Western and West Midland, at a rent guaranteeing 6% on the capital. Thus that railway became the joint line it remained until the end of 1947.

This transaction gave the North Western the long sought access to South Wales by means of the Shrewsbury & Hereford's running powers over the Newport, Abergavenny & Hereford line, which enabled them to reach the Monmouthshire, with whom they made a traffic agreement, and also the Merthyr, Tredegar & Abergavenny Railway. This line had been authorized in 1859 from a junction with the Newport, Abergavenny & Hereford, a mile north of Abergavenny through the coal and iron district towards Merthyr, leasing from the Newport Company the surviving 2 miles of the old Llanvihangel Railway. It passed into the hands of the London & North Western in 1862 and was opened as far as Brynmawr in the same year. That company also made its first step in the direction of Swansea this year by taking over the Knighton Railway from Craven Arms, hitherto worked by Brassey on behalf of the Shrewsbury & Hereford, leading to the Central Wales Railway, with which they had already made traffic arrangements, though no part of it was yet open.

At the same time the West Midland took over from Brassey the working of the Leominster & Kington Railway, a single line of some 13 miles, opened in 1857, from the Shrewsbury & Hereford to the little town of Kington.

The only remaining extension of the West Midland was the portion of the Stourbridge Railway from Stourbridge Junction to Cradley in the Black Country, with two short branches to neighbouring ironworks, opened on 1st April 1863.

The Bill to effect the amalgamation of the Company with the Great Western was deposited in time for the 1863 Session of Parliament, and, though it met with strenuous opposition, was eventually passed, the chief opponents being pacified with special clauses and scheduled traffic agreements, as related elsewhere. The Act came into force on 1st August 1863, from which date the West Midland Railway Company was dissolved. Its shareholders, however, remained a distinct class, designated 'Great Western (West Midland) Proprietors', and separate accounts of both capital and revenue were kept, the net revenue of the whole system continuing to be divided in the proportions laid down by the Amalgamation

Acts. The West Midland share was again divided between the three sections of West Midland shareholders, the Worcester & Hereford first getting their guaranteed 5%, and then the Oxford, Worcester & Wolverhampton and the Newport, Abergavenny & Hereford people sharing the residue in the proportions of 72 and 28 respectively, as provided by the West Midland Act of 1860. This arrangement remained in force till 1870, when the Oxford proprietors were allotted £70 and the Newport £60 of Great Western consolidated ordinary stock for each £100 of their former holdings.

Six Directors were elected by their colleagues to join the Great Western Board, among them Edward Watkin, late General Manager and soon to be Chairman of the Manchester, Sheffield, & Lincolnshire Railway, and the redoubtable John Parson himself.

The latter gentleman was not, however, destined long to occupy a seat in the Board Room of the Company he had fought so fiercely in the past. He was also Chairman of the Hammersmith & City Railway Company, and in this capacity was publicly accused by a shareholder, Surgey by name, of having purchased, in conjunction with a co-director named Blake, the Portobello Estate of 130 acres, through which they knew the Hammersmith line was to run, for £107,000, and then demanded, through solicitors of course, no less than £20,000 for the 2 acres required by the Company.[1] He brought an action for libel against Surgey and was awarded nominal damages, but the Lord Chief Justice made such scathing remarks on his conduct that the Great Western Directors felt compelled to allude to them in their Report to the Half-yearly Meeting of March 1864, at which he with others came up for re-election. Parson defended himself at great length to the assembled shareholders, but finding the feeling of the Meeting strongly against him eventually withdrew his candidature. He also disappeared from the Hammersmith & City Board.

At the time of its dissolution the West Midland Company owned about 190 miles of railway, besides the Stratford & Moreton Railway, and leased or worked 77 miles more. As we have seen, the whole of the Oxford, Worcester & Wolverhampton section, except the Chipping Norton and Stratford branches, was laid with bridge rails, some 70 some 60 lbs to the yard, on longitudinal timbers, while most if not all of the Newport, Abergavenny & Hereford section consisted of Barlow rails. On the former there were no less than 76 timber viaducts and bridges carrying the railway, all north of Evesham, besides numerous over-bridges, most of which had to be renewed with more durable materials in the course of the next twenty years. The locomotive stock consisted of 131 engines of various descriptions, 59 of which had belonged to the Oxford, Worcester & Wolverhampton Company, 26 to the Newport, Abergavenny & Hereford, and 17 to the Shrewsbury & Hereford, and there were 305 passenger

---

[1] It is interesting to note that the Great Western bought some of this land in 1837 for £112 an acre.

train vehicles, all four-wheeled, and 4,064 goods and mineral waggons to be added to the Great Western narrow-gauge stock.

The Chairman of the Company, W. Fenton, became Deputy Chairman of the Great Western; while of the officers, the General Manager, A. C. Sherriff, joined the Boards of the Metropolitan and several other railways and went into Parliament, the Superintendent and Goods Manager, P. Morris, became General Manager of the North Staffordshire, the Engineer, E. Wilson, stayed on for a time under the Great Western regime, and the Secretary and former Superintendent, W. T. Adcock, devoted himself to the affairs of the Stourbridge Railway, of which also he was Secretary, till 1870, when it was discovered that he had been imitating Lionel Redpath of the Great Northern by issuing spurious stock to the extent of £52,000, and so, needless to say, he disappeared from the railway world.

Swansea Station, South Wales Railway, on opening day

Part of Landore Viaduct, South Wales Railway

Llansamlet Flying Arches, erected by Brunel to resist slips in the cutting

Llansamlet Station, South Wales Railway, about 1867, showing " Fantail " signal at *Danger* and (*right*) capstan for working the Auxiliary Signal

# XI

# *The South Wales Railway*

In the summer of 1844 the Prospectus of the South Wales Railway Company with a capital of £2,500,000 in £50 shares was issued from the Great Western office in Princes Street. It proposed a railway from the Cheltenham Branch of the Great Western at Standish, where the Bristol & Gloucester joined the latter, to cross the Severn estuary at Hock Cliff between Fretherne and Awre and follow the coast by Chepstow to Newport, thence on through Cardiff and by Bridgend, Aberavon, Neath, Swansea, and Carmarthen to Fishguard, with a branch from the neighbourhood of Whitland direct to Pembroke. The importance of communication with the whole of the South of Ireland is much dwelt on, and many Irish names appear among the Provisional Committee, together with representatives of South Wales and Great Western Directors. Brunel was the Engineer and Messrs Hunt, the Great Western Solicitors, solicitors for the new Company. It was in fact entirely a Great Western project, for which most of the canvassing was done as usual by Saunders and Brunel. Their efforts were so successful that the Great Western Directors were able to announce in the following February that they had secured 'the formation of a substantial Company to make the South Wales Railway by a promise to contribute one-fifth of the Capital, or £500,000, in the same manner as was arranged with the South Devon Railway Bill carried in the last Session of Parliament. The other shares of the South Wales Railway Company have been subscribed for, and there can be no doubt of the Bill being carried, as a great national undertaking to connect the South of Ireland as well as South Wales with the Metropolis.'

No competing project was proposed, and the course of the line west of Newport met with general approval, but east of that town there was considerable opposition to be faced. The Monmouthshire people objected to the coast line as affording no local accommodation to the County, and urged that the railway should be carried from Newport up the valley of the Usk by Caerleon to Monmouth and so to Gloucester, a course entailing an additional 18 miles to London and much worse gradients. They were of course supported in this by the citizens of Gloucester. The strongest opposition was to the proposed bridge over the Severn as impeding navigation, although as a matter of fact this was conducted above Sharpness almost entirely along the Gloucester and Berkeley Canal, which was to be crossed by a swing-bridge. To disarm this Brunel proposed to make a new navigable cut across the Arlingham promontory, with the approval of the Severn Navigation Commissioners. However, the Admiralty decided against the Severn bridge, and the eventual result of the application to Parliament was the sanction of the line as far as Chepstow only, leaving the Company to come again with fresh proposals for crossing the Severn.

The Act of 1845 therefore incorporated the South Wales Railway Company with a capital of £2,800,000, of which the Great Western were to subscribe £600,000, to make a railway from Fishguard and Pembroke Dock to Chepstow, with a branch, evidently added to conciliate the Monmouthshire opposition, from Newport through Caerleon and Usk to Monmouth, where it was to join the Monmouth & Hereford Railway of the Great Western.[1] There were to be a swing-bridge over the River Loughor and a drawbridge over the Towy at Carmarthen, while the viaduct over the Tawe at Swansea was to be at least 75 feet above high-water mark. Powers to lease or sell the undertaking to the Great Western were given, and the latter was to appoint six of the eighteen Directors. The Act is silent as to the gauge of the railway, but the general Gauge Act of the following year provided that this should be 7 feet, as had of course always been intended.

The Great Western Chairman became Chairman of the new Company, and one N. Armstrong its Secretary.

Next year the Company came to Parliament with alternative plans for crossing the Severn at the point originally proposed between Awre and Fretherne, one by a larger bridge, the other by a tunnel, as suggested by James Walker, who had been employed by the Admiralty to report on the subject. Both being rejected, they were obliged to abandon the direct line to Standish and fall back on a detour through Gloucester.

To provide for this eventuality, the Directors had already arranged with the Gloucester & Dean Forest Railway Company, a local project under Great Western auspices formed in 1844 to connect Gloucester with the Monmouth & Hereford Railway in the neighbourhood of Grange Court, which had been postponed at the suggestion of the Board of Trade, to extend their line from Grange Court some 7 miles to Hagloe Farm 2 miles south-west of Awre Village, there to meet a South Wales extension from Chepstow. This was approved by Parliament and both Companies obtained the necessary powers in 1846.

The South Wales Act of this year also authorized branches from Landore into Swansea and from about the present Clarbeston Road Station to Haverfordwest, as well as certain deviations of the main line. Two extensive deviations had been applied for; one between Carmarthen and Kidwelly to carry the line by the coast and so improve the gradients and lessen the earthwork, which would have included a tunnel, at the expense of an additional 3 miles; the other between Aberavon and Bridgend with exactly the opposite effect, to avoid the coast and the shifting sands of Newton Nottage and pass inland by Pyle and Margam, 3 miles shorter

[1] Apart from some earthworks near Caerleon, there appears to be no evidence that work on this line was started.

but with worse gradients. The latter was not sanctioned till the following Session.

Soon after the passage of this Act the Company came to an agreement with the Gloucester & Dean Forest that instead of subscribing £100,000 to that undertaking they should take over the extension line between Grange Court and Hagloe and make it themselves, thus establishing the eastern terminus of the South Wales Railway at Grange Court within 8 miles of Gloucester.

About the same time negotiations with the Great Western took place, resulting in December 1846 in a perpetual lease of the railway to that Company at a guaranteed rent of 5% on a capital of £3 millions in shares and £1 million on loans, together with half the surplus profits, to commence from the completion of the line from Gloucester to Fishguard. Any portions previously opened were to be worked by the Great Western on behalf of the South Wales.

The works were begun in the summer of 1846 at Swansea, Neath, Newport, and Chepstow, where there was most to be done, and by August 1847 the whole line was in progress from the Gloucester & Dean Forest to within 7 miles of Fishguard.[1] Very soon afterwards the general financial difficulties, which affected all railways in the country, began, obliging the Directors to suspend or delay operations, and eventually causing them to decide to concentrate the funds at their disposal on the line east of Swansea. The principal works on this, besides the Chepstow Bridge, which had not been begun, were the large timber viaducts at Landore and Newport, the Newport Tunnel, and the rock cuttings near Chepstow. The Newport Viaduct over the Usk, 1,200 feet long, had been nearly completed, when on 31st May 1848 it caught fire from the driving of an iron bolt and was entirely destroyed. When rebuilt, wrought-iron bow-string girders were substituted for timber in the centre span, the remaining ten spans being renewed in timber as before. In many places along the line the contractors were delayed by difficulties in obtaining possession of land, which Brunel reported had been greater on the South Wales than on any line with which he had been connected.

By 1849 the effects of the Great Famine in Ireland and the general scarcity of money had made it plain that a railway to Fishguard for Irish traffic was a hopeless undertaking, and its abandonment was proposed. The Irish lines with which it had been intended to work were either abandoned or most unlikely to be made, consequently the prospects of cross-channel traffic were very small. One of these lines, the Waterford, Wexford, Wicklow & Dublin Railway, had been promoted chiefly by people connected with the Great Western, Brunel being its engineer, and assisted by a subscription of over £33,000 of South Wales capital. It was soon cut down to the modest Dublin & Wicklow Railway, destined many years later to grow again into the Dublin, Wicklow & Wexford. Brunel's

---

[1] The first permanent rail was laid at Rumney, near Cardiff, on 6th August 1849.

other Irish railway, the Cork & Waterford, to which the South Wales contributed £6,000, also drew in its horns and became the Cork & Youghal, ultimately to be swallowed up by the Great Southern & Western. All hope of either reaching Waterford or Wexford in the near future was in 1849 quite vain.

In their desire to stop their line at Swansea, or at any rate Carmarthen, the South Wales Directors were faced with the difficulty that the Great Western 5% guarantee, on which so much depended, was conditional on completion of the railway to Fishguard. They therefore approached the Great Western Board with the suggestion that the guarantee should be modified so as to come into operation on the opening of the line to Swansea. The latter Board were, however, by no means as ready to incur any avoidable liabilities as they had been in the spacious days of 1846, and firmly declined to alter the existing agreement.

The position is well summed up in the Report of a Committee of Sohut Wales shareholders appointed at the August General Meeting to confer with the Directors on the course to be adopted, and the following extract is of interest in these days when Fishguard has at last become a cross-channel port.

Even if the Irish Railways, which were expected to bring traffic to the western extremity of the South Wales Railway, had not been abandoned, we apprehend that, looking at the matter through the more sober medium which recent experience has afforded for the estimation of such projects, no company governed by ordinary prudence would entertain the notion of carrying a line to Fishguard. Indeed, on this point, there really is and can be no difference of opinion; and if there were no guarantee in the case, the Directors of the Great Western Company would, as holders of more than one fourth of the paid-up Shares, be the first to urge upon the South Wales Company the abandonment of this portion of the undertaking. That they do not openly take this wise course, by meeting our advances to that end, is attributable, we believe, partly to the erroneous supposition that the South Wales Company will break down in the attempt to reach Fishguard, and thus be unable to bring the guarantee into operation, and partly to the very natural disinclination which they feel to present to their Proprietors, in the existing difficulties of railway property, any positive and immediately pressing liability.

In the event of the Great Western Board maintaining their uncompromising attitude, the Committee considered the Company must take vigorous measures to provide the funds required for the completion of the whole line, and showed that this could be easily done without exceeding the £4 millions, for interest on which the Great Western would then be responsible. They conclude by expressing great confidence in the new Chairman, C. R. M. Talbot of Margam Park, Lord Lieutenant of Glamorganshire—Russell had naturally resigned as soon as the interests of the two Companies clashed—but declared 'their conviction that up to the time of his accession to that office, our Directors as a body were too much under the influence of the Great Western Railway Company, and we do not remember a single instance in which any of them supported the Shareholders in opposing the investment of their property in schemes foreign to the originally proposed undertaking'. In spite of this and other rebukes the Report was adopted by the Directors, and later by a General Meeting in December.

About the same time that Russell resigned the Chair, the Secretary Armstrong took an opportunity of absconding with some £5,000 of the Company's money, whereupon Frederick George Saunders, Secretary of the Vale of Neath Railway, a young nephew of Charles Saunders of the Great Western, was appointed to the post. The Head Office of the Company was at 449 West Strand, London, till 1852, when it was moved to 10 Eastbourne Terrace, Paddington. General Meetings were held at Paddington Station till the opening of the Great Western Hotel, and then in the hotel.

On 18th June 1850 the first portion of the South Wales Railway, from Chepstow to Swansea High Street Station, 75 miles, was opened for traffic. It was a double line throughout of bridge rails on longitudinal timbers in Brunel's usual style and furnished with disc-and-cross-bar signals. The most notable engineering works were the timber viaducts already mentioned, of which the biggest, over the River Tawe and its marshes at Landore, was exactly a third of a mile long with thirty-seven spans varying from 40 to 100 feet each. The only tunnel was at Newport, 742 yards long.

Engines and rolling stock were provided by the Great Western, having been shipped across from Bristol. Frederick Clarke resigned his post of Great Western Superintendent at Bristol to become Superintendent of the South Wales Railway, and all the station masters, clerks, guards, police-men, and porters, in fact the whole staff except the enginemen, were South Wales employés under him.

At first no goods traffic was carried; up to the end of the year it produced only £1,575 out of a total of £26,400, and for the whole of 1851 only £7,380 out of £66,000. Minerals did not even figure in the accounts till the end of 1853.

Very soon after the opening a considerable slip occurred in the deep cutting near Llansamlet between Neath and Swansea. To put a stop to this, and at the same time avoid the enormous amount of excavation which would have been necessary to flatten the slope on the hillside, Brunel adopted the original plan of throwing four flying arches across the cutting at short intervals, weighted with heavy copper slag to resist the thrust of the side.

Negotiations with the Great Western for the modification of the leasing Agreement having led to no result, Brunel took on himself to act as peacemaker, and in a letter to the Great Western Chairman suggested a basis of settlement, which led to a new agreement being made between the two Boards and approved by the Great Western shareholders in November. The South Wales Shareholders, however, would have none of it, and urged their Directors to press on with the completion of the line to Fishguard. Instructions were accordingly given to the contractors for the line west of Swansea, whose operations had been suspended since the autumn of 1848, to proceed with the works.

This may have had its effect in inducing the Great Western to give better terms; at any rate, a new agreement was come to in March 1851, which was accepted by both Companies. This provided for the eventual completion of the South Wales Railway to Milford Haven instead of Fishguard, and a lease of the whole undertaking to the Great Western for 999 years, to take effect when the line was opened from Grange Court to Swansea, and on the rest as completed. It was not, however, a lease in the ordinary sense of the term. The line was to be worked and managed by a Joint Committee of five Directors from each Company, the Great Western providing engines and rolling stock, and the South Wales accommodation for the traffic. After payment of working expenses and debenture interest the South Wales were to receive two-thirds of the net profits, and the Great Western the remaining one-third. For this the latter were to pay the former as fixed rent for the line from Grange Court to Swansea £30,500, to Carmarthen £38,500, and to Milford Haven £46,000. The staff, other than the Locomotive Department, remained South Wales Railway servants.

After this, for the time being, happy termination of the first quarrel with the parent Company all work on the line to Fishguard beyond the point of junction with the branch to Haverfordwest was finally stopped, and progress westward concentrated on that between Swansea and Carmarthen. Eastward, although the contractor for the Chepstow Bridge was much in arrear with his work, the railway thence to Grange Court was nearly ready for opening in the summer, while beyond Grange Court the Gloucester & Forest of Dean Railway was in an equally forward state and only delayed by the opening bridge over the Severn and the junction arrangements with the Great Western Station at Gloucester.

These having been completed, the line was opened on 19th September 1851 from Gloucester to a temporary station, entitled 'Chepstow East', at the road bridge close to the present junction of the Wye Valley Branch, about a mile east of Chepstow Station. Passengers were conveyed in omnibuses between the two stations, but, needless to say, no through goods traffic worth mention was attempted.

The following description of the great bridge over the Wye is extracted from Brunel's Life:

At the part of the River Wye where it is crossed by Chepstow Bridge, a cliff of limestone rock rises on the left bank to a height of 120 feet above the bed of the river, forming the precipitous ledge of a broad table-land; while on the right bank the ground slopes gently for a considerable distance, rising only a little above high water, and is composed partly of clay and partly of loose shingle interspersed with large boulder stones. As it was necessary to leave a clear headway of 50 feet above high water for the navigation, the line on one side of the river is on an embankment of great height, and on the other side it penetrates the cliff about 20 feet below the top. The whole space to be bridged over, 600 feet wide, was divided into a river span of 300 feet and three land spans of 100 feet each. At one end of the great span a secure abutment was offered by the cliff; but at the other end and under the piers of the smaller spans, the ground throughout was soft and full of water. There was, however, rock at a depth of 30 feet below the bed of the river. To reach this foundation with masonry, by means of a coffer dam. was almost impracticable, as it was 84 feet below high water. . . .

Brunel ultimately decided on forming the piers of cast-iron cylinders forced down by loading and afterwards filled with concrete, and the work was commenced in the spring of 1849.

.  .  .  .  .  .  .  .  .  .

The bridge is for two lines of way; each line is carried between two longitudinal girders. The girders over the three land spans of 100 feet are in one piece 300 feet long, supported at two intermediate points. Those across the main span are also 300 feet long, and are supported by the main truss.

The truss for each line of way consists of two suspension chains, one on each side of the roadway, hung from either side of the ends of a horizontal circular tube [9 feet in diameter], arched slightly for the sake of appearance, which rests on piers rising about 50 feet above the level of the rails. The pier at the land end is of masonry, and the upper part of the middle pier is of cast iron, resting on the cylinders already mentioned. Each pier has two archways for the trains to pass through. The chains carry the roadway girders at four points, and the tube is supported at two intermediate points in its length by upright standards resting on the chains. Thus, while the weight of the structure is supported somewhat in the same manner as in a suspension bridge, the inward drag of the chains is resisted by the tube. To prevent the framework from being distorted by unequal loading, it is made rigid by diagonal chains connecting the upper and lower ends of the two upright standards.[1]

One side of the bridge was at length finished, and a single line over it opened for traffic on 19th July 1852,[2] exactly ten months after the opening of the railway from Gloucester. This completed through communication from London to Swansea, and brought the Great Western Lease of the South Wales Railway into operation. The second line over the bridge was not ready till 18th April 1853.

The flexible nature of the main spans (the trusses are quite independent for each rail track), made them unsuitable for high-speed running and a severe speed restriction over the bridge was in force for many years. Following extensive corrosion of the cross and track girders, the main river spans were replaced in 1962 with modern steel trusses; the land spans had been re-girdered 14 years earlier.

Soon after the through connection with the Great Western system had been thus established, Swansea ceased to be the western terminus by the extension of the main line for 30 miles from Landore to Carmarthen on 11th October 1852. Owing to delay in the delivery of the rails this was only a single line beyond Pembrey until the following February. Barlow rails were used throughout this extension, laid on the ballast without any timber or other supports, for the sake of economy, which led to trouble later on. The more important engineering works were the Cockett Tunnel, 789 yards long, and the

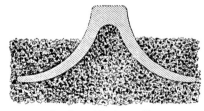

Section of Barlow rail

timber viaducts at Loughor and Kidwelly, each with a wrought-iron opening bridge, the former a swing-bridge of 30 feet opening, the latter a lifting bridge of 20 feet. The Llanelly Railway and several mineral lines

---

[1] Further interesting details of this bridge and its construction are given in L. T. C. Rolt's *Isambard Kingdom Brunel* (Longmans, Green 1957).

[2] A ceremonial opening took place on the 14th.

worked by horses were crossed on the level, the crossings being protected by heavy timber gates.

Communication with the Docks at Swansea was established in the summer by the opening in June 1852 of the 'Swansea Coal Branch', as it was called, from a junction outside the High Street Station to the North Dock, and the provision of 'coal drops' for the shipment of coal.

Meanwhile the western terminus of the South Wales Railway had at last been decided on, and an Act was obtained this same year for an extension from Haverfordwest to Neyland Point on Milford Haven and the abandonment of 14 miles of the original line between Fishguard and the junction of the Haverfordwest Branch.

The Great Western Lease had not been in force six months before a dispute arose as to the charges to be made by that Company for supplying rolling stock and working the traffic; this was referred to the arbitration of Sir William Cubitt. At the General Meeting of the South Wales Company in February 1853 the Chairman stated his belief that 'the bargain with the Great Western was a very bad one for the South Wales, but at the same time he did not mean to say it was a very good one for the Great Western. The traffic continued to increase and would have increased to a much greater extent if the Great Western had been able to supply a sufficient number of trucks. They were not carrying one-tenth of the goods and mineral traffic that they would carry if they had sufficient stock for bringing it on the line. During the last year the goods traffic had increased about 300 per cent. To meet the difficulty it was proposed that private parties should become truck owners, and there were already on the railway a great many trucks thus supplied.'

Sir William Cubitt's Award came out at the end of the year, and gave the Great Western more than they had expected or even asked for. Without going into details, the result was that Mr Talbot told the shareholders at the August Meeting of 1854, when the effect of the Award had been worked out, that the accumulation of authorized charges raised a doubt in his mind whether the South Wales were not carrying the whole of their goods traffic at a loss. He had, however, reason to believe the Great Western authorities were willing to modify these charges, and found no fault with them on the subject of the Award. As regards passenger traffic the position was not quite so bad, but he pointed out one serious disadvantage of the Great Western method of working it. If an excursion train were run from Swansea to London and back the engine and carriages were sent down from Swindon and returned there afterwards, and the South Wales had to pay for all this empty mileage over their line. This was no advantage to the Great Western and was a loss to the South Wales. The worst feature of the whole arrangement was that the Great Western had no inducement to keep down the working expenses.

Though the Great Western did agree to modify some of the charges authorized by the Award, and a friendly settlement was after much negotiation arrived at, the position remained far from satisfactory, and the South Wales Company eventually gave notice to terminate the Award at the earliest opportunity—30th June 1857. In the meantime they had loyally observed its onerous conditions, and had to some extent overcome the chronic shortage of mineral trucks by purchasing stock on their own account.

On the termination of the Cubitt Award a new arbitration took place, F. G. Saunders being appointed on behalf of his Company to settle matters with D. Gooch on the part of the Great Western. They soon disagreed, so Captain Galton was named by the Board of Trade to act as umpire. His Award, published in 1859, was more favourable to the South Wales, but, though extremely detailed and complicated, left room for further disputes, which were never really settled till the two Companies agreed in 1861 to amalgamate. Indeed, the whole of the quasi-independent life of the South Wales Railway was clouded with disputes and arbitrations with the Great Western, whose interests as contractors for locomotive power and rolling stock constantly conflicted with those of the owning Company. The disputes were, however, always conducted in a more or less friendly fashion, and the two Companies never became really hostile to each other.

Carmarthen—a temporary station near the present Junction— remained the western terminus till 2nd January 1854, when a single line of Barlow rails was extended to Haverfordwest. This included the Carmarthen Drawbridge, which Brunel made with three wrought-iron girders 116 feet long for a double line; these covered two spans and were opened by hydraulic machinery lifting one end and then rolling the bridge back on the rails, so as to leave a clear waterway of 50 feet.[1]

Meantime the only connections with other railways were at Llanelly, where an apparatus for the transfer of coal from the old Llanelly Railway of 1828 was installed; Neath, to which station the Vale of Neath Railway from Aberdare had been opened in September 1851; and Newport, where a so-called junction branch to the Western Valley line of the Monmouthshire Railway was made a year later. As the latter was narrow-gauge, like the Llanelly, no real junction was possible.

The Taff Vale Railway, opened throughout from Cardiff to Methyr Tydvil in 1841, two months before the Great Western itself, was enjoying an independent and prosperous existence, undisturbed by the advent of its broad-gauge neighbour. Though Brunel was its Engineer he had made it narrow-gauge because, as he told the Gauge Commissioners, he then thought that gauge more suitable to the many sharp curves he was obliged to adopt. In 1851 the South Wales obtained Parliamentary powers to make a junction with it at Bute Street, Cardiff, and the endeavoured to induce the Company to add broad-gauge rails on its system. The Taff, however, remained impervious to all blandishments and firmly refused to do anything of the sort, with the result that the South Wales, being of the two the more anxious for the connection, had to make the necessary

[1] It was replaced in 1911 by the present rolling lifting bridge. This is still operated by the original electric motor built in 1908.

short branch and even lay narrow-gauge rails on their main line from the Bute Street Junction for ½ mile westward through Cardiff Station, where the traffic had of course to be transferred. This, the only piece of Mixed Gauge on the South Wales Railway, was completed with the junction branch in January 1854, and sanctioned for passenger trains by the Board of Trade at the end of February. Two years later the mineral traffic had so increased that 'extensive sidings and tipping stages' were established for its transfer.

The Forest of Dean Branch from the main line near Newnham to Churchway and other collieries in the neighbourhood of Bilson and Cinderford, as well as the short branch to the wharf on the Severn at Bullo Pill, were completed as broad-gauge lines and opened for coal traffic on 24th July 1854.

As early as 1845 the South Wales Company had agreed to buy the old tramway there, known as the Forest of Dean or Bullo Pill Railway, but the purchase was not completed till September 1850. The purchase and reconstruction were authorized by the South Wales Railway Act of 2nd July 1847, the relevant clauses being dropped from the earlier Act due to Severn & Wye Railway opposition. Reconstruction included two inclined planes and steep gradients, but these were eliminated by revised powers in the Act of 3rd July 1851.

Even in 1850 the tramway was carrying a considerable coal traffic, more than enough to pay in tolls 5% on the purchase money. A connection was made soon after the opening of the main line, and early in the next year the alteration of most of it to a broad-gauge railway was begun. This involved the enlargement of a very small tunnel, over 1,000 yards long, without stopping the coal traffic, described by Brunel as 'a tedious and difficult work', and the construction of two short tunnels near Soudley. The branch to the wharf at Bullo Pill included another drawbridge, of wrought iron on a timber framework and 30 feet span.

The Bullo Pill Railway had been opened on the 4-foot gauge in 1809. The troublesome tunnel is still in regular use (1962) and seems to have been the first on a public railway in the British Isles, probably in the world. Its length is now 1,064 yards.

Not far off, at Lydney, another ancient tramway from the Forest crossed the South Wales Railway on the level. This was known as the Severn & Wye Railway. Its story is told in Volume II.

Another horse-worked tramway, the Llynvi Valley Railway, destined later to be replaced by a proper railway, brought coal to a transfer station at Stormy, about a mile east of Pyle; while farther west between Llansamlet and Landore the Swansea Vale Railway crossed the South Wales on the level. At first the two lines were not connected, but in 1855 steps were taken to divert the Swansea Vale, abolish the dangerous crossing, and form a junction. These works were completed and the crossing done away with in February 1857; as if to show their necessity, a destructive collision between two mineral trains occurred at it in the previous

October. About this time broad-gauge rails were added to the Swansea Vale from the junction to their Swansea terminus on the east side of the North Dock.

Neither of the branches which formed part of the original South Wales Railway of 1845 was ever made. That from Newport to Monmouth was postponed in view of the suspension and ultimate abandonment by the Great Western of their Monmouth & Hereford Railway, with which it was to connect. At last an application to Parliament in 1853 for a further extension of time and a new line to Pontypool was rejected, and no further attempt to reach Monmouth was made. The original power to make the Pembroke Branch having been kept alive, an Act was obtained in the same year to deviate nearer to Tenby and extend it to some proposed Docks at Pennar Mouth, and the Directors entered into what they thought was a definite contract with some well-known contractors, Wythes and Treadwell, to complete it within two years. But the contractors soon repented of their bargain, and succeeded in defeating the Company's attempt to enforce it in the Law Courts. Upon this the Directors tried in 1855 to get an extension of time, but were defeated by the landowners' opposition. As they then allowed their powers to lapse without doing anything, one of the disappointed landowners, Allen by name, brought an action in Chancery and obtained an injunction stopping the payment of any dividend by the Company, under the 'Cardwell clause' inserted in all Railway Acts at that time to enforce the making of lines for which powers were given. The dividend of $3\frac{1}{2}\%$ for the second half of 1857 was therefore suspended; and the Directors were obliged to introduce a Bill in the following session to revive their powers. At the same time they brought in another for a shorter branch. The latter only was passed by the Commons, to the discomfiture of Mr Allen; but the House of Lords Committee decided that the public need for a railway to Pembroke was not sufficient to justify the expense involved. So the Company was relieved of the obligation they had once willingly undertaken to make a branch to Pembroke, and enabled to pay the suspended dividend. It was not till 1864 that the independent Pembroke & Tenby Railway Company of 1859 was authorized to extend their line to Whitland and so, in effect, provide the branch.

Meanwhile the main line of the South Wales Railway, which the former Haverfordwest Branch had become, had been extended to Neyland on the opposite side of Milford Haven, whence passengers and goods were ferried across to Pembroke Dock. This was opened as a single line from Haverfordwest, where yet another opening bridge, a 30 feet wrought-iron lifting span, crossed the River Cleddau, on 15th April 1856. Unlike the rest of the railway west of Landore, it was laid with the ordinary bridge rails on timber baulks and not with Barlow rails. The latter had already been found unsatisfactory for heavy traffic and liable to spread. Early in the next year their replacement by bridge rails and timbers between Landore and Loughor was begun, to be continued by degrees on the rest of the line to Haverfordwest. This was insisted on by the Great Western, who also claimed that the whole expense should be borne by the South Wales Company, thereby raising a new point of dispute between the Companies.

The port at Neyland owed its creation entirely to Brunel, who selected it as being sheltered and always having deep water for the largest vessels. At first only a couple of wharves were provided, though a steamboat service twice a week to Waterford was begun almost immediately after the opening of the railway. In August 1856 Brunel reported to the South Wales Board:

A temporary Passenger Station was erected, and provision has been made for carrying on a certain amount of Goods Traffic across the Harbour by lighters.

A fixed Pier, extending a certain distance into deep water, and the deepening of the shore where the Coal Shipping Staithes are to be placed, have been commenced and are now nearly completed.

The designing and constructing the Terminus of a Railway upon the shores of a Haven, at a point where no trade of any sort at present exists, although there is every prospect of a very large trade being created, must necessarily be progressive and must mainly consist of expedients contrived from time to time to keep pace with each requirement as it may grow. Such has been our commencement at Milford Haven and such must, for some time to come, be the character of our proceeding. The Wharf accommodation provided for the Lighter trade is already found insufficient and is about to be extended, while the success of the Steam Boat communication with Ireland has shown that a portion, if not the whole, of the Floating Pier, as originally designed, is not only desirable but essential for carrying on the trade, particularly in Cattle, which promises to be considerable. Accordingly a portion has been ordered and will be immediately proceeded with.

The portion he referred to consisted of a wrought-iron pontoon 150 feet long by 40 wide, connected with the shore by a landing bridge 12½ feet wide in one span of 205 feet formed by plate-iron girders. It was brought into use in the spring of 1857, and two years later extended by the addition of four pontoons purchased from the Cornwall Railway Company, which had been used for the floating of Saltash Bridge. Hydraulic truck lifts between the pier and pontoons were installed about the same time.

Already a second boat had been put on the Waterford service, which now worked each way thrice a week, and in May 'a fast and powerful Vessel of 1,400 tons and 500 horse power, named *Pacific*', began to run twice weekly to and from Cork. Both services were provided by Messrs Ford & Jackson, a London shipping firm. The voyage to Waterford took about 9 hours, and night boat trains were put on between the terminus and Gloucester, where they connected with London trains, the journey between London and Milford Haven taking just over 8 hours.

The new port was called 'Milford Haven' till 1859, then for a few months by its proper name of Neyland; but by the end of that year the Railway Company christened it 'New Milford', which it retained for more than forty years till after the resurrection of its ancient rival Fishguard, when its real name was restored in the hour of defeat.[1]

[1] The new name was first used in the timetables for September 1906.

The second line was completed between Carmarthen and Neyland on 1st July 1857, making a double broad-gauge line throughout from Paddington of 285¼ miles, of which 164 belonged to the South Wales Company.[1]

The only additions to the system made after this time were the Bute Docks Branch at Cardiff, and a short extension of the Swansea Coal Branch to connect with the Swansea Harbour Railway opened in September 1859. The Bute Docks Branch was begun in the summer of 1856 and would, according to Brunel's Report of the following February, have been completed by that time, 'but for an accident to the adjoining embankment of the Rhymney Railway Company, which has for a time completely arrested our progress'. This must have been a very extensive slip, for it was not made good for more than six months and delayed the opening of the South Wales branch till 19th April 1858.

Four small independent Companies made broad-gauge lines of their own in connection with the South Wales, all of which eventually came into the hands of the Great Western and are dealt with elsewhere. The South Wales Mineral Railway of 1853 undertook a line of about 12 miles from Briton Ferry to Glyncorrwg Colliery and opened a portion of it for mineral traffic in 1860. It had already been leased to the Glyncorrwg Coal Company, and remained in the hands of them and their successors as a colliery line till after 1921. The Carmarthen & Cardigan Railway Company of 1854 opened their line, which never reached Cardigan, from the South Wales station, thereupon renamed Carmarthen Junction, to the town in March 1859 and as far as Conwil on 3rd September 1860. The old Llynvi Valley Railway Company obtained power in 1855 to convert their tramway into a broad-gauge locomotive line and connect it with the South Wales at Bridgend; they accomplished the work from Bridgend to Tywith[2] and Porthcawl in August 1861, but for goods and mineral traffic only. Lastly, the Ely Valley Railway Company of 1857 opened a mineral line from Llantrissant to Tonyrefail in August 1860 and on to Dinas (alias Penygraig) two years later, with branches to Gellyrhaidd and Brofiskin Collieries. This was worked by the Great Western and became practically part of their system under a long lease in July 1861.

These short lines brought some addition to the mineral traffic, which had hitherto come almost entirely from the Vale of Neath. Very little originated on the South Wales system, the Forest of Dean being almost the only district where it had direct access to collieries. The Vale of Neath traffic was considerable, but the bulk of it, destined for the ports of Swansea and Briton Ferry, used only short portions of the South Wales and was worked through by Vale of Neath engines and men. One coal train a day from Swansea to London sufficed for the through eastbound traffic during the lifetime of the South Wales Railway and remaining ten years of the

---

[1] As an economy measure, the Clarbeston Road–Neyland section was converted to single line in 1917. The double line between Clarbeston Road and Johnston was restored in 1921–22.

[2] Renamed Nantyffyllon in 1903.

Broad Gauge. That gauge alone was a heavy handicap. The necessity for transfer of all coal coming by the Monmouthshire, Taff Vale, and other mineral lines and tramways precluded any effective competition with sea transport, while the traders as a rule refused to provide themselves with trucks for use only on the limited broad-gauge system, and the lighter and handier narrow-gauge trucks were preferred to the heavy broad-gauge waggons at the collieries and docks. Complaints and agitation begun soon after the opening of the line and increased in volume as time went on. As early as 1860 the Ely Valley Company promoted a Bill in Parliament for power to change their gauge to narrow and make an independent line to Cardiff parallel to the South Wales. The latter Company then offered to lay the Mixed Gauge from Llantrissant, but the Great Western refused to consent to this and eventually induced the Ely Company to withdraw their Bill.

Notwithstanding all impediments, the traffic both in passengers and goods continued to increase year by year. A fair amount of Irish traffic, chiefly cattle, came to the new port on Milford Haven, but the expectations of transatlantic services were not realized. At the autumn General Meeting of 1859 Mr Talbot suggested that monetary inducements would be necessary to induce shipping companies to come there, whereupon a cynical shareholder expressed his opinion that the Company might as well start farming in Pembrokeshire in order to carry the produce over their line. However, the next Half-yearly Report triumphantly announced that the 'Anglo-Luso-Brazilian Royal Mail Steam Navigation Company' had begun to use Milford Haven for a monthly boat to Portugal and Brazil under arrangements with the Company, and that the traffic was important. Important or not, it soon ceased, the Anglo-Luso-Brazilian boats betaking themselves to Liverpool after a few months. Brunel's famous but unfortunate ship, the *Great Eastern*, arrived at the end of August 1860 on her return from her first trip to New York and was laid up in the Haven for repairs till the following May, when she sailed again for New York, returning to Liverpool. The following autumn saw her back at Milford for further repairs, and there she stayed till May 1862. In the course of the four years 1860 to 1863 she made only nine voyages across the Atlantic and back, after which she did some useful work in laying the Atlantic and other telegraph cables.

Relations with the Great Western were but little improved by the Galton Award of 1859, on the interpretation of which numerous disputes at once arose between the two Companies. To the February General Meeting of 1860 the South Wales Directors reported that the traffic of the district was much injured by the existing arrangements for working it and that any course would be preferable to a continuance of the existing Agreement of 1851. The Chairman explained that the Award provided for no less than fifteen different engine loads on as many inclines, resulting in light loading and much empty engine mileage, and that the demurrage on trucks charged by the Great Western was £9,000 in the half-year more than their own reckoning. The Board had proposed yet another arbitration, but the Great Western refused unless the question of sufficiency of accommodation provided by the South Wales was also submitted. The Company's Auditors suggested cancelling the lease, and one of the Great Western Auditors agreed with them. The Meeting then passed a resolution 'that the present Agreement for a lease from the South Wales to the Great Western is injurious to the interests of both Companies, and that it would be desirable to put an end to it'.

By the following August, though some matters had been settled, new disagreements were constantly arising, so the Directors recommended an application to Parliament in the following Session. Out of over £170,000 received in the half-year only £24,000 was available for dividend, 33 % of the whole receipts being absorbed by locomotive expenses alone. For this Mr Talbot, in his speech to the Half-yearly Meeting, blamed Gooch's instructions to the enginemen, which, he said, only allowed them to take about half the loads the engines were capable of, and led to the unnecessary use of many additional engines. The delays and consequent injury to the traffic were so great that it was really impossible to carry it on under existing conditions, the entire alteration of which would benefit the Great Western as well as the South Wales. Apart from this, questions involving large sums of money, including that of the replacement of the Barlow rails west of Swansea, were by this time in dispute. The Board therefore proposed to promote a Bill for additional capital to enable them to work the line themselves. Lord Shelburne, the Great Western Chairman, who was present in his capacity of a nominated Director of the South Wales, agreed in condemning the existing state of things between the Companies and the method of working the railway, but defended Gooch, who, he said, was acting with the full authority of the Great Western Board. Eventually the Meeting resolved that the two Chairmen should consult with a view to settling a scheme for the working of the South Wales line which would be free from the faults of the present system.

The result was a third arbitration, this time before a lawyer, C. S. Whitmore, Q.C., on all matters in dispute between the Companies but before he was able to come to any decision the case had been submitted to another tribunal. Urged on by a large and influential portion of the shareholders, the South Wales Directors were obliged to proceed with their proposed application to Parliament, and accordingly introduced a Bill in the 1861 Session to alter certain provisions of the Agreement and empower the Company to provide its own rolling stock. Although the Great Western Board admitted losing money under the existing arrangement, they opposed the Bill and a long inquiry ensued before the Commons Committee, who were eventually convinced that it was in the interest of the public as well as that of both Companies that the Agreement should be annulled in part, and so declared the preamble of the Bill proved. They suggested, however, that as there was no chance of its reaching the House of Lords in time to pass all its stages there during the current session it should be withdrawn, in the hope that the Companies would be able to arrive at a satisfactory settlement. The Bill was accordingly withdrawn for the time and the Great Western Board, influenced by the Committee's opinion, proposed an amalgamation with the South Wales on the lines of their own recent arrangement with the West Midland Company, under which the net receipts of the united railways would be appropriated to the respective Companies in fixed proportions. The terms first offered were not considered good enough by the elected South Wales Directors, and it was not until the autumn that an agreement was effected.

This Agreement of 15th November 1861 provided that the Great Western should take a lease of the South Wales Railway from 1st January 1862 for six years, or until the Great Western and West Midland amalgamation had been sanctioned by Parliament, at a rent of £170,000 a year, and work the line as part of their own system. After that amalgamation had been sanctioned, the lease at the fixed rent was to be changed into a division of net receipts, the South Wales receiving a proportion rising from 10·7% in 1864 to 10·9 in 1869 of the united Great Western, West Midland, and South Wales net receipts, but in no case less than £170,000. Four South Wales Directors were to join the joint Board of the three Companies, and all plant belonging to the South Wales was to be paid for by the Great Western and West Midland. The Barlow rail controversy was decided in favour of the South Wales, all renewal expenses up to the commencement of the new lease being charged against the joint revenue and not against that Company only.

A more formal Agreement between the three Companies was drawn up and sealed in February 1862, and its terms were embodied in a Bill promoted in the next year's session of Parliament, together with that for the amalgamation of the Great Western and West Midland. The South Wales Bill was opposed by the Vale of Neath and Taff Vale Companies, but they were pacified by scheduled agreements, and it received the Royal Assent on 21st July. The Act provided for the dissolution of the South Wales Railway Company and its amalgamation with the united Great Western and West Midland on 1st August 1863.

As in the case of the latter, the South Wales shareholders remained a class by themselves till 1870, and owing to the guarantee of £170,000 received a considerably better dividend than either of their partners, never less than $3\frac{1}{4}$%. In that year, when the fusion of the various classes of shareholders was effected, they acquired £108 of Great Western consolidated stock for each £100 they held.

C. R. M. Talbot continued Chairman of the Company till the end, when he became and long remained a Great Western Director. F. G. Saunders, the Secretary, succeeded his uncle as Great Western Secretary in October 1863, and Frederick Clarke, the Superintendent, became Secretary of the London & South Western Company in 1862. W. G. Owen, who had succeeded Brunel as the Company's Engineer, remained on as Engineer for this district of the Great Western.

Wye Bridge—Chepstow, South Wales Railway

Disc-and-Crossbar at *All right*

Board or Fantail at *Caution*

Up Disc-and-Crossbar at *Danger*

Down Disc-and-Crossbar at *Danger*

# XII

# Signals and Telegraph

When the Railway was opened to Maidenhead in June 1838, the need for fixed signals had not yet been generally recognized. Evidently it was thought that the Company's Police, posted at the stations and level crossings or patrolling their beats, into which the whole line was divided, would be able to control the traffic by hand signals, just as police constables do at some road junctions to-day. For the first three months or more they had not even the means of making such signals after dark, but on 24th August the London Committee ordered 'Lamps for the Police', and at the same time asked for estimates for 'Police Boxes'. These were wooden sentry boxes just big enough for a man to stand up in, furnished with a seat but of course no door. If not at first, very soon they were mounted on a pivot so that they could be turned back to the wind. Until the advent of 'locking-gear boxes' many years later they remained as a rule the signalmen's only shelters.

On the Great Western, point indicators were established before fixed signals. The first mention of them is found in the following notice issued on the opening to Twyford.

NOTICE TO ENGINE MEN

On and after the 1st of July the 10 o'clock M$^g$ & the 6 o'clock Ev$^g$ Twyford Trains will not call at Maidenhead up or down. The down Trains will pass through the shed without going into the siding. The Attention of the Engine men is called to a Signal, applied to the Lever of the Switches, to denote whether they be open or shut. Two Targets are so attached that if both be seen the Switch is open, but if both range in a line so that one only can be seen the Switch is right for the Straight Line.

Before coming to the Shed in either direction the steam must be shut off at a sufficient distance to allow the Engine to be perfectly in command and able to be stopped in case of anything being wrong.

SEY$^r$ CLARKE

Ch$^f$ Sup

Paddington
26th July [*sic*] 1839.

In the following month Saunders, at the request of Lord Granville Somerset, gave some evidence on the subject before the Select Committee on Railways. He said that on the Great Western the switches generally had an 'index' by which no doubt he meant a target, as he afterwards added 'We have not a target at every switch or crossing'. Self-acting switches, common on other railways, which were weighted to stand right for the main line and had to be held over during the passage of vehicles to or from the branch or siding, had been tried and rejected. The best policemen were chosen to attend to switches, and were called 'switchmen', to distinguish them from 'common constables'; they received higher pay and also a bonus for good conduct. Asked as to signals, he said: 'The

Policemen make signals with their arms; by this the Engine men are principally governed.' Hence it is plain that there were still no fixed signals more than a year after the opening.

Capstans, as they were called from their shape, designed by Brunel for working points and at the same time indicating their position, came into use this same year, during which we find that Slaughter & Co. of Bristol supplied many 'Sets of switches complete with capstan, disc and quadrant' for £50 each. These appliances, stood close beside the points. The horizontal lever worked in a quadrant frame on the short hollow cast-iron column, moving the points, by means of an iron spindle and the connecting rod at the base, and also the large disc or target fixed on the upper part of the spindle. It was held in either position by a pin, which could be secured by a padlock. The face of the target always denoted that the points were set for the main line; it was turned edgeways for the branch or siding. These capstans were generally confined to facing points, or meeting points as they used to be called, and exits from sidings to running lines, trailing points being worked by an ordinary ground lever. For the former purpose they became standard on the Great Western and Brunel's other railways and remained so until after 1865. They were painted dark green, and the target white with—on the Great Western— a red ring.

The earliest mention of a fixed signal is found in Gooch's 'Regulations for the Engines working the Trains on and after the 30th March 1840', issued for the opening to Reading on that day. This manuscript document gives the daily working of the various engines, and concludes:

A Signal Ball will be seen at the entrance to Reading Station when the Line is right for the Train to go in. If the Ball is not visible the Train must not pass it.[!]

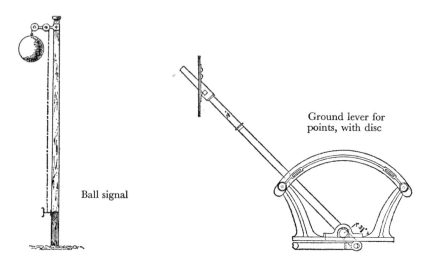

Ground lever for
points, with disc

Ball signal

R. C. Rapier, who read a paper 'On the Fixed Signals of Railways' before the Institution of Civil Engineers in 1874,[1] stated:

On the Great Western Railway a ball signal was introduced about 1837 [*sic*]. The ball drawn up to the top of the post, after the manner of a high-water signal, indicated 'safety' and a common stable lantern was hooked on at night instead of the ball.

He gave a figure of this Ball signal, from which the annexed drawing is taken, but its accuracy cannot be guaranteed, and no confirmation of the asserted use of a 'common stable lantern' has been discovered. That some signal was raised and lowered, and when lowered meant 'Stop', is shown by the following extracts from the Minutes of the General Traffic Committee of the Board in 1840:

*November 18th*—Switchman at Slough dismissed for neglecting to *lower* the Signal.
*December 9th*—Engineman fined £5 for passing Southall with a red light shown to him and the Station Signal being also *down* at the time.

but whether this signal was a sphere, as Rapier suggests, or a disc is distinctly doubtful in view of Sir Frederic Smith's contemporary report (8th December) on the new section of line between Faringdon Road and Hay Lane, in which he says:—

The Signal *Disks* and lamps, which are of a very satisfactory character on that part of the Railway at present open, are not yet up.

Moreover, the rules suggested for adoption by all Companies at the abortive conference of railway officers held at the instance of the Government at Birmingham in January 1841,[2] speak of 'Ball Disc' Signals, as if the words were synonymous.

In view of the standard of education of the enginemen in those days—Brunel told the Select Committee in March 1841 that the best of them could neither read nor write—it is possible that Gooch used the word 'Ball' in his notice as more likely to be understood by the men than 'Disc'.[3]

Whether Balls or Discs, these first signals had a very short life. Already on 3rd November 1840 Saunders had submitted to the Board a 'Code of Regulations for the Management of Signals at all Stations and for the Policemen on the Line', which was approved and ordered to be adopted as soon as the requisite apparatus and lamps had been obtained. It came into force in the following February, by which time the new signals had been erected throughout the railway then open. These were Brunel's once well-known Disc-and-Crossbar signals, for many years standard on the Great Western and all other broad-gauge lines,[4] some of which survived almost to the end of the century.

---

[1] Published in book form by Clowes & Sons, 1874.
[2] Russell, Saunders, and Brunel represented the Great Western at this conference.
[3] Many years later old drivers often spoke of the Disc *All right* signal as 'the Ball'.
[4] They were also adopted on some narrow-gauge lines, for example the Furness Railway. The last one on the Somerset and Dorset Joint Railway, near Blandford, lasted until 1902, and a solitary example on the former Bristol Port Railway & Pier Company's line at Boulter's Crossing, until 1907.

The signal consisted of a tall round mast with a large disc at the top to show *All right* and a crossbar immediately below and at right angles to the disc to show *Danger*, both of sheet iron and generally perforated with round and oblong holes respectively to lessen the wind pressure. The signal was reversed by turning it a quarter of a circle by means of a lever at the foot of the mast, which worked on a pivot and was supported by a short square post let into the ground beside it. These signals were generally very high, 40 to 60 feet or so, and, the disc being 3 or 4 feet in diameter and the crossbar 8 feet by 1 foot 3 inches,[1] were visible at a great distance. They were specially praised by the Board of Trade Inspectors because they gave a positive

Green      Red

*Left:* Flag signal
(Caution)

*Right:* Disc-end-
crossbar signal
(Original form)

*All right* signal, which no others did, the *All right* signal on other railways consisted merely of the absence of a *Danger* or *Caution* signal.

On the other hand, having only two positions they were of course incapable of showing *Caution*; so to meet this requirement Brunel adopted a subsidiary signal of the form illustrated, with green and red canvas curtains on either side of the post attached to rings travelling on an iron bow frame and worked by cords and pulleys. These were known officially as 'Flag Signals', and by the men as 'Fantails' or 'Kites'.

The Regulations of February 1841, after giving under the title of 'Line Signals' woodcuts of policemen making the same hand signals as are in

[1] Later on some were of smaller dimensions and much lower.

use to-day, and directions as to night signals with the white, green, and red glasses of their hand lamps, proceed:

### STATION, TUNNEL, AND GATE SIGNALS

Signals by means of a round disc, and a cross-bar on a mast, and also by flags in the day-time and lights by night on a separate flag-staff, are provided at each station, at the entrances to long tunnels, and at all the gates which shut across the line, to be used for the purposes described.

The cross-bar seen along the line is the signal To stop.

The red flag on the flag-staff by day and the red light by dusk or at night, is also the DANGER signal To stop, and must be shown in every instance of the line being obstructed, or of any accident or stoppage at the station, in the tunnels, or on the line, and also for *three minutes* after the passage of any engine or train in the same direction along the line.

The green flag on the flag-staff by day, and the green light at night, is the CAUTION signal To SLACKEN SPEED, and must be shown, after *three minutes* shall have elapsed from the passing of an engine or train in the same direction, as well as in any case where it may seem proper to recommend a reduced speed.

The disc shown full along the line implies 'ALL RIGHT'.

The white light at night also implies 'ALL RIGHT'.

The disc must always be reversed (so as not to be seen along the railway) and the cross-bar must be shown whenever the *Danger* signal is indicated upon either flag-staff, whether by red flag or by red light; and consequently the full disc will only be seen when the line is perfectly clear and no engine or train shall have passed for three minutes previously.

The flag-staff to show signals for engines or trains on the down line is always on the south and left-hand side of the down train; and for the up line is always on the north and left-hand side of the up train; but when necessary to give *Caution* or *Danger* signals to the engines in each direction, the flags or lights must of course be shown on both flag-staffs at the same time, as well as by the cross-bar.

In the case of a fog, both the day and night signals must be used simultaneously.

Brunel was very pleased with these new signals. Giving evidence before the Select Committee on Railways at the end of March, he said that the Great Western signals had been changed in the last few weeks, and were totally different from those which Sir F. Smith had thought so good. They were 'very much improved in construction, and the code and mode of signalling was also greatly improved'.

**DANGER**      **CAUTION**      **ALL RIGHT**

"Line Signals"

The Flag signals, however, did not last long, as might have been expected; they were one of Brunel's curiously unpractical inventions; he had forgotten the wind. We find the Bristol Superintendent, Frederick Clarke, writing to Saunders on 19th October:

The consumption of flags on the Exeter Line[1] is enormous. The flags will not stand a week. These last few windy days have, I believe, put every flag on the Line out of repair. They are flying from the mast head in streamers. Two or three of the large masts[2] have also been blown down.

In consequence of this and, doubtless, other like complaints, the Traffic Committee ordered on 27th October 'new signals in tin, corrugated iron, or wood to be substituted for the present flags on account of the expense in constant repairs as well as the difficulty of keeping them on the staff during tempestuous weather', at a cost estimated by Brunel of £2 10s each.

The result was an arrow-shaped wooden board, red on one side, green of the other, on a revolving post, to take the place of the double flags. Like the latter, these signals were always fixed on the left of the line to which they applied,[3] the red side, when turned on, pointing towards it, and the green away from it; when neither was required the board was turned edgeways, *All right* being shown by the disc of the main signal. They were established in January 1842, when the notice reproduced on page 315 was issued, and remained in use for rather more than a quarter of a century.

Board (or 'Fantail') signal (Original form)

Officially they were variously called 'Caution', 'Board', or 'Ten Minute' signals; unofficially they inherited the title of 'Fantails', by which later on they became generally known. On their introduction the lamps for night signals, which had been on the flag-staffs, were transferred to separate staffs of their own. These early lamps were square, somewhat like the street lamps of the period with red and green slides, which reposed in sockets when not in use, and were not as yet constructed to show the different lights by being turned. Both Fantail and Lamp generally stood close to the taller Disc-and-Crossbar signal. In station yards a large bell hanging on a roofed wooden frame was fixed near each policeman's sentry box, to be rung to give warning of the approach of a train.

At first the disc of the signal was painted white and the crossbar black, but it was soon found these did not show up well against some backgrounds, and eventually a bright sealing-wax red was adopted for both, as being most conspicuous in all situations. Questioned before a Parliamentary Committee as to the abnormal feature of a red disc indicating *All right*, Saunders replied that the colour was of no consequence and was only

---

[1] Then open as far as Bridgwater, and much exposed in the flat country.
[2] Of the Disc-and-Crossbar signals.
[3] In spite of this definite rule, they were sometimes fixed on the outside of the opposite line, for example, on sharp curves; but this was very exceptional.

adopted for the sake of visibility; the disc was the signal of safety and the crossbar of danger, the colour of either being quite immaterial.

### Great Western Railway,

#### LIST OF SIGNALS.

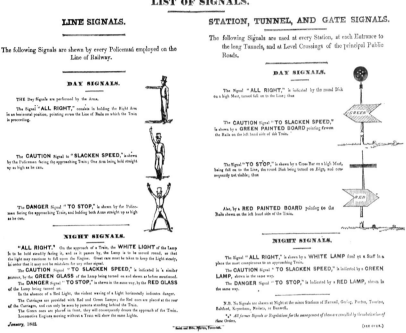

| LINE SIGNALS. | STATION, TUNNEL, AND GATE SIGNALS. |
|---|---|
| The following Signals are shewn by every Policeman employed on the Line of Railway. | The following Signals are used at every Station, at each Entrance to the long Tunnels, and at Level Crossings of the principal Public Roads. |

**LINE SIGNALS.**

The following Signals are shewn by every Policeman employed on the Line of Railway.

**DAY SIGNALS.**

THE Day Signals are performed by the Arms.

The Signal "ALL RIGHT," consists in holding the Right Arm in an horizontal position, pointing *across* the Line of Rails on which the Train is proceeding.

The CAUTION Signal to "SLACKEN SPEED," is shewn by the Policeman facing the approaching Train; One Arm being held straight up as high as he can.

The DANGER Signal "TO STOP," is shewn by the Policeman facing the approaching Train, and holding both Arms straight up as high as he can.

**NIGHT SIGNALS.**

"ALL RIGHT." On the approach of a Train, the WHITE LIGHT of the Lamp is to be held steadily facing it, and as it passes by, the Lamp is to be moved round, so that the light may continue to fall upon the Engine. Great care must be taken to keep the Light steady, in order that it may not be mistaken for any other signal.

The CAUTION Signal "TO SLACKEN SPEED," is indicated in a similar manner, by the GREEN GLASS of the Lamp being turned on and shewn as before mentioned.

The DANGER Signal "TO STOP," is shewn in the same way, by the RED GLASS of the Lamp being turned on.

In the absence of a Red Light, the violent waving of a Light horizontally indicates danger.

The Carriages are provided with Red and Green Lamps; the Red ones are placed at the rear of the Carriages, and can only be seen by persons standing behind the Train.

The Green ones are placed in front, they will consequently denote the approach of the Train. Locomotive Engines moving without a Train will shew the same Lights.

*January,* 1842.

**STATION, TUNNEL, AND GATE SIGNALS.**

The following Signals are used at every Station, at each Entrance to the long Tunnels, and at Level Crossings of the principal Public Roads.

**DAY SIGNALS.**

The Signal "ALL RIGHT," is indicated by the round Disk on a high Mast, turned full on to the Line; thus

The CAUTION Signal "TO SLACKEN SPEED," is shewn by a GREEN PAINTED BOARD pointing from the Rails on the left hand side of the Train.

The Signal "TO STOP," is shewn by a Cross Bar on a high Mast, being full on to the Line, the round Disk being turned on Edge, and consequently not visible; thus

Also, by a RED PAINTED BOARD pointing to the Rails shewn on the left hand side of the Train.

**NIGHT SIGNALS.**

The Signal "ALL RIGHT," is shewn by a WHITE LAMP fixed on a Staff in a place the most conspicuous on an approaching Train.

The CAUTION Signal "TO SLACKEN SPEED," is indicated by a GREEN LAMP, shewn in the same way.

The DANGER Signal "TO STOP," is indicated by a RED LAMP, shewn in the same way.

N.B. No Signals are shewn at Night at the minor Stations of Hanwell, Goring, Purton, Turston, Saltford, Keynsham, Madeca, or Banwell.

⁎⁎⁎ *All former Signals or Regulations for the management of these are cancelled by the substitution of these Orders.*

(SEE OVER.)

The need for distinctive signals at junctions, of which the first were those at Swindon and the Harbour Bridge outside the Bristol Terminus, both opened in 1841, soon made itself felt and was met by the adoption of double discs, the upper generally somewhat smaller than the lower, and double crossbars on one mast for the branch trains, main line trains continuing to be controlled by the ordinary single disc and crossbar. At night double lamps, one above the other, were used for the branch signal.

These signals, both single and double, have never been surpassed for visibility from afar, but their great fault lay in their liability to be blown down, a by no means unusual event, the wind pressure on the large crossbars and discs at such a height being enormous, although both were perforated to lessen it as much as possible. This defect was partially overcome later by making the mast a fixture—sometimes with stay-wires attached to the top—and mounting the signal on a long iron spindle revolving in brackets fixed to it. At the same time lamp cases were attached to these spindles and revolved with them, the separate lamp staffs being abolished. These lamp cases were square, with 8 inch lenses in two adjacent sides and small lenses opposite them. The lamps, which were of course removable for trimming purposes, had two opposite sides of red and green glass respectively, and another of plain[1] glass facing the rape oil container, which formed the fourth side and had a round opening through its centre to show a back-light. Hence the back-lights of the *Danger* and *All right* positions were green and white respectively. Some of the lamp cases were provided with chain and pulley hoisting gear with guide-rods attached to the revolving spindle; others were reached by an iron ladder and small platform fixed to the supporting mast.

The Fantail signals were also mounted on spindles in the same way, but were not usually fitted with lamps, save when they were used independently of the Disc-and-Crossbars. This was generally in station yards, where they acted as inner home signals, the approach to the yard being protected by the usual Disc-and-Crossbar. Such lamps showed red and green lights only.

To enable Saunders to reply to certain enquiries of the Railway Commissioners as to the visibility of the signal lights, Gooch wrote to him in April 1848:

The Station signal lights are the most powerful we have and are made with Argand Burners[2] one inch in diameter having a reflector about 8 inches in diameter. These lights may be seen in a clear night several miles distant. We have in fact no straight line of sufficient length for the distance to prevent our seeing the lights. Our Twyford signals are seen very distinctly at a distance of between 4 and 5 miles. I cannot say what are the comparative distances at which the various colours in use may be seen, but the order in which they stand may be stated as follows—1st White, 2nd Red, 3rd Green. I think Red and Green are the best colours to use for coloured lights as producing the greatest contrast with each other and with White.

In thick or foggy weather the distance the lights are seen depends entirely upon the density of the fog. I have known it so bad that they could not be seen until within a few yards of them. There is also a difficulty in a fog in distinguishing at a distance a White light from a Red one. The fog gives the White light a Red appearance.

To return to the Disc-and-Crossbar signals, at first there was only one at each 'road station', as the smaller stations were called, which was to show the crossbar 'whenever the *Danger* Signal is indicated upon *either* flagstaff'. This continued for some time after the substitution of boards for flags, but eventually separate Up and Down Disc-and-Crossbars were provided at all signal stations. The next step found necessary was to distinguish the Down from the Up *Danger* signal, and this was done by the addition of short pieces projecting downwards at the ends of the crossbar the plain bar being henceforth confined to the Up line. The new form makes its first appearance in the Rule Book of 1852; it is not found in that of 1848, which, by the way, was the first Traffic Department book; previously all regulations had been issued on foolscap sheets. The Locomotive Department on the other hand had a Rule Book of its own much earlier, notwithstanding the fact that many of the drivers could not read.

---

[1] White lights at junctions, termini, and certain large stations being abolished at some date in the late 'fifties, a green glass was then substituted for this on the signals at such places.

[2] These were soon superseded by flat-flame burners.

Another innovation in this 1852 book is the adoption of red and green flags for hand-signals. Hitherto these hand-flags, in common use on most, if not all, other railways, had not been seen on the Great Western. The white hand-flag followed three years later.

Yet another variety of the crossbar was introduced between 1852 and 1855: the 'Level Crossing Signal where one mast is used and applicable to both lines Up and Down'. This had T-pieces at each end of the crossbar to distinguish it. It was obviously adopted to save the expense of two signals at each crossing.

Auxiliary, now known as Distant, signals are first mentioned in 1852. Owing to the visibility of the main Disc-and-Crossbars they were seldom needed on the Great Western, and for many years were only erected at exceptional places where the distant view of the main signal was obstructed. They were of the usual Up or Down form as the case required, and were worked at first by double wires from a capstan similar in appearance to that for points but differing in its lever travelling a whole semicircle instead of a quadrant; later a single wire and counterweight worked by a 'Worcester' lever were substituted.

All Fixed Signals within sight of each other and Auxiliary Signals must be made to repeat the same signal. In case of DANGER being shown by any Auxiliary Signal, the Engineman must pull up so as to stop at such Signal; but if he then sees the Line clear ahead, he must take his train slowly on towards the Station. (Rule 54 of 1852.)

The Windsor 'Drum' or 'Tambourine' signal remains to be noticed. Owing to the right-angle curve of the railway approaching Windsor Station an ordinary Disc-and-Crossbar was found to be useless, as the *Danger* signal would appear when first sighted to be an *All right* one, and *vice versa*. So Brunel designed a modification which when at *Danger* would show a crossbar in all directions. In the *All right* position it showed the driver first an upright bar and then, as he came round the bend, the usual disc. This signal seems to have been unique; so far as can be discovered there was no other of the kind on the system. It remained in use till the end of the 'eighties.[1]

Until the acquisition of the Shrewsbury Railways in 1854 there was only one Semaphore signal on the Great Western. This was the Midland Company's signal at the Tramway Crossing outside Gloucester Station, where the two lines crossed each other on the level. The early Rule Books give a full description and crude drawings of this strange foreign signal.

On the common line to Cheltenham there were Disc-and-Crossbars for Great Western and Semaphores for Midland trains side by side at Lansdown Junction and, as long as it existed, at Barnwood Junction also.

From 1855 for the next ten years the Rule Books say:

The Disc and Crossbar Signal is used on all the Line south of the Priestfield Junction, near Wolverhampton, with the exception of the Tramway Crossing at Gloucester Station. The Semaphore Signal is used on all the Lines north of the Priestfield Junction and at the Tramway Crossing at the Gloucester Station.

[1] A Fine set of models of the principal earlier types of signals is exhibited at the Great Western Railway Museum, Swindon opened in 1962.

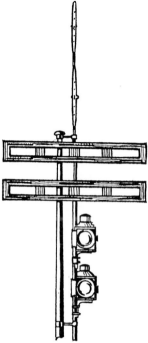

Up junction signal at DANGER

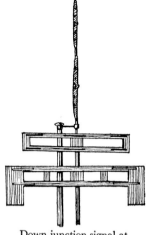

Down junction signal at
DANGER

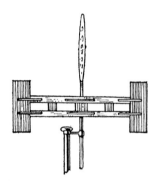

Level crossing signal for both
lines at DANGER

Up or down junction
signal at ALL RIGHT

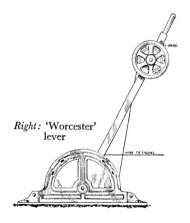

*Right:* 'Worcester'
lever

Not until 1865 did Semaphores appear elsewhere south of Priestfield. The first were brought into use on 1st April in that year throughout Paddington Yard as far as Kensal Green, and soon afterwards the rule was altered to—

The Disc Signal is used principally on the Broad Gauge system; the Semaphore Signal principally on the Narrow Gauge lines, but in some case also on the Broad Gauge.

Like the permanent way, the fixed signals were maintained and repaired by district contractors until 1859, when the Company took over the plant of one of these, long established at Slough, and set up works of their own on a small scale at Reading.

The time intervals governing the use of the signals remained 3 minutes *Danger* followed by 7 minutes *Caution* after the passage of any train

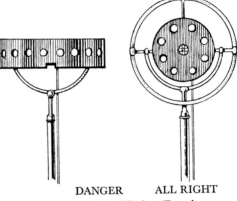

DANGER     ALL RIGHT

The Windsor 'Drum'

*Signals.*     29     30     *Signals.*

### Description of the Semaphore Signal at the Tram-way Crossing.

### By Day.

37. The Signals are constructed with either one or two Semaphore Arms.

The Signal is invariably made on the **Left-hand** side of the post as seen by the approaching engine-driver.

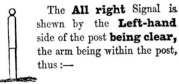

The **All right** Signal is shewn by the **Left-hand** side of the post **being clear,** the arm being within the post, thus :—

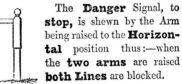

The **Caution** Signal, to **slacken speed,** is shewn by the Semaphore Arm on the **Left-hand** side being **raised to an angle of 45 degrees,** thus:

The **Danger** Signal, to **stop,** is shewn by the Arm being raised to the **Horizontal** position thus:—when the **two arms** are raised **both Lines** are blocked.

Extract from 1852 Rule Book

till 1852, when they were altered to 5 minutes *Danger* and 5 more *Caution* after a passenger train, and 8 minutes *Danger* and 7 more *Caution* after a goods train. After the whole 10 or 15 minutes, as the case might be, had elapsed, the signals were restored to their normal position of *All right*, provided of course no obstruction existed within sight of the signalman, except at Slough, Reading, Didcot, Swindon, Bath, Gloucester, and all junctions and terminal stations, where the normal position was *Danger*, only altered to admit a train. At junctions, approaching branch trains gave two whistles for the double signal to be turned off.

These intervals remained unaltered till 1877. The sensible distinction between passenger and slow-moving goods trains was peculiar to the Great Western; on most other railways the intervals were 5 minutes *Danger* and 5 *Caution* after all trains.

The new Electric Telegraph was first made use of on 1st December 1847 for signalling trains through Box Tunnel, and as this was the very first attempt at Block Telegraph on the Great Western, the rather quaint instructions are worth recording. Unfortunately no specimen of the instrument used has been preserved. It evidently had a large dial with an outer circle of letters and an inner one of numbers, to which the long and short ends respectively of the hand could be made to point by the sending station, the motive power being clockwork released by electricity.

### GREAT WESTERN RAILWAY
#### BOX TUNNEL—ELECTRIC TELEGRAPH

*December 1st, 1847.*

After this date the old orders for working this Tunnel will be suspended, as the Telegraph will be in use, and the knowledge thereby obtained as to whether trains have passed through the Tunnel will render the precautions hitherto taken unnecessary.

The instructions for the management of the instruments and for the regulation of the Batteries are in the hands of the parties in charge of the different instruments at Box, Corsham and the Tunnel mouths.

The following instructions must be particularly attended to.

As soon as a Train has entered the Tunnel, the Policeman must turn on his Cross Bar or Red Light, and then the information will be first communicated by him to the man at the further Tunnel mouth, in the following manner, he is to ring the bell the number of times specified to call attention, wait till the same number of Bells is returned, then pull out the stop, turn the right-hand index to T., push in the stop, and work the hand round till the short end points to the number on the dial referring to the desired message, the party receiving the message then works the hand round to the letters Q.S. to signify the signal has been understood, after which the party who sent the signal works round to the M., pulls out the stop, turns the right-hand index to B., pushes in the stop, and the instrument is then ready for another communication.

The Cross Bar or Red Light, remains on till information is received that the Train has passed out of the Tunnel. The Policeman will then turn on his caution signal, and admit the next train, without waiting the customary ten minutes as at present with the down trains to ensure the Tunnel being clear. At the proper time (see Police Instructions) the green light will be turned off, and the white light put on.

If intelligence is received that an Up Train which has taken the Bank Engine, is clear of the Tunnel, it will not be necessary to wait the return of the Bank Engine, if the Train then due is able to go through without its assistance.

For all trains that do not stop at Box, and which consequently will not be able to know from the clerk if the Tunnel is clear, a Red and Green Board and Light have been erected on the Up Line abreast of the Upper signals at Box. These signals will repeat those shown at the Tunnel mouth and if 'all right' or caution be shown, the drivers will then know that the Tunnel is clear and they may proceed up the Bank, otherwise they will stop until the proper signals are made.

As the greatest accuracy in receiving and transmitting these messages will be required, the attention of all parties is particularly called to the necessity of abstaining from sending trivial or useless messages, as in this case some important telegraphic communication may be interrupted or misunderstood.

The efficiency of the Batteries will be under the care of the Clerks at Box and Corsham, the one taking the Battery at the upper and the other the one at the lower end under their care, as well as those of their respective stations.

In all cases of interrupted messages where the instrument is thrown out of connection, the greatest care must be taken to observe what station the party throwing the instrument our of gear wishes to communicate with, this is known by the number of bells, and when this is ascertained no other communication must be attempted until this is concluded.

When any communication is going on, no other person must interfere or touch the instrument except in cases of importance or urgency.

In the event of any doubt arising in the mind of the person receiving a message, the letters Q.R. being given will signify 'it is to be repeated'.

If it is requisite to send a message not contained in signals, the letters may be used on the dial, and the party receiving the communication will understand the intention by the hand being worked round from starting point A. until the short end of the hand points to the small star on the centre of the dial, this directs the attention to the longer end of the hand and to the letters.

The numbers from 1 to 20 will refer only to the Tunnel signals, for which see list annexed. In the event of sending any other numbers or spelling, it is advisable to intimate where the message is coming from, which is to be done by working from the A. to the key letter signifying the station, and then to the number, or star if spelling is to be used.

| | Bells | Letters | | Bells | Letters |
|---|---|---|---|---|---|
| Box | 2 | R. | Corsham end of Tunnel | 4 | P. |
| Box end of Tunnel | 3 | Q. | Corsham | 5 | O. |

The proportions for making the Battery mixture is, one part Sulphuric Acid, and nine of Water. The Mixture will require to be renewed about once a month, and occasionally the Zinc plates will require renewing, which is very easily done, a few extra plates being kept on hand. A little quicksilver is also necessary for the small contact caps, and for amalgamating the plates.

FRED CLARKE.

LIST OF SIGNALS

| | (No. on Dial) |
|---|---|
| Up Train has entered Tunnel | 12 |
| Up Train is through Tunnel | 5 |
| Down Train has entered Tunnel | 9 |
| Down Train is out of Tunnel | 3 |
| Bank Engine has entered Tunnel | 17 |
| Bank Engine is through Tunnel | 15 |
| Waggons[1] are coming through Tunnel on Up Line | 19 |
| Waggons are coming through Tunnel on Down Line | 18 |
| Waggons are through Tunnel on Up Line | 10 |
| Waggons are through Tunnel on Down Line | 7 |

FRED CLARKE.

In August 1849 the telegraph through the tunnel was reported as out of order; whether it was then repaired or time-interval working reverted to does not appear. Three years later, in June 1852, the Electric Telegraph Company's representative found it quite useless, owing to defective insulation caused by the wires being 'in a water drain for half-a-mile and hung on the damp wall the rest of the way', and wrote that two new wires throughout were necessary. His Company were then ordered to put it to rights at once.

The next section to be worked by telegraph was that between Tetbury Road and Brimscombe with its steep inclines and the Sapperton Tunnels.

[1] Doubtless ballast or stone waggons duly attached to an engine are meant. That loose waggons were run down through the tunnel on either road indiscriminately seems quite incredible.

A collision occurred near the former station in December 1851 between some runaway trucks and a Down passenger train, which Captain Galton of the Board of Trade said could have been averted if the telegraph had been in use, so it was installed in the following year.

The mile of new line between Birmingham Station and Hockley was worked by telegraph from the opening in 1845, and soon afterwards the section through Snow Hill Tunnel to Bordesley. It was also brought into use between Gloucester Station and the junction with the Docks Branch at Over early in 1855, and the Shrewsbury & Birmingham Company is said to have used it for signalling trains through their short tunnel at Oakengates before that line was taken over.

With these few exceptions the time interval system remained in force on practically all double lines till the early 'seventies. Some portions of the West Midland and South Wales Railways were worked by telegraph before the amalgamation,[1] and a few trifling additions were made in the later 'sixties, but no serious extension of Block Telegraph was undertaken till after 1870, and even then progress was very gradual.

Between Paddington and Twyford trains were indeed signalled by telegraph as early as 1861, but with no idea of ensuring space intervals between them. Though the regulations—reproduced on the next page—provided for 'Line Blocked' being sent, this only meant that the approaching train was to be stopped and cautioned, while below Ealing its use was expressly forbidden 'except in cases of Break-downs or disablement of Trains'.

Down to 1855 the few single lines were each worked by one engine only, which generally carried a target or other distinguishing mark. Save for the 24 mile stretch from Oxford to Banbury during its two years of single existence, these were all quite short branches. The first to be worked by telegraph was that from Grange Court to Hereford in June 1855, with Ross as the only crossing station. Then came the long single lines in the Wilts and Somerset District opened in 1856 and 1857, all worked by single-needle telegraph and telegraphic crossing orders.

The Wycombe Branch, on its extension to Thame in 1862, seems to have been the first on which the Train Staff and Ticket system was introduced. This had been in force for some time before the amalgamation on the single lines of the West Midland Railway, except those between Colwall Tunnel and Shelwick Junction near Hereford, Crumlin and Quaker's Yard, and the Severn Valley Line from Hartlebury to Shrewsbury, which were worked by telegraph alone.

Detonators were adopted on the Great Western within a year or two of their invention in 1841 by E. A. Cowper. The Rule Book of 1848 prescribes their use in case of a breakdown: 'A policeman, if one should be within call, or underguard of the train or other person' was to go back fixing them on the rails at the same distances as now—one at a quarter,

---

[1] For instance, between Kidderminster and Wolverhampton and between Hereford and Pontypool, where 'Permissive Block' with Tyer's Instruments was established.

# Great Western Railway.

## SPECIAL REGULATIONS

### FOR WORKING THE

# SIGNALS,

### AND ALSO THE

# TELEGRAPH,

### BETWEEN

## PADDINGTON & EALING,

### For giving information of approaching Trains.

THE FOLLOWING SIGNALS WILL BE USED:—

A TRAIN APPROACHING ......Needle to be moved "Right" "Left," "Right" "Left," until replied to in like manner.

LINE CLEAR.......................Needle held for a few seconds over to the "Left."

LINE BLOCKED...................Needle held for a few seconds over to "Right."

All Signals are to be repeated back to shew that they are understood.

These movements must be made steadily and distinctly.

Care must be taken that the Bells are wound up as often as required, and turned on immediately the signalling is completed.

### LINE BLOCKED.

On receipt of the Signal "Line Blocked," the Signals are to be set at "Danger," and any Train or Engine proceeding to the point from which this Signal has been received is to be stopped, and the Driver cautioned to proceed cautiously, so as to render assistance, if necessary, in case of failure to the preceding Train.

# Great Western Railway.

## REGULATIONS

### FOR

### Working the Single Needle and Bell Telegraph

### BETWEEN

# EALING AND TWYFORD INCLUSIVE,

### For giving information of approaching Trains.

CODES DENOTING CHARACTER OF TRAINS.

| | | | | |
|---|---|---|---|---|
| ROYAL TRAIN ... ... ... | **R** | EXCURSION ... ... ... ... | **U** |
| EXPRESS, OR FAST ... ... | **X** | SPECIAL ... ... ... ... | **L** |
| STOPPING PASSENGER ... ... | **P** | BALLAST ... ... ... ... | **B** |
| COALS, GOODS, AND CATTLE... | **G** | ENGINE ... ... ... ... | **Q** |

The Narrow Gauge Trains will be Signalled with the Letter **N** before the above Letters, thus—Narrow Gauge Express or Fast **N X**.

Line Clear . . . . . Hold Needle over to the left.

Line Blocked . . . . Hold Needle over to the Right.

The signals "Line Clear" and "Line Blocked" are NOT to be used, except in cases of Break-down, or disablement of Trains, and are to be sent back when given to shew that they are understood.

Where it is necessary to give the Signal "Line Blocked," the time of sending it is to be entered in the Train Book; and the time of its receipt must also be entered by the person receiving it.

2

### UP TRAINS.

The approach of all Up Trains must be signalled from Ealing to the next Telegraph Station in advance, and from that point on again until the Signal is received at the Paddington Station, as follows:—

The FAST TRAINS as soon as the Signal is received FROM HANWELL.

The STOPPING TRAINS as soon as they are in sight of EALING STATION.

The Up Signal at the Green Lane Bridge is the Main Station Signal for the Paddington Station, and all Trains must stop "Dead" outside it until signalled to come in.

The Switchman at Green Lane Bridge will keep his Signals at "Danger," until he gets the "All Right" Signal from the Switchman at the Engine House Crossing.

If the Line is clear between Green Lane Bridge and the Up Signal at the Engine House Crossing, the Switchman at the Green Lane Bridge must inform the Driver, and allow him to proceed slowly to the next Signal.

The Engine Drivers (particularly those of the Express and Fast Trains), must approach the Station at such a rate of speed as will enable them to stop at any of the Signals which may be against them.

### DOWN TRAINS.

The Down Trains are to be signalled from the Engine House, and on from Station to Station in advance.

### NOTE.—During the Day,

Between the Hours of 6.0 a.m. and 7.0 p.m. the Telegraph communications will be as follows :—

EALING to WEST LONDON JUNCTION, WEST LONDON JUNCTION to GREEN LANE BRIDGE, and vice versa.

### During the Night,

Between the hours of 7.0 p.m. and 6.0 a.m. the Telegraph communications will be from EALING to GREEN LANE BRIDGE, and vice versa, WEST LONDON JUNCTION being cut out of circuit during the night.

N.B.—This order cancels all previous instructions on the same subject.

JAMES KELLEY,
*Superintendent of Traffic.*

C. E. SPAGNOLETTI,
*Telegraph Superintendent.*

PADDINGTON STATION,
21st OCTOBER, 1861.

3

As soon as the Line is Clear again, the Signal "Line Clear" is to be given to the Station to which "Line Blocked" has previously been sent, and the time this Signal is given is to be entered in the Train Book by both the Sender and the Receiver of the Signal.

All these movements must be made with steadiness and regularity.

Care must be taken that the Bells are wound up as often as required, and turned on immediately the signalling is completed.

The Down Trains will commence to be signalled from Ealing, and the Up Trains from Twyford Station.

To call the attention of a Station, the Bell should be turned off, and the Needle steadily shaken to and fro, which will have the effect of ringing the Bell at the other end, and will likewise denote Train APPROACHING; this must be continued until replied to in like manner.

Then the Letter denoting the character of the approaching Train is to be sent, and returned by the Station signalled to, to denote that it is understood.

If the Code letter should be misunderstood, and wrongly returned, the Needle is to be again shaken to and fro, and the correct letter sent, which must likewise be repeated by the Station receiving the signal.

Should a Train become disabled near, or at, your Station, before passing it, the Policeman must send the "Line Blocked" signal back to the Station from which the Train was signalled to him; but if a Train break down after passing your Station within sight, or nearer to your Station than the next in advance to which your Signal, it will be in the power of your Policeman to stop the approaching Train himself; but he may, as a safeguard, give "Line Blocked" to the Station in the rear.

If a break down should foul both lines, the "Line Blocked" signal is to be sent to the next Station in advance, as well as to the one in the rear.

On receiving the "Line Blocked" signal, all Trains and Engines are to be stopped by the usual signals, and the Drivers desired to proceed slowly and cautiously, and keep their Trains under control, so as to render assistance if necessary.

This order cancels all previous instructions on the same subject.

(Signed) C. E. SPAGNOLETTI,
*Telegraph Superintendent.*

(Countersigned) JAMES KELLEY,
*Superintendent,*
*Great Western Railway, Paddington.*

7th NOVEMBER, 1861.

one at half, and two at three-quarters of a mile from the train. During fogs an obstruction at a station was considered sufficiently protected by one detonator at 300 yards, or 500 if a train was nearly due. 'Men who move about the line will be provided with a quantity in a tin case, which they must carry with them.' Very soon these distances of ¾ mile and 300 yards were found insufficient for safety, and both were increased in 1852 to the full mile, which remained standard on the Great Western for many years. Most of the other Companies were content with ¾ mile or even less, in spite of the objurgations of Board of Trade Inspectors when collisions occurred, as they often did in those days of insufficient brake-power.

Fusee signals, resembling the fireworks known as Roman candles, carried in long tin cases[1] by all guards, were introduced in 1852, and remained in use till 1865.

> They are fixed in the ballast between the rails, and upon being smartly struck ignite and burn for fifteen[2] minutes, and can be seen at a considerable distance from an approaching train. They are to be considered as signals of *Caution*, and indicate that a train has moved on from the spot where they are burning within fifteen[2] minutes. (1852 Rule Book.)

A guard who had been protecting his train, stopped from any cause outside fixed signals, was directed to light and fix one at the mile and another at ½ mile behind it when he picked up his detonators to rejoin the train.

Sidings were not furnished with any safety appliance to prevent vehicles fouling the running lines, hand-scotches under the wheels being thought sufficient, until after a collision at Wootton Bassett one night in September 1850, when an empty horse-box was blown out of a siding on to the Down main line by the wind of one passing excursion train and run into by the next. The Directors then decided to provide safety points and dead ends with buffer stops to all sidings where there was room for them, and elsewhere permanent scotch-blocks to be kept locked across the rail when not in use. The latter were forthwith installed in most cases, dead ends not becoming general till the 'seventies.

The illustration of Llansamlet Station facing page 333 gives the back view of a Fantail (at *Danger*) used independently as a Station Signal and so furnished with a lamp. Owing to the sharp curve, the signal is abnormally placed on the outer side of the other line so as to be seen under the bridge from an approaching train. The capstan at the end of the opposite platform is for working the Auxiliary Signal, which is out of sight beyond the bridge.

### TELEGRAPH

Some months before the first opening of the railway the Directors, on the advice of Brunel, made an agreement with W. F. Cooke for the trial of his and Professor C. Wheatstone's new Electric Magnetic Telegraph

---

[1] In 1862 110 passenger vehicles of all sorts and 26 goods guards' vans were fitted with brackets to carry these.
[2] Altered to ten in 1855.

Spagnoletti-type single-needle telegraph instrument. This remained standard equipment on nearly all G.W.R. lines until replaced by telephones

Cooke & Wheatstone's double-needle two wire telegraph instrument installed at Paddington in 1843

Paddington Station, by W. P. Frith, R.A. 1862.    One of the best-known railway paintings.    On a canvas 8 feet 5 inches by 3 feet 10 inches, it is celebrated for the remarkable amount of accurate and authentic detail

between Paddington and West Drayton, a distance of 13 miles. The agreement was confirmed on 24th May 1838. According to Saunders' evidence before the Select Committee on Railways in February 1840, it provided that the Great Western Company should lay the wires at their own expense, and that after a certain period they might call on the patentees to give them a free licence to instal the invention throughout the railway. He added:

> The Company's idea is that the telegraph will be simplifying the working tend to diminish the amount of stock of every description such as engines and carriages, as well as producing other advantages and greater security in working the railway. It is proposed that guards shall have portable telegraphs capable of operating at a distance of every quarter mile, but this has not been carried out up to the present. There are places where portable telegraphs may be applied, but the men have not been instructed in it yet.

The telegraph was working as far as Hanwell by April 1839, for on 6th of that month Seymour Clarke wrote to Saunders:

> The Telegraph has been of use to-day. Mr. Brunel, with whom I fell in at Maidenhead, asked me to stop the 12 o'clock at Hanwell, and after looking at Peto and Grissells proposal for the Bridge we were waiting at the Hanwell Station and playing on the Telegraph when we found that the Altas had dropped her fire bars at Bourne farm and stopped. We sent word what to do and stopped the down train at 2 to caution it.

Saunders told the Committee it was finished to West Drayton in the following July; but, as will be seen, all through messages had to be transmitted at Hanwell. The line consisted of five wires, insulated with cotton and gutta-percha, in an iron pipe fixed above ground at the side of the line, and the instruments were thus described by Professor Wheatstone to the aforesaid Committee:

> Figure A is what may be called a dial with five vertical magnetic needles; upon the dial twenty letters are marked and the various letters are indicated by the mutual convergence of two needles when they are called to move. If the first needle deviates to the right and the fourth to the left, then the letter B is indicated. If the same needles converge downwards the letter V is pointed to.
>
> These magnetic needles are acted upon by electrical currents passing through coils of wire placed immediately behind them. Each of the coils forms a portion of a communicating wire may be extended to any distance. These wires are extended to a communicator by which the signals are made. It consists of five longitudinal and two transverse metal bars fixed on a wooden frame, the latter are united to the two poles of a voltaic battery, and in the ordinary condition of the instruments have no metallic connections with the longitudinal bars, which are each connected with a different length of the line. On each of the longitudinal bars two stops are placed, forming together two parallel rows. When a stop of the upper row is pressed down the bar upon which it is placed forms metallic connection with the transverse bar below it, which is connected with one of the poles of the battery; and when one of the stops on the lower row is touched another to the longitudinal bars forms a connection with the other pole of the battery, and the current flows through the two wires connected by the longitudinal bars. There is a communicator and a dial at each end.
>
> An alarm on the principle of a clock alarm is provided to call attention. This alarm is wound up and a current worked through an electro-magnet pulls the stop of the alarm out and causes the bell to ring.
>
> This sort of telegraph is not in operation on any other railway, but the Blackwall Company shortly intend to have it.

The cost of the installation to the Company was stated by Saunders as between £250 and £300 a mile, including the charge for the instruments.

The telegraph at Paddington at once became one of the sights of London. We find Seymour Clarke writing to Saunders on 24th August:

The Duke of Wellington, Lord Bathurst, Lord Fitzroy Somerset, and some ladies, and afterwards Lord Howick came. The telegraph worked capitally. Mr Sims and Mr Gibbs were here. The Duke appeared much pleased, and I think he will go to Twyford with us on Monday. He seems mightily afraid of having his wheels stick fast. I said all I could to convince him of the error of his conclusion, and said that one or two cases had occurred of the many thousand carriages we had carried.

Gibbs noted the event in his Diary:

*August 24th*—Sims and I received the Duke of Wellington at Paddington and showed him the Electro-Magnetic Telegraph and the station.

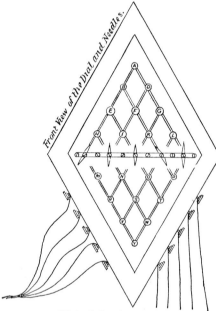

Dial of 1839 instrument

Besides its attractions for the public, the new telegraph became very useful for advising the Superintendent of the constant engine troubles of those days and other emergencies and conveying his orders. On 10th December he writes to Saunders:

I was speaking to Mr Cooke about having the connection established between Paddington and Drayton direct, without the necessity of using the instrument at Hanwell, which is now the case. Mr Cooke said he was in communication with you on the matter.

Whether Hanwell was 'switched out' after this has not been ascertained, neither has any further item of interest as to the telegraph been noted for nearly three years, by which time the wires had been damaged and the apparatus presumably had ceased working.

On 24th November 1842 the General Traffic Committee of the Board, meeting at Steventon, accepted the terms proposed by Mr Cooke for the repair of the telegraph and its extension to Slough. These were shortly:

Cooke to continue at his own expense the Electro-Magnetic Telegraph from West Drayton to Slough, and to repair and replace on an improved plan the injured portions between Paddington and West Drayton, and keep the whole in order and give it up to the Company at the end of a lease to be granted him for fourteen years at a peppercorn rent.

Two separate wires, instruments and alarms for the Company to use for their own purposes but not for hire, to be provided at Paddington, Slough, and all intermediate stations, free of charge, and Cooke's clerks to aid transmission for the Company's purposes.

The 'improved plan' consisted of double-needle instruments requiring only two wires, and, instead of being incased in an iron pipe, these were 'suspended separately in the air by a series of upright standards of cast iron, varying from ten to twenty-five feet in height and placed sometimes as much as 150 yards apart'.[1]

The new system was installed between Paddington and Slough in 1843, and acquired considerable fame by its speedy announcement to the Ministers of the Crown and the Metropolis generally of the birth of the Queen's second son, known later as the Duke of Edinburgh, at Windsor on 6th August 1844. A few months later it achieved still greater fame by effecting the arrest of a murderer.

On New Year's Day 1845 a scoundrel named John Tawell travelled down to Slough with cyanide of potash in his pocket for the purpose of poisoning a discarded mistress then living in a cottage at Salthill. He successfully administered the poison in a glass of stout, but to his horror, immediately after drinking, the victim gave a piercing scream, which alarmed the neighbours. He at once made off to the station at Slough, caught an evening train, and arrived safely at Paddington, where he took a sixpenny bus to the Bank, and after visiting a couple of coffee-houses, doubtless with a view to proving an alibi if necessary, strolled home to his lodgings in Scott's Yard, Cannon Street. Next morning, to his astonishment, he was arrested, and in due course tried and hanged at Aylesbury.

His train had not left Slough many minutes when news of the murder was brought from Salthill, and the murderer's appearance described by one who had seen him leave the cottage. A message for Paddington was forthwith handed in at the telegraph office telling of the murder and that 'a man in the garb of a Quaker' wearing a long brown greatcoat in a specified compartment was the suspected murderer. The telegraphic code of the day did not include the letter Q, so the clerk, not to be outdone, promptly spelled the word 'Kwaker', and his equally bright colleague at Paddington understood. The train was met by a sergeant of the Company's Police in plain clothes and the 'Kwaker' spotted, but apparently the telegram was not thought a sufficient ground for arresting him. So the sergeant shadowed the man till he was safely bestowed for the night at his lodgings and then returned to Paddington to meet an emissary from Slough, with whom he made the arrest.

Sir Francis Head, who relates the story in his *Stokers and Pokers*,[2] adds:

A few months afterwards, we happened to be travelling by rail from Paddington to Slough in a carriage filled with people all strangers to one another. Like English travellers they were all mute. For nearly fifteen miles no one had uttered a single word, until a short-bodied, short-necked, short-nosed, exceedingly respectable-looking man in the corner, fixing his eyes on the apparently fleeting posts and wires of the electric telegraph, significantly nodded to us as he muttered aloud—'Them's the cords that hung John Tawell'.

This dramatic arrest of the murderer was of course a great advertisement, and many more people flocked to inspect the wonderful new invention, to the no small profit of Cooke's licensee.

[1] Bourne's *History*.
[2] John Murray, 1849.

The novelty having worn off in the course of the next year or two, the telegraph seems to have fallen largely out of use, for in May 1848 the Electric Telegraph Company, who had taken over Cooke's rights, proposed to close the line between Paddington and Slough 'as now of very little importance' to them and not paying. Four months later they gave formal notice to close it at the end of September, whereupon the Great Western Directors replied that they would take possession of the whole apparatus if the Telegraph Company ceased to maintain it. Finally, in June 1849, we find that the telegraph had been removed, owing to the Railway Company having claimed compensation for damage to an engine caused by a fallen post.

By this time the telegraph had been established on most of the other railways of the country, so that from having been a pioneer in the enterprise the Great Western had now become one of the last to make any permanent use of it.

At length, in the autumn of 1850, the Directors came to an agreement with the Electric Telegraph Company for a line between Oxford and Banbury; and in the following year arranged with them for a general installation, as we have already seen. The telegraph was completed between London and Bristol in May 1852, and from this time onwards it was rapidly extended all over the system and on all new lines of importance, but many more years elapsed before there was an instrument and a man capable of using it at every station.

The first instruments were all of the double-needle kind, but the new branches opened in the later 'fifties were equipped with single needles, and in August 1860 the Directors ordered that the latter sort should be substituted for all existing double needles.

It is said that for the first fifteen years or so some at any rate of the telegraph posts on the Great Western were painted white with tarred bases.

In May 1855 the Company appointed a Telegraph Superintendent of their own, C. E. Spagnoletti, a former employé of the Electric Telegraph Company, being the person chosen; but the small importance attached to the new office in the minds of the Directors may be gathered from the salary allotted to him—£100 a year! Spagnoletti was soon to distinguish himself by patenting the Disc Block Telegraph Instrument, of which more will be said hereafter. It was first introduced on the Metropolitan Railway at the opening thereof in January 1863, and later became standard on practically all the double lines of the Great Western.

# XIII

# *Train Service*

## TRAIN SERVICE

The advertisement of the opening to Maidenhead showed eight trains each way daily on weekdays and six on Sundays, all stopping at West Drayton and Slough. Later in 1838 the weekday trains were increased to nine each way, and in December four 'short trains' between Paddington and Drayton were put on to serve the newly opened stations at Ealing and Hanwell.

The earliest official Train Bill, as these notices were called, which has survived, is that issued for the opening of a station at Southall on 1st May 1839.

It will be observed that the 'Posting Carriage' fares of the opening have disappeared, but that there were still two distinct 'Second Class' fares. This ceased on 1st July when the line was extended to Twyford, the 'Second Class Close' being then abolished. Some of the closed carriages were altered into firsts, but twenty-three of them were still in stock in October 1840, when they were ordered to be used 'for the Night Long trains in place of the Open Carriages', of course at the ordinary fares.

The reason that no proper time-tables were issued in those early days was explained by Saunders to the Parliamentary Committee on Railways in April 1841:

At the opening in 1838 we found the engines were so inefficient that time-table working was hopeless; one or two engines might keep time, the other eight or ten were always out of time. So we suspended time-tables till the locomotive power became sufficient.

It was not till the end of 1840 that a sufficient number of Gooch's engines had been delivered to work the traffic properly and so enable a real time-table to be issued for the opening to Wootton Bassett Road in December.

The following extracts from a series of reports made by Seymour Clarke to Saunders in 1839, apparently whenever the latter happened to be absent from Paddington, which have fortunately been preserved, shed much light on the difficulties under which the traffic was carried on in those early days and the troubles of the first London Superintendent.

*8th January*—I have again been suffering for the want of a reserve water tank. No water came in during the night. We had enough for the 8 o'clock but the expected supply not having come by 9 I was obliged to get the fire engine out and had recourse to a little well near my cottage and by this means send off the 9, 9½ and 10 o'clock trains, taking those engines that had most in their tenders. I now have men pumping at the old Saw Pit. . . . The Morning Star is unloading to-day.

*11th January*—The 2 o'clock train up from Maidenhead was coming at about 40 miles an hour on the new piece at Southall Bridge when a Hunter without his rider came along in the opposite direction on the other line at full gallop; on seeing the train he turned short

# Great Western Railway.
## LONDON TO MAIDENHEAD.

**On and after the 1st of May, the SOUTHALL STATION will be opened**
*For Passengers and Parcels.*

An **Extra Train** to **Slough** will leave Paddington on **Sunday Mornings,** at **half-past 9 o'clock,** calling at Ealing, Hanwell, Southall and West Drayton.

**Horses and Carriages,** being at the Paddington or Maidenhead Station ten minutes before the departure of a Train, will be conveyed upon this Railway.

*Charge for 4-wheel Carriage,* 12s. *Two-wheel ditto,* 8s. *For 1 Horse;* 10s. *Pair of Horses,* 16s.

**Post Horses** are kept in readiness both at Paddington and Maidenhead, and upon sufficient notice being given at Paddington, or at the Bell and Mouth Office, St. Martin's-le-Grand, would be sent to bring Carriages from any part of London to the station, at a moderate charge.

## TRAINS.

| From Paddington To Maidenhead. | From Maidenhead To Paddington. |
|---|---|
| **8** o'clock morn. calling at - - Southall and Slough | **6** o'clock morning, calling at - - Slough *(and on Wednesday Morning at Southall)* |
| **9** do. - - - Slough | **8** do. - Slough and West Drayton |
| **10** do. - West Drayton and Slough | **9** do. - Slough and West Drayton |
| **12** do. - West Drayton and Slough | **10** do. - - Slough and Southall |
| **2** o'clock afternoon - West Drayton and Slough | **12** do. - Slough and West Drayton |
| **4** do. - - - Slough | **2** o'clock afternoon - - Slough and Southall |
| **5** do. - - Hanwell and Slough | **4** do. - - - Slough |
| **6** o'clock evening Ealing, West Drayton and Slough | **5** do. - - Slough and Hanwell |
| **7** do. - Southall and Slough | **6** o'clock evening - Slough and West Drayton |
| **8** do. - - Slough | **7** do. - - Slough and Ealing |

The **six o'clock up Train will call at Southall on Wednesday mornings, for the convenience** of persons attending the market on that day).

### SHORT TRAINS.

| From Paddington To West Drayton. | From West Drayton To Paddington. |
|---|---|
| ¼ past **9** o'Clock Morning, ⎫ calling at ⎰ **Ealing,** | ¼ before **9** o'Clock Morning, ⎫ calling at ⎰ **Southall,** |
| ¼ past **1** do. Afternoon, ⎬ ⎨ **Hanwell,** | ¼ before **11** do. ⎬ ⎨ **Hanwell,** |
| ¼ past **4** do. do. ⎬ ⎨ AND | ¼ before **3** Afternoon ⎬ ⎨ AND |
| ¼ past **8** do. Evening ⎭ ⎱ **Southall,** | ¼ before **7** o'Clock Evening ⎭ ⎱ **Ealing.** |

☞ *There are no second class close carriages in the short Trains.*

Passengers and Parcels for Southall and Maidenhead will be conveyed from all the stations by means of the short Trains, waiting to be taken on by the succeeding long Train, as above; and in like manner they will be conveyed from Maidenhead and Slough, to every station on the Line.

## On SUNDAYS,

| From Paddington To Maidenhead. | From Maidenhead To Paddington. |
|---|---|
| **8** o'clock Morn. calling at - - Ealing and Slough | **6** o'clock morn. calling at - - - - Slough |
| ¼ past **8** do. do. - - West Drayton and Slough | **8** do. do. - Slough Southall and Ealing |
| **9** do. do. - - Southall and Slough | **9** do. do. Slough West Drayton and Hanwell |
| **5** afternoon do. Hanwell West Drayton and Slough | **5** afternoon do. - - - Slough and Hanwell |
| **6** evening do. Ealing West Drayton and Slough | **6** evening do. - Slough and West Drayton |
| **7** do. do. - - Southall and Slough | **7** do. do. - - - Slough and Ealing |

### SHORT TRAINS,
## PADDINGTON TO SLOUGH.

**Half-past Nine o'Clock Morning,** - - - calling at **Ealing, Hanwell, Southall, and Drayton.**

| To West Drayton. | From West Drayton. |
|---|---|
| ¼ past **9** o'Clock Morning, ⎫ *Ealing, Hanwell, & Southall.* | ¼ before **8** o'Clock Morning, ⎫ calling at ⎰ *Southall, Han-* |
| calling at ⎬ *and proceeding to Slough* | ¼ before **7** do. Evening, ⎬ ⎱ *well & Ealing.* |
| ¼ past **8** do. Evening, ⎭ *Ealing, Hanwell & Southall* | |

## FARES.

| Paddington. | 1st. Class. | Second Class. | | Maidenhead. | 1st. Class. | Second Class. | |
|---|---|---|---|---|---|---|---|
| | Coach. | Close. | Open. | | Coach. | Close. | Open. |
| To Ealing ..... | 1 6 | 1 0 | 0 9 | To Slough ..... | 2 0 | 1 6 | 1 0 |
| Hanwell ... | 2 0 | 1 6 | 1 0 | West Drayton | 3 0 | 2 6 | 2 0 |
| Southall .... | 2 6 | 1 9 | 1 3 | Southall .... | 4 0 | 3 0 | 2 6 |
| West Drayton | 3 6 | 2 0 | 1 6 | Hanwell ... | 4 6 | 3 6 | 3 0 |
| Slough ..... | 4 6 | 3 0 | 2 6 | Ealing ..... | 5 0 | 4 0 | 3 6 |
| Maidenhead. | 5 6 | 4 0 | 3 6 | Paddington. | 5 6 | 4 0 | 3 6 |

*The same Fares will be charged from Slough to West Drayton as from Maidenhead to Slough.*

OMNIBUSES and Coaches start from Princes Street, Bank, one hour before the departure of each Train, calling at the Angel Inn, Islington; Bull Inn, Holborn; Moore's Green Man and Still, Oxford Street; Golden Cross, Charing Cross; Chaplin's Universal Office, Regent Circus; and Gloucester Warehouse, Oxford Street; to the Paddington station.—**Fare 6d.** without Luggage.

round and being knocked down threw the whole train off the rails. The Star[1] is standing upright in the ditch—up to the gearing in mud—the tender with her and the open carriage; the close carriage is standing with her hind wheels in the air; the 1st Class was got on to the road and was pushed up by the short train. Mr Gooch has gone to see after the engine. I sent Carr to get the coaches on the Line and Russell to see to shifting the passengers from the train but this latter was done before they arrived. Not a soul was hurt, the passengers scarcely felt the shock. Mr Mill's brother was among the number of dismounted Horsemen who took our fence. The killed Horse belongs to some Lord. But I know not who—he did not come up to see after it, but someone in scarlet shook his head and said 'It belongs to Lord——'. The Directors and their friends were not in the train. There was not a delay of more than 1½ hours. Appleby says the Star is not injured; the 2nd Class Coach is slightly injured.

*25th January*—The Duke of Lucca came to-day to go to Windsor in a great hurry. I went with him, we started at ¼ to 1 and arrived[2] at 1¼; he had four friends with him. We had the Star and one 6 wheeled carriage. He was very much pleased. The engine was not expected to go till 1¾ so her steam was low. I charged him £10. He is coming back by regular train. . . . The Vulcan Engine driving wheel broke badly to-day on the way up—all to pieces; it had been temporarily mended before.

*4th February*—The Eagle Engine and 9 o'clock train have all been off the line at Maidenhead just beyond the Engine House owing to the points being wrong. The Engine is now in the ditch, the carriages are all on the line again not much damaged; the engine is, as far as they can tell, not much injured. The three stage coaches are gone on their journey. The 10 o'clock train up could not start till 11 o'clock—then through the Engine House. No passengers injured and hardly any one alarmed. The Engineman Almond saw the points were wrong but could not stop in time.

*5th February*—We had an eccentric on that unfortunate Bacchus break to-day at Slough which detained us an hour. There were not many passengers and no complaints.

*7th February*—Last evening 8 o'clock train, Premier took 42 mins, she was pushed by the Bacchus, which was going to take her place for this evening.
Morning Star—36 mins. up this evening from Engine House, 4 coaches.
Bacchus—43 mins.
Vulcan—47 mins. All going well. .

*23rd February*—The turntable on Arrival line is not complete, which materially adds to the labour of the Station. The wet weather does not improve the Traffic; Thursday was only £142 14s 0d.

*5th March*—All is well to-day and the traffic very fair. The 8 o'clock last evening did not arrive till 9.45. The joint of the Steam pipe of the Atlas failed at Southall, and she could not proceed. The Pilot Engine brought it up. Mr Gooch seems to think the Engineman was in fault, and has fined him a week's pay. It was not the proper Engineman, he [Jas. Almond] was in the shed getting the Eagle ready, which is at work to-day.

*12th March*—I am sorry to be obliged to detail a delay that occurred last evening. The 7 o'clock train down had gone as far as Ranelagh Bridge when the Hurricane and the carriages all got off in consequence of the switch from the Engine House being wrong. Goodlad, the man who was pardoned before, is the person; I have of course finished his service here. None of the 3 trucks came off. I got out another train of carriages and the Neptune engine, passed them over the Westbourne switches, then ran back the trucks with them and got them all over Lord Hill's Crossing. The 8 and 8½ o'clock managed this way also. Nothing was broken, the engine was on again by 12 o'clock. The carriages were pulled on by the Eagle. The delay was about 1 hour in consequence of the time it took to arrange the passengers, get out the new train, &c, &c, which brought us so near 8 o'clock that we deemed it prudent to wait till the last train had come in before we used Lord Hill's switches.

*19th March* All has gone well to-day. I have not heard much comment about our delays of yesterday. The troops went down in fine style—429 people, 8 6 wheelers and 1 truck in 38 minutes.

*2nd April*—The Viper went, after the last train, to Bull's Bridge to fetch a load of timber. She was returning at about 1 o'clock, coming at about 12 to 15 miles an hour, when, owing to the points west of the Engine House being open, she ran into it. Broke one pair of doors all to pieces and much damaged the western ones. The Morning Star

[1] North Star.                    [2] At Slough.

was standing to go out the first thing this morning and she received the first shock, her cylinder covers are both broken in and the end of her frame destroyed. The Vulcan was next, she received very little damage, and the Thunderer third, which had only the Hand Rail bent. All these Engines were driven out of the Engine House. The two latter are at work and the Star will be a week off the Line.

*6th April.*—We had 6 Stage Coaches, 1 private Carriage, and an empty truck per 9 o'clock, and from the time that the trucks stopped till the last coach was off 11½ minutes elapsed, and I think of this 5 at least were occupied in running the trucks back to the Traversing Frame along the curve of the siding. I made the men divide the lot into two parts of 3 and 4, the 3 were taken off at the Turn Table and the 4 at the Traversing Frame. The Frame works capitally, I pulled it by myself, walking backwards, empty and pushed it with the truck on it.

*7th June.*—We are badly off again for engines. The North Star broke her Cranked Axle at Drayton Engine House at 10 going down. The Thunderer is as you know damaged; the Hurricane is in dock; and the Lion with the levers of her Weigh Bar broken. The Morning Star—Cylinder split and the cover gone. We have a spare cranked axle for the North Star and Gooch says she will be out on Monday, also the Hurricane.

We have the Atlas, the Eagle, the Ajax, the 3 small Vulcans[1] and the Vulcan. The Apollo is on the Short train, the Neptune and Venus working together. The trains have been later in consequence of these accidents, but no one hurt by anything, nor is there much grumbling. We certainly have been a long while free from accidents and now as usual they come together.

*22nd July.*—The 9 o'clock down yesterday did not get in[2] till ¼ to 12, the Vulcan pushed them on to Slough and the Neptune met them at Maidenhead but very much time was lost in getting the Cheltenham coach off at Maidenhead in consequence of the Engine being in the rear. After you left yesterday I changed my mind about sending the Hurricane after them as I recollected that the short train returns from Slough to Drayton *on the wrong line* so I thought it more prudent to run the chance of delay than the danger of a concussion. Would it not be better for the 9 o'clock to go on to Maidenhead and come back to Drayton on its proper line? All the rest of the trains and the up ones went very well.

The Morning Star brought up a very long train this evening at ¼ to 8 from Twyford and the 9 is in in capital time 5 mins. past 10.

*31st July.*—The short train last evening did not reach Maidenhead till ¼ to 10. They were 1¼ hours going to Drayton owing to the steam in the Vulcan being low. The engine had been under repair and the fire had not been in sufficiently long before starting. They stopped for the coke too. The coaches when let off at the Traversing Frame ran on to the Station in consequence of the rain having made the brakes so slippery that they would not hold. It was ½ past 10 before the coaches went through Maidenhead. Mr Andrews ordered the Aeolus out to push but a cold engine being in the way it could not be after the train in time to be of use. We had pretty good trains considering the weather —7 private carriages in the first two trains.

*15th August.*—You will be sorry to hear that the North Star with the 9 o'clock train broke her connecting strap and the piston has forced out the end of the cylinder. The Planet with the short train pushed her on to Drayton and would then go on to Twyford. This occurred at Ealing. Mr Gooch says the North Star will be in shed for 6 weeks.

*15th September.*—We have not been fortunate to-day. In the first place the 9 o'clock up from Twyford was late. The Vulcan burst one of her tubes—this so frightened the Fireman that he fainted off the Engine at the Thames Junction while she was running—he struck against the Bridge and injured his skull; this threw him back and he has a compound fracture of the leg. He is a little hunchbacked man, Isaac Robson by name, you may recollect that he injured his hand with the Ajax one day at Slough. He usually went on the Planet. I fear he will die. I sent him to St. George's Hospital.

Then this evening the North Star got off the line, and the 5 o'clock did not start till 20 to 6, and the 6 at 13 to 7, the 7 went at proper time. All have come in well.

*3rd October.*—All went quite well yesterday. I received intelligence per Telegraph that the 8 o'clock this evening has broken down, the cylinder head of the Planet having broken. I sent word that the 9 would push them on. It occurred at Bull's Bridge. The Telegraph is in excellent order.

In September 1839, soon after the opening to Twyford, goods traffic began, chiefly by carriers, who also took 'persons in lower stations of life'

---

[1] *Apollo, Neptune,* and *Venus.*　　　　　　　　　　　　　　　[2] To Twyford.

with the goods, as they had been accustomed to do in their road waggons. The Company made no attempt to accommodate such people till after the line was opened to Reading, when they announced that 'The Goods Train Passengers will be conveyed in uncovered Trucks by the Goods Trains only, and 14 lbs of luggage allowed for each', and advertised the starting of two goods trains and the stations they stopped at.

The passenger trains, according to Saunders' evidence before the Select Committee on Railways at the end of July 1839, usually consisted in summer of three open seconds and three firsts, capable of taking 216 and 92 people respectively.[1] He said nothing of the guards or luggage. At first some, at any rate, of the luggage was carried on the roofs of the coaches as on the London & Birmingham Railway, but this practice was soon abandoned. The Stock List of October 1840 includes 'Luggage Waggons with Tarpaulins running with Passenger Trains', and in October 1841 the General Traffic Committee of the Board ordered that 'one Body in each of ten 2nd Class carriages be closed up to convey Bridgwater luggage without being exposed to loss or injury by wet weather'. After this we hear no more of luggage on the roofs till 1859, when the practice was resumed for some ten or twelve years. Great Western guards were never perched on the roofs to be blinded and stifled by cinders and smoke, as were those of the London & Birmingham and some other railways. They sat with the passengers in certain compartments of the second-class carriages in command of brakes, which Brunel described to another Select Committee in March 1841 as 'tolerably useless'. The firsts had no brakes at all, and as yet there were no regular brake vans; in fact the only efficient brakes were on the tenders, and even these were an afterthought in 1840. The light carriage trucks, on the other hand, always had lever brakes for use in shunting. There were generally two or three of these with private carriages and their occupants on most trains, sometimes with guards on them, but their brakes, if used at all, would have had little effect on the train.

The Post Office continued to send the bulk of the mails by road till 4th February 1840,[2] when a Night Mail train to and from Twyford, also carrying passengers, was established, to be extended with or soon after each extension of the railway. The first sorting carriages (four) were ordered, on the requisition of the Postmaster-General, in July 1841, and four second-class carriages altered to carry the Day Mail bags and their guard sheltered from the weather.

The last of the Train Bills, with the service to Faringdon Road in August 1840, and the first real time-table, with that to Wootton Bassett Road in December,[3] are reproduced.

[1] Each second had six compartments holding twelve, and each first four holding eight. $3 \times 6 \times 12 = 216$, but $3 \times 4 \times 8 = 96$. Perhaps 92 is a misprint; the guards were certainly never in the firsts.

[2] The Cheltenham Mail Coach was sent on a truck by one of the evening trains before this.

[3] As this section was not actually opened till 17th December the latter must be a proof.

When the line was opened throughout to Bristol the fastest train, the Down Night Mail, was allowed 4 hours and 10 minutes for the 118¼ miles with ten stops, and inclusive speed of just over 28 miles an hour; the rest in both directions took anything from 4¼ to 4¾ hours. The goods train passengers, now called third-class, left Paddington in their open trucks at 4.30 a.m. or 9.30 p.m. and reached Bristol in 9½ hours or 8 hours 10 minutes respectively, the corresponding Up goods trains starting from Bristol at 3 and 9.30 p.m. and taking 9 hours 10 minutes and 10 hours 10 minutes on the journey.

It was to one of these goods trains, the 4.30 a.m. Down on Christmas Eve 1841, that the first bad Great Western accident occurred. The train consisted of the *Hecla* engine and tender, two 'third-class Carriages', one on six wheels the other on four, a station truck[1] and 17 goods waggons mostly four wheeled, in the order given. In the middle of Sonning Cutting the engine ran into a slip which had covered the rails to a depth of 4 feet; the goods waggons of course crushed the 'carriages' against the tender, smashing one and considerably damaging the other, and of the 38 passengers 8 were killed on the spot and 17 more or less severely injured. The verdict at the Inquest was accidental death 'with a deodand[2] of £1,000 on the engine, tender and carriages'. Sir Frederic Smith, in his report to the Board of Trade, attributed the slip to the excessive rainfall, and after stating the vertical depth of the cutting at the slip as 58 feet and the slope as two to one, said: 'I do not imagine that any engineer would have thought it necessary to give the sides of this cutting a greater slope than two to one, and therefore there has been, in my opinion, no error in the construction.'

Besides not having spring buffers—

The third class carriages have seats 18 inches high, but the sides and ends are only two feet above the floor, so that a person standing up, either when the train is unexpectedly put in motion or stopped, is, if near the side or end, in great danger of being thrown out of the carriage, and those sitting near the sides are also in danger of falling; besides which, the exposure to the cutting winds of the winter must be very injurious to the traveller, who, if proceeding from London to Bristol, often remains exposed for ten or twelve hours a great part of which is in the night-time.

It so happened that the Directors had already ordered on 6th December four 6-wheeled third-class trucks with spring buffers and higher sides; but in the meantime all those in use were at once boarded up to 4 feet 6 inches from the floor, and four more ordered on 4th January.

This accident caused the Board of Trade to make enquiries of all the Companies as to their method of conducting the third-class traffic. The replies received show that only the Great Western and London & South Western sent the passengers by loaded goods trains, though the London & Birmingham sometimes combined them with cattle, horses, and empty

[1] A station truck is one, generally covered, containing parcels of goods for different stations.

[2] By the old Common Law, any chattel causing the death of a man was *Deo Dandum* (to be given to God) and forfeited to the Crown for pious uses. Its value was fixed by the Coroner's Jury. In this case the £1,000 would have gone, under an old Crown Grant, to Mr Palmer, the Lord of the Manor, but the Company appealed and got it reduced to a nominal sum. Deodands were abolished by Act of Parliament in 1846.

waggons, which would probably be almost as destructive in case of accident.[1] The average fare per mile varied from ·82 of a penny on the Chester & Birkenhead to 1½*d* on the London & Birmingham, the Great Western figure being 1·83*d*.

Third-class passengers on the Great Western continued to be carried by goods trains only till Gladstone's Railway Regulation Act came into force on 1st November 1844, compelling the provision of at least one train a day each way at a speed of not less than 12 miles an hour including stops, which were to be made at all stations, and of carriages protected from the weather and provided with seats; for all which luxuries not more than a penny a mile might be charged.

'Cheap Trains' were then put on, leaving Paddington at 7 a.m. and Bristol at 9.30 a.m., and taking respectively 9 hours 20 minutes and 9½ hours on the journey. The night goods trains (9.30 from Paddington and 10 p.m. from Bristol) continued for some years to convey third-class passengers, and afforded them the only means of making the journey beyond Bristol without spending a night there, as the third-class trains to and from the west left Bristol at 7 a.m. and arrived at 7.30 p.m.

After this, second-class passengers of course had also to be protected from the weather, so the open seconds, of which bitter complaints had long been rife, disappeared and 'Second Class Close' were reverted to. The opens were now not even eligible for third-class on the new 'Parliamentary Trains', so most of them were closed up with windows in the doors, and the rest reserved for use on goods and excursion trains. Later on the few survivors were sold to other Companies, such as the South Devon and Vale of Neath.

All this time no improvement had been made in the speed of the passenger trains. In January 1845 the fastest train on the line, the Night Mail, took 4 hours and 20 minutes to Bristol and 7 hours 10 minutes to Exeter. In fact the Broad Gauge had done nothing in the way of speed, with regular trains at any rate, to justify its existence, especially when its splendidly straight and level road is considered. It did not even lead in the snails' race of the period. The following table from a paper read before the Statistical Society in 1843 is taken from Acworth's *Railways of England*.[2]

LINES ON WHICH THE TRAINS TRAVEL AT THE GREATEST SPEED

| *Railways* | Average speed exclusive of *stoppages* | | |
|---|---|---|---|
| Northern & Eastern (London to Bishop's Stortford) . . . | 36 | miles | per hour |
| Great Western . . . . . . . . . | 33 | ,, | ,, ,, |
| Newcastle & North Shields . . . . . . . | 30 | ,, | ,, ,, |
| North Midland (Leeds to Derby) . . . . . | 29 | ,, | ,, ,, |
| Birmingham & Derby . . . . . . . | 29 | ,, | ,, ,, |
| Midland Counties (Derby to Rugby) . . . . | 28 | ,, | ,, ,, |
| Chester & Birkenhead . . . . . . . . | 28 | ,, | ,, ,, |
| London & Birmingham . . . . . . . | 27 | ,, | ,, ,, |
| Manchester & Birmingham . . . . . . . | 25 | ,, | ,, ,, |

The average speed (exclusive of stoppages) on all the lines is 21½ miles an hour.

[1] The London & Birmingham commenced carrying third-class passengers on 5th October 1840, one train in each direction calling at all stations being put on for this purpose.

[2] John Murray, 1889.

# Great Western Railway.

## READING, STEVENTON, AND THE FARINGDON ROAD.

TEN MILES FROM OXFORD.

## EXTENSION OF THE LINE TO THE FARINGDON ROAD.

SIXTY-THREE MILES FROM LONDON.

The LINE is now OPEN to the FARINGDON ROAD, for the Conveyance of Passengers, Carriages, Horses, Goods, and Parcels.

This Station, which is on a Turnpike Road, is distant from CHELTENHAM, 38 Miles; GLOUCESTER, 41 Miles; BATH, 48 Miles.

The MOULSFORD and PANGBOURNE Stations are now Opened for Carriages, Horses, and Goods.

HORSES and CARRIAGES being at the under-mentioned Stations, 10 minutes before the time specified for the departure of a Train, will be conveyed on this Railway, at the following Charges:—

| BETWEEN | | Carriages. 4-WHEEL. | Carriages. 2-WHEEL. | Horses. EACH. | Horses. PER PAIR, being the same Property. |
|---|---|---|---|---|---|
| PADDINGTON | and FARINGDON ROAD ...... | 36s. | 27s. | 32s. | 56s. |
| ,, | and STEVENTON ........ | 32s. | 24s. | 28s. | 48. |
| ,, | and MOULSFORD ........ | 28s. | 21s. | 24s. | 40s. |
| ,, | and PANGBOURNE ........ | 24s. | 18s. | 20s. | 32s. |
| ,, | and READING ........ | 20s. | 15s. | 16s. | 28s. |
| ,, | and TWYFORD ........ | 16s. | 12s. | 14s. | 24s. |
| ,, | and MAIDENHEAD ........ | 12s. | 9s. | 10s. | 16s. |
| ,, | and SLOUGH ........ | 11s. | 8s. | 9s. | 14s. |

POST HORSES are kept in readiness at the above Stations; and upon sufficient notice being given at Paddington, or the Bull and Mouth Office, St. Martin's-le-Grand, would be sent to bring Carriages from any part of London, to the Station, at a charge of 9s. west of St. Martin's Lane, and 10s. 6d. beyond it, both including Post-boy.

## TRAINS, (*Daily, excepting Sundays,*)

**DOWN TO** — CALLING AT

| DOWN TO | Hour. H. M. | | | | | | | | | | | | | |
|---|---|---|---|---|---|---|---|---|---|---|---|---|---|---|
| Faringdon Road | 8 | . . | . . | . . | . . . | Slough | Maidenhead | . . | Reading | Pangbourne | . . | . . . | Steventon | Faringdon Road |
| Slough ...... | 8.30 | Ealing | Hanwell | Southall | West Drayton | Slough | | | | | | | | |
| Faringdon Road | 9 | . . | . . | . . | . . . | Slough | . . . . | wyford | Reading | . . . | . . | Moulsford | Steventon | Faringdon Road |
| Faringdon Road | 10 | . . | . . | . . | . . . | Slough | Maidenhead | . . | Reading | Pangbourne | Goring | . . . | Steventon | Faringdon Road |
| Maidenhead . | 10.30 | Ealing | Hanwell | Southall | West Drayton | Slough | Maidenhead | | | | | | | |
| Faringdon Road | 12 | . . | . . | . . | West Drayton | Slough | Maidenhead | Twyford | Reading | Pangbourne | . . | Moulsford | Steventon | Faringdon Road |
| Slough ...... | 1.30 | Ealing | Hanwell | Southall | West Drayton | Slough | | | | | | | | |
| Faringdon Road | 2 | . . | . . | . . | . . . | Slough | Maidenhead | Twyford | Reading | . . . | Goring | . . . | Steventon | Faringdon Road |
| Slough ...... | 3.30 | Ealing | Hanwell | Southall | West Drayton | Slough | | | | | | | | |
| Faringdon Road | 4 | . . | . . | . . | . . . | Slough | Maidenhead | Twyford | Reading | Pangbourne | . . | Moulsford | Steventon | Faringdon Road |
| Maidenhead . | 4.30 | Ealing | Hanwell | Southall | West Drayton | Slough | Maidenhead | | | | | | | |
| Reading .... | 5 | . . | Hanwell | . . | West Drayton | Slough | Maidenhead | Twyford | Reading | | | | | |
| Slough ...... | 5.30 | Ealing | Hanwell | Southall | West Drayton | Slough | | | | | | | | |
| Maidenhead . | 6 | Ealing | . . | Southall | West Drayton | Slough | Maidenhead | | | | | | | |
| Faringdon Road | 7 | . . . | . . | . . | . . . | Slough | . . . . | . . | Reading | Pangbourne | Goring | Moulsford | Steventon | Faringdon Road |
| Reading .... | 8 | Ealing | Hanwell | Southall | West Drayton | Slough | Maidenhead | Twyford | Reading | | | | | |
| (*Mail.*) Faringdon Road | 8.55 | . . | . . | . . | West Drayton | Slough | Maidenhead | . . | Reading | . . . | . . | Moulsford | Steventon | Faringdon Road |
| **GOODS.** | | | | | | | | | | | | | | |
| Faringdon Road | 4 A.M. | . . | . | . . | West Drayton | Slough | Maidenhead | Twyford | Reading | Pangbourne | . . | . . . | Steventon | Faringdon Road |
| Faringdon Road | 9 P.M. | . . | . . | . . | . . . | Slough | Maidenhead | . . | Reading | . . . | . . | Moulsford | Steventon | Faringdon Road |

**UP FROM** — CALLING AT

| UP FROM | Hour. H. M. | | | | | | | | | | | | | |
|---|---|---|---|---|---|---|---|---|---|---|---|---|---|---|
| (*Mail.*) Faringdon Road | 3 | Steventon | Moulsford | . . | . . . | Reading | . . | Maidenhead | Slough | West Drayton | . . | . . | . . | Paddington |
| Reading .... | 7.30 | . . . | . . . | . . | . . . | Reading | Twyford | Maidenhead | Slough | West Drayton | Southall | Hanwell | Ealing | Paddington |
| Faringdon Road | 8 | Steventon | Moulsford | . . | Pangbourne | Reading | Twyford | Maidenhead | Slough | . . . | . . | . . | . . | Paddington |
| Slough ...... | 9 | . . . | . . . | . . | . . . | . . | . . | . . . . | Slough | West Drayton | Southall | Hanwell | Ealing | Paddington |
| Faringdon Road | 9 | Steventon | . . . | Goring | . . . | Reading | . . | Maidenhead | Slough | . . . | . . | . . | . . | Paddington |
| Slough ...... | 10 | . . . | . . . | . . | . . . | . . | . . | . . . . | Slough | West Drayton | Southall | Hanwell | Ealing | Paddington |
| Reading .... | 10.30 | . . . | . . . | . . | . . . | Reading | Twyford | Maidenhead | Slough | West Drayton | Southall | Hanwell | Ealing | Paddington |
| Faringdon Road | 11 | Steventon | Moulsford | . . | Pangbourne | Reading | . . | . . . . | Slough | . . . | . . | . . | . . | Paddington |
| Maidenhead . | 12 | . . . | . . . | . . | . . . | . . | . . | Maidenhead | Slough | West Drayton | Southall | Hanwell | Ealing | Paddington |
| Faringdon Road | 1 | Steventon | . . . | Goring | . . . | Reading | Twyford | Maidenhead | Slough | West Drayton | . . | . . | . . | Paddington |
| Faringdon Road | 3 | Steventon | Moulsford | . . | Pangbourne | Reading | . . | Maidenhead | Slough | . . . | . . | . . | . . | Paddington |
| Slough ...... | 4 | . . . | . . . | . . | . . . | . . | . . | . . . . | Slough | West Drayton | Southall | Hanwell | Ealing | Paddington |
| Faringdon Road | 5 | Steventon | . . . | Goring | Pangbourne | Reading | Twyford | . . . . | . . | . . . | . . | . . | . . | Paddington |
| Maidenhead . | 6 | . . . | . . . | . . | . . . | . . | . . | Maidenhead | Slough | West Drayton | Southall | . . | Ealing | Paddington |
| Slough ...... | 7 | . . . | . . . | . . | . . . | . . | . . | . . . . | Slough | West Drayton | Southall | Hanwell | Ealing | Paddington |
| Faringdon Road | 7 | Steventon | Moulsford | . . | Pangbourne | Reading | Twyford | Maidenhead | Slough | . . . | . . | . . | . . | Paddington |
| Maidenhead . | 9.30 | . . . | . . . | . . | . . . | . . | . . | Maidenhead | Slough | West Drayton | . . . | Hanwell | . . | Paddington |
| **GOODS.** | | | | | | | | | | | | | | |
| Faringdon Road | 4 A.M. | Steventon | Moulsford | . . | . . . | Reading | . . | Maidenhead | Slough | West Drayton | Southall | On Wednesdays only | | Paddington |
| Faringdon Road (Except on Saturdays) | 8 P.M. | Steventon | Moulsford | | Pangbourne | Reading | Twyford | Maidenhead | Slough | . . . | . . | . . | . . | Paddington |

## ON SUNDAYS,

**DOWN TO** — CALLING AT

| DOWN TO | Hour. H. M. | | | | | | | | | | | | | |
|---|---|---|---|---|---|---|---|---|---|---|---|---|---|---|
| Faringdon Road | 8 | . . | . . | . . | . . . | Slough | Maidenhead | Twyford | Reading | Pangbourne | . . | Moulsford | Steventon | Faringdon Road |
| Slough ...... | 8.30 | Ealing | Hanwell | Southall | West Drayton | Slough | | | | | | | | |
| Reading .... | 9 | . . | . . . | Southall | West Drayton | Slough | Maidenhead | Twyford | Reading | | | | | |
| Slough ...... | 9.30 | Ealing | Hanwell | . . | West Drayton | Slough | | | | | | | | |
| Reading .... | 5 | Ealing | Hanwell | Southall | West Drayton | Slough | Maidenhead | Twyford | Reading | | | | | |
| Slough ...... | 6 | Ealing | Hanwell | Southall | West Drayton | Slough | | | | | | | | |
| Faringdon Road | 7 | . . | . . | . . | . . . | Slough | Maidenhead | . . | Reading | Pangbourne | Goring | Moulsford | Steventon | Faringdon Road |
| Maidenhead . | 8 | Ealing | Hanwell | Southall | West Drayton | Slough | Maidenhead | | | | | | | |
| (*Mail.*) Faringdon Road | 8.55 | . . | . . | . . | West Drayton | Slough | Maidenhead | . . | Reading | | . . | Moulsford | Steventon | Faringdon Road |
| **Goods.** Faringdon Road | 4 A.M. | . . | . . | . . | West Drayton | Slough | Maidenhead | Twyford | Reading | Pangbourne | . . | . . . | Steventon | Faringdon Road |

**UP FROM** — CALLING AT

| UP FROM | Hour. H. M. | | | | | | | | | | | | | |
|---|---|---|---|---|---|---|---|---|---|---|---|---|---|---|
| (*Mail.*) Faringdon Road | 3 | Steventon | Moulsford | . . | . . . | Reading | . . | Maidenhead | Slough | West Drayton | . . | . . | . . | Paddington |
| Reading .... | 7.30 | . . . | . . . | . . | . . . | Reading | Twyford | Maidenhead | Slough | West Drayton | Southall | Hanwell | Ealing | Paddington |
| Faringdon Road | 8 | Steventon | Moulsford | Goring | Pangbourne | Reading | Twyford | Maidenhead | Slough | . . . | . . | . . | . . | Paddington |
| Slough ...... | 9 | . . . | . . . | . . | . . . | . . . | . . | . . . . | Slough | West Drayton | Southall | Hanwell | Ealing | Paddington |
| Slough ...... | 5 | . . . | . . . | . . | . . . | . . . | . . | . . . . | Slough | West Drayton | Southall | Hanwell | Ealing | Paddington |
| Faringdon Road | 5 | Steventon | Moulsford | Goring | Pangbourne | Reading | Twyford | Maidenhead | Slough | . . . | . . | . . | . . | Paddington |
| Slough ...... | 7 | . . . | . . . | . . | . . . | . . . | . . | . . . . | Slough | West Drayton | . . | Hanwell | . . | Paddington |
| Reading .... | 7 | . . . | . . . | . . | . . . | Reading | Twyford | Maidenhead | Slough | West Drayton | Southall | Hanwell | Ealing | Paddington |
| Maidenhead . | 9.30 | . . . | . . . | . . | . . . | . . . | . . | Maidenhead | Slough | West Drayton | Southall | Hanwell | Ealing | Paddington |
| **GOODS.** | | | | | | | | | | | | | | |
| Faringdon Road | 4 A.M. | Steventon | Moulsford | . . | . . . | Reading | . . | Maidenhead | Slough | West Drayton | . . | . . | . . | Paddington |
| Faringdon Road | 8 P.M. | Steventon | Moulsford | . . | Pangbourne | Reading | Twyford | Maidenhead | Slough | . . . | . . | . . | . . | Paddington |

Passengers and Parcels between the long and short Stations, can proceed in either direction to Slough and be taken on by the succeeding Train.

**The Goods' Train,** which leaves Faringdon Road at 4 o'clock in the Morning, will, for the present, start from Reading at 6 o'clock, by which Train, Passengers, Carriages, &c., &c., will be conveyed to Paddington and other Stations.

## FARES.

| Paddington | 1st Class. | 2nd Class. Open Carriage. | Goods' Train. |
|---|---|---|---|
| To Ealing ........ | 1 6 | 0 9 | . . |
| ,, Hanwell ...... | 2 0 | 1 0 | . . |
| ,, Southall ...... | 2 6 | 1 3 | 0 9 |
| ,, West Drayton.. | 3 0 | 1 6 | 1 0 |
| ,, Slough ........ | 4 6 | 2 6 | 1 6 |
| ,, Maidenhead.... | 5 6 | 3 6 | 2 0 |
| ,, Twyford ...... | 7 0 | 5 0 | 2 6 |
| ,, Reading ...... | 8 0 | 5 6 | 3 0 |
| ,, Pangbourne.... | 9 6 | 6 6 | 3 6 |
| ,, Goring ........ | 10 6 | 7 0 | . . |
| ,, Moulsford .... | 11 6 | 8 0 | 4 6 |
| ,, Steventon...... | 12 6 | 8 6 | 5 0 |
| ,, Faringdon Road | 14 0 | 10 0 | 6 0 |

| Reading | 1st Class. | 2nd Class. Open Carriage. | Goods' Train. |
|---|---|---|---|
| To Paddington .... | 8 0 | 5 6 | 3 0 |
| ,, Ealing ........ | 7 6 | 5 0 | . . |
| ,, Hanwell ...... | 6 6 | 4 6 | . . |
| ,, Southall ...... | 6 6 | 4 6 | 2 9 |
| ,, West Drayton.. | 5 6 | 4 0 | 2 6 |
| ,, Slough ........ | 4 6 | 3 0 | 2 0 |
| ,, Maidenhead .... | 3 0 | 2 0 | 1 6 |
| ,, Twyford ...... | 1 6 | 1 0 | 0 9 |
| ,, Pangbourne .... | 1 6 | 1 0 | 0 9 |
| ,, Goring ........ | 2 6 | 1 6 | . . |
| ,, Moulsford...... | 3 6 | 2 6 | 1 6 |
| ,, Steventon .... | 4 6 | 3 0 | 2 0 |
| ,, Faringdon Road | 6 0 | 4 6 | 3 0 |

| Faringdon Road | 1st Class. | 2nd Class. Open Carriage. | Goods' Train. |
|---|---|---|---|
| To Paddington ...... | 14 0 | 10 0 | 6 0 |
| ,, Ealing .......... | 13 6 | 9 6 | . . |
| ,, Hanwell ........ | 12 6 | 9 0 | . . |
| ,, Southall ........ | 12 6 | 9 0 | 5 9 |
| ,, West Drayton.... | 11 6 | 8 6 | 5 6 |
| ,, Slough .......... | 10 6 | 7 6 | 5 0 |
| ,, Maidenhead...... | 9 0 | 6 6 | 4 6 |
| ,, Twyford ........ | 7 6 | 5 6 | 4 0 |
| ,, Reading ........ | 6 0 | 4 6 | 3 0 |
| ,, Pangbourne ...... | 5 0 | 4 0 | 2 6 |
| ,, Goring .......... | 4 0 | 3 0 | . . |
| ,, Moulsford........ | 3 0 | 2 0 | 1 6 |
| ,, Steventon........ | 2 0 | 1 6 | 1 0 |

**The Goods' Train Passengers** will be conveyed in uncovered Trucks by the Goods' Trains only, and 14-lbs. of Luggage allowed for each.

The Charge for Goods between Paddington and the Faringdon Road Station, will be 18s. per Ton; and between Paddington and Reading, 12s. per Ton, including loading and unloading. The Charge to the other Stations in proportion. Sheep, Beasts, &c., are conveyed by the Goods' Trains.

Conveyances will run between the FARINGDON ROAD Station and Cheltenham; STEVENTON Station and Oxford, through Abingdon; between the TWYFORD Station and Henley; the MAIDENHEAD Station and Marlow and Wycombe; the WEST DRAYTON Station and Uxbridge; and Windsor Omnibuses meet every Train at Slough.

OMNIBUSES start from Princes Street, Bank, one hour before the departure of each Train, calling at the Angel Inn, Islington; Bull Inn, Holborn; Moore's Green Man and Still, Griffin's Green Man and Still, Oxford Street; Golden Cross, Charing Cross; Chaplin's Universal Office, and Bull and Mouth, Regent Circus; and Gloucester Warehouse, Oxford Street, to the Paddington Station. **Fare Sixpence,** without Luggage.

**Parcels** may be booked at the Railway Office, Princes Street, Bank; all the London Parcels Delivery Company's Receiving Houses, and the above established Booking Offices; for Cheltenham, Gloucester, Witney, Burford, Cirencester, Cricklade; Oxford, Abingdon, Reading, Newbury, Windsor, &c., at which places, and all the Railway Stations, they will be received for conveyance. FOUR DAILY DELIVERIES will be made at all parts of London, and in the Country.

W. SNELL, Printer, 30, Newcastle Place, Edgware Road, London.

Train Bill, August 1840

# GREAT WESTERN RAILWAY.
# LONDON TO BRISTOL.

On and after *MONDAY, the 7th of December,* 1840, *the Line will be* FURTHER EXTENDED *to the* **Wootton Basset Road Station,** (*80 Miles from London,*) *for the Conveyance of Passengers, Carriages, Horses, Goods, and Parcels. The* SHRIVENHAM STATION *will also be Opened.*

NOTICE.—London Time is kept at all the Stations, and will regulate the Arrivals and Departures throughout the Line.

| | |
|---|---|
| LONDON TIME is | Minutes before READING Time. |
| Ditto | ditto   STEVENTON Time. |
| Ditto | ditto   SWINDON Time. |

And the intermediate distances are in proportion thereto.

## HOURS OF DEPARTURE AND TIME TABLE.

### Down Trains, (Daily, excepting Sundays.)

| DOWN From Paddington | Departure from Paddington | Ealing | Hanwell | Southall | West Drayton | Slough | Maidenhead | Twyford | Reading | Pangbourne | Goring | Wallingford Road | Steventon | Faringdon Road | Shrivenham | Wootton Basset Road |
|---|---|---|---|---|---|---|---|---|---|---|---|---|---|---|---|---|
| | h. m. | h. m. | h. m. | h. m. | h. m. | h. m. | h. m. | h. m. | h. m. | h. m. | h. m. | h. m. | h. m. | h. m. | h. m. | h. m. |
| To Wootton Basset Rd. A.M. | 8. 0 | | | | | | 8.35 | | 9.13 | 9.26 | 9.34 | | 9. 59 | 10.17 | 10.34 | 10.53 |
| — Maidenhead | 8.30 | 8.41 | 8.45 | 8 50 | 8.59 | 9.10 | 9.20 | | | | | | | | | |
| — Wootton Basset Road | 9. 0 | | | | | 9.35 | | 10. 3 | 10.15 | | | 10 39 | 10.59 | 11.16 | | 11.50 |
| — Wootton Basset Road | 10. 0 | | | | | 10.35 | 10.47 | | 11.15 | | | | 11.57 | 12.14 | 12.31 | 12.50 |
| — Slough | 10 30 | 10.41 | 10 45 | 10.50 | 10.59 | 11.10 | | | | | | | | | | |
| — Wootton Basset Road | 12. 0 | | | | | 12.26 | 12.38 | 12.50 | 1. 9 | 1.21 | 1.34 | | 1.48 | 2. 8 | 2.26 | 3. 0 |
| — Slough   P.M. | 1.30 | 1.41 | 1.45 | 1.50 | 1.59 | 2.10 | | | | | | | | | | |
| — Wootton Basset Road | 2. 0 | | | | | 2 35 | 2.47 | 3. 5 | 3.17 | | 3.37 | | 4. 1 | 4.19 | 4.36 | 4.55 |
| — Wootton Basset Road | 4. 0 | | | | | 4.35 | 4.47 | | 5.15 | 5.28 | | 5.42 | 6. 1 | 6.19 | | 6.53 |
| — Slough | 4.30 | 4.41 | 4.45 | 4.50 | 4.59 | 5.10 | | | | | | | | | | |
| — Reading | 5. 0 | | 5.13 | | 5.26 | 5 28 | 5.49 | 6. 7 | 6.20 | | | | | | | |
| — Maidenhead | 6. 0 | 6.11 | 6.15 | 6.20 | 6.29 | 6 40 | 6.50 | | | | | | | | | |
| — Wootton Basset Road | 7. 0 | | | | | 7.35 | | | 8.13 | 8.25 | 8.35 | 8.42 | 9. 1 | 9.19 | 9.36 | 9.55 |
| — Reading | 8. 0 | 8.11 | 8.15 | 8.20 | 8.29 | 8.41 | 8.53 | 9.12 | 9.25 | | | | | | | |
| — Wootton Basset Road (Mail Train) | 8.55 | | | | | 9.20 | 9.32 | 9.44 | 10.12 | | | | 10.37 | 10.56 | 11.14 | 11.48 |

### Sunday Down Trains.

| DOWN From Paddington | Departure from Paddington | Ealing | Hanwell | Southall | West Drayton | Slough | Maidenhead | Twyford | Reading | Pangbourne | Goring | Wallingford Road | Steventon | Faringdon Road | Shrivenham | Wootton Basset Road |
|---|---|---|---|---|---|---|---|---|---|---|---|---|---|---|---|---|
| | h. m. | h. m. | h. m. | h. m. | h. m. | h. m. | h. m. | h. m. | h. m. | h. m. | h. m. | h. m. | h. m. | h. m. | h. m. | h. m. |
| To Wootton Basset Rd. A.M. | 8. 0 | | | | | 8.36 | 8.48 | 9. 7 | 9.19 | 9.32 | 9.39 | 9.46 | 10. 6 | 10.23 | 10.41 | 11.0 |
| — Slough | 8.30 | 8.41 | 8.46 | 8.52 | 9. 2 | 9.15 | | | | | | | | | | |
| — Reading | 9. 0 | | | 9.20 | 9.30 | 9.42 | 9.54 | 10.13 | 10.25 | | | | | | | |
| — Slough | 9.30 | 9.42 | 9.48 | | 10. 2 | 10.15 | | | | | | | | | | |
| — Wootton Basset Rd. P.M. | 2. 0 | | 2.14 | | 2.28 | 2.40 | 2 52 | | 3.21 | 3.34 | | 3.48 | 4. 8 | 4.25 | | 5. 0 |
| — Reading | 5. 0 | 5.11 | 5.16 | 5.22 | 5.32 | 5.45 | 5.58 | 6.18 | 6.30 | | | | | | | |
| — Slough | 7. 0 | 7.11 | 7.16 | 7.22 | 7.32 | 7.45 | | | | | | | | | | |
| — Wootton Basset Road (Mail Train.) | 8.55 | | | | | 9.20 | 9.32 | 9.44 | 10.12 | | | | 10.37 | 10.56 | 11.13 | 11.48 |

### Up Trains, (Daily, excepting Sundays.)

| UP To Paddington | Wootton Basset Road | Shrivenham | Faringdon Road | Steventon | Wallingford Road | Goring | Pangbourne | Reading | Twyford | Maidenhead | Slough | West Drayton | Southall | Hanwell | Ealing | Paddington |
|---|---|---|---|---|---|---|---|---|---|---|---|---|---|---|---|---|
| | h. m. | h. m. | h. m. | h. m. | h. m. | h. m. | h. m. | h. m. | h. m. | h. m. | h. m. | h. m. | h. m. | h. m. | h. m. | h. m. |
| From Wootton Basset Rd. A.M (Mail Train.) | 2.30 | | 3. 1 | 3.18 | 3.36 | | | 4. 0 | | 4.29 | 4.40 | 4.52 | | | | 5.20 |
| — Reading | | | | | | | | 7.30 | 7.39 | 7.56 | 8. 6 | 8.18 | 8.28 | 8.33 | 8.38 | 8.50 |
| — Slough | | | | | | | | | | | 9. 0 | 9.10 | 9.19 | 9.24 | 9.28 | 9.40 |
| — Maidenhead | | | | | | | | | | 9.50 | 10. 0 | 10.10 | 10.19 | 10.24 | 10.28 | 10.40 |
| — Wootton Basset Road | 8.30 | 8.47 | 9. 3 | 9.19 | 9.37 | 9.46 | 9.54 | 10. 6 | 10.19 | 10.37 | 10.49 | | | | | 11.26 |
| — Reading | | | | | | | | 11. 0 | | 11.25 | 11.35 | 11.47 | 11.57 | 12. 3 | 12. 8 | 12.20 |
| — Wootton Basset Road | 10.15 | 10.32 | 10.48 | 11. 5 | 11.23 | | | 11.47 | 12. 0 | 12.27 | | | | | | 1. 5 |
| — Wootton Basset Road | 11.30 | | 12. 1 | 12.18 | | 12.42 | 12.50 | 1. 2 | | 1.31 | 1.42 | | | | | 2.20 |
| — Slough | | | | | | | | | | | 3. 0 | 3.10 | 3.19 | 3.24 | 3.28 | 3.40 |
| — Wootton Basset Rd. P.M. | 1.15 | 1.32 | 1.49 | 2. 6 | 2 25 | | | 2.49 | 3. 3 | | 3.31 | | | | | 4.10 |
| — Wootton Basset Road | 2.30 | | 3. 2 | 3.19 | | 3.49 | 4. 2 | 4.30 | 4.48 | | | | | | | 5.20 |
| — Slough | | | | | | | | | | | 6. 0 | 6.10 | 6.19 | 6.24 | 6.28 | 6.40 |
| — Wootton Basset Road | 4.30 | 4.47 | 5. 3 | 5.19 | 5.37 | 5.46 | | 6. 4 | 6.17 | 6.35 | | | | | | 7.20 |
| — Maidenhead | | | | | | | | | | 7.45 | 7.54 | 8. 6 | 8.16 | 8.22 | 8.27 | 8.40 |
| — Wootton Basset Road | 6.30 | | 7. 0 | 7.16 | | | 7.46 | 8.35 | | | | | | | | 9.10 |

### Sunday Up Trains.

| UP To Paddington | Wootton Basset Road | Shrivenham | Faringdon Road | Steventon | Wallingford Road | Goring | Pangbourne | Reading | Twyford | Maidenhead | Slough | West Drayton | Southall | Hanwell | Ealing | Paddington |
|---|---|---|---|---|---|---|---|---|---|---|---|---|---|---|---|---|
| | h. m. | h. m. | h. m. | h. m. | h. m. | h. m. | h. m. | h. m. | h. m. | h. m. | h. m. | h. m. | h. m. | h. m. | h. m. | h. m. |
| From Wootton Basset Rd. A.M (Mail Train.) | 2.30 | | 3. 1 | 3.18 | 3.36 | | | 4. 0 | | 4.29 | 4.40 | 4.52 | | | | 5.20 |
| — Reading | | | | | | | | 7.30 | 7.39 | 7.56 | 8. 6 | 8.18 | 8.28 | 8.33 | 8.38 | 8.50 |
| — Slough | | | | | | | | | | | 9. 0 | 9.10 | 9.19 | 9.24 | 9.28 | 9.40 |
| — Wootton Basset Rd. P.M. | 2. 0 | 2.17 | 2.34 | 2.49 | 3. 8 | | 3.22 | 3.34 | 3.48 | 4. 7 | 4.18 | | | | | 5. 0 |
| — Slough | | | | | | | | | | | 5. 0 | 5.10 | 5.21 | 5.28 | | 5.45 |
| — Wootton Basset Road | | 5.32 | 5.47 | 6. 6 | 6.14 | 6 22 | 6.34 | | | | 6.30 | 6.46 | | 6.55 | 7. 1 | 7.15 |
| — Wootton Basset Road | 5. 0 | 5.34 | 5.49 | 6. 8 | 6.16 | 6.24 | 6.36 | 6.48 | 7. 8 | 7.28 | 7.34 | | | | | 9.10 |
| — Reading | | | | | | | | 8. 0 | 8.27 | 8.39 | 8.52 | 9. 3 | 9.10 | 9.16 | | 9.30 |

*Passengers and Parcels, between the long and short Stations, can proceed in either direction to Slough, and be taken on by the succeeding Train.*

Time-table, December 1940. (Proof)

# Great Western Railway.

## ALTERATION OF TRAINS.

## LONDON to CIRENCESTER, BATH, BRISTOL and BRIDGEWATER.

In compliance with directions received from Her Majesty's Postmaster General, for the conveyance of the Mails, the Trains on and after FRIDAY, the 30th July, will run as specified below:—

N.B. BRIDGEWATER is 11 miles from TAUNTON, 42 miles from EXETER, & 90 miles from PLYMOUTH: CIRENCESTER is 15 miles from CHELTENHAM, 12 miles from STROUD, & 17 miles from GLOUCESTER.

HORSES and CARRIAGES being at those Stations, which are distinguished by Black Letter Type, ten minutes before the time specified for the departure of a Train, will be conveyed on this Railway.

POST HORSES are kept in readiness at the Principal Stations, and upon sufficient notice being given at Paddington, or at the Bull and Mouth Office, St. Martin's-le-Grand, would be sent to bring Carriages from any part of London to the Station, at a charge of 9s. west of St. Martin's Lane, and 10s. 6d. beyond it, both including Post Boy. Similar Notice may be given at Bristol for Carriages to be brought from Clifton, or the neighbourhood to the Bristol Station.

## TIME TABLE.

LONDON TIME is kept at all the Stations on the Railway, which is about 4 minutes earlier than READING time; 5½ minutes before STEVENTON time; 7½ minutes before CIRENCESTER time; 8 minutes before CHIPPENHAM time; 11 minutes before BATH and BRISTOL time; and 14 minutes before BRIDGEWATER time.

| Dis-tance. | Down Trains. | DOWN TRAINS DAILY (excepting on Sundays). | | | | | | | | | | | | | | | | | | Every Day. GOODS. | | TRAINS ON SUNDAYS ONLY. | | | | | | | | |
|---|---|---|---|---|---|---|---|---|---|---|---|---|---|---|---|---|---|---|---|---|---|---|---|---|---|---|---|---|---|---|
| | | | | DAY MAIL From Bristol to Bridgewater. | | | | DAY MAIL. | | | | | | | | | | | MAIL. | | | | DAY MAIL From Bristol to Bridgewater. | | DAY MAIL. | | | | | MAIL |
| | *Starting from* | a. m. | a. m. | a. m. | a. m. | a. m. | a. m. | a. m. | a. m. | a. m. | a. m. | p. m. | p. m. | p. m. | p. m. | p. m. | p. m. | p. m. | p. m. | a. m. | p. m. | a. m. | a. m. | a. m. | a. m. | p. m. | p. m. | p. m. | p. m. | p. m. |
| miles | **Paddington** | — | — | 6. 0 | — | 8. 0 | 9. 0 | 10.15 | 11. 0 | 11.30 | 12. 0 | 1.30 | 2. 0 | 4. 0 | 4.30 | 5. 0 | 5.30 | 7.30 | 8.55 | 4.30 | 9.30 | 8.30 | 9. 0 | 9.30 | 10.15 | — | 2. 0 | 5. 0 | 7. 0 | 8.55 |
| 5¼ | *Calling at* Ealing | — | — | — | — | — | 9.11 | — | — | 11.41 | — | 1.41 | — | — | 4.41 | — | 5.41 | 7.41 | — | — | — | 8.41 | — | 9.42 | — | — | — | 5.11 | 7.11 | — |
| 7¾ | Hanwell | — | — | — | — | — | 9.15 | — | — | 11.45 | — | 1.45 | — | 4.13 | 4.45 | — | 5.45 | 7.45 | — | — | — | 8.46 | — | 9.48 | — | — | 2.14 | 5.16 | 7.15 | — |
| 9 | Southall | — | — | — | — | — | 9.20 | — | — | 11.50 | — | 1.50 | — | — | 4.50 | — | 5.50 | 7.50 | — | *5. 0 | — | 8.52 | — | 9.54 | — | — | — | 5.22 | 7.20 | — |
| 13 | West Drayton | — | — | — | — | — | 9.29 | — | — | 11.59 | — | 1.59 | — | 4.26 | 4.59 | — | 5.59 | 7.59 | 9.20 | 5.24 | — | 9. 2 | — | 10. 4 | — | — | 2.28 | 5.32 | 7.29 | 9.20 |
| 18 | **Slough** | — | — | 6.35 | — | 8.40 | 9.40 | 10.50 | 11.35 | 12.10 | 12.40 | 2.10 | 2.38 | 4.37 | 5.10 | 5.35 | 6.10 | 8.10 | 9.50 | 5.44 | 10.30 | 9.15 | 9.40 | 10.18 | 10.50 | — | 2.40 | 5.45 | 7.40 | 9.30 |
| 22½ | **Maidenhead** | — | — | 6.45 | — | — | 9.50 | 11. 2 | — | — | 12.55 | — | 2.50 | 4.48 | — | — | 6.20 | 8.20 | 9.40 | 6. 0 | — | — | 9.50 | — | 11. 2 | — | 2.52 | 5.58 | 7.50 | 9.40 |
| 30½ | **Twyford** | — | — | — | — | 9. 5 | — | — | 12. 0 | — | — | — | [illegible] | 5. 6 | — | — | — | 8.38 | — | 6.30 | — | — | 10.10 | — | — | — | 3.10 | — | 8. 8 | — |
| 35¾ | **Reading** | — | — | 7.15 | — | 9.20 | — | 11.35 | 12.13 | — | 1.25 | — | [illegible] | 5.18 | — | 6.15 | — | 8.50 | 10.10 | 6.50 | 11.36 | — | 10.29 | — | 11.35 | — | 3.21 | — | 8.20 | 10.10 |
| 41½ | **Pangbourne** | — | — | — | — | 9.35 | — | — | — | — | 1.42 | — | — | — | — | 6.27 | — | 9. 5 | — | 7.40 | — | — | — | — | — | — | 3.36 | — | 8.35 | — |
| 44½ | Goring | — | — | 7.34 | — | — | — | — | 12.30 | — | — | — | — | — | — | — | — | 9.12 | — | — | — | — | — | — | — | — | — | — | 8.42 | — |
| 47½ | **Wallingford Road** | — | — | — | — | 9.49 | — | — | 12.40 | — | — | — | 3.45 | — | — | 6.40 | — | 9.20 | 10.35 | — | 12.19 | — | — | — | — | — | 3.50 | — | 8.50 | 10.25 |
| 56½ | **Steventon** | — | — | 7.55 | — | 10. 8 | — | 12.18 | 12.58 | — | 2.10 | — | 4. 3 | — | — | 6.58 | — | 9.35 | 10.50 | 8.30 | 12.50 | — | — | — | 12.18 | — | 4.10 | — | 9. 5 | 10.50 |
| 63½ | **Faringdon Road** | — | — | 8.10 | — | — | — | 12.33 | — | — | 2.30 | — | — | — | — | 7.14 | — | 9.50 | 11. 5 | — | 1.19 | — | — | — | 12.33 | — | 4.28 | — | 9.20 | 11. 5 |
| 71½ | **Shrivenham** | — | — | — | — | 10.38 | — | — | 1.30 | — | — | — | 4.34 | — | — | — | — | 10. 5 | — | — | 1.49 | — | — | — | — | — | 4.44 | — | 9.35 | — |
| 77 | **Swindon (Junction)** | — | — | 8.35 | — | 10.50 | — | 1. 0 | 1.43 | — | 2.58 | — | 4.48 | — | — | 7.40 | — | 10.20 | 11.30 | 10. 0 | 2.15 | — | — | — | 1. 0 | — | 4.55 | — | 9.50 | 11.30 |
| | *Departure for* **Cheltenham** | — | — | 8.55 | — | 11. 0 | — | 1.10 | — | — | 3. 8 | — | 4.58 | — | — | 7.50 | — | — | 11.40 | 11. 0 | 8.55 | — | — | — | 1.10 | — | 5. 5 | — | — | 11.40 |
| | 81 Purton | — | — | 9. 5 | — | 11.10 | — | — | — | — | 3.18 | — | 5. 8 | — | — | — | — | — | — | 11.10 | 9. 5 | — | — | — | — | — | 5.15 | — | — | — |
| | 85 **Minety** | — | — | 9.15 | — | 11.20 | — | 1.30 | — | — | — | — | 5.18 | — | — | 8. 5 | — | — | — | 11.20 | 9.15 | — | — | — | 1.30 | — | 5.25 | — | — | — |
| | 95 **Cirencester** | — | — | 9.50 | — | 11.40 | — | 1.55 | — | — | 3.48 | — | 5.40 | — | — | 8.30 | — | — | 12.25 | 11.40 | 9.50 | — | — | — | 1.55 | — | 5.50 | — | — | 12.25 |
| — | **Swindon,** *Junc. (Depar.* | — | — | 8.45 | — | 11. 0 | — | 1.10 | 1.53 | — | 3. 8 | — | 4.58 | — | — | 7.50 | — | — | 11.40 | 10.20 | 2.30 | — | 8.45 | — | 1.10 | — | 5. 5 | — | — | 11.40 |
| 82¾ | **Wootton Basset** | — | — | 8.59 | — | — | — | — | 2. 5 | — | — | — | 5.10 | — | — | 8. 2 | — | — | — | 11.50 | 3. 0 | — | 8.58 | — | — | — | 5.17 | — | — | — |
| 93¾ | **Chippenham** | — | — | 9.23 | — | 11.32 | — | 1.40 | 2.27 | — | 3.42 | — | 5.33 | — | — | 8.25 | — | — | 12.10 | 12.40 | 3.45 | — | 9.23 | — | 1.40 | — | 5.40 | — | — | 12.10 |
| 98¼ | Corsham | — | — | 9.33 | — | 11.42 | — | — | 2.37 | — | — | — | — | — | — | 8.35 | — | — | — | — | — | — | 9.33 | — | — | — | 5.50 | — | — | — |
| 101½ | Box | — | a. m. | 9.43 | a. m. | — | p. m. | — | 2.48 | — | — | — | 5.50 | p. m. | — | — | p. m. | — | — | — | — | a. m. | 9.43 | — | 1.55 | p. m. | 6. 2 | — | p. m. | — |
| 106½ | **Bath** | — | 8.45 | 9.55 | 11. 0 | 12. 3 | 1. 0 | 2. 5 | 3. 0 | — | 4.10 | 5. 0 | 6. 5 | 7.45 | — | 8.55 | 10. 0 | — | 12.40 | 1.20 | 5. 0 | 8.45 | 9.55 | — | 2. 5 | 5. 0 | 6.13 | — | 9.30 | 12.40 |
| 108¼ | Twerton | — | — | 10. 0 | — | — | 1. 5 | — | — | — | — | 5. 5 | — | — | — | — | 10. 5 | — | — | — | — | — | 10. 0 | — | 2.10 | 5. 5 | — | — | 9.34 | — |
| 111¼ | Saltford | — | 8.58 | — | 11.13 | — | 1.13 | — | — | — | — | 5.13 | — | — | — | — | — | — | — | — | — | 8.58 | — | — | — | 5.13 | — | — | 9.42 | — |
| 113¾ | Keynsham | — | 9. 5 | 10.15 | 11.20 | — | 1.20 | — | 3.20 | — | — | 5.20 | — | 8. 3 | — | — | 10.18 | — | — | — | — | 9. 5 | 10.15 | — | 2.20 | 5.20 | 6.35 | — | 9.48 | — |
| 118¼ | **Bristol,** arrival | a. m. | 9.15 | 10.25 | 11.30 | 12.30 | 1.30 | 2.30 | 3.30 | — | 4.40 | 5.30 | 6.33 | 8.13 | — | 9.20 | 10.28 | — | 1. 5 | 2. 0 | 5.40 | 9.15 | 10.25 | — | 2.30 | 5.30 | 6.45 | — | 10. 0 | 1. 5 |
| | **Bristol,** departure | 8. 0 | 9.25 | 10.50 | — | 12.40 | — | 2.40 | — | — | 4.50 | — | 7. 0 | — | — | — | — | — | 1.15 | 7. 0 | 8. 0 | 9.25 | 10.50 | — | 2.50 | — | 7. 0 | — | — | 1.15 |
| 126¼ | *Calling at* **Nailsea** | 8.18 | 9.45 | 11. 8 | — | — | — | — | — | — | 5. 8 | — | 7.18 | — | — | — | — | — | — | 7.18 | 8.18 | 9.45 | — | — | — | — | 7.18 | — | — | — |
| 130¼ | **Clevedon Rd,** at Yatt. | 8.28 | 9.55 | 11.18 | — | 1. 5 | — | 3. 3 | — | — | 5.16 | — | 7.27 | — | — | — | — | — | — | 7.27 | 8.27 | 9.55 | — | — | 3.15 | — | 7.27 | — | — | — |
| 133¼ | Banwell | 8.35 | — | 11.25 | — | — | — | — | — | — | — | — | 7.35 | — | — | — | — | — | — | 7.35 | 8.35 | 10. 3 | — | — | — | — | 7.35 | — | — | — |
| 136½ | **Weston Su.Mare** *(Junc)* | 8.42 | 10.15 | 11.35 | — | 1.20 | — | — | — | — | 5.30 | — | 7.42 | — | — | — | — | — | — | 7.42 | 8.42 | 10.15 | — | — | 3.30 | — | 7.42 | — | — | — |
| 145¾ | **Highbridge** | 9.10 | 10.35 | 11.53 | — | — | — | 3.30 | — | — | 5.46 | — | 8.10 | — | — | — | — | — | — | 8.10 | 9.10 | 10.35 | — | — | 3.48 | — | 8.10 | — | — | — |
| 151½ | **Bridgewater** | 9.30 | 10.50 | 12.10 | — | 1.50 | — | 3.45 | — | — | 6. 0 | — | 8.30 | — | — | — | — | — | 2.25 | 8.30 | 9.30 | 10.50 | 12.10 | — | 4. 5 | — | 8.30 | — | — | 2.25 |

| Dis-tance. | Up Trains. | UP TRAINS DAILY, (excepting on Sundays.) | | | | | | | | | | | | | | | | | | EVERY DAY. GOODS. | | Trains on Sundays only. | | | | | | | | |
|---|---|---|---|---|---|---|---|---|---|---|---|---|---|---|---|---|---|---|---|---|---|---|---|---|---|---|---|---|---|---|
| | | | | | | | DAY MAIL. | | | | | | DAY MAIL From Bridgewater to Bristol | | | | | | MAIL. | | | | | DAY MAIL. | | DAY MAIL From Bridgewater to Bristol | | | | MAIL. |
| | *Starting from* | a. m. | a. m. | a. m. | a. m. | a. m. | a. m. | a. m. | a. m. | a. m. | a. m. | p. m. | p. m. | p. m. | p. m. | p. m. | p. m. | p. m. | p. m. | a. m. | p. m. | a. m. | a. m. | a. m. | p. m. | p. m. | p. m. | p. m. | p. m. | p. m. |
| miles | **Bridgewater** | — | — | — | — | — | — | 8. 0 | 9.30 | — | 11.30 | — | 12.44 | — | 3.30 | 5. 0 | — | 7. 0 | 11.40 | 8. 0 | 7. 0 | — | — | 7.15 | — | 12.44 | 2.30 | — | 7. 0 | 11.40 |
| 6¼ | *Calling at* **Highbridge** | — | — | — | — | — | — | 8.14 | 9.44 | — | — | — | 12.59 | — | 3.44 | 5.14 | — | 7.16 | — | 8.14 | 7.16 | — | — | 7.29 | — | — | 2.44 | — | 7.15 | — |
| 16¼ | *Starting from* **Weston SuMare** (Station) | — | — | — | — | — | — | 8.20 | 9.50 | — | 11.25 | — | 1. 5 | — | — | 5.20 | — | 7.25 | — | 8.20 | 7.24 | — | — | 7.35 | — | 1. 5 | 2.50 | — | 7.20 | — |
| 17½ | *Calling at* **Banwell** | — | — | — | — | — | — | 8.42 | — | — | — | — | — | — | 4.12 | — | — | 7.45 | — | — | — | — | — | 7.50 | — | 1.27 | — | — | 7.48 | — |
| 21 | **Clevedon Rd.** (Yatton) | — | — | — | — | — | — | 8.50 | 10.18 | — | 12.20 | — | 1.35 | — | 4.20 | 5.50 | — | 7.55 | — | 8.50 | 7.55 | — | — | 7.58 | — | 1.35 | 3.20 | — | 7.56 | — |
| 25 | Nailsea | — | — | — | — | — | — | 8.58 | 10.26 | — | — | — | 1.43 | — | — | 5.58 | — | 8. 5 | — | 8.58 | 8. 5 | — | — | 8. 6 | — | 1.43 | 3.28 | — | 8. 5 | — |
| 33 | **Bristol,** arrival | — | — | — | a. m. | a. m. | a. m. | 9.20 | 10.46 | — | 12.50 | — | 2. 4 | — | 4.50 | 6.20 | — | 8.30 | 12.50 | 9.20 | 8.30 | — | — | 8.28 | — | 2. 4 | 3.50 | — | 8.30 | 12.50 |
| | **Bristol,** departure | — | — | — | 7. 0 | 8. 0 | 8.40 | 10. 0 | 11. 0 | 12. 0 | 1. 0 | — | 2.30 | 4. 0 | 5. 0 | 6.30 | 7. 0 | 9. 0 | 1. 0 | 3. 0 | 9.30 | 8. 0 | — | 8.40 | — | 2.30 | 4. 0 | 6.30 | 8.40 | 1. 0 |
| 38 | *Calling at* Keynsham | — | — | — | — | 8.10 | — | 10.10 | — | 12.10 | — | — | 2.40 | 4.10 | — | 6.40 | 7.10 | 9.10 | — | — | — | 8.10 | — | — | — | 2.40 | 4.10 | 6.40 | 8.50 | — |
| 40 | Saltford | — | — | — | — | — | — | 10.15 | — | 12.16 | — | — | — | 4.15 | — | — | 7.15 | — | — | — | — | 8.15 | — | — | — | — | 4.15 | — | — | — |
| 43 | Twerton | — | — | — | — | 8.20 | — | — | — | 12.22 | — | — | — | 4.22 | — | — | — | 9.20 | — | — | — | 8.23 | — | — | — | — | 4.22 | — | 9. 5 | — |
| 44½ | **Bath** | — | — | — | 7.25 | 8.28 | 9. 5 | 10.28 | 11.25 | 12.30 | 1.25 | — | 2.55 | 4.28 | 5.25 | 7. 0 | 7.28 | 9.28 | 1.20 | 3.45 | 10.30 | 8.30 | — | 9. 5 | — | 2.55 | 4.30 | 7. 0 | 9.15 | 1.20 |
| 49½ | Box | — | — | — | 7.40 | — | — | — | 11.40 | — | — | — | — | — | 5.40 | — | — | — | — | — | — | — | — | — | — | — | — | 7.12 | — | — |
| 53 | Corsham | — | — | — | 7.53 | — | — | — | 11.53 | — | — | — | 3.26 | — | — | 7.26 | — | — | — | — | — | — | — | — | — | 3.26 | — | 7.26 | — | — |
| 57½ | **Chippenham** | — | — | — | 8. 5 | — | 9.40 | — | 12. 5 | — | 1.55 | — | 3.38 | — | 6. 0 | 7.40 | — | — | 1.50 | 4.40 | 11.20 | — | — | 9.40 | — | 3.28 | — | 7.40 | — | 1.50 |
| 68¼ | **Wootton Basset** | — | — | — | 8.30 | — | — | — | 12.30 | — | — | — | 4. 3 | — | — | 8. 0 | — | — | — | 5.20 | 12.20 | — | — | — | — | 4. 5 | — | 8. 0 | — | — |
| 94½ | *Starting from* **Cirencester** | — | — | — | 7.50 | — | 9.35 | — | 11.55 | — | 1.40 | — | 3.30 | — | 5.45 | — | — | — | 1.40 | 5.45 | 1.40 | — | — | 9.35 | — | 3.30 | — | — | — | 1.40 |
| 82½ | *Calling at* **Minety** | — | — | — | 8.15 | — | — | — | 12.18 | — | 2. 5 | — | 3.55 | — | 6.10 | — | — | — | — | 6.10 | — | — | — | 9.58 | — | 3.53 | — | — | — | — |
| 78½ | Purton | — | — | — | 8.23 | — | — | — | 12.28 | — | 2.15 | — | — | — | 6.20 | — | — | — | — | 6.20 | — | — | — | 10. 8 | — | 4. 3 | — | — | — | — |
| 74½ | **Swindon** } Arrival | — | — | a. m. | 8.40 | — | 10.20 | — | 12.40 | — | 2.30 | — | 4.15 | — | 6.35 | 8.10 | — | — | 2.25 | 6.35 | 2.25 | — | a. m. | 10.20 | — | 4.15 | — | 8.10 | — | 2.25 |
| | **Junction** } Departure | — | — | 7.30 | 8.50 | — | 10.30 | — | 12.50 | — | 2.40 | — | 4.25 | — | 6.45 | 8.20 | — | — | 2.35 | 6.50 | 2.40 | — | 7. 0 | 10.30 | — | 4.25 | — | — | — | 2.35 |
| 80 | **Shrivenham** | — | — | 7.42 | — | — | 10.42 | — | 1. 3 | — | — | — | — | — | 6.57 | — | — | — | — | 7.15 | — | — | 7.14 | 10.42 | — | 4.37 | — | — | — | — |
| 87¼ | **Faringdon Road** | — | — | 7.58 | — | — | 10.55 | — | — | — | 3. 3 | — | [illegible] | — | — | 8.46 | — | — | 3. 0 | 7.45 | — | — | 7.30 | 10.55 | — | 4.53 | — | — | — | 3. 0 |
| 95 | **Steventon** | — | — | 8.12 | 9.30 | — | 11.10 | — | 1.32 | — | 3.12 | — | [illegible] | — | 7.25 | 9. 0 | — | — | 3.12 | 8.15 | 4. [illegible] | — | 7.50 | 11.10 | — | 5. 8 | — | — | — | 3.16 |
| 103½ | **Wallingford Road** | — | — | 8.30 | 9.47 | — | — | — | 1.50 | — | — | — | [illegible] | — | 7.43 | — | — | — | 3.36 | 8.45 | 4.50 | — | 8.10 | — | — | 5.26 | — | — | — | 3.36 |
| 106½ | Goring | — | — | 8.38 | — | — | — | — | — | — | — | — | 5.29 | — | — | 9.25 | — | — | — | — | — | — | 8.18 | — | — | — | — | — | — | — |
| 110 | **Pangbourne** | a. m. | — | 8.46 | — | — | — | — | — | — | 3.45 | — | [illegible] | — | 7.55 | — | — | — | — | 9.10 | — | — | 8.26 | — | — | 5.40 | — | — | p. m. | — |
| 115¼ | **Reading** | 7.30 | — | 9. 0 | 10.12 | — | 11.50 | — | 2.15 | — | 4. 0 | — | 5.48 | — | 8. 5 | 9.45 | — | — | 4. 0 | 9.30 | 5.10 | — | 8.40 | 11.50 | — | 5.55 | — | — | 8. 0 | 4. 0 |
| 120¼ | **Twyford** | 7.40 | — | 9.10 | 10.22 | a. m. | — | — | 2.28 | — | — | — | 6. 0 | p. m. | — | — | — | — | — | 10.15 | — | — | 8.49 | — | — | 6.10 | p. m. | — | 8. 9 | — |
| 128¼ | **Maidenhead** | 7.56 | a. m. | 9.30 | — | 11.15 | 12.20 | p. m. | 2.46 | — | — | p. m. | 6.17 | 7.25 | — | 10.15 | — | — | 4.25 | — | 6. 0 | a. m. | 9. 6 | 12.20 | p. m. | 6.28 | 7.30 | — | 8.27 | 4.25 |
| 133¼ | **Slough** | 8. 6 | 9. 0 | 9.40 | 10.45 | 11.25 | 12.30 | 2. 0 | 2.56 | — | 4.35 | 5.36 | 6.27 | 7.54 | 8.40 | 10.25 | — | — | 4.40 | 10.55 | 6.30 | 8. 0 | 9.16 | 12.30 | 5. 0 | 6.38 | 7.45 | — | 8.39 | 4.40 |
| 138¼ | West Drayton | 8.18 | 9.10 | 9.53 | — | 11.37 | — | 2.10 | — | — | — | 5.40 | — | 8. 6 | — | — | — | — | 4.52 | — | 6.50 | 8.10 | 9.28 | — | 5.12 | — | 7.57 | — | 8.52 | [illegible] |
| 142½ | Southall | 8.28 | 9.19 | 10. 3 | — | 11.46 | — | 2.19 | — | — | — | 5.49 | — | 8.16 | — | — | — | — | — | 11.40 | — | 8.19 | 9.38 | — | 5.21 | — | 8. 6 | — | 9. 3 | — |
| 144 | Hanwell | 8.33 | 9.24 | 10. 9 | — | 11.51 | — | 2.24 | — | — | — | 5.54 | — | 8.22 | — | — | — | — | — | — | — | 8.24 | 9.43 | — | 5.27 | — | 8.12 | — | 9.10 | — |
| 145¾ | Ealing | 8.38 | 9.28 | 10.14 | — | 11.56 | — | 2.28 | — | — | — | 5.58 | — | 8.27 | — | — | — | — | — | — | — | 8.28 | 9.48 | — | 5.32 | — | 8.18 | — | 9.16 | — |
| 151¼ | **Paddington** | 8.50 | 9.40 | 10.30 | 11.25 | 12. 8 | 1. 5 | 2.40 | 3.40 | — | 5.15 | 6.10 | 7. 5 | 8.40 | 9.20 | 11. 0 | — | — | 5.20 | 12.10 | 7.40 | 8.40 | 10. 0 | 1. 5 | 5.45 | 7.20 | 8.30 | — | 9.30 | 5.20 |

N.B. The Time Table is calculated throughout at London Time.

Passengers, Parcels, &c. from Bridgewater, Bristol, Bath, and Chippenham, proceeding to Gloucester, Cheltenham, &c., may be booked for Cirencester by the UP TRAINS to "**Swindon Junction**," proceeding by the DOWN TRAINS to Cirencester. In like manner, Passengers from Gloucestershire, &c., can proceed "WEST" by coming from Cirencester to the "**Swindon Junction**," and thence by the DOWN TRAINS to Chippenham, Bath, Bristol, and Bridgewater, as explained on the other side.

The GOODS' TRAIN PASSENGERS will be conveyed in uncovered Trucks by the Goods' Trains only, and 14-lbs of Luggage allowed for each.

* The time entered for the Goods Trains calling at Southall, applies only to Wednesday Morning "Down," and Tuesday Night "Up" for the convenience of the Cattle Market, as the Trains will not stop there except on those days.

The "UP" Sunday Evening Goods' Train will leave Cirencester at 3.30, instead of 5.45 p. m.; and the "DOWN" Goods' Trains on Sunday, will leave Swindon at 1.10, instead of 8.55 a.m., or 11.0. a. m.

Coaches will run from Bridgewater to Exeter, Plymouth, Devonport, Barnstaple, &c.; and places may be secured for those Coaches at Princes Street Office, or at Paddington Station. Coaches also run from Chippenham to Devizes, and from Bath to Frome, Wells, Shepton Mallet, and Glastonbury. There are Coaches from Cirencester for Cheltenham, from every Train; also Coaches during the day for Gloucester, Stroud, Dursley, &c.; from the Steventon Station to Oxford, through Abingdon; between the Twyford Station and Henley; the Maidenhead Station and Marlow and Wycombe; the West Drayton Station and Uxbridge. And Windsor Omnibuses meet every Train at Slough.

Omnibuses start from Princes Street, Bank, one hour before the departure of each Train, calling at the Angel Inn, Islington; Bull Inn, Holborn; Moore's Green Man and Still, Griffin's Green Man and Still, Oxford Street; Golden Cross, Charing Cross; Chaplin's Universal Office, and Bull and Mouth, Regent Circus; and Gloucester Warehouse, Oxford Street, to the Paddington Station, Fare Sixpence, without Luggage. Omnibuses leave the Station at Bristol for Clifton Hot-wells, &c. & the Bath Station for all parts of that City on the arrival of every Train.

Parcels may be booked at the Railway Offices, Princes Street, Bank, and Paddington; at the Coach Offices, Spread Eagle, Gracechurch Street, and Regent Circus; the Bull and Mouth, St. Martin's-le-Grand, Golden Cross, Charing Cross, and Regent Circus; Gr[illegible]'s Green Man and Still, and Moore's Green Man and Still, Oxford Street; Bull Inn, Holborn; George and Blue Boar, Holborn; Angel Inn, St. Clements, and Islington; Swan with two Necks, Lad Lane; Cross Keys, Wood Street; White Horse, Fetter Lane; [illegible] White Horse Cellar, Piccadilly; and the Western Office, corner of Portman Street, for Bristol, Bath, Bridgewater, Taunton, Exeter, Devonport, Plymouth, and Cirencester, and all parts of the West of England, Gloucestershire and Wales, and the Towns and Villages right and left of the Line of Railway, at which places, and all the Stations, they will also be Received for Conveyance. Four Daily Deliveries will be made in London, Bath, Bristol and Bridgewater.

GOODS and CATTLE are Conveyed on the Railway, Particulars of which can be had at all the Stations.

TURN OVER.

Time-table, 30th July 1841

## DOWN TRAINS leave PADDINGTON STATION, all calling at Slough, Reading, Steventon, Swindon, and Chippenham Stations.

| For Cirencester. | | For Bath & Bristol. | | For Bridgewater. | |
|---|---|---|---|---|---|
| h. m. | h. m. | h. m. | h. m. | h. m. | h. m. |
| 6 0 a. m. | 2 0 p. m. | 6 0 a. m. | 12 0 a. m. | 6 0 a. m. | 12 0 a. m. |
| 8 0 „ | 5 0 „ | 8 0 „ | 2 0 p. m. | 8 0 „ | 2 0 p. m. |
| 10 15 (Mail) | 8 55 (Mail) | 10 15 (Mail) | 5 0 „ | 10 15 (Mail) | 8 55 (Mail) |
| 12 0 a. m. | | 11 0 a. m. | 8 55 (Mail) | | |
| ON SUNDAYS. | | ON SUNDAYS. | | ON SUNDAYS. | |
| 10 15 a.m. Mail | 8 55 p.m. Mail | 10 15 a.m. Mail | 8 55 p.m. Mail | 10 15 a.m. Mail | 8 55 p.m. Mail |
| 2 0 p.m. | | 2 0 p.m. | | 2 0 p.m. | |

### SHORT TRAINS DOWN,

*Calling at Intermediate Stations, as per Train Bill.*

**From Paddington.**

| | h. m. |
|---|---|
| For Maidenhead | 9 0 a. m. |
| For Slough | 11 30 „ |
| For do. | 1 30 p. m. |
| For Reading | 4 0 „ |
| For Slough | 4 30 „ |
| For Maidenhead | 5 30 „ |
| For Swindon | 7 30 „ |
| **ON SUNDAYS.** | |
| For Slough | 8 30 a. m. |
| For Reading | 9 0 „ |
| For Slough | 9 30 „ |
| For Maidenhead | 5 0 p. m. |
| For Swindon | 7 0 „ |

**From Bath.**

| | h. m. |
|---|---|
| For Bristol & Bridgewater | 8 45 a. m. |
| For Bristol | 11 0 „ |
| For do. | 1 0 p. m. |
| For do. | 5 0 „ |
| For do. | 7 45 „ |
| For do. | 10 0 „ |
| **ON SUNDAYS.** *Leave Bath* | |
| For Bristol & Bridgewater | 8 45 a. m. |
| For do. do. | 9 55 „ |
| For Bristol | 5 0 p. m. |
| For do. | 9 30 „ |

**From Bristol.**

| | h. m. |
|---|---|
| For Bridgewater | 8 0 a. m. |
| For do. | 9 25 „ |
| For do. (Mail) | 10 50 „ |
| For do. | 7 0 p. m. |
| **ON SUNDAYS.** *Leave Bristol* | |
| For Bridgewater | 9 25 a. m. |
| For do. (Mail) | 10 50 „ |
| For do. | 7 0 p. m. |

From Swindon, on Sundays, at 8 45 a. m. for Bath, Bristol, and Bridgewater.

## UP TRAINS, all calling at Chippenham, Swindon, Steventon, Reading, and Slough Stations.

**From Bridgewater.**

| | H. M. |
|---|---|
| To Bristol | 5 0 a. m. |
| To London and Cirencester | 9 30 „ |
| To London and Cirencester | 11 30 „ |
| To London & Cirencester (Mail) | 12 44 p. m. |
| To London and Cirencester | 3 30 „ |
| To London | 5 0 „ |
| To Bristol and Bath | 7 0 „ |
| To London (Mail) | 11 40 „ |
| **ON SUNDAYS.** | |
| To London | 7 15 a. m. |
| To London & Cirencester (Mail) | 12 44 p. m. |
| To Bristol and Bath | 2 30 „ |
| To do. do. | 7 0 „ |
| To London (Mail) | 11 40 „ |

**From Bristol calling at Bath.**

| | H. M. |
|---|---|
| To London (Mail) | 1 0 a. m. |
| To London and Cirencester | 7 0 „ |
| To London and do. (Mail) | 8 40 „ |
| To London and do. | 11 0 „ |
| To London and do. | 1 0 p. m. |
| To London and do. | 2 30 „ |
| To London and do. | 5 0 „ |
| To London | 6 30 „ |
| Short Trains to Bath at | 8 0 a. m. |
| „ do. | 10 0 „ |
| „ do. | 12 0 „ |
| „ do. | 4 0 p. m. |
| „ do. | 7 0 „ |
| **ON SUNDAYS.** | |
| To London (Mail) | 1 0 a. m. |
| To London (Mail) | 8 40 „ |
| To London and Cirencester | 2 30 p. m. |
| To Swindon, calling at intermediate Stations | 6 30 „ |
| Short Trains to Bath at 8 a.m. & 4 p.m. | |
| „ do. | 8 40 p. m. |

**From Cirencester.**

| | H. M. |
|---|---|
| To London (Mail) | 1 40 a. m. |
| To London, Bath, Bristol, and Bridgewater | 7 50 „ |
| To London, Bath, Bristol, & Bridgewater (Mail) | 9 35 „ |
| To London, Bath, Bristol, and Bridgewater | 11 55 „ |
| To London, Bath, Bristol, & Bridgewater | 1 40 p. m. |
| To London, Bath, Bristol, and Bridgewater | 3 30 „ |
| To London | 5 45 „ |
| **ON SUNDAYS.** | |
| To London (Mail) | 1 40 a. m. |
| To ditto (ditto) | 9 35 „ |
| To London, Bath, Bristol, and Bridgewater | 3 30 p. m. |

### SHORT TRAINS UP TO PADDINGTON,

*Calling at Intermediate Stations, as per Train Bill.*

| | h. m. | | h. m. | | h. m. |
|---|---|---|---|---|---|
| From Reading | 7 30 a. m. | From Maidenhead | 11 15 a. m. | From Slough | 9 0 a. m. |
| From Swindon | 7 30 „ | From do. | 7 45 p. m. | From do. | 2 0 p. m. |
| | | | | From do. | 5 30 „ |
| **ON SUNDAYS.** | | **ON SUNDAYS.** | | **ON SUNDAYS.** | |
| From Swindon | 7 0 a. m. | From Maidenhead | 7 30 p. m. | From Slough | 8 0 a. m. |
| From Reading | 8 0 p. m. | | | From do. | 5 0 p. m. |

## DOWN from CIRENCESTER.

*Passengers travelling from Cheltenham, Gloucester, &c. can take their places "through" to Bath, Bristol, Bridgewater, &c. at the following hours:*

| FROM Cirencester. | FROM Swindon. |
|---|---|
| H. M. | H. M. |
| 7 50 a. m. | 8 45 a. m. |
| 9 35 „ | 11 0 „ |
| 11 55 „ | 1 10 p. m. |
| 1 40 p. m. | 3 8 „ |
| 3 30 „ | 4 58 „ |
| **On Sundays.** | **On Sundays.** |
| 3 30 p. m. | 5 5 p. m. |

*To the Swindon Junction, proceeding thence by the London DOWN Trains at*

## FARES.

| PADDINGTON to | PASSENGERS. First Class. s. d. | Second Class. s. d. | Third Class. s. d. | CARRIAGES. 4-wheel s. d. | 2-wheel s. d. | HORSES. Each. s. d. | Per Pair belonging the same Property. s. d. |
|---|---|---|---|---|---|---|---|
| Ealing | 1 6 | 0 9 | ... | ... | ... | ... | ... |
| Hanwell | 2 0 | 1 0 | ... | ... | ... | ... | ... |
| Southall | 2 6 | 1 3 | 0 9 | ... | ... | ... | ... |
| West Drayton | 3 0 | 1 6 | 1 0 | ... | ... | ... | ... |
| Slough | 4 6 | 2 6 | 1 6 | 11 0 | 8 0 | 9 0 | 14 0 |
| Maidenhead | 5 6 | 3 6 | 2 0 | 12 0 | 9 0 | 10 0 | 16 0 |
| Twyford | 7 0 | 5 0 | 2 6 | 16 0 | 12 0 | 14 0 | 24 0 |
| Reading | 8 0 | 5 6 | 3 0 | 20 0 | 15 0 | 16 0 | 28 0 |
| Pangbourne | 9 6 | 6 6 | 3 6 | 24 0 | 18 0 | 20 0 | 32 0 |
| Goring | 10 6 | 7 0 | ... | ... | ... | ... | ... |
| Wallingford Road | 11 6 | 8 0 | 4 6 | 28 0 | 21 0 | 24 0 | 40 0 |
| Steventon | 12 6 | 8 6 | 5 0 | 32 0 | 24 0 | 28 0 | 48 0 |
| Faringdon Road | 14 0 | 10 0 | 6 0 | 36 0 | 27 0 | 32 0 | 52 0 |
| Shrivenham | 17 0 | 12 0 | 7 6 | 39 0 | 29 0 | 35 0 | 55 0 |
| Swindon | 20 0 | 14 0 | 9 0 | 42 0 | 32 0 | 38 0 | 58 0 |
| Purton | 21 6 | 15 0 | ... | ... | ... | ... | ... |
| Minety | 23 0 | 16 0 | 10 0 | 45 0 | 35 0 | 41 0 | 61 0 |
| **Cirencester** | 25 0 | 18 0 | 11 0 | 48 0 | 38 0 | 44 0 | 64 0 |
| Wootton Basset | 22 0 | 15 6 | 9 6 | 44 0 | 34 0 | 40 0 | 60 0 |
| Chippenham | 24 6 | 17 6 | 10 6 | 47 0 | 37 0 | 43 0 | 63 0 |
| Corsham | 25 6 | 18 6 | ... | ... | ... | ... | ... |
| Box | 26 6 | 19 0 | ... | ... | ... | ... | ... |
| **Bath** | 27 6 | 19 6 | 11 6 | 53 0 | 43 0 | 48 0 | 68 0 |
| Twerton | 28 6 | 20 0 | ... | ... | ... | ... | ... |
| Saltford | 29 0 | 20 6 | ... | ... | ... | ... | ... |
| Keynsham | 29 6 | 20 6 | ... | ... | ... | ... | ... |
| **Bristol** | 30 0 | 21 0 | 12 6 | 58 0 | 48 0 | 53 0 | 73 0 |
| Nailsea | 32 0 | 22 0 | 13 0 | ... | ... | ... | ... |
| Clevedon Road | 33 0 | 22 6 | 13 6 | 61 0 | 51 0 | 56 0 | 76 0 |
| Banwell | 34 0 | 23 6 | ... | ... | ... | ... | ... |
| Weston Super Mare | 35 0 | 24 0 | 14 6 | 64 0 | 54 0 | 59 0 | 79 0 |
| Highbridge | 36 6 | 25 6 | 15 0 | 68 0 | 57 0 | 63 0 | 83 0 |
| **Bridgewater** | 38 0 | 26 6 | 16 0 | 72 0 | 60 0 | 65 0 | 85 |
| **From Bristol to** | | | | | | | |
| Nailsea | 2 0 | 1 0 | 0 9 | ... | ... | ... | ... |
| Clevedon Road | 3 0 | 1 6 | 1 0 | 8 0 | 6 0 | 7 0 | 12 0 |
| Banwell | 4 0 | 2 6 | ... | ... | ... | ... | ... |
| Weston Super Mare | 5 0 | 3 0 | 2 0 | 12 0 | 9 0 | 10 0 | 16 0 |
| Highbridge | 6 6 | 4 6 | 3 0 | 16 0 | 12 0 | 14 0 | 24 0 |
| Bridgewater | 8 0 | 5 6 | 3 6 | 20 0 | 15 0 | 16 0 | 28 0 |

## FARES.

| BRIDGEWATER to | PASSENGERS. First Class. s. d. | Second Class. s. d. | Third Class. s. d. | CARRIAGES. 4-wheel s. d. | 2-wheel s. d. | HORSES. Each. s. d. | Per Pair belonging the same Property. s. d. |
|---|---|---|---|---|---|---|---|
| **Highbridge** | 2 0 | 1 0 | 0 9 | 8 0 | 6 0 | 7 0 | 12 0 |
| Weston Super Mare | 3 6 | 2 6 | 1 6 | 12 0 | 9 0 | 10 0 | 16 0 |
| Banwell | 4 6 | 3 0 | ... | ... | ... | ... | ... |
| Clevedon Road | 5 6 | 4 0 | 2 0 | 16 0 | 12 0 | 14 0 | 24 0 |
| Nailsea | 6 6 | 4 6 | 3 0 | ... | ... | ... | ... |
| Bristol | 8 0 | 5 6 | 3 6 | 20 0 | 15 0 | 16 0 | 28 0 |
| Bath | 10 6 | 7 0 | 4 6 | 28 0 | 21 0 | 24 0 | 40 0 |
| Cirencester | 20 0 | 14 0 | 8 0 | 40 0 | 32 0 | 35 0 | 52 0 |
| **Paddington** | 38 0 | 26 6 | 16 0 | 72 0 | 60 0 | 65 0 | 85 0 |
| **From Bristol to** | | | | | | | |
| Keynsham | 1 6 | 0 9 | ... | ... | ... | ... | ... |
| Saltford | 2 0 | 1 0 | ... | ... | ... | ... | ... |
| Twerton | 2 3 | 1 3 | ... | ... | ... | ... | ... |
| **Bath** | 2 6 | 1 6 | 1 0 | 8 0 | 6 0 | 7 0 | 12 0 |
| Box | 3 6 | 2 0 | ... | ... | ... | ... | ... |
| Corsham | 4 6 | 2 6 | ... | ... | ... | ... | ... |
| Chippenham | 5 6 | 3 6 | 2 0 | 12 0 | 10 0 | 11 0 | 17 0 |
| Wootton Basset | 8 0 | 5 6 | 3 0 | 16 0 | 14 0 | 15 0 | 22 0 |
| Purton | 10 6 | 7 6 | ... | ... | ... | ... | ... |
| Minety | 11 0 | 8 0 | 4 0 | 20 0 | 17 0 | 19 0 | 27 0 |
| **Cirencester** | 12 0 | 8 6 | 4 6 | 22 0 | 18 0 | 20 0 | 29 0 |
| Swindon | 10 0 | 7 0 | 3 6 | 20 0 | 17 9 | 19 0 | 27 0 |
| Shrivenham | 13 0 | 9 0 | 5 0 | 24 0 | 20 0 | 22 0 | 32 0 |
| Faringdon Road | 16 0 | 11 0 | 6 6 | 28 0 | 23 0 | 25 0 | 37 0 |
| Steventon | 17 6 | 12 6 | 7 6 | 32 0 | 26 0 | 28 0 | 42 0 |
| Wallingford Road | 18 6 | 13 0 | 8 0 | 36 0 | 29 0 | 32 0 | 46 0 |
| Goring | 19 6 | 14 0 | ... | ... | ... | ... | ... |
| Pangbourne | 21 0 | 14 6 | 9 0 | 40 0 | 32 0 | 35 0 | 50 0 |
| Reading | 22 0 | 15 6 | 9 6 | 43 0 | 35 0 | 38 0 | 54 0 |
| Twyford | 23 0 | 16 0 | 10 0 | 47 0 | 38 0 | 42 0 | 58 0 |
| Maidenhead | 24 6 | 17 6 | 10 6 | 51 0 | 42 0 | 46 0 | 63 0 |
| Slough | 25 6 | 18 6 | 11 0 | 54 0 | 45 0 | 49 0 | 67 0 |
| West Drayton | 27 0 | 19 6 | 11 6 | ... | ... | ... | ... |
| Southall | 27 6 | 20 0 | 12 0 | ... | ... | ... | ... |
| Hanwell | 28 0 | 20 6 | ... | ... | ... | ... | ... |
| Ealing | 29 0 | 21 0 | ... | ... | ... | ... | ... |
| **Paddington** | 30 0 | 21 0 | 12 6 | 58 0 | 48 0 | 53 0 | 73 0 |

## UP to CIRENCESTER.

*Passengers travelling from Plymouth, Exeter, Bristol, Bath, &c. to Cheltenham, Gloucester, &c. can take their places "through" to Cirencester at the following hours:*

| FROM Bridgewater. | FROM Bristol. |
|---|---|
| | H. M. |
| | 7 0 a. m. |
| H. M. | 8 40 „ |
| 9 30 a. m. | 11 0 „ |
| 11 30 „ | 1 0 p. m. |
| 12 44 p. m. | 2 30 „ |
| 3 30 „ | 5 0 „ |
| **On Sundays.** | |
| 12 44 p. m. | 2 30 p. m. |

*To the Swindon Junction, proceeding thence by the DOWN Train to Cirencester at*

| FROM Swindon. |
|---|
| H. M. |
| [illegible] |
| **On Sundays.** |
| 5 5 p. m. |

Back of time-table opposite

As we have seen, the poor speed of the Great Western trains was one of the reasons which led the 'Five Kings' at the Board of Trade to report in January 1845 against broad-gauge lines from Oxford to Rugby and Wolverhampton. Their report roused the Broad Gauge champions to action, and on 10th February the Great Western Board resolved:

That it is expedient to commence on Monday 10th March with a quick train daily from Paddington down to Exeter, from Didcot to Oxford, and from Swindon to Cirencester, and another train daily up from those places—the whole journey 194 miles being performed in five hours.

Accordingly trains began running at the times shown on page 342 on 10th March 1845. They were easily the fastest trains in the world.

After about a month's experience Saunders and Gooch came to the conclusion that ½ hour might be saved on the journey, partly by reducing the stop at Swindon to 1 minute; so the time was cut down to 4½ hours on 12th May, while the Gauge battle was raging in the Committee Room at Westminster.

Needless to say, these trains, at 43 miles an hour, including stops, caused a sensation in the year 1845, and doubtless did their share in winning the Parliamentary fight for the Broad Gauge, besides making its cause popular with the general travelling public. But one person looked askance at them, Griffiths of Cheltenham, the tenant of Swindon Refreshment Rooms, who, as soon as he heard of the proposal to cut the time at Swindon, complained to his landlords, Messrs Rigby; and they, getting no satisfaction from Saunders, filed a Bill in Chancery against the Company to compel stoppage of the trains for the covenanted 10 minutes.

Rigby's Lease provided that:

All trains carrying passengers, not being Goods trains or *trains to be sent express* or for special purposes, and except trains not under the control of the Great Western Railway Company, which shall pass the Swindon Station either up or down, shall, save in case of emergency or unusual delay arising from accidents, stop there for refreshment of passengers for a reasonable period of about ten minutes.

The Company's lawyers of course maintained stoutly that an express train was 'a train sent express', but the Court decided that the latter term was intended to mean a private special, and certainly not a train carrying the general public, however fast it might run. Although the original Bill had been filed two days before the acceleration of the trains in May, the final judgment against the Company was staved off till the middle of the following January, so for all the intervening eight months the 1 minute stop remained in force. The 10 minutes for refreshments was enforced from 26th January 1846, and again Gooch came forward and undertook that his engines, still the 7 foot singles of 1840, should make up the time lost. The trains were of course very light, according to modern ideas at any rate, seldom exceeding 50 tons although they carried second as well as first-class passengers.

A new 4½ hour time-table was accordingly drawn up and remained in force till the end of November 1847.

At this time the fight for the Broad Gauge to Birmingham was pending, and, moreover, seven of Gooch's great 8 foot singles—*Great Western, Iron Duke, Great Britain, Lightning, Emperor, Pasha,* and *Sultan*—were already on the road. So, by way of showing what they could do, a further acceleration of 13 minutes to Bristol was arranged, making the time exactly 2¼ hours from London. Below Bristol 8 minutes were absorbed by a new stop at Bridgwater, so the time to Exeter was only reduced to 4 hours 25 minutes.

For the 52⅞ miles from the old station at Paddington to Didcot only 55 minutes were allowed, involving a speed of over 57 miles an hour, and on one occasion at least—on 11th May 1848—the distance was covered by the *Great Britain* in 47½ minutes![1]

These new times were adopted on 1st December 1847, and, as far as the 55 minutes run to Didcot was concerned, remained in force till April 1852, but a stop at Chippenham, added on the opening of the branch to Westbury in September 1848, made the time to Bristol 2 hours 35 minutes, and to Exeter the even 4½ hours again. When the Bristol & Exeter Company took charge of their own line in May 1849 stops were put in at Weston and Tiverton Junctions, adding a further 10 minutes to the journey to Exeter.

Though the Up train covered the whole distance, with the same stops, in the 4½ hours, it had no such sensational timing as that from London to Didcot. It was allowed 2 hours 46 minutes from Bristol, and its fastest run was the short one from Swindon to Didcot in 27 minutes, rather over 53½ miles an hour. The Bristol & Exeter Company made it a quarter of an hour slower on their line in May 1849 by the same two extra stops as the Down train, but the Great Western maintained the timing from Bristol till the end of 1852.

The story of these once famous Exeter expresses has been told somewhat fully on account of their historical interest as the first really fast trains in the world, and to show what was done on the Broad Gauge in the best days of Brunel, Saunders, and Gooch. The last named indeed claims in his *Diaries* to be 'the father of Express trains'.

It was the Down train, with its 57 miles an hour run to Didcot, that was first nicknamed 'Flying Dutchman', after a very famous horse which won both the Derby and the Leger in 1849.

The times of the trains at the different periods are shown in the table on page 342.

Two other 4½ hour expresses began to run in April 1846, leaving Paddington at 5.30 p.m. and Exeter at 6.30 a.m. respectively; these stopped at Reading instead of Didcot, and also at Chippenham and Bridgwater.[2] The Up train was discontinued west of Bristol in November

---

[1] Gooch's statement in Proceedings of the Institute of Civil Engineers, 1848—'repeatedly in 48 to 50 minutes, and once in company of several engineers at 67 m.p.h. start to stop, *i.e.* in 47½ minutes'.

[2] The fact that these trains were allowed only 3 and 2 minutes respectively at Bristol shows that the Express Platform there was already in use by both Up and Down trains. It was situated on the Up side of the B. & E. curve on a site later covered by part of No. 4 (now No. 9) Platform.

EXETER EXPRESSES, 1845–1852

| Miles from Paddington | | | 10 Mar.—10 May 1845 | 12 May 1845—24 Jan. 1846 | 26 Jan. 1846—Nov. 1847 | Dec. 1847—Sept. 1848 | Oct. 1848—April 1849 | May 1849—Mar. 1852 | April—Dec. 1852 |
|---|---|---|---|---|---|---|---|---|---|
| | | | *Down Train* | | | | | | |
| | Paddington | dep. | 9 30 | 9 45 | 9 45 | 9 50 | 9 50 | 9 50 | 9 45 |
| 52⅞ | Didcot | arr. | 10 43 | 10 53 | 10 50 | 10 45 | 10 45 | 10 45 | 10 43 |
| | | dep. | 10 45 | 10 55 | 10 52 | 10 47 | 10 47 | 10 47 | 10 45 |
| 77 | Swindon | arr. | 11 20 | 11 27 | 11 23 | 11 15 | 11 15 | 11 15 | 11 15 |
| | | dep. | 11 30 | 11 28 | 11 33 | 11 25 | 11 25 | 11 25 | 11 25 |
| 93¾ | Chippenham | | — | — | — | — | 11 45 | 11 45 | 11 45 |
| 106⅝ | Bath | arr. | 12 10 | 12 6 | 12 9 | 12 0 | 12 5 | 12 5 | 12 10 |
| | | dep. | 12 12 | 12 8 | 12 11 | 12 2 | 12 7 | 12 7 | 12 12 |
| 118¼ | Bristol | arr. | 12 30 | 12 25 | 12 28 | 12 20 | 12 25 | 12 25 | 12 30 |
| | (Express Platform) | | | | | | | B.& | E.R. |
| | | dep. | 12 35 | 12 30 | 12 33 | 12 25 | 12 30 | 12 30 | 12 35 |
| 151⅜ | Bridgwater | | — | — | — | 1 5 | 1 9 | * 1 15 | * 1 15 |
| 163 | Taunton | arr. | 1 35 | 1 26 | 1 27 | 1 27 | 1 31 | | |
| | | dep. | 1 37 | 1 28 | 1 29 | 1 29 | 1 33 | 1 40 | 1 40 |
| 193¾ | Exeter | arr. | 2 30 | 2 15 | 2 15 | 2 15 | 2 20 | * 2 30 | * 2 30 |
| Miles. Intermediate | | | *Up Train* | | | | | | |
| | Exeter | dep. | 11 45 | 12 0 | 12 0 | 12 0 | 12 30 | 12 40 | |
| 30¾ | Taunton | arr. | 12 30 | 12 41 | 12 41 | 12 40 | 1 9 | * 1 27 | |
| | | dep. | 12 32 | 12 43 | 12 43 | 12 42 | 1 11 | 1 29 | |
| 11½ | Bridgwater | | — | — | — | 12 58 | 1 27 | 1 45 | |
| 33¼ | Bristol | arr. | 1 35 | 1 40 | 1 36 | 1 40 | 2 10 | * 2 35 | |
| | (Express Platform) | | | | | | | G.W.R. | |
| | | dep. | 1 40 | 1 45 | 1 41 | 1 44 | 2 14 | 2 39 | |
| 11⅝ | Bath | arr. | 1 55 | 2 2 | 1 56 | 2 0 | 2 30 | 2 55 | |
| | | dep. | 1 57 | 2 4 | 1 58 | 2 2 | 2 32 | 2 57 | |
| 13 | Chippenham | | — | — | — | — | 2 52 | 3 17 | |
| 16⅝ | Swindon | arr. | 2 45 | 2 46 | 2 43 | 2 45 | 3 20 | 3 45 | |
| | | dep. | 2 55 | 2 47 | 2 53 | 2 55 | 3 30 | 3 55 | |
| 24½ | Didcot | arr. | 3 28 | 3 18 | 3 22 | 3 22 | 3 57 | 4 22 | |
| | | dep. | 3 30 | 3 20 | 3 24 | 3 25 | 4 0 | 4 25 | |
| 52⅞ | Paddington | arr. | 4 45 | 4 30 | 4 30 | 4 30 | 5 0 | 5 25 | |

It is uncertain whether the Chippenham and Bridgwater times are arrival or departure.

* Stops at Weston Junction and Tiverton Junction.

1848, starting thence at 8.10 and reaching Paddington at 11 as before, and the Down was made 40 minutes earlier as far as Bristol at the same speed (4.50–7.32); below Bristol it became a stopping train.

It remains to be noticed that by means of a train from Swindon off the 9.50 a.m., stopping at Tetbury Road, Stroud, and the T Station at Gloucester, the journey from Paddington to Cheltenham (120¼ miles) was accomplished in 2 hours 47 minutes, and that the three other Expresses had connections to or from that town giving a 3 hour service. Oxford[1] was reached in $1\frac{1}{4}$ hours from London.

During all the years these fast trains were running there is only one serious accident to record. On 10th May 1848 the 12 o'clock express from Exeter, drawn by *Sultan*, and consisting of a van, three second and three first-class carriages, all six-wheeled, with upwards of 200 passengers and an estimated weight of 120 tons, ran at full speed into a cattle truck and horse-box at Shrivenham. These had just been pushed out foul of the main line by a couple of porters to enable them to use a turn-table in the siding to shift a goods waggon, regardless of the fact that the signal showed *All right* for the overdue express, and without the knowledge of the policeman on duty, who was stationed at the level crossing at the other end of the station. *Sultan* hit the trucks up on to the platform and passed on almost undamaged with the van, but the debris fell back on the leading second-class coach, killing six passengers and injuring thirteen.

A second accident, not so serious, occurred to the morning train from Bristol on 24th February 1853, after its booked speed had been much reduced. Consisting in order of a van, two seconds and three firsts, it had passed Ealing when the three first-class carriages left the rails and ran up the side of the cutting to the left. Of the twenty-one passengers in the leading coach no one was seriously injured, though the body was separated from the frame and capsized, but in the next one passenger was killed. This was James Gibbs, a Great Western Director and former Chairman of the Bristol & Exeter Railway, on his way to attend the Board. The cause was never ascertained, but was thought to be the fracture of some portion of the frame of the leading first.

For some reason or other, probably the need for economy, all this brilliant exhibition of speed came to an end with the year 1852. From 1st January 1853 the best train took $3\frac{1}{4}$ hours to Bristol and $5\frac{1}{4}$ to Exeter, and in the opposite direction the same or more; the time of the 'Dutchman', no longer 'Flying', from Paddington to Didcot was increased to 68 minutes. So things remained with little or no improvement for more than nine years.

Meantime, on the opening to Birmingham in October 1852, two trains were put on to do the 129 miles in $2\frac{3}{4}$ hours, stopping only at Oxford and Leamington, 70 minutes being allowed for the $63\frac{1}{4}$ miles to Oxford new station (via Didcot Station) and 55 for the $42\frac{1}{2}$ thence to Leamington. They had a very short life. The autumn was the wettest for many years, and the heavy rain did much damage to the new cuttings and embankments. Round Oxford the country was under water for weeks, and at Kennington the railway was flooded in November to such an extent that engines could not pass. Captain Galton, of the Board of Trade, reporting on a trifling collision at Heyford, which occurred on 26th November, describes how the trains were got through.

[1] Old station, $62\frac{1}{2}$ miles from Paddington.

On the evening in question the trains from London were unusually late. The delay was caused at Oxford in consequence of the floods from the very great quantity of rain which had fallen having rendered a portion of the line impassable for engines, in consequence of which it was necessary to draw the trains through the water by means of horses. The trains from London were stopped at Kennington Crossing between 2 and 3 miles south of the Oxford Station and about a quarter of a mile south of the water. The engine was here shifted to the rear of the carriages, which it pushed to the water's edge; horses were then harnessed to them, and the carriages drawn by them through the water. At the other side the engine which was to take the train on from Oxford was in waiting; this engine was accompanied by a pilotman, who received his instructions from an Inspector of Police, who was stationed on the south side of the water. The actual time required to pass a train through the water was about 12 minutes.

Similar floods recurred at the same place in November 1875 and November 1894, stopping the traffic altogether for some days, the expedient of horses not being tried. After the latter of these, several openings were made to give the flood-water freer passage under the railway, and the line was raised as much as the Abingdon Road Bridge would allow.

The result of the floods was that an extra $\frac{1}{4}$ hour was allowed to Birmingham in December, and in January 1853 the trains were combined with Bristol trains between London and Didcot and took 3 hours 25 minutes. Though they again became independent in May, no further attempt was made for some years to beat the London & North Western time of 3 hours for their 113 miles.

Fast express trains having appeared and disappeared, the next special feature of the Great Western programme was the first Postal Train in the world.

From February 1840 to the end of 1854 the night mails for the West had left Paddington together with passengers at 8.55 p.m. and taken 4 hours and 20 minutes to Bristol, while the Up train took 5 minutes longer (11.50–4.15). Being heavy trains with frequent stops, they appear to have kept bad time, especially in the winter. General complaints of the irregularity of the postal service throughout the three kingdoms culminated in an inquiry by a Committee of the House of Commons into the whole subject in 1854, with the result, as far as the Great Western was concerned, that Rowland Hill of famous memory, Secretary of the Post Office and father of the now defunct Penny Postage, arranged with Saunders for special trains to be run between London and Bristol, exclusively for the use of the Post Office, from 1st February 1855.

The Down train was timed to leave Paddington at 8.46 p.m. and reach Bristol, after stopping at Slough, Maidenhead, Reading, Steventon (for Oxford), Swindon, Chippenham, and Bath, at 12.30, where it overtook the passenger train, which had started at 8.10, and, combined with it, proceeded westward at 12.40, reaching Exeter at 3.20 and Plymouth at 5.45, $\frac{3}{4}$ hour earlier than before. In the opposite direction the train from the west (7.10 from Plymouth and 9.45 from Exeter) having arrived at Bristol at 12.25, the mail vans were detached and left at 12.35, reaching Paddington with the same seven stops at 4.19 a.m., followed at 12.50 by the passengers[1]. The train was a very light one, consisting as a rule of two sorting carriages and a van, and was usually worked by one of the old 7 foot single engines. It was known officially as the 'Special Mail', and among the men as the 'Little Mail'.

Eleven years later the apparatus for picking up and delivering bags without stopping was used at Slough and Maidenhead[2]; so from 1st March 1866 the trains were altered to leave Paddington at 9 o'clock and arrive at 3.55 respectively. In June 1869 the Post Office was persuaded to allow one first-class coach to be attached in each direction for a limited number of passengers between London and Bath and Bristol only. So strict was the limit that even Directors' passes were not available; any Director wishing to travel by the train had to apply for a special pass, which was only issued if there was room for him in the carriage. With this innovation, the trains of course ceased to be 'Special' and became 'Limited' Mails, like those already running on the London & North Western Railway.

Slip carriages made their appearance on the Great Western on 29th November 1858, carriages being detached at Slough and Banbury off the 9.30 a.m. Down Birmingham train. Beyond the fact that the slip guard pulled a rope attached to the coupling, the exact method of detaching the coach is not recorded. The practice was soon extended, and in the course of the next decade slips became fairly common.

Two curious instances are worth notice. In the summer of 1864 the morning express from Bristol, due into Paddington at 11.15, slipped a carriage at West London Junction, which was forthwith worked specially to Kensington and Victoria, where it was due at 11.30. This attempt to make use of the new London Terminus, which the Company had acquired at no small expense, evidently was not a success, for after five months' trial the through service was discontinued, never to be revived. The other instance was and will doubtless remain unique—a slip at Paddington itself! In June 1866 a morning broad-gauge train from Windsor to Bishop's Road and the Metropolitan Line began to slip carriages for Paddington just short of the junction, then at Westbourne Bridge Box, and continued to do so for two years. The slip portion appears from the Service Time Book to have run on by its own impetus into the terminus, where it was due 3 minutes after the main train had arrived at Bishop's Road. As this station was practically part of Paddington, the need for such an exploit is inconceivable.

The practice of diverting a slip coach from the line on which the train passed was quite usual in those days and for long afterwards. As the coach was detached a mile or more from the station and followed the train at a very respectful distance, there was generally no difficulty in changing the points between them. For several years from 1869 onwards the evening express to Birmingham via Didcot Loop used to slip a carriage

---

[1] Until September 1858 the night passenger train left Bristol at 11.30 p.m., Shunted for the Mail at Reading and reached Paddington at 4.50 a.m.

[2] It had been installed at West Drayton, Slough, Maidenhead, Wallingford Road and Faringdon Road in September 1858.

for Didcot, which ran on into the station and connected with a slow train to Swindon, while the Reading slips off Up trains were diverted across the Down line into the Up station there.[1]

The speed of Great Western trains, though better than that on the other English lines, remained distinctly poor till almost the end of the 'fifties. After 1852 no further effort was made to show the superiority of the Broad Gauge, and for more than six years there was no 50 miles an hour run on the system, while both Bristol and Birmingham were over 3 hours from Paddington.

The Birmingham service was the first to be improved. From May to August 1857, the 9.15 a.m. from Paddington, calling at Reading, Oxford and Leamington, reached Birmingham at 12.5; in September and October it was given 3 hours, thence more until 1859. In May 1859 two Down trains were timed to cover the 129¼ miles from Paddington, with three stops, in 2 hours 50 minutes, 10 minutes less than the best train from Euston over a route 16½ miles shorter. One of them (6.30 p.m.) ran to Didcot, 53⅛ miles,[2] in the even hour, and continued to do so until the second general slackening of speed in June 1864. The other (9.50 a.m.) stopped at Reading instead of Didcot and nowhere exceeded 48 miles an hour; it relapsed to 3 hours a year later, and to 3 hours 20 minutes in October 1861, when it became a narrow-gauge through train to Birkenhead. In the opposite direction the North Western time of 3 hours was not improved on.

The spur of competition was evidently needed to effect any acceleration of the Bristol and West of England service. This came at last in February 1862, when the London & South Western authorities, without any notice to the Broad Gauge Companies, suddenly altered their express, 12 noon from Waterloo, to run their 171½ miles to Exeter in 4¾ hours, 25 minutes quicker than the best train from Paddington. This alarmed the Bristol & Exeter Directors, and a conference was held at their request between Saunders, Gooch, Kelley, and Graham of the Great Western, Dykes of the Bristol & Exeter, and Cockshott of the South Devon, which resulted in a recommendation to the two Boards concerned that the 4½ hours of 1845–9 should be re-established. New expresses were accordingly put on on 1st March to do the 194 miles in this time, leaving Paddington at 11.45 and Exeter at 10.30 a.m. respectively. The Down train stopped at Didcot, Swindon, Bath, Bristol, where it backed into the Bristol & Exeter Express Platform, and Taunton, and was allowed only 57 minutes to Didcot, 2 minutes more than its 1848 predecessor, but with a heavier train and an extra ¼ mile to run—which meant a start to stop speed of 56 miles an hour. The Up had an additional stop at Chippenham, but

---

[1] At Reading, this practice, begun with the first slip in 1864, continued till 1898. In July 1897 no less than thirteen Up trains slipped carriages there daily.

[2] The opening of the new station at Paddington in 1854 had made all distances thence a quarter of a mile longer.

EXETER EXPRESSES, 1862–1867

| Miles from Paddington | | | | 1862 March | 1864 June | 1865 December | 1867 June to October |
|---|---|---|---|---|---|---|---|
| | | | Down Train | | | | |
| | — | Paddington | dep. | 11 45 | 11 45 | 11 45 | 11 45 |
| | 53⅛ | Didcot | arr. | 12 42 | — | — | — |
| G.W.R. | | | dep. | 12 45 | — | — | — |
| | 77¼ | Swindon | arr. | 1 15 | 1 15 | 1 20 | 1 30 |
| | | | dep. | 1 25 | 1 25 | 1 30 | 1 40 |
| | 106⅞ | Bath | arr. | 2 2 | 2 2 | 2 9 | 2 19 |
| | | | dep. | 2 5 | 2 5 | 2 13 | 2 23 |
| | 118½ | Bristol | arr. | 2 25 | 2 25 | 2 33 | 2 43 |
| | | (B. & E. Station) | dep. | 2 30 | 2 30 | 2 38 | 2 50 |
| B.&.E.R. | — | Bridgwater[1] | | — | — | — | 3 38 |
| | 163¼ | Taunton[1] | | 3 30 | 3 30 | 3 34 | 3 55 |
| | | Tiverton Junction[1] | | — | — | — | 4 31 |
| | 194 | Exeter | arr. | 4 15 | 4 15 | 4 15 | 4 50 |

| Miles. Intermediate | | | | 1862 March | 1864 June | 1865 December | 1867 June to October |
|---|---|---|---|---|---|---|---|
| | | | Up Train | | | | |
| B.&.E.R. | | Exeter | dep. | 10 30 | 10 30 | 10 30 | 10 20 |
| | 30¾ | Taunton[1] | | 11 8 | 11 8 | 11 8 | 11 5 |
| | — | Bridgwater[1] | | — | — | — | 11 25 |
| | 44¾ | Bristol | arr. | 12 12 | 12 12 | 12 12 | 12 15 |
| | | (B. & E. Express Platform) | dep. | 12 15 | 12 15 | 12 20 | 12 20 |
| | 11⅝ | Bath | arr. | 12 32 | 12 32 | 12 37 | 12 37 |
| | | | dep. | 12 35 | 12 35 | 12 40 | 12 40 |
| G.W.R. | 13 | Chippenham | arr. | 12 53 | 12 53 | 12 59 | 12 59 |
| | | | dep. | 12 55 | 12 55 | 1 2 | 1 2 |
| | 16⅝ | Swindon | arr. | 1 20 | 1 20 | 1 27 | 1 30 |
| | | | dep. | 1 30 | 1 30 | 1 37 | 1 40 |
| | 24⅛ | Didcot | arr. | 1 58 | — | — | — |
| | | | dep. | 2 0 | — | — | — |
| | — | Reading (Slip) | — | — | (2 18) | (2 25) | (2 32) |
| | 53⅛ | Paddington | arr. | 3 0 | 3 0 | 3 10 | 3 20 |

used the Express Platform at Bristol and so saved time there; its fastest run was from Didcot to Paddington in the even hour.

Like their predecessors, these trains were far and away the fastest in the world, and soon inherited the old more or less dormant title of 'Flying Dutchman', by which they were generally known for more than forty years.

Unfortunately the speed soon began to deteriorate. It seems that in bad weather or with a strong side wind the drivers could not, or perhaps from coal economy motives would not, keep time to Swindon, so in June 1864, after the trains had been running for over two years, the Didcot stop was cut out, while the 90 minutes to and from Swindon remained unaltered, thereby reducing the fastest booked speed from 56 to 51½ miles an hour.

During the next three years the trains were twice further slowed by the Great Western till at last they took 3 hours between London and Bristol

[1] The B. & E.R. 'Working Time Books' give one time only at these stations, and do not state whether it is arrival or departure.

and so ceased to be expresses, according to the now generally accepted definition of 40 miles an hour including stops. At first the Bristol & Exeter made up for its partner's deficiencies and preserved the 4½ hours to Exeter by the Down train, but on the second occasion it was evidently sickened, and followed suit by inserting stops at Bridgwater and Tiverton Junction and taking 2 hours to cover its 75½ miles, thus helping to make the time from London to Exeter as much as 5 hours and 5 minutes. Needless to say, 'Express Fares' continued to be charged by both Companies, as indeed they were by two still slower trains.[1] The London & South Western best times at this period were 4 hours 58 minutes Down and 5 hours 22 minutes Up. Evidently the three Companies had agreed not to 'race' too hard!

After this debacle it is almost a relief to find that the 'Dutchman' ceased to fly in November 1867, to begin a longer and more auspicious life eighteen months later. Its times during this, its second incarnation, are given in the following table. The trains usually consisted of seven 6-wheeled coaches each of Swindon (one each for Cheltenham and Weymouth) and five beyond, alternatively Great Western and Bristol & Exeter stock, three to and from Torquay, and two to and from Plymouth.

The rest of the train service throughout the 'fifties and 'sixties calls for little comment; though up to the general standard of the period, it was anything but fast. The West Midland and South Wales amalgamations made no difference in this respect. There were, it is true, a few trains on those sections which did not stop at all stations, and even some in South Wales by which express fares were charged, but none that could be called fast. The two or three new narrow-gauge trains of 1861 between London and the Northern and West Midland Lines were timed very easily, it being an axiom at Paddington that narrow-gauge trains could not possibly run as fast as broad-gauge.

The 'lowest order of passengers', as Saunders called them in 1839, who travelled third-class, were not encouraged. In the later 'fifties two, or sometimes three, through trains conveyed such people from Paddington: the 'Plymouth Cheap' at 6 a.m. for stations beyond Highbridge (later Bath), Frome, and Gloucester; the 'Cheap' at about 7 a.m.[2] for Great Western stations in general; and the 'Northern Cheap' at about 7.40 a.m. for stations beyond Birmingham; the last two were often combined as far as Didcot. The 'Plymouth Cheap' ran 'fast' to Swindon in 2 hours 40 minutes, stopping only at Reading and Didcot, and reached Bristol in a little less than 5 hours, but the other or others stopped at all stations and took about 7 to Bristol and Birmingham and 12 to Chester. Not till 1860 did third-class passengers get a chance of starting at a reasonable hour— between 11 and 12—for such distant stations as Exeter, Birmingham, Shrewsbury, and Birkenhead; while during 1861 those for Gloucester and

---

[1] To Exeter these were 5s more than the ordinary fares of 35s First and 25s Second. To Bristol they were respectively 26s 1d and 18s 3d as against 20s 10d and 15s 8d.

[2] A note in the time-tables announced that 'The Booking Office Doors will be closed at 6.50 in order that this train may start punctually at 7.0'.

Cheltenham only were for some obscure reason, probably North Western and Midland competition, actually allowed to travel as far as Didcot at 53 miles an hour by the fastest train on the line, the 6.30 p.m. Birmingham Express! Locally and on branches, one or sometimes two trains each way were marked 1, 2, 3, in the time-tables; it was only between Birmingham and Wolverhampton that the 3 was at all common. Matters had only slightly improved by the end of 1869. There were then generally two or sometimes three third-class trains between the more important places, but even between towns so close together as London and Windsor, or Bristol and Bath, there were only five. In fact they were exceptional, by far the greater number of trains being first and second only. It by no means followed because trains had third-class carriages that anyone might use them. Far from it; many carried such passengers between certain specified stations only, and the time-tables are full of voluminous notes to this effect. The necessity for such complicated restrictions, which were common on many larger railways, is not apparent and has not been fully explained.

## ROYAL TRAINS

The Great Western had been open for four years between London and Slough before Queen Victoria ventured on her first railway journey. Meanwhile her suitor, as he then was, Prince Albert, made his on 14th November 1839, when, accompanied by his elder brother, he took the train from Slough to Paddington, proceeding thence by road to Dover on his return home from a visit to Her Majesty at Windsor. After his marriage in the following year he soon became a frequent traveller, several specials being run for him in the autumn of 1840, one of which, on 21st September, drawn by *Sun*, one of Gooch's 6 foot single class, is recorded to have covered the 18¼ miles in 22½ minutes. Anticipating that the Queen must soon be converted, the Directors had their first Royal Saloon built.[1] This was ready in July 1840, and was first used, not by Queen Victoria, but by the Dowager Queen Adelaide, from Wallingford Road to Slough on 15th August. The Queen of England was not even the first reigning Sovereign to use the English railways. On 24th January 1842 the King of Prussia, Frederick William IV, who had come to Windsor for the christening of the Prince of Wales, went up to London by the Great Western for a day's sightseeing.

At last the Queen suddenly made up her mind, and on a Saturday afternoon Saunders was notified that Her Majesty, with Prince Albert and their suite, desired to travel from Slough to Paddington on the following Monday, 13th June 1842. In spite of the short notice all was got ready in good time, and before noon the Royal Train, consisting of *Phlegethon*—one of the 7 foot singles—an open second-class carriage with brakes, a saloon, the Royal Saloon, another saloon, and three carriage trucks, was waiting in Slough Station.

[1] See Chapter XVI.

At Slough the Royal party, on their arrival at the station a few minutes before 12 o'clock in six carriages, were received by Mr C. Russell the Chairman, Mr F. P. Barlow one of the Directors, and Mr C. A. Saunders the Secretary of the Company, and conducted to the splendid apartments at the station designed for the reception of Royalty. Her Majesty, however, during the delay necessarily occasioned by the placing of the carriages of the attendants on the trucks, proceeded to examine the line and the Royal Saloon, enquiring very minutely into the whole of the arrangements. Precisely at 12 o'clock the train left Slough for Paddington, Mr Gooch, the Superintendent of the Locomotive Department, accompanied by Mr Brunel, the Engineer, driving the Engine.[1]

At Paddington by 11 o'clock the centre of the wide space apportioned for the arrival of trains was parted off and carpeted with a crimson carpet, which reached from one end of the platform to the other. The whole of the arrangements for the reception of the Royal party were under the superintendence of Mr Seymour Clarke, the Superintendent of the line, assisted by Supt. Collard of the Company's Police. Capt. Hay, Assistant Commissioner of Metropolitan Police, and Supt. Lincoln and a large body of the D Division were also present.

Before 12 o'clock large numbers of elegantly dressed ladies consisting of the families and friends of the Directors and Officers of the Company were arranged on each side of the part apportioned for the arrival of the Royal train, and at five minutes before 12 o'clock Her Majesty's Carriage drawn by four horses arrived from the Royal Mews at Pimlico, and a few minutes afterwards a detachment of the 8th Royal Irish Hussars under the command of Capt. G. Brown arrived from the Barracks at Kensington for the purpose of acting as an escort to Her Mejesty.

Precisely at 25 minutes past 12 o'clock the Royal Special train entered the Terminus having performed the distance in 25 minutes, and on Her Majesty alighting she was received with the most deafening demonstration of loyalty and affection we have ever experienced. H.R.H. Prince Albert alighted first. Her Majesty, on being handed out of the Saloon, in a most condescending manner returned the gratulations of the assembly present. The cheers were re-echoed by the numerous persons who crowded the Bridge over the Terminus leading to Paddington Green and lined the avenue towards the Junction Road, along which the Royal cavalcade passed. Her Majesty reached Buckingham Palace shortly before one o'clock, round which a large assemblage of respectable persons was waiting her arrival, by whom she was loudly cheered.

So much for Queen Victoria's first railway journey. She was evidently pleased with the experience, for on 23rd July she returned from Paddington to Slough with Prince Albert, the Princess Royal, and the Prince of Wales, aged eight months—his first trip. This time the three carriage trucks were dispensed with, and the train consisted of the usual open 'brake second' and the Royal Saloon between two firsts, drawn by *Mentor*, another of the 7 foot singles. After this Her Majesty used the Great Western constantly between Slough or Windsor and Paddington during the rest of her long reign.

On 19th July 1843 Prince Albert made what was then considered a fast journey from Paddington to Bristol and back, the occasion being the launch of the *Great Britain* steamship, designed by Brunel. In the early portion of the *Diaries of Sir Daniel Gooch*, written some thirty years later, the return journey is stated to have been made in the surprising time of 2 hours and 4 minutes. Contemporary accounts, however, record it with details as 2 hours and *forty* minutes! The engine was *Damon* and the load four coaches. The Down journey took 3 hours 6 minutes with a special

---

[1] It is as well to state here, in view of legends to the contrary, that Brunel told the Parliamentary Committee on Railways in March 1841: 'I never dare drive an engine, although I always go upon the engine; because if I go upon a bit of the line without anything to attract my attention I begin thinking of something else'. Nothing has been found to suggest that he ever changed his attitute; he was not a locomotive engineer.

stop of 7 minutes at Bath, where an address was presented; the other stops in both directions were at Reading and Swindon.

The first of the Queen's northern journeys affecting the Great Western appears to have been that made in the autumn of 1849 from Scotland to the Isle of Wight. It afforded her personal experience of the inconvenience of a break of gauge, of which she had doubtless heard and read much. Arriving at Gloucester by the Midland from Derby, where she had spent the night, Her Majesty was of course obliged to change on to the Broad Gauge, and it may be that the new and luxurious saloon lately built to supersede the original of 1840 consoled her to some extent for the trouble. In charge of Saunders and Seymour Clarke, the Royal Train then proceeded to Reading and Basingstoke, where the Queen had to change back to the Narrow Gauge for Gosport. Next year she used the London & North Western and Midland Lines from and to Euston via Rugby, Derby, and York, and in 1851 Seymour Clarke was responsible for her train in his new capacity of General Manager of the Great Northern, then open from Maiden Lane to Doncaster via Lincoln.

At the end of August 1852 the Royal party once more adopted the route from Gosport to Scotland via Basingstoke, Reading, and Gloucester, in spite of the two inevitable changes it involved.

It was on this occasion that Saunders received from Her Majesty's Equerry, the Hon. Alexander Gordon, instructions as to the speed of the Royal Train, which he was commanded to convey to the other Companies.

OSBORNE<br>
*Aug.* 26. 1852.

My dear Sir

I am desired to intimate Her Majesty's wish that the speed of the Royal Train on the 30th & 31st should on no account be increased at any one part of the line in order to make up for the time lost by an unforseen delay at another, so that if any unexpected delay does take place no attempt is to be made to regain the time by travelling faster than what has been agreed upon in the Time-bill you have sent me.

This order has probably arisen from one of the Directors telling Her Majesty last year that they had been driving the Train at the rate of <u>60 miles</u> an hour, a gratuitous piece of information which very naturally alarmed Her Majesty, although it was probably incorrect.

I have to request you will communicate Her Majesty's wishes to the Secretarys of the other Railways concerned.

I remain,<br>
Yours truly<br>
ALEX GORDON.

Returning from Balmoral on 12th October, the Queen, Prince Albert, and the Prince of Wales paid a visit of inspection to Robert Stephenson's famous Britannia Tubular Bridge over the Menai Straits, then lately opened, spending a night at Bangor for the purpose. After the inspection, the Royal Train returned over the Chester & Holyhead Railway to Saltney Junction, whence the Shrewsbury & Chester Company took it to Shrewsbury, and, after luncheon there, the Shrewsbury & Birmingham Company on to Wolverhampton (High Level Station). There the London & North Western took charge, and the train proceeded over the Stour Valley line, through Birmingham, to the point on the Midland Railway towards Gloucester where the newly opened Great Western passed under it close to the present Bordesley Junction. Temporary platforms had been set up there on both railways, and Her Majesty walked down to the low level and travelled on the Broad Gauge direct to Windsor. Thus the Queen used all she could of the future Great Western route from Chester, and patronised the Birmingham and Oxford line within a fortnight of its opening.

Next year Leamington was tried as the point of exchange between the broad- and narrow-gauge systems, Her Majesty with Prince Albert and their family travelling from Southampton via Basingstoke, where she of course had to change from narrow to broad, in August, and returning to Windsor in October. After this she seems to have had enough of these breaks of gauge, and for the next seven years adopted the Great Northern route to and from Scotland, at first going by train between Windsor and Paddington, and driving to King's Cross, and later using the South Western, North & South Western Junction, London & North Western, and North London Railways between Windsor and King's Cross Goods Station, via Kew, Willesden, and Chalk Farm.

For the return journey to Osborne in September 1860 a new route was arranged, London & North Western from Carlisle to Bushbury Junction near Wolverhampton, thence by the West Midland and the Great Western narrow-gauge rails via Birmingham and Oxford and the Didcot and Reading Loops direct to Basingstoke and the South Western Railway. This at once became the regular route between the Isle of Wight and Scotland, but the Great Northern continued to be used from and to Windsor till April 1862, when, narrow-gauge rails having recently been completed between Reading and Windsor, the widowed Queen was enabled to make the first of her many journeys thence via Bushbury to the North without change of carriage. From this time onwards to the end of her reign Her Majesty travelled regularly by the Bushbury route to and from Balmoral—usually four times a year—from Windsor about 20th May, returning in June, then from Gosport at the end of August, and back to Windsor in November, the narrow-gauge Royal Train for these journeys being provided by the London & North Western Company. Between Windsor and Osborne, she used to 'go Great Western' to and from Basingstoke, of course on the narrow-gauge rails.

Special care was of course always taken of the Royal Train. The Company's police, reinforced by porters and permanent way men, were stationed all along the line; goods trains on the opposite road were stopped; and a pilot engine was dispatched $\frac{1}{4}$ hour in front of the train, nothing being allowed to foul the line after the passing of the pilot. Later, after the general introduction of the telegraph, a special instrument was carried in the train, by means of which a connection with the wires could be established anywhere on the line in case of emergency.

## SPECIAL AND EXCURSION TRAINS

The first special trains were run on the very next day after the opening to Maidenhead. The *Times* of the opening day contains an advertisement that 'On Tuesday, 5th June there will be two extra trains for the convenience of persons visiting Eton Montem', giving the times of starting from Paddington and Maidenhead, and concluding, 'These extra trains will not call at West Drayton'.

In 1839 there were some for Ascot Races, and in connection with the return trains in the evening there was trouble at Slough. Saunders told a Parliamentary Committee about it afterwards: how, the train being full, many passengers climbed on to the roofs of the carriages and refused to come down, whereupon the staunch conductor refused to start the train till they did, and so kept it more than ½ hour, for which very proper conduct the Secretary commended him.

In April 1841 he told a similar Committee that there had been frequent extra trains last summer but few since, save several in the autumn for Prince Albert. In the winter of 1839 on several nights there had been 'express engines up on the occasion of the Monmouth trials', presumably with news of the results of these trials of Chartist rioters from Newport.

When the first special excursion train was run has not been ascertained; the point is hardly of much interest.[1] On Michaelmas Day 1842 between six and seven hundred persons were brought up from Bristol, Bath, Chippenham, and Swindon at half the usual fares for a day in the Metropolis by an early morning train—a regular one, however—but whether this was the first instance of excursion bookings seems very doubtful. Soon after this, if not before, excursion trains became a normal feature of the summer season.

An interesting insight into excursion train working in later but still early days is afforded by a Board of Trade Report on an accident which befell one of these trains, full of passengers returning from the Great Exhibition, at Fox's Wood near Bristol on 10th August 1851.

The train consisted of 28 carriages drawn by an engine; it left London about 8.20 p.m.; the superintendent of police and a porter occupied a break-van in the centre of the train, and another porter was placed in the last carriage in charge of another break; this arrangement lasted to Swindon, but thence to Chippenham the porter riding with the superintendent got into a carriage having a break, so that there were three breaks going down the Wootton Bassett incline, The train arrived at Reading about 9.30 and reached Swindon a little before the mail, which is due there at 11.40. Here there were some passengers to discharge, and ten carriages to take on, full of passengers who had been forwarded by a preceding excursion train going to Cheltenham [which had left London at 7.35]. A delay of about an hour occurred before again starting. The train then proceeded to Chippenham [with 38 carriages, be it noted!], where it arrived at 1.15 and left at 2.15, a delay of nearly [*sic*] another hour, caused, it is stated, by the number of passengers to be discharged, stopping at and proceeding on from Chippenham, and having to detach ten carriages. The train then proceeded to Bath, where it arrived at 2.50. A detention of 10 minutes occurred there, when the train proceeded on its journey. About five miles from Bath it slackened speed very much, and at about three miles farther it

---

[1] The first special excursion train in Britain at really cheap fares, appears to have been run by the little Bodmin & Wadebridge Railway in Cornwall, on 14th June 1836. The 'attraction' was a public hanging at Bodmin.

came to a standstill a short distance from the Brislington Tunnel. The driver's account of the stoppage is that after leaving Bath, finding that but one of his pumps would work, and that the water was getting low in his boiler, he reduced his steam so low that for fear of a stoppage in the tunnel he pulled up at the entrance, intending to wait till his steam should get up. The train had hardly come to a standstill when it was run into by a pilot engine, which had left Bristol at 12.45 that morning to assist a goods train up the Box incline and was then on its return from Corsham; it had been detained at Bath for 23 minutes after the excursion train had started, and the driver was aware of the cause of his detention.

The amount of damage is not stated, but apparently no one was killed. The Inspector 'supposes' that the driver and fireman of the pilot engine were asleep, and has some nasty remarks to make about the Company's excursion arrangements.

# XIV

# *Staff, Organization, and Early Methods*

## STAFF

The original staff, wherewith the Company began work in June 1838, consisted, besides the necessary clerks, of Police, Conductors, Guards, Porters, some 'Boys to attend on the First Class Passengers', and of course Engine-drivers and Firemen. Save the last two, who were engaged by Gooch subject to Brunel's approval, all were appointed by the Board of Directors, or a committee thereof, after a personal interview, and continued to be so appointed until 1865.

The Police formed the most important class, and were all sworn constables. It is not strictly accurate to say they were appointed by the Board, for the Incorporation Act of 1835 provided that they should be appointed by 'two or more Justices of the Peace acting within their Jurisdiction' on the nomination of any three Directors of the Company, and should forthwith take an oath 'duly to execute the office of constable within the said Railway and other Works'. Having been so sworn, they were invested with all such powers 'as constables duly appointed now have by the Laws and Statutes of this Kingdom', subject to dismissal by the Justices or any three or more Directors. They had their Inspectors, Sub-Inspectors, and Sergeants, and were modelled on the Metropolitan Police Force of the day, wearing a similar uniform, even to the 'on duty' wristlet as shown in the illustration on page 313. Each man was provided with a constable's staff or truncheon, about 18 inches long, on which a large crown was elaborately hand-painted in gold, picked out with red, green, and white, with 'GWR' in gold letters beneath; and each Inspector carried a short hollow brass and ebony baton surmounted by a crown and containing his warrant of authority on a small parchment scroll.

Some of these constables were posted at the stations while the remainder patrolled their beats, into which the whole line was divided. Their duties are described in the following extract from the Rules of February 1841:

The duties of the Police may be stated generally to consist in the preservation of order in all the stations and on the line of railway. They are to give and receive signals; to keep the line free from casual or wilful obstructions; to assist in case of accidents; to caution strangers of danger on the railway; to remove intruders of all descriptions; to superintend and manage the crosses or switches; to give notice of arrivals or departures; to direct persons into the entrance to the stations or sheds; to watch movements of embankments or cuttings; to inspect the rails and solidity of the timber; to guard and watch the company's premises; and to convey the earliest information on every subject to their appointed station or superior officer.

They were indeed men of all work, and several present-day grades of railwaymen, apart from Signalmen and Special Police, are descended from them. Very soon they were relieved of the duties of permanent way inspection, but on the other hand those at stations were about the same time made responsible for the collection of tickets; the special grade of Ticket Collector was a later growth.

We learn from Saunders' evidence before the Select Committee on Railways in August 1839 that already some of the best policemen had been chosen to manage the switches, and were called 'switchmen' and received higher pay than 'common constables', as well as a bonus of £3 or £5 a year for managing their switches correctly. Four bonuses entitled the recipient to wear a red chevron on his left sleeve. Brunel told the same Committee in March 1841 that the number of police on the Great Western averaged $1\frac{1}{2}$ per mile, including all policemen at the stations, at each of which there were several; the number on the line varied greatly, apparently according to the likelihood of trespassing in the locality; for instance, on the $7\frac{1}{2}$ miles between Maidenhead and Twyford there were only two.

At first there was only one Inspector of Police—in early days he was sometimes referred to as 'Superintendent'—who covered the whole of the London Division as it gradually extended. When the line was opened throughout another was appointed at Bristol for that Division, followed thirteen years later by a third for the new Northern Division. When the number of Divisions was greatly increased after the 1863 amalgamations, an Inspector was appointed for each, who soon became known as Chief Inspector, to distinguish him from his Sub-Inspectors, who by this time had dropped the sub- and were called District Inspectors. As early as November 1838 each Sub-Inspector was ordered to patrol his district, and for the next forty years the current rules bade him 'from time to time, at uncertain intervals, and both by day and night, to walk through his district, and to report to his Superintendent any irregularity he may detect, either in the conduct of the men or in the state of the signals, switches, etc.' There is an old Great Western story of a conscientious and unpopular Sub-Inspector carrying out this rule one dark night in the middle 'fifties, soon after the installation of the telegraph, and being nearly brained by one of his own policemen, who sprang out of his lonely sentry-box and smote him sorely with his truncheon, taking him—so the man afterwards declared—for one of a gang of wire-cutters he had been warned to look out for.

The Conductors can be best described as 'train-masters', similar in their way to station masters. Each train was in the charge of one of them, who was responsible for its general working and the safe delivery of the passengers at their destinations, as well as for seeing that they all provided themselves with proper tickets. Although we read of a fracas at Paddington on one occasion when a passenger tried to insist on taking possession of the 'Conductors Box'[1] and had to be forcibly ejected therefrom, it seems that these functionaries as often as not travelled on the engine, the driver being placed by the rules 'under the order of the Conductor in all matters

[1] No description of the early carriage stock discloses the whereabouts of this 'box'.

affecting the starting, stopping or motions of the train'. Saunders told the aforesaid Committee of Parliament in April 1841 that a way-bill was made up by the clerk at the starting station and handed to the Conductor in charge of the train, who entered thereon all irregularities and eventually gave it in to the Superintendent of the finishing station; also that the Conductors and not the Station Clerks were responsible for getting the trains away from the stations. That these Conductors were very superior persons is shown by the facts that they got nearly double the wages of the Guards, and did not wear uniform. They had a short life, being taken off the trains in June 1842, when some were set to collect tickets at Paddington, Bristol, Bath, and Bridgwater, and Saunders was directed to arrange for the transfer of the rest to other duties.

The Guards, of whom there seem to have been at least two with every train, occupied themselves in opening and shutting doors, seeing to the stowage of luggage and parcels, attending to such brakes as there were on the train, and generally carrying out the Conductor's orders. When the Conductors disappeared, the senior Guards took over such of their duties as were not transferred to the Station Superintendents and Station Clerks, and had their wages considerably increased, though not to the Conductors' scale; so the change was an economical one.

The Porters need no comment; the duties of their ancient calling were much the same in 1838 as they are to-day.

The 'Boys to attend on the First Class Passengers' must remain mysterious. What they did and where and how they did it is not recorded. Their attendance seems to have been of very short duration; in fact, we hear no more of them, except that they wore 'common close jackets and trowsers'. Some of them at any rate were Conductors' sons.

Last but not least, the first woman on the staff remains to be noticed. On 25th May 1838 the Directors appointed Mary Coulsell 'Female Attendant at Paddington'.

Early in the same month they had decided on the uniform, or livery as they called it, by adopting the following Minutes of a special Sub-Committee:

Upon consideration of the Livery, IT WAS RESOLVED

That the Coats and Waistcoats be made of dark rifle green edged with scarlet of the patterns now chosen.

That the trowsers be made of dark Oxford mixture of the pattern also chosen.

That the Buttons be gilt and of the size now exhibited as a Pattern.

That the Inspector of Police be distinguished by a red stripe of an inch and a quarter on the Trowsers.

That the Sub-Inspectors be marked by an edging on the Trowsers of the same width as the edging of the Coat.

That the Policemen have G.W.R. with a number marked on the stand-up collar in scarlet cloth.

That the Hats of the Policemen be precisely similar to those of the Metropolitan Police.

That the Conductor be required to wear a small Badge on the button hole of his Coat with the Buttons of G.W.R., not having any Livery.

That the Guards have a Frock Coat and Waistcoat with G.W.R. on the fall of the Collar.

Trowsers of Oxford Mixture plain.

The boys to have a common close Jacket with Trowsers.

The Porters to have sleeved Jackets with G.W.R. painted on the Glazed Hats and a badge with G.W.R. and a number on the arm.

In the following September it was decided that the Porters should be clothed in 'green plush'; and green plush or corduroy they continued to wear till 1852, when the green was changed to brown, on account of its liability to fade and look dirty from exposure to the weather. After this common brown corduroys remained the Great Western porters' uniform until 1859, when green was resumed.

All the men, even the Porters, wore top-hats, those of the Police being of beaver with a leather crown and leather sidestays.

Guards are required to wear their proper uniform with their *hats* and not caps, while on the platform at any station.

is a rule appearing in the book of 1848. Four years later caps were substituted, the Board having decided, in March 1851, on caps instead of hats for Guards after the current year's contract. The glazed top-hats of the Porters had already gone.

In 1852 the clothing provided by the Company was as follows:

PASSENGER GUARDS. 1 great coat, 1 frock coat, 2 waistcoats, 2 pairs of trowsers, 2 pairs of boots,[1] and 1 cap yearly.

GOODS GUARDS. 1 great coat, 1 jacket, 1 waistcoat, 2 pairs of trowsers, 2 pairs of boots,[1] and 1 cap yearly.

POLICE. 1 great coat, and 1 cape every two years; and 1 dress coat, 2 pairs trowsers, 2 pairs of boots,[1] 1 stock and 1 hat yearly.

PORTERS. 1 cape every two years; and 2 jackets, 2 pairs of boots,[1] and 1 cap yearly.

Not till 1859 did the Police get rid of their heavy leather-crowned top-hats. At a Board Meeting early in March of that year 'the advantages of substituting caps for hats in the case of policemen were discussed, and it being considered that such alteration would be productive of comfort to the men as well as economy to the Company', the Directors decided to carry it into effect. A fortnight later they went further and, after ordering the frock coats of Guards to be made of West of England cloth, instructed the contractor to prepare a new pattern of a single-breasted dress coat for the police. This was produced at the next meeting and approved, and the new caps were ordered to be made of green cloth of the same shade as the coats. Thus the Police were at last relieved not only of their heavy hats but also of their tightly belted coats and leather stocks. The great majority of them, being really nothing more or less than signalmen, had already ceased to be sworn in as constables.

The Engine-drivers and Firemen seem at first to have been all gathered by Gooch from the North of England. They were chosen for mechanical rather than literary attainments, many of them being unable to read or write. Brunel told the Committee of 1841 that non-reading men were the best drivers as their minds were not so liable to wander. 'The best Engine-driver, now a foreman at Reading, can neither read nor write; he has a clerk.'

[1] The issue of boots, save to men already appointed, ceased in 1868.

As to dress, the Rule Books till 1855 laid down:

Every Engineman and Fireman must appear on duty dressed in white fustian clothes, which are to be clean every Monday morning, or on Sunday, when he may be required to work on that day.

Like the switchmen, the drivers were, from the beginning, given bonuses for good conduct and the economical working of their engines.

The Great Western Railway Provident Society was established in December 1838, 'for the purpose of affording relief to its members in sickness, providing a pension in case of permanent incapacity for labour through sickness, accident, or old age, and the means of decent burial for themselves and wives'. Membership was at first voluntary, but by 1848 it had been made a condition of the service. A widows and orphans fund was subsequently established in connection with the Society.

## ORGANIZATION

### TRAFFIC DEPARTMENT

Brunel's chief clerk at 18 Duke Street, Seymour Clarke, was chosen early in 1837 to be the first traffic officer of the Great Western Railway. He thereupon left Brunel's service and went, as he told the Gauge Commissioners later, to Belgium and the North of England and other places to see the different systems of traffic working and learn the business. Having spent more than a year in this way he entered on his duties at Paddington with the title of Chief Superintendent some few months before the opening to Maidenhead.

Two years later a younger brother, Frederick Clarke, was appointed Superintendent at Bristol in anticipation of the opening thence to Bath in August 1840.

Seymour Clarke's authority went forward with the successive openings till at last it reached Chippenham and Cirencester, but on the opening throughout at the end of June 1841 he gave up the main line west of Swindon to his brother of Bristol, who also had charge of the successive sections of the Bristol & Exeter Railway. Meanwhile, in November 1840 the Directors had appointed Saunders 'General Superintendent of the Line', which made him what he had been from the first in all but name— the chief traffic officer. Less than a year later the Clarke brothers were directed to act 'in the capacity of Assistants to the General Superintendent of the Line for their respective districts'. They were therefore the first Divisional Superintendents, and Saunders the first Superintendent of the Line.

Under them were several 'District Superintendents', as the officers in charge of the principal stations were styled, each being responsible for a varying number of small stations, at which subordinate 'Station Clerks' were posted. In 1854 these local districts averaged six to eight stations and about 28 miles of line. For example, the Oxford District, one of the largest, then included Wallingford Road, Shrivenham, and Aynho; and the

Reading District, another large one, Twyford, Goring, Hungerford, and Basingstoke.

By the end of 1848 the London Division extended to Cheltenham, Oxford, Hungerford, and Basingstoke, and the Bristol Division from the confines of Swindon to Exeter and Westbury. In the following May the loss of the Bristol & Exeter Railway cut the latter off short at Bristol and so reduced it to very modest dimensions.

We have seen[1] that the general reduction of salaries recommended by the Committee of Consultation and unwillingly effected by the Board early in 1850 caused many of the officers and principal clerks to seek other employment 'in despair of improving their position in the present service'. Among these were the two Clarkes, who left in June, Seymour to become General Manager of the new Great Northern Railway, and Frederick for the post of Superintendent of the South Wales Railway, just about to be opened.

The new superintendent of the London Division, now cut down to the lines east of Swindon, was George Nugent Tyrrell, who entered the service as station clerk at Keynsham in December 1842, and after being at Exeter and Gloucester became superintendent of the Cirencester District in January 1850. The Bristol Division, increased by the addition of Swindon and the Cheltenham Branch, was placed under Thomas Graham, who joined at Cirencester when the railway opened in May 1841 and was the first superintendent at Gloucester, going thence to Reading in January 1848.

At the beginning of 1855, when the Shrewsbury Railways were absorbed into the system, a new Northern Division was constituted with headquarters at Shrewsbury, the two old divisions being at the same time renamed Southern and Western respectively. The Northern Division then took Birmingham and all north of it, the Southern all south of Birmingham and east of Swindon, and the Western Swindon and the rest. The new superintendent at Shrewsbury was James Kelley, a booking clerk at Paddington on the opening in 1838, and afterwards district superintendent successively at Steventon (1840), Oxford (1844), and Birmingham (1852). No further alteration was made till after the amalgamations of 1863, save that in November 1860 Kelley came to London in place of Tyrrell, who went to the Northern Division, and a month later, doubtless on account of the acquisition of the Birkenhead Railway, moved its headquarters from Shrewsbury to Chester, where they remained to the end of the Company's existence.

The petty local superintendents with their station clerks continued throughout this period and down to the general reorganization in 1864–5, when their districts were gradually abolished and they became either full-blown Divisional Superintendents or mere station masters with authority limited to their own stations. Long before this the station clerks

[1] Page 161.

had come to be generally called station masters, and the title was officially adopted about 1860. Until 1865 they, and of course the superintendents also, wore plain clothes with the inevitable top-hat, but apparently no badge of office.

In the course of the 'fifties some of the least important stations, mostly on newly opened country branches, were placed in the charge of policemen styled 'Booking Constables' instead of clerks. It is interesting to note that this economical plan was revived in the late 1920's. From that time many smaller stations were placed in charge of senior porters and supervised in groups by the station master at a nearby larger station. In some cases he was responsible for four stations.

Under a clause in the original Act of 1835 the Christian name and surname of every 'Collector of the Rates or Tolls' had to be painted in letters at least 2 inches high on a board 'in front of the Toll House or other building whereat he shall be on duty'. Hence down to within living memory the name of the officer in charge of a station used so to appear over the Booking Office door as that of the 'Collector'.

### GOODS DEPARTMENT

For the first ten years or so the goods traffic was part of the work of the Traffic Department, and no one seems to have taken any particular interest in it. We hear of a 'Goods Superintendent', W. Massey by name, at Paddington in 1845, and possibly there was another at Bristol, but elsewhere goods traffic came under the local passenger superintendents and station clerks. At last in 1850 as a result of the Consultation Committee's Report, A. J. Drewe was appointed Goods Manager. Four years later, just before the Shrewsbury amalgamation, we find that Drewe was outdoor manager and J. S. Forbes indoor manager of goods traffic for the whole line, and that there were goods clerks at the principal stations subject both to the local Superintendent and to the Goods Manager.

Then in January 1855 a Goods Manager was appointed for each division, Drewe taking the Southern, Forbes the Western, with head-quarters at Gloucester, and a new man from the recently formed North Eastern Railway, W. L. Newcombe, the Northern. In September the last named was appointed the first Great Western delegate to the Railway Clearing House in response to an invitation from that institution, which the Company had hitherto had no occasion to join owing to the difference in gauge and lack of through booking. These three officers were independent of one another, and there was no co-ordinating authority save Saunders and the Board until February 1856, when Newcombe was made Chief Goods Manager, and as such moved to Paddington, Drewe's duties being then limited to the London business and the canal traffic. The Northern division was split up between James Grierson, who took the South Staffordshire district and the line as far as Ruabon, and W. English, who took the remainder from Wrexham northward.

When Newcombe left in September 1857 to become General Manager of the Midland Railway, Grierson succeeded him as Chief Goods Manager at Paddington, Drewe retired, and J. S. Forbes resigned to go to the Dutch Rhenish Railway, whence he returned to become General Manager of the London, Chatham & Dover in 1861, and later Chairman of that and the Metropolitan District Companies. After this clearance the goods districts were subdivided and several local managers appointed.

During all this early period the receipts from goods and mineral traffic were very much less than those from passengers, mails and parcels; even in the later 'fifties they were little more than half the latter on the Great Western proper, while on the Shrewsbury lines the proportions were about equal. Not until towards the end of the next decade did the goods receipts reach the level of the coaching traffic, after the mileage, especially of narrow-gauge lines, had vastly increased.

In August 1842 the Directors reported that they had 'still to contend against a vigorous competition in water carriage both by canal and sea', especially as to stone and coal. They had, however, recently arranged with the owners of two quarries close to the line to carry their stone, and were also 'about to send coals to their principal stations for sale, with a view to encourage that traffic on the Line, for which purpose they mean to select the larger coal from the stock supplied to their coke ovens'.

Competition with other railways did not begin until Gloucester and Cheltenham were reached, when the London & North Western and the Midland did their best to keep the London traffic of those places, both goods and passengers, to their route via Birmingham by reducing rates and fares to scarcely remunerative figures. They also made a strong attack on the Bristol goods traffic as soon as the Narrow Gauge reached there in 1854, and this in the Great Western's own goods station at Temple Meads, which the Midland continued to use till 1865. Although competition for passenger traffic soon ceased, goods between Bristol and London was secured by the Midland in steadily increasing quantity. Its successor, the London, Midland & Scottish, was able to use the shorter SMJ route via Broom and Olney, giving a much quicker transit. As a wartime economy. the competition finally ceased from 4th October 1941 and was not resumed.

Reading became a competing point as soon as the South Eastern gained access to it in 1849, and the competition was intensified on the arrival of the London & South Western seven years later. This was put an end to by a pooling agreement in 1858.

The opening of the northern line and acquisition of the Shrewsbury Railways of course meant general competition at all important places, but by this time the days of rate-cutting were nearly over.

### ENGINEERING DEPARTMENT

Save on the section between London and Maidenhead, the maintenance of the works and permanent way was from the very first let to contractors.

Seymour Clarke told the Gauge Commissioners in October 1845 that the line was then almost entirely under contract. Brunel was of course responsible, but having much constructive work on hand, both at home and abroad, delegated the Great Western maintenance to one of his assistants, with District Engineers under him at Reading, Swindon, and Bristol, each with a small staff of inspectors. J. W. Hammond was the assistant in charge till his death in 1847, and then T. H. Bertram and Michael Lane successively, the latter taking the work while Bertram was engaged on the construction of the line from Oxford to Birmingham or on new works elsewhere.

In 1853 a permanent engineering establishment was for the first time located at Paddington, still of course under Brunel as the chief engineer. The contract system, however, remained in force for several years after this.

As an example of one of these contracts, Brotherhood of Chippenham undertook 'the repair and maintenance of the earthwork and ballasting, the permanent way, sidings, station buildings, bridges and viaducts, tunnels and culverts, drains, level crossings, roads, fences and other works' from Reading to Bristol, Oxford, Frome, Radstock, and Warminster, excepting the station buildings at Didcot, Swindon, Chippenham, and Bristol, for five years from July 1856.

The new branches opened in this and the following year, most of them in the Wilts & Somerset district, were not let to contractors, but taken over directly by the Company as soon as the construction contracts expired; and in August 1858 Bertram, as Resident Engineer in Brunel's absence abroad, recommended in his half-yearly report to the Board that such portions of the main line and older branches as had not already been taken over should in future be maintained 'by the employment of labourers under the direct supervision of Assistant Engineers and District Inspectors', as the existing contracts expired. This policy had evidently already been adopted to some extent, and it is probable that Brotherhood's contract, which expired at the end of June 1861, was the last of them.

Practically all the broad-gauge lines consisted of bridge rails on longitudinal timbers, but a few exceptional forms of permanent way were tried during Brunel's regime. Of these, the Barlow and MacDonnell rails, as well as the 'T' rails on cross-sleepers of the Bathampton Branch, have already been described. Another kind of rail experimentally laid during the 'fifties was Seaton's patent 'safety rail'. Its form appears in the drawing, but its claim to the title does not.

Seaton's Rail

The general reconstruction in masonry or iron of the numerous timber viaducts and bridges all over the system began in 1858 and proceeded more or less continuously for many years.

On Brunel's death Bertram became Principal Engineer, but resigned in 1860 and was succeeded by Michael Lane, John Fowler being appointed Consulting Engineer about the same time.

In February of this same year the Directors reported that they had decided to establish a Rolling Mill at Swindon 'for the working up of the worn or damaged iron, in order to be converted, with the aid of fresh material of the very best quality, into new rails, which would possess a longer and therefore more economical existence than any which have yet been manufactured for them'. The cost of the mill and machinery was estimated at £20,000, which they proposed should be paid off in fourteen years. They had been advised to do this by Gooch, who records in his *Diaries* that the new rail mill was started in May 1861 and cost £25,000. But before the fourteen years had elapsed the use of steel instead of iron rails had become general, so, as no steel-making plant was installed, the rolling mill gradually fell out of use, for this purpose at any rate.

### TRAIN WORKING

On the first opening of the railway in 1838 and for some time afterwards the traffic seems to have been conducted very much in the go-as-you-please style. Trains were not even always confined to the proper Up or Down road, and the difficulties of the police in 'preserving order on the line' must have been immense. Moreover, in September and October 1838 Dr Dionysius Lardner's experimental train was literally 'knocking about' in the midst of the regular service. Gibbs records that on 26th September 'the 8 o'clock train ran into the experimental train this morning and injured three of the carriages very much'; whereupon the enraged Dionysius wrote 'a very improper letter' to the Board. Exactly a month later—'A very distressing accident occurred on the line, by which a pupil of Dr Lardner's was killed on the spot'. Fortunately the sage himself was elsewhere at the moment.

Scientific friends of Brunel's seem also to have been allowed to play about with experimental trains. Professor Charles Babbage, of calculating machine fame, arriving at Paddington one Sunday morning, desired the official placed at his disposal to 'order out my train immediately', and was about to start off *on the Up line* at the instigation of the same official, the Down being blocked, when he fancied he heard an engine approaching in the distance. Sure enough, a light engine presently arrived, from which Brunel himself 'covered with smoke and blacks' descended, having posted up from Bristol to Maidenhead and ordered out an engine he found there in steam.[1]

Seymour Clarke's letter of 22nd July 1839, already quoted, in which he states that a certain train 'returns from Slough to Drayton on the wrong line', seems to show that this dangerous practice was officially recognized. Recognized or not, it continued till one day in October 1840 Brunel got a fright and wrote to Gooch:

On Saturday I saw an engine on the line near the Scrubbs sent to look for the 3 o'clock train, in which I was and which was very late. This engine started after the 6 o'clock out and without any special orders from anyone in authority, but authorised by a general

[1] Babbage's Memoirs, quoted in *Temple Bar* for July 1892.

order which is issued, and returned on the wrong line. I cannot contemplate the dreadful results that might have happened, and there must be an immediate revision of our locomotive arrangements.

The immediate revision is evidenced in the *Rules for Enginemen and Firemen* approved by the Board on 3rd November:

10. No engine must ever, on any account whatever, be moved from any of the stations on to the main line, except when the engine-man is proceeding in his turn and at the proper time to take his place in front of a train: or, when on the main line, he must never run beyond the limits which may be fixed at each station without a regular despatch-note, filled up and signed by the proper superintendent or foreman, and he must then follow strictly the orders contained in such despatch-note, both as regards the time of starting and the place and time of returning.

11. The engines are never to run forward on the right-hand road, but always to move on the south road from Paddington towards Bristol, and on the north road from Bristol towards Paddington, except when specially ordered to do otherwise upon accident or emergency by the conductor of a train; and then the engineman must always ascertain from the conductor, and also satisfy himself, that the police have been made aware of the circumstance for the whole distance which he proposes to run; and he must proceed slowly and continue to sound his whistle by beats the whole time.

In his reminiscences of these early days Gooch wrote some thirty years later:[1]

When I look back upon that time, it is a marvel to me that we escaped serious accidents. It was no uncommon thing to take an engine out on the line to look for a late train that we expected, and many times have I seen the train coming and reversed the engine and run back out of its way as quickly as I could. What would be said of such a mode of proceeding now?

The practice of sending a pilot engine to look for an expected train continued till the general introduction of the telegraph and even later, for it was long before there was a man capable of using the instrument always in attendance at the smaller stations. It was provided for by the rules in force as late as 1876, but the pilot ran only on the proper road and, having found the train, went on to the next crossing and returned to render any necessary assistance or merely to follow it home.

Later in this same October of 1840 we find Brunel writing to Gooch:

J. Hill brought the 'Cyclops' up on Monday in 27 minutes from Slough, following the short train into Paddington within three minutes. This work must be put a stop to effectually, and the Directors have determined to fine him ten shillings. I have spoken severely to him and will see him myself about the fine. I should wish the 'Cyclops' tried alone with the 3 o'clock up; it might do it.

It is highly probable that the kind-hearted Engineer himself gave Hill the wherewithal to pay the fine; save for the annoying proximity of the wretched short train, such an exploit would have appealed to him. Moreover, the man had shown what his engine could do, and so suggested a means of overcoming the trouble with the '3 o'clock up', evidently the heavy train of the day. No fault seems to have been found with the police, who usually came in for it on such occasions, which suggests that time intervals between trains were not yet in force. They were introduced soon afterwards.

After dark engines carried green headlights, and the carriages— apparently all of them—lamps showing green to the front and red to the

[1] *Diaries*, p. 39.

rear, but after a few years' experience all these green lights were altered to white ones, and a red tail-lamp was added behind the last vehicle of the train. Side-lamps were then carried on the first as well as the last carriage of a train till 1855, when the former were dispensed with. Side-lamps on passenger trains were discontinued from 1st June 1933. From 1848 till 1865 special trains were distinguished by 'a red and green double signal board placed on the tail-lamp iron, and at night a corresponding green and red double tail lamp'. The more useful and still surviving double red discs or lamps on the train preceding a special run without notice were introduced in 1852. Goods trains carried two tail-lamps behind till 1855, when the fashion changed to one with two new side-lamps.

Returning to 1841, we find that the duty of protecting broken-down trains devolved on the policeman on the beat, who was ordered to hasten back a mile and stay there showing a *Danger* signal. In the event of an accident fouling the opposite road after dark, in addition to showing red lights in both directions and sending word to the next policeman, the engineman 'must rake out and make up a fire on the other line, for the purpose of forming an additional signal'. The introduction of detonators a year or two later did away with the need for this rather drastic proceeding.

The first attempt at a communication between guards and driver was established in 1847 in the shape of a 'Travelling Porter' on the back of the tender.

The business of the Travelling Porter is to ride on the seat placed for him on the tender, and to keep a steady and vigilant look-out along the side and top of the train, so that in case of accident to any of the carriages or of any signal from the guard, or any apparently sufficient cause that may come to his observation, he may at once communicate with the engineman, and if necessary stop the train.

He was also made responsible for the lamps and general equipment of the carriages and for keeping the axle-boxes filled with grease. At first these porters were confined to the expresses, but later they were appointed to other long-distance trains, and most of the passenger engine tenders were provided with hooded seats for them, commonly called 'iron coffins' by the men. They were finally abolished in 1864, a cord from the front van to a large gong on the side of the tender close to the footplate being substituted.

As regards the precedence of trains, the old Rule Books laid down that 'Ordinary Trains must make way for Express; Third Class for Ordinary; and Goods for Passenger Trains'. In pre-telegraph days there was of course considerable difficulty in carrying this out when the superior train happened to be late; how late no one knew till it appeared. The procedure ordered was that the slower train should be sent on after being kept waiting, if an Ordinary 15 minutes, if a Third Class 20 minutes, and if a Goods ½ hour, the *Danger* signals of course being shown to stop the late train. Subject to the proviso that 'no information can be obtained by Electric Telegraph', this crude method persisted for many years.

PASSENGER ARRANGEMENTS

In 1838 and for several years afterwards passenger tickets were of paper with counterfoils. Booking clerks were provided with separate books of them for each class, and on issuing a ticket stamped it and the counterfoil with the passenger's destination, the date, and the time of the train. Armed with one of these tickets the passenger proceeded to the platform, gave it up to the conductor of the train, and was shown into the coach, or 'body' as a compartment was called, appropriated to his destination, and locked in. As soon as all the passengers for a train had been booked, the clerk made up the way-bill from his counterfoils showing the number of passengers for each station, and handed it to the conductor, who might then start the train. At intermediate stations it appears to have been the duty of the clerk to enter his passengers and their destinations on the conductor's way-bill, the latter meanwhile unlocking the doors of the 'bodies' for that station and letting out the passengers arriving. The weaknesses of this system were soon pointed out in the following anonymous letter, which happens to have been preserved.

LONDON,
*6th September* 1838.

— Hammond, Esq.
  Maidenhead.
Sir,
    Having been a frequent traveller by the Great Western Railway I am induced to notice the system of Tickets which is adopted on it, under the impression that it is incomplete in so far as it affords the Public an opportunity of imposing on the Railway Company by paying a short distance fare and travelling farther than the sum paid entitles, also by putting it in the power of a Guard to draw the additional fare from a passenger while the repayment of the same to the Company by the Guard is optional, it not having been drawn under the surveillance of any superior. The bad effect of this need not be traced further by me.
    You seem to have only 2 Colours of Tickets Blue for the 2nd train and Grey for the first, both of which are stamped with the Hour of the Train. The Passenger for instance pays the 2nd Class fare from Maidenhead to Slough, and if he choose he may sit still and pass on to London for that sum unchallenged. The only check being the Memory of the Guard who received the ticket, and his recollection is almost none at all as in many cases the passengers are unavoidably mixed in the Coaches although they are labelled with their destination before starting, but not unfrequently even the Names of the Places are removed before the Train starts. I have witnessed the above in so far as on the arrival at Slough the Guard did not know who intended to leave the Train at that point, and it was only by request the Door was opened. Further it is notorious that such frauds have been effected.
    Allow me to suggest 1st That you should have Tickets of Different Colours for your different fares on the line or Tickets of the same colour for the same amount of fare in the same Class—2nd That there should be an obvious difference in the appearance of the Tickets of the 1st and 2nd Class—3rd That all the Tickets of the same Class and amount from any Station should have a running Number and that these Tickets bear either the name of the Station or a Colour which will indicate readily the price and place from which it may have been received—4th That the Tickets in all cases should only be exhibited by the Passenger on entering the Coach and delivered on leaving it either to the Guard or a person or persons at the different stations, of whose duty the receipt of all the Tickets will form a part. Expertness at this point is of service.
    The Delivery on arrival you will observe is a chief part of the Cheque, and those Tickets once received you may adopt a thorough system of cheque over every point of your receiving department on the Line, which over and above being satisfactory would be most useful in drawing your attention to the influence of particular fares or Hours of Departure.

The Management of this cheque over the Receipts ought to be a distinct department at Paddington or Maidenhead, and the Tickets drawn at the Country Stations should be sent to the Office of the Department daily in order to be assorted and compared with periodical Returns from the different Stations showing the Tickets sold daily and amounts.

While so small a portion of your Line is open you have the means of introducing a complete system before your Receipts and Stations increase, moreover your Receipts now cannot fail to influence the Credit of the concern, while any want of management is also discreditable. In the hope that this Hasty Hint from one who has witnessed the good effect of such management in similar undertakings may be of service.

I am Sir,<br>
Your obedient Servant,<br>
A RAILWAY TRAVELLER.

These sensible suggestions were not as yet adopted. In the following April Saunders told the Select Committee on Railways that the tickets were taken before the passengers were let into the carriages and the doors locked; that there were different carriages for the different stations; and incidentally that the fares averaged—First Class $3\frac{1}{8}d$ per mile, Second Class Closed $2\frac{1}{8}d$, Second Class Open $1\frac{3}{4}d$. He added that there was a 'Complaint Book' at Paddington, but no entry had yet been made in it. Such books had previously been suggested by the same Committee to be provided at the London termini for the use of aggrieved passengers. As we have seen, the Second Class Closed fares were abolished in July on the opening to Twyford.

It seems from the following undated letter from Clarke to Saunders that small children were at first carried free and that later the Board ordered a charge to be made.

The late order about infants is, I fear, doing us much harm; so much so that I have troubled you with this in order that I may have your permission at any rate to suspend the execution of it until reconsidered, so that not any more departures may take place with it in force. I hear from Mr Bill that Judge Pattison came in his carriage to-day with his family, fare amounting to 40/-. Upon the demand being made for his infant, he at once ordered horses and posted. Others have gone by coach, etc.

Probably as a result of this, the Directors decided on 10th April 1839 that no charge should be made for children under three, and half-fare for those between three and ten years of age.

In August 1838 the Company, in General Meeting assembled, made its first By-laws, as it was empowered to do, without the need of any confirmation, by the Incorporation Act. They are worth reproduction if only for their barefaced attempt to get rid of all liability for passengers' luggage, and the same hard-and-fast penalty imposed on an innocent ticket loser and a fraudulent rogue.

BYE-LAWS

1. No person will be allowed to travel upon the Railway without first having paid his fare and received a ticket.

2. If any passenger shall refuse to produce or deliver up his ticket, when required to do so by the conductor, guard, or other attendant on the train, he shall be chargeable with the fare for the entire journey, and shall be subject to the penalty of 40s.

3. Every first-class passenger will be allowed 112 lbs, and every second-class passenger 56 lbs of luggage, free of charge; but the Company will not be responsible for the care of the same, unless booked and paid for accordingly. All surplus luggage and merchandize of every description will be charged for. The Company's porters will load and unload the luggage at the different stations, free of charge.

4. No dogs will be permitted to accompany passengers in the carriages; but they will be conveyed separately and charged for.

5. No smoking will be allowed in any of the carriages or stations of the Company, under a penalty of 40*s* and the liability of removal from the Company's premises or carriages.

6. If any passenger conducts himself improperly, or shall be intoxicated to the annoyance of the passengers, or wilfully obstructs any of the Company's officers in the discharge of their duty, he shall be subject to a penalty of 40*s*, and be immediately removed from the Company's premises or carriages and shall forfeit any fare which he may have paid.

7. If any passenger shall wilfully damage any part of the Company's carriages, stations, or other property, he shall be fined five pounds, over and above the cost of repairing such damage; and all accidental damage shall be paid for by the party committing the same.

8. If any passenger shall attempt to force his way into a carriage, without having previously procured a ticket; or, shall occupy (without permission) a superior class carriage to that for which he has obtained a ticket; or, shall continue his journey in the Company's carriages beyond the place for which he shall have paid his fare, he shall be liable to a fine of 40*s*, in addition to the full fare of the entire journey.

9. Every train is provided with guards, and a conductor who is responsible for the order and regularity of the journey.

10. No fee or gratuity is permitted to be taken by any guard, porter, or other servant of the Company, under pain of immediate dismissal.

These by-laws did not remain in force very long. A clause was inserted in the Company's Act of the following year making them invalid unless allowed by a Judge of the High Court, the Middlesex Quarter Sessions, or the Recorder of Bristol; but another clause of the same Act gave the Company better protection against fraudulent travelling. They were replaced by new by-laws at the General Meeting of February 1840, and these in their turn were made subject to the approval of the Board of Trade by Lord Seymour's Act of the same year, after which a standard code for all railways was gradually evolved.

The locking of the carriage doors was continued for four years, until the terrible accident at Versailles on 8th May 1842, when fifty-three imprisoned passengers were burned to death, caused a public outcry. Even after this the Directors were very loth to alter the practice, but a circular from the Board of Trade in June caused them to change their minds and give orders that in future only the off-side doors should be locked, and that the stations should be fenced in.

Other changes made at this time were the abolition of conductors, whose places were taken by senior guards, the collection of tickets by the station staff at arrival stations, and the tentative introduction of roof-lamps in the carriages, six first-class coaches being ordered to be fitted with them in August.

The date when paper tickets with counterfoils gave way to cardboard without them has not been definitely ascertained; they were still in use in August 1842. Way-bills for the guards were being prepared by the Paddington booking-clerks as late as October 1845, when Seymour Clarke told the Gauge Commissioners: 'We do not start exactly at the time though we close the door at a certain minute. We have to make up the way-bill and so on.'

In these early days great care was taken that first-class passengers should not be incommoded by contact with their inferiors of the second class, in the principal stations at any rate. At Bath, for example, the two flocks were penned separately. Brunel writes to Saunders in June 1842:

> Bath Station. I have only fenced off pens for the 2nd and 1st Class on the up platform. On the down platform I have not done anything yet because I could not satisfy myself as to the best mode, and it appears to me that as there are waiting rooms below for both classes, you could manage for a short time. Chippenham is doing or done by this time.

The letter includes a sketch plan of the Up platform at Bath showing a railed-in pen for the second-class people and a larger one with a waiting-room for the first class, each with its separate staircase from the ground floor; separate exits are also shown at either end of the platform. Third-class travellers are not provided for; doubtless they were loaded and unloaded at the adjacent goods shed, or on the platform at times when respectable people were not about.

Ladies' Compartments were provided from an early period. The 1848 Rule Book says:

> One body in that first class coach of the long trains which is going the longest distance is to be devoted to the use of ladies only, and is to have a board indicating such appropriation put up on the door.

On the other hand, no accommodation for persons smoking tobacco was provided till Parliament forced it on the unwilling Directors in 1868. Until then any miscreant persisting in committing such a nuisance either in the trains or stations was ordered to be ejected from the Company's premises, and might think himself lucky if he was not prosecuted for breach of the by-laws.

Persons of quality, who preferred to travel in their own carriages on trucks, had the privilege of paying first-class fares in addition to the charge for the carriage. For the first few years they were exceptionally numerous on the Great Western, but by degrees they discovered that the Company's first-class carriages were more comfortable, especially in bad weather, and so gave up the practice altogether.

Luggage was dealt with much as it is to-day, except that for London, which was specially provided for in the last-mentioned Rule Book.

> All articles of London luggage not taken charge of by the passengers themselves are to have red labels pasted on showing the initial letter of the owner's surname, and the porters at Paddington are, on the arrival of the trains, to take care that the luggage thus labelled is placed in the proper bins or divisions of the barrier on the platforms, and delivered only to the proper owners.

The ancient tale of the Paddington porter who told the Rev Mr L——, enquiring for his luggage, to go to 'L', and was forthwith reported for insolence, is well known. The system remained in force for many years, and a somewhat similar plan prevails to-day for the registered luggage of Ocean passengers.

A cloak-room existed at Paddington in 1848, and is referred to as the depot for all property lost on the system. The first cloak-room is said to have been established at Bath Station two years earlier.

Through first-class carriages were run between London and Oxford and Gloucester from the opening of those branches, as well as through luggage vans to the latter place, but second-class branch passengers had to change at Didcot or Swindon, and Oxford luggage was usually transferred at Didcot, until extensions made both branches into main lines.

The system of Return Tickets, available for two or three days according to the length of the journey, which had been adopted on these Lines in more prosperous times as a means of augmenting that branch of traffic, having ceased to create the progressive increase of revenue which was anticipated, and being discovered to give rise to fraud, was discontinued in November last.

By a careful examination of the traffic during the six subsequent months it was ascertained that while the receipts had increased by the abolition of those tickets for passengers travelling the long journeys, there had been a falling off not only in the number of but also in income from passengers travelling shorter distances between intermediate stations.

The result of this investigation induced the Board to introduce single day tickets, limited to an allowance of 25 per cent upon the double fare, which have been in operation since the 1st May; and the encouragement given to a description of traffic which has been always considerable on the Great Western Railway seems at present to have answered the purpose.

So runs a passage in the Directors' Report of August 1849, interesting in casting a light on the methods of those days and in showing how all such matters were solemnly debated and decided by the Directors. The day of return tickets available for a reasonable period had not yet come.

Season tickets, already common on nearly every other railway in the kingdom, were unknown on the Great Western till June 1851, when they were at last adopted between Paddington, Windsor, and Maidenhead.

Through booking of passengers to foreign lines, other than the Bristol & Exeter, South Devon, and South Wales, does not seem to have begun until the end of the 'fifties.

It remains to be noticed that foot-warmers for first-class passengers were introduced in 1856. Their use was not, officially at any rate, extended to the second class until fourteen years later.

# XV

# *The Locomotive Department*

## FIRST PERIOD, 1837–1839

It may be safely stated, without exaggeration, that in the whole history of British railways there has never existed such an extraordinary collection of freak locomotives as those which were built for the Great Western and delivered during a period of about eighteen months from November 1837. The following preliminary observations may help to supply a partial explanation of the reasons which led to some of their peculiarities.

Although these were the early days of railways, nevertheless the locomotive had by 1836 made such rapid progress in design that on the principal narrow-gauge railways there was not only a distinct tendency in favour of certain types, the survival up to that time of the fittest, but also a general consensus of technical opinion in regard to proportional dimensions. For passenger engines driving wheels of 5 feet 6 inches diameter were then the largest in use, though the usual size was 5 feet. The cylinders of the more recent engines varied between the limits of 11 inches to 12½ inches diameter by 16 inches to 18 inches stroke of piston. The effect on the tractive effort of a locomotive caused by varying these leading dimensions was by 1836 well understood, partly as the result of the exhaustive published researches and experiments made by the Comte de Pambour on the Liverpool & Manchester Railway. The passenger locomotives of the Grand Junction Railway, which were contemporary with the earliest Great Western engines, had 5 feet 6 inch driving wheels and 13 inch by 18 inch cylinders, and their tractive force per pound of effective steam pressure on the pistons was 46 lb.

With a 7-feet gauge larger engines were not only possible but were also intended, and the principal object which Brunel and the Directors had in view was the attainment of speeds greater than those hitherto achieved on other railways. To this end the diameter of the driving wheels of the locomotives could have been enlarged to 6 feet or 6 feet 6 inches, in which case, to obtain a greater speed, the cylinders could have been made 15 inches or 16 inches in diameter by 18 inch piston stroke without departing from what was even then orthodox practice.

In a report of 1836 submitted to the Great Western shareholders it was stated:

> Difficulties and objections were at first supposed by some persons to exist in the construction of engines for the increased width of rails, but the Directors have pleasure in stating that several of the most experienced locomotive engine manufacturers in the North have undertaken to construct these, and several are now contracted for, adapted to the peculiar track and dimensions of this railway, calculated for a minimum velocity of thirty miles an hour.

The expression 'minimum velocity' is somewhat quaint, more especially since some of the original engines probably never even attained a maximum velocity at the rate mentioned.

On 8th August 1836 Brunel wrote to Messrs Tayleur, of the Vulcan Foundry, near Warrington, confirming a verbal order for two engines of the class described in their letter of 23rd July with cylinders 14 inch diameter by 16 inch stroke of piston and driving wheels 8 feet diameter, to have 'a force of traction of 800 pounds on a level at 30 miles per hour', and also for two engines having the same piston stroke and size of driving wheels, 'but of such reduced dimensions of cylinders and capacity of boiler as may be sufficient to maintain a force of traction of 500 pounds at the same speed'. He added: 'I understand Mr Loom said he expected they would weigh 10 or 10½ tons.'

The tractive force at the circumference of the driving wheels of the larger engines with 14 inch cylinders was 32·6 lb, and that of the smaller 12 inch engines only 24 lb per pound of effective steam pressure in the cylinders.

*Ajax* with 10 feet driving wheels and 14 inch by 20 inch cylinders also had a tractive force of 32·6 lb per pound of effective steam pressure. This engine was built by Mather, Dixon & Co. of Liverpool. The power of these locomotives, which carried a steam pressure of 50 lb, similar in amount to that of other engines of that day, was therefore from about 20 to 50 per cent less than the power of engines running upon many of the narrow-gauge railways.

When the engines were contracted for the Company had not yet appointed a locomotive superintendent, and the technical responsibility for the orders rested upon Brunel. In a later report to the Directors, dated 15th August 1838, which dealt with the construction of the line and carriages as well as with the locomotives, he wrote:

The next point I shall consider is the construction of the engines; the modifications in which, necessary to adapt them to higher speeds than usual, have like the increased width of gauge, been condemned as innovations. I shall not attempt to argue with those who consider any increase of speed unnecessary. The public will always prefer that conveyance which is the most perfect, and speed within reasonable limits is a material ingredient in perfection in travelling.

A rate of 35 to 40 miles an hour is not unfrequently attained at present on other railways in descending planes, or with light loads on a level, and is found practically to be attended with no inconvenience. To maintain such a speed with regularity on a level line, with moderate loads, is therefore quite practicable and unquestionably desirable. With this view the engines were constructed, but nothing new was required or recommended by me; a certain velocity of the piston is considered the most advantageous.

The engines intended for slow speeds have always had the driving wheels small in proportion to the length of stroke of the piston. The faster engines have had a different proposition, the wheels have been larger, or the strokes of the piston shorter. From the somewhat clamorous objections raised against the large wheels, and the construction of the Great Western Railway engines, and the opinions rather freely expressed of my judgment in directing this construction, it would naturally be supposed that some established principle had been departed from, and that I had commended this departure. The facts are, that a certain velocity of piston being found most advantageous, I fixed this velocity so that the engines should be adapted to run 35 miles an hour, and capable of running 40—as the Manchester and Liverpool Railway engines are best calculated for 20 to 25, but capable of running easily at 30 and 35 miles an hour; and fixing also the load which the engine was to be capable of drawing. I left the form of construction and the proportions entirely to the manufacturers, stipulating merely that they should submit detail drawings to me for my approval.

This was the substance of the circular which, with your sanction, was sent to several of the most experienced manufacturers. Most of these manufacturers of their own accord, and without previous communication with me, adopted the large wheels as a necessary consequence of the speed required. The recommendation coming from such quarters, there can be no necessity for defending my opinion in its favour; neither have I now the slightest doubt of its correctness. As it has been supposed that the manufacturers may have been compelled or induced by me to adopt certain modes of construction or certain dimensions in other parts by a specification—a practice which has been adopted on some lines—and that these restrictions may have embarrassed them, I should wish to take this opportunity to state distinctly that such is not the case. I have, indeed, strongly recommended to their consideration the advantages of having very large and well-formed steam passages, which generally they have adopted, and with good results; and with this single exception, if it can be considered one, they have been left unfettered by me (perhaps too much so) and uninfluenced, except, indeed, by the prejudices and fears of those by whom they have been surrounded, which have by no means diminished the difficulties I have had to contend with.

The principal proportions of these engines being those which have been recommended by the most able experimentalists and writers, and these having been adopted by the most experienced makers, it is difficult to understand who can constitute themselves objectors or what can be their objections. Even if these engines have not been found effective, at least it must be admitted that the best and most liberal means had been adopted to procure them; but I am far from asking such an admission. The engines, I think, have been proved to be well adapted to the particular task for which they were calculated, namely high speeds—but circumstances prevent their being beneficially applied to this purpose at present, and they are, therefore, working under great disadvantages. An engine constructed expressly for high velocity cannot, of course, be well adapted to exert great power at a low speed; neither can it be well adapted for stopping frequently and regaining its speed. But such was not the intention when these engines were made, neither will it be the case when the arrangements on the line are complete; in the meantime our average rate of travelling is much greater than it was either on the Grand Junction or the Birmingham Railway within the same period of the opening.

I have but one serious objection to make to our present engines, and for this, strange as it may seem, I feel that we are mainly indebted to those who have been most loud in their complaints. I refer to the unnecessary weight of the engines; there is nothing in the wide gauge which involves any considerably increased weight in the engines. An engine of the same power and capacity for speed, whether for four feet eight inch rail or for a seven feet rail, will have identically the same boiler, the same firebox, the same cylinder and piston, and other working gear, the same side frames and the same wheels; the axles and the cross framing will alone differ, and upon these alone need there by any increase, but if these were doubled in weight the difference upon the whole engine would be immaterial; but the repeated assertion, frequently professing to come from experienced authorities, repeated until it was supposed to be proved, that the increased gauge must require increased strength and great power, was not without its indirect effect on the manufacturers. Unnecessary dimensions have been given to many parts, and the weight thereby increased rather tending, as I believe, to diminish than to add to the strength of the whole. I thought then, and I believe now, that it would have been unwise in this case to have resisted the general opinion and taken upon myself the responsibility which belonged to the manufacturers; but I need not now hesitate to say that a very considerable reduction may be effected, and that no such unusual precautions are necessary to meet these anticipated strains and resistances—such being, in fact, imaginary. . . .

In his evidence in 1845 before the Gauge Commission Brunel said that in regard to the diameter of the driving wheels his original proposal was to have 7 feet and 8 feet for passenger engines. Two or three of the engines had 10 foot driving wheels. In regard to these he added:

The idea did not originate with me, but was proposed by certain manufacturers, and although I expressed some fear of the feasibility of constructing 10 feet wheels, I thought it worth the trial. They were made, and it so happened that the three engines, to which they were applied, totally failed in other respects, and the whole was cast aside. . . . I take the whole responsibility of having allowed the 10 ft. wheel to be made, . . . and the construction of the wheels was one which we should certainly never again adopt; it was an entire plate, and that with such a diameter is heavy, and offers such an enormous surface to the side wind that it certainly would not do to adopt it.

If Brunel's statements be impartially analyzed in the light of definite historical knowledge of the locomotive practice of that day, it is difficult to acquit him of a great part of the responsibility for the very large proportion of freak locomotives obtained by the Company, and it is impossible to come to any other conclusion than that his first instructions had considerably greater influence over several of the manufacturers than he really intended. In stating that the principal proportions of these engines were those which had been recommended by the most able experimentalists and writers, and that *these had been adopted by the most experienced makers*, he seems to have been badly advised, and to have mistakenly stated what was not the case. There had been no locomotives previously constructed by any firms which could be compared with most of these early Great Western engines, either in relative dimensions or in the general design of several of them. His views in regard to the weights of the engines also proved to be completely wrong, as will be seen later.

The key to the trouble is to be found in the circular letter which Brunel sent out to the locomotive builders in June 1836, when asking for tenders. In this he certainly stated that the particular form and construction of the engines would be left to their own judgment, but he added the following clauses:

Drawings of the proposed engines to be submitted to me as the Engineer of the Company before execution, and if, during execution, any material alteration is proposed, it will be necessary that I should have an opportunity on the part of the Company of objecting to it if I should consider it an experiment not worth the making.

The following are a few conditions *which must be complied with*: A velocity of 30 miles an hour to be considered as the standard velocity, and this to be attained *without requiring the piston to travel at a greater rate than 280 ft. per minute*. The engine to be of such dimension and power as to exert and maintain without difficulty—with the pressure of steam in the boiler not exceeding 50 lbs. upon the square inch, and with a velocity of 30 miles an hour—a force of traction equal to 800 lbs. upon a level, independent of the power required to move its own weight and that of the tender with a supply of fuel and water for one hour's consumption. The weight of the engine, exclusive of the tender, but in other respects supplied with water and fuel for work, *not to exceed* 10½ *tons*, and if above 8 tons, to be carried on six wheels.[1]

The condition in regard to limit of weight could, of course, be decided only by Brunel himself, as the engineer responsible for bridges and track. But the limit of 10½ tons was extremely low, and less than the weights then usual in the case of narrow-gauge engines on six wheels. Evidently the manufacturers were unable to meet it and at the same time comply with the other conditions, since we find that the officially recorded weights in working order of the Great Western engines, other than those on Harrison's patent in which the boiler was carried on a separate frame, varied from 14½ to 18¾ tons. The specified maximum piston speed of 280 feet per minute at 30 miles per hour was ridiculously low. Narrow-gauge passenger

[1] The italics are ours.

engines with 5 foot driving wheels and 18 inch stroke had a piston speed of 504 feet per minute at 30 miles per hour. There is no doubt whatever that Brunel wished to leave as much as possible to the builders, but the result of his limitation of piston speed was such that the latter were forced to combine a stroke of medium length with excessively large driving wheels. These wheels added very considerably to the weight, and to prevent the engine from being too heavy the boilers had to be made too small. But in respect of the 10 foot wheels of *Ajax* the makers must bear the greater part of the responsibility, as will be shown later.

Daniel Gooch was appointed Locomotive Superintendent of the Great Western and began his duties on 18th August 1837, a few days before his twenty-first birthday, having been born at Bedlington in Northumberland on 24th August 1816. In 1831 his father removed to Tredegar Ironworks in Monmouthshire, and young Gooch started his professional career by working in the foundry at the works. In January 1834, after the death of his father, he obtained work at the Vulcan Foundry near Warrington. This concern, which grew into one of the largest locomotive building firms in this country, was founded by Charles Tayleur and Robert Stephenson, and the works were not quite finished when Gooch went there. He remained about eight months, at the end of which his health began to give way, but after remaining at home for three months he obtained a temporary draughtsman's post under Messrs Stirling of East Foundry, Dundee. Early in January 1836 he joined Messrs Robert Stephenson & Co, the celebrated locomotive builders of Newcastle-on-Tyne. At the time of his appointment on the Great Western he was engaged in the engineer's office of the Manchester & Leeds Railway, then under construction.

In his *Diaries* Gooch wrote that on his arrival in London none of the engines had been delivered, although several, of which he enumerated eighteen, had been ordered. He added:

I was not much pleased with the design of the engines ordered. They had very small boilers and cylinders and very large wheels. Those made by the Vulcan Company had wheels 8 ft. in diameter, and three of them only 12 inch cylinders . . .; two of Mather Dixon's had 10 ft wheels and 14 inch cylinders with very small boilers. Those made by Hawthorn were on a patent plan of Tom Harrison's, having the engine and boiler on separate carriages, and coupled with ball-and-socket steam pipes. These were immense affairs, the boilers were large. . . . In one the cylinders were coupled direct to the driving wheels, which were 10 ft diameter, and the other had a spur and pinion 3 to 1, with 6 ft wheel, making the wheel equal to 18 ft diameter. The same plan of gearing was used in the two engines built by the Haigh Foundry; their wheels were 6 ft diameter, and the gearing 2 to 1,[1] but the cylinders were small. I felt very uneasy about the working of these machines, feeling sure that they would have enough to do to drive themselves along the road.

Of several of the earliest engines the known particulars are incomplete, but such as exist are of considerable historical interest.

The first to be mentioned were two by Robert Stephenson & Co of Newcastle, *North Star* and *Morning Star*, which may be described as of

---

[1] Gooch, writing long after 1837, seems to have been in error in regard to the gear ratio of 2 to 1. The official records state that it was 3 to 2.

orthodox design. Both had been built for the New Orleans Railway, U.S.A., of 5 feet 6 inches gauge, but owing to a financial panic the two engines were left on Messrs Stephenson's hands. The driving wheels had a diameter of 6 feet 6 inches, and the cylinders were 16 inch diameter by 16 inch stroke. The Great Western having purchased them they were altered by Messrs Stephenson to suit the 7 foot gauge, and in the case of *North Star*, in order to meet Brunel's requirements as far as was reasonably possible, new driving wheels 7 feet diameter were made. *North Star* was delivered at Maidenhead on 28th November 1837, and had the honour of working the Directors' train on 31st May 1838, preparatory to the opening of the line, when it conveyed a train of carriages containing nearly 200 passengers, and ran the 22½ miles in 47 minutes, at the rate of 28 miles per hour.

The following extract from a letter written by Brunel to T. E. Harrison on 5th March 1838 shows the importance he attached to the general appearance of an engine, and his admiration of *North Star*:

Lastly let me call your attention to the appearance—we have a splendid engine of Stephenson's, it would be a beautiful ornament in the most elegant drawing room and we have another of Quaker-like simplicity carried even to shabbyness but very possibly as good as engine, but the difference in the care bestowed by the engine man, the favour in which it is held by others and even oneself, not to mention the public, is striking. A plain young lady however amiable is apt to be neglected. Now your engine is capable of being made very handsome, and it ought to be so.

In December 1838 Brunel made experiments with *North Star*, and altered the blast-pipe. On the 29th of that month G. H. Gibbs recorded a trial run to Maidenhead with a train weighing 43 tons. The average rate of speed was 43 miles per hour, and the coke consumption 0·95 lb per ton of net weight per mile.

*North Star* was a very successful engine. In 1854 it was rebuilt at Swindon with a new boiler and 16 inch by 18 inch cylinders; the wheel base was lengthened by 1 foot. After these alterations it remained in service until December 1870, and was subsequently stored at Swindon until early in 1906, when it was broken up owing to the space occupied being required for other purposes.

On 3rd May 1838 Brunel wrote to Robert Stephenson:

My dear Stephenson:—In reply to yours of the 30th relating to the second engine, I have to request that you will lose no time in proceeding with it for us. I should wish it to be in every respect, except the double firebox, a duplicate of the North Star, certainly not smaller cylinders.

This engine, *Morning Star*, was not despatched from Newcastle until December 1838, and was accepted by the Company in January 1839. It differed from *North Star* in that the original 6 feet 6 inch driving wheels were retained, but in other respects was generally similar.

Whishaw in *The Railways of Great Britain and Ireland* (1840) gave the weight in working order as 12 tons 12 cwt 2 qr, and empty as 11 tons 9 cwt; these figures were stated to have been taken from Messrs Stephenson's list, but there must have been a serious error. Seeing that Brunel had specified a maximum weight of 10 to 10½ tons for the engines, it is not unlikely that *Morning Star* retained its original wheels in order to keep the weight as low as possible. *North Star,* according to the Company's records, weighed 18 tons 15 cwt 2 qr 14 lb 'without water, fire, or men', and cost £2,150. *Morning Star* can hardly have weighed much less than 18 tons. The latter with tender and some spare parts cost £2,825 2s 6d.

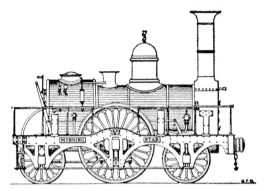

*Morning Star* 1838

Some interesting correspondence between Gooch and Messrs Stephenson during November and December 1839 on the subject of a broken leading axle of *Morning Star* shows that, when the above two engines were altered from 5 feet 6 inches to 7 feet gauge, new ends were scarf-welded by the makers on the old axles to lengthen them. Messrs Stephenson's usual practice, as shown by the letters, was to forge four square bars placed longitudinally the whole length of the axle.

The two engines by Messrs Stephenson have been mentioned first, for the reason that they do not come within the category of freaks, and further, since *North Star* may be considered as the Great Western No. 1, having worked the first passenger train. But the first engine actually tried in steam was *Vulcan.* It was shipped by Messrs Tayleur to London Docks, whence it came by canal to West Drayton, arriving at the latter place, together with *Premier,* from Mather, Dixon & Co, about 10th November 1837. Gooch had to get them and two other engines, which arrived later, from the wharf to the engine-house about a mile distant. An elm tree, which happened to be handily situated, was used to support the tackle for lifting the engines from the barge.[1]

*Vulcan* was tried on 28th December 1837 between mileposts 14 and $15\frac{1}{2}$ near Iver, and this length was therefore the first section of the Great Western line on which a locomotive actually ran. The sister engines to *Vulcan,* named *Æolus* and *Bacchus* were delivered on 30th November and 2nd December 1837. All three came from Charles Tayleur & Co, The Vulcan Foundry, near Warrington, and were the first freaks, having 8 foot driving wheels and 14 inch by 16 inch cylinders, as previously

[1] The official recorded date of delivery of both *Vulcan* and *Premier* is 25th November 1837, three days earlier than that of *North Star*; this was probably the date when the parts had been assembled in the Drayton engine-house.

mentioned. Their other dimensions are given in the table on page 396, from which it will be seen that the boilers were very small. *Vulcan* and *Æolus* cost £1,669 11s each, and *Bacchus*, in virtue of an arrangement made with Brunel, £1,769 11s. The price of the tenders was £400 each.

The three later engines delivered by the same firm in 1838, *Apollo*, *Neptune*, and *Venus*, were similar in type, and although they also had 8 foot driving wheels, the boilers and the cylinders, 12 inches by 16 inches, were even smaller, in accordance with the instructions quoted previously. Their weight in working order was about 2 tons less than that of the *Vulcan* class. There does not appear to be any record of the reasons which induced Brunel to order less powerful engines, but it may be surmised that he either wished to use them for lighter trains, or was afraid that the larger engines might too greatly exceed the limit of $10\frac{1}{2}$ tons which he had in mind in 1836. As it was, the *Vulcan* class weighed $18\frac{1}{4}$ tons and the *Apollo* class $16\frac{1}{4}$ tons in working order, and it is clear from the correspondence that he had never intended to use engines as heavy as this.

*Vulcan* 1837

Amongst the spare parts which were delivered by Messrs Tayleur we find two pairs of 8 foot driving wheels at £120 each pair, two crank axles at £100 each, two pairs of carrying wheels, 4 feet 6 inch diameter, at £50 each, and two straight axles for the latter, complete with keys and keyed on to the wheels, at £12 each.

A very interesting item in Messrs Tayleur's account, dated 19th October 1838, reads: 'To ironwork in part finished for Mr Melling's friction rollers.' John Melling, who was one of the chief locomotive officials of the Liverpool & Manchester Railway, had in 1837 patented an arrangement in which a friction roller was placed on each side of the engine between the small leading and the large driving wheel. By means of small steam cylinders, placed vertically at the sides of the smoke-box, and a system of levers the friction could be brought to bear against the tyres of the wheels at the will of the driver, who was thus able to convert the single engine temporarily into the equivalent of a coupled engine in that the tendency of the single pair of driving wheels to slip was avoided.

Whether these friction wheels were actually fitted to any of the engines is doubtful, since on 7th September 1837 Brunel wrote to Gooch, then in Manchester:

If the addition of Melling's wheels is to cause much delay, I must do without them, although for command of stopping and starting I should have liked them.

Although it does not appear in the drawings of the Vulcan Foundry, the correspondence shows that some at least of the engines by this firm had a casing of sheet iron on each side immediately inside the wheels with space for the enginemen to pass to get at the motion. This may have been the equivalent of the back of the splashers, to which there was no front, but it must have extended beyond the wheels for Brunel evidently thought of putting the name-plates on it and in October 1837 wrote to Robert Stephenson to ask whether he had ever done anything of the sort.

Another interesting suggestion is contained in one of Brunel's letters to Tayleur & Co: 'A bow or round front to take off the direct action of the air against the flat surface of the smokebox.' Nothing appears in the correspondence or other papers to show whether this was actually fitted to any engines, though it seems likely to have been tried.

Although Gooch in his *Diaries* mentioned that the Vulcan Foundry engines were more reliable than most of the other early locomotives except those by Stephenson, they were nevertheless very far from successful. Whishaw recorded a run by *Vulcan* from Paddington to West Drayton with a load of 18 tons only, the mean speed, deducting time taken for three stops, being 28·3 miles per hour. On the return journey with a train weighing 14½ tons the mean speed, deducting four stops, was 21 miles per hour. The maximum speed on this trip was 50 miles per hour. A sister engine, *Æolus*, on 4th June 1838 worked the first train run for the public. On 21st July following Whishaw tested the speed of this engine when conveying a train weighing slightly less than 43 tons, and recorded his experience thus:

Leaving Paddington the first mile was performed at the rate of 6.49 miles per hour, and the second mile at the rate of 6.16 miles per hour. About the 2½ mile standard the train was suddenly stopped, and remained 'in statu quo' for 21.75 minutes. In the meantime *Æolus* moved slowly away to recover his strength; and having sufficiently exercised himself, returned after a lapse of 21.75 minutes to lead the train forward.

The highest speed attained during the remainder of this journey was about 24 miles per hour for a length of 1½ miles. Nicholas Wood, in his report of 1838 to the Board, stated that *Æolus* was capable of drawing 32 tons at 50 miles per hour.

At the end of 1838 Gooch was requested by the Directors to report upon the state of the locomotive stock as it then was. The circumstances which gave rise to this request will be mentioned later, but the narrative will be rendered more intelligible if the extracts from this report, which is dated 2nd January 1839, are given in connection with the descriptions of the engines to which they refer. Dealing with Messrs Tayleur's six engines, the report reads:

VULCAN—has just had completed a thorough repair, in doing which I found the centres of the engines very much out of truth, not only causing in her very much friction but a serious increase of wear and tear. The manufacturer was to blame for building her in this state; it has now been rectified at our expense and the Engine has been doing much better since, and should no serious accident occur to her she may run 9 or 10 thousand miles without any repair of consequence, but will then require the wheels re-turning, and probably the tubes will be principally worn out.

At the end of this report I adjoin the consumption of coke with her work done for 2 days since the repairs, and the same previous to that time.[1]

ÆOLUS. Hitherto this engine has done her work very well, and is certainly the best engine Tayleur has delivered to us; she has now run about 15 thousand miles and requires a heavy repair. The principal part of the tubes, I fear, are bad but until the Ferriles are taken out I am unable to state the real state of them. The wheels are also very bad, particularly the large wheels, and the joint between the steam duct and cylinder has failed, to remedy which I fear it will be necessary to take out the cylinder and remake it; there is a chance, however, of making it tight without, and in which I have succeeded with Apollo; should I find it necessary to take the cylinder out, that with the tubes and large wheels will require 3 or 4 weeks to put her in good order again. These are the principal repairs required in the Æolus; she will run as she is now doing by a little attention to her for a few weeks longer until we are enabled to lay her up.

BACCHUS. This engine has never been a fortunate engine for us. There is some very serious strain upon one of the valve gears, owing to which several stoppages have taken place from either the levers or weigh bar breaking. I have in vain tried to trace the cause to untruth in the work, the little I have discovered and put right, but the same accident occurred last Saturday. I can now only attribute it to the nature of the metal on the face of the valve causing a serious friction from being soft, as I have known a similar case.

I am now having new valves cast and I hope after they are in the engine will be very well as this is the only serious thing about her.

NEPTUNE. She is at present generally in a very good state of repair, and has hitherto worked very well and at little cost for repairs; she will probably run about 7 to 8 thousand miles without any heavy repairs.

APOLLO. This engine is also in very good order with the exception of one lever which is now making, and it will only require about one day to put it on. She will do fully as much work as the Neptune before any great repairs may be necessary.

VENUS. This, I may say, is the worst engine delivered by Tayleur; I have been unable to make any use of her as a regular train engine, but we have kept her as a Pilot at Maidenhead. The great fault about her is the Boiler which is not tight, to remedy which it will be necessary to take the under casing off and caulk the boiler afresh; this is not a work of much expense and ten days or a fortnight would put her into very good order.

There is one great source of expense in all the engines delivered by Tayleur & Co, and that is in the steam pipes in the smokebox; all the joints ought to have been made by facing the metal true, and not using any Compo or other substance between them, the heat being too great. Lead or canvas is soon burnt and the steam escapes through, not only destroying the blast but wasting a considerable portion of the steam. In repairing the Vulcan I put new pipes and had all the flanches faced and so far they are perfectly tight. I propose doing them all soon as they come in for heavy repairs when we will have time to do it. The whole of Tayleur's tenders have been very badly constructed; they have all had a good deal done to them, the axles also have nearly all broken and the whole of the fractures have shown either very bad iron or unsound work. The springs also both in engines and tenders, have been too weak and broken and a considerable amount has been spent upon them in replacing the springs.

The above report deals entirely with faults of workmanship, and does not touch the almost equally important question of proportional leading

---

[1] The figures referred to show that on 23rd August 1838, one month before the repairs, *Vulcan* ran 192 miles with 50 tons at 24 miles per hour, consuming 96 cwt. of coke or at the rate of 1.1 lb. per ton per mile. On 1st January, after the repairs, the engine ran 192 miles with 38 tons at 29½ miles per hour, consuming 56 cwt. of coke, or 0.86 lb. per ton per mile.

dimensions. This appears to have come up shortly afterwards, for in May 1839 Brunel wrote to Saunders enclosing a copy of Gooch's estimate for 'altering the three 8 ft. engines with small cylinders, *Venus*, *Apollo*, and *Neptune*, and reducing the driving wheels to 6 ft. 2 in. diameter. The alteration will, I think, render them serviceable engines'.

In accordance with this scheme *Apollo* was shortly afterwards altered, retaining the old frames which had the axle guards placed above them. The lowering of the frames also necessitated a reduction in size of the leading wheels to about 3 feet diameter. *Venus* was recorded in 1843 as one of the old engines not at work but must have been similarly modified, possibly shortly afterwards, since it appears thus in later records of the locomotive stock. *Neptune* was taken out of service before 1843, and evidently not considered worth the expense of alteration.

Of the larger engines *Vulcan* was converted to a tank engine but retained the 8 foot driving wheels and ran until 1868. *Æolus* was altered to have

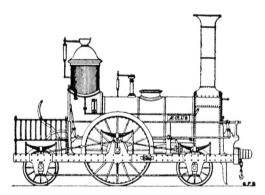

*Aeolus* 1838 (after alteration of driving wheels to 6 feet)

6 foot wheels in 1843 but *Bacchus*, who was always in trouble, disappeared from the effective list, together with *Neptune*, about 1841–2, though they were not disposed of until later. *Æolus*, *Apollo*, and *Venus* with 6 foot wheels, were converted to tank engines and ran until about 1867–1870.

The next engines to be described are those by Mather, Dixon & Co of Liverpool, of which there were six in all, but unfortunately full particulars are not available. The first of these, *Premier*, was delivered on the same day as *Vulcan* and therefore shared with the latter the distinction of being one of the two first engines received by the Great Western. *Ariel* arrived in March 1838. Both engines were intended to be alike, as shown by the table of dimensions, but for some reason the cylinders of *Premier* were $14\frac{1}{2}$ inch diameter by $14\frac{1}{2}$ inch stroke, whilst those of *Ariel* were 14 inches by 14 inches. The driving wheels had a diameter of 7 feet. The peculiar feature was the short stroke, which was less than that of any other engine on the line, but the ratio, 6 to 1, of diameter of driving wheel to stroke of piston in the case of *Premier* was the same as that of Tayleur's 8 feet engines. The 14 inch stroke was calculated to give a piston speed of exactly 280 feet per minute at 30 miles per hour, as specified by Brunel, but it appears from correspondence with another firm that Brunel was not in favour of a short stroke, and Mather Dixon's later engines were therefore made with larger driving wheels instead.

On 19th June 1838 Brunel wrote to Mather, Dixon & Co:

> Ariel has faulty springs and too narrow wheels, so that they are constantly going off the line at the crossings. The tenders are altogether too slight and shockingly noisy and only holding 200 to 300 gallons.

In the same letter he stipulated that the other engines to be supplied by the firm should have 8 foot wheels, 16 inch cylinders, and increased steam capacity.

No authentic illustration of these engines is known to exist, and one which has been published as *Premier* is obviously that of a later engine of Gooch's 1840 type. Judging from correspondence between Brunel and Mather, Dixon & Co on the subject of extra payment for adding an outside frame to the later engine *Ajax*, it seems probable that *Premier* and *Ariel* had inside frames and bearings only. The chimneys were of oval shape, 17 inches by 13 inches. Some very interesting particulars are contained in two reports by Gooch, of which the first forms a portion of the one referred to previously, and reads as follows:

> ARIEL and PREMIER. Both these engines are at work and in good repair; they are however not adapted to our fast trains owing to two causes, the principal one of which is her having only single eccentrics and in consequence the engine works without any lead, is in fact a little the reverse, and to attain high speed lead is indispensable, the construction of the boilers is also much against them from the difficulty or impossibility of preventing the engine priming or throwing the water into the cylinders of the out boiler with the steam, the tendency to do which increases as the speed. I therefore think that even should we put 2 more eccentrics in, a high speed could only be attained at great risk of burning the box or tubes, as it could only be done by running with the water very low in the boiler. There is also another thing in the engines much against them and that is the slide valves themselves, they are made upon a plan once tried upon the Liverpool line 5 years ago—commonly called a double slide—the great evil attending them is great increase of rubbing surface; in the above engines the total quantity in two cylinders amounts to 300 square inches, and which with a pressure of 50 lbs on the square inch amounts to an enormous friction against the engine. This has been the cause of the great destruction to the valve gear, a single slide would not have had above 100 square inches, only half of what it now is. To put a new sort of valve gear would cost about £70 or £80.

The type of slide valve to which Gooch refers was one which had been tried by R. Stephenson & Co in 1832 and almost immediately abandoned. It is sometimes termed the divided valve. The steam ports are near the ends of the cylinder, and there are two openings into the central exhaust port. Each of the two slides on one spindle controlled the admission and exhaust at one end only of the cylinder.

It appears that the report of these two engines was considered to be so serious that Gooch was asked to submit further particulars. These are given in the following letter to Saunders, dated Paddington, 21st January 1839.

> According to your request I send you a report upon the alterations required to be made to Messrs Mather & Dixon's engines in order to make them such engines as we require for our trains. In the first place one great defect lies in the construction of the boiler. The

accompanying sketch will more clearly show you where the fault lies and I have given another sketch showing the best plan in my opinion of curing the evil.

In the present boiler the height from the crown of the firebox A to the top of the barrel or cylindrical part of the boiler BB containing the tubes is only 9⅜ inches, and from the crown A to the top of the outside box C is 20 inches. The pipe D is the pipe conveying the

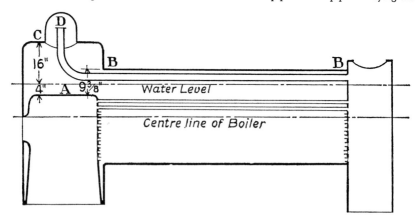

steam to the cylinders, open at the end in the dome, the mouth of which is 26 inches from A; now when the engine in in working order or taking a train we should never have less than 4 inches of water on the crown of the firebox as shown by the blue line, which only leaves 5⅜ inches of steam room in the barrel and in the box 16 inches. The steam pipe almost fills up this little in the barrel and the remaining quantity is so small compared with the quantity required to fill each cylinder that there is in consequence (when the engine runs at any speed) a very great agitation of the water in the box, and there being so small a stock, as it may be called, the part next the water is required, and giving a strong current along the barrel of the boiler it must inevitably carry the water with it. The remedy which I should propose as the cheapest is to put a sugar loaf top to the box as shown in sketch No. 2, and so form a reservoir for the steam when of course the agitation will be much less. And I think it would be able to run with water in the boiler sufficient for safety, which is not the case at present, for often when the Ariel and Premier are running with a light train and get to any speed the engineman is not able to shut the steam off at the stations or the water would fall below the top of the firebox—he is obliged to bring her up by reversing and allowing a portion of the steam to remain upon her. The top of the sugar loaf should be carried at least 3 feet 6 inches above the top of the box A and kept as large as is consistent with safety.

The other principal defect lies in the valves and valve gear, in the first place the valves are much too large or rather there are two of them when one would do as well, causing a very great increase of friction and strain upon the gear which works it, without having any advantage of consequence to recommend it—and secondly there are only two fixed eccentrics, one for each slide; upon this plan it is quite impossible to give any lead to the slides, but on the contrary they must be much behindhand in giving steam to the piston, for even with our small valves after an engine has worked a few weeks there is a degree of straining in the levers, etc., driving them, and when we set them with $\frac{5}{16}$ths to ⅜ths of an inch lead we do not get more than half this when running. Therefore if instead of having ⅜ths when no strain is on the gear we have $\frac{1}{16}$th the other way (or what we call lap) how will the valve be placed when working with the full pressure on, particularly when the valves are very heavy as in this case? They must be at least ⅜ths of an inch behindhand—and without we can have lead in the slide high speeds cannot be attained. I have tried several of our 8 feet wheel engines and also the Star with various quantities of lead and have found the engines do best with about $\frac{5}{16}$ths. To remedy the present evil of Mather & Dixon's engines it would be necessary to put in the four eccentrics or let the present two be loose. The last is a plan, I however should not recommend, loose eccentrics have been found very troublesome. The expense of putting gear with four would not be much upon each engine, something between £70 and £80, and it would be by far the most complete job when finished, as at present upon the engines I have seen the gear is much too light and such as I do not consider is to be depended upon.

The above letter is of great interest both from the personal and the historical aspects. Although Gooch was not yet twenty-three years of age it shows keen powers of observation, and an early ability to discern the causes of trouble. It also shows that many of the faults of the engines were due to the manufacturers and to causes for which Brunel, who in respect of the design of details had left them a free hand, was in no way responsible.

The firm of Mather, Dixon & Co had not had the experience in loco-motive building which was possessed by R. Stephenson & Co and in a lesser degree by Vulcan Foundry. The history of Mather Dixon's engines on other railways shows that nearly all of them had exceedingly short careers and were removed from service before contemporary engines by other leading firms.

Whether *Premier* and *Ariel* were altered in accordance with Gooch's suggestions does not appear, but as *Ariel* ran only 7,840 miles before being withdrawn from service it seems likely that it remained in its original condition. *Premier* may have had some modifications, but its total mileage was only 14,789. Both appear in the 1843 statement of locomotive stock as 'old engines not at work'. The mileage accounts show that they did not run after 1840.

Following the above came several engines from other firms, but Mather, Dixon & Co's next engine was *Ajax*, delivery of which was accepted in December 1838. This remarkable locomotive had driving wheels no less than 10 feet diameter, and cylinders 14 inches by 20 inches, and all the wheels, instead of having spokes, were formed of pieces of boiler plate, cut to shape and riveted together. The form was not unlike that of the disc wheels of some types of racing motor-cars of to-day.

The dimensions given in Brunel's official record of the Company's locomotives differ in most important respects from those given in Whishaw's book. The latter gives the driving wheels as 8 feet, and the two pairs of carrying wheels as 4 feet in diameter. Brunel's list shows the latter to have been 5 feet. Whishaw also gives the piston stroke as 18 inches instead of 20 inches. The latter figure must be accepted, since at 30 miles per hour the piston speed would in this case be 280 feet per minute, the amount specified by Brunel. Whether the driving wheels were subsequently reduced to 8 feet is uncertain, since there is no record of any such alteration; nevertheless, it is not unlikely that a spare pair of 8 foot wheels, which existed at the end of 1839, may have been used under *Ajax*, and the leading wheels correspondingly reduced.

Both Brunel's and Whishaw's records show that the boiler was of the same dimensions as those of *Premier* and *Ariel*, and of ridiculously small size.

Beyond his stipulation as to piston speed Brunel was not responsible for the extraordinary dimensions of this engine, which were decided by the makers. On 27th July 1837 he wrote to J. Grantham, the representative of Mather, Dixon & Co:

> I have never received any plan of the large plate wheel, . . . I am very anxious to see these large sheels, particularly as by your letter you have gone boldly to 10 feet, instead of 9 feet, which we talked of.

The following letter to Grantham, dated 13th July 1838, seems to show that Brunel had, perhaps reluctantly, accepted wheels 10 feet diameter for one engine, as a *fait accompli.*

> I shall be glad to hear from you exactly what dimensions you have adopted in the four engines now making by you, as regards the cylinders and wheels particularly, as I have not heard from you since my letter of 19th June, in which I left you to decide on your own suggestion of increasing the cylinders to 16 inches.
>
> As regards the wheels, I understand that one has 10 feet wheels, the second to have 8 feet, the third the same, and the fourth wheels not begun.

But the question of payment for the larger wheels brought forth the following letter from Brunel, dated 1st January 1839:

> As to the original construction of the engine proposed by you and described in your letter of yesterday, I agree, also as to the subsequent proposal on your part to increase the stroke of the cylinder, and my reply consenting, provided the wheel were increased. But the 10 ft wheel was not then thought of, because the increase of stroke referred to by you in your letter of July 8th was only to 16 inches. . . . The subject of the 10 ft. wheel was then discussed and no particular objections that I can recollect were urged on either side. I think you had not arrived at the conclusion that outside framing would be necessary, indeed the 10 ft. wheel was never mentioned by me till after I had received this letter of yours of the 26th of July.

Brunel was prepared to advise the Directors to share the additional cost of larger wheels and outside framing, but left the firm to address the Board directly 'if the 10 foot wheel and the consequences which you say arise from its adoption are to be considered by you as *ordered by me*'.

Gooch's report to the Directors stated:

> AJAX. This is an engine lately delivered by Mather, Dixon & Co, she has worked a few days on trial, but the same faults exist in her as in the Ariel and Premier; the present gearing in her is much too light to drive the valves and has already failed upon one engine. They have sent two others which are in the yard, but not having seen the work of them I cannot report upon it. The boilers are the same as those previously mentioned; part of a third is also come but I cannot speak as to her work or dimensions.

As a result of this Brunel seems to have paid special attention to the working of *Ajax* and on 23rd April 1839 wrote the following report to the Directors, which directly traverses Gooch's brief condemnation.

> Gentlemen. Within the last ten days I have had several opportunities of examining the working of the Ajax. All the gearing of the engine appear to me to work very smoothly, indicating sufficient strength and good workmanship. There is no priming and plenty full supply of steam with a train consisting of three railway carriages, three loaded carriage trucks and a horse box; an average speed of 30 miles an hour was maintained exclusive of stoppages, and it appeared to me that when the engine was better known and understood by the engineer that the performance would be improved, as in that experiment there was an excess of steam but the engine appeared throttled.   During the high gales of last week this engine has been much more delayed than the others, but the comparison has been made only with the two 'Stars', the 'Atlas' and 'Lion', engines of greater power—and which have been longer running[1]—to what extent this delay is to be

---

[1] As regards *Morning Star* he was in error. This engine was delivered one month after *Ajax*.

attributed to want of power or to increased resistance from the surface exposed[1] I am not yet prepared to say, but from the performances of the engine in fair weather I think that in power and speed it will be about on a par with the Vulcan large engines, while the workmanship is very superior and the consumption of coke singularly small.

There are some trifling alterations required in unimportant parts of the engine but which can be better done when it is thrown off work for a day or two, at present it is necessarily in constant use.

I am, Gentlemen,
Your obedient Servant
I. K. BRUNEL.

*Ajax* 1838

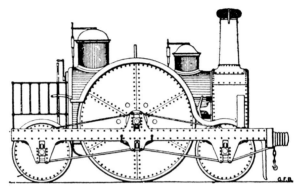

The illustration of *Ajax*[2] shows a large dome over the firebox casing in addition to a smaller one on the boiler barrel. This arrangement with two domes must have been due to Gooch's report on Mather, Dixon's boilers and substituted for his original suggestion of a 'sugar-loaf' (i.e., Gothic) form of firebox casing. The chimney was oval in section, 17 inches by 13 inches, as in *Premier*. The last mileage entry against *Ajax* in the books was for the half-year ending 30th June 1840, and its total mileage was 15,264. The boiler was subsequently used for stationary work.

Gooch's report of 2nd January 1839, quoted above, makes reference to two other engines and part of a third, which had just been delivered by Mather, Dixon & Co and were then standing in the yard. One of these, probably the last mentioned, was *Mars*, with which another pair of 10 foot wheels had been sent. For this and possibly other causes the engine was not accepted by the Company, and a new pair of 8 foot driving wheels had to be substituted by the makers, who may also have had to make alterations to the boiler, which was originally similar to those of *Premier* and *Ajax*. *Mars* was not finally passed for acceptance until 20th April 1840, after which it ran 10,500 miles, almost entirely with goods and ballast trains, but was recorded in the June 1843 return as already on the shelf. There is no mileage entry after December 1840 and the engine was sold in 1845.

The remaining two engines by Mather, Dixon & Co, *Planet* and *Mercury*, would appear from the above to have been in the Great Western

---

[1] This has reference to the large plate wheels.

[2] Drawing by the late Mr G. F. Bird derived from an original contemporary sketch in a notebook by E. T. Lane, who was in the Great Western Railway Locomotive Department in the early days.

yard by December 1838. If so, and since they were not accepted by the Company until 1st August and 26th September 1839 respectively, they must also have required considerable alterations, probably to boilers and valve gear, since the 8 foot driving wheels, which they always had, had been agreed upon beforehand. Very little information concerning these engines has been preserved, and whether they were enlargements of the *Premier* type or, as is more likely, designed on the lines of *Ajax*, is not known. Whishaw has recorded the leading dimensions, from which we find that the boilers were of similar dimensions to those of the preceding engines. Brunel's record of Mather, Dixon's boilers show that they originally had 111 $1\frac{5}{8}$ inch tubes, but Whishaw's list, which was of a later date, gives the number as 96. Whether Whishaw's dimensions were incorrect or, as is possible, the alterations for the purpose of obtaining the much needed extra steam space included the lowering of the firebox roof and a consequent reduction in the number of tubes, we do not know.

The cylinders of *Planet*, as given by Whishaw, were 16 inches by 20 inches, and there is evidence that this size may be correct since Brunel wrote to Grantham on 19th June 1838:

> I think 8 ft. wheels will be large enough for the other engines which you can alter and if you feel confident about the capacity for steam, which I do not, I should certainly prefer 16 inch cylinders.

Judging from the size of the boiler it is probable that Brunel's opinion was correct; nevertheless, *Planet* ran a total mileage of 25,290, a figure greater than that reached by any other of the six engines built by the firm. In June 1843 it figured amongst the old derelicts 'out of work'. Its last mileage entry was for the half-year ending 30th June 1840.

*Mercury*, according to Whishaw, had cylinders only 14 inches by 18 inches, and it is possible that smaller cylinders may have replaced those 16 inches in diameter, owing to the small boiler. It was the only engine by Mather, Dixon & Co which was reported in June 1843 as 'in good order and ballasting', having run 16,969 miles. But something seems to have happened to it, for it ran only 40 additional miles during the next twelve months, and before July 1844 had joined the happy band of unemployables.

When Mather, Dixon & Co asked for payment for their engines there was more trouble. On 31st May 1839 they wrote to Saunders:

> Your letter of the 25th is before us and we cannot conceal our astonishment at the view you have taken of our responsibility as to the first two engines [*i.e.*, *Premier* and *Ariel*] supplied by us. It is the first instance which has come to our knowledge where a Company, having given its approval of the plans and construction of an engine, and having had the use of it between one and two years, has requested the manufacturers to undertake the repairs for an indefinite period at their own cost.

The firm certainly appears to have had some cause for grievance, not only in that its drawings had been approved by Brunel, but that the engines had been worked, even if unsatisfactorily, on regular trains for some time. On 11th July Mather, Dixon & Co agreed to alter *Premier* and *Ariel*, and put them into a complete state of repair at their own cost, except that certain sums were to be paid by the Company. Nevertheless, negotiations dragged on, though the Great Western paid £1,777 on account, and on 17th October 1840 a long letter pleading for a final settlement of the account was written by the firm. In this the following significant passages occur:

> It is a source of deep regret to us that our engines have caused them [*i.e.*, the Directors] disappointment, but for this we can only *share* the blame, and we have expressed our willingness to share the loss. The circumstances which led to the defects of the engines are well known to you, and we would merely enquire whether, as a matter of justice, individuals should be made to bear *all* the weight of the losses incurred in making experiments for the benefit of a public Company to carry out a principle originating with themselves, and progressing under their sanction and by their desire. . . .
>
> We make these statements in the hopes that the Directors upon consideration will see that our case is one of peculiar hardship, and if they recollect that most of the defects arose from our desire, at Mr Brunel's request, to avoid weight, a point in which other makers were not so much restricted, they will view the matter more favourably.

Three engines by Sharp, Roberts & Co of Manchester were of much more ordinary and modest dimensions, and although they had certain peculiarities, none of them can with fairness be included amongst the regiment of freaks. In the first place the driving wheels were only 6 feet in diameter, and in this respect the correspondence shows that the manufacturers had an absolutely free hand. There are some very interesting letters relating to these engines. On 22nd September 1836 Messrs Sharp, Roberts & Co wrote to the Directors:

> It will be seen, however, on reference to the sketch, that we propose to make the propelling wheels 6 feet in diameter, the cylinders 14 ins, diameter, and the stroke 12 ins., the fire box (which is intended to be of copper) 2ft. 6 in. long by 4 ft. 4½ in. broad, the boiler 8 ft. long by 3 ft. 6 in. in diameter, proposed to be fitted up with about 120 brass tubes, 1¾ in, diamr.
>
> We propose to make the steam valves and the wheels on our patent principle; the former having been proved to work almost free from friction, and the latter, we may venture to state, are the most approved wheels now in use, and such as we are making for the Grand Junction and other railways.
>
> The price at which we should be disposed to make one engine only, as described above and similar to the sketch, would be from £1300 to £1400, if ordered immediately, and the time in which we would undertake the delivery, eight to twelve months.
>
> The engine tenders made by us are entirely of metal, and consequently much more durable than those made of wood. We have not however had time to make drawings of one adapted to your line, and therefore cannot name an exact price, but we presume it will be from £220 to 250.

The first point to be noted in the above is that the makers, in order to meet Brunel's views as to limited piston speed, proposed a very short stroke of 12 inches, similar to that then being tried on the Liverpool & Manchester engines, which with a 6 foot driving wheel would have given the specified piston speed of 280 feet per minute. The firm's standard engines which they were then building for the Grand Junction Railway had a stroke of 18 inches. In the second place they refer to their patent valves. These can only mean Roberts's piston valves, which consisted of long hollow bronze pistons having inner and outer chambers.[1]

Later in 1836 Brunel wrote asking Sharp, Roberts & Co to increase the diameter of the steam 'passages', and that he had determined to have two fire-doors 'or one of not less than 18 inches wide. I should prefer the

---

[1] These piston valves are illustrated in Colburn's *Locomotive Engineering*, page 40.

former.' Subsequently on 2nd June 1837 he wrote disapproving of the short stroke, although reiterating his desire to keep the piston speed down to 280 feet per minute at 30 miles per hour.

As you have adopted 6 feet driving wheels I think there is a difficulty—but if no delay will arise from the alteration, I think with 14 or 15 inch stroke and a 13 inch piston the engines would be more serviceable but not so fast as the others which you are making. I will leave you the option, provided a change will not delay the delivery and shall be glad to hear what you decide.

Actually a compromise was made between the 12 inch stroke originally proposed and Sharp & Co's standard of 18 inches, and the engines were built with cylinders 14 inch diameter by 15 inch stroke. In other respects they conformed generally to the firm's standard design, but owing to the width of the gauge the frames were placed between instead of outside the wheels. The weight empty, as given by Whishaw, was 16 tons. The three engines of this class were *Lion* (May 1838), *Atlas* (June 1838), and *Eagle* (November 1838).

A letter to the builders appears to show that *Lion* was delivered with a single central buffer. On 13th July 1838 Brunel wrote:

Three successive accidents have happened to the same valve of the 'Lion'.
Upon my referring to my correspondence with you, I cannot find any mention of a single central buffer. How did the mistake arise?

The above also shows that the piston valve had already given much trouble before the engine had been two months at work.

Gooch's report of January 1839 refers to these engines as follows:

EAGLE. This engine is working very well but the consumption of coke is very much greater than in the large-wheeled engines in the proportion to the Vulcan, as she has been running for the last 2 or 3 days, of 48 to 30, and to the Æolus of 48 to 38—this quantity of bags or cwts, is consumed in 4 trips. I think it is mainly owing to the smallness of the firebox and the consequent diminution in the blast pipe which ought to be larger in proportion to the size of the cylinders than in the Vulcan from the rapid succession of blasts and consequently keeping the chimney better exhausted; there is also much more loss in the cylinders from the short stroke and small wheel—it was found on the Liverpool line, when they tried the 12 inch stroke instead of a 16, one third more fuel was consumed to run the same distance from the same cause to which I attribute the loss in the Eagle. It would however be remedied by putting a greater quantity of fire surface in the box; otherwise the machinery of the engine is very compact and substantial and I think we will find her a serviceable engine as regards repairs.[1]

ATLAS. The new cylinders are now in this engine and I expect to have her ready in about 2 weeks, should nothing unforeseen occur to delay the work when she is ready. I expect her to be much such an engine as the Eagle.

LION. This engine has been constantly at work ballasting or assisting in some way, but as I have previously reported to you the cause of her not working the trains it is useless recounting them. However, as soon as the Atlas is ready I propose bringing her into the shed, after which in about 7 weeks I hope to have her ready the same as the Eagle and Atlas.

As to *Lion*, G. H. Gibbs has the following entry in his diary under date 25th July 1838:

Went in the evening to Englefield via Slough. The 'Lion' did not appear equal to the work and was 57 minutes on the road.

---

[1] Although Gooch makes no mention of it, it is very likely that the long piston valves, which had no packing rings, allowed a considerable quantity of steam to leak past them into the exhaust, thereby causing much waste in addition to the loss due to excessive proportion of clearance space.

Gooch in the above report refers to new cylinders for *Atlas*, and Whishaw in his tabulated dimensions of the engines gives the cylinders of all three as 14 inch by 18 inch stroke. Probably the old cylinders with piston valves were removed and new ones with longer stroke, in accordance with Sharp & Co's usual practice, were then substituted. Later official records of the engines show 15 inch by 18 inch cylinders.

*Lion* 1838

After their alterations they appear to have been reliable engines. In the June 1843 returns their recorded mileages to date were: *Lion*, 71,621; *Atlas*, 78,304; and *Eagle*, 51,285. The last two were 'rebuilt' in 1860, though whether any of the originals remained is extremely problematical.

So far we have described engines, the dimensions of the majority of which were abnormal. But there were in addition four others, which may be described as 'super-freaks', in that not only their dimensions but also their construction were of the wild-cat order. Of these, three were arranged with toothed gear wheels between the crank-shaft and the driving axle, in order to obtain a high wheel velocity in conjunction with the low piston speed which Brunel desired.

The first of them, *Thunderer*, was built by R. & W. Hawthorn of New-castle to the general arrangement and patents of T. E. Harrison, who in later years was well known as the Chief Engineer of the North Eastern Railway. The main feature of the design was the complete separation of the engine from the boiler, each forming an independent vehicle. The whole constituted a sort of procession. First came the engine, the cylinders of which were placed at the back, and the driver took his stand in an exposed position in front of them. The second vehicle carried the boiler only, which was of the usual locomotive type with smokebox and chimney in front, conveniently arranged so that the steam and exhaust pipes passed directly from the smokebox end to the cylinders on the first vehicle. The connections were made by means of gland pipes with ball and socket joints at each end. The fireman, who was separated from the driver, stood on a footplate in the usual place at the rear of the boiler carriage. The third vehicle was an ordinary tender, and finally there came the train 'at the back of beyond'. One of the objects of the arrangement was to obtain a large boiler, at the same time avoiding excessive weight on the engine wheels, but there was the disadvantage of making the adhesive weight of the engine too small. It was also claimed that the boiler carriage could always be uncoupled when the engine was under repairs, and used with another similar engine, or *vice versa*.

The engine of *Thunderer*[1] was carried on four wheels, 6 foot diameter, coupled together. The cylinders were 16 inches by 20 inches, and the connecting rods drove a crank shaft which had bearings in the carriage frame vertically above the leading axle of the latter, the shaft and the axle being connected by gearing in the ratio of 27 to 10.[2] The equivalent diameter of a driving wheel was therefore over 16 feet. The boiler, which had a six-wheeled carriage, was certainly a good one with a very large fire-box. The latter had a longitudinal 'midfeather' or intermediate water space, which divided it into two portions, each having a separate fire-door. This caused inconvenience, since one fire tended to go out when the other was burning briskly after lighting up, and sometimes delayed the engine before joining the train.

We can imagine that such an engine would appeal to Brunel, who not only obtained thereby his low piston speed but also an engine weight nearer to the 10½ tons limit than that of any other on the line. Nicholas Wood gave the weight of the engine portion as 12 tons. G. H. Gibbs records that on 12th July 1838 Brunel explained to the entire satisfaction of the Board the grounds on which he had originally recommended Harrison's engine. The arrangement made with Harrison in June 1837 was that the latter should furnish drawings and directions to Messrs Hawthorn, but the firm shortly afterwards wrote that his tracing contained only the principle. It seems, therefore, that the details of the design were made by the firm. No price was fixed when the order was given on 1st July 1837[3] and Brunel wrote:

> I am willing to trust to the respectability of your firm. . . . I am most anxious that these engines should be amongst the earliest to run upon our line, . . . the success of the experiment will depend much upon this [*i.e.*, the workmanship], and if it be successful great numbers of similar engines will certainly be immediately required.

The 'Thunderer' was accepted by the Company on 6th March 1838. G. H. Gibbs mentions in his diary, under date 12th May 1838, that he had a double trip on the footplate. 'Along the greater part of the 4 miles the engine ran beautifully smooth and for some way we cleared 60 miles an hour.' But Gooch's report of January 1839 contains the following:

> THUNDERER. This engine has been at work some time but it does not work so favourably in point of speed or cost as the Vulcan engine or the Star. She has required a considerable

---

[1] Illustrations purporting to represent *Thunderer* and Harrison's second Great Western engine *Hurricane* have been widely published, but are certainly apocryphal and contain some glaring anachronisms. A good idea of the general arrangement of the former engine may be obtained from a sectional diagram in Colburn's *Locomotive Engineering*, page 48.

[2] This, as given by Acworth in his *Railways of England*, is believed to have been the true ratio; though it is stated in the note to Brunel's table on p. 396, as 2 to 1, and by Gooch in his *Diaries* as 3 to 1.

[3] Saunders told the Select Committee in 1839 that Harrison's engines cost £3,000 each.

amount of repair and is now laid up by one of the eccentrics breaking, to repair which it has been necessary to lift out the larger open wheels; the repairs generally upon her are many.

Part of these repairs were due to the use of copper instead of brass for the tubes, of which Gooch reported that most were worn out, several being burnt through.

*Thunderer* was a complete failure and its total mileage was only 9,882, the last entry recording 680 miles during the second half of 1839. It was afterwards sold, but the boiler being good was utilized for a stationary engine.

Two other locomotives, named *Viper* and *Snake*, in which motion was communicated to the driving wheels by means of toothed gearing, were built by the Haigh Foundry Company of Wigan in 1838. What they were originally like or how the gearing was arranged is not known. The cylinders are shown in the list prepared at the end of 1838 as $14\frac{3}{4}$ inch diameter by 18 inch stroke, the diameter of the driving wheels as 6 feet 4 inches, and the ratio of the gearing as 3 to 2.

No sooner had they arrived than there was trouble. On 16th July 1838 Brunel wrote to the makers and stated that in the original drawing submitted to him the lowest point of the gearing was shown 17 inches above the rails, and that he 'was surprised to find it very different, the teeth of the driving wheel being within 10 inches of the rails, so that when the springs yielded this would probably be reduced to $8\frac{1}{2}$ inches'. For this reason he did not consider them safe. On 6th August he wrote again that he had been instructed by the Directors to say that 'they cannot allow the engines to run in their present state'. In the Directors' Report of the 12th it was stated that they were under the necessity of declining to receive them, but on the 30th the Board agreed to take them under certain conditions.

On 25th October Brunel informed the builders that the Company had not yet succeeded in making the two engines 'perform the regular work of the trains, so as to be used at all for this purpose', and added that Gooch reported the regulator work so weak as to require renewing and that the valve gear had also to be altered. In Gooch's report of January 1839 they are referred to as follows:

SNAKE and VIPER. Neither of these engines are sufficiently to be depended upon to run the trains. The causes I have previously reported to you. As they are, they can only be used for ballasting, to alter them so as to make efficient engines of them would cost about £350 to £400 per engine—the boiler and wheels would do again very well and perhaps parts of the engine might be brought in. I think the cylinders are very defective in having the steam so much throttled in the eduction. I think a pair of 13 inch cylinders with 18 inch stroke and 6 ft. wheel would make the engines good useful engines. As they are, the repairs they will require to keep them at work will soon swallow up their value.

Further correspondence during March–May 1839 shows that the alterations which were to be made included new cylinders and steam pipes, new valve gear and regulator, and also new outside framing. These were subsequently carried out, probably in 1839 or 1840, and the gearing removed. *Viper* appears in the list of June 1843 with a recorded mileage of 28,410, and *Snake* of 20,513. In July 1844 both were reported 'in perfectly good order, having been repaired for the Oxford line'. In 1846 they were re-christened *Teign* and *Exe* respectively,[1] but both resumed their old names by 1852, after which both were at work until 1868. They then had 6 foot driving wheels and 15 inch by 18 inch cylinders and were probably complete renewals, though this cannot be definitely stated with certainty.

*Teign* alias *Viper*

Of the freaks, one more engine, *Hurricane*, built by R. & W. Hawthorn and accepted by the Company in October 1838, remains to be described. This was also constructed in accordance with a portion of Harrison's patent, in so far as engine and boiler were on independent vehicles, but the spur gearing was omitted.

The engine portion was carried on six wheels, with the driving pair, 10 feet in diameter, in the middle. As in *Thunderer*, the cylinders, 16 inch diameter by 20 inch stroke, were at the back, and similarly connected by jointed pipes to the front of the boiler. The latter was exactly similar to that of *Thunderer*.

The 10 foot driving wheels were made with spokes and not as plated discs like those of *Ajax*. But shortly after the engine had been put into service a water-tank dropped off the frame and became entangled in the spokes, some of which were broken.[2]

Gooch's January 1839 report refers to this engine as follows:

HURRICANE. During the short time this engine was at work she worked very well, fully equal to any we have, she has not, however, done enough work to judge at what cost she will do it for us; she is certainly a much better engine than the Thunderer. From a letter received from Hawthorn & Co. I expect the new wheels up here in a fortnight.

When put into regular service on the trains to and from Twyford it was found that *Hurricane's* coke consumption was exceedingly heavy. For the six months ending 31st December 1839 the average was 57·3 lb per mile, compared with a mean of 43·6 lb per mile for all other engines at work. The mileage book shows that it must have been laid aside by the end of the year, having run a total of 10,527 miles.

---

[1] These names suggest that they were sent to the South Devon Railway, which the Great Western supplied with locomotives from 1846 to 1851.

[2] Acworth states in his *Railways of England* (Murray 1889) that the boss of one of these wheels 'was used as a counterweight to balance a coal crane outside Swindon Station'.

In September 1845 we find Gooch offering two pairs of 10 foot driving wheels for sale to Mr Stubbs of Llanelly Dock. 'One pair are plate wheels, the other open wheels on Locke's[1] pattern, both are perfectly new and have never been under an engine. The cost to the Company was £240 each pair, and I should think are now worth £150 the pair, delivered in Bristol.'

The wheels in question must have been those delivered with *Mars*, and a spare pair for *Hurricane*. Apparently Mr Stubbs did not buy, for in 1846 two pairs of 10 foot wheels, corresponding to the above, were lent to Messrs Grissell & Peto for the purpose of transporting the equestrian statue of the Duke of Wellington from the sculptor's studio in Harrow Road to Hyde Park. *Hurricane's* boiler was used for the second *Bacchus* built in 1849.

The dimensions of most of the preceding engines are given in the table on page 396, which is a copy of the original in the possession of the Company. The drawings of the engines were made by the late Mr G. F. Bird from the original sketches by E. T. Lane, now in the possession of the Science Museum, South Kensington.

Gooch recorded in his *Diaries* that after the line was opened to the public on 4th June 1838—

my difficulties with the engines began. The 'North Star' and the six from the Vulcan Foundry Company were the only ones I could at all depend upon. The result was I had to begin in a measure to rebuild one half of the stock I had to work with. For many weeks my nights were spent in a carriage in the engine-house at Paddington, as repairs had to be done to the engines at night to get them to do their work next day. The 'North Star' being the most powerful one, and in other respects the best, was my chief reliance, but she was often getting into trouble from other causes.

Gooch did not escape blame and criticism which was unfairly thrown upon him on account of the behaviour of all these engines. G. H. Gibbs made the following entry in his diary on 26th December 1838: 'Our engines are in very bad order, and Gooch seems to be very unfit for the superintendence of that department.' Again, on the 28th he wrote of 'the total unfitness of Gooch for his situation'.

Quoting once more from Gooch's *Diaries*:

The failure of so many engines made the Directors very anxious, and they called upon me, apart from Mr Brunel, to make them a report on each engine, I had hitherto done all I could to get them into working order, and had reported to Mr Brunel alone, as my chief; but the directors having called upon me for a separate report, I felt I was placed in a great difficulty, as I could only tell what I believed to be the facts. I, however, had no choice, and had to make this report, in which I condemned the construction of the engines. This alarmed the Directors, and obtained for me rather an angry letter from Mr Brunel. I will, however, do him the justice to say that he only showed it in his letter, and was personally most kind and considerate to me, leaving me to deal with the stock as I thought best. His good sense told him that what I said was correct, and his kind heart did me justice.

The greater portion of this report has already been given in connection with the various engines, and it may be noted that most of it dealt with workmanship, and very little, if any, could be said to have implicated Brunel.

[1] Probably a clerical error for Losh's.

## GREAT WESTERN RAILWAY LOCOMOTIVES
[1st January 1839]

| Name | Diameter of Cylinder | Length of Cylinder | Diameter of Boiler | Length of Boiler | Dimensions: Tubes: No. | Tubes: Diam. | Tubes: Length | Tubes: Area | Fire Box: Length | Fire Box: Width | Fire Box: Height above Bars | Fire Box: Area | Fire Box: Area of Grate | Diameter of Chimney | Wheels: Driving: No. | Driving: Diam. | Small: No. | Small: Diam. | Steam Way: Length | Steam Way: Width | Weight empty | Weight working Condition | Tender empty | Tender full |
|---|---|---|---|---|---|---|---|---|---|---|---|---|---|---|---|---|---|---|---|---|---|---|---|---|
| | In. | In. | Feet | Feet | | In. | Feet | Sq. ft. | Feet | Feet | Feet | Sq. ft. | Sq. ft. | In. | | Feet | | Feet | In. | In. | Cwt. | Cwt. | Cwt. | Cwt. |
| North Star | 16 | 16 | 4 | 8.6 | 167 | 1⅝ | 9 | 654.7 | 3.5¾ | 3.11 | 3.9¾ | 70.1 | 13.6 | 16⅝ | 2 | 7 | 4 | 4 | | | 321.5 | 364.5 | 130 | 240 |
| Vulcan<br>Æolus<br>Bacchus | 14 | 16 | 3.6 | 8.2 | 147 | 1⅝ | 8.6½ | 534 | 2.6 | 3.10 | 3.6 | 50.3 | 9.5 | 12 | 2 | 8 | 4 | 4.6 | 1¾ | 9¾ | 323 | 365 | 116 | 226 |
| Neptune<br>Apollo<br>Venus | 12 | 16 | 3.3 | 8.2 | 127 | 1⅝ | 8.6½ | 464.5 | 2.3 | 3.10½ | 3.2 | 45 | 8.71 | 10½ | 2 | 8 | 4 | 4.6 | 1¾ | 8½ | 293 | 325 | 116 | 226 |
| Lion<br>Atlas | 14 | 15 | | 8 | 112 | 1⅝ | 8.4¾ | 399.8 | 2.5 | 4.4 | 3.6 | 55.3 | 10.4 | 15 | 2 | 6 | 4 | 3.6 | | | 257.5 | 290 | 104 | 224 |
| Premier<br>Ariel | 14½<br>14 | 14½<br>14 | 3 | 8.6 | 111 | 1⅝ | 9 | 420.9 | 2.8½ | 3.9 | 3.9 | 55.2 | 10.15 | 17×13 | 2 | 7 | 4 | 4.6 | 1½ | 10 | 270 | 303 | 106 | 216 |
| Snake<br>Viper | 14¾ | 18 | 3.6 | 9 | 96 | 2 | 9.6 | 477.1 | 2.5½ | 3.5 | 3.3 | 42.5 | 8.33 | 13 | 2 | 6.4 | 4 | 3.5 | | | | | | |
| Thunderer | 16 | 20 | 3.8 | 8.8½ | 135 | 1⅝ | 9 | 516.7 | 3.8½ | 5 | 3.11 | 108.2 | 17.12 | 18 | 4 | 6 | 6 | 4.6 & 2 4.0 | 1½ | 9 | | | | |
| Ajax | 14 | 20 | 3 | 8.6 | 111 | 1⅝ | 9 | 420.9 | 2.8½ | 3.9 | 3.9 | 55.2 | 10.15 | 17×13 | 2 | 10 | 4 | 5 | 1½ | 10 | | | | |

N.B. In the Thunderer the velocity of the wheel is multiplied as 2 to 1.
In the Snake and Viper " " " as 3 to 2.

*Note.*—This list is a copy of the original among Brunel's papers at Paddington (Brunel Collection, vol. 10). *Hurricane* and *Eagle* are conspicuous by their absence; the former's driving wheels were broken (see p. 394), and the latter was evidently not on the active list at this date.

Specific instances of trouble with the engines are recorded in Seymour Clarke's reports to Saunders in Chapter XIII.

The above early period in the history of the locomotive department has been dealt with at some length, since not only is it of considerable historical technical interest, but it also brings into prominence the opinions and joint early work of those giants of the Great Western, Isambard Kingdom Brunel and Daniel Gooch.

## Second Period, 1839–1845

In consequence of the failure of so many of the Company's engines it was decided, with the full assent of Brunel, that Gooch should prepare complete drawings for future locomotives, and that the locomotive builders were to construct these in strict accordance with Gooch's designs and instructions. From his *Diaries* we learn that he took great pains over these designs, to every detail of which he gave much thought and consideration. The chief draughtsman responsible under Gooch for the drawings was Thomas Russell Crampton, who subsequently made his mark as a celebrated Locomotive Engineer, more particularly in connection with the well-known Crampton locomotives so long used on the French and other Continental railways. The drawings were lithographed and specifications printed, and, in addition, sheet-iron templates were made for those parts which it was essential to have interchangeable. Both lithographs and templates were supplied to all the locomotive builders with whom contracts for the supply of engines were made, and Gooch frequently visited the various works in the north of England during the progress of the work.

The Great Western was the first railway in the country to initiate and adopt such a system of standardized locomotives with interchangeable parts.

Before describing these standard engines, others built by R. Stephenson & Co, known as the 'Star' class, must be mentioned. *North Star* and *Morning Star* have already been described, and of the early locomotives were the only really reliable ones in service. An order was given to Messrs Stephenson for ten additional generally similar engines, delivery of which was spread over a period of nearly two and a half years. The first two, *Evening Star* and *Dog Star*, arrived in July and September 1839, but the remaining eight engines were only delivered between July 1840 and November 1841, after a considerable number of the new standard engines had been placed in service. In January 1840 the following friendly note was written by Brunel to Robert Stephenson:

My Dear Stephenson,—We have given out that we shall open our line 30 miles further by May 1st. Our line will be ready, but we shall be short of steam power. Another 'Star' would make us comparatively easy, particularly the Directors, who consider the 'Stars' double 'Stars'; I suppose as they always reckon them for two. Now can you by any extra exertions deliver us one in March?

Messrs Stephenson were apparently unable to complete this engine by the date required, for *Polar Star* did not leave their Newcastle works until

4th June 1840, to be followed by *Red Star* on 3rd July. The Great Western records show that these two engines started work in July and August respectively. They were the first to have flanges on the driving wheels.

The 'Stars' were not all alike, though the general design of framing and boilers was similar and all of them had driving wheels 7 feet in diameter, as in the case of the original *North Star*. The cylinders of seven of the engines were 15 inch diameter by 18 inch stroke, but *Polar Star* had cylinders 15½ inch diameter. The last two engines had 15½ inch cylinders by 19 inch stroke, according to Messrs Stephenson's drawings. Since the

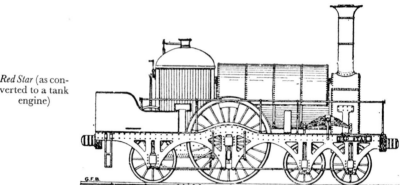

*Red Star* (as converted to a tank engine)

piston speed with 18 inch stroke at 30 miles per hour was about 361 feet per minute, Brunel's limit of 280 had already been wisely discarded, and this length of stroke was made the standard for Gooch's engines of all classes and sizes of driving wheels until 1846. All the 'Star' class had 4 foot leading and trailing wheels, but the lengths of wheel base varied in different engines, as also did the dimensions of the boilers and tubes. The mean total heating surface was about 662 sq. feet, and the pressure 50 to 55 lb per sq. inch.

Several of the 'Star' class were rebuilt in later years as eight-wheeled saddle tank engines for branch line traffic, the tenders being removed. The boilers were lengthened and in place of a single pair of leading wheels two pairs were substituted, both axles being rigid.

Gooch's standard passenger engines of 1840–1842 were direct derivatives of Messrs Stephenson's 'Stars', and if the general drawings of both classes be compared, it will be found that in most essential particulars the designs were very similar, though there were differences in dimensions, modifications in the latter having been made as a result of experience gained in the working of the 'Stars' already in service. It is in no way derogatory to Gooch's high merit as a Locomotive Engineer of great ability to state that he took Stephenson's engines as his model; on the contrary, he acted in the best interests of the Company in basing his designs upon engines which had proved generally efficient in service, at the same time improving their details. The Company had already had more than enough of experimental failures.

In all, 105 six-wheeled standard tender engines were built during the years 1840–1842. These consisted of four classes, as follows:

(1)  62 passenger engines with single 7 foot driving wheels.
(2)  21 passenger engines with single 6 foot driving wheels.
(3)  18 goods engines with four-coupled 5 foot wheels.
(4)  4 goods engines with six-coupled 5 foot wheels.

The 62 engines of Class (1) were built by the following firms:

| | |
|---|---|
| Jones, Turner & Evans of Newton-le-Willows . . . . | 6 |
| Sharp, Roberts & Co of Manchester . . . . . . | 10 |
| Fenton, Murray & Jackson of Leeds . . . . . . | 20 |
| Nasmyth, Gaskell & Co of Patricroft . . . . . . | 16 |
| R. B. Longridge & Co of Bedlington . . . . . . | 6 |
| Stothert & Slaughter of Bristol . . . . . . . | 2 |
| G. & J. Rennie of Blackfriars, London . . . . . . | 2 |

Gooch stated that all the makers did their work well, though the best engines were built by Fenton, Murray & Jackson of Leeds.

The peculiar design of slotted outside sandwich framing may be noted, a pattern which appeared in *North Star* and all the other Stephenson-built engines on the line. Sandwich frames, which were the usual practice at that period, consisted of ash or oak planking, about 3 inches thick, covered on each side with $\frac{1}{2}$-inch iron plates bolted on. Gooch used ash planking in these early engines. The triangular apertures were slotted out to lighten the structure, and this form rarely appeared in the engines of railways other than the Great Western. This design of frame was used on the line long after all other companies had discarded it, principally for the reason that the engines ran with less vibration on the old longitudinal sleeper road. The inside frames, of which there were four, were formed of wrought-iron slabs bolted to the cylinders in front and to the firebox casing at the back, and may be described as centre stays for supporting the crank axle rather than as frames. The crank axle had two outside and four inside bearings. The high dome-shaped firebox casing often termed the Gothic shape, though very common until about 1850, has long since gone out of use. The tender frames were similar to those of the engines, and their water tanks were raised above the frames, upon which they rested through the intermediary of bearers.

These engines had 7 foot flanged driving wheels, as in the 'Star' class, a diameter 1 foot larger than that of any narrow-gauge engines of that day. In later years the original 15 inch by 18 inch cylinders were replaced by larger ones 16 inches by 20 inches.

Some of the details shown in the complete specification dated 10th September 1840, which was probably a revised copy of the earlier one issued in 1839, are of considerable interest, and not only exhibit the great care taken over every part of the engines, but also the deep insight already possessed by Gooch at the age of twenty-four in respect of practical locomotive design. The straps of the connecting rods, we find, were to have wrought-iron syphons forged solid with them. It was the usual practice at that time, and for many years afterwards, to screw brass syphon oil cups into the straps. Experience proved that the latter sometimes worked loose and were thrown off when running.

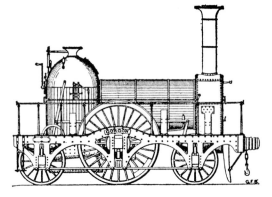

*Gorgon* 1841 (one of the 7 foot singles.)

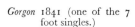

The following paragraph quoted from the specification relates to the valve gear, and attention may be drawn to the steeling and hardening of the wearing surfaces.

*Valve Gear.* The Valves shall be worked by fixed eccentrics upon the crank shaft, one to be fixed upon each side of each crank; the two inner ones shall drive the forward gear, and the outside ones the back. The eccentrics shall be made of cast iron, and fastened by two steel set bolts; there shall also be a tightening strap, as shown in drawing No. 12. The eccentric straps shall be made of best wrought iron, and welded to the eccentric rod—the Valves shall be reversed by fork ends, made as shown in drawing No. 12, the face of the fork being well steeled, and the hollow to be bushed with steel and hardened. The forks will be lifted by links attached to a steel pin on the fork; the eyes of the links being also well steeled. The Valve shafts and weigh bars shall be 2 inches in diameter at the bearings, and made of best fagotted iron well twisted. The bearings being turned to templates in order that they may all fit each other, all the levers and other parts of the Valve Gear to be well fitted and neatly made; all the pins to be steel and the eyes well steeled and hardened. Drawings Nos 14 and 15 shew the particular shape and strength of the different parts; the bearings shall work in carriages welded to the inside frame.

The steam pipe in the boiler between the regulator and the smokebox was of copper, $6\frac{1}{2}$ inch inside diameter, and the two pipes from the T-piece in the smokebox to the cylinders were $4\frac{1}{2}$ inches in diameter and made of best rolled brass. The bottom of the chimney was to be 'formed by a square box containing a grating', obviously a spark-arresting device. This is not shown in the original drawings, and may have been a later addition which first appeared in the amended specification of 1840.

Probably as a result of Brunel's earlier differences with Mather, Dixon & Co, to which reference has been made, the following sentence occurs in the concluding paragraph:

The Manufacturer is to deliver, put together, and start the engines in complete working order, upon the line of the Great Western Railway Company either at London or Bristol, as may be directed by the Company and shall be held liable for any breakages that may occur, either from bad materials or bad workmanship, until each engine has performed a distance of 1,000 miles with proper loads; at the end of which time, should the engines be perfect, the Manufacturer will be relieved from any further responsibility.

It is interesting to note that the 1,000 mile trial period was specified to the end of the Company's existence in 1947, and may have been derived from the Great Western specification of 1840.

The first engine delivered was *Firefly*, built by Jones, Turner & Evans, which arrived on 12th March 1840, and on the 25th ran from Paddington to Reading in 46½ minutes with a load of three vehicles. On the return journey a maximum speed of 56 miles per hour was attained. One of the class, *Ixion*, by Fenton, Murray & Jackson, was selected by Gooch for the speed trials before the Gauge Commissioners, to which reference is made elsewhere.

*Orion*, another of the class, was used for the opening of the Bristol & Exeter Railway on 1st May 1844, when Gooch himself drove the engine from London to Exeter and back, a total distance of 388 miles. On the return journey the train left Exeter at 5.20 p.m. and stopped at Paddington platform at 10.0.

These engines, known at first as the 'Firefly', and later for no very obvious reason as the 'Priam'[1] class, were very successful and performed excellent work for many years. A number were rebuilt between 1859 and 1864 with domeless boilers, to accommodate which the engine frames were lengthened. After 1870 they were rapidly broken up; not only had they then become too light for the increased train loads, but their services were no longer required when many broad-gauge sections of the railway were converted to narrow-gauge. The last, *Ixion*, rebuilt in 1863, disappeared in July 1879.

Of the twenty-one 6 foot single engines (Class 2), known from the first of them as the 'Sun' class, sixteen were ordered by the Great Western, eight from R. & W. Hawthorn of Newcastle, and eight from Stothert & Slaughter of Bristol; they were intended for working passenger trains between Swindon and Bristol. The remaining five of identical design had been ordered from Sharp, Roberts & Co by the Bristol & Exeter Company before the lease to the Great Western was contemplated, and were taken over from the makers by the latter Company. After some years they were all found to lack adhesive weight and were converted to tank engines by the substitution of saddle tanks over the boilers for the original tenders.

Of the goods engines (Class 3), which had the driving and trailing wheels coupled, three came from R. & W. Hawthorn, three from Fenton, Murray & Jackson, and twelve from Rothwell & Co of Bolton, Lancashire. All were built in 1841-2. They soon proved too light for the increasing loads, and like the preceding class were altered to saddle-tank engines.

The four six-coupled goods engines of 1842 were an afterthought on the part of Gooch, who instructed the builders, Nasmyth, Gaskell & Co. to

[1] *Priam* was one of the last to arrive—March 1842.

construct the last four of an order for passenger engines as trial goods engines by altering the frames and wheels to suit. They were the only six-coupled engines on the Broad Gauge to have the frames outside the wheels.

The leading dimensions of the above standard classes are given in the table opposite, and a complete list on pages 467 to 472.

After the delivery in December 1842 of the last of the 7 foot single engines, no further locomotives were built for the Company until Swindon Works produced its first engine in February 1846.

The big deep-toned Brake Whistle still carried in addition to the ordinary whistle by all ex-Great Western engines was introduced by Brunel and Gooch in the autumn of 1841 as a safety appliance to cause the instant application of brakes by the guards, and generally to indicate danger. Its sound, nowadays confined to emergencies, is quite unmistakable.

Coke was the fuel used on all railways at this time. The principal companies made their own coke, and for this purpose the Great Western had established coke ovens at West Drayton. Whishaw wrote that 'they were conveniently placed on the level of the railway, which saves much labour in filling the waggons'. As we have seen, these ovens were superseded by the larger establishment at Bristol very soon after the opening of the railway throughout.

The coke consumption of the early engines was exceedingly high, and according to one of Gooch's weekly reports, dated November 1838, varied from 40·6 to 71·6 lb per mile, in spite of the light weights of the trains.

In 1842 Gooch made a series of careful tests of the coke consumption of his new standard engines, the results of which showed that a considerable reduction had been effected. In great part this was due to the addition of lap on the slide valves of the engines.

Brunel made experiments with anthracite coal at an early date, but found that it was reduced to powder, which was carried through the tubes to the smokebox, so that after running a few miles the engine had to be stopped and the smokebox cleared. It took many years of experiment on various railways before the problem of burning bituminous coal in locomotive fireboxes was successfully solved, and it was not until 1857 that coal finally replaced coke in locomotives with ordinary fireboxes.

In 1841 Gooch, who seems to have worked in conjunction with Lord Willoughby D'Eresby in the matter, tried peat as fuel. This was tested in various ways, some samples being caked, and others merely compressed, but it was found that although steam could be maintained, the consumption was so great that the fuel proved unprofitable.

In 1854, during the Crimean War, the Company became possessed of a coal mine of their very own—the Gyfeillon Colliery near Pontypridd on the Taff Vale Railway. Its acquisition was due to the failure of a contractor for the supply of the Bristol coke ovens; it was worked by the Company till 1865 and then sold.

DIMENSIONS OF GOOCH'S STANDARD ENGINES, 1840 TO 1842

| Class of Engine | Cylinders Diameter × Stroke | Diameter of Driving Wheels | Diameter of Carrying Wheels | Wheel Base | Tubes Number and Diameter | Heating Surface | | | Grate Area sq. ft. |
|---|---|---|---|---|---|---|---|---|---|
| | | | | | | Tubes sq. ft. | Firebox sq. ft. | Total sq. ft. | |
| FIREFLY 2-2-2 | 15″ × 18″ | 7′ 0″ | 4′ 0″ | 6′ 7″ + 6′ 7″ | 131  2″ | 602 | 97 | 699 | 13·5 |
| SUN 2-2-2 | 14″ × 18″ (some 15″ × 18″) | 6′ 0″ | 3′ 6″ | 6′ 10″ + 6′ 10″ | 120  2″ | 519 | 88·7 | 607·7 | 12·5 |
| LEO 2-4-0 | 15″ × 18″ | 5′ 0″ | 3′ 6″ | 6′ 4″ + 6′ 5″ | 94  2″ | 396 | 71 | 467 | 11·5 |
| HERCULES 0-6-0 | 15″ × 18″ | 5′ 0″ | 5′ 0″ | 6′ 3″ + 6′ 3″ | 131  2″ | 602 | 97 | 699 | 13·5 |

The original standard pressure was 50 lb. per square inch, but was subsequently raised in the case of many of the engines. *Ixion*, an engine of the " Firefly " class, was worked during the Gauge Commission experiments in 1845 at a pressure of 75 lb. per square inch.

One of the difficulties which Locomotive Engineers have had to face from the earliest days of railways has been the heavy wear of tyres and the consequent cost of renewal. Gooch was the first to attempt to solve the problem, and in November 1840 patented a method of steeling the treads, either by cementing them after manufacture, or by welding a slab of steel on the wrought-iron bars from which the tyres were then made. The latter was the method used in practice, and Gooch records in his *Diaries* that good sound tyres were made, containing about one-fifth part of best shear steel. Although expensive to make, they were used for all Great Western engines and tenders, and resulted in a large economy, many of them having a life of more than 200,000 miles. The surfaces were so hard that the tyres could not be turned, but had to be ground in the lathe by means of revolving grindstones.

Another but less successful experiment was the trial of copper fireboxes with corrugated plates. Gooch's intention was thereby to increase the heating surface area of the plates, but he admitted subsequently that this form of construction was not beneficial from the heating surface standpoint, as the bulk of the fire was not increased. A strong firebox resulted, but the expense was so great that only two engines were fitted.

In 1843 Gooch produced his well-known stationary link motion, which took the place of the older 'gab' motion, and allowed the steam to be cut off in the cylinders at varying points of the stroke according to requirements. Gooch's gear differed from that of Stephenson and Howe, which had been invented in 1842, in that the curved quadrant link, to which the eccentric rods were attached, was suspended from above, and the die block to which the valve rod was connected, could be moved up and down within the link. In the Stephenson link motion the die block is stationary and the quadrant link with eccentric rods attached are moved together. The Gooch link motion was fitted to most broad-gauge engines, as well as to the earlier narrow-gauge engines of 1855 to 1859.

Of the evidence given before the Gauge Commissioners in 1845, it is remarkable what a large proportion dealt with the comparative efficiency of locomotives. In regard to this part of the enquiry Gooch was practically the sole champion of the Broad Gauge, and had a single-handed fight against such powerful antagonists as Robert Stephenson, Joseph Locke, J. E. McConnell, G. P. Bidder, and others. Much of the evidence was concentrated upon the comparative power and boiler evaporation obtainable in the engines of both gauges. At the end of nearly three months of fierce argument Brunel threw out a challenge that the merits of the respective engines should be put to a practical test and to this the Commissioners, nothing loth to have a change of scene, assented.

The engine selected by Gooch was *Ixion*, one of the standard type with 7 foot driving wheels and cylinders enlarged to 15¾ inch diameter. The pressure was raised to 75 lb per sq. inch, an amount agreed to as the maximum permissible. Three double trips were made between Paddington and Didcot, the distance being 53 miles. On the first down journey with a load of 8 carriages, each weighing 10 tons, the maximum speed attained was 53 miles per hour, and on the return journey 60 miles per hour, and the second trips, with a load of 70 tons, gave similar figures. The exact starting and arrival times were not recorded. The third down journey, with 60 tons (6 carriages), was performed from start to stop in 63 minutes 34 seconds, at the average rate of 50, and a maximum speed of 60 miles per hour. The up journey to the fifty-second mile-post took 57 minutes 55 seconds; average speed 53·9, maximum speed 61 miles per hour.

The performances of the narrow-gauge engines, the trials of which took place between York and Darlington, were by no means equal in merit, and a maximum speed of $53\frac{3}{4}$ miles per hour only was reached with a load of 50 tons.

There were some distinctly humorous features in connection with the carrying out of these trials. The three Commissioners were Lt.-Col. Sir Frederic Smith, R.E., late Inspector-General of Railways, Prof G. B. Airey, Astronomer Royal, and Prof P. Barlow of the Royal Military Academy, Woolwich. The first and last named, with great foresight and prudence, deputed the Astronomer Royal to ride on the engines, possibly for the reason that, in case of accidents, he certainly could claim greater experience in seeing stars. It actually happened that the trials came to an abrupt conclusion owing to one of the narrow-gauge engines suddenly leaving the rails and turning over, though the Astronomer seems to have been somewhere else when this occurred, and his post of observation on the engine had been taken by Gooch's chief assistant, W. Martley, afterwards Locomotive Superintendent of the London, Chatham & Dover Railway.

Perhaps the most amusing side of the trials was the manner in which Gooch in the Broad Gauge and Bidder in the Narrow Gauge interests vied with one another in their applications of the science of thermo-dynamics as enunciated by 'The Heathen Chinee'. In the first run of the Great Western engine *Ixion* the feed water, as recorded by the Commissioners, was 'hot in the tender', the presumption being that it had been heated previously. In the subsequent runs its temperature varied from 'slightly warmed' to 'hot'. Bidder went one better, thereby exciting Gooch's strong protest as duly recorded in the latter's report. Not only did the Narrow Gauge champion heat up the water in the tender before the start, but at the end of the journey and before beginning the return trip a 'powerful stationary engine blast' was employed at Darlington, for the purpose not only of getting very hot water, but also a very bright fire. In this connection it should be explained that the quantity of water evaporated per pound of coke burnt during the runs was one of the most important quantities to be ascertained. It was an extraordinary omission on the part of the Royal Engineer Colonel, the Astronomer Royal, and the Professor of Mathematics that they 'jointly and severally' neglected to lay down any conditions in regard to initial feed-water temperatures.

Nevertheless, although the advocates of the Broad Gauge lost their case, the Great Western locomotive department, and Gooch in particular, won theirs. The report of the Commission contained the following:

> We consider them [*i.e.*, the trials] as confirming the statements and results given by Mr Gooch, in his evidence, proving, as they do, that the Broad Gauge Engines possess greater capabilities for speed with equal loads, and, generally speaking, of propelling greater loads with equal speed; and moreover, that the working of such engines is economical where very high speeds are required, or where the loads to be conveyed are such as to require the full power of the engine.

### THIRD PERIOD, 1846–1866

It was expected that a renewal of the Gauge War would occur during the next session of Parliament, and in order to be prepared for further tests, the results of which were to show a still greater superiority of the broad-gauge locomotives, Gooch designed and built at Swindon a very remarkable express engine, named *Great Western*. Being urgently required, the work of construction proceeded both day and night, and the engine was completed and tried at the end of April 1846, in thirteen weeks from the date of the order. There was no time in which to make detailed drawings, and the engine was built from a few centre-line drawings and rough dimensioned sketches. *Great Western* was the first engine built entirely at Swindon, though a goods engine had been turned out during the previous February, being the first of an order for which the boilers were made outside.

In *Great Western* a return was made to 8 foot driving wheels, but the large cylinders, 18 inches by 24 inches, and the boiler were in proportion, so that no comparison lay between it and the freaks of 1837–8. As originally built it ran on six wheels, but the weight on the leading wheels was somewhat too great for that day, and after it had been at work for several

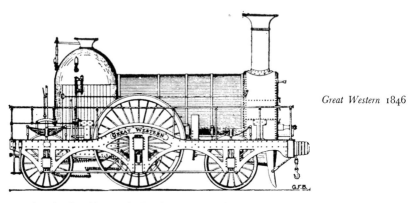

*Great Western* 1846

months the leading axle broke near Shrivenham. An alteration was then made by lengthening the framing and placing the front end on two axles, thus producing an eight-wheeled engine. The diameter of the leading wheels, which had been 4 feet 6 inches, was reduced to 4 feet for both new pairs. The boiler, which carried 100 lb pressure, was provided with a large Gothic firebox. The tube heating surface was 1,582 sq. feet, firebox surface 151 sq. feet, total 1,733 sq. feet; grate area 22·6 sq. feet, dimensions which were far in excess of those of any engine then running.

Before the addition of the extra axle *Great Western* had on 1st June 1846 run from Paddington to Exeter, 194 miles, in 208 minutes, returning in 211 minutes, both being the running times exclusive of stoppages. Gooch stated that on 13th June the engine, with a train of 100 tons, ran to Swindon in 78 minutes. It was broken up in December 1870, after completing 370,687 miles.

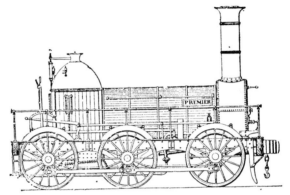

*Premier* 1846

The first locomotive to be built at Swindon Works was *Premier*, which was turned out in February 1846. This name had previously been borne by one of the early freaks, already withdrawn from service. *Premier* formed one of an order for twelve six-coupled goods engines, built during 1846 and 1847, but, as stated above, their boilers were made by an outside firm. These engines marked a considerable advance upon goods engines hitherto used. The frames were of the sandwich pattern, placed inside the wheels, and the trailing axle was behind the firebox. The inside cylinders were 16 inch diameter by 24 inch stroke, coupled wheels 5 feet diameter. The boiler, which had the Gothic form of firebox, used on the Great Western until 1847, had a total heating surface of about 1,081 sq. feet.[1] The engines, which were afterwards generally referred to officially as the 'Ajax' or 'Fury' class, weighed 26·6 tons loaded. The subsequent 0-6-0 goods engines of 1847–8, known as the 'Pyracmon' or 'Alligator' class, consisted of six engines, which differed from *Premier* in that the wheel base was longer by about 1 foot, and the boiler was larger and of a different pattern with firebox casing of the raised round-topped shape in place of the Gothic form, which was henceforth discarded. The total heating surface was about 1,373 sq. feet, grate area 18·4 sq. feet, and the boiler

[1] This and other heating surfaces given differ from those stated in the early official records, for the reason that they are calculated for the water side of the tubes as is usual in British practice. During a great part at least of Gooch's superintendency of the locomotive department the heating surfaces were calculated for the 'fire side.'

pressure 115 lb per sq. inch. The sizes of cylinders and wheels remained as in *Premier*.

Returning to the passenger engines, we find that Gooch wisely decided to give the large 8 foot engine *Great Western* an extended trial before building others of a similar class. In the meantime six smaller engines, the 'Prince' class were constructed at Swindon from August 1846 to March

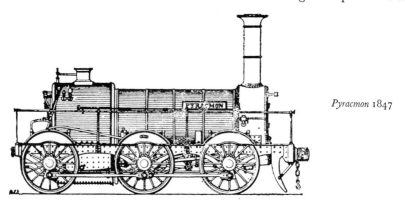

*Pyracmon* 1847

1847, of which five had 7 feet, and the remaining engine *Witch* 7 feet 6 inch driving wheels. The design was different from that of the earlier engines of 1840–2 in that the wheels were outside the sandwich frames, and all bearings were inside as in the goods engines. The boilers had Gothic firebox casings. The cylinders were 16 inches by 24 inches, and the wheel base was 14 feet 10 inches. The boilers were of the same dimensions as those of the goods engines of the 'Premier' class. The approximate weight was 26·2 tons, of which 11·5 tons were carried on the driving wheels. They ran the Exeter Expresses until superseded by the class next described, and from 1852 onwards worked almost exclusively between Didcot and Birmingham. All six were scrapped in 1870.

*Great Western* had by this time proved very successful, and Gooch decided upon a similar but improved design of eight-wheeled express engine, resulting in the appearance in April 1847 of the first of the celebrated 'Iron Duke' or 'Great Britain' class, which, with slight modifications, continued to be the standard express engines until the abolition of the Broad Gauge in 1892. In size and power they greatly exceeded all locomotives hitherto built for any railway. There were six engines of the first series of 1847, all built at Swindon. The first ran its trial trip on the anniversary of the Duke of Wellington's birthday, 29th April, and on that account received the name *Iron Duke*.

The large domeless boiler had a raised firebox casing, on which a brass safety-valve cover was mounted. This shape of cover, which from now onwards remained the standard pattern during Gooch's superintendency, earned the nickname on the part of the Swindon men of 'squashed bonnet-box'. After discarding the Gothic firebox casing, Gooch always used domeless boilers, steam being taken from a long perforated pipe, Hawthorn's patent, which extended longitudinally the whole length of the inside of the boiler at the top, and terminated at a gridiron slide valve regulator in the smokebox. Steam entered the pipe through a large number of holes or slits in the top of the pipe, whence it passed through the regulator to the cylinders. The sandwich frames were outside the wheels, and of a similar pattern to those of Stephenson's *North Star*. The two pairs of leading wheels had a single inverted spring on each side of the engine. The two inside plate frames were fastened to the back of the cylinders and extending backwards to the front of the firebox casing. In addition, there was a third inside frame or 'centre stay' so that the cranked driving axle had five bearings, two outside and three between the wheels. The carrying axles had outside bearings only. The steam chest was placed between the cylinders; and the slide valves, which were vertical, were balanced by small pistons, to which they were connected by means of horizontal pinned links. This latter arrangement, which caused considerable rattling when the engine was running, was subsequently abandoned. The firebox had a deep transverse water partition. The draught in Gooch's engines of this period was regulated by means of a set of louvres placed immediately in front of the smokebox tubeplate, the opening and closing of which could be controlled by the driver.

The cylinders were 18 inch diameter by 24 inch stroke, the flangeless wheels 8 feet, and the six carrying wheels 4 feet 6 inch diameter. The total wheel base was 18 feet 6 inches. The boiler contained 303 tubes, 2 inch outside diameter, the heating surface of which was 1,797 sq. feet. The firebox and water partition added 147·8 sq. feet, giving a total of 1,944·8 sq. feet. The original boiler pressure was 100 lb per sq. inch, subsequently increased to 115 lb. The weight in working order was 35·5 tons, of which 12·3 tons were carried on the driving wheels.

A new design of tender with iron frames was provided for these engines. It was carried on six 4 foot wheels and had a water capacity of 1,800 gallons and a fuel capacity of about 1½ tons of coke. These and other passenger engine tenders were usually provided with a covered seat at the back for the use of a porter, whose duty was to keep observation on the train. New tenders with outside sandwich frames like the engines themselves were substituted for the above in the late 'fifties, and in 1864 their water capacity was increased to upwards of 2,700 gallons to enable the engines to run through between London and Swindon without a stop. Owing to the width of the gauge, these tenders had a very low free-board—to borrow a nautical expression—which caused the engines with their 8 foot wheels to look much bigger than they really were.

Sixteen similar engines known as the 'Courier' class, were also built at Swindon between June 1848 and March 1851. These differed from the 'Iron Duke' class in that the wheel base, 18 feet 8½ inches, was slightly longer, and that the boiler, 4 feet 9⅜ in diameter outside the largest ring, had a tube heating surface of 1,757·5 sq. feet, a firebox surface of

162 sq. feet; total 1,919·5 sq. feet. The grate area was 25·47 sq. feet. They also differed from all the earlier engines in being the first to have the wood lagging of their boilers cased with sheet iron.

The celebrated *Lord of the Isles* was originally named *Charles Russell*, but at Russell's request the name was replaced by the one by which it has always been known, and with which it appeared in the Great Exhibition of 1851 in London. The engine did not start work until July 1852, and subsequently ran with its original boiler until June 1884, when it had completed 789,300 miles. It was then withdrawn from service and kept at Swindon, and in 1890 appeared at the Edinburgh Exhibition. In 1893 it was sent across the Atlantic to the Chicago Exhibition, and subsequently was again exhibited at Earl's Court. It was finally broken up in 1906 together with *North Star*.

More engines of the class being required to run the Birmingham Expresses, seven were built in 1854–5 by Rothwell & Co of Bolton, Lancashire, and named after battles and places celebrated during the Crimean War.

These differed slightly in boiler dimensions and heating surface from the 'Courier' class, the total surface being 1,883 sq. feet. Their weight in working order was 39·3 tons, of which the driving wheels carried 12·35 tons. As originally built the driving and trailing wheel springs were connected by compensating levers, which were subsequently removed.

In the early morning of 8th November 1862 the boiler of *Perseus* exploded in Westbourne Park engine shed. The engine itself was thrown 30 feet to the east, and a large piece of the boiler, weighing about $\frac{3}{4}$ ton, blown through the roof into the carriage sidings 100 yards away, striking and destroying two trucks. Unfortunately, the 'lighter up' and two cleaners working on the engine were killed. On examination the bottom plates of the barrel were found to have wasted down to $\frac{1}{8}$ to $\frac{1}{16}$ inch thick. There was at that time no regular system of examining and testing boilers at fixed periodic intervals. The Government Inspector stated that it was dangerous to allow a boiler to work for seven years without being tested. *Perseus* afterwards received a new boiler and ran until 1880.

The total number of these 8 feet single engines, including *Great Western*, was thirty, the list of which is given on page 473. When the Broad Gauge was abolished in 1892 three of them, perhaps containing portions of the old frames and some other parts, were still at work. Most of the remainder had been replaced by entirely new engines of similar design but different wheel base and boiler dimensions.

Detailed particulars of actual measured performances of the above engines were published in D. K. Clark's well-known work, *Railway Machinery* (*see opposite page*).

The above tables are interesting as showing the high average rates of speed attained by the express trains of 1847 to 1849. But the loads were extremely light, since none of the trains, after deducting the weights of engine and tender, attained 60 tons. For these loads the coke consumption was high.

The highest known *maximum* speed ever recorded with these engines in the old days was about 78·2 miles per hour down the Wootton Bassett bank of 1 in 100, and this was registered when Brunel and Gooch were testing the engines at the time they were new. There are reasons why the maximum speeds of the present century are higher than they were fifty to seventy years ago, amongst which are the greater strength of the

### I. RESULTS OF PERFORMANCES WITH EXPRESS TRAINS BETWEEN PADDINGTON AND SWINDON DURING AUGUST AND SEPTEMBER 1847.

| | Speed and Weight | | Consumption of Water and Coke | | |
|---|---|---|---|---|---|
| Name of Engine | Average Speed. | Average Gross Weight of Engine, Tender and Train. | Average Coke per mile. | Water per Pound of Coke. | Temperature of water in Tender. |
| | Miles per hour | Tons | Pounds | Pounds | Deg. Fahr. |
| GREAT BRITAIN | 51 | 103.5 | 34.4 | 8,23 | 109° |
| IRON DUKE | 53·4 | 105 | 36.6 | 8.4 | 91° |
| GREAT WESTERN | 53 | 106 | 36.2 | 7·4 | 144° |

### II. RESULTS OF PERFORMANCES WITH EXPRESS TRAINS BETWEEN PADDINGTON AND BRISTOL DURING MARCH AND APRIL 1849.

| | | | | | |
|---|---|---|---|---|---|
| WIZARD | 50.19 | 108.7 | 38.51 | 7.04 | |
| DRAGON | 51.5 | 104.2 | 31.1 | 7·37 | |
| HIRONDELLE | 51.5 | 101 | 35·4 | 6.8 | tempera- |
| TARTAR | 50.19 | 100.7 | 37·3 | 6.28 | ture |
| LIGHTNING | 50.23 | 101 | 34·58 | 7.65 | not |
| ROUGEMONT | 44.54 | 101 | 31.07 | 7.55 | given |
| EMPEROR | 51.3 | 104.2 | 38.16 | 7·36 | |
| PASHA | 49.6 | 101 | 37.7 | 8.1 | |
| COURIER | 50.19 | 106 | 34.26 | 7·55 | |
| WIZARD | 53.1 | 101 | 34.4 | 7.2 | id. |
| WARLOCK | 51 | 101 | 32.1 | 8.04 | |
| DRAGON | 50.3 | 101 | 29.4 | 7.8 | |
| EMPEROR | 49.37 | 109.2 | 39 | 7.28 | |
| SULTAN | 50.1 | 104.2 | 34.4 | 7.8 | |
| LIGHTNING | 52.3 | 104.7 | 36.1 | 7.68 | id. |
| PASHA | 50.9 | 106 | 38.7 | 6.9 | |
| ROUGEMONT | 51.9 | 101 | 34·3 | 7.2 | |
| COURIER | 51.4 | 104.2 | 38.16 | 6.64 | |

The average weight of engine and tender was 50 tons. The three sections of Table II refer to tests with three different qualities of coke.

permanent way, the heavier and harder rails, and the harder tyres of to-day. Before the year 1890, or thereabouts, there were very few authentic instances on any railway of maximum speeds of over 76 to 78 miles per hour, and 80 to 81¼ were just attained on one or two extremely rare occasions.

The experiments which Gooch conducted in 1848 for the purpose of estimating train resistances under various conditions have already been referred to in Chapter VI. They were the most complete experiments made in this country for fifty years, and formed the basis from which D. K. Clark constructed his well-known formulae for train resistance. In his *Diaries* Gooch wrote that they cost him a vast amount of labour and that it was a difficult task to sit on the buffer beam of the engine and take indicator readings at speeds of 60 miles an hour. In later years a specially designed shelter was erected at the front of the engine to protect the men engaged upon such work.

For the above purpose Gooch designed and constructed at Swindon a special dynamometer car, probably the first which was ever made. The traction spring was 7 feet 6 inches long and consisted of five plates carefully tapered and maintained at a distance of ½ inch apart in the middle, the distance pieces at the ends being made to act as rollers. A pencil was carried from this spring to a table above, upon which a roll of paper was moved by a measuring wheel on the rail. This measured and recorded on the paper each $\frac{1}{16}$ of a mile travelled over. A clock was provided to register intervals of one-fifth of a second. To record the force and direction of the wind a wind-gauge was placed 5 feet above the top of the dynamometer carriage, with the necessary connections brought down to pencils on the table. All the results required were recorded automatically upon a large scale, opposite to each other on a continuous roll of paper.

In addition to the above, Gooch designed a novel form of steam-engine indicator, which produced a continuous diagram on a long sheet of paper which passed over rollers.

The ingenuity displayed in the design of the apparatus and the care taken in making the experiments show throughout the work of one who was a great engineer.

In May 1849 a six-coupled goods engine, *Bacchus*, was turned out from Swindon Works, and replaced 'the unfortunate one', whose roystering days were over. The second *Bacchus* was not an entirely new engine, since the boiler was that of *Hurricane*. The inside frames, judging from an old but indistinct photograph, were not of Gooch's usual type, and may in part have also been derived from the boiler carriage of one of the latter engines. *Bacchus* had wheels 5 feet in diameter and cylinders 16 inches by 24 inches. It was the only engine of its class, and was characterized by completely closed-in splashers and a manhole cover over the middle of the boiler.

A new class of passenger saddle tank engine with driving and trailing wheels coupled and a leading bogie was built at Swindon in 1849 for use on the heavy gradients of the South Devon Railway. The main frames, which were of the sandwich type and placed inside, extended only from the immediate front of the driving wheels to the back buffer beam. The leading bogie, which, as in all Gooch's engines of this type, was placed with its centre behind the smokebox, was of the swivelling ball and socket type with rigid pivot. A peculiarity of the design was that the boiler formed the connection between the cylinders and the main frames, though there was in addition a central bearing for the crank axle. The piece of framing, which formed the 'hornplate' for this bearing, was

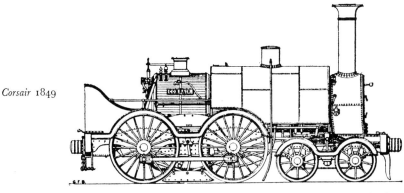

*Corsair* 1849

rivited to the underside of the boiler and was stayed by rods to the firebox casing at the back and to the gusset plate supporting the bogie pin at the front. The sandbox was on the top of the saddle tank, and the sand had to be ladled down the pipes by hand. The cylinders were 17 inches by 24 inches, the coupled wheels 6 foot diameter, and the total wheel base 18 feet 2 inches.

A sledge brake, which acted on the rails, was placed between the driving wheels. This form of brake tended to lift the body of the engine at the back, and was also unsatisfactory in that there was danger of the sledge blocks fouling points and crossings. These engines had the peculiar form of splashers round the tops only of the wheels, a design which appears in all broad-gauge coupled engines from about 1847 onwards. Being without a platform it made the driver's task of getting round the engine, when running, very awkward. Only two engines were built of this class, *Corsair* and *Brigand*. In the latter the sledge brake was dispensed with and brake blocks on the backs of the trailing wheels substituted.

In 1854–5 thirteen somewhat similar engines, but with 5 feet 9 inch coupled wheels, were built by R. & W. Hawthorn of Newcastle. These were named after classical poets, and with *Corsair* and *Brigand* were known as the 'Bogie' class.

In 1851 eight six-coupled goods engines, known as the 'Caesar' class, were built at Swindon. In general dimensions they were similar to the earlier engines of the 'Pyracmon' class, and were the last broad-gauge goods engines to have 16 inch cylinders. In outward appearance and general design they were very similar to the later design of 1852 to 1863. The latter engines, 102 in number, of the 'Ariadne' and 'Caliph' classes, had inside sandwich frames,[1] but the cylinders were 17 inches by 24 inches, and the boilers larger with a diameter of 4 feet 6 inches and a total heating surface of 1,599·8 sq. feet. The grate area was 19·2 sq. feet and the pressure 120 lb per sq. inch. The 'Caliph' class, which differed principally in minor details from the 'Ariadne' class, and were somewhat heavier, weighed 32 tons 6 cwt in working order

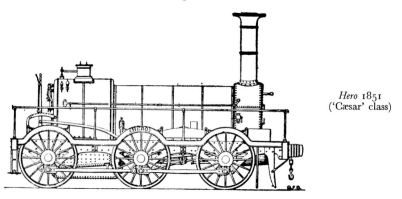

*Hero* 1851
('Cæsar' class)

All the foregoing Swindon built goods engines of 1846–63 disappeared from service between 1870 and 1884, with the exception of *Europa*, which received a new boiler in 1869 and lasted until May 1892.

There were also five banking engines which differed from the main line goods engines in having no tenders, the water being carried in a short saddle tank over the boiler barrel. Of these, *Avalanche* was built in 1846 by Stothert & Slaughter of Bristol; *Juno* and *Jago* were built at Swindon

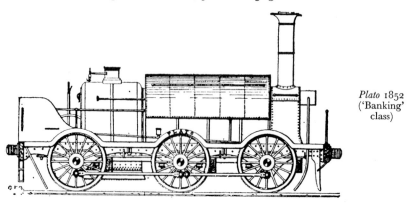

*Plato* 1852
('Banking' class)

in 1852, and *Plato* and *Bithon* in 1854. *Avalanche* was of an older design, but the remaining four were of similar dimensions to the goods engines. The sandbox was placed in front near the top of the smokebox and the fireman

[1] The later engines of the 'Caliph' class had welded plate frames.

had to go to the front and ladle the sand down a small funnel in the box, from which it dropped into the sand pipes.

In 1855 ten 8-wheeled four-coupled express engines were built by Robert Stephenson & Co, all of which, save the first, took their names from Scott's Waverley novels. Like the 8 foot singles, the leading end was carried on two axles with bearings in the main frames, which were inside and of the usual sandwich pattern. The cylinders were 17 inches by 24 inches, diameter of coupled wheels 7 feet, total wheel base 17 feet 11⅝ inches, boiler diameter 4 feet 6 inches, total heating surface 1,574 sq. feet. The weight in working order was 37 tons 5 cwt, of which 22 tons 1 cwt were available for adhesion. These engines were all stabled at Swindon till 1872 and worked thence chiefly to Bristol, and after 1862 to South Wales. Two of them were broken up in 1872 and the remainder in 1876, after an average mileage for each engine of nearly ½-million.

The 'Waverley' class which had a somewhat long rigid wheel base for running over any other section than the main line between London and Bristol, was not repeated, and the subsequent coupled engines of 1856–64 were of the six-wheeled 2-4-0 type and of smaller dimensions. These were known as the 'Victoria' class and all were built at Swindon, the first eight of 1856 being named after then reigning European monarchs,[1] and the later ten of 1863–4 after celebrated British engineers, beginning with Brunel. The cylinders were 16 inches by 24 inches, and the coupled wheels 6 feet 6 inches. The boiler was 4 feet in diameter, and had a total heating surface of 1,263 sq. feet. The total weight in working order was 30 tons 13 cwt, of which the coupled wheels carried about 20 tons. These engines, like the six-coupled banking engines, had the peculiarity of being provided with compensating levers between the springs of all three axles.

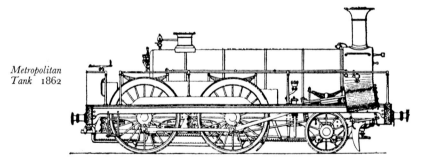

*Metropolitan Tank* 1862

In 1862 Gooch designed some 2-4-0 broad-gauge tank engines for the Metropolitan service between Bishop's Road and Farringdon Street. These were the first engines in the country to be fitted with condensing apparatus for working in tunnels. Some years previously Gooch had made experiments to test the distance which a locomotive would run without

---

[1] These engines were originally provided with four-wheeled tenders of the outside sandwich frame type.

any blast upon the fire. The new engines, of which six were built by Kitson & Co of Leeds, six by The Vulcan Foundry, Lancashire, in 1862, and ten at Swindon in 1863–4, were the only broad-gauge locomotives with outside cylinders, which owing to the great width were spaced at about 8 feet 2½ inch centres. To clear the leading wheels the cylinders had to be steeply inclined. Their outside position was necessitated in order to make room for the water tanks and condensing apparatus, which were placed underneath the boiler, with the addition of a supplementary tank beneath the footplate. Flap valves, worked by rods from the footplate, directed the exhaust steam either up the chimney when the engine was running in the open, or into the tanks when working in the tunnels. The connecting pipe from the right-hand cylinder crossed over to the left-hand side of the tank, and *vice versa*. The pipes were prolonged within the tank, inside which they were perforated with holes to distribute the exhaust steam. To prevent the water from being drawn into the cylinders owing to the production of a vacuum, additional automatic flap valves were placed in the exhaust pipes, but there was great difficulty in keeping these water-tight and the pipe joints air-tight. Very often it was necessary to exhaust into the atmosphere inside the tunnels, as the tanks were too small and the water became overheated. The cylinders of these engines were 16 inches by 24 inches, and the coupled wheels 6 feet in diameter. Solid welded plate and not sandwich frames were used. There were two similar narrow-gauge engines built at Swindon in 1864; these had 5 feet 6 inch coupled wheels.

During 1868–70 nearly all the above engines had the tanks and condensing apparatus removed and some were also altered to tender locomotives, after which they ran for a few years on the Windsor services and on various branches.

They were the last locomotives designed by Gooch, who resigned the chieftainship of the locomotive department at the end of September 1864. There were, in addition, a number of narrow-gauge engines constructed to his designs from 1855 onwards. These will be described subsequently, and in the meantime the three classes of broad-gauge engines, built by his successor, Joseph Armstrong, during 1865–6, may be conveniently included here, since they bring to a close a definite epoch in the history of Great Western locomotives.

Armstrong's broad-gauge engines differed in two important respects from most of those designed by Gooch. The valve gear was of Stephenson's shifting link in place of Gooch's stationary link type, and the inside frames were solid plates, the built-up sandwich type being abandoned. The dome-less boiler was retained in the case of the passenger and goods tender engines, but six tank engines of 1866 had domed boilers, the first which had been made since the very early days. The brass safety valve covers were of a somewhat clumsy design, by no means so neat as the previous 'squashed bonnet-boxes', now abandoned.

Twenty-six four-coupled 2-4-0 passenger engines, known as the 'Hawthorn' class, came out in 1865-6, of which six, built at Swindon, took the names of older engines broken up, and the remaining twenty, constructed at Bristol by the Avonside Engine Co, were named after well-known locomotive engineers. The coupled wheels, which had wrought-iron tyres of Gooch's type with steel faces, were 6 feet in diameter; the cylinders were 16 inches by 24 inches, and the pressure 130 lb per sq. inch. In 1877 ten of these engines were converted to 2-4-0 saddle tank locomotives for service west of Exeter, when the diameter of the driving wheels was reduced to 5 feet and the cylinders were enlarged to 17 inch diameter. These tank engines and many of those which retained their tenders, remained in service until the abolition of the Broad Gauge in 1892.

The fourteen goods engines of the 'Swindon' class, built by the Company in 1865-6, were named after the principal cities and towns on the system. These had solid plate frames, 5 foot wheels, and 17 inch by 24 inch cylinders. In 1872-4 they were all sold to the Bristol & Exeter Railway, when the names were removed and numbers substituted; in 1876 they reverted to the Great Western and were then renumbered 2077 to 2090. Five were provided with standard narrow-gauge boilers in 1885-6, and one survived until May 1892.

The six 0-6-0 goods tank engines, 'Sir Watkin' class, were built at Swindon in 1865-6. Originally they had very long side tanks, which made the motion inaccessible for examination and oiling, but in the 'eighties saddle tanks were substituted. Three of them, *Bulkeley*, *Fowler*, and *Saunders*, were sold to the South Devon Railway in 1872, returning to the Great Western in 1876, when they were numbered 2157 to 2159, though still retaining the original names

All the broad-gauge engines built by and for the Great Western had names but no numbers. Some of these names were certainly curious and others had a distinctly though unintentionally humorous side. Those of some of the early engines of 1837-9 appear to have been suggested by the makers who would of course have obtained Brunel's sanction and approval. *Atlas* must certainly have been proposed by Sharp, Roberts & Co, the builders of this engine, after the title of their works, and many of their early engines on other railways bore this name. In the case of *North Star*, Brunel originally suggested the name *Stephenson*, but Robert Stephenson demurred and proposed *North Star*, a favourite appellation for many of his firm's early engines. The eleven later engines by Messrs Stephenson were named 'Stars', in virtue, as Brunel stated, of the good reputation which *North Star* had acquired. Owing to some inadvertence there were a couple of Venuses, but the name of neither was changed, and they appeared for many years in the lists as *Venus No. 1* and *Venus No. 2*.

The classical and other names of the engines of 1840-2 were appropriate, as such names go, and were probably selected by Russell, Brunel, or Saunders, but many of the ultra-classical names of later years smack largely of having been forcibly extracted from a dictionary of Greek and Roman antiquities, which must have proved extremely useful. The staff of this department did not always exercise moderation and select names with due regard to the limited knowledge of the man in the train. Jupiter he knew, likewise Hercules, and of Ajax he had a more or less hazy idea, but who, for example, was Salus? Careful research reveals that this individual was a Latin goddess who seems to have presided over the Roman Ministry of Health, and caused the citizens so little trouble that we hear very little about her. The Great Western *Salus* was an exceedingly prosaic goods engine.

Included in the output of the Company's classical department may be noticed *Zina*, *Nora Creina*, *Telica*, and others of the same tribe. *Hades*, another goods engine, might perhaps be described as the nearest concrete form of the abstract idea conveyed by the American aphorism 'H—l on wheels'. Other goods engines received the ridiculous names *Flirt* and *Coquette*, very likely aftermaths of a dance attended by a disappointed member of the staff of the nomenclature office the night before the names were selected.

But the classics occasionally went sadly awry. The department extracted Laocoön from the dictionary of antiquities, and presumably, in railway clerical parlance, 'duly noted same' on a paper, which was despatched to the shops for execution. What happened on its way there has never come to light, but the name of the engine eventuated as *Lagoon*! However, one name is almost as good as another, so *Lagoon* remained.

On one occasion the departmental exponents of Homer and Virgil ran amok in French, a language for which the dictionary of antiquities was of no assistance. One of the 8 foot express engines of the 'Iron Duke' class was to have been named Estafette, which is French for courier. They got most of it right in the shops, but the f's and t's were not sorted out properly and the engine ran for thirty-four years as *Astaffete*. There was also an English *Courier* of the same class, as well as a *Swallow* and a *Hirondelle*.

A number of engines built in 1841–2 received names of lethal weapons, such as *Stiletto*, *Creese*, *Javelin*, etc. Included amongst them was Assegai, which appeared on the engine in the plural as *Assagais*. This error was probably made by the makers of the engine, but the official record of 1843 went one better and made it 'Assaigis'. A later plural, probably conceived by the wise men of Swindon, was *Magi*, the name of a goods engine. Of the Metropolitan 'Flower' class, Azalea was spelt *Azalia*, and Camellia, *Camelia*.

In 1865–6 twenty engines were named after locomotive engineers— past and present—and one had the nameplate *Wood*, which was doubtless intended for Woods;[1] Blenkinsop was misspelt *Blenkensop* on another.

Of the same class was *Peacock*, a name which had no immediate connection with the bird, but was that of a very well-known locomotive engineer

---

[1] Edward Woods, at one time of the Liverpool & Manchester Railway, and in later years President of the Institution of Civil Engineers.

in Manchester, who, in his young days about 1840–1, had been a Great Western driver. A story in the Great Western Magazine (1890) relates that Peacock was once driving a new engine under test and omitted to see a trolley on the line. The consequences were bad for both trolley and engine, and Peacock, after contemplating the remains, and feeling a strong objection to facing Gooch, made an immediate strategical retreat across the fields for the north of England.

Another of these engines was named *Slaughter* after the head of the then well-known Avonside Engine Company of Bristol. The story goes that one of the Directors, happening to travel in a train drawn by *Slaughter*, strolled up to look at the engine. Apparently he was horrified at the appalling suggestion of the name, for shortly afterwards it was removed and *Avonside* substituted.

Complete lists of the names, dates, and other particulars of the broad-gauge locomotives built for the Great Western Railway down to the end of 1866 are given on pages 466 to 480.

## NARROW-GAUGE LOCOMOTIVES

The first narrow-gauge locomotive stock of the Great Western consisted of the engines taken over in 1854 with the Shrewsbury & Chester and Shrewsbury & Birmingham Railways, of which those from the former line retained their original numbers and became Great Western Railway Nos. 1 to 35 (omitting 33). The Shrewsbury & Birmingham engines were renumbered 33 and 36 to 56 on the Great Western. These locomotives formed a miscellaneous assortment, all designed by various well-known makers, generally of their standard types. A few of the passenger engines had names such as No. 13 *Prince of Wales*, and 21 *Victoria and Albert*, from the Shrewsbury & Chester Railway, and 37 *Queen*, 54 *Salopian*, 55 *Vulcan*, and 56 *Wrekin* from the Shrewsbury & Birmingham Railway. The names were afterwards removed, and with the exception of about ten later engines it was not the practice to give names to any narrow-gauge locomotives until after the abolition of the Broad Gauge in 1892.

## SHREWSBURY & CHESTER ENGINES

Edward Jeffreys was Locomotive Superintendent of the Shrewsbury & Chester Railway, the works of which were at Saltney, near Chester. He was not responsible for the design of any of the engines, though he probably gave the locomotive builders general instructions in regard to the class of work for which they were intended. In 1853 the engines of both the Shrewsbury & Chester and Shrewsbury & Birmingham were pooled under a joint committee, and Jeffreys left to take charge of the locomotive department of the Shrewsbury & Hereford Railway for Mr Brassey.

The earliest engines, Nos. 1 to 6, of the Shrewsbury & Chester Railway were of Stephenson's long boiler type with inside cylinders, built in 1846–7 by R. B. Longridge & Co of Bedlington, Northumberland. No. 1 was a six-wheels coupled goods engine and the others were for passenger work. Of the latter Nos. 5 and 6 were of the 2-4-0 type with 5 foot coupled wheels and 14½ inch by 24 inch cylinders. The boilers had domed Gothic fireboxes similar to Stephenson's and Gooch's patterns. Long boiler engines of this type with all the wheels in front of the firebox, resulting in a very short wheel base, were very unsteady, and No. 5 earned an unenviable notoriety. In June 1865 it was the leading one of two engines on a heavy excursion train of 32 carriages for the south from Birkenhead, and at Rednal it ran off the rails, the driver and 12 passengers being killed. The road was under repair at the time, the only warning being a green flag on a pole stuck in the bank of the cutting. No. 5 ran off to the left, and the second engine, No. 72, to the right, the coaches being piled up and four of them destroyed. Two of the above engines were subsequently rebuilt about 1868 at Wolverhampton, when they were provided with boilers having an internal flue of the Cornish type, without fireboxes of the usual pattern.

A notable locomotive was No. 14, one of Sharp Brothers' single passenger engines. No. 14, which had 5 foot driving wheels and 14 inch by 20 inch cylinders, was built in July 1848. On being taken out of service it was preserved at Wolverhampton for many years, and was probably the last of a formerly well-known class to remain in existence.

Engine No. 15 deserves special mention. This was a small four-wheeled shunting saddle tank engine with haystack firebox and bar frames, which had been built by Bury, Curtis & Kennedy in November 1847, and had a surprisingly long life. It was partially rebuilt at Wolverhampton Works in 1866, and again in 1887, retaining the bar frames and copper firebox, and was not broken up until August 1904 after fifty-eight years of constant work in the Chester and Wrexham districts. There were several other bar-framed passenger and goods engines by Bury & Co among the early locomotives of the Shrewsbury & Chester Railway, all of which were six-wheeled.

An interesting express engine, No. 32, was built in November 1852 by Jones & Potts of Viaduct Foundry, Newton-le-Willows. Apparently it was ordered for the Shrewsbury & Birmingham Railway though it appears in the locomotive stock of the Shrewsbury & Chester, possibly as a result of the transference of several engines by the joint committee from one line to the other. This engine, which was nicknamed by the Permanent Way people 'The Flying Flogger', was of 2-2-2 type with inside frames and inside cylinders 15½ inches by 20 inches, and driving wheels 6 feet 6 inch diameter. The steam chests, eccentrics, and the whole of the Stephenson link motion were outside, the crank axle being extended outside the wheels to form bosses for the eccentric sheaves. The boiler had the usual raised firebox casing on which a peculiarly shaped dome, somewhat like a cottage loaf, was placed. 'The Flying Flogger' was stationed at Shrewsbury and worked fast trains both to Chester and to Wolverhampton until 1872.

*North Star* as rebuilt and preserved at Swindon 1870–1906

*Firefly*, 1840. The first engine designed by Daniel Gooch, then 24 years of age

Broad-gauge carriages outside Paddington Station, about 1865

Narrow-gauge first class carriage from one of the Shrewsbury Railways, believed to have been built by Wright of Birmingham in 1846

Two remarkable engines, Nos. 34 and 35, were built by The Vulcan Foundry in 1848, according to the firm's records, though the Great Western official particulars give March 1853 as the date when they began work. They were large four-wheeled tender engines with 16 inch by 24 inch inside cylinders, 5 feet 3 inch coupled wheels and a wheel base

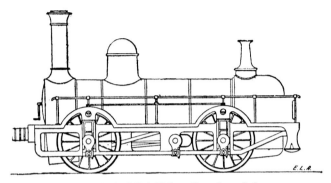

No. 34 (S. & C.R.) Vulcan Foundry, 1848

11 feet 5 inches in length. The inside cylinders drove an intermediate cranked shaft, sometimes referred to as a 'dummy' shaft. This was, in effect, a crank axle without wheels which had bearings in the main frames. The movement of rotation was transmitted from the shaft to the front and back wheels through the coupling rods. The outside frames were of a heavy bar pattern, and there were both inside and outside bearings. The springs above the axle-boxes were enclosed in boxes and appear to have been of a helical or volute type. The boilers were very large, oval in section, and had a total heating surface of 1,293 sq. feet.

### SHREWSBURY & BIRMINGHAM ENGINES

The majority of the Shrewsbury & Birmingham locomotives were of the long boiler type. Four of the original passenger engines by R. Stephenson & Co, 1849, were of the 2-4-0 type with outside cylinders 15 inches by 22 inches, and coupled wheels 6 feet 1½ inch diameter. Three or four years afterwards they were completely reconstructed as 0-4-2 mixed traffic engines with 5 foot coupled wheels and inside cylinders 15 inches by 24 inches, only the original Stephenson's boilers being retained. The long boiler 0-6-0 goods engines with inside cylinders, built by the firms of Stephenson and Longridge, did very good service for many years in their original condition.

Four express engines, all different, may be mentioned. No. 3, *Queen*, which became No. 37 on the Great Western Railway, was a 2-2-2 engine with inside cylinders 15 inches by 22 inches, inside bearings for the driving and outside bearings for the carrying axles. This engine was built by R. Stephenson & Co in 1849 and had the steam chests and valve gear outside, an arrangement which the makers adopted in the case of several engines of that day. The diameter of the driving wheels, which were without flanges, was 6 feet $1\frac{1}{4}$ inches, according to the makers' drawings, though the Great Western Railway records show 5 feet 6 inches. The firebox casing, like many of those of the Shrewsbury & Birmingham engines, was of the raised Gothic type.

No. 21 (GW 54), *Salopian*, was a 2-2-2 engine by E. B. Wilson & Co of Leeds, 1849, and of this firm's enlarged 'Jenny Lind' type. The cylinders, $15\frac{1}{2}$ inches by 22 inches, were inside, and the driving wheels, which had inside bearings only, were 6 feet 6 inch diameter. The carrying wheels had outside bearings. *Salopian* was the largest passenger engine on the Shrewsbury & Birmingham Railway, and the boiler had the large heating surface for that day of 1,271 sq. feet.

*Vulcan*, No. 22 (GW 55), by W. Fairbairn & Sons, 1849, was a double-framed 2-2-2 engine, of very similar design to Sharp Brothers' standard type. The driving wheels were 5 feet 6 inch diameter, and the cylinders were 15 inches by 20 inches. Heating surface was $1,185\frac{1}{2}$ sq. feet.

No. 23 (GW 56), *Wrekin*, was delivered by Bury, Curtis & Kennedy in July 1850, and appears to have been the last locomotive built by this once celebrated firm. It had inside bar framing, and all the bearings were inside. The inside cylinders were 15 inches by 20 inches, and the diameter of the driving wheels 5 feet 7 inches, though they seem to have been increased to 5 feet 9 inches by the Great Western Railway. The boiler was without dome, the steam being taken from an internal pipe with slits as in Hawthorn's and Gooch's engines.

Such locomotive shops as the Shrewsbury & Birmingham Company had were at Stafford Road, Wolverhampton. These became the headquarters of the Northern or Narrow Gauge Division under the management of Joseph Armstrong, who had lately been Locomotive Superintendent to the joint committee of the two Shrewsbury Railways, and on their absorption was appointed Assistant Superintendent under Gooch, in charge of the narrow-gauge stock.

In May 1855 Swindon Works turned out its first narrow-gauge engine. This was No. 57, built to Gooch's designs, the first of an order for twelve 0-6-0 goods engines, Nos. 57 to 68. Until narrow-gauge rails reached Swindon in 1872 all such engines were conveyed on special broad-gauge trucks to Wolverhampton,[1] after which Swindon saw them no more for many years; in fact it is doubtful whether some of them ever returned there, at least while anything whatever of the original engines remained. In 1855 and for many years afterwards Swindon considered a narrow-gauge engine as something beneath contempt, and having built it, packed it off with a blessing of the 'good riddance, bad rubbish' order.

[1] To Didcot only from 1869.

Nos. 57 to 68 had double frames, the outside ones being of the slotted-out sandwich type similar to those of the earlier broad-gauge engines. The cylinders were 15½ inches by 22 inches, diameter of coupled wheels 5 feet, wheel base 15 feet 6 inches, total heating surface 1,111·8 sq. feet, and weight in working order 29·6 tons. These engines had all the main features of Gooch's designs, including the domeless boiler and stationary link motion. Compensating levers were arranged between the springs of all axles. Similar goods engines, Nos. 79 to 90 and 119 to 130, but with 4 feet 6 inch wheels and 16 inch by 24 inch cylinders, were built at Swindon during 1857 to 1862. The subsequent class of 1862 of which 131 to 136 were built at Swindon, and 137 to 148 by The Avonside Engine Company, Bristol, though generally like the 57 class, had Stephenson's instead of Gooch's link motion. These had 5 foot coupled wheels and 16 inch by 24 inch cylinders.

Whilst the first engines of the 57 class were in course of construction at Swindon, the first narrow-gauge 2-2-2 passenger engines of Gooch's design, Nos. 69 to 76, were constructed during 1855–6 by Beyer, Peacock & Co, Manchester, and were the first engines built by that firm. These also had outside sandwich frames, and Gooch's stationary link motion. The cylinders were 15½ inches by 22 inches, diameter of driving wheels 6 feet 6 inches, and the boilers were of similar dimensions to those of the 57 class goods engines. For a few years these engines were employed on the fast trains between Birmingham and Chester, but were transferred to the Paddington service, when narrow-gauge trains began to run from London to the North. The first of these was worked from Paddington by engine No. 75 on 1st October 1861. T. Houghton Wright, subsequently District Locomotive Superintendent at Neath, was on the engine and afterwards described the great excitement at Paddington, adding that 'some of the Broad Gauge bigots wondered whether the train would ever reach its destination'. It arrived at Oxford 5 minutes late, and changed engines there, No. 76 of the same class coming on. At Leamington a vehicle with a hot box had to be put off; nevertheless the arrival at Birmingham was only 3 minutes late,[1] but the driver had heated the smokebox and the lower half of the chimney. The train was a curiosity; no two of the carriages, all of which were four-wheeled, were alike either in design or size.

Engines 69 to 76 were completely reconstructed at Wolverhampton in 1872–5, then becoming, in fact, new engines with 17 inch by 24 inch cylinders and larger boilers. Afterwards they were transferred to Swindon and worked thence to Paddington in one direction and to Neath, via Gloucester, in the other.

Two 0-6-0 goods engines, Nos. 77 and 78, were purchased in 1857, of which the makers, Beyer, Peacock & Co, designed the frames and engine portion and Gooch the boilers.

---

[1] The train was allowed 3 hours 20 minutes for the 129¼ miles.

## THE BIRKENHEAD ENGINES

The locomotives of the Birkenhead Railway were taken over by the Great Western and London & North Western Railways in November 1860. The Great Western share was twenty-one of those then at work, which Gooch reported as in a bad state of repair, together with two additional engines, which had been ordered from R. Stephenson & Co, but were not delivered until 1861. This stock was numbered 95 to 116 and 118 on the Great Western Railway.

Before the original Chester & Birkenhead Railway was opened for traffic in 1840, a number of locomotives were ordered from Mather, Dixon & Co of Liverpool, and R. Stephenson & Co of Newcastle to be shared equally with the Chester & Crewe Railway. The position was complicated by the Chester & Crewe line being taken over by the Grand Junction Railway and of the engines ordered only two, by Mather Dixon, became the property of the Birkenhead Company. Four others were supplied by Tayleur & Co in 1840–41.

The two engines by Mather, Dixon & Co, which began work in 1840, were of the 2-2-2 type, having outside sandwich frames, inside cylinders 12 inches by 18 inches, and 5 feet 6 inch driving wheels. A characteristic feature was the use of two steam domes, one immediately behind the chimney and the other over the raised firebox casing. This arrangement, which appeared in the narrow-gauge engines built by this firm in 1839–40 for other railways, is not unlikely to have been the direct result of Gooch's strictures on the unfortunate engines, *Premier*, etc., which Mather, Dixon & Co had previously built for the Great Western. Lack of sufficient steam space in the boiler was one of the defects of the latter, and the second dome was provided in later engines to remedy the trouble.

One of these Mather Dixon engines, No. 3, *Touchstone*, survived to be taken over by the Great Western, on which it was the oldest narrow-gauge engine in service, though it had been so completely reconstructed by the Birkenhead Railway in 1853 as to be practically new. In this condition the cylinders had been enlarged to 13 inch diameter, but the new boiler had the old arrangement of two domes. About 1863 it became GWR No. 1, and remained in service until 1873.

There were also two 2-2-2 engines purchased from Tayleur & Co in 1845 which, according to the Great Western Railway records, had been built in 1843. As rebuilt in 1857 and 1858 by the Birkenhead Railway they had the peculiarity that the carrying wheels had elliptical bent spokes similar to those formerly used on railway wagons.

Of the later 2-2-2 passenger engines, one built in 1851 by B. Hick & Son of Bolton, became GWR No. 110. It had a domeless boiler, outside cylinders 15 inches by 22 inches, and 6 foot single driving wheels.

Other passenger and mixed traffic engines were of the 2-4-0 type by the firms of Stephenson, Hick,[1] and Fairbairn. The two engines by the latter

---

[1] The three Hick engines (GWR Nos. 111–113) are recorded at Swindon as 2-2-2 type, but when withdrawn in 1863 as 0-4-2 with 6 foot coupled wheels.

firm, GWR Nos. 106 and 107, built in 1855, had an exceedingly long career on the Great Western. They were rebuilt at Wolverhampton in 1875 and 1873 respectively, and again about twenty years later, when outside bearings for the front carrying axle were substituted for the original inside bearings. The coupled wheels were 5 feet in diameter and the inside cylinders 15 inches by 22 inches. These two engines finished their career on the Severn Valley line between Worcester and Shrewsbury after a total service of about fifty years.[1]

Two very neat 2-4-0 passenger side tank engines, *Volante* and *Voltigeur*, built by R. Stephenson & Co in 1856, had 5 feet 3 inch coupled wheels and 14 inch by 20 inch cylinders. They became GWR Nos. 97 and 98, and were subsequently transferred to London for the local trains between Victoria, Addison Road, and Southall.

Of the six-coupled goods engines, two were by B. Hick & Son, 1849, and were amongst the first 0-6-0 engines of standard British type with inside cylinders and plate frames and trailing axle behind the firebox. The remaining four engines which became Great Western property were built by R. Stephenson & Co, 1856 and 1861, and had double frames. Two of the latter, Nos. 101 and 102, were part of an order for the Midland Railway, but had been purchased from the makers by the Birkenhead Company. One of them exploded at Chester in 1865 and was afterwards rebuilt at Wolverhampton.

Mention may lastly be made of two small 0-4-0 saddle tank shunting engines, which were built by Sharp, Stewart & Co, Manchester, in 1856–7. They became GWR Nos. 96 and 95 respectively, and their claim to special recognition rests upon the fact that since the Great Western acquired them they certainly earned their keep. They were very insignificant-looking four-wheeled engines, having coupled wheels 4 foot diameter, and cylinders 14 inches by 18 inches. They were rebuilt at Wolverhampton in 1888 and 1890, much of the originals then being retained; 95 lasted till March 1925, and 96 till November 1935. During their long careers they nearly always worked in the Chester district, principally on the colliery branches near Wrexham.

In the meantime new locomotive construction had begun at Wolverhampton Works, where the first two passenger tender engines, Nos. 7 and 8, were built in September and October 1859. These were followed by a similar engine, No. 30, in March 1860. All three were designed by Armstrong, and had single driving wheels 6 feet in diameter with inside bearings only. The leading and trailing wheels had outside bearings, and the cylinders were $14\frac{1}{2}$ inch diameter by 22 inch stroke. The boilers were domeless, probably in accordance with Gooch's instructions, though the engines bore no resemblance to his designs. These engines replaced old Shrewsbury & Chester stock, broken up.

---

[1] No. 106 was scrapped in 1900 after running 665,470 miles, and 107 in 1905, mileage 815,454.

Two other designs by Gooch remain to be mentioned, of which the first consisted of eight fast passenger engines of the 2-4-0 type with four coupled wheels 6 feet 6 inch diameter, and 16 inch by 24 inch cylinders. These, Nos. 149 to 156, were built by George England & Co of Hatcham Ironworks, London, in 1862. They had the usual Gooch pattern of outside sandwich frames and domeless boilers, but the link motion was of Stephenson's type. They were the only coupled engines with wheels as large as 6 feet 6 inches which ran on the Great Western narrow-gauge sections for many years, and were always employed on the northern section except in the case of occasional excursion trains between Wolverhampton and Paddington. A striking feature in their outward appearance, as in that of the earlier 69 and contemporary 157 classes, was the broad polished brass bands which formed the open driving splashers. The boilers were of large dimensions for that period, and contained 195 2-inch tubes, which provided a heating surface of 1,091 sq. feet. The total heating surface, inclusive of firebox, was 1,240·8 sq. feet. These engines were completely reconstructed at Wolverhampton during 1878–83 with 17 inch by 24 inch cylinders and domed boilers, and one of them, No. 154, was then named *Chancellor* in honour, it was stated, of a visit which the late Sir Stafford Northcote, Chancellor of the Exchequer, paid to Wolverhampton Works. When the West and North express services between Bristol and Shrewsbury, via the Severn Tunnel, were first instituted on 1st July 1888, four of these engines were stationed at Shrewsbury to run some of the trains through to Bristol.

The single express engines, Nos. 157 to 166, built by Sharp, Stewart & Co in 1862, were also very handsome engines, which for a long time worked the northern expresses between Paddington and Wolverhampton. The chief characteristics were similar to those of Nos. 149 to 156, and the principal dimensions were: cylinders 16 inches by 24 inches, single driving wheels 7 foot diameter, tube heating surface 1,126 sq. feet, total heating surface 1,248 sq. feet. Their total weight was 29·8 tons, of which 12·84 tons were carried on the driving wheels. In later years they became too light for the increasing train loads, and were broken up during 1879 to 1881, when they were replaced by somewhat similar but larger engines built at Swindon.

In connection with the 149 and 157 classes the generous boiler dimensions may be noted. The stinting of heating surface was never a characteristic of Great Western designs, and the boilers were generally larger than those of contemporary engines of most other leading railways.

### West Midland Engines

In 1863 the locomotives of the West Midland Railway, which included the former Oxford, Worcester & Wolverhampton and Newport, Abergavenny & Hereford Railways, were taken over, and became Nos. 171 to 301.

When the Oxford, Worcester & Wolverhampton Company was ready to begin operations in the spring of 1852 it had no engines and no money to buy any, so the Directors arranged with Charles Williams, a carriage builder of London, to provide locomotive power by contract. Williams at once engaged David Joy to represent him at Worcester, and the latter's first job was to travel post haste round the country to beg, borrow, or appropriate any old engines upon which he could lay his hands. He succeeded in obtaining a miscellaneous assortment consisting of half a dozen nondescript locomotives, two of which were borrowed from the North Staffordshire Railway, and the remainder obtained from various contractors at places as far apart as Pontefract, Welwyn, and Offord. Only one of these, a 2-4-0 mixed traffic engine, by E. B. Wilson & Co of Leeds, 1849, which Joy subsequently, in 1855, converted into an express engine with single driving wheels, came into the possession of the Great Western Railway as No. 206. Fortunately, it had just received a complete overhaul at the works of the makers, and being in good condition was immediately purchased for £1,250, making its first trial trip on the line on 29th April 1852, only two days before the public opening.

For about six months the railway had to do the best possible with the above engines, and it was not until November 1852 that those on order from R. & W. Hawthorn of Newcastle began to arrive. These 2-4-0 passenger engines had outside sandwich frames, 5 feet 9 inch coupled wheels, and 16 inch by 20 inch cylinders, and engines of similar dimensions but of different appearance were also supplied in 1853 by E. B. Wilson & Co. The latter firm also built in 1856 two express engines of the celebrated 'Jenny Lind' type, one of which was named *Will Shakespere* (sic). These had 6 feet 4 inch driving wheels and 15 inch by 22 inch cylinders. Eight of the coupled passenger engines, Nos. 178 and 180 to 186, worked for about fifty years, having been provided with new boilers at Wolverhampton.

The six-wheels coupled goods engines, also with sandwich frames, were designed by the makers, Messrs Hawthorn, Wilson, Kitson, etc., the majority being of E. B. Wilson's standard type.

There were also two very pretty little branch line well-tank engines by R. Stephenson & Co, 1859, with large canopied American type cabs of a somewhat ornamental appearance. These had outside cylinders 12 inch diameter by 18 inch stroke, and 5 feet 6 inch single driving wheels. One of them, afterwards GWR No. 223, was named *Ben Jonson* and worked the branch line between Chipping Norton Junction and Chipping Norton. The other (GWR No. 224) was not named, but was known to the staff as 'Mrs Jonson'; it worked between Chipping Norton Junction and Bourton-on-the-Water.

In 1860 two goods engines, which had just been built at Derby, were purchased from the Midland Railway. These were of Matthew Kirtley's standard design with double plate frames, 5 feet 2 inch wheels, and 16 inch by 24 inch cylinders, and carried 140 lb pressure. They became GWR

Nos. 280 and 281, and were followed in 1861 by twelve exactly similar engines (later GWR Nos. 282 to 293), part of a lot which W. Fairbairn & Sons of Manchester were then building for the Midland. These engines appeared to find favour on what by amalgamation with the Newport, Abergavenny & Hereford had now become the West Midland Railway, for a number of similar engines (GWR Nos. 260–263), but with a shorter wheel base, were built in 1862 at the Company's Works at Worcester. Until 1885–7, when they were broken up, these engines of the 260 and 280 classes worked main line goods trains, including the Droitwich salt trains, between Worcester and London.

The engines of the Newport, Abergavenny & Hereford Railway, 25 in number, were mostly of E. B. Wilson's design and build, very similar to those of the Oxford, Worcester & Wolverhampton.

The best passenger engines of the West Midland Railway were of the 2-2-2 and 2-4-0 types, six of each, by Beyer, Peacock & Co, Manchester, 1861 and 1862. The single express engines, GWR Nos. 209 to 214, had 6 feet 6 inches, and the coupled engines, GWR Nos. 196 to 201, 6 foot driving wheels. The cylinders of both classes were 16 inches by 20 inches. The driving or coupled wheels had inside bearings only, those of the carrying wheels being outside.

Williams' contract on the Oxford, Worcester & Wolverhampton Railway and with it Joy's employment were brought to an end in 1856, and that Company took over its own locomotive department with Frederic Haward as Superintendent. He was succeeded two years later by Edward Wilson, who combined the office with that of Permanent Way Engineer, first of the Oxford, Worcester & Wolverhampton and afterwards of the whole West Midland Railway, and remained in charge at Worcester till the summer of 1864. The Locomotive Superintendents of the Newport, Abergavenny & Hereford during its six years' life were successively Mark Carr and Alexander McDonnell.

### Shrewsbury & Hereford Engines

The first six passenger engines of the Shrewsbury & Hereford Railway, built by the Vulcan Foundry, near Warrington, in 1853–4, were of an extraordinary design with inside cylinders 15 inches by 20 inches, and single driving wheels 5 feet 6 inch diameter. The outside framing was a very light built-up construction and the steam chests, eccentrics, and Stephenson's link motion were placed outside it. The pumps were placed at each side of the firebox and driven from lugs attached to the back-gear eccentric sheaves.

The goods engines, also by the Vulcan Foundry, 1853–5, were of the outside framed 0-4-2 and 0-6-0 types. The latter, of which four were taken over by the Great Western Railway, were large heavy engines with 5 foot wheels and $15\frac{3}{4}$ inch by 24 inch cylinders. Unlike the passenger engines, they had the usual inside motion, but the steam chests were beneath the cylinders and arranged in ∧ form.

Most of the remaining later engines were of the London & North Western 'Crewe' type of that day, 2-4-0 with outside cylinders, and with the exception of three tank engines by Jones & Potts of Newton-le-Willows were built by Brassey & Co of Canada Works, Birkenhead.

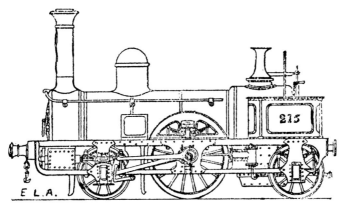

No. 215 (S. & H. R.) Vulcan Foundry, 1853

When the locomotive stock was divided in December 1862 between the West Midland, Great Western, and London & North Western Railways, the last-named company took over fourteen engines, of which thirteen were the newest Brassey-built stock. The three engines by Jones & Potts, and the fourteen older engines were taken by the Great Western and West Midland jointly and left for the time in the hands of the latter. After the amalgamation they were numbered with the West Midland stock. Four completely new 0-6-0 goods engines on order from Beyer, Peacock & Co, dated December 1861 were taken over direct from the makers by the Great Western as Nos. 167 to 170.

# XVI

# Carriages and Wagons

As in the case of locomotives, Brunel had views regarding the designs of railway carriages which differed from those held by his contemporaries, though one at least of his ideas was adaptable only to broad-gauge vehicles, and could not have been carried out in the construction of those for the Narrow Gauge. He wished to obtain a mechanical advantage by increasing the diameter of the wheels without raising the bodies of the carriages. Nicholas Wood, in his report, wrote:

> This comprehends, what is deemed by Mr Brunel the most important part of the advantage of an enlarged width of gauge, viz.: the reduction of friction by the increased diameter of wheels, by which, at the same time, by being enabled to place the body of the carriage within the wheels, the centre of gravity of the carriage is kept low, and greater stability and steadiness of motion is expected to be attained. Four-feet wheels have been put upon the carriages at present in use upon the line; but Mr Brunel states 'that he looks forward to the employment of wheels of a larger diameter, and that he has been influenced to a considerable extent in recommending the increased width of gauge by its capabilities of prospective improvements which may take place in the system of railroads.'

Brunel himself reported:

> We see that there is a diminution of friction by the increase in the diameter of the wheels; but it is doubtful to what extent this is modified by elevating the bodies of the carriages; a broad gauge, by allowing the bodies of the carriages to be placed within the wheels, and thus to reduce the height of the carriages, and consequently diminish the area of the frontage, is an advantage, considering the great amount of resistance arising from the atmosphere. To effect this, with the most convenient form of body, similar to that ordinarily adopted on railways, does require, as I have frequently stated in previous reports, a width of at least 6 feet 10 inches.

Only two classes of vehicles, both four-wheeled, were constructed on the above principles. One of these was the 'posting carriage', or, as it would now be termed, saloon carriage. The length was 18 feet 6 inches, and the

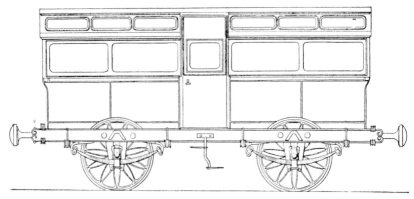

Posting carriage

width of the body down to the level of the seats 7 feet 6 inches, but below this level the width was diminished in a curve to 6 feet at the bottom, so that the wheels, which were 4 feet in diameter, could be placed outside the body. Whishaw, in *The Railways of Great Britain and Ireland*, gives the following description:

> The posting-carriage, which is calculated to hold eighteen persons, is fitted up in a style of elegance not met with in any other railway-conveyance in the Kingdom (save only the royal railway-carriage); it is furnished with cushioned seats all round except at the doorways, and a table extending down the middle, so that for a family party or a party of friends it is a most excellent contrivance. . . . In the middle of each side there is a glass door 2 feet 4 inches wide and 6 feet high, the glass square being 19 inches high and 21 inches wide. On each side of the door there are two lights ranging in height with that of the door, and above these are three smaller lights, which fill up the whole of the top spaces between the door and the ends of the body.

The centre of the roof was raised, forming what is now termed the clerestory roof. The reason given for this construction was that the passengers were thereby enabled to walk about the carriage. Between the body and the frame were interposed eight air cushions in india-rubber cases, which were placed upon two longitudinal pieces covered with sheet iron and fixed to the frame by bolts. The air cushions were kept in place by iron plates fixed to the framing of the body, and were finally secured by bands fastened to the frame. The framing and cross-bearers were finished at the ends in the shape of ornamental scrolls. The wheel-base was 10 feet and the weight nearly 5 tons 6 cwts.

The London newspaper, *Sun*, of 2nd June 1838, describes these carriages as 'Extra First Class' with 'luxurious couches, cushions and sofas, even tables on which people may eat read or play chess'.

The posting carriages were subsequently found to be of 'little general use'. Three were still in service at the end of 1849, and the last one disappeared during the second half of 1856.

The other vehicles with bodies inside the wheels were the Carriage Trucks. In the early days carriage trucks were used not only for the conveyance of empty private carriages, but also as passenger vehicles, since 'persons of the first quality' often preferred to travel on the railway in their own carriages. The Great Western carried a quite unusually large proportion of such persons; hence the great number of carriage trucks— there were 161 in 1845 and 224 in 1849—and the ample provision originally made for dealing with private carriages at most of the stations.

These carriage trucks had 4 foot wheels and weighed 3 tons 13 cwts. They were specially mentioned in Gooch's evidence before the Gauge Commissioners in 1845; he then stated that 'they were put inside the wheels altogether; they do not overhang at all', and added that as thus made they were wide enough for the purpose of a private carriage or anything else that was carried upon them. In reply to the question whether he was of opinion that private carriages travel with less oscillation in consequence of being within the wheels, he replied that the carriage trucks were remarkably easy.

Whishaw describes the general arrangement of the four-wheeled carriages as similar to those with six wheels, and the latter had wide laterally overhanging bodies. When Gooch was asked by the Gauge Commissioners in 1845 whether the bodies of the passenger carriages were placed between the wheels, he replied in the negative, giving as the reason that four passengers were carried abreast, and that this, as far as the Company was concerned, was the cheapest way of carrying them.

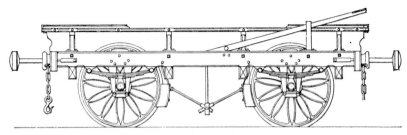

Carriage truck

That the posting carriages were the only vehicles, other than carriage trucks, with their bodies between the wheels is shown by the following extract from Major-General Pasley's Report to the Board of Trade, dated 10th March 1843,[1] recommending the gauge of 5 feet 3 inches for all Irish Railways instead of the 6 feet 2 inches previously proposed by the Irish Railway Commissioners:

> Secondly, to use very large wheels for railway carriages and place them outside as proposed by the Commissioners, which they give as a chief reason for recommending the 6 feet 2 inches gauge, would require all the passengers to ride omnibus fashion, instead of the present more comfortable mode, because the doors of railway carriages of the present commodious form would be blocked up by such wheels. Accordingly this very inconvenient arrangement of the wheels has never been attempted, except in a very few of what are termed posting carriages on the Great Western Railway, which have only one door in the centre of each side, and yet carry fewer passengers by one third than their other first-class carriages of the same length, which are all fitted up in the usual manner, with wheels under the body of each.

Wheels running loose upon the axles appear to have been designed for the Great Western. The late Sir Frederick Bramwell made the following remarks before the Institution of Mechanical Engineers in 1875:

> With respect to the question of loose wheels, he feared that the works in which he had himself been an apprentice had had something to do with the discredit attaching to them. Some loose wheels had actually been made there for Brunel, intended for the Great Western Railway; but they were so badly designed by the maker and so defectively made, that they never did work, and never could have worked for any length of time, and they therefore brought discredit upon the whole system. If haply in those days the manufacture of the loose wheels, the value of which Brunel appreciated, had fallen into the hands of some one who would have spent more pains to make a good job of them, he could not help thinking that railways would not now be suffering from having equal-sized wheels rigidly keyed upon parallel axles, which had to go round curves, and which ought therefore to be capable of having differential velocities.

But whatever ideas Brunel, according to the above, may have entertained at first on the subject of loose wheels, he had certainly relinquished

---

[1] Gauge Commission Report, Appendix, p. 379

them before 1845, when he expressed himself to the Gauge Commissioners as satisfied that the coning of the treads of fixed wheels was far greater than was required to counteract the effects of the slip of the wheels round curves.

Dealing now with carriages of the usual form of construction with laterally overhanging bodies, the four-wheeled first-class, according to Whishaw, had three compartments, each seating eight persons. Their length over bodies was 18 feet, and their weight $4\frac{3}{4}$ tons. The four-wheeled second-class carriages were similar, but open at the sides, and divided into four compartments, each accommodating twelve passengers. The weight of these was 3 tons 17 cwts. When the railway was first opened there was another type of closed second-class carriage, but as we have seen elsewhere, it was abandoned as early as July 1839. The diameter of the wheels was 4 feet, and this size, which is 6 inches larger than that usually adopted for railway carriages down to the present day, became standard until about 1875 for all Great Western broad-gauge coaching stock, except horse-boxes and a number of eight-wheeled carriages built in 1862–3 for the Metropolitan Railway. Horse-boxes had 3 feet wheels to allow the floors to be made lower.

Some at least of the above-mentioned four-wheeled carriages had the defect of much too short a wheel-base, the two axles being bunched together under the middle at a distance of only about 6 feet 6 inches to 7 feet apart. Immediately after the opening of the line there were strong complaints about the jolting, and two of the causes were given in the Chairman's circular of 22nd June 1838, as due to the springs of the carriages and 'a defect in the position of the axles under the bodies'. Gibbs records in his diary under date 12th July 1838, that 'Melling's four-wheel carriages were ordered off the line', and although he does not give the reasons, it is not too much to believe that the above defect may have been partly responsible for such a drastic decision within a few weeks of the opening of the railway.

The early carriages, built from 1837 to 1842, came from the following builders: Beard, D. Davies, Dell, Gower, R. Jeffreys, R. Melling, J. Perry, W. Shackleford, Mather & Chantler, and Williams. The first appear to have been made in 1837 by Richard Melling & Co of Manchester, but the greater number of the best first-class carriages were made by David Davies of Wigmore Street, London. Davies, Perry, and Shackleford continued to have a long connection with the Company, especially the last named, who had works at Benson near Wallingford, and after about 1850 at Cheltenham, where the firm built carriages for the Great Western until 1860.

The number of four-wheeled carriages originally built is uncertain, since in addition to those 'ordered off the line', others were altered. As early as August 1837 Brunel submitted plans to the London Committee for six-wheeled carriages, and was instructed to arrange for the alteration of some already ordered from four- to six-wheels. Of the four-wheeled type there were in service in June 1845 only 28 first-class and 6 second-class carriages. Two still existed in 1862.

The standard passenger carriages, if they may be so termed, were six-wheeled from the first.[1] Brunel told the Gauge Commissioners that carriages with three axles conduced to the public safety, and Gooch, at the same time, said that the four-wheeled carriages left the rails, and 'we attributed it to the lightness of the carriage . . . We found that we could not use four-wheeled carriages at high velocities.'

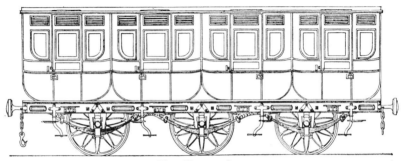

First Class carriage

The large or six-wheeled first-class carriages had wheels 4 foot diameter, placed 7 feet apart between centres of axles. Whishaw gives the following description:

> [They] are in four compartments, each calculated to hold eight persons, or thirty-two in all; some of these compartments are subdivided by a central partition, in the middle of which is a glass door furnished with a roller-spring blind. This arrangement is found to be attended oft-times with considerable advantage, in affording ladies and small families the means of travelling, as it were alone. The fittings of the interior are of the most comfortable description, including the stuffed leather cushions, elbows, and linings, added to the additional height given to all the Great Western carriages. Each compartment has side-lights ranging with the sashes of the doors; and above these lights, and corresponding in width, are as many shallow blinds. The length of a large first-class body is 24 feet, the width 9 feet 6 inches, and the height 6 feet. . . . The distance from centre to centre of buffers is 5 feet 10 inches. The weight of a large first-class carriage is 15,232 lbs. [= 7 tons 16 cwt.].

The official dimensions of the standard first-class six-wheeled carriages, as recorded in the tables produced to the Gauge Commissioners in 1845, agree with the above, save that the extreme width is given as 9 feet, and the weight as 7 tons 9 cwt 17 lbs. Gooch, in his evidence, also stated that the extreme width was 9 feet, and that the maximum lateral overhang on each side of the gauge was 12 inches, so the width and weight given by Whishaw must have been inaccurate.

The six-wheeled second-class carriages, open at the sides, were longer, the axles being 9 feet apart. The wheels were 4 feet in diameter. The carriages were divided into six compartments, each accommodating

---

[1] The train of 1839 shown facing page 365 is made up of one of each sort—Open 2nd, Closed 2nd, First, and Posting Carriage (of which only a bit of the roof appears), in the order given.

twelve passengers on seats 15 inches wide. The length of the body was 27 feet 2½ inches and the extreme width 9 feet. These carriages were provided with brakes, as shown, which were applied by a guard, who sat among the passengers in a nice sociable sort of way. The weight of the carriages as given by Whishaw, was 6 tons 13 cwt 2 qrs. The design appears to have been slightly modified before 1845, and the wheel-base increased from 18 feet to 18 feet 4 inches, after which the weight became 7 tons 5 cwt 2 qrs.

Passengers in these vehicles, especially those near the sides, were of course exposed to the wind and driving rain; and very soon this began to be bitterly complained of, even by people who had been used to long journeys on the outside of stage coaches. A coroner's jury is said once to have returned a verdict that—'the Deceased died from cold and exposure from travelling in a second-class carriage on the Great Western Railway'! As we have seen, these carriages disappeared from ordinary trains in 1844.

In June 1845 there were 78 six-wheeled first-class, and 97 six-wheeled second-class carriages, the costs of which were £730 10s 11d and £437 1s 4d respectively.

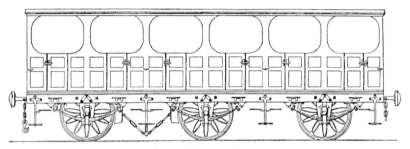

Second Class carriage

It may be mentioned here that the large 4 foot wheels projected upwards through the floors of the carriages, and were encased in 'paddle-boxes', which sometimes coincided, at any rate partially, with a door-way, and these were liable to cause an unwary or flustered passenger to make an undignified and sometimes painful exit from the carriage. This arrangement was not unusual in the case of narrow-gauge carriages of that day even with their smaller wheels.

The third-class carriages were open trucks, and appear to have been so called in official correspondence. Before the Gauge Commissioners Seymour Clarke referred to them as 'common waggons'.

The Sonning accident of 24th December 1841 and the consequent improvement of these 'common waggons' have already been described. Three years later the 'Cheap Trains Act' compelled the provision of carriages protected from the weather to the satisfaction of the Board of Trade, and in June 1845 an official return was published, which contained lithographed drawings of 'the carriages already sanctioned, recommended or most approved by the Railway Department of the Board of Trade for the conveyance of third-class passengers'.

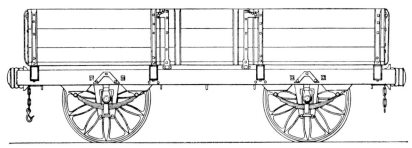

Third class 'carriage' 1840

The accompanying drawings of the Great Western third-class carriage show that it had the general appearance of a milk-van with small venetian ventilators at the top, which admitted a moderate amount of air, and in hot weather the small sliding shutters could be opened, if desired. The Company's officials of that day evidently considered that the third-class passenger was not likely to be interested in the scenery, so they encased him in a box without windows, only permitting such light to penetrate into the interior as could find its way through the top venetians. Anyhow the passenger could not fall out, and this was the main thing. He must also have experienced considerable difficulty in falling in, since there was only one narrow door on the platform side, which a percentage of stout would-be patrons of the Company might have failed to negotiate even sideways.

This carriage was 20 feet 9 inches long, 8 feet 6 inches wide, and 6 feel 9 inches high, and accommodated fifty-nine passengers on transversely arranged seats, the sixtieth seat being reserved for the brakesman. Clasp brakes actuated by a system of levers were applied to all wheels, and took the place of the 'tolerably useless' toggle-joint brakes of the old second-class carriages. The return shows that the Company was the proud possessor of eight of these vehicles, which had cost £282 6s 6d each. They were used on the down and up Parliamentary trains between Paddington and Bristol, and lasted until 1856.

It may be with a sigh of relief that the reader will turn his attention from these third-class vehicles to the Royal Saloon, which, from a chronological standpoint, should have been described earlier, since it was constructed in 1840. It was originally a four-wheeled carriage with a clerestory roof. A contemporary newspaper contained the following flamboyant description:

The Great Western Railway Company, anticipating the Patronage of the Queen and her illustrious Consort, Prince Albert, and of the Members of the Royal Family, have just had built a splendid railway carriage for their accommodation. It is a very handsome vehicle 21 feet in length and divided into three compartments, the two end ones being four feet six inches long and nine feet wide, while the centre forms a noble saloon, twelve feet long, nine feet wide, and six feet six inches high. The exterior is painted of the same

The Queen's Carriage, 1848. A small disc-and-Crossbar was provided on the roof to convey signals and instructions to the footplate

Charles Alexander Saunders, Secretary and General Superintendent 1833–1863, " a remarkable man who was destined to do more towards founding the Great Western Railway system than any other single individual, Brunel himself not even excepted "

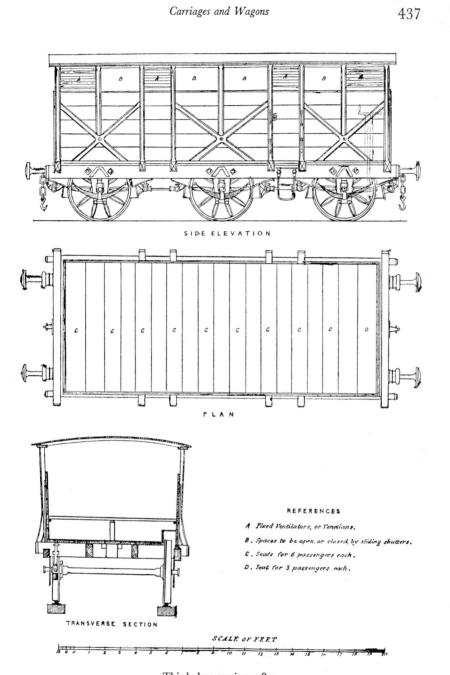

SIDE ELEVATION

PLAN

TRANSVERSE SECTION

REFERENCES

A . *Fixed Ventilators, or Venetians.*

B . *Spaces to be open, or closed, by sliding shutters.*

C . *Seats for 6 passengers each.*

D . *Seat for 5 passengers each.*

*SCALE OF FEET*

Third class carriage 1844

brown colour as the others of the Company's carriages, and at each end is a large window affording a view of the whole of the line. The interior has been most magnificently fitted up by Mr Webb, upholsterer, Old Bond Street. The saloon is handsomely arranged with hanging sofas of carved wood in the rich style of Louis XIV, and the walls are panelled out in the same elegant manner, and fitted up with rich crimson and white silk and exquisitely executed paintings representing the four elements by Parris. The end compartments are also fitted up in the same style, each apartment having in the centre a useful and ornamental rosewood table; and the floors of the whole are covered with chequered India matting.

The carriage itself was built by David Davies of London, and judging from an old woodcut appears to have been of a type similar to that of the posting carriages with body inside the wheels. In this condition it was probably used only by Queen Adelaide and Prince Albert, for on 19th January 1842, a minute of the General Traffic Committee records that the 'Queen's Carriage' was likely to be required for a journey by the King of Prussia, and that it needed improvement, being less easy and not so safe on four wheels as the first-class carriages. Brunel recommended a new frame with eight wheels, an alteration which was sanctioned and apparently made before Queen Victoria herself made her first journey in it on 13th June 1842.

This seems to have been the first eight-wheeled carriage in the country, ante-dating those by Adams for the London & Woolwich Railway by about five years. It was altered in 1851 to an ordinary saloon and broken up in 1879.

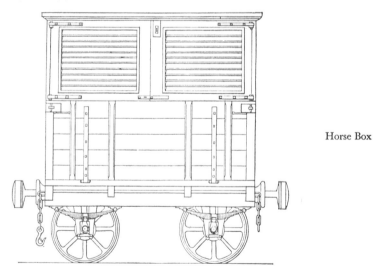

Horse Box

The original horse-boxes were strange vehicles, wider than they were long. Their dimensions were 9 feet 8 inches long (12 feet 8 inches over buffers) by 10 feet 8 inches wide by 7 feet 6 inches high. They ran on four 3 foot wheels with a wheel-base of only 6 feet, and weighed about 4 tons 2 cwt. Robert Stephenson commented unfavourably on this to the Gauge

Commissioners, adding: 'I have observed upon that line that the motion of the horse-boxes is sometimes fearful, from the side motion because they want length with reference to their width.' Joseph Locke did not agree with him as to this proportion affecting the rocking motion, and incidentally stated that the horses travelled sideways on the Great Western. Evidently this mode of progression or the form of the boxes themselves—probably both—was found to be objectionable, for, a little later, Gooch told the Commissioners: 'Our old horse-boxes are wider, they are about 10 feet, but some new horse-boxes we are making are narrower; we are putting three horses instead of four.' This seems to imply that the three were carried with their heads foremost in the usual way.

Before leaving the period, which may be said to end in 1842, a few details may be added. In 1841 Brunel reported that the best carriages had elastic hair and not spring buffers. In November 1841 the Board directed that the second-class carriages were to have the partitions boarded up to the top rails, and in August 1842 gave instructions that six first-class carriages were to be fitted with inside roof lamps.

Both bodies and frames were at first made of wood, as was the usual practice for many years on most railways, though the nature of the timber is not recorded. Gooch was asked by the Gauge Commissioners in October 1845 whether long use caused the timber to deteriorate, and replied:

We find that the timber suffers very much, and we have made and continue to make our waggons entirely of iron. We have made carriage frames for some time all of iron.

The luggage vans of 1841–2, built by Braby and Carr[1] were four-wheeled, and had bodies and frames of wood. But in 1844 a number of four-wheeled vans were built by 'Gooch', i.e., probably at Swindon, some of which had both bodies and frames of iron. These not only mark the first appearance of vehicles built at Swindon, but also the earliest use of iron bodies for coaching vehicles. Iron frames for carriages were not new, the earliest coaching stock of the London & Greenwich Railway, of about 1836, having had them.

The following table, from the returns made by the Company to the Gauge Commissioners, gives some particulars of the rolling stock in the summer of 1845:

| Class | Number | Diameter of Wheels Feet | Average Weight T. c. q. | Average Cost £ s. d. |
|---|---|---|---|---|
| | | *Six-wheeled Stock* | | |
| First | 78 | 4 | 7 9 0 | 730 10 11 |
| Second | 97 | 4 | 7 4 2 | 437 1 4 |
| Third | 8 | 4 | 7 5 1 | 282 6 6 |
| Royal Mails | 4 | 4 | 7 3 0 | 391 6 6 |
| Goods Waggons | 3 | 4½ | | |
| „    „ | 44 | 4 | 5 5 3 | 247 12 11 |
| „    „ | 2 | 3 | | |

[1] Braby and Carr seem to have been employees of the Company at Paddington.

*History of The Great Western Railway*

| Class | Number | Diameter of Wheels Feet | Average Weight | | | Average Cost | | |
|---|---|---|---|---|---|---|---|---|
| | | | T. | C. | Q. | £ | s. | d. |
| *Four-wheeled Stock* | | | | | | | | |
| First | 28 | 4 | 4 | 15 | 0 | 534 | 13 | 10 |
| Second | 6 | 4 | 3 | 17 | 0 | 227 | 11 | 0 |
| Third | — | — | | — | | | — | |
| Carriage Trucks | 161 | 4 | 3 | 13 | 1 | 151 | 15 | 3 |
| Horse Boxes | 96 | 3 | 4 | 1 | 3 | 198 | 17 | 9 |
| Luggage Vans { | 15 | 4 | | | | | | |
| | 9 | 3½ | } 4 | 12 | 2 | 169 | 15 | 0 |
| Goods Waggons | 237 | 4 | | | | | | |
|     ,,   ,, | 84 | 3½ | } 4 | 0 | 0 | 133 | 8 | 7 |
|     ,,   ,, | 20 | 3 | | | | | | |

The third-class passenger was promoted in 1845 from a glorified milk-van to an 'armoured train', out of which also he was effectually prevented from falling, except through the doors. The first ten of these all-iron third-class carriages were built in September and October 1845 by the Company. All of them were converted to luggage vans in 1859–1860. Ten more of a later design, built in 1848 by Stothert & Slaughter of Bristol, were of the form shown on the opposite page. The bodies were made of thin sheets riveted to angle irons. Instead of the ventilating venetians of the older third-class carriages, small four-pane attic windows were thoughtfully provided in the doors, so that by standing up and pressing its nose against the panes, the 'proletariat' might perchance catch fleeting glimpses of the scenery. The carriage was open from end to end and was provided with transverse seats. The 'compartments' were separated only by the backs of the seats, 15 inches high, and one oil lamp did duty for a carriage 26 feet 8 inches long inside. All wheels were provided with brake blocks actuated through levers and rods by a guard who sat among the passengers in the middle compartment, which had a seat on one side only. In 1871 most of the above ten carriages were converted into goods brake vans.

When the third-class passenger used one of the carriages just described, he travelled in luxury, but when he journeyed by excursion train he was not so fortunate. In August 1850 forty goods box-wagons were ordered to be fitted up temporarily for use in excursion trains during the season; and we find that nine third-class carriages were 'transferred' in 1850 from *stone trucks* (!), and in 1855 were 're-transferred' for goods service.

D. K. Clark, in his well-known work, *Railway Machinery*, gives drawings of the first-class carriage of the 1848–53 period, which are reproduced on page 442 and may be compared with the earlier one on page 434. The style of the old stage coach was still retained, though two lamps were now provided for the four compartments. The bodies, 24 feet long by 9 feet wide over all, were of timber, but the majority of the under-frames were of iron plates and angles riveted together. Each compartment accommodated eight

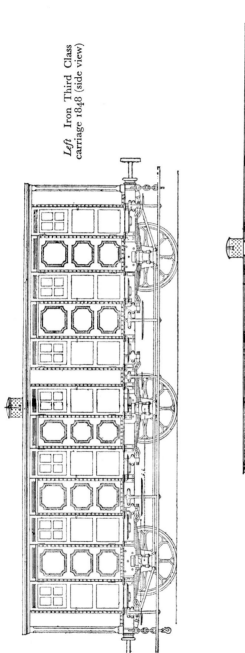

*Left* Iron Third Class carriage 1848 (side view)

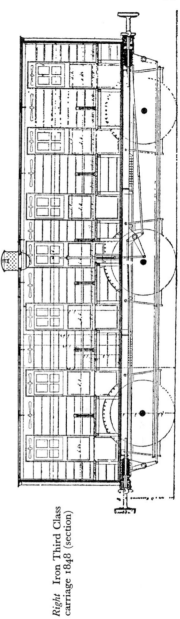

*Right* Iron Third Class carriage 1848 (section)

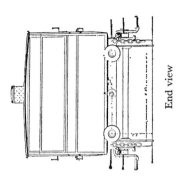

End view

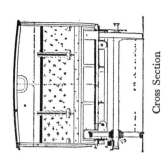

Cross Section

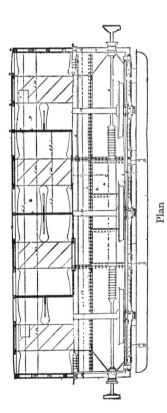

Side View

Plan

First Class Carriage, c. 1851

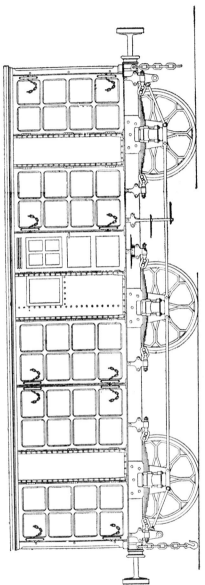

Passenger Luggage Van 1848 with Guard's Compartment (Brake gear omited)

passengers. The length of wheel-base was 15 feet, divided equally by the middle axle, and the springs and axle boxes, were of improved design.

Although iron frames were generally used, in 1846–7 the Great Western Railway made a number of wood frames for first-class carriages, the bodies of which were built by David Davies of London, Messrs Wright of Saltley, Birmingham, and by Shackleford. There also seem to have been a few carriages of which the wood bodies were made by the Great Western at Paddington in 1851–2, and the iron frames by Hennett.

The luggage vans were entirely of iron, and of very similar construction to that of the iron third-class carriages. The brake gear is omitted from the illustration, which represents vans constructed in 1848–9 by Stothert & Slaughter, Bristol, and in 1852 by The Vulcan Foundry, near Warrington. Incidentally it may be added here that there were a few four-wheeled vans by Shackleford in 1847, which had 3 foot wheels, and with the exception of the standard horse-boxes were then the only coaching vehicles with wheels less than 4 foot diameter.

Until 1846 there does not appear to have been any officer specially in charge of the rolling stock. In the early days the carriages were under the Traffic Superintendents at London and Bristol, both for working and maintenance, and we find Brunel writing to Saunders in August 1842 that the maintenance and repairs should be supervised by someone of mechanical training. Whether the letter had any immediate result has not been ascertained, but in 1846 J. Gibson was appointed Superintendent of the Carriage and Waggon Department, which post he retained till his resignation in 1864.

The second Royal Saloon, known as the 'Queen's Carriage', was built in 1848,[1] the wood body being made by Davies and the iron frame at Swindon. The body was 30 feet 8 inches long, 10 feet wide, and 7 feet 7 inches high, and contained one saloon, one end compartment and one lavatory. The carriage ran on eight wheels, 3 feet in diameter, the total wheel-base being 22 feet. The illustration apparently shows that the two pairs of axles did not form swivelling bogies; the weight at each end was carried on two laminated springs, each 8 feet long, and from these was transferred to compensating beams, the ends of which rested upon the axle-boxes. The buffer and drawbar springs were of indiarubber. A disc-and-crossbar signal was fitted on the roof to enable the Queen's attendants to convey her behests as to speed or stoppage to the look-out man in the 'iron coffin' on the tender, and so to the officer in charge of the engine. In 1887 the automatic vacuum brake and, apparently, new bogies were fitted. In December 1889 the carriage was altered to Narrow Gauge and broken up in 1903.

---

[1] This date has usually been stated as 1850, but the official List of Stock for the half-year to 30th June 1849—the earliest extant—includes the 'Queen's Carriage' as well as the 'Old Royal'—both eight wheeled—and does not specify the former as an addition during the half-year; hence it already existed.

In July 1850 a first-class carriage was made by the Company, in which the body panels were of papier maché instead of wood. Evidently this was in the nature of an experiment, which seems to have been successful, for from June 1851 to 1858 we find that the panels of nearly all the first and second-class carriages, including composites, were made of this material. Most of these were constructed by Messrs Wright of Birmingham, J. Ward of Exeter, Shackleford of Cheltenham, and Perry & Co of Wolverhampton. Some were also built by the Company at Paddington during the 1857–1863 period. As a result of a decision of the Board in April 1853 most of the iron frames for Ward's, Shackleford's, and Perry's coaches were made at Swindon, but in 1856 a large number were contracted for, to be built by Ashbury of Manchester.

Papier maché bodies do not seem to have been made for third-class carriages, but about 1852 wood was substituted for iron, and in 1855 luggage vans were also made with wood bodies.

In 1852 the Company introduced the first eight-wheel carriages to be employed on regular express passenger services by a British railway, a set of six first- and second-class composites for the broad-gauge London and Birmingham service. These remarkable vehicles, known to contemporary railwaymen as 'Long Charleys', were 38 feet long, the four axles, though not arranged in bogies, were equalized in pairs with large outside compensating beams between each, and a pivotal action in these gave limited side play. The seating capacity was 24 first - and 48 second-class in three and four compartments respectively.

After a main line life of eleven years, they were fitted with gas lighting in place of the miserable pot lamps and put to work on the Metropolitan Railway when it opened in 1863. They were broken up in 1875-7.

It was the practice in those days to adorn the insides of second-class carriages with advertisement bills; in June 1853 a letter was read to the Board calling attention to their dirty state, 'which Gibson represented to be caused by the billposters'. Some discussion ensued on discontinuing the practice, without immediate result, but it was eventually abandoned at the beginning of 1855.

From 1854 nearly all the new carriages of superior class were composites with five compartments, two first-class, two second-class, and one for luggage. In July of this year it was decided that all second-class compartments should carry ten passengers only in each 'body' instead of twelve.

After 1856 the only new six-wheeled third-class carriages consisted of ten constructed by Shackleford in 1860. From this time onwards, with exception of some special stock for Metropolitan service, no new broad-gauge thirds were built for many years, and when carriages of this class were required, the oldest seconds were altered for the purpose. The latter were of such a nature that they lent themselves to almost anything, for in 1861 there is a record that 'four old second class, which had been renewed during the previous half-year, were altered to carry fish'!

The above alterations coincided with the first recorded improvements to the interiors of the seconds, for in 1859–60 100 second-class carriages were provided with stuffed cushion seats and backs, and also with hat cords in the roofs. As these latter have long disappeared from the carriages, it may be as well to remind the present generation that in those good old days no really respectable British citizen travelled or even appeared in public without a tall cylindrical top-hat on his head. Needless to say, these erections were extremely inconvenient in the low railway carriages of the period, so some genius invented a quite simple contrivance for disposing of them during the journey. It consisted of a thick cord forming an oblong parallelogram, suspended about an inch from the roof of the carriage by brass hooks at the corners, and of such size and elasticity as to admit the insertion of the brim of an inverted top-hat, which, until the adoption of this beneficent appliance, its owner had been obliged to place on the seat at some risk, hold in his hands, or replace on his head after safely assuming a sitting posture, it being most rash for a man of average height to attempt to stand erect with the hat on.

About this same period several minor additions are recorded, of which the most important was the fitting of top rails and luggage covers for carrying luggage on the carriage roofs. This practice, almost, if not quite, universal on the narrow-gauge lines, had been abandoned after a very short trial on the Great Western nearly twenty years before. Its revival on the 'Long Charleys' of 1852 was suggested but not effected. Captain Wynne of the Board of Trade, reporting in May 1854 on a method of communication between guard and driver, by means of a rope along the tops of the carriages, in use on the Bristol & Exeter Railway, wrote:

The Carriages on the Great Western lines are not constructed as on the narrow-gauge lines to carry luggage on their roofs, hence there is a facility for applying a rope as a means of communication on the former lines which does not exist on the latter.

Probably to economise stock, the practice was now adopted, and in two years from the autumn of 1859 140 broad-gauge passenger roofs were fitted with rails and tarpaulins. The narrow-gauge carriages taken over with the two Shrewsbury Railways had always had them. After this, luggage on the roofs became a daily nuisance to the staff till it was finally abandoned in the early 'seventies. It may be mentioned that the air resistance of a train is greatly increased by it.

In 1854 a royalty was paid to a Mr Williams for 'pendant balance window springs used in the carriages', and in October 1856 we meet with the first mention of foot-warmers on the Great Western, when a tender for the supply of these was submitted to the Board. They were supplied to first-class passengers in that year, extended to the second-class in 1870 and to third-class three years later.

An experiment in lighting a carriage by gas, proposed by Mr George Knox, who had been Secretary and afterwards a Director of the Shrewsbury & Birmingham Railway, was authorized by the Board in December 1857. One of the saloon carriages was selected, the arrangements being under the supervision of Mr Knox. No details of the system are available.

Other novel additions were the fitting in 1860–1 of brackets for destination or label boards, and the fixing of enamel number plates inside first-class carriages.

For working the Metropolitan Railway, 45 eight-wheeled broad-gauge carriages were provided in 1862–3. Six of these were our old friends, the 'Long Charley' composites, now ten years old, whose second-class compartments were converted into thirds, doubtless without much difficulty. The remainder—6 firsts, 9 composites (1st and 2nd), 10 seconds, and 14 thirds—were constructed by Messrs Brown & Marshall of Birmingham to an entirely new design, for which John Fowler is said to have been responsible. These had teak bodies 39 feet long, 10 feet 6 inches wide, and 7 feet 2 inches high, and iron frames with 3 feet 3 inch wheels, the axles of which, though grouped in pairs at each end, did not form bogies in the usual sense of the term as there were no centre pins. The attachment to the under-frames was merely through the medium of links suspended from the ends of the springs at an angle of about 30 degrees. The other ends of the links were attached to brackets riveted to the frames. The end axles were maintained parallel to each other by means of stay rods connecting the axle-boxes, and although there were hornplates, the latter did not act as guides for the axle-boxes, but merely limited the movements of the trucks. The comparatively flexible connections between axle-boxes, springs, and links allowed the trucks to radiate at each end, and permitted the long wheel base to adjust itself to the curves. All these carriages were lighted by gas, carried in encased indiarubber bags on the roof, from which it would seem that Knox's experiment had proved successful. In addition, ten old second-class six-wheeled coaches were altered to thirds as a temporary arrangement.

When the Company gave up working the Metropolitan in August 1863 all this new stock was, of course, left on their hands after no more than seven months' use on the service it had been built for. It came in later for the Main Line and City trains and the Hammersmith and Kensington services, and subsequently for local trains elsewhere.

A curious and somewhat inexplicable entry occurs in the stock report for the second half of 1862 as follows: 'One wood box altered to mixed gauge.' Unfortunately further details are missing, and the reader must be left to guess the nature of the mechanical sleight-of-hand which made the 'box' so amazingly adaptable. Was it perhaps an experimental revival of the old idea of loose wheels sliding laterally upon the axles, which has already been mentioned? Or was it a dummy vehicle with wide buffers for the purpose of being sandwiched between broad- and narrow-gauge coaches? The latter is the more probable explanation.

A list of the broad-gauge carriage stock at the time of the West Midland amalgamation in 1863 will be found on page 450.

In general appearance the carriages of this period looked like huge oblong flat boxes, the width of the bodies being considerably greater than their height; all the outside woodwork of the almost flat sides was painted dark brown.

After 1863 very few broad-gauge carriages were constructed for more than ten years. In 1865 three composites (first and second) were built by the Company at Paddington, followed by one second-class carriage in the early part of 1868. These were the last of the old stock with six 4 foot wheels.

Before concluding the story of the broad-gauge carriage stock to 1863, there are one or two details which may be mentioned. All carriages had spoked wheels of various forms, the majority until about 1860 being of the forms shown in the illustrations. It will be noticed that the earlier carriages had Losh's wheels with twelve open elliptical spokes. The carriages of the 1848–54 period had open spokes of a different pattern, as illustrated on pages 434–443. The first-class carriages had Hague's type of wheel, but the third-class coaches and vans had wheels of a peculiar pattern, the origin of which is not known, though it may have been due to Gibson, the Carriage Superintendent during this later period. The number of spokes in each wheel was reduced to eight only. Probably this number did not provide sufficient support for the tyre, and we find that in October 1854 the Board ordered that 'an extra spoke be placed in all the carriage wheels constructed'. Generally, these spoked wheels were formed of wrought-iron bars bent to shape, the naves being cast in the foundry.

The original method of securing the tyres to the wheels, both being of wrought iron, was to rivet them on. The rivets, which passed right through both wheel rim and tyre, had a deep countersink in the tread. The rivet holes were a source of weakness, and several bad accidents resulted from the breakages of tyres through these holes. An improved tyre fastening, which did away with the holes, was invented by Gibson, and used on the Great Western from 1855 onwards. This consisted of a continuous ring which was dovetailed into the tyre, the projecting outer portion abutting against a bevelled surface on the inside of the rim of the wheel. The dovetailed part of the ring was let into a rectangular groove in the tyre, and the inner edge of the latter was then hammered down upon it.

### NARROW-GAUGE CARRIAGE STOCK

By the absorption of the Shrewsbury lines in 1854 the Great Western Company became possessed of 188 narrow-gauge coaching vehicles, including carriage trucks and horse-boxes, of which 108 had belonged to the Shrewsbury & Chester and 80 to the Shrewsbury & Birmingham. With the exception of four first-class carriages, which had six wheels, the whole of this stock was four-wheeled and, as the first portion of the two railways was only opened in 1846, must have been comparatively new when taken over. There were two classes of vehicles which were not represented amongst the broad-gauge stock of that period, viz.: second and third-class composite carriages, of which there were two, and a 'composite' consisting of a first-class compartment and hound van, of which there was one solitary example.

The makers of the above carriages were entirely different from those who had been building stock for the Great Western, and amongst them were the well-known firms in the Birmingham district, such as Brown, Marshall & Co, the Railway Carriage Company of Oldbury, and J. Wright & Son. Other names, not so well known, were Quadling & Co, Adams & Co, and Tudor.

In March 1855 a return of the narrow-gauge stock was submitted to the Board by Mr Truss, carriage superintendent of the Shrewsbury lines, and it was resolved on his recommendation to order 24 first and second-class carriages, 6 passenger luggage vans, 20 horse-boxes and 10 carriage trucks, and also to convert 16 'open sided' carriages into second-class and 4 'stand-up' carriages into thirds. Evidently these last were some sort of 'fourths', though in the return they were classed as thirds. The alteration consisted in closing them in with the addition of seats. The 24 new coaches, many of which had teak bodies, were built by the firms of Shackleford and Dickson. All were four-wheeled, and in this respect the Great Western did not imitate its broad-gauge policy in adopting six-wheeled carriages for the Narrow Gauge until many years later.

In November 1857 Mr Kelley, traffic superintendent of the northern division, wishing to reduce the number of carriages in the through trains between Birmingham and Birkenhead, put in a plea for six first- and second-class composites. He did not get them, and had to be content with permission to convert four of the *smallest* first-class carriages into 'compos'. In those days there was only one gauge that counted for anything, and that was the Broad, which was easily first. The best that might be said of the Narrow was that it 'also ran'. As it was then far away 'at the back of beyond', and did not make an appearance at Paddington until 1861, the powers that were took only a very mild interest in it.

In December 1860 a moiety of the Birkenhead Railway stock was taken over, in a very bad state of repair according to Gibson.

For the new through service between London and Birkenhead 200 narrow-gauge passenger carriages and brake vans, all four-wheeled, were purchased from the three Birmingham firms already named and Shackleford of Cheltenham in 1861-2. West Midland Company's carriages also worked through to Paddington from October 1861 till the amalgamation in August 1863.

Until this event, the only repairing shops for the narrow-gauge stock were those of the late Shrewsbury & Chester Railway at Saltney.

At the moment of this amalgamation, 1st August 1863, the stock of the two Companies, including the moiety of that of the Shrewsbury & Hereford Railway, was as follows:

| | G.W.R. | | W.M.R. | S & H.R. |
|---|---|---|---|---|
| | B.G. | N.G. | N.G. | N.G. |
| Royal Saloons | 2 | — | — | — |
| First Class | 186 | 87 | 35 | 4 |
| Composite | 93 | 54 | 65 | 3 |
| Second Class | 240 | 142 | 43 | 4 |
| Third Class | 112 | 95 | 75 | 4 |
| Luggage, Brake, Parcel, and Mail Vans } | 73 | 63 | 40 | 4 |
| Carriage Trucks | 207 | 33 | 14 | 4 |
| Horse Boxes | 184 | 40 | 33 | 3 |
| Total | 1,097 | 514 | 305 | 26 |

Thus the new Great Western Company began work with 1,097 broad-gauge and 845 narrow-gauge vehicles.

### GOODS WAGONS

Of these there were two sorts—open box wagons and tilt wagons, the latter generally known in later years as 'bonnet-end trucks'. Some of the former had six wheels, and were the only six-wheeled wagons in the country. Whishaw (1840) does not record their length, but gives the width at the top as 8 feet 3 inches, and the tare weight as about 4½ tons. Most of them were four-wheeled, 17 feet long by 8 feet 3 inches wide, and weighed about 3 tons 3 cwt. All the wagons, both box and tilt, were of wood with 4 foot wheels, dead buffers, and drawbars provided with spiral springs.

Between 1841 and 1845 iron was substituted for wood, owing to the rapid deterioration of the latter, and for many years iron was the only material used both for frames and bodies. Most if not all of these iron wagons, which, by the way, had spring buffers, were built at Swindon. According to a table which Gooch handed into the Gauge Commissioners in October 1845, the dimensions, etc., of the wagons then in use were:

| | Wheels | Length | | Width[1] | | Tare | | Load | Cost |
|---|---|---|---|---|---|---|---|---|---|
| | | ft. | in. | ft. | in. | T. | C. | T. | £ |
| Tilt | 4 | 17 | 6 | 8 | 9 | 5 | 2 | 6 | 136 |
| Box | 6 | 20 | 0 | 8 | 6 | 5 | 2 | 9 | 179 |
| Box | 4 | 17 | 6 | 8 | 6 | 5 | 0 | 6 | 131 |

On the same occasion he stated that the six-wheeled wagons were 'probably the most economical we have for carrying loads'.

Brake vans were as yet unknown. Some of the box wagons, mostly those on six wheels, were provided with brakes, and the guards travelled on these without any protection from the weather; the brake wagon was by no means necessarily the last on the train. The Rule Book of 1848 says:

Each goods guard is furnished with a basket containing a lamp-iron, available for the wooden and iron waggons, a tail-lamp and a hand-lamp. At dusk, each guard[2] must hang his tail-lamp on the end waggon, one on each side.

No train may start without one break waggon at the least.

No goods waggons are to be attached to the passenger trains, or even to the third class trains, excepting in cases of necessity.

[1] These are the inside measurements; the extreme width outside was at least 9 feet.
[2] There were always two on every train.

Four years later vehicles at any rate called 'vans'—whether they were all necessarily closed is another matter—had been provided, for the rule of 1852 reads:

No Goods Train may start without at least one efficient brake Van, which must invariably be the last vehicle on the Train. When there are two Break Vans, the second should be placed about the centre of the Train, and a Guard must ride in each.

Like the wagons, the brake vans were mostly of iron, and later on many of them were old disembowelled passenger vehicles.

The development, such as it was, of the goods stock does not present many features of interest. The wagons seem to have attained a standard pattern before 1850, and many of these remained in use till the end of the Broad Gauge in 1892, by which time they looked very antiquated indeed.

There were no proper cattle wagons till after 1853, the tilts being used for this purpose. In September of that year we find Brunel representing to the Board the detriment to wagons caused by their being used indiscriminately for cattle and goods, and proposing that trucks for the conveyance of cattle should be built; this seems to have been done soon afterwards.

The 2,600 narrow-gauge wagons taken over in 1854, 1,849 of them from the Shrewsbury & Chester and 751 from the Shrewsbury & Birmingham, call for no comment.

The broad-gauge stock then numbered about 3,200 wagons of all sorts. Nine years later, at the time of the West Midland amalgamation, it consisted of 1,076 open goods wagons and cattle trucks, 2,023 covered goods wagons, 2,194 coal, coke, and permanent way and locomotive department trucks, 284 timber trucks, 31 furniture van trucks, and 81 goods brake vans, making a total of 5,689.

Of narrow-gauge trucks, the Company then owned 4,072, to which were added 4,220 from the West Midland Railway, and 148 from the Shrewsbury & Hereford; total 8,284.

# APPENDIX I

## TABLE OF OPENING DATES, MILEAGE, AND GAUGE

NOTE.—Italics indicate changes of gauge or loss of mileage. B.G. = Broad Gauge.
M.G. = Mixed Gauge. N.G. = Narrow Gauge.

### GREAT WESTERN RAILWAY

(INCLUDING LINES WORKED)

| Date | Section of Line | B.G. | |
|---|---|---|---|
| | | M. | C. |
| 1838<br>June 4 | Paddington (Old Station)—Maidenhead (Old Station) | 22 | 43 |
| 1839<br>July 1 | Maidenhead (Old Station)—Twyford .. .. .. | 8 | 18 |
| | 31 December 1839 | 30 | 61 |
| 1840<br>Mar. 30 | Twyford—Reading .. .. .. .. .. | 4 | 77 |
| June 1 | Reading—Steventon .. .. .. .. .. | 20 | 44 |
| July 20 | Steventon—Faringdon Road (now Challow) .. .. | 7 | 29 |
| Aug. 31 | Bristol (Old Terminus)—Bath .. .. .. .. | 11 | 43 |
| Dec. 17 | Faringdon Road—Hay Lane (80¼ M.P.) .. .. .. | 16 | 29 |
| | 31 December 1840 | 91 | 43 |
| 1841<br>May 31 | Hay Lane—Chippenham .. .. .. .. .. | 13 | 57 |
| ,, ,, | Cheltenham & Great Western Union Railway,<br>Swindon Junction—Kemble .. .. .. .. | 13 | 58 |
| ,, ,, | Kemble—Cirencester .. .. .. .. .. | 4 | 17 |
| June 14 | B & ER Bristol, Harbour Bridge Junction[1]—Bridgwater | 33 | 20 |
| ,, ,, | Weston Junction—Weston-super-Mare .. .. | 1 | 38 |
| June 30 | Chippenham—Bath .. .. .. .. .. | 12 | 73 |
| | 31 December 1841 | 170 | 66 |
| 1842<br>July 1 | B & ER Bridgwater—Taunton .. .. .. | 11 | 45 |
| | 31 December 1842 | 182 | 31 |
| 1843<br>May 1 | B & ER Taunton—Beambridge (171 M. 52 C.) .. | 8 | 40 |
| | 31 December 1843 | 190 | 71 |

[1] See note on page 71

452

## GREAT WESTERN RAILWAY—*(continued)*

| Date | Section of Line | B.G. | | M.G. | |
|---|---|---|---|---|---|
| | | M. | C. | M. | C. |
| | Brought forward | 190 | 71 | | |
| 1844 May 1 | B & ER Beambridge—Exeter      .. | 22 | 23 | | |
| June 12 | Didcot Junction—Oxford (Old Station) .. | 9 | 57 | | |
| | 31 December 1844 | 222 | 71 | | |
| 1845 May 12 | Kemble Junction—Gloucester   ..      .. (Standish Junction to Gloucester (7 M. 30 C.) opened by Bristol & Gloucester Railway 8 July 1844). | 23 | 9 | | |
| | 31 December 1845 | 246 | — | | |
| 1847 July 28 | B & ER Yatton—Clevedon      ..      .. | 3 | 45 | | |
| Oct. 23 | Gloucester, Tramway Junction—Cheltenham, Lansdown Junction. GW portion .. (Narrow-gauge, Tramway Junction—Lansdown Junction, opened by Birmingham & Gloucester Railway 4 November 1840.) | | | 3 | 11 |
| ,,  ,, | Cheltenham, Lansdown Junction—St James' Station   ..   ..   ..   .. | 1 | 6 | | |
| ,,  ,, | Gloucester Avoiding Line (Millstream Junction—Barnwood Junction) ..   .. | | 56 | | |
| ,,  ,, | Gloucester T Line (Tramway Junction—T Station) ..   ..   ..   ..   .. | | 20 | | |
| Dec. 21 | Reading—Hungerford   ..   ..   .. | 25 | 32 | | |
| | 31 December 1847 | 276 | 79 | 3 | 11 |
| 1848 June 12 | B & ER Tiverton Road—Tiverton      .. | 4 | 60 | | |
| Sept. 5 | Wilts, Somerset & Weymouth Railway, Thingley Junction—Westbury   ..   .. | 13 | 54 | | |
| Nov. 1 | Southcot Junction—Basingstoke  ..   .. | 13 | 49 | | |
| | 31 December 1848 | 309 | 2 | 3 | 11 |
| 1849 May 1 | *B & ER Company took over their own Line* .. | 85 | 31 | | |
| Oct. 8 | Slough—Windsor, and West Curve at Slough  ..   ..   ..   ..   .. | 3 | 5 | | |
| | 31 December 1849 | 226 | 56 | 3 | 11 |

GREAT WESTERN RAILWAY—*(continued)*

| Date | Section of Line | B.G. | | M.G. | |
|---|---|---|---|---|---|
| | | M. | C. | M. | C. |
| **1850**<br>Sept. 2 | Brought forward | 226 | 56 | 3 | 11 |
| | Oxford, Millstream Junction (62 M.P.)—<br>Banbury (Single Line)  ..    ..    .. | 24 | 15 | | |
| Oct. 7 | Westbury—Frome (Single Line) ..    .. | 5 | 61 | | |
| | 31 December 1850 | 256 | 52 | 3 | 11 |
| **1851**<br>Sept. 9 | Westbury—Warminster (Single Line)  .. | 4 | 73 | | |
| ,,  19 | Gloucester & Dean Forest Railway,<br>Gloucester—Grange Court (Junction<br>with South Wales Railway)    .. | 7 | 36 | | |
| | 31 December 1851 | 269 | 1 | 3 | 11 |
| **1852**<br>Oct. 1 | Oxford, Millstream Junction—Birmingham<br>(Narrow Gauge began at Isis River<br>Bridge, 63 M.P.) ..    ..    ..    .. | 1 | — | 66 | 24 |
| ,,  ,, | *Oxford, Millstream Junction—Banbury, mixed<br>and doubled ..    ..    ..    ..    ..* | *24* | *15* | | |
| | 31 December 1852 | 245 | 66 | 69 | 35 |
| **1853**<br>July 11 | Hereford, Ross & Gloucester Railway,<br>Grange Court—Hopesbrook    ..    .. | 5 | 5 | | |
| | 31 December 1853 | 250 | 71 | 69 | 35 |
| **1854**<br>Jan. 16 | Paddington New Station. Departure Side .. | | 20 | | |
| Mar. 20 | Over Junction—Gloucester Docks ..    .. | 1 | 16 | | |
| May 29 | Paddington New Station. Arrival Side    .. | — | — | | |
| ,,  ,, | *Bristol, Midland Junction to Terminus..    ..* | | *34* | | *34* |
| Aug. 1 | Wycombe Railway, Maidenhead, Wycombe<br>Junction—High Wycombe    ..    .. | 9 | 71 | | |
| | Carried forward | 261 | 64 | 69 | 69 |

## GREAT WESTERN RAILWAY—(*continued*)

| Date | Section of Line | B.G. | | M.G. | | N.G | |
|---|---|---|---|---|---|---|---|
| | | M. | C. | M. | C. | M. | C. |
| | Brought forward | 261 | 64 | 69 | 69 | | |
| 1854 Sept. 1 | Shrewsbury & Birmingham Railway (page 459) .. .. .. .. | | | | | 22 | 59 |
| ,, ,, | Shrewsbury & Chester Railway (page 459) | | | | | 54 | 58 |
| Nov. 14 | Birmingham—Priestfield Junction with OW & WR .. .. .. .. | | | 10 | 72 | | |
| ,, ,, | Wolverhampton, Cannock Road Junction —Stafford Road Junction .. .. | | | | 56 | | |
| ,, ,, | *Stafford Road Junction—Oxley Viaduct and Victoria Basin* .. .. .. .. | | | 1 | 10 | 1 | 10 |
| ,, ,, | Frome—Radstock (Mineral Line) .. | 8 | 19 | | | | |
| | 31 December 1854 | 270 | 3 | 82 | 47 | 76 | 27 |
| 1855 June 2 | Hereford, Ross & Gloucester Railway, Hopesbrook—Hereford (Barr's Court) .. | 17 | 46 | | | | |
| | 31 December 1855 | 287 | 49 | 82 | 47 | 76 | 27 |
| 1856 June 2 | Abingdon Railway, Abingdon Junction— Abingdon .. .. .. .. .. | 1 | 70 | | | | |
| ,, 30 | Warminster—Salisbury .. .. .. | 19 | 50 | | | | |
| Sept. 1 | Frome—Yeovil .. .. .. | 25 | 62 | | | | |
| ,, 8 | West Drayton—Uxbridge.. .. .. | 2 | 51 | | | | |
| Dec. 22 | *Oxford, Isis Bridge (63 m.p.)—Didcot, North Junction* .. .. .. .. .. | 9 | 4 | 9 | 4 | | |
| ,, ,, | Didcot Loop, North Junction—East Junction .. .. .. .. .. | | | 1 | 2 | | |
| | *Didcot, East Junction—Reading, West Junction* | 15 | 66 | 15 | 66 | | |
| ,, ,, | Reading Loop, West Junction—Oxford Road Junction .. .. .. .. | | | | 45 | | |
| | *Reading, Oxford Road Junction—Basingstoke* | 14 | 50 | 14 | 50 | | |
| | 31 December 1856 | 298 | 2 | 123 | 54 | 76 | 27 |
| 1857 Jan. 20 | Yeovil—Dorchester Junction .. .. | 20 | 66 | | | | |
| ,, ,, | Dorchester Junction—Weymouth .. | | | 6 | 49 | | |
| | Carried forward | 318 | 68 | 130 | 23 | 76 | 27 |

## GREAT WESTERN RAILWAY—(*continued*)

| Date | Section of Line | B.G. | | M.G. | | N.G. | |
|---|---|---|---|---|---|---|---|
| | | M. | C. | M. | C. | M. | C. |
| | Brought forward | 318 | 68 | 130 | 23 | 76 | 27 |
| **1857** | | | | | | | |
| Feb. 2 | Bradford Junction—Bathampton.. .. | 9 | 12 | | | | |
| June 1 | Twyford—Henley .. .. .. .. | 4 | 47 | | | | |
| July 1 | Holt Junction—Devizes .. .. .. | 8 | 17 | | | | |
| Nov. 12 | Bridport Railway, Maiden Newton—Bridport .. .. .. .. .. | 9 | 21 | | | | |
| | 31 December 1857 | 350 | 5 | 130 | 23 | 76 | 27 |
| **1858** | | | | | | | |
| Nov. 9 | East Somerset Railway, Witham—Shepton Mallet .. .. .. .. .. | 9 | 3 | | | | |
| Dec. 1 | Reading, West Junction—Junction with Staines & Wokingham Railway (SER) (Single Line) .. .. .. .. | | | | | 1 | 45 |
| | 31 December 1858 | 359 | 8 | 130 | 23 | 77 | 72 |
| **1859** | | | | | | | |
| June 1 | Wednesbury, Branch to S. Staffordshire Railway .. .. .. .. .. | | | | 14 | | |
| July 18 | Great Western & Brentford Railway, Southall—Brentford .. .. .. (Goods only; Passengers 1 May 1860.) | 3 | 77 | | | | |
| | 31 December 1859 | 363 | 5 | 130 | 37 | 77 | 72 |
| **1860** | | | | | | | |
| Aug. 2 | Ely Valley Railway, Llantrissant—Tony-refail (Goods) .. .. .. .. | 4 | 77 | | | | |
| Oct. 10 | Stratford-on-Avon Railway, Hatton—Stratford (Old Station) .. .. | | | | 9 | 43 | |
| Nov. 20 | Birkenhead Railway. Joint with L & NWR (page 464).. .. .. .. | | | — | — | — | — |
| | 31 December 1860 | 368 | 2 | 140 | — | 77 | 72 |
| **1861** | | | | | | | |
| July 1 | Wellington & Severn Junction Railway, Ketley Junction—Lightmoor .. .. (Opened 1 May 1857, Ketley Junction —Horsehay; remainder after March 1858, and worked by Coalbrookdale Iron Co till 1 July 1861.) | | | | | 4 | 41 |
| July 24 | Stratford-on-Avon Railway, connecting line to West Midland Railway at Stratford .. .. .. .. .. | | | | 32 | | |
| | Carried forward | 368 | 2 | 140 | 32 | 82 | 33 |

GREAT WESTERN RAILWAY—*(continued)*

| Date | Section of Line | B.G. | | M.G. | | N.G. | |
|---|---|---|---|---|---|---|---|
| | | M. | C. | M. | C. | M. | C. |
| | Brought forward | 368 | 2 | 140 | 32 | 82 | 33 |
| 1861 Oct. 1 | *Reading, West Junction—Paddington* .. .. | 36 | 78 | 36 | 78 | | |
| ,, ,, | *Single Line, West Junction to east of Reading Station superseded as running line* .. .. | | | | | 1 | 17 |
| ,, ,, | *Southall—Brentford (Up line only)* .. | 3 | 77 | 3 | 77 | | |
| Nov. 1 | Bordesley Junction Branch to Midland Railway .. .. .. .. .. | | | | 21 | | |
| | 31 December 1861 | 327 | 7 | 181 | 48 | 81 | 16 |
| 1862 Jan. 1 | South Wales Railway (page 460) .. .. | 174 | 65 | | 40 | | |
| ,, 8 | Ely Valley Railway (Goods) Mwyndy and Brofiskin Branch .. .. .. .. | 2 | 63 | | | | |
| | Branch to Gellyrhaidd .. .. .. | 1 | 24 | | | | |
| Mar. 1 | East Somerset Railway, Shepton Mallet—Wells .. .. .. .. .. | 4 | 62 | | | | |
| Mar. | *Slough—Windsor, and West Curve at Slough* .. | 3 | 5 | 3 | 5 | | |
| ,, | *Reading, Station Junction—Oxford Road Junction* .. .. .. .. .. | | 59 | | 59 | | |
| May 22 | Wrexham & Minera Railway, Croes Newydd Junctions—Junction with old branch from Wheatsheaf at Brymbo .. | | | | | 3 | 33 |
| | *Old line between Moss and Brymbo abandoned (about)* | | | | | | 60 |
| June 2 | Vale of Llangollen Railway, Ruabon, Llangollen Line Junction—Llangollen .. (Goods June 1863.) | | | | | 5 | 40 |
| July 1 | Shrewsbury & Hereford Railway. Joint (Half GW and WM, half L & NW, page 464) .. .. .. .. .. | | | | | — | — |
| ,, ,, | Leominster & Kington Railway (page 461) | | | | | — | — |
| Aug. 1 | Wycombe Railway, High Wycombe—Thame .. .. .. .. .. | 13 | 72 | | | | |
| Nov. 11 | Berks & Hants Extension Railway, Hungerford—Devizes .. .. .. | 24 | 32 | | | | |
| Dec. | Ely Valley Railway, Tonyrefail—Dinas (Penygraig) .. .. .. .. | 2 | 10 | | | | |
| | 31 December 1862 | 547 | 31 | 185 | 72 | 89 | 29 |

## GREAT WESTERN RAILWAY—(*continued*)

| Date | Section of Line | B.G. | | M.G. | | N.G. | |
|------|-----------------|------|------|------|------|------|------|
| | | M. | C. | M. | C. | M. | C. |
| | Brought forward | 547 | 31 | 185 | 72 | 89 | 29 |
| 1863 Jan. 10 | Metropolitan Railway, Bishop's Road—Farringdon Street (Old Station), 3 M. 60 C., worked by GWR until 10 August 1863 .. .. .. .. .. | | | — | — | | |
| April 1 | West London Junction—North Pole Junction .. .. .. .. .. | | | | 34 | | |
| ,, ,, | West London, and West London Extension Railways. Joint (page 465).. .. | | | — | — | | |
| June 1 | *Didcot Station, East Junction—North Junction* | *1* | *12* | 1 | 12 | | |
| | 1 August 1863 | 546 | 19 | 187 | 38 | 89 | 29 |
| Aug. 1 | West Midland Railway (page 461) .. | | | 2 | 9 | 280 | 67 |
| | Combined Mileages | 546 | 19 | 189 | 47 | 370 | 16 |

TOTAL MILEAGE[1] 1ST AUGUST 1863

| | | M. | C. |
|---|---|---|---|
| Great Western Railway | .. | 823 | 6 |
| West Midland Railway | .. | 282 | 76 |
| | | 1,106 | 2 |
| Joint Lines (page 465) | .. | 116 | 33 |

[1] Including lines worked.

## SHREWSBURY LINES

| Date | Section of Line | N.G. | |
|------|-----------------|:---:|:---:|
| | | M. | C. |
| | **SHREWSBURY & BIRMINGHAM RAILWAY** | | |
| 1849 June 1 | Shrewsbury—Wellington .. .. .. .. .. <br> Joint with Shropshire Union Railway (L & NW) (page 464) | — | — |
| ,, ,, | Wellington—Oakengates .. .. .. .. .. | 2 | 42 |
| Nov. 12 | Oakengates—Wolverhampton, High Level, and Victoria Basin .. .. .. .. .. .. .. .. | 16 | 21 |
| 1854 June 1 | Madeley Junction—Lightmoor .. .. .. .. | 3 | 76 |
| | Mileage, 1 September 1854 (to page 455) | 22 | 59 |
| | **SHREWSBURY & CHESTER RAILWAY** | | |
| 1846 Nov. 4 | Chester, Saltney Junction—Ruabon (with powers over Chester & Holyhead Railway, Chester Station to Saltney Junction 1 M. 67 C.) .. .. .. .. .. .. | 15 | 8 |
| ,, | Branch to Saltney Quay .. .. .. .. .. | | 56 |
| 1847 July | Wheatsheaf Junction—Minera .. .. .. .. | 6 | 20 |
| Nov. | Short branches to collieries and works at Ffrwd, Brynmally, Westminster, South Sea, Brymbo, and Vron; in all about | 5 | — |
| 1848 Aug. 1 | Chester General Station (Joint) .. .. .. .. | — | — |
| Oct. 14 | Ruabon—Shrewsbury .. .. .. .. .. | 25 | 23 |
| Dec. 23 | Gobowen—Oswestry .. .. .. .. .. .. | 2 | 31 |
| | Mileage, 1 September 1854 (to page 455) | 54 | 58 |

## SOUTH WALES RAILWAY

| Date | Section of Line | B.G. | | M.G. | |
|---|---|---|---|---|---|
| | | M. | C. | M. | C. |
| 1850 June 18 | Chepstow—Landore .. .. .. | 73 | 28 | | |
| ,, ,, | Landore—Swansea, High Street .. .. | 1 | 25 | | |
| 1851 Sept. 19 | Grange Court (Junction with GWR)—Chepstow East .. .. .. .. | 18 | 70 | | |
| 1852 June | Swansea, Branch to North Dock .. .. | | 34 | | |
| July 19 | Chepstow East—Chepstow. (Single line; doubled 18 April 1853) .. .. .. | 1 | — | | |
| Oct. 11 | Landore—Carmarthen. (Single from Pembrey; doubled 8 February 1853) .. .. | 30 | 14 | | |
| 1854 Jan. 2 | Carmarthen—Haverfordwest. (Single: doubled 1 July 1857) .. .. .. | 31 | 14 | | |
| ,, 17 | *Cardiff, Bute Street Junction (with TVR)—Station* .. .. .. .. .. | | 40 | | 40 |
| July 24 | Forest of Dean, Bullo Pill—Churchway, etc. (Tramway converted) .. .. | 7 | 20 | | |
| ,, ,, | Bullo Pill Dock Branch .. .. .. | | 53 | | |
| 1856 April 15 | Haverfordwest—'New Milford' (Neyland). (Single; doubled 1 July 1857) .. .. | 9 | 16 | | |
| 1857 Feb. | Branch to Swansea Vale Railway .. .. | | 30 | | |
| 1858 April 19 | Cardiff, Bute Docks Branch.. .. .. | 1 | 19 | | |
| 1859 Sept. | Swansea, North Dock Branch extended .. | | 22 | | |
| | Mileage, 1 January 1862 (to page 457) | 174 | 65 | | 40 |

## WEST MIDLAND RAILWAY
### (Including Lines Worked)

| Date | Section of Line | M.G. | | N.G. | |
|------|-----------------|------|------|------|------|
| | | **M.** | **C.** | **M.** | **C.** |
| 1860<br>July 1 | Oxford, Worcester & Wolverhampton Railway (page 462) .. .. .. | 2 | 9 | 109 | 17 |
| ,, ,, | Newport, Abergavenny & Hereford Railway (page 463) .. .. .. .. | | | 52 | 6 |
| | Worcester & Hereford Railway (page 463) | | | 9 | 51 |
| July* | Worcester, Rainbow Hill Junction—Shrub Hill *probably 23rd. .. .. .. | | | | 17 |
| | 31 December 1860 | 2 | 9 | 171 | 11 |
| 1861<br>July 1 | Coleford, Monmouth, Usk & Pontypool Railway .. .. .. .. .. (Little Mill Junction—Usk opened 2 June 1856. Usk—Monmouth (Troy) opened 12 October 1857. Monmouth (Troy)—Wyesham opened 1 July 1861.) | | | 17 | 2 |
| Sept. 13 | Malvern Wells—Shelwick Junction (with Shrewsbury & Hereford Railway) .. | | | 18 | 5 |
| Nov. 14 | Witney Railway, Yarnton—Witney .. | | | 8 | 13 |
| | 31 December 1861 | 2 | 9 | 214 | 31 |
| 1862<br>Feb. 1 | Severn Valley Railway, Hartlebury—Sutton Bridge Junction (with Shrewsbury & Hereford Railway) .. .. .. | | | 39 | 44 |
| ,, ,, | Much Wenlock & Severn Junction Railway, Buildwas—Much Wenlock .. .. | | | 3 | 40 |
| Mar. 1 | Bourton-on-the-Water Railway, Chipping Norton Junction—Bourton-on-the-Water .. .. .. .. .. | | | 6 | 47 |
| July 1 | Shrewsbury & Hereford Railway. Joint with GW and L & NW (page 464) .. | | | — | — |
| ,, ,, | Leominster & Kington Railway, Leominster Junction—Kington .. .. (Opened 20 August 1857, and worked by Brassey till June 1862, then leased by WM) | | | 13 | 28 |
| | 31 December 1862 | 2 | 9 | 277 | 30 |
| 1863<br>April 1 | Stourbridge Railway, Stourbridge Junction—Cradley .. .. | | | 2 | 21 |
| | Cradley—Corngreaves Yard (Goods) .. | | | | 34 |
| June | Lye—Hayes Lane (Goods) .. .. | | | | 62 |
| | Mileage, 1 August 1863 | 2 | 9 | 280 | 67 |

WEST MIDLAND RAILWAY—*(continued)*

| Date | Section of Line | M.G. | | N.G. | |
|---|---|---|---|---|---|
| | | **M.** | **C.** | **M.** | **C.** |
| | **OXFORD, WORCESTER & WOLVERHAMPTON RAILWAY** | | | | |
| 1850 | | | | | |
| Oct. 5 | Worcester—Norton .. .. .. .. | | | 3 | 8 |
| ,, ,, | Norton—Abbot's Wood Junction (with Midland) .. .. .. .. .. | | | | 66 |
| 1852 | | | | | |
| Feb. 18 | Worcester—Droitwich .. .. .. | | | 5 | 49 |
| ,, ,, | Droitwich—Stoke Works Junction (with Midland) .. .. .. .. .. | | | 4 | 3 |
| May 1 | Droitwich—Stourbridge .. .. .. | | | 16 | 37 |
| ,, ,, | Norton Junction—Evesham .. .. | | | 10 | 48 |
| Nov. 16 | Stourbridge—Dudley (for passengers Dec. 20) .. .. .. .. .. .. | | | 5 | 46 |
| 1853 | | | | | |
| June 4 | Evesham—Wolvercot Junction (with GWR) (Single Line) .. .. .. Doubled: Wolvercot—Handborough 18 Nov. 1853. Handborough—Charlbury 1 Aug. 1854. Campden—Evesham 20 March 1855. Charlbury—Campden 2 August 1858. | | | 40 | 48 |
| Dec. 1 | Dudley—Tipton .. .. .. .. | | | 1 | 4 |
| ,, ,, | Tipton—Junction with Stour Valley Railway (L & NW) .. .. .. .. | | | | 52 |
| 1854 | | | | | |
| April | Tipton—Priestfield (passengers 1 July) .. | | | 3 | 17 |
| ,, | Priestfield—Wolverhampton, Cannock Road (passengers 1 July) .. .. .. .. | 2 | 9 | | |
| July | Cannock Road—Bushbury Junction (with L & NWR) for goods; passengers 1 January 1864 .. .. .. .. | | | | 75 |
| 1855 | | | | | |
| Aug. 10 | Chipping Norton Junction—Chipping Norton .. .. .. .. .. | | | 4 | 42 |
| Oct. | Priestfield—Walsall Street (Goods) .. | | | 1 | — |
| 1858 | | | | | |
| Nov. 14 | Kingswinford Junction—Bromley Basin .. | | | 1 | 45 |
| 1859 | | | | | |
| July 12 | Honeybourne—Stratford-on-Avon .. | | | 9 | 37 |
| | Mileage, 1 July 1860 (to page 461) | 2 | 9 | 109 | 17 |

## WEST MIDLAND RAILWAY—*(continued)*

| Date | Section of Line | N.G. | |
|------|-----------------|------|------|
| | | M. | C. |
| | **NEWPORT, ABERGAVENNY & HEREFORD RAILWAY** | | |
| 1854 Jan. 2 | Hereford, Barton—Pontypool, Coedygric Junction (with Monmouthshire Railway) .. .. .. .. | 33 | 59 |
| ,, 16 | Hereford, Barton Station—Barton (now Barr's Court) Junction (with Shrewsbury & Hereford Railway) .. | 1 | 7 |
| 1855 Aug. 20 | Pontypool Road—Crumlin (Junction) .. .. .. | 5 | 41 |
| Sept. 3 | Crumlin (Junction)—Llanhilleth (Goods) .. .. | 1 | 25 |
| Oct. 20 | Llanhilleth Junction (with Monmouthshire Railway) .. | — | — |
| 1857 June 1 | Crumlin Junction—Tredegar Junction (now Pontllanfraith) .. .. .. .. .. .. .. | 3 | 27 |
| 1858 Jan. 11 | Tredegar Junction—Quaker's Yard (Low Level) Junction (with Taff Vale Railway) .. .. .. .. | 7 | 7 |
| | Mileage, 1 July 1860 (to page 461) | 52 | 6 |

## WORCESTER & HEREFORD RAILWAY

| Date | Section of Line | N.G. | |
|------|-----------------|------|------|
| 1859 July 25 | Henwick—Malvern Link .. .. .. .. .. | 6 | 8 |
| 1860 May 17 | Worcester, Tunnel Junction—Henwick .. .. .. | 1 | 33 |
| ,, 25 | Malvern Link—Malvern Wells .. .. .. .. | 2 | 10 |
| | Mileage, 1 July 1860 (to page 461) | 9 | 51 |

## JOINT LINES

| Date | Section of Line | N.G. | |
|------|-----------------|------|------|
| | **SHREWSBURY & WELLINGTON LINE**<br>(Constructed jointly by Shrewsbury & Birmingham and Shropshire Union Companies.) | | |
| 1849<br>June 1 | Shrewsbury—Wellington, Stafford Junction .. .. | 10 | 48 |
| | **BIRKENHEAD RAILWAY**<br>(Vested in Great Western and London & North Western Companies jointly as from 1 January 1860, though possession was not actually taken till 20 November 1860.) | | |
| 1840<br>Sept. 23 | Chester—Birkenhead, Grange Lane .. .. .. | 14 | 29 |
| 1844<br>Oct. 23 | Birkenhead, Branch to Monk's Ferry .. .. .. | | 43 |
| 1847<br>April 5 | Birkenhead, Grange Lane—Cathcart Street Junction (with Docks Lines) .. .. .. .. .. | 1 | 10 |
| 1848<br>— | Birkenhead, Brook Lane Junction—Boundary .. .. | | 26 |
| Aug. 1 | Chester, West Loop .. .. .. .. .. | | 16 |
| 1850<br>Dec. 18 | Chester—Walton Junction .. .. .. .. | 17 | 10 |
| 1855<br>Aug. 18 | Birkenhead, Cathcart Street—Goods Shed .. .. | | 12 |
| | 1 January 1860 | 33 | 66 |
| 1863<br>July 1 | Hooton—Helsby .. .. .. .. .. .. | 8 | 69 |
| | 1 August 1863 | 42 | 55 |
| | **SHREWSBURY & HEREFORD RAILWAY**<br>(Leased to London & North Western (½) and Great Western and West Midland (½) Companies jointly from 1 July 1862.) | | |
| 1852<br>April 21 | Shrewsbury—Ludlow .. .. .. .. .. | 27 | 43 |
| 1853<br>Dec. 6 | Ludlow—Hereford, Barr's Court (through goods traffic commenced 30 July 1852) .. .. .. .. | 23 | 40 |
| 1861<br>Aug. 1 | Tenbury Railway, Woofferton—Tenbury .. .. | 5 | 9 |
| | 1 July 1862 | 56 | 12 |

## JOINT LINES—(*continued*)

| Date | Section of Line | M.G. | | N.G. | |
|---|---|---|---|---|---|
| | | **M.** | **C.** | **M.** | **C.** |
| | **WEST LONDON AND WEST LONDON EXTENSION RAILWAYS** (As to ownership, etc., see pages 231–233.) | | | | |
| 1863 March 2 | North Pole Junction—Longhedge Junction (LC & DR) .. .. .. .. | 5 | 36 | | |
| ,, ,, | Latchmere Junction—Clapham Junction (LB & SCR) .. .. .. .. | | | | 59 |
| ,, ,, | Latchmere Junction—Clapham Junction (L & SWR) .. .. .. .. | | | | 38 |
| ,, ,, | Chelsea Basin Branch .. .. .. | | 25 | | |
| | | 5 | 61 | 1 | 17 |
| | *Summary*, 1 *August* 1863 | | | | |
| | Shrewsbury & Wellington Line .. .. | | | 10 | 48 |
| | Birkenhead Line .. .. .. .. | | | 42 | 55 |
| | Shrewsbury & Hereford Line .. .. | | | 56 | 12 |
| | West London Lines .. .. .. .. | 5 | 61 | 1 | 17 |
| | | 5 | 61 | 110 | 52 |

## Total Mileage of Joint Lines 116M 33C

# APPENDIX II

## LIST OF BROAD-GAUGE LOCOMOTIVES OF THE GREAT WESTERN RAILWAY
### 1837-1866

*Note.*—The column headed 'Ceased Work' gives the dates when the engines were withdrawn from service, as nearly as they can be ascertained from the existing records. These dates do not necessarily correspond with the official 'condemnation' of the engines. Tank engines are so described; all others had tenders.

### MISCELLANEOUS ENGINES, 1837–1840
19 in all, excluding the 4 'Stars'.

| Name | Builders | Delivered[1] | Ceased Work |
|---|---|---|---|
| PREMIER | Mather Dixon & Co | Nov. 25, 1837 | Dec. 1840 |
| VULCAN | Tayleur & Co | ,, ,, ,, | April 1868 |
| NORTH STAR | R. Stephenson & Co | ,, 28 ,, | Dec. 1870 |
| ÆOLUS | Tayleur & Co | ,, 30 ,, | April 1867 |
| BACCHUS | ,, | Dec. 2 ,, | June 1842 |
| APOLLO | ,, | Jan. 16, 1838 | Aug. 1867 |
| NEPTUNE | ,, | Mar. 5 ,, | June 1840 |
| ARIEL | Mather Dixon & Co | ,, ,, ,, | Dec. 1840 |
| THUNDERER | R. & W. Hawthorn | ,, 6 ,, | Dec. 1839 |
| LION | Sharp, Roberts & Co | May 6 ,, | June 1847 |
| ATLAS | ,, | June 6 ,, | June 1872 |
| VIPER | Haigh Foundry | Aug. 30 ,, | Jan. 1868 |
| SNAKE | ,, | Sept. 7 ,, | Nov. 1869 |
| VENUS (No. 1) | Tayleur & Co | ,, ,, ,, | July 1870 |
| HURRICANE | R. & W. Hawthorn | Oct. 6 ,, | Dec. 1839 |
| EAGLE | Sharp, Roberts & Co | Nov. 8 ,, | 1871 |
| AJAX | Mather Dixon & Co | Dec. 12 ,, | June 1840 |
| MORNING STAR | R. Stephenson & Co | Jan. 24, 1839 | Nov. 1869 |
| EVENING STAR | ,, | July 25 ,, | June 1871 |
| PLANET | Mather Dixon & Co | Aug. 1 ,, | June 1840 |
| DOG STAR | R. Stephenson & Co | Sept. 18 ,, | 1869 |
| MERCURY (No. 1) | Mather Dixon & Co | ,, 26 ,, | Dec. 1843 |
| MARS (No. 1) | ,, | April 20, 1840 | Dec. 1840 |

[1] According to the Company's records. In several cases the dates are those of *acceptance*, often much later than the dates shown in the makers' books.

## STANDARD TYPES, 1839–1842

### 'STAR' CLASS

12 Engines. 2-2-2. Cylinders: (*a*) 16 inch by 16 inch; (*b*) 15 inch by 18 inch; (*c*) 15½ inch by 19 inch. Diameter of Driving Wheels, 7 feet.

| Name | Delivered | Ceased Work |
|------|-----------|-------------|
| Built by R. Stephenson & Co, Newcastle. | | |
| NORTH STAR (*a*)[1] | Nov. 1837 | Dec. 1870 |
| MORNING STAR (*a*)[2] | Jan. 1839 | Nov. 1869 |
| EVENING STAR (*b*) | July ,, | June 1871 |
| DOG STAR (*b*) | Sept. ,, | 1869 |
| POLAR STAR (*b*) | July 1840 | July 1870 |
| RED STAR (*b*) | Aug. ,, | Feb. 1865 |
| LOAD STAR (*b*) | Jan. 1841 | July 1870 |
| RISING STAR (*b*) | Mar. ,, | April 1871 |
| BRIGHT STAR (*b*) | April ,, | ,, 1864 |
| SHOOTING STAR (*b*) | Aug. ,, | Sept. 1871 |
| WESTERN STAR (*c*) | Nov. ,, | Oct. 1866 |
| ROYAL STAR (*c*) | ,, ,, | June 1871 |

Some of the 'Star' class were rebuilt as eight-wheeled saddle tank engines, having two leading axles, the frames being lengthened.

[1] *North Star* was rebuilt in 1854 as a six-wheeled engine.
[2] *Morning Star* had 6 feet 6 inch wheels.

### 'FIREFLY' CLASS

62 Engines. 2-2-2. Cylinders: 15 inch by 18 inch, later enlarged to 16 inch by 20 inch. Diameter of Driving Wheels, 7 feet.

| Name | Delivered | Rebuilt | Ceased Work |
|------|-----------|---------|-------------|
| Built by Jones, Turner & Evans, Newton, Lancs. | | | |
| FIREFLY | Mar. 1840 | — | Nov. 1870 |
| WILDFIRE | April ,, | — | July 1867 |
| SPITFIRE | ,, ,, | April 1861 | Oct. 1878 |
| FIREBRAND | May ,, | — | April 1866 |
| FIRE KING[1] | ,, ,, | Jan. 1861 | June 1875 |
| FIREBALL[1] | ,, ,, | — | Nov. 1866 |

[1] *Fire King* and *Fireball* were converted to 2-2-2 saddle tank engines with 6 foot driving wheels.

STANDARD TYPES, 1839–1842—*(continued)*

'FIREFLY' CLASS—*(continued)*

| Name | Delivered | Rebuilt | Ceased Work |
|---|---|---|---|
| | | | |

### Built by Sharp, Roberts & Co, Manchester.

| Name | Delivered | Rebuilt | Ceased Work |
|---|---|---|---|
| TIGER | April 1840 | Nov. 1864 | Dec. 1873 |
| LEOPARD[1] | May ,, | Aug. 1859 | Jan. 1879 |
| PANTHER | June ,, | — | Dec. 1869 |
| LYNX | July ,, | — | ,, 1870 |
| STAG | Sept. ,, | — | ,, 1863 |
| VULTURE | Oct. ,, | — | ,, 1870 |
| HAWK | ,, ,, | — | ,, 1865 |
| FALCON | Nov. ,, | — | ,, 1867 |
| OSTRICH | Dec. ,, | — | ,, 1865 |
| GREYHOUND | Jan. 1841 | — | July 1866 |

### Built by Fenton, Murray & Jackson, Leeds.

| Name | Delivered | Rebuilt | Ceased Work |
|---|---|---|---|
| CHARON | May 1840 | Oct. 1864 | June 1878 |
| CYCLOPS | Oct. ,, | — | ,, 1865 |
| CERBERUS | June 1841 | — | Feb. 1866 |
| HARPY | Aug. ,, | Nov. 1864 | June 1873 |
| PLUTO | ,, ,, | — | Oct. 1870 |
| MINOS | Sept. ,, | — | Aug. 1870 |
| IXION | Oct. ,, | Sept. 1863 | July 1879 |
| HECATE | Nov. ,, | — | April 1867 |
| GORGON | ,, ,, | Feb. 1863 | Oct. 1878 |
| VESTA | Dec. ,, | — | Dec. 1864 |
| ACHERON | Jan. 1842 | — | Feb. 1866 |
| EREBUS | Feb. ,, | Sept. 1865 | June 1873 |
| MEDEA | Mar. ,, | Oct. 1863 | Dec. 1873 |
| HYDRA | April ,, | — | July 1865 |
| LETHE | ,, ,, | Feb. 1862 | Oct. 1878 |
| PHLEGETHON | May ,, | — | Jan. 1866 |
| MEDUSA | June ,, | — | Nov. 1864 |
| PROSERPINE | ,, ,, | Nov. 1865 | June 1873 |
| GANYMEDE | July ,, | April 1863 | Aug. 1878 |
| ARGUS | Aug. ,, | July 1864 | June 1873 |

### Built by R. B. Longridge & Co, Bedlington.

| Name | Delivered | Rebuilt | Ceased Work |
|---|---|---|---|
| JUPITER | April 1841 | — | July 1867 |
| SATURN | June ,, | Oct. 1864 | June 1878 |
| MARS (No. 2) | July ,, | — | Sept. 1868 |
| LUCIFER | Aug. ,, | — | May 1870 |
| VENUS (No. 2) | Oct. ,, | — | July 1870 |
| MERCURY (No. 2) | ,, ,, | — | Feb. 1865 |

[1] Exploded at Bristol 1857.

## STANDARD TYPES, 1839–1842—*(continued)*

### 'FIREFLY' CLASS—*(continued)*

| Name | Delivered | Rebuilt | Ceased Work |
|---|---|---|---|
| *Built by Nasmyth, Gaskell & Co, Manchester.* | | | |
| ACHILLES | June 1841 | — | April 1867 |
| MILO | ,, ,, | — | Feb. 1866 |
| HECTOR | July ,, | — | Nov. ,, |
| MENTOR | Aug. ,, | — | Nov. 1867 |
| CASTOR | ,, ,, | Sept. 1865 | June 1874 |
| BELLONA | Nov. ,, | — | July 1870 |
| ACTÆON[1] | Dec. ,, | Aug. 1856 | Mar. 1868 |
| CENTAUR | ,, ,, | — | Nov. 1867 |
| DAMON | Mar. 1842 | — | July 1870 |
| PRIAM | ,, ,, | — | June 1864 |
| ELECTRA | ,, ,, | — | Jan. 1867 |
| ORION[2] | ,, ,, | — | July 1870 |
| POLLUX | July ,, | — | Feb. 1866 |
| PHŒNIX | Aug. ,, | — | July 1870 |
| STENTOR | Dec. ,, | — | Dec. 1867 |
| PEGASUS | ,, ,, | — | June 1868 |
| *Built by Stothert & Slaughter, Bristol.* | | | |
| ARROW[3] | July 1841 | — | Dec. 1864 |
| DART | ,, ,, | — | ,, 1870 |
| *Built by G. & J. Rennie, Blackfriars, London.* | | | |
| MAZEPPA | Mar. 1841 | — | Mar. 1868 |
| ARAB | May ,, | — | July 1870 |

[1] Exploded at Gloucester, February 1855.

[2] *Orion* was converted to an eight-wheeled saddle tank engine, similar to some of the 'Star' class.

[3] The dates of *Arrow* and *Dart* are given as above in the official records, but *Arrow* is recorded as having run from Bristol to Bath on 21st August 1840, and *Dart* was delivered in time for the opening.

## STANDARD TYPES, 1839–1842—(*continued*)

### 'SUN' CLASS

21 Engines. 2-2-2. Cylinders: 14 inch by 18 inch and 15 inch by 18 inch. Diameter of Driving Wheels, 6 feet.

| Name | Delivered | Rebuilt | Ceased Work |
|------|-----------|---------|-------------|
| *Built by R. & W. Hawthorn, Newcastle.* | | | |
| SUN | April 1840 | July 1863 | June 1873 |
| SUNBEAM | May ,, | — | July 1870 |
| ECLIPSE | Aug. ,, | — | June 1864 |
| MERIDIAN | ,, ,, | — | Dec. 1870 |
| COMET | Oct. ,, | — | June 1871 |
| METEOR | Nov. ,, | — | Jan. 1864 |
| AURORA | Dec. ,, | — | Dec. 1866 |
| HESPERUS | Jan. 1841 | April 1857 | Aug. 1876 |
| *Built by Sharp, Roberts & Co, Manchester.* | | | |
| GAZELLE | March 1841 | Jan. 1864 | June 1879 |
| WOLF | July ,, | April 1859 | ,, 1873 |
| ANTELOPE | Aug. ,, | — | July 1870 |
| ZEBRA | ,, ,, | — | June 1871 |
| GIRAFFE | Sept. ,, | — | ,, 1872 |
| *Built by Stothert & Slaughter, Bristol.* | | | |
| JAVELIN | July 1841 | — | Dec. 1870 |
| DJERID | ,, ,, | — | July 1870 |
| LANCE | Aug. ,, | — | Dec. 1870 |
| YATAGHAN | ,, ,, | — | June 1871 |
| ASSAGAIS [*sic*] | Sept. ,, | Jan. 1864 | ,, 1875 |
| ROCKET | Nov. ,, | — | July 1870 |
| STILETTO | Dec. ,, | — | ,, ,, |
| CREESE | Jan. 1842 | — | Mar. 1866 |

These were all converted to 2-2-2 saddle tank engines, and were then sometimes called the 'Wolf' class. *Fire King* and *Fireball* of the 'Firefly' class were also altered to this class.

## STANDARD TYPES, 1839–1842—(*continued*)

### 'LEO' CLASS

18 Engines. 2-4-0. Cylinders: 15 inch by 18 inch.
Diameter of Coupled Wheels, 5 feet.

| Name | Delivered | Ceased Work |
|------|-----------|-------------|
| *Built by R. & W. Hawthorn, Newcastle.* | | |
| ELEPHANT | Jan. 1841 | Dec. 1870 |
| DROMEDARY | Mar. ,, | ,, 1866 |
| BUFFALO | ,, ,, | April 1865 |
| *Built by Fenton, Murray & Jackson, Leeds.* | | |
| STROMBOLI | April 1841 | July 1870 |
| HECLA | ,, ,, | Sept. 1864 |
| ETNA | June ,, | Dec. 1870 |
| *Built by Rothwell & Co, Bolton, Lancs.* | | |
| ARIES | June 1841 | June 1871 |
| TAURUS | July ,, | Dec. 1870 |
| GEMINI | Sept. ,, | Mar. 1866 |
| CANCER | Oct. ,, | June 1874 |
| LEO | ,, ,, | Dec. 1870 |
| VIRGO | Dec. ,, | ,, ,, |
| LIBRA | Feb. 1842 | June 1871 |
| SCORPIO | ,, ,, | Dec. 1872 |
| SAGITTARIUS | April ,, | June 1871 |
| CAPRICORNUS | ,, ,, | July 1870 |
| AQUARIUS | June ,, | ,, ,, |
| PISCES | July ,, | June 1874 |

These were all converted to 2-4-0 saddle tank engines.

## STANDARD TYPES, 1839–1842—(*continued*)

### 'HERCULES' CLASS

4 Engines. 0-6-0. Cylinders: 15 inch by 18 inch.
Diameter of Coupled Wheels, 5 feet.

| Name | Delivered | Ceased Work |
|------|-----------|-------------|
| *Built by Nasmyth, Gaskell & Co, Manchester.* | | |
| HERCULES | July 1842 | July 1870 |
| SAMPSON [*sic*] | ,,   ,, | ,,   ,, |
| GOLIAH[1] | Aug.  ,, | June 1871 |
| TITYOS | Oct.  ,, | July 1870 |

[1] Exploded at Plympton, July 1849.

## PASSENGER ENGINES, 1846-1866

### 'PRINCE' CLASS

6 Engines. 2-2-2. Cylinders: 16 inch by 24 inch.
Diameter of Driving Wheels, 7 feet.

| Name | Built | Ceased Work | Name | Built | Ceased Work |
|------|-------|-------------|------|-------|-------------|
| *Built by GWR, Swindon.* | | | | | |
| PRINCE | Aug. 1846 | June 1870 | WITCH* | Dec. 1846 | May 1870 |
| ELK | ,,   ,, | Sept.  ,, | QUEEN | Feb. 1847 | Jan.   ,, |
| PERI | Nov.  ,, | July   ,, | SYLPH | Mar.  ,, | April  ,, |

* *Witch* had 7 feet 6 inch driving wheels.

PASSENGER ENGINES, 1846–1866—(*continued*)

'IRON DUKE' CLASS

30 Engines. 4-2-2. Cylinders: 18 inch by 24 inch.
Diameter of Driving Wheels, 8 feet.

| *Name* | *Built* | *Rebuilt* | *Ceased\* Work* | *Mileage in Original Condition* |
|---|---|---|---|---|
| Built by GWR, Swindon. | | | | |
| GREAT WESTERN .. | April 1846 | — | Dec. 1870 | 370,687 |
| IRON DUKE .. .. | April 1847 | — | Oct. 1871 | 607,412 |
| GREAT BRITAIN .. | July ,, | July 1870 | Sept. 1880 | 567,760 |
| LIGHTNING .. .. | Aug. ,, | — | April 1878 | 816,601 |
| EMPEROR .. .. | Sept. ,, | — | June 1873 | 690,225 |
| PASHA .. .. .. | Nov. ,, | — | Feb. 1876 | 613,038 |
| SULTAN .. .. .. | ,, ,, | — | June 1874 | 727,300 |
| COURIER .. .. | June 1848 | — | Nov. 1877 | 746,120 |
| TARTAR .. .. .. | July ,, | — | Aug. 1876 | 731,817 |
| DRAGON .. .. | Aug. ,, | — | Dec. 1872 | 670,757 |
| WARLOCK .. .. | ,, ,, | — | June 1874 | 639,410 |
| WIZARD .. .. .. | Sept. ,, | — | Nov. 1875 | 711,908 |
| ROUGEMONT .. | Oct. ,, | — | Aug. 1879 | 772,401 |
| HIRONDELLE .. | Dec. ,, | — | May 1873 | 605,010 |
| TORNADO .. .. | Mar. 1849 | — | Mar. 1881 | 687,997 |
| SWALLOW .. .. | June ,, | — | Sept. 1871 | 569,232 |
| TIMOUR .. .. | Aug. ,, | — | Nov. ,, | 569,893 |
| PROMETHEUS .. | Mar. 1850 | May 1870 | Oct. 1887 | 538,025 |
| PERSEUS .. .. | June ,, | —† | Dec. 1880 | 722,458 |
| ESTAFFETE [*sic*] .. | Sept. ,, | June 1870 | ,, 1884 | 505,544 |
| ROVER .. .. .. | ,, ,, | — | Aug. 1871 | 461,344 |
| AMAZON .. .. | Mar. 1851 | — | July 1877 | 729,841 |
| LORD OF THE ISLES .. | ,, ,,‡ | — | June 1884 | 789,309 |
| Built by Rothwell & Co, Bolton. | | | | |
| ALMA .. .. .. | Nov. 1854 | — | June 1872 | 444,608 |
| BALAKLAVA .. .. | Dec. ,, | — | Oct. 1871 | 406,425 |
| INKERMANN .. .. | Mar. 1855 | — | ,, 1877 | 650,220 |
| KERTCH .. .. .. | April ,, | — | Dec. 1872 | 326,246 |
| CRIMEA .. .. .. | May ,, | — | Nov. 1876 | 605,701 |
| EUPATORIA .. .. | ,, ,, | — | Oct. ,, | 618,275 |
| SEBASTOPOL .. .. | July ,, | — | ,, 1880 | 707,148 |

\* Most of them were replaced by new engines of the same names, as will appear later.
† Exploded 1862 and reboilered 1863.
‡ *Lord of the Isles* commenced work July 1852.

PASSENGER ENGINES, 1846–1866—*(continued)*

### 'BOGIE' CLASS

15 Bogie Saddle Tank Engines. 4-4-0. Cylinders: 17 inch by 24 inch.
Diameter of Coupled Wheels, 6 feet and 5 feet 9 inches.

| Name | Built | Ceased Work | Name | Built | Ceased Work |
|---|---|---|---|---|---|
| | | | | | |
| Built by GWR, Swindon. 6 foot Wheels. | | | | | |
| CORSAIR | Aug. 1849 | June 1873 | BRIGAND | Sept. 1849 | June 1873 |
| | | | | | |
| Built by R. & W. Hawthorn, Newcastle. 5 feet 9 inch Wheels. | | | | | |
| SAPPHO | June 1854 | Dec. 1873 | LUCRETIUS | Dec. 1854 | Mar. 1872 |
| HOMER | Aug. ,, | ,, ,, | THEOCRITUS | ,, ,, | Dec. 1873 |
| VIRGIL | Sept. ,, | ,, ,, | STATIUS | Jan. 1855 | Oct. 1871 |
| HORACE | ,, ,, | ,, 1880 | EURIPIDES | Feb. ,, | Dec. ,, |
| OVID | Oct. ,, | Mar. 1872 | HESIOD | Mar. ,, | Feb. 1872 |
| JUVENAL | Nov. ,, | Dec. 1873 | LUCAN | ,, ,, | Mar. ,, |
| SENECA | ,, ,, | Mar. 1872 | | | |

### 'WAVERLEY' CLASS

10 Engines. 4-4-0. Cylinders: 17 inch by 24 inch.
Diameter of Coupled Wheels, 7 feet.

| Name | Built | Ceased Work | Name | Built | Ceased Work |
|---|---|---|---|---|---|
| | | | | | |
| Built by R. Stephenson & Co., Newcastle | | | | | |
| LALLA ROOKH | Feb. 1855 | Dec. 1872 | CŒUR DE LION | May 1855 | June 1876 |
| IVANHOE | Mar. ,, | Sept. 1876 | PIRATE | ,, ,, | ,, ,, |
| ROBIN HOOD | ,, ,, | Nov. ,, | ABBOT | June ,, | Oct. ,, |
| ROB ROY | April ,, | Feb. 1872 | RED GAUNTLET | ,, ,, | Nov. ,, |
| WAVERLEY | ,, ,, | June 1876 | ANTIQUARY | ,, ,, | June ,, |

PASSENGER ENGINES, 1846–1866—*(continued)*

## 'VICTORIA' CLASS

18 Engines. 2-4-0. Cylinders: 16 inch by 24 inch.
Diameter of Coupled Wheels, 6 feet 6 inches.

| Name | Built | Ceased Work | Name | Built | Ceased Work |
|------|-------|-------------|------|-------|-------------|
| | | | Built by GWR, Swindon. | | |
| VICTORIA | Aug. '56 | Jan. '79 | BRUNEL | May '63 | Mar. '79 |
| NAPOLEON | ,, ,, | Dec. '80 | LOCKE | June ,, | June '81 |
| LEOPOLD | Sept. ,, | Jan. '77 | STEPHENSON | ,, ,, | Dec. '78 |
| OSCAR | ,, ,, | Dec. '80 | TREVETHICK[1] | July ,, | ,, ,, |
| ABDUL MEDJID | Oct. ,, | ,, '77 | SMEATON | Aug. ,, | Feb. '77 |
| VICTOR EMANUEL | ,, ,, | June '78 | FULTON | Jan. '64 | Nov. '76 |
| ALEXANDER | Nov. ,, | ,, ,, | WATT | Feb. ,, | Feb. '80 |
| OTHO | ,, ,, | Dec. '80 | TELFORD | April ,, | ,, '79 |
| | | | RENNIE | ,, ,, | Dec. '78 |
| | | | BRINDLEY | May ,, | Mar. '79 |

[1] *sic*

## 'METROPOLITAN' CLASS

22 Condensing Tank Engines. 2-4-0. Cylinders (outside): 16 inch by 24 inch
Diameter of Coupled Wheels, 6 feet.

| Name | Built | Ceased Work | Name | Built | Ceased Work |
|------|-------|-------------|------|-------|-------------|
| | | | Built by Vulcan Foundry, Newton-le-Willows. | | |
| HORNET* | June 1862 | June 1873 | MOSQUITO | Aug. 1862 | Dec. 1875 |
| BEE | July ,, | Dec. 1874 | WASP | ,, ,, | June 1877 |
| GNAT | ,, ,, | June ,, | LOCUST | ,, ,, | Dec. 1876 |
| | | | Built by Kitson & Co, Leeds. | | |
| SHAH | June 1862 | June 1872 | MOGUL* | Aug. 1862 | June 1872 |
| BEY | July ,, | ,, ,, | KAISER | Sept. ,, | ,, ,, |
| CZAR | Aug. ,, | ,, 1871 | KHAN | ,, ,, | Dec. ,, |
| | | | Built by GWR, Swindon. | | |
| FLEUR-DE-LIS | July 1863 | Dec. 1872 | AZALIA [sic]* | April 1864 | June 1872 |
| ROSE | Aug. ,, | Oct. 1877 | LILY* | May ,, | Dec. ,, |
| THISTLE | Sept. ,, | June 1874 | MYRTLE* | ,, ,, | ,, 1873 |
| SHAMROCK | Nov. ,, | Dec. 1877 | VIOLET* | July ,, | ,, 1872 |
| CAMELIA [sic] | Dec. ,, | June 1876 | LAUREL* | Oct. ,, | June ,, |

These were all converted to non-condensing engines in 1868–1870, and those marked *
to tender engines.

## PASSENGER ENGINES, 1846–1866—(*continued*)

### 'HAWTHORN' OR 'AVONSIDE' CLASS

26 Engines. 2-4-0. Cylinders: 16 inch by 24 inch.
Diameter of Coupled Wheels, 6 feet.

| Name | Built | Ceased Work | Name | Built | Ceased Work |
|---|---|---|---|---|---|
| **Built by Avonside Engine Co, Bristol.** | | | | | |
| HAWTHORN | April 1865 | Mar. 1876 | DEWRANCE | July 1865 | May 1892 |
| HACKWORTH | May ,, | May 1892 | FOSTER | Aug. ,, | Sept. 1876 |
| JOHN GRAY | ,, ,, | Mar. 1876 | BLENKENSOP | Dec. ,, | May 1892 |
| MELLING* | ,, ,, | May 1892 | AVONSIDE‡ | ,, ,, | Jan. ,, |
| MURDOCK† | ,, ,, | ,, ,, | BEYER* | ,, ,, | April 1887 |
| GOOCH | ,, ,, | ,, ,, | PENN* | Jan. 1866 | May 1892 |
| ROBERTS* | June ,, | ,, ,, | STEWART* | ,, ,, | ,, ,, |
| HEDLEY*† | ,, ,, | ,, ,, | WOOD | ,, ,, | ,, ,, |
| FENTON | July ,, | ,, ,, | PEACOCK | Feb. ,, | Dec. 1875 |
| BURY* | ,, ,, | ,, ,, | SHARP | ,, ,, | June 1887 |
| **Built by GWR, Swindon.** | | | | | |
| HAWK | Dec. 1865 | May 1892 | CERBERUS* | Feb. 1866 | May 1892 |
| OSTRICH* | ,, ,, | ,, ,, | ACHERON | ,, ,, | June 1887 |
| PHLEGETHON | Jan. 1866 | June 1887 | POLLUX*† | ,, ,, | May 1892 |

\* These ten were converted to saddle tank engines with 5 foot wheels and 17 inch by 24 inch cylinders in 1877.

† *Murdock* and *Hedley* were rebuilt with new boilers in August 1891 and November 1890 respectively, *Pollux* in August 1890.

‡ Originally named *Slaughter*, after a founder of the Avonside Company.

## GOODS ENGINES, 1846–1866

All 0-6-0; and all, save one, built at Swindon. Diameter of Coupled Wheels, 5 feet, except the last class. Tank engines are so described; the rest had tenders.

### 'PREMIER' OR 'AJAX' CLASS

12 Engines. Cylinders: 16 inch by 24 inch.

| Name | Built | Ceased Work | Name | Built | Ceased Work |
|---|---|---|---|---|---|
| PREMIER | Feb. 1846 | Nov. 1869 | DREADNOUGHT | Oct. 1846 | April 1871 |
| AJAX | May ,, | Aug. 1871 | FURY | Dec. ,, | Feb. ,, |
| ARGO | July ,, | Mar. 1866 | BERGION | Jan. 1847 | Nov. 1870 |
| BELLEROPHON | ,, ,, | April 1870 | BRIAREUS | Feb. ,, | Dec. ,, |
| VESUVIUS | Sept. ,, | ,, ,, | BRONTES | May ,, | June 1872 |
| TELICA | Oct. ,, | July ,, | JASON | ,, ,, | Sept. 1870 |

## GOODS ENGINES, 1846–1866—(*continued*)

### 'PYRACMON' OR 'ALLIGATOR' CLASS

7 Engines. Cylinders: 16 inch by 24 inch

| Name | Built | Ceased Work | Name | Built | Ceased Work |
|---|---|---|---|---|---|
| PYRACMON | Nov. 1847 | Mar. 1872 | MAMMOTH | April 1848 | July 1872 |
| STEROPES | Jan. 1848 | Aug. 1871 | ALLIGATOR | July ,, | Dec. 1873 |
| CALIBAN | Feb. ,, | June 1873 | BACCHUS* | May 1849 | Nov. 1869 |
| BEHEMOTH | Mar. ,, | Dec. ,, | | | |

* *Bacchus*, though included in this class, was different from the rest, parts of older engines having been used in its construction.

### 'CÆSAR' CLASS

8 Engines. Cylinders: 16 inch by 24 inch.

| Name | Built | Ceased Work | Name | Built | Ceased Work |
|---|---|---|---|---|---|
| DIDO | June 1851 | Dec. 1872 | FLORENCE | Nov. 1851 | June 1874 |
| VOLCANO | ,, ,, | June 1874 | NORA CREINA | Nov. ,, | May 1872 |
| THUNDERER | July ,, | ,, ,, | HERO | Dec. ,, | June 1871 |
| CÆSAR | Aug. ,, | ,, 1880 | DRUID | Feb. 1852 | Mar. 1879 |

The cylinders of the 'Caesar' class were subsequently increased to 17 inches by 24 inches.

### 'ARIADNE' CLASS

26 Engines. Cylinders: 17 inch by 24 inch.

| Name | Built | Ceased Work | Name | Built | Ceased Work |
|---|---|---|---|---|---|
| GIAOUR | May 1852 | Dec. 1880 | MINERVA | Aug. 1853 | Nov. 1877 |
| HEBE | ,, ,, | July 1877 | PSYCHE | Oct. ,, | June 1874 |
| FLIRT | ,, ,, | Mar. 1874 | CUPID | ,, ,, | Nov. ,, |
| PEARL | ,, ,, | Feb. 1878 | COQUETTE | ,, ,, | Dec. 1875 |
| ARIADNE | Nov. ,, | June 1879 | HECUBA | Nov. ,, | June 1873 |
| LEANDER | Dec. ,, | ,, 1875 | WELLINGTON | ,, ,, | Dec. ,, |
| EUROPA* | Mar. 1853 | May 1892 | ROMULUS | ,, ,, | Nov. 1877 |
| CATO | ,, ,, | June 1871 | REMUS | ,, ,, | May 1879 |
| NELSON | April ,, | Dec. 1873 | MONARCH | Dec. ,, | Dec. ,, |
| TRAFALGAR | June ,, | Jan. 1871 | ZINA | ,, ,, | June 1874 |
| ULYSSES | July ,, | Dec. 1872 | CERES | Jan. 1854 | Dec. 1877 |
| CICERO | ,, ,, | Jan. 1871 | BRUTUS | ,, ,, | June 1874 |
| DIANA | Aug. ,, | Dec. 1877 | RUBY | ,, ,, | ,, 1881 |

* *Europa* was rebuilt in June 1869 and alone survived till the end.

GOODS ENGINES, 1846–1866—(*continued*)

'CALIPH' CLASS

76 Engines. Cylinders: 17 inch by 24 inch.

| Name | Built | Ceased Work | Name | Built | Ceased Work |
|------|-------|-------------|------|-------|-------------|
| FLORA | Feb. 1854 | Dec. 1872 | ESK | June 1857 | July 1880 |
| THAMES | ,, ,, | ,, 1877 | AVON | ,, ,, | Mar. 1877 |
| VESPER | Mar. ,, | Mar. 1879 | LIFFEY | Aug. ,, | ,, 1872 |
| IRIS | ,, ,, | ,, 1874 | BOYNE | ,, ,, | ,, 1874 |
| NEPTUNE | ,, ,, | Aug. 1881 | SHANNON | ,, ,, | Jan. 1880 |
| CYPRUS | April ,, | Dec. 1878 | FORTH | ,, 1858 | Feb. 1878 |
| JANUS | May ,, | ,, 1880 | CLYDE | ,, ,, | June 1872 |
| CALIPH | ,, ,, | ,, 1878 | TAY | Sept. ,, | Mar. 1881 |
| ORSON | June ,, | June 1874 | WEAR | April 1859 | Dec. 1879 |
| VIXEN | ,, ,, | May 1879 | TYNE | May ,, | April 1877 |
| SALUS | Aug. ,, | Mar. 1877 | WYE | ,, ,, | Dec. 1879 |
| SIBYL | ,, ,, | Dec. 1878 | RHONDDA | June ,, | Aug. 1877 |
| SPHINX | Sept. ,, | ,, 1873 | TAMAR | ,, ,, | Jan. 1880 |
| BANSHEE | ,, ,, | ,, 1879 | PLYM | ,, ,, | June 1875 |
| CAMBYSES | Nov. ,, | Nov. 1877 | WARRIOR | Mar. 1861 | Dec. 1872 |
| MIDAS | ,, ,, | June 1875 | WARHAWK | ,, ,, | June 1877 |
| NIMROD | ,, ,, | Nov. 1877 | GLADIATOR | ,, ,, | Nov. ,, |
| GERYON | Dec. ,, | ,, 1876 | LAGOON [sic]* | ,, ,, | May 1876 |
| NEMESIS | Jan. 1855 | ,, 1877 | TALBOT | ,, ,, | Dec. 1877 |
| NERO | ,, ,, | ,, ,, | SIRIUS | June ,, | ,, 1880 |
| PLUTUS | Feb. ,, | Mar. 1874 | SEVERUS | ,, ,, | Nov. 1878 |
| ZETES | ,, ,, | Dec. 1877 | PIONEER | July ,, | June 1877 |
| OCTAVIA | ,, ,, | ,, 1873 | HADES | Aug. ,, | Nov. 1878 |
| METIS | Mar. ,, | Nov. 1877 | ORPHEUS | Sept. ,, | Oct. 1877 |
| RHEA | April ,, | Feb. 1872 | CHRONOS | ,, ,, | Dec. 1878 |
| TYPHON | ,, ,, | Dec. 1879 | OLYMPUS | Oct. ,, | Sept. 1879 |
| OSIRIS | May ,, | Nov. 1877 | PLUTARCH | Sept. 1862 | Aug. 1875 |
| PELOPS | ,, ,, | Mar. 1876 | REGULUS | Oct. ,, | June 1883 |
| CREON | Mar. 1856 | May 1872 | THESEUS | Nov. ,, | Dec. 1880 |
| PANTHEA | ,, ,, | Nov. 1878 | TANTALUS | ,, ,, | June 1876 |
| AMPHION | April ,, | Dec. 1877 | COSSACK | ,, ,, | ,, 1880 |
| MAGI | May ,, | ,, 1879 | CHAMPION | Dec. ,, | Mar. 1878 |
| PALLAS | ,, ,, | Feb. ,, | SYLLA | ,, ,, | Dec. ,, |
| GYFEILLON | June ,, | Aug. ,, | XERXES | Jan. 1863 | ,, 1882 |
| MERSEY | Jan. 1857 | July ,, | LEONIDAS | ,, ,, | June 1881 |
| SEVERN | Feb. ,, | Dec. 1873 | PANDORA | ,, ,, | Mar. 1880 |
| TWEED | ,, ,, | Nov. 1874 | LUNA | Feb. ,, | Dec. ,, |
| HUMBER | June ,, | Dec. 1883 | ETHON | Mar. ,, | ,, 1883 |

* Probably meant for Laocoön.

## GOODS ENGINES, 1846–1866—(*continued*)

### BANKING CLASS

5 Saddle Tank Engines. Cylinders: 17 inch by 24 inch.

| Name | Built | Rebuilt | Ceased Work |
|------|-------|---------|-------------|
| | Built by Stothert & Slaughter, Bristol. | | |
| AVALANCHE | Feb. 1846 | — | Aug. 1865 |
| | Built by GWR, Swindon. | | |
| JUNO* | Oct. 1852 | Mar. 1869 | June 1889 |
| IAGO | ,, ,, | — | July 1881 |
| PLATO | Sept. 1854 | — | Dec. 1883 |
| BITHON | Oct. ,, | — | June 1871 |

\* Sold to South Devon Railway in June 1872 and renamed *Stromboli*. GWR number 2138 added in 1876.

### 'SWINDON' CLASS

14 Engines. Cylinders: 17 inch by 24 inch.

| Name | Built | Sold to B & ER | B & E No. | 1876 GWR No. | Rebuilt (N.G. Boiler) | Ceased Work |
|------|-------|----------------|-----------|--------------|----------------------|-------------|
| SWINDON | Nov. 1865 | Sept. 1874 | 109 | 2090 | Aug. 1886 | Dec. 1888 |
| LONDON | Dec. ,, | June 1873 | 100 | 2081 | Jan. ,, | ,, ,, |
| BRISTOL | ,, ,, | July ,, | 101 | 2082 | Aug. ,, | ,, ,, |
| WINDSOR | Jan. 1866 | April ,, | 99 | 2080 | — | June 1889 |
| READING | ,, ,, | May 1874 | 107 | 2088 | — | May 1892 |
| BATH | ,, ,, | Mar. ,, | 105 | 2086 | Dec. 1885 | June 1888 |
| OXFORD | ,, ,, | July ,, | 108 | 2089 | — | Dec. 1889 |
| BIRMINGHAM | ,, ,, | Aug. 1873 | 103 | 2084 | — | June ,, |
| WOLVERHAMPTON | Feb. ,, | Feb. 1874 | 104 | 2085 | — | Dec. ,, |
| SHREWSBURY† | ,, ,, | July 1872 | 97 | 2078 | Feb. 1886 | ,, 1888 |
| CHESTER | Mar. ,, | April 1873 | 98 | 2079 | — | June 1887 |
| GLOUCESTER | ,, ,, | July ,, | 102 | 2083 | — | Dec. 1891 |
| HEREFORD† | ,, ,, | ,, 1872 | 96 | 2077 | — | June 1887 |
| NEWPORT | ,, ,, | May 1874 | 106 | 2087 | — | ,, 1889 |

† *Shrewsbury* may have become B & E No. 96, and *Hereford* No. 97 (GWR Nos. 2077 and 2078) being withdrawn in June 1887 and December 1888 respectively. Both versions occur in Great Western contemporary records and it is uncertain which is correct.

GOODS ENGINES, 1846–1866—*(continued)*

### 'SIR WATKIN' CLASS

6 Side Tank Engines. Cylinders: 17 inch by 24 inch.
Diameter of Coupled Wheels, 4 feet 6 inches.

| Name | Built | Ceased Work | Name | Built | Ceased Work |
|------|-------|-------------|------|-------|-------------|
| BULKELEY* | Dec. 1865 | Dec. 1890 | FOWLER* | Sept. 1866 | June 1887 |
| MILES | Aug. 1866 | June 1888 | SAUNDERS* | ,, ,, | May 1892 |
| SIR WATKIN | Sept. ,, | May 1892 | WHETHAM | ,, ,, | June 1889 |

\* Sold to South Devon Railway in June 1872. In 1876 they were given GWR numbers 2157–9 in addition to their original names. All six were altered to saddle tanks about 1885.

*Note.*—In or about 1865 several of the above classes were renamed in the Swindon books on no apparent principle, sometimes after one of the latest built engines in the class. Thus the 'Firefly' and 'Prince' classes were amalgamated as the 'Priam Class', the 'Sun' (6 foot tanks) became the 'Wolf Class'; and the 'Iron Duke' and 'Waverley' classes were re-christened 'Alma' and 'Abbot' respectively. Of the goods engines, the older 'Hercules' and 'Premier' classes, with the addition of *Bacchus*, became the 'Fury Class', and the remaining 'Pyracmon', 'Caesar', 'Ariadne', and 'Caliph' classes together the 'Caesar Class'.

# *Index*